A History of Chile, 1808–20c

A *History of Chile* chronicles the nation's political, social, and economic evolution from its independence until the early years of the Lagos regime. Employing primary and secondary materials, it explores the growth of Chile's agricultural economy, during which the large landed estates appeared; the nineteenth-century wheat and mining booms; the rise of the nitrate mines; their replacement by copper mining; and the diversification of the nation's economic base. This volume also traces Chile's political development from oligarchy to democracy, culminating in the election of Salvador Allende, his overthrow by a military dictatorship, and the return of popularly elected governments. Additionally, the volume examines Chile's social and intellectual history: the process of urbanization, the spread of education and public health, the diminution of poverty, the creation of a rich intellectual and literary tradition, the experiences of middle and lower classes, and the development of Chile's unique culture.

Simon Collier (1938–2003) was a professor of history at Vanderbilt University. He is the author of numerous books and articles on Latin American history, including *Tango!: The Dance, the Song, the Story* (1997) and *Chile: The Making of a Republic, 1830–1865* (Cambridge, 2003).

William F. Sater is Emeritus Professor of History at California State University in Long Beach. He has published six books, edited and co-edited two others, and written numerous articles that have appeared in Chile, Great Britain, the United States, Italy, and Mexico.

CAMBRIDGE LATIN AMERICAN STUDIES

General Editor
Herbert S. Klein, Columbia University

82
A History of Chile, 1808–2002
Second Edition

For a list of other books in the Cambridge Latin American Studies Series,
see the pages following the Index.

A History of Chile, 1808–2002
Second Edition

SIMON COLLIER

Vanderbilt University

WILLIAM F. SATER

California State University, Long Beach

PUBLISHED BY THE PRESS SYNDICATE OF THE UNIVERSITY OF CAMBRIDGE
The Pitt Building, Trumpington Street, Cambridge, United Kingdom

CAMBRIDGE UNIVERSITY PRESS
The Edinburgh Building, Cambridge CB2 2RU, UK
40 West 20th Street, New York, NY 10011-4211, USA
477 Williamstown Road, Port Melbourne, VIC 3207, Australia
Ruiz de Alarcón 13, 28014 Madrid, Spain
Dock House, The Waterfront, Cape Town 8001, South Africa

http: // www.cambridge.org

First edition first published 1996
Second edition first published 2004

Printed in the United States of America

Typeface Garamond 11/12 pt.   *System* LATEX 2ε   [TB]

A catalog record for this book is available from the British Library.

Library of Congress Cataloging in Publication Data

Collier, Simon.
A history of Chile, 1808–2002 / Simon Collier, William F. Sater. – 2nd. ed.
p.   cm. – (Cambridge Latin American studies ; 82)
Includes bibliographical references and index.
ISBN 0-521-82749-3 (hbk.) – ISBN 0-521-53484-4 (pbk.)
1. Chile – History – 1810- 2. Chile – History – 1565-1810.   I. Sater, William F.   II. Title.
III. Series.
F3093.C65   2004
983′.04 – dc22   2003065454

ISBN 0 521 82749 3 hardback
ISBN 0 521 53484 4 paperback

In memoriam

HAROLD BLAKEMORE
(1930–1991)

SIMON COLLIER
(1938–2003)

My friends, and Chile's

Contents

Maps

Preface to the Second Edition

For this second edition of the book originally entitled *A History of Chile 1808–1994* (Cambridge, 1996), we have added a new final chapter, to take account of developments since 1990 in a broad sweep, and we have made some minor revisions to the rest of the text to correct a few factual errors and to update the story. Our aim in this book is to present a general account of Chile's history as an independent nation-state for English-language readers, although we hope that Chileans, too, will enjoy it. It is our firm belief that the main task of writing Chilean history belongs to Chileans. Yet we also believe that a fresh eye can sometimes be cast over the changing Chilean scene from outside, and hopefully our effort has been worthwhile. As foreigners, we can never claim the intimate knowledge of Chilean society and culture that Chileans themselves grow up with, but we have both had a long personal connection with the country, going back to the presidency of the unforgettable Jorge Alessandri, and this book expresses, we trust, our strong affection for Chile and the Chileans. We have both enormously enjoyed Chile's undoubted charm, its scenery, its literature, its music, its people's notable humor, and, not least, its admirable wines – the finest, our upper nasal cavities tell us, in the Americas. Our lives have been enriched and sometimes frustrated by Chilean virtues and failings. We hope that something of this is communicated to the reader.

In writing the book, we wanted to combine a basic narrative of political events (bearing in mind A. J. P. Taylor's remark that the historian's first duty is "to answer the child's question 'What happened next?'")[1] with descriptions of the broader economic and social tendencies that have molded Chilean life and that underlie the outward "story." Our panoramic (and doubtless very incomplete) economic and social overviews for the mid-nineteenth century (Chapter 4) and the mid-twentieth (Chapter 10) are supplemented by shorter overviews for the so-called Parliamentary period (a section in Chapter 7) and for the end of the twentieth century (a section in Chapter 14). Three short sections on "culture" at different phases are

---

[1] A. J. P. Taylor, *A Personal History* (London, 1984), p. 301.

included in Chapters 7, 10, and 14. We are only too aware of what we have had to leave out. There is so much more that we could have said, especially about the vast anonymous production of that intangible, unquantifiable quality, "national character." It stems, no doubt, from Chile's long isolation in colonial times, during which Chileans, distinctive members of the great Hispanic family, devised their own ways of doing things, their own idiosyncratic form of the Spanish language, their own highly developed sense of humor. Little of this can be dealt with in a history book of this kind, which has mostly to deal with what can most simply be termed *national performance*. On this score, we are sure that Chileans have more than a little of which to be proud. Despite setbacks, some of them serious and prolonged, their story over the past two centuries has generally been one of progress and improvement. By the same token, we have no wish to present an idealized or "Whig" version of Chile's past. Our duty as historians is to tell the truth as we see it – warts and all.

Footnotes in this book are confined to (1) sources of quotations, except where these are so well known for referencing to be pointless, (2) references for unusual facts that might seem to need them, and (3) minor points of explanation or elaboration that do not belong in the main text. We have provided a note on further reading (emphasizing English-language materials), a glossary of Spanish terms, and a list of acronyms and initialisms, of which, in our era of alphabet soup, there are far too many. As a matter of principle, we use (where they exist) the time-honored English forms for South American names. The classic cases here are Valparaiso, always properly spelled in English *without* its Spanish accent, and River Plate, not Río de la Plata.

Acknowledgments

Our greatest debt is to the late Harold Blakemore. He was to have been our co-author. His death (February 20, 1991) was a severe personal blow to both of us. There are many others who could say the same, not least in Chile. Although fate denied Harold his part in writing this book, his influence on it was not small. He commented in detail on all the chapters in first draft up to the time of his death (roughly half the eventual text), and the book greatly benefited from many of his ideas and suggestions.

We wish to acknowledge the numerous friends, in Chile and elsewhere, who advised us (even if just by sparking off ideas) or who gave us help and support in other ways, in some cases over many years. In particular, we express our gratitude to Patricia Arancibia, Christon Archer (Calgary, Canada), the late Mario Bronfman, his widow Nana and their children as well as their respective spouses, Eduardo Cavieres, Ricardo Couyoumdjian,

Baldomero Estrada, the late Patricio Estellé (director of the Archivo Nacional at the time of his sadly premature death in 1975), Cristián Gazmuri, the late Mario Góngora, the late Gonzalo Izquierdo, Iván Jaksić (Mishawaka, Indiana), the late Álvaro Jara, the late Rolando Mellafe, Gonzalo Mendoza (former Chilean Consul General in Los Angeles) and his wife Verónica, the late Claudio Orrego Vicuña (whose far-too-early death in 1982 was a real loss to Chilean politics), Luis Ortega, the late Dr. Arturo Prat E. and his widow Elena Walker Martínez vda de Prat, Jaime and Linda Rodríguez (Los Angeles), Sol Serrano, the late Richard Southern (whose understanding of Chile was unique among English-speaking scholars), the late Juan Uribe-Echeverría, Michael Varley (*Rector* of Wenlock School, Santiago), and Sergio Villalobos R. (whose intellectual tenacity has been a constant inspiration to us). Ricardo Donoso, Guillermo Feliú Cruz, and Eugenio Pereira Salas – Chilean scholars of a now vanished generation – gave much unwitting stimulation; it was a privilege to have known them. Our warm gratitude is also due to the friendly staffs of the Biblioteca Nacional de Chile (Sala Medina, Sala Matta Vial, Newspaper and Microfilm sections in particular), where we have both passed non-trivial portions of our adult lives, as well as (far from Chile) those of the Albert Sloman Library (University of Essex) and the Jean & Alexander Heard Library (Vanderbilt University). Simon Collier thanks the Catholic University of Valparaiso and the Pontifical Catholic University of Chile (Santiago) for their generous hospitality to him as visiting professor in 1994 and 2002. Norma Antillón (Center for Latin American & Iberian Studies, Vanderbilt University) gave us eagle-eyed assistance in the final preparation of the original manuscript. Finally, we are both extremely grateful to the original two anonymous readers for Cambridge University Press for some valuable comments and to Frank Smith (Publishing Director, Social Sciences, Cambridge University Press) for inveigling us into doing this second version of our book.

For permission to quote two lines from W. H. Auden's classic poem "Letter to Lord Byron," first published in W. H. Auden and Louis MacNeice, *Letters from Iceland* (London, 1937), the authors thank Faber and Faber Ltd., London.

S. C.
Nashville, Tennessee

Postscript

Regrettably, Simon Collier unexpectedly succumbed to cancer in February 2003. As much as Simon loved fine wine and the tango, he loved Chile more. His loss is a personal tragedy for me, his colleagues at Vanderbilt, particularly Professors Michael Bess, Marshall Eakin, and Jane Lander, as well as his many friends in Chile, Great Britain, and the United States.

W. F. S.
Beverly Hills, California

March 2003

A note on geography

Nobody who looks at the map of the western hemisphere can fail to be struck by the unusual shape of the Republic of Chile. "The worst-located and worst-shaped nation on the planet" – this verdict by the Argentine writer Ezequiel Martínez Estrada[1] is no doubt exaggerated. Yet there is no denying that the country is about 2,600 miles (4,200 kilometers) long and on average about 90 miles (140 kilometers) wide, and hence indisputably *una larga y angosta faja de tierra,* a long thin sash of land, as Chileans themselves often say. How the sash came to be so long is part of the story unfolded in this book.

In area (292,257 square miles/756,946 square kilometers) Chile is somewhat larger than either France or Texas, but it stretches out across no less than thirty-eight degrees of latitude, its southernmost point, Horn Island (where the cape is), lying almost exactly on the 56th parallel. Thus part of Chile falls inside the tropics, and part is the closest continental land on earth to the snowy expanse of Antarctica, a section of which is claimed by Chile. So large a span of latitude is bound to contain great variations in climate. In the desert north there is scarcely any rainfall; Santiago, the capital, has what is often called "Mediterranean" weather; in the south the dampness is of British or Irish proportions; the southernmost part of Chile is as windy as New Zealand. Arid deserts, valley-oases, tranquil green pastures, rain-forests, mountain-framed lakes, icy glaciers, rocky archipelagos – the range of scenery is also impressive, and the scenery itself often a delight to the eye.

Geographers sometimes divide the republic into zones, slicing the map along lines of latitude – Desert Chile, Mediterranean Chile, Forest Chile, and so on. We avoid this terminology in our book, although certain commonly used expressions will recur: Norte Grande ("the greater North"), Norte Chico ("lesser North"), Central Valley, South, Far South. A basic, underlying physical configuration is common to all zones, though sometimes disguised. To the east the skyline is always dominated

---

[1] *Radiografía de la pampa,* 8th ed. (Buenos Aires, 1976), p. 81.

xix

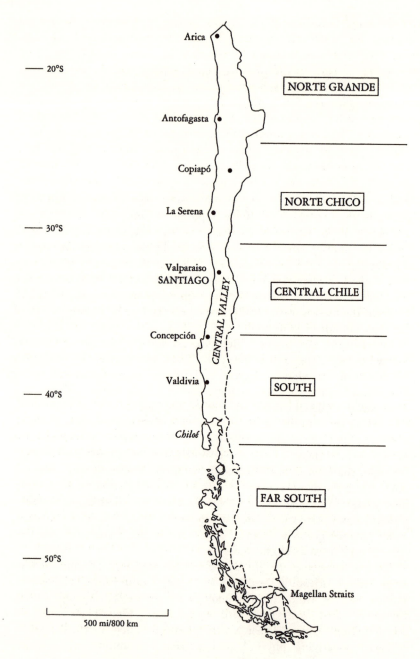

20°S

NORTE GRANDE

Arica

Antofagasta

Copiapó

NORTE CHICO

La Serena

30°S

Valparaiso
SANTIAGO

CENTRAL CHILE

CENTRAL VALLEY

Concepción

Valdivia

SOUTH

40°S

Chiloé

FAR SOUTH

50°S

Magellan Straits

500 mi/800 km

General sketch map of Chile

by the huge Cordillera of the Andes, whose highest peak, Aconcagua (23,000 feet/7,000 meters), rises on the Chilean-Argentine border less than 100 miles from Santiago. To the west, of course, there is the ocean: its specks of land include Easter Island, Chile's toehold in Polynesia (spontaneously annexed by a naval officer in 1888), fully five hours in a jet airliner from the South American mainland. Immediately behind the coast for much (though not all) of the length of the country there rises a coastal cordillera, much lower than the main Andean chain, but in places (near Santiago, for instance) rising to elevations of more than 6,000 feet. (The wild Cordillera de Nahuelbuta, the section of this lesser chain to the south of Concepción, is a bit lower.) At around 42°S., some 600 miles south of Santiago, the coastal range sinks beneath the sea, reappearing above the water farther south to form islands such as Chiloé. Between the two ranges there lies a shallow depression. In the Norte Chico this is broken up by hills and river-valleys; in the Norte Grande it is more a sloping shelf connecting the coastal range (here rising in huge cliffs straight from the ocean) to the main Cordillera. Between Santiago (33°S.) and Puerto Montt (42°S.), however, a continuous series of intermontane basins forms the so-called *valle central* or Central Valley, the northern half of which, the 300 or so miles between Santiago and Concepción, has been the true Chilean heartland for more than four centuries. The South can be said to begin roughly at the latitude of Concepción, and the Far South somewhere below Chiloé.

The first Europeans to be seen and heard in any part of what is now Chile were Ferdinand Magellan and the members of his expedition, some of whom were later to complete the first circumnavigation of the globe. In October and November 1520 three of Magellan's ships made their way through the straits now bearing his name (a distance of 310 nautical miles) and out into the ocean Magellan decided (in hopes of a calm crossing) to call the Pacific. This event, whatever its intrinsic interest, has no real connection with the story of Chile. It was not until Francisco Pizarro's conquest of the Inca empire of Peru in the early 1530s that the Spaniards (now sweeping across the newly named American continent in the most spectacular and ruthless invasion the continent has ever experienced) mounted their first incursion into Chile (1536), with an expedition led by Diego de Almagro, Pizarro's principal lieutenant. Almagro's men beat a retreat to Peru after reconnoitering a part of the Central Valley. In 1540 the Spanish conquistadors returned to Chile. This time they came to stay.

CAMBRIDGE LATIN AMERICAN STUDIES

PART I

Birth of a nation-state, 1800s–1830s

Established by Spanish conquistadors in the 1540s, the "captaincy-general" of Chile developed as a small and neglected agrarian colony on the fringe of the Spanish American empire, its isolation enhancing what became after two-and-a-half centuries a distinctive embryonic national culture. The formation of great landed estates sharply stratified colonial society, the predominantly mestizo laboring poor dominated by an upper class modified by eighteenth-century immigration, much of it Basque (Chapter 1). The wars of independence brought the Chilean nation-state into being: its soldiers and sailors played a key role in the emancipation of the viceroyalty of Peru. The quest of the new nation's early leaders for a suitable political order culminated in a comprehensive settlement by Conservative politicians in the 1830s. This gave the country a record of institutional continuity unusual in the upheaval-prone Spanish America of the nineteenth century (Chapters 2 and 3).

GOVERNMENTS

1817–1823	General Bernardo O'Higgins
1823–1826	General Ramón Freire
1827–1829	General Francisco Antonio Pinto
1829–1830	Junta
1830	Francisco Ruiz Tagle
1830–1831	José Tomas Ovalle
1831	Fernando Errázuriz
1831–1841	General Joaquín Prieto

1

Colonial foundations, 1540–1810

The kingdom of Chile, without contradiction the most fertile in America and the most adequate for human happiness, is the most wretched of the Spanish dominions.

— Manuel de Salas (1796)

The first Europeans arriving in Chile were charmed and captivated by its natural beauty and generally moderate climate. "This land is such that for living in, and for settling, there is none better in the world," wrote Pedro de Valdivia, the Spanish conquistador who opened up the fertile Central Valley of Chile to European colonization in 1540.[1] It is easy enough to see how Valdivia and his men, coming from a fairly arid homeland, having marched southward from Peru through endless desert, should have taken pleasure in the softer tones of the Chilean landscape. From the first, however, the colonizers' enjoyment of this scenery was bought at the price of isolation from the rest of the world. At no time was this truer than during the two and a half centuries that followed Valdivia's successful invasion, the period when the deep foundations of modern Chilean culture and nationality were laid. If Chileans form, as they do, a distinctive branch of the Spanish American family, the key to understanding their distinctiveness is, precisely, their long isolation – mitigated to an extent by the steamship in the second half of the nineteenth century, and more so by the jet airliner in the second half of the twentieth.

Aside from the Philippines, Chile was the most remote of all the Spanish possessions. When, in March 1796, a flotilla sailed into Talcahuano Bay in southern Chile after a voyage of ninety-five days from Cadiz, this was commented on at the time as an unusually fast passage. Before the Cape Horn route came into use in the 1740s, the journey (by way of Panama or Buenos Aires) took much longer. Moreover, Chile's isolation was not merely a matter of distance from the imperial metropolis. Even

[1] To Emperor Charles V, September 4, 1545. J. T. Medina, ed., *Cartas de Pedro de Valdivia* (Santiago, 1953), p. 42.

in South America the "long thin land" was lonely – separated from the Viceroyalty of Peru to the north by hundreds of miles of unfriendly desert, and from the pampas of the River Plate to the east by the towering Cordillera of the Andes. To the west, beyond the colony's beautiful coastline, the widest of the world's oceans was a fearsome expanse to be discreetly skirted rather than boldly navigated, although in 1574 the sea-captain Juan Fernández ventured farther from the coast than usual on a voyage from Peru and discovered the islands that now bear his name (400 miles offshore). Fernández later worked out how to take advantage of the wind systems in order to reduce the sailing time between Chile and Peru.

Only in the south did man rather than nature fix the boundaries of the new Spanish colony. For here the invaders were eventually checked by the indigenous inhabitants whose land they had come to conquer. The exact size of the native population of Chile at the time of Valdivia's arrival will never be known with certainty: Rolando Mellafe's judicious estimate puts the figure at between 800,000 and 1,200,000. Nor were the native Americans encountered by Valdivia's men a single nation, though most of them shared a common language. In the northern Central Valley, the Picunche peoples had earlier been assimilated into the great Inca empire of Peru, but full Inca rule stopped at the Maipó River (though exercised more tenuously at least as far as the Maule River, 160 or so miles farther south). In the more densely populated country south of the Maule, the Mapuche and other groups had fought off the Inca army and retained their independence. Here the peoples were proto-agricultural, living together in rather loosely organized, dispersed communities whose basic unit was the extended family. They were not concentrated in villages, still less in cities, and had none of the treasures which so excited the plundering instincts of the soldiers of Cortés and Pizarro in Mexico and Peru.

The Spaniards came to refer to the native peoples of southern Chile as "Araucanians." Their military prowess (they soon adopted the horse and became formidable cavalrymen) was extolled by Alonso de Ercilla, the soldier-poet whose epic of the conquest, *La Araucana* (3 parts, 1569–89), was the first literary work (in fact the first work of any kind) to bring Chile to the attention of Europe. Praising the adversary, of course, is not uncommon in the literature of imperialism, but thanks in part to Ercilla's poetic skill, Caupolicán and Lautaro, the two outstanding Araucanian leaders of the time, were long remembered in story and song far beyond the boundaries of Chile. Their names and those of other Araucanian heroes such as Galvarino and Tucapel, are still sometimes given to Chilean boys (and Chilean girls have sometimes been called Fresia, an "Araucanian" name almost certainly invented by Ercilla). Such names are much better recognized today than those of the Spanish governors who ruled Chile after the death of Pedro de Valdivia at the hands of the Mapuche in December 1553.

The overriding preoccupation of Valdivia's immediate successors was warfare, in a colony that was not only outnumbered but also over-extended. It was the great Araucanian offensive after December 1598 that fixed the final dimensions of colonial Chile, by closing off the well-watered southern half of the Central Valley, and forcing the Spaniards to abandon their main settlements, their "seven cities" south of the Bío Bío River. The last to be evacuated was Osorno, in March 1604. From then onward the gently curving Bío Bío (a "river of history" if ever there was one) became a stable if at times bloody "Frontier" between unconquered, independent Araucania and the Spanish colony growing up farther north. "Indomitable Araucania" was in effect a separate country (reluctantly recognized as such by Spain) which outlasted Spanish imperial rule.

The Chilean colony was never important enough, strategically or economically, for the imperial government to contemplate a full-scale invasion of the trans–Bío Bío territory. From the early seventeenth century a small standing army (rather unusual for the Spanish empire) was stationed in the south to patrol the Frontier, repelling Indian raids (*malones*) while often staging profitable little forays of its own (*malocas*). Chile came to enjoy the reputation of being "the Flanders of the New World," as the Jesuit chronicler Alonso de Ovalle put it in the 1640s, "the arena and dueling-ground of greatest valor in America, both for the Spaniard in his conquest and for the Araucanian in his resistance."[2] There was a touch of hyperbole here. Warfare along the Frontier lessened in intensity during the seventeenth century, and still more in the eighteenth. Cross-frontier trade developed rapidly during these centuries, the Mapuche supplying cattle, horses, and ponchos (among other things) in exchange for hardware, wine, or a variety of European manufactures. Missionaries (Jesuits, and later Franciscans) attempted to win Araucanian hearts and minds, with much persistence but without much success.

Development of rural society

If the Amerindians below the Bío Bío retained their independence, those to the north were altogether less fortunate. We do not know how many made their way across the Frontier to freedom. Those who remained took their place in the developing pattern of colonial society, and it was to be a strictly subordinate place. The conquistadors were the arrogant and confident champions of an empire fast approaching its peak. They did

[2] *Histórica relación del Reyno de Chile,* ed. Walter Hanisch SJ (Santiago, 1974), p. 101.

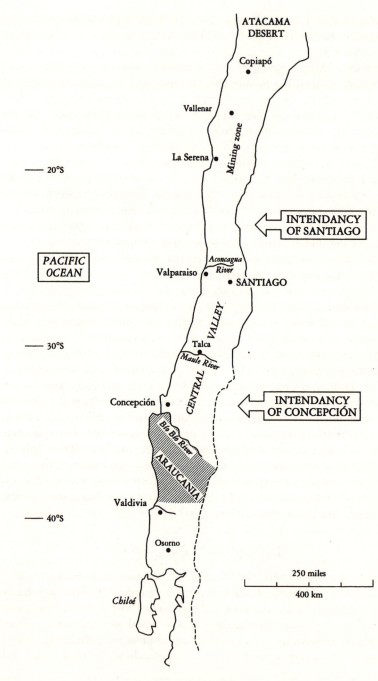

ATACAMA
DESERT

Copiapó

Vallenar

Mining zone

La Serena

—— 20°S

INTENDANCY
OF SANTIAGO

PACIFIC
OCEAN

Aconcagua
River

Valparaiso

SANTIAGO

CENTRAL VALLEY

—— 30°S

Talca

Maule River

Concepción

INTENDANCY
OF CONCEPCIÓN

Bío Bío River

ARAUCANIA

Valdivia

—— 40°S

Osorno

250 miles

400 km

Chiloé

Late-colonial Chile

not doubt that the fact of conquest gave them rights over the peoples and lands they had conquered. Valdivia's lieutenants and their successors aspired to a seigneurial way of life patterned on that of Spain. Their Spanishness had given them a preference for urban life: hence the urban nuclei that formed the pattern of Spanish colonization, as everywhere in America, and the importance the invaders gave to founding townships ("cities") – establishing them with prescribed ceremony, forming the first *cabildos* (municipal councils), and tracing out urban blocks for division among themselves. Santiago, the capital of the new Chilean colony, was founded by Valdivia in just this way on February 12, 1541, at the northern end of the Central Valley, on the then densely forested banks of the Mapocho River, at the foot of a hill the natives called Huelén and the conquerors the Cerro Santa Lucía. The colony's two other main townships were established soon afterward: La Serena (December 1543) some 300 miles to the north, in the semi-desert country of what we now call the Norte Chico, and Concepción (March 1550) in the south, on the shores of Talcahuano Bay, close to the Frontier itself.

No less urgent for the conquerors was the mobilization of Amerindian labor. Valdivia, like all conquistadors in America, apportioned natives among his followers in what were known throughout the empire as *encomiendas:* each *encomendero* (holder of an encomienda) was, in theory, to civilize and Christianize his natives, in return for (and this was no theory) their tribute or work. Initially, "work" chiefly meant panning gold from the rivers. Respectable amounts of gold were panned (and later mined) in sixteenth-century Chile, but the exhaustion of many deposits (and the loss of others after 1599) forced the settlers to fall back on agriculture and (especially) ranching as their mainstay. This set in motion what we must underline as one of the fundamental processes of Chilean history: the formation of great estates ruled by a land-owning elite and worked by a semi-servile rural population. This theme lies at the heart of the growth of Chilean culture and nationality. As Mario Góngora has wisely observed, "the configurations called 'colonial' are . . . the basic structures that underlie all the happenings of the 'national' period."[3]

The great landed property did not make its appearance in the Central Valley overnight. Its beginnings can no doubt be seen in the land-grants (*mercedes de tierras*) made by Valdivia and his successors. In the mind of the imperial government, there was no connection between a grant of land and the encomienda, technically a "grant" of people. In the minds of the conquerors of Chile the distinction may well have been blurred, as encomiendas became incorporated into large seigneurial landholdings.

[3] "Vagabundaje y sociedad fronteriza en Chile (siglos XVII a XIX)," *Cuadernos del Centro de Estudios Socio-Económicos,* No. 2 (1968), p. 29.

Our picture of these is not by any means clear. What *is* clear is that the impact of the encomienda on the native population, as in other parts of the Spanish empire, was little short of catastrophic. Much more catastrophic, however, was the effect of Old World diseases (against which the natives had no built-up resistance). Indigenous society outside Araucania rapidly disintegrated. By the end of the sixteenth century, Amerindian numbers were in sharp decline to the north (and also, as far as we can tell, to the south) of the Bío Bío, probably by around four-fifths.

A third factor that affected the fate of the natives in the Spanish colony was miscegenation, the interbreeding of Spaniards and natives, producing the new mestizo component in the population. Given the near-total absence of European women in the early colonial period, such a development was unavoidable. Some conquistadors were positively boastful of their efforts on this score. The most picturesque case is that of the larger-than-life Francisco de Aguirre, the conqueror of the Norte Chico (and a large part of what is now northwest Argentina), who fathered scores of children, some fifty of whom he recognized. Aguirre was censured by the Church for his hyperactive sexual conduct and distinctly heterodox opinions. One of the many heretical propositions he was required to recant in a ceremony at La Plata (the modern Sucre, Bolivia) in April 1569 was that "more service is rendered to God in engendering mestizos than sin is incurred in so doing."[4] Anybody who consults the telephone directory of today's Norte Chico will find more than a few Aguirres.

The process of miscegenation in Chile occurred over several generations, but its end result was clear well before the end of colonial times. By the close of the eighteenth century few communities of Amerindians survived north of the Bío Bío, and those that did were no longer completely native in either genes or culture. The new and constantly expanding mestizo component was the dominant component of the Chilean population of 700,000 or so in 1800. The evidence of baptismal records shows not only that Amerindian names had largely vanished by then, but that mestizos were to a great extent passing themselves off (or were being passed off) as "Spaniards." Here, in this remote corner of the caste-conscious Spanish empire, there grew up a relatively homogeneous population in which only one vague ethnic division was of importance: the division between the predominantly mestizo (Spanish-Amerindian) majority and the more definitely European upper class consisting of "creoles" (Spanish-Americans) and *peninsulares* (Spaniards from Spain). The culture of the upper class was fundamentally Spanish, though inevitably affected in many small ways by the more mixed mestizo culture, where indige-

---

[4] Luis Silva Lezaeta, *El conquistador Francisco de Aguirre* (Santiago, 1953), pp. 376–77.

nous influence survived in popular sports, superstitions, diet, and vocabulary – all of which played their part in the formation of the Chilean nationality.

The decline in the number of natives available for encomiendas led in due course to a variety of alternative methods of mobilizing labor. One was the enslavement of Mapuches captured in the warfare along the Frontier – a practice well under way before King Philip III legalized it in 1608. Slaves from the south were used throughout the seventeenth century (on paper the practice was abolished in 1674). Frontier garrisons regarded the sale of captured Amerindians as a standard perquisite. The Huarpe natives from the encomiendas of Cuyo (the sparsely populated region across the Andes which was formally part of Chile until 1778) were also drafted for forced labor and brought across the mountains to the Central Valley. African slavery, much relied on farther north in the Spanish empire, made less of an impression: the colony's poverty precluded its development on any great scale. In the eighteenth century, thousands of slaves passed through Chile on their way from Buenos Aires to Peru, but relatively few stayed. In 1800 there were between 10,000 and 20,000 blacks and mulattoes in the colony: some 5,000 were slaves, many of these house-slaves.

The mainstay of the Chilean economy by the seventeenth century was ranching. Its scale must not be exaggerated. Markets for produce were very limited. Locally, there were the small Frontier garrisons to be supplied – not least with the tough, wiry horses for which Chile was soon noted. A modest inter-colonial trade also grew up with the Viceroyalty of Peru. In addition to "opulent Lima," the impressive viceregal capital, the vital silver-mining city of Potosí acted as an economic magnet or "growth-pole" for much of southern South America. The Potosí miners' insatiable demand for mules was partly met from the Central Valley – the mules sent in long trains to the great annual fairs at Salta. The main Chilean offerings throughout this period, however, were cattlehides (among other things used for shoemaking), *charqui* (jerked beef), and tallow (used mostly for candlemaking and soap). The common description of Chile's seventeenth century as "the tallow century" is not too strong an exaggeration.

It was ranching, above all, that consolidated the settlers' lands into the form of the great estate, the *estancia* as it was usually termed at this early stage. The needs of ranching gave the great estates their natural shape: a section of the Central Valley floor (the core of each property usually was located there), and pastures in the better-watered lands of the coastal range and main Cordillera. While no detailed account of the build-up of the estancia yet exists, it is clear that a tendency to concentration was

under way by the mid-seventeenth century. It was reinforced soon afterward by the rise of a new Chilean staple, with the development of a
wheat trade with Peru.

Wheat-growing in Peru was badly affected by an earthquake in 1687
and by disease thereafter. Once established in the Peruvian market, Chilean
wheat (cheaper and of better quality) never lost its popularity. Domestic demand also grew with the expansion of the mestizo population, with
its preference for European rather than native food. Chilean estates, hitherto mostly ranches, now turned to cereal cultivation, and from then on
were referred to as *haciendas*. (The common alternative term, *fundo*, came
into use only later.) Once again, we should not exaggerate the scale of
the wheat trade. In Peru, to be sure, it came to be regarded as vital:
"without Chile, Lima would not exist," wrote a Viceroy in 1736.[5] Even
so, production in the middle and late eighteenth century was modest in
comparison with the levels of one hundred years later. By nineteenth-
century standards, only a relatively small acreage was brought under
the plow. Large sections of every estate lay fallow from year to year.
Cultivation, however, was sufficient to maintain a reasonable trade and,
more important, to give the Central Valley the fundamental social shape
it retained until well into the twentieth century.

With the decline of the encomiendas (which survived mostly in outlying areas such as the north, or on the island of Chiloé, until abolished
in 1791 by Governor Ambrosio O'Higgins), landowners were forced to
look elsewhere for reliable labor. During the ranching phase, they often
found it useful to allow families of "poor Spaniards" (sometimes veterans) or mestizos to settle on estates as "renters," in return for services
such as watching the herds, guarding against rustlers, and helping with
the annual round-up and slaughter. Such short-term contracts (*arriendos*
or *préstamos,* as they were called) gradually hardened into the more permanent arrangement whereby the "renters," in return for their little plots
of land and other perquisites, supplied regular labor all year round – an
obvious need with the spread of wheat-growing. Opportunities for such
people were in any case narrowing. The open, military camaraderie of
the decades of conquest was steadily being supplanted by a more consciously hierarchical order in which the best land was already in the hands
of the colonial elite. Indeed, the connection between cereal cultivation,
miscegenation, and a developing social hierarchy seems inescapable.

The "renters" on the haciendas came in time to form a distinctive rural class, becoming known as *inquilinos*. (The specialized Chilean use of
the common Spanish term for "tenant" was becoming widespread by the
second half of the eighteenth century.) Inquilino tenancies in effect be-

[5] Quoted in Diego Barros Arana, *Historia general de Chile,* 16 vols. (Santiago, 1884–1902), VI, 74.

came hereditary. With the spread of agriculture, the estate owners, the *hacendados,* placed heavier demands on these tenant-laborers, and their original status was correspondingly diminished. When Charles Darwin observed the arrangement in the 1830s, it struck him as "feudal-like," although the inquilino was not legally bound to the land, *adscriptus glebae,* in the manner of the European serf. Inquilinos and other peasant cultivators who acquired horses (great rural status symbols) became known, additionally, as *huasos* – later to form a standard rural stereotype, much evoked by writers and musicians, and not without its effects on the life styles of landowners themselves. For two hundred years the *huaso* was most commonly to be seen in the area between Santiago and the Maule River: in 1842 the writer José Joaquín Vallejo was to describe Colchagua as "our Cossack province."[6]

By 1800, the institution of *inquilinaje* was a main feature of rural society in the Central Valley. Yet neither the hacienda nor *inquilinaje* was at any stage universal in Chile, either in colonial times or later. Smaller properties, some no more than tiny subsistence plots, abounded. These seem to have come into existence in a variety of ways: from simple squatting, from the smaller land-grants of the conquest, from concessions of municipal land to deserving peons, and from the subdivision of larger properties – a common practice under Spanish law. The most prosperous smaller farms were to be found in areas like the Aconcagua Valley, close to the urban market, such as it was, of Santiago. In the immediate neighborhood of the towns, small farms known (from a Quechua term) as *chacras* were also common; many of these belonged to hacendados, but a modestly flourishing semi-independent peasant economy seems to have existed also, supplying meat and vegetables to the townships and contributing wheat to the export trade. In the long run, this potential "bold peasantry" found its scope greatly reduced by the growing predominance of the hacienda.

The hacienda was to prove one of the most stable and enduring of Chilean institutions, leaving long-lasting marks on the national psychology. It is difficult to say exactly how many estates there were by 1800 or so: there is no Chilean Domesday Book to help us. Arnold Bauer's educated guess gives a figure of 500 or so estates larger than 1,000 hectares (2,470 acres) in the "core" region between Santiago and Concepción. Of these, perhaps slightly fewer than half contributed to the grain trade. Some were enormous, extending from the Andean foothills across the valley to the coastal range. In many ways each estate was a self-contained community, growing its own food, weaving its own coarse clothing, organizing its own bucolic jollifications – given the high num-

---

[6] José Joaquín de Vallejo, *Obras de don José Joaquín Vallejo* (Santiago, 1911), p. 140.

ber of saints' days in the year, these were not infrequent. The Central
Valley countryside had few if any European-style villages; the new townships which were founded in the 1740s did not amount to much, with
the possible exception of Talca; the hacienda was the natural social nucleus. At certain times of the year it drew on the casual labor of peons
from outside the estate. There were always far more peons than jobs. Off
the hacienda, indeed, life for the rural poor was distinctly precarious.
Throughout the eighteenth century (and for much of the nineteenth)
a large "floating population" of peons and vagabonds roamed up and
down the Central Valley in search of subsistence, sometimes squatting on
neglected land, sometimes turning to petty theft, cattle-rustling or banditry. The numbers of such people were a repeated concern to the authorities in the second half of the eighteenth century, and a concern regularly
expressed throughout the nineteenth.

But with most of the best land already covered by the estates, with
only a limited chance of becoming an inquilino or successful peasant
cultivator, with no "frontier" to colonize, the peon was compelled to
wander. A love of roaming the world is sometimes taken to be a distinctive aspect of the Chilean national character. If so, its roots may well
lie here. Those peons who drifted into casual labor in the towns became
known as *rotos* ("ragged men"), a term later applied to the urban lower
class as a whole. Here a second standard Chilean stereotype was born:
the *roto,* like the *huaso,* has come to be regarded (and idealized) over the
years as supposedly embodying certain perennial features of the Chilean
character – cheeriness, improvidence, a strong gambling instinct, and an
almost miraculous ability to improvise.

The "classical" Chilean countryside had, by 1800 or so, taken on its
clearest shape (though not in all respects its later appearance, for the nowadays ubiquitous poplar was introduced only at the very end of colonial
times) in the area between the Aconcagua Valley and the Maule River.
This area was within easy reach of Santiago and Valparaiso, the tiny
port through which most of the colony's external trade was conducted.
It was here that the majority of the 700,000 or so Chileans lived in 1800.
To either side of this heartland, outlying regions showed a somewhat different socio-economic pattern. One such region lay between the Maule River
and the Frontier, and here the economic value of the great estates was more
limited, except for those within easy reach of Concepción. Concepción,
apart from being the garrison town for the Frontier, was the focus
of a minor regional economy, with its wheat shipped directly to the
Peruvian market from Talcahuano.

The Frontier itself, we should note here, remained stable until the end
of colonial times. The standing army was gradually reduced in size: after
Governor Agustín Jáuregui's reorganization in 1778 it stood at around

1,500. The Frontier defenses were maintained or rebuilt. The somber grey trapezoidal fortress at Nacimiento (at the confluence of the Bío Bío and Vergara) still stands as a memorial to the presence of Spain's empire on its uttermost frontier. Seen under the rainy skies so common in the south, it has a remarkable atmosphere, though its appearance was somewhat marred by the addition in 1975 of an unsightly brick balustrade placed on the ramparts.

Araucanian attacks were much less frequent in the later colonial period (the offensives of 1723, 1766, and 1769–70 were the most serious of the eighteenth century). Relations between Spanish Chile and the Amerindian territory were entrusted to specially appointed officials, the so-called *comisarios de naciones* ("commissioners of nations") and their subordinate *capitanes de amigos* ("captains of friends"). There were also regular *parlamentos* ("ceremonial parleys") between colonial officials and the Mapuche, the first of which occurred in 1641. By the end of colonial times there may have been as many as 150,000 Araucanians. Their way of life had changed as a result of continuous contact with the Spanish colony, especially through the flourishing cross-frontier trade mentioned earlier. (The Mapuche request for peace terms in 1723 was probably spurred by the disruption of this trade.) Agriculture and livestock-raising became much more widespread south of the Bío Bío. While Araucania never developed a centralized state, some caciques came to exercise authority over particular regions, though the four *butalmapus* or "provinces" represented at parleys may have existed more strongly in the Spanish mind than in reality. By the mid-eighteenth century the Araucanians also had spread over the Andes on to the plains of the River Plate, often raiding the isolated Spanish settlements on the fringes of the pampa, thus playing an important part in the early history of Argentina as well as Chile.

Three tiny enclaves of the Spanish empire survived to the south of Araucanian territory in 1800. Two were of long standing: the tiny settlement at Valdivia, and Chiloé with its 25,000 or so people. Valdivia, one of the "seven cities" lost in the Mapuche offensive of 1599, was resettled and fortified in the 1640s, soon after a Dutch corsair expedition had disturbingly appeared there. Chiloé was made directly dependent on the Viceroyalty of Peru after 1767. In most respects the island was the poor relation of a poor colony: the *chilotes,* waging constant battle against their impenetrable forest, and subjected to the exactions of unscrupulous Lima merchants, were in a peculiarly miserable position. At the very end of colonial times, Governor Ambrosio O'Higgins organized the resettlement of Osorno (1796), thus showing a renewed official interest in the area which was to be taken up more seriously by the governments of the nineteenth century.

Mining, manufacturing, trade

So far we have focused mostly on the Central Valley. Far fewer Chileans
lived at the northern end of the colony – the area now called the Norte
Chico. Its semi-desert terrain confined agriculture to a few valley-oases.
The eighteenth century brought limited growth to this thinly settled
area. Its population doubled (from 30,000 to 60,000 between 1763 and
1813) with its development as a specialized mining zone. The effective
northern limit of Chile now shifted to the southern fringes of the Ata-
maca desert: Copiapó, a tiny staging-post on the little-used land route
to Peru, was given city status in 1744. There were mines in the Central Valley heartland, too, but it was the north that now set the pace.
Gold-mining led the way: production, which registered a ninefold increase in the eighteenth century, averaged about 3,000 kilograms per year
in the first decade of the nineteenth. (Between 1800 and 1820 Chile accounted for nearly one-sixth of the world supply.) Gold-mining accounted
for 60 to 70 percent of all mineral production. Silvermining also developed
steadily, though hampered by an uncertain supply of the mercury so vital
for the separation of silver from its ore by means of the "patio" process
common in the Spanish colonies since the sixteenth century. Copper was
also extracted in the north – used for domestic utensils and for artillery,
the imperial government placing orders through the governor – a practice
that occasionally led to speculative hoarding by traders.

As with agriculture and ranching, it is important not to over-emphasize
the extent of mining. Its growing commercial role, admittedly, warranted
the creation (in 1787) of a mines tribunal modeled after the one in Mexico.
In value, output came to between 1 million and 2 million pesos per
year at the end of the colonial era. This was not a huge amount. Taking the colonial period as a whole, Chile's production of precious metals, while of great importance to Chile itself, amounted to only about
one thirty-third of the Spanish-American total.

The Norte Chico abounded in high-grade ores, the mining of which
required little in the way of capital, and whose processing required only
simple technical methods. Some of these were ingenious: the *trapiche,* the
ore-grinder for gold and silver, seems to have been a local innovation.
(Elsewhere in Spanish America the word means sugar-mill.) The mines
themselves were numerous (several hundred), small, shallow, and short-
lived: the sinking or cutting of shafts or adits was rare. They were usually clustered in groups known as *minerales* (of which there were around
eighty), while several *minerales* in close proximity constituted a recognized
mining district, the classic example being Copiapó – "the most brilliant
abode of the mineral kingdom," as Juan Egaña put it, with a certain

exaggeration.[7] Egaña was the secretary of the mines tribunal who attempted a complete enumeration of Chile's mines, though his list is incomplete.

Mines at this period (and for long afterward) were operated mostly by individuals or small partnerships with the help of a few laborers, the *barretero*, who dug the ore, and the *apir*, who shifted it from the mine, being the two most familiar types. Marginal operations of various kinds were also very common. The most widespread was the so-called *pirquén* system by which a lessee (*pirquinero*) worked a mine section or even an entire mine on his own account in return for a rent or royalty paid to the mineowner. It is probable, in fact, that most mining in the north in the eighteenth century was done in this way. This particular pattern – numerous small enterprises, simple technology, marginal activity – was to remain fundamental even when the scale of mining greatly expanded in the nineteenth century.

Mining was the only "industry" to speak of in colonial Chile. We should not, however, ignore the level of domestic industry in the countryside – weaving, pottery, and carpentry. Given that only the small creole-*peninsular* upper class could afford imported European merchandise, local weavers, potters, and carpenters had to meet most of the colony's needs. There were a few small tanneries in the Central Valley. Ships (mostly smallish craft by 1800) were constructed at various points along the coast. In the towns the usual arts and crafts could be found, though evidently they were not noted for their quality: "uncouth craftsmen, silversmiths without taste, carpenters without standards, painters who cannot draw, copycat tailors, stick-in-the-mud tinsmiths, swindling shoemakers" – such was the much-quoted verdict, in the 1790s, of Manuel de Salas on the colony's "gang of artisans."[8] The artisan class in the urban population, small and poorly trained as it was, needs to be included in any picture of colonial life. It was to remain in place in the nineteenth century, and indeed well beyond, for Chile is still a land where small workshops are common.

The mainstays of Chile's external trade, as we have indicated, were agriculture and (toward the end of the colonial era) mining. Back in the seventeenth century the pattern of trade had been simple, and highly disadvantageous to Chile. The carefully regulated mercantilist system of the Spanish empire prescribed a single monopoly port in Spain (Seville

[7] Egaña, *Informe anual que presenta la secretaría de este Real Tribunal...Año de 1803* (Santiago, 1894), p. 5.

[8] *Escritos de don Manuel de Salas y documentos relativos a él y a su familia*, 3 vols. (Santiago, 1910–14), I, 171.

and later Cadiz), annual transatlantic convoys, and a select number of
monopoly ports on the American continent. Thus all trade to and from
Chile had to be funneled through the Panama isthmus and Peru. As can
easily be imagined, the cost of importing goods from Spain was very
high. Moreover, the powerful merchant interest of Lima, organized in
its *Consulado* (trading guild), had a decisive hold over the much feebler
trading interest in Chile. Chilean dependence on the Viceroyalty at this
stage was extreme.

Here, too, the eighteenth century brought noticeable changes, especially with the onset of the Bourbon reforms (from the 1710s onward) in
the Spanish empire, administrative and commercial reforms designed to
reverse Spain's obvious national decline and to loosen up the empire's internal commercial system. Their effect was to widen Chile's commercial
horizons while greatly lessening the Peruvian stranglehold. From 1740
onward ships were allowed to use the direct Cape Horn route from Spain.
Chile's growing trade with the neighboring River Plate provinces (raised
to Viceroyalty status in 1776) was now legalized. The notable decrees on
liberalized trade issued by King Charles III in February and October 1778
merely confirmed all of these trends. All such changes were strongly resented by the Consulado of Lima, which was especially worried by the
rise of Buenos Aires as the focus of a commerce "ever perilous to that
of Peru," as it claimed in 1774.[9] In fact, while Lima's general influence
was much reduced, its own trade greatly benefited from the Bourbon
reforms.

By the close of the century, therefore, Chile's external trade was increasingly diversified. Most of the highest positions in commerce were
held by recently arrived *peninsulares,* some forty or so traders forming
the mercantile elite – most working in Santiago, a few in Concepción.
The commercial link with Spain was still the most important. Peru remained the only market for Chilean wheat and tallow, but now sent trop-
ical products (notably sugar) in return, since European merchandise came
direct from Spain. The River Plate's chief export to Chile was *yerba mate*
(Paraguayan tea), an infusion of which was the colony's most popular non-
alcoholic drink – still common enough in Chile, though less so than in
Argentina. The old Peruvian "domination" was by this stage mostly confined to the edge Lima enjoyed in the important wheat trade: most of
the twenty-five or thirty ships that plied the trade between the colonies
were owned by Peruvians. This was a definite grievance in Chile and
the cause of several acrimonious disputes. These left an effect on the way
Chilean creoles saw the outside world (their fear of and respect for Peru,
in particular), but in practical terms every commercial reform of the

---

[9] Quoted in Manfred Kossok, *El virreynato del Río de la Plata* (Buenos Aires, 1959), p. 68.

eighteenth century brought greater Chilean independence vis-à-vis Peru. The creation of a local mint in Santiago (1750), and the foundation of a separate Consulado (1796) set the seal on this process.

The liberal historians of the nineteenth century sometimes blamed the "odious Spanish monopoly" for having constricted Chile's colonial trade. Modern research by Sergio Villalobos and others has undermined this view. Quite apart from the Bourbon liberalization, a number of short-term concessions (to offset the dislocation of trade in wartime) enabled Chilean merchants to trade with the vessels of allied or neutral powers, with foreign colonies, and even, under certain circumstances, with foreign countries. One Chilean merchant even planned to buy goods from far-away Sweden.[10] After 1796, it must be remembered, Spain was almost continuously at war, and such concessions were far from being merely formal.

In addition to legal trade, there was also contraband, which must at times have been considerable, if for obvious reasons unquantifiable. During the first two decades of the eighteenth century (when restrictions were briefly relaxed by the new Bourbon dynasty), French ships had flocked to the Chilean and Peruvian coasts, and a handful of French traders settled in the captaincy-general (one of them a Guillaume Pinochet from Brittany). Toward the end of the eighteenth century, British and American vessels regularly sailed in Chilean waters: Eugenio Pereira Salas, in a well-known study, has identified 257 such ships from the United States alone between 1788 and 1810.[11] That smuggling was a highly organized business seems certain. The ill-fated *Scorpion,* an English ship whose brutal capture by the authorities in September 1808 aroused a famous furor in Chile, was on her third trip to the coast. According to the depositions of the arrested sailors, her owners had reliable local contacts and were well informed about the state of the market.

The real problem with late-colonial trade, therefore, was not one of supply but of demand. The odious Spanish monopoly was much less to blame than the social structure of the colony. Given the general poverty, the domestic market was quickly saturated: the mercantile elite was thus anxious to restrict, not expand, the flow of trade. Unlike the new Viceroyalty of the River Plate, Chile was not well placed to take advantage of the Bourbon reforms. There was no great flow of trade *through* the colony, and, apart from wheat, no commodity that earned very much in the external market. The annual deficit, inevitably, was covered by shipments of metal or coin. Here the importance of mining shows up in its true light. Quite apart from being seen as pernicious from the standpoint of

---

[10] Sergio Villalobos R., *El comercio y la crisis colonial* (Santiago, 1968), p. 209.

[11] Eugenio Pereira Salas, *Buques norteamericanos en Chile a fines de la era colonial* (Santiago, 1936).

mercantilist orthodoxy, this practice also had the effect of draining Chile of money. The lack of small change, in particular, was to be a constant complaint well into the twentieth century, a minor economic ailment of long duration.

The colonial elite and its urban setting

Almost from the beginning, a small upper class of creoles and *peninsulares* took its place at the head of this isolated, agrarian colony. In the tumultuous early decades, the conquistadors and their followers stood out as the dominant group by virtue of their European origin and the power they commanded. Social distinctions within the conquering group were probably blurred and unclear. Later on, as the great estates were consolidated, the dividing line between a dominant land-owning class and everybody else became much thicker. A typical upper-class Chilean by the mid-seventeenth century held an encomienda and owned an estancia and a *chacra*. He often lived in Santiago some of the time, perhaps served a term or two on the *cabildo* (municipal council), and possibly held a public office of some kind. It was not always "he," either, as is shown in the case of the widow Catalina de los Ríos Lisperguer, better known by her nickname, La Quintrala. This sadistic and probably murderous seventeenth-century La Ligua valley landowner (an image of powerful female character, it should be noted) was to become one of Chile's most enduring national legends.

The composition of this colonial elite changed discernibly in the eighteenth century. With growing commercial opportunities, thousands of Spaniards migrated to the colony – approximately 24,000 between 1700 and 1810. Roughly half of these came from the Basque country or Navarre – hence Miguel de Unamuno's celebrated remark that the two greatest creations of the Basques were the Society of Jesus and the Republic of Chile. The most successful members of this migratory group made enough money (normally in trade) to buy themselves haciendas and to take their place in the upper class. Many older creole families (Carrera, Cerda, Covarrubias, Irarrázaval, Ovalle, and Toro spring to mind) retained their position, but others yielded their places to the new arrivals. In this way there came into being the so-called "Basque-Castilian aristocracy" that looms so large in so many Chilean history books. While most of its families did, indeed, come from northern or central Spain, other parts of Spain were also represented, and there was even a very small tinge of foreign blood. Despite the official prohibition of foreigners in the Spanish empire (with the exception of Catholic Irishmen, a number of whom were to be found in late-colonial Chile as army officers and traders), a few succeeded in putting down roots in the colony. Several Portuguese, a few

French, and one or two Italian families clearly formed part of the upper class by the end of the eighteenth century, by which time we can make out rather more than 300 families constituting the colonial elite. Their surnames are writ large over all the subsequent history of the country. One such surname (Errázuriz) was among those of the presidential candidates of 1989.

Whether there have ever been genuine traditions of aristocracy in the Western world outside Europe is not something we can enter into here. But the self-image of the colonial elite was undoubtedly aristocratic. There were various ways in which this sense could be enhanced. For the richest creoles, the most desirable status symbols were the establishment of *mayorazgos* (strict entails, binding estate-ownership through the successive generations of a family) and the securing of titles of nobility. Chile, being a poor colony, had only seventeen *mayorazgos* in 1800, and no more than twelve noble titles (seven *marqueses*, marquises, and five *condes*, counts) – many titles and *mayorazgos* overlapping. (Lima at this period had forty titled families; the parvenu colony of Cuba in 1796 had more than twenty.) For those who could not aspire to a title, membership in one of the great Spanish orders of chivalry (Santiago, Calatrava, Alcantará, Montesa) was sometimes an option. A larger number took commissions in the colonial militias – reorganized (and made more decorative) under the Bourbons.

As elsewhere in the Spanish empire, the upper-class sense of family was also very notable. Many leading families were linked; some had very extensive ramifications. The most celebrated case, no doubt, is that of the Larraín clan, whose Basque founder arrived in Chile in the 1680s. By 1800 it was divided into two main branches, one headed by a *mayorazgo*-holding *marqués*, the other less well-to-do, but so large that it became known as the "Ottoman" house or "the eight hundred." The Larraíns (with their connections to other notable families such as Errázuriz and Vicuña) were to appear and reappear on the political stage when independence came. An understanding of these family networks is inseparable from any appreciation of the course of Chilean history.

Economically and socially, this colonial elite held unchallenged sway in the colony. Its political influence was necessarily somewhat less direct, given the Spanish imperial policy of excluding creoles from high office. Nevertheless, late-eighteenth-century creole families seem to have been successful in forming marriage alliances with well-placed civil or military officials, and certainly by 1800 several creoles were themselves in good positions. Jacques Barbier's study of the period indicates that there were always "close ties between the local elite and administrative cadres."[12]

---

[12] *Reform and Politics in Bourbon Chile, 1755–1796* (Ottawa, 1980), p. 192.

The most effective eighteenth-century governors were those who worked with, rather than against, the creole elite.

How rich were the richest creoles? In general the creole elite was markedly less well-to-do than its counterparts in the great Viceroyalties. A Spanish visitor in 1796 listed seven men in Chile with incomes of "much more than" 100,000 pesos, along with twenty others who had incomes at around that level – roughly £25,000, or about US$100,000. The list was incomplete.[13] Earnings from agriculture were not very high except for a favored few. In 1796 Manuel de Salas reported that the countryside was "full of people with illustrious names" embittered by economic hardship.[14] If it is difficult to assemble a composite picture of upper-class incomes in late-colonial times, it is even more difficult to do so for wages further down the social scale. In the countryside money wages were rare. A carpenter in Santiago might earn 200 to 300 pesos in a good year, a mason rather more.

The colonial elite, though prizing rural property, preferred an urban setting. Eighteenth-century governors were interested in creating new townships and offered creoles incentives to settle there. Some of the familiar modern towns of the Central Valley (Talca, San Fernando, Rancagua, Curicó) were founded by Governor Manso de Velasco in the early 1740s; others (Linares, Parral) were founded in the 1790s. None of these (Talca, at the mid-point between Santiago and Concepción, was the largest), amounted to much more than a few streets coated or caked with dust or mud, depending on the season. Practically all the main towns in Chile were villages by European standards. Valparaiso, the main port (memorably sacked by Francis Drake back in 1578), was a small cluster of houses and ramshackle warehouses on an untidy beach. Its population in 1800 cannot have exceeded 4,000. La Serena, focus of life in the north, was somewhat larger and more of a small town with its own atmosphere. Because of its military role and direct links to Peru and Spain, the second city of the colony, Concepción, destroyed by earthquake in 1751 and rebuilt on a new site alongside the Bío Bío, regarded itself, not altogether convincingly, as the rival of Santiago.

In fact, only the capital itself was much of a town in 1800. Most of its one-story houses were built of adobe. Its population that year was around 30,000 (2,000 houses, 179 blocks). A few of its streets were paved. Toward the end of colonial times, limited embellishment took place: in 1765 an imposing eleven-arched stone bridge (the Puente de Cal-y-Canto) was built over the Mapocho. The Mapocho was dry for much of

[13] Juan Ricardo Couyoumdjian, "Los magnates chilenos del siglo XVIII," *Revista Chilena de Historia y Geografía*, No. 136 (1968), 315–22.

[14] *Escritos de don Manuel de Salas*, I, 155.

the year – hence the popular colonial catchphrase, "Either sell the bridge or buy a river!" (The bridge was demolished in 1888 as part of President Balmaceda's urban improvements.) At other times the river could flood disastrously, as it still regularly does: a new embankment running thirty blocks down one side of the town was opened in 1804. The poverty of Chile, as well as its earthquakes (Santiago's worst was in May 1647), delayed the appearance of anything more than the simplest architecture, but by 1800 the capital was endowed with a few respectable buildings. The most respectable, undoubtedly, was the Casa de la Moneda (more simply "La Moneda"), the austerely beautiful neoclassical palace which from 1805 housed the colonial mint and from 1846 the republican president – the Chilean White House. Its Italian architect, Joaquín Toesca, also left his mark on the city with the cathedral (which long remained unfinished) and public buildings (one is still there) on the north side of the main square, the Plaza de Armas.

If Chile was isolated from the world, colonial townships were in many ways isolated from each other. Roads worthy of the name scarcely existed. Governor O'Higgins built an adequate highway from Santiago to Valparaiso, though Captain George Vancouver, who saw it (as it was being completed) on his visit in 1795, was struck by how little it was used. The overland journey from Santiago to Concepción was laborious: eight days to Talca, another eight days from there to Concepción.[15] Until the advent of the railroads, the easiest way of traveling up and down the country was by ship. (In the case of the northern provinces this remained true until the twentieth century.) But in late-colonial times, the number of regular upper-class travelers was in any case very small.

The horizons of the creole upper class, therefore, were narrow. The colony had no proper printing press, and therefore no newspapers, even of the limited kind that were published in Lima or Buenos Aires. Although a small theater opened in Santiago in 1802, most social life was confined to the soirées and *tertulias* (conversational gatherings) held in the richer households. Dances (fandangos and boleros in this pre-*cueca* era) and musical evenings were enlivened, toward the end of the eighteenth century, by flutes, clarinets, and even a few imported pianos. Higher education of a rather traditional kind was provided for the sons of the upper class by the Royal University of San Felipe, which opened in 1758. Between 1758 and 1813 it educated some 1,837 students and conferred 299 doctorates (including 128 in law, 106 in theology, and 5 in medicine). The Academia de San Luis, formed in 1797 on Manuel de Salas's initiative to provide a more technical education, did not prosper. The somnolence of the urban scene was rarely interrupted unless by public

[15] Diego Barros Arana, *Historia general de Chile,* 16 vols. (Santiago, 1884–1902), VII, 406.

festivities (the arrivals and departures of governors; births, marriages, and deaths in the royal family) or by the feast-days of the Catholic Church. These were numerous, the most extensively celebrated being the annual festival of St. James (July 23–25) – from whom, after all, the city took its quintessential Spanish name.

Church and state

The Catholic Church, so important in the pattern of public ceremonial, was inescapable in colonial times, at least in the towns; in the country-side the ministrations of the clergy were much more intermittent. Chile's two bishoprics, Santiago and Concepción, dependent on Peru, dated from the earliest period of settlement (1561 and 1603 respectively). In 1800 some 220 secular clergy worked in the Santiago diocese, about 90 in Concepción. There were also around 1,000 religious, distributed among the five main orders (Franciscans, Augustinians, Dominicans, Mercedarians, and Hospitallers of San Juan de Dios). The Church was active in education, such as it was, and ran the colony's six hospitals. It was not, however, an important landowner. The one religious order that had ever owned land on any scale was conspicuous by its absence in 1800. As elsewhere in the Spanish empire, the Society of Jesus (present in Chile from 1593) had earlier built itself up as the most powerful order of all. The Jesuits had owned and worked over fifty estates, the only pharmacies in Chile, work-shops turning out glassware, pottery and textiles, and even a small ship-yard at the mouth of the Maule River. The best wine of the period is said to have come from their vineyards. This imposing economic role, combined with their suspiciously ultramontane opinions, was their even-tual undoing: in 1767 the order was abruptly expelled from the Span-ish empire. Of the 400 Jesuits deported from Chile by Governor Guill y Gonzaga, half were priests and three-quarters creole. It was perhaps the single most dramatic occurrence in eighteenth-century Chile. "Do you remember the expulsion of the Jesuits?" was a question asked by census-takers in 1854, when trying to establish the number of centenarians in the country. Apart from leaving a wide gap in education, the expulsion also placed a fair number of well-run haciendas on the market. These were auctioned off by a committee from 1771 onward, and more than a few passed into the hands of the "Basque-Castilian aristocracy."

Quite apart from its religious function, the Church was also a land-mark in the panorama of imperial authority. The government saw the hierarchy and the clergy as agents of the state, duly inculcating loyalty and obedience to the distant monarch. Most Chileans who thought about such things at all were loyal enough, and accepted the hierarchical system of government at whose apex the king sat in all his majesty. In this system, Chile was a captaincy-general, a minor province of the king's huge empire. Its administrative subordination to the Viceroyalty of Peru never amounted to very much (the Viceroy could intervene only in "very serious cases of great importance") and was formally abandoned in 1798. The colony was ruled by a governor and (from 1609 onward) an *Audiencia,* whose judges, as well as hearing appeals, also advised the governor on administrative matters. Its president was the governor himself. (*Presidente* was in fact the title by which he was most commonly known.) Below governor and *Audiencia,* a number of *corregidores* presided over the unevenly sized local districts into which the colony was divided until the administrative changes of the 1780s.

King Charles III's reforms did not, of course, affect the authoritarian, hierarchical system; indeed, they were consciously designed to strengthen it. In 1786–87, following a now standard Bourbon pattern, Chile was reorganized into two Intendancies, Santiago and Concepción (the boundary lying along the Maule River), and twenty-two inferior jurisdictions (fourteen for Santiago, eight for Concepción) known as *partidos,* each governed by a *subdelegado.* The governor himself became the senior of the two Intendants. These measures probably enhanced the local pride of Concepción, watering seeds of regionalism that were to germinate briefly in early republican times. The new system did not operate long enough to enable us to assess its merits. Nor is it easy to evaluate the quality of government in late-colonial times. Most governors of the period later rose to viceregal rank, in either Peru or the River Plate, a reasonable sign of professional ability. One of the most industrious of these governors, the Irishman Ambrosio O'Higgins, left his mark on Chile in several practical ways, even, with true Irish sentiment, commemorating his distant native heath in naming the new northern town of Vallenar: it is a hispanicized form of Ballinary (County Sligo).

The authoritarian structure of the empire did not permit the kind of tradition of political debate and dissent (still less religious nonconformity) that was to be found, for instance, in the colonies of Great Britain. Yet although creoles were excluded from the highest levels of government, they did not lack their own forum. This was the *cabildo* or municipal council. By the end of the eighteenth century, the Santiago *cabildo,* for obvious reasons the most important in Chile, consisted of twelve permanent *regidores* (councillors), a secretary, and a *procurador* (attorney). There was no element of popular election here: councillorships, like so many offices in the empire, were bought and sold when vacancies arose. Tradition, however, assigned the cabildo an important role in times of emergency, when it could summon a *cabildo abierto,* or open assembly of leading citizens. In normal times, the regular institutions of government greatly outweighed any influence the cabildo could bring to bear.

This emphatically does not mean that creoles were incapable of expressing discontent. The introduction of an *estanco* (state tobacco monopoly) in 1753, designed to finance the Frontier garrisons, provoked a flurry of agitation, which recurred thirteen years later. The government's attempts to raise money through new taxes (in 1776) and by other means (1781 and 1805) also brought episodes of tension between creoles and the governor.[16] The crisis (if that is what it was) of 1776 seems to have been potentially quite serious. These grievances were ephemeral, and did not call in question the absolutist political structure of the empire.

A more serious latent issue, beyond doubt, was the creole desire to win access to the highest levels of administration. This can be seen in the sporadic attempts by creoles to bar *peninsulares* from provincialships in the religious orders and to keep them off the *cabildo* of Santiago. Despite such signs, relations between creoles and *peninsulares* seem on the whole to have been very harmonious. However, creole awareness of the defects of colonial society was evidently sharpening by the close of the eighteenth century. Educated and "enlightened" creoles (not that there were very many) laid bare in a variety of writings the economic and social ills they saw around them: the high number of vagabonds and beggars, the problems of trade, the backwardness of education. They were never diffident in appealing for reform. At the root of all such discussions lay an optimistic belief in the colony's potential. "Chile could be the emporium of the earth," wrote Anselmo de la Cruz, secretary of the new Consulado, and a rare advocate of freer trade, in 1808.[17] It is not difficult to detect, here, the growth of a mild proto-nationalism, reflected in some of the writings of the period, not least the loving descriptions of Chile compiled by a few of the exiled Jesuits, notably the great Juan Ignacio Molina, for whom his native land was "the garden of South America." Throughout his long Italian exile, Molina never ceased to wish "to return to the homeland and . . . to die amongst my own."[18] His wish was not granted.

---

[16] The *estanco* became the biggest single source of revenue for the captaincy-general. Colonial taxes included duties on metals, customs dues (*almojarifazgos*), several kinds of sales tax (*alcabalas*), and bridge and road fees. A tithe (*diezmo*) was also collected (in kind) on behalf of the Church. Most colonial taxes were abolished or replaced in the decades after independence.

[17] Miguel Cruchaga Tocornal, *Estudio sobre la organización económica y la hacienda pública de Chile,* 2 vols. (Santiago, 1878–81), I, 343.

[18] Charles E. Ronan SJ and Walter Hanisch SJ, eds., *Epistolario de Juan Ignacio Molina SJ* (Santiago 1979), p. 218.

A nationality in embryo?

But who *were* Father Molina's "own"? What prompted his eloquent self-identification with the land he had lost? We need to ask to what extent Chile's colonial isolation, combined with the ethnic mix resulting from the conquest, had meant the gradual formation of a distinctive nationality in Spanish America. Too much, yet, should not be made of the term "nationality." We cannot argue that a developed, deep-rooted sense of Chilean nationhood (certainly not in a political sense) existed in the eighteenth century. It must be questioned how clearly any marked sense of "Chilean" identity was assimilated by the hacienda populations or by the poorer inhabitants of the colonial towns. The patriotic strand in the propaganda of the revolution for independence, and the moderately systematic invention of national tradition that occurred in the early republic – these things naturally lay in the future. But when they came, they built on something real, something already there. Consciously or unconsciously, a Chilean nationality *was* being born in colonial times, and we need to consider this, however cursorily.

It may be objected that the deep social stratification of the period (not to mention later on) makes any suggestion of an incipient "national" culture meaningless. By the same token, however, we could argue that a *sense* of social hierarchy was itself an important component of the embryonic national culture. Certain patterns of deference and snobbery became deeply ingrained in Chilean life in the colonial period, patterns which have only begun to dissolve in very recent times, and which were (as we shall see) possibly evoked at a subconscious level during the military regime of the 1970s and 1980s.

Let us concentrate, however, on two basic matters whose importance to any culture is undeniable: food and language. Man may or may not be what he eats, but what he eats is certainly a vital part of his culture. And nothing is more fundamental to a culture than language itself. As far as food is concerned, we at least know that Father Molina was interested in the subject: he was an enthusiast for cooking, and left numerous recipes among his private papers.

While it obviously took time for anything like a distinctively Chilean cuisine to develop (the first real Chilean cookbook, a mere twenty-nine pages long, was published in 1851), its main components were there from the sixteenth century, as the Spaniards introduced European crops and livestock, while at the same time including native American foods in their diet. From this original combination stemmed everything that was later to give Chilean cuisine its special character, and while few perhaps would rank the culinary tradition of the country as the greatest in the

world, it has always had its delights. Although wheat and other Old
World crops spread rapidly in the Central Valley after the conquest,
the conquerors were not slow to adopt such local foods as maize, the
potato, and the ubiquitous *poroto* bean. (The word *poroto* itself, from
the Quechua *purutu*, was long disdained by purists, who preferred the
more Spanish *fréjol*. But it could not be kept down. So it is that the phrase
"As American as apple pie" has "As Chilean as *porotos*" as its often-used
Chilean counterpart.) From the great ocean came the fish (the corvina,
the congrio, and others) and shellfish that are still in all likelihood the
modern visitor's most enduring gastronomic memory of Chile – not forgetting the *cochayuyo* (seaweed) soon taken up by the sixteenth-century
settlers, and still easy enough to find (not least on a Sunday afternoon
walk along the coast road north of Viña del Mar).

Maize, potatoes, and *porotos* became as fundamental to the creole-mestizo
diet as they had been to the Mapuche, and they have remained fundamental ever since, as has the use of animal fat in cooking. At the
same time, Spanish dishes were gradually adapted to make use of local
ingredients: the classic Chilean *cazuela,* for instance, evolved from the
Spanish *olla podrida* (stew), and the *empanada* (pastry) which in Chile received a filling of minced meat and onions. Beef for a long time was
often consumed in jerked form, *charqui,* which itself became the basis
of long-enduring popular dishes such as *charquicán* and the *Valdiviano.*
A standard condiment for many such dishes was, as it remains, *ají* (chili).
The scarcity and high cost of sugar delayed the appearance of desserts for
the sweet-toothed, but pastry-making developed (often at the hands of
nuns) in the seventeenth century, and there was always an abundance of
fruits, both imported and indigenous, including the native Chilean *frutilla (Fragaria chilensis),* eventually taken to Europe and cultivated at Ver-
sailles. Wine was made in Chile from the first years of settlement, from
País and Muscat grapes, and was later supplemented by *chicha* (from the
fermented juice of grapes, apples or *frutillas*). Overindulgence in wine
and chicha was as normal in colonial times as it was to be at subsequent stages of Chilean history. Among other drinks, *mate,* Paraguayan
tea, as we have mentioned already, became popular by the later seventeenth century, and chocolate (for those who could afford it) arrived in the
eighteenth.

The valuable pioneering work of Eugenio Pereira Salas and others has
given us a good picture of the various dishes known to have been created and eaten by better-off creoles and mestizos, many of which have
survived to the present day. We know much less about the eating habits
of the rural or urban poor, whose diet was altogether more monotonous
and unvarying than that of the better-off. What evidence we have indicates
that maize, wheat, potatoes, *porotos,* and (sometimes) *charqui* formed the

standard mix. For the better-off themselves, we might note, mealtimes followed an essentially Spanish pattern in the colonial era: an early lunch (*almuerzo*), a one o'clock dinner (*comida*), and an evening supper (*cena*) not later than 6:30 P.M. Refreshments were also taken at around 11:00 A.M. – *las once*, comparable to the English "elevenses." During the nineteenth century, in ways that have not been adequately documented, the modern Chilean timetable somehow established itself: breakfast (*desayuno*), a one o'clock lunch, and a late-evening (by American or British standards, very late-evening) dinner. One of the more mysterious shifts (though it was a logical one) was that "elevenses" was transferred to the afternoon – to coincide with (and somewhat resemble) the English "tea-time."

Turning from what people eat to how they talk, there seems little doubt that the main distinguishing features of Chilean Spanish were well in place by the end of colonial times. It has become recognized as one of the five main variants of the Spanish language in the Americas. Modern linguists, in fact, classify Chile as a "dialect area" in its own right. The dialect in question has not invariably had a good press. The great grammarian and polymath Andrés Bello railed (to no great effect) against the hasty, garbled speech he heard around him when he settled in the country in 1829. In the 1870s the journalist and politician Zorobabel Rodríguez wrote: "The incorrectness with which the Spanish language is written and spoken in Chile is an ill as generally recognized as it is justly deplored."[19] Since that time education has done much to improve standards of grammar and spelling in the written language (though we have seen *cigarrillo,* cigarette, spelled as *sigario* on Chilean shop-fronts), but the distinctive Chilean pronunciation and many peculiarities of syntax (and vocabulary) have survived and (happily) show no signs of disappearing.

Chilean Spanish shares many features with other American forms, on which the influence of Andalusia has been especially marked. (The Mapuche impact on accent and intonation does not seem to be very notable, except possibly in the south.) As elsewhere in Spanish America, the soft "c" and "z" become "s"; the "ll" is no more than a "y," lacking its more liquid Castilian sound, though at times it comes close to the distinctive River Plate "zh." The use of the second-person singular *vos* instead of *tú* (still universal across the mountains in Argentina and Uruguay, and also in Costa Rica, and widespread among the less lettered elsewhere in America) has tended to decline in more recent times in Chile. Visitors to today's Chile who are accustomed to the strict canons of Castilian Spanish will note (among many other things) the rather musical intonation, the disappearance of the "s" in plurals (and its virtual disappearance before consonants), the marked glide given to the vowel "e" after "g" or "j," and

[19] *Diccionario de Chilenismos* (Santiago, 1875), p. vii.

the very distinctive "tr" sound (also much heard in Costa Rica). This can be vividly appreciated when a Chilean tackles the tricky tongue-twister *tres tristes tigres trigo trillado tragaron en un trigal* ("Three sad tigers swallowed threshed wheat in a wheat-field").

The rich local vocabulary (not least an extensive slang vocabulary) includes elements from Mapuche (*poncho,* "poncho," *pichanga,* "party," etc.) and Quechua (*papa,* "potato," *palta,* "avocado pear," and so on) as well as from English, French, and German. We are getting ahead of the story here, for most of the borrowings from other European languages (a particularly well-known example is *gásfiter,* from the English "gas-fitter," meaning "plumber") have obviously occurred since colonial times, when the lexical mix must have been more exclusively Spanish-Mapuche. We might also note here that Chileans tend to use diminutives (and indeed augmentatives) more than most other Spanish-speakers. And, while it is hard to measure such things, the Chilean tendency to employ coarse language may possibly be the most pronounced in the Spanish-speaking world. The nouns *huevón* and *huevada* (and the associated verb *huevear*) – often considered gross elsewhere – have been so widely used that they have lost much of whatever force they originally possessed: they are perhaps less shocking in polite society nowadays than the classic four-letter word in English. The great Chilean linguist Rodolfo Oroz, noting in the mid-twentieth century that these swear-words were universal among the urban poor, suggested that they had penetrated even "certain sections of the middle class."[20] This strikes us as an example of Chilean understatement.

It would be interesting to generalize about the psychology of the embryonic Chilean nationality, but few scholars have yet given serious attention to the subject. Certain aspects (Chilean humor, for instance, the sharpest in Latin America) seem peculiarly unamenable to investigation. Rolando Mellafe, one of the few historians to address such themes at all, has suggested that regular natural disasters, especially earthquakes, have left their mark on the Chilean mind-set. (Mellafe computes 282 disasters between 1520 and 1906: 100 earthquakes, forty-six episodes of serious flooding, fifty droughts, eighty-two epidemics, and four plagues of plant- and tree-devouring insects.)[21] Modern visitors to Chile as different as Albert Camus and Stephen Clissold have speculated along these lines as

---

[20] *La lengua castellana en Chile* (Santiago, 1966), p. 403.
[21] *Historia social de Chile y América* (Santiago, 1986), pp. 279–88. For a more recent list of disasters, 735 in all between 1541 and 1992 (260 fires, 136 epidemics and famines, 166 earthquakes and volcanic eruptions, 173 floods and droughts), see Rosa Urrutia de Hazbún and Carlos Lanza Lazcano, *Catástrofes en Chile 1541–1992* (Santiago, 1993). Not all the disasters catalogued strike one as having been major.

well. The great French writer, on a short visit in 1949, detected "a psychology of instability" probably deriving from earthquakes and leading, he thought, to a propensity for gambling.[22] Chileans, or many of them anyway, *are* born gamblers. The Englishman Clissold, a longer-term resident during the same period, and the author of perhaps the most charming book about Chile in English, asks rhetorically: "is not all life something of a gamble…for those who live in a land where serious earthquakes may at any moment rob them of all worldly possessions, and even of life itself?"[23] The question is a very fair one.

If we cannot pursue these themes very far, we can nonetheless argue that they are well worth following up, and deserve to be integrated into the general historical record much more thoroughly than has yet been the case. They surely will be.

Reformers and revolutionaries

However isolated and remote, the captaincy-general of Chile could not remain entirely unaffected by the new trends beginning to spread through the Western world in the later eighteenth century, in particular the liberal critiques being mounted in Europe against absolute monarchy and the principle of colonial subordination. A few creoles became acquainted with the literature of the European Enlightenment, and sometimes imported prohibited books, with or without permission. The successful rebellion of the thirteen English colonies in North America (supported, we must remember, by Spain among others) did not pass unnoticed. Within a few years zealous Americans, imbued with revolutionary patriotism, were distributing translations of the Declaration of Independence or the new federal Constitution on whaling or smuggling trips to the Chilean coast. The French Revolution, too, made its mark in the minds of a few creoles. Yet whatever the impact of these novel ideas and great events may have been elsewhere in the Spanish empire, no historian has ever been able to make a convincing case for the existence of serious creole conspiracies against the established order in Chile. About the best that we can come up with is the case of an eccentric priest, Fr. Clemente Morán of Coquimbo, whose pronouncements in favor of the French Revolution won him confinement to the monastery of Santo Domingo in Santiago, and death in obscurity (October 1800). Nobody took him very seriously.

It is indisputable, however, that there *was* a handful of out-and-out separatists in Chile at the very end of colonial times. Bernardo Riquelme,

[22] *American Journals* (London, 1990), p. 132.   [23] *Chilean Scrapbook* (London, 1952), p. 143.

the bastard son of Governor O'Higgins, sent to England for part of his education (and the first Chilean to study there), learned revolutionary ideals at the feet of no less a figure than the tireless Venezuelan plotter Francisco de Miranda, greatest of all the acknowledged "precursors" of Spanish-American independence. This did not prevent Riquelme, on returning to Chile to inherit his 64,000-acre estate on the Frontier, from attempting (unsuccessfully) to assume his famous father's marquisate and barony as well as his surname. But he did not forget Miranda's teachings. Separatists like the young O'Higgins were necessarily discreet in spreading their views. The most enlightened creoles of the time, men such as Manuel de Salas and Juan Egaña, were powerful advocates of economic and even social reform, and put forward practical schemes, in the best traditions of the Enlightenment. Their writings can be seen, in retrospect, as exemplifying the proto-nationalism already mentioned. But hindsight should not make us draw the wrong conclusions. Most reform-minded creoles (like their counterparts in Spain) were "neo-mercantilists" who looked to the imperial monarchy as the agency of change – not to some hypothetical national revolution which might never occur. The leaders of creole society followed, from afar (and with a time lag of three or four months), the tumultuous events in revolutionary and Napoleonic Europe, events into which Spain itself was only too quickly drawn. They strongly disapproved of the Terror in France – "the worst scandal of all ages," wrote the *mayorazgo*-holding José Antonio de Rojas,[24] himself possibly a secret separatist and certainly an enlightened skeptic who had visited Europe and brought back prohibited books. Creoles sent donations to help the Spanish war effort (127,988 pesos between 1793 and 1806), but the great world of Europe, with its tramping legions, its navies, its Bonapartes and Pitts, seemed reassuringly distant. And so it was.

In 1806–7, however, that world came disconcertingly closer, when a British expedition from South Africa suddenly captured Buenos Aires. Though repelled by a hastily mustered creole force, the British returned in strength and seized Montevideo, finally withdrawing from the River Plate only after a second unsuccessful assault on Buenos Aires. These dramatic happenings in a neighboring province struck a chord of imperial patriotism in Chilean creole hearts, chiefly expressed in a burst of enthusiasm for militia drills. Most creoles were sure that the main danger came from the Spanish empire's traditional enemy, England. Such fears, no doubt heightened by ancestral memories of daring raids on the Chilean coast by English sea-dogs in the sixteenth and seventeenth centuries, were well justified: a British expedition to Chile was in fact both planned and sent off, only to be diverted to the bungled operations in the River

---

[24] Quoted in Jaime Eyzaguirre, *Ideario y ruta de la emancipación chilena* (Santiago, 1957), p. 76.

Plate. By an ironic twist of fate, Great Britain was soon to go to the aid of Spain herself, in the dire emergency of 1808. As a consequence of that surprising turn of events, the remote and isolated captaincy-general of Chile became the independent nation whose story is the theme of our book.

2

Independence, 1808–30

Live with honor, or die with glory!

– Bernardo O'Higgins (1813)

The timing of the independence of the captaincy-general (and most of the rest of Spanish America) was due entirely to the great upheaval of the Napoleonic wars in Europe. In May 1808, having forced the Spanish King Charles IV to abdicate, Napoleon deposed and banished the new king, Ferdinand VII, and placed his own brother Joseph on the Spanish throne. Spaniards rose in ferocious resistance to the "intruder king" and the French armies pouring into their country. Authority in what was left of free Spain passed spontaneously to a series of local juntas, a Central Junta at Cadiz emerging as the effective government, though early in 1810 this was replaced by a Council of Regency. Spanish radicals and reformers (the first politicians in the world to bear the honorable name of *liberals*) seized this opportunity to secure a constitution (1812) transforming Spain into a constitutional monarchy. These extraordinary political changes were overshadowed by the shifting fortunes of the Peninsular war, as Spanish guerrillas and their newfound British allies set about driving the French from Spain, a task completed in 1814.

The news of these events spread consternation throughout Spanish America. In Chile, where the news of Ferdinand VII's dethronement arrived in September 1808, the immediate reaction was to express intense, fervent loyalty to the motherland in its hour of catastrophe. Creoles again sent donations to help the war effort; the young bloods of Santiago (Francisco Antonio Pinto, a future president of Chile, among them) sported pictures of Ferdinand VII on their hats. As the months passed, however, this loyalist mood underwent a shift. With Spanish liberal propaganda hinting at a new and more equitable relationship between metropolis and colonies, with Spain itself in grave danger of extinction by Napoleon, a number of creoles began to ponder the desirability of taking control of the colony's affairs. Novel as this thought was, it quickly gained ground.

Pressure in this direction came from three main sources. Those educated creoles who had earlier promoted economic and social reform now sensed that this change could best be achieved by creating an autonomous Chilean government, albeit within the Spanish empire. A larger number, perhaps, saw home rule as a means of securing the long-desired prize of easier access to public office. (The Larraíns of the "eight hundred" branch seem to have grasped the point very quickly.) Then, too, there was that tiny handful of separatists, for whom Spain's difficulty was Chile's opportunity, eager for any change that might lead to the goal of an independent republic. To the governor and the Audiencia, needless to say, even the mildest of such proposals smacked of subversion. As it happened, the incumbent governor, Francisco Antonio García Carrasco, was a blunderer, ill-suited to deal with the rising tide of creole aspirations. Yet these were obviously universal in Spanish America. In April 1810 the captaincy-general of Venezuela became the first colony to depose its governor and set up a creole Junta. A month later, amidst turbulent crowd scenes, Buenos Aires followed suit. This news from next door was especially dramatic in its effects on creole opinion in Santiago.

The first creole governments

As in other Spanish-American capitals, it was the cabildo that played the main part in furthering the emerging creole program. García Carrasco's arrest of three prominent creoles on suspicion of plotting in May 1810 opened a three-way tussle among the cabildo, the governor, and the *Audiencia.* The tension grew to the breaking point when two of the three men were deported to Peru. To allay a dangerous public outcry, the *Audiencia* swiftly deposed García Carrasco, appointing in his place the rich octogenarian creole Mateo de Toro Zambrano, Conde de la Conquista. The *cabildo* was only briefly outflanked by this maneuver. With the new governor's assent, it summoned a *cabildo abierto* to consider the imperial emergency. This assembly, attended by some 400 leading citizens, was held in the Consulado building on September 18, 1810. The cabildo's clever young attorney, José Miguel Infante, analyzed the legal precedents for a creole Junta. The crowded hall rang with shouts of *"¡Junta queremos!"* ("We want a Junta!"). A Junta was duly chosen (six men, presided over by the Conde de la Conquista himself) to defend and preserve Chile for the "unfortunate monarch" Ferdinand VII, and to govern the colony until a congress could be summoned to Santiago. September 18, the *dieciocho,* became the Chilean national holiday, starting in 1811, and has remained so ever since.

As far as we can tell, the Junta's protestations of loyalty to Ferdinand VII were mostly sincere. Yet the cautious autonomism of September 1810 could easily be transformed into a more radical posture. By its very existence (not least by its call for a congress) the Junta marked a decisive break with the past. Its most active member, the lawyer Juan Martínez de Rozas, certainly held separatist views. Under his influence the new government swiftly created the nucleus of a small army. Events elsewhere reminded Chileans that their fortunes were linked to a much wider drama: on the bleak plateau of Upper Peru, soldiers from the new United Provinces of the River Plate (Argentina) were already fighting against the Viceroyalty of Peru, where no creole initiative had developed in 1810. The battle-lines between creole "patriots" and Spanish (or pro-Spanish) "royalists" were now being drawn all over the continent. The 400 men which the Junta offered to Buenos Aires were a clear sign of its solidarity with the general patriot cause. That the struggle ahead might be a bloody one was shown, too, in an abortive royalist rising in Santiago (April 1811) which claimed more than fifty victims. Its Spanish ringleader, Colonel Tomás de Figueroa, went before a firing squad. The Audiencia, which had taken few pains to disguise its hostility to the Junta, now swiftly dissolved.

Creole opinion, however, was not yet ready to move as fast as Rozas and other radicals wanted. When the promised congress (elected by the various cabildos) assembled in Santiago in July 1811, its majority consisted of cautious moderates. Rozas withdrew to Concepción in disgust. The undeterred reformers of Santiago, led by the "eight hundred" Larraíns, next established an unfortunate precedent by enlisting the support of the military to further their cause, with the help of an impetuous young officer just back from the war in Spain, José Miguel Carrera. A purge of congress followed without delay. But Carrera's passionate nature did not incline him to accept a subaltern role, least of all for the Larraíns. Two months later (November 15, 1811) he placed himself at the head of a new Junta, and dissolved congress altogether. The early months of 1812 were taken up with a tussle between Carrera in Santiago and the still defiant Rozas in Concepción. Rozas was eventually unseated and deported to Mendoza (July 1812). For the moment at least, Chile was under the rule of a single master – a caudillo.

Writers were later to depict Carrera as the great romantic figure of the creole revolution. His father had been a member of the first Junta; the family was an old one. Carrera himself was a handsome and dashing young man of unquestionable popularity and reforming ardor. Under his aegis the pace of reform quickened. Revolutionary doctrines were disseminated in the pages of *La Aurora de Chile,* the first Chilean newspaper, printed on a recently imported press and edited by the radical cleric Fray Camilo Henríquez. The ceremonious reception of Joel R. Poinsett as consul of the United States, and the creation of a distinctive "national" flag (yellow, blue, and white) showed how far the creole leadership was now traveling from the loyalism of 1810. Nevertheless, Carrera stopped well short of declaring independence. His short "provisional constitution" (October 1812) still affected a formal show of loyalty to Ferdinand VII. He could hardly fail to ignore the widespread hostility which the new ideas aroused. Even among creoles, royalist feeling was still strong, while the Larraín clan, with its numerous connections and associates, opposed him from the patriot side – a division within the revolutionary ranks that was to have fateful consequences soon enough. Though the first patriot governments had discovered reforming zeal, they had not yet discovered the vital importance of unity.

The wars of independence

The embryonic Chilean state now had to face its sternest test. The viceroy of Peru, José Fernando Abascal, staunchest and stubbornest champion of Spain's cause in South America, was no longer prepared to tolerate the evident subversion of Chile. Early in 1813 he sent a small task force under Brigadier Antonio Pareja to Chiloé and Valdivia, royalist strongholds whose garrisons remained loyal to Spain. Within a matter of weeks Pareja recruited an army of 2,000 and won control of much of the province of Concepción, where his army became still larger. The wars that now opened were to a large extent fought between Chilean and Chilean; only later did Spanish regulars play any real part, the viceroy's strategy focusing on the royalist south as a base of operations.

On hearing the news of Pareja's invasion, Carrera handed over the government to a new Junta and dashed south to Talca to rally the patriot forces. The opening campaign revealed both patriot and royalist incapacity. Both armies were constantly plagued by desertion, something that was to remain true throughout the war. The royalists' success at Yerbas Buenas (April 1813), the first action to rank as more than a skirmish, was followed by the indecisive battle of San Carlos. Mortally ill with pneumonia, Pareja decided to concentrate his strength at Chillán and winter there. The patriots invested the town, but were unable to dislodge the enemy. The war soon settled into stalemate.

But war it was, nevertheless, with predictable effects on the creole revolution. It was now harder for creoles to remain neutral; the patriot-royalist clash was fully in the open. Families were sometimes divided: if the "eight hundred" Larraíns were fervently patriot, the other branch of the family was not; most, but not all, Spaniards were royalist. The coming of war certainly stiffened the resolve of the patriot leadership in Santiago. The labors of Henríquez and other publicists (outstanding among them were Bernardo de Vera and the Guatemalan-born Antonio

José de Irisarri) did much to disseminate revolutionary ideology. More-over the creation of a new Instituto Nacional (for secondary and higher education) and of a new National Library were eloquent signs that the reforming impulse was being maintained.

As time passed, however, the new Junta (Larraín-influenced) became increasingly critical of Carrera's failures before Chillán. In October 1813 it moved to Talca, and soon afterward appointed Bernardo O'Higgins to succeed Carrera as commander-in-chief. O'Higgins, a former ally of Ro-zas, had fought bravely in the first campaign, but his elevation, briefly resisted by Carrera, merely deepened divisions in the patriot ranks. The change of command (February 1, 1814) came not a moment too soon. A second royalist task force, under Brigadier Gabino Gainza, was now sweeping north. The panic-stricken Junta fled from Talca. Gainza's army thrust rapidly to the Maule, but O'Higgins's ragged troops, victorious in the actions of El Quilo and Membrillar, barred its way to Santiago. It was at this juncture that an English naval officer, Captain James Hillyar, with the apparent encouragement of the viceroy of Peru, offered to mediate between the two sides. The resulting agreement, the Treaty of Lircay (May 3, 1814), provided for a degree of Chilean autonomy within the Spanish empire, but among other concessions the patriots agreed to sacrifice the new national flag.

With the royalists still controlling much of the south, the last thing the patriots needed was further dissension. But the quarrel between Carreras and Larraíns was as bitter as ever. Carrera himself, briefly impris-oned by the royalists, escaped, returned to Santiago, and overthrew the government (July 1814). O'Higgins repudiated the new regime, and a few desultory clashes between the two rival patriot armies had taken place when news came that the viceroy had rejected the Treaty of Lircay and that a third expedition, under General Mariano Osorio, was advanc-ing toward Santiago. O'Higgins reconciled himself with Carrera, but it was too late. He decided to make a last-ditch stand at Rancagua, fifty miles south of the capital. It was a ferocious, heroic defense (October 1–2, 1814), but in vain: no reinforcements arrived from Carrera, and O'Hig-gins had to fight his way into retreat. As the patriot armies disintegrated, panic took hold of the capital. O'Higgins, Carrera, and some 2,000 others made their laborious way across the high Andean passes to the safety of Argentina. Osorio entered Santiago in triumph, to the applause of the crowd and the gratitude of those creoles (among them all those who had titles and most of the *mayorazgo*-holders) who had remained loyal to the king.

Osorio himself was not a vindictive man, but he was obliged to take a stern line with Chile. King Ferdinand VII, now restored to his throne, was determined to destroy all traces of liberalism in Spain and America alike; by 1816 the patriot cause was in ruins everywhere except in the River Plate provinces. In Chile, most of the patriot reforms of 1810–14 were swept away; Instituto Nacional and National Library alike disappeared; the Audiencia was restored. Both Osorio himself and his more vengeful successor as governor, Francisco Casimiro Marcó del Pont, strove hard to extirpate patriot support. Some forty prominent creoles were banished to the Juan Fernández Islands, where they lived miserably in caves; others were incarcerated, exiled from Santiago, required to pay forced loans, deprived of their properties. The brutal murder of a number of patriot prisoners by the Spanish soldiers of the Talavera Regiment was a particularly sickening episode of this unhappy period.

The Spanish "reconquest" of Chile and its accompanying repression did much to transform creole hearts and minds. To most creoles, independence now seemed the only practical course. The most fervent patriots, needless to say, continued the struggle. The legendary Manuel Rodríguez, a young lawyer who had once been Carrera's secretary, organized an elusive guerrilla band, an example imitated by others, though it is Rodríguez who remains to this day the archetypal guerrilla for Chileans. The patriots' main hopes, however, lay on the far side of the Andes, where the powerful governor of Cuyo, General José de San Martín, had long been planning to use a liberated Chile as the base for a seaborne assault on the Viceroyalty of Peru – the key to the expulsion of Spain from South America. The arrival in Mendoza of numerous Chilean refugees in 1814 gave San Martín some valuable new allies: O'Higgins in particular became his close friend. By the start of 1817, San Martín's Army of the Andes (over 4,000 men) was ready to undertake its liberating mission. Mostly Argentine in composition, it nonetheless had a small Chilean contingent, and O'Higgins commanded one of its divisions.

The crossing of the bleak and icy passes of the Andes by San Martín's army was one of those supreme feats of war which are constantly re-evoked. Distracted by guerrilla actions, the royalists were caught largely off guard. At the battle of Chacabuco (February 12, 1817), a risky and unauthorized cavalry charge by O'Higgins won the day for the patriots and opened the way to Santiago, where an assembly of notables offered the government to San Martín. His mind was now firmly fixed on Peru, and he declined. The only alternative was O'Higgins, who was thus chosen as Supreme Director of the State of Chile. From its first moments the new regime was overwhelmingly occupied with the prosecution of the war. Within nine days of Chacabuco, O'Higgins decreed the formation of a military academy, and by the end of the year the new Army of Chile (nearly 4,800 men) was larger than the Army of the Andes. The royalists, meanwhile, had impregnably fortified themselves on the Talcahuano peninsula and could not be expelled. Abascal's successor as viceroy of Peru now ordered General Osorio to lead yet another expedition to Chile; its arrival at Talcahuano was the signal for a new and powerful royalist offensive. In defiance, and while withdrawing his soldiers to the north once more, O'Higgins took the long overdue step of proclaiming the independence of "the mainland territory of Chile and its adjacent islands" (February 1818).

For a few tense weeks nothing could have seemed less appropriate. At Cancha Rayada, near Talca (March 19, 1818), the royalists fell by night on the patriots; O'Higgins was badly wounded. In Santiago, confusion reigned: a number of patriots even fled across the mountains to Mendoza for a second time. The ex-guerrilla Manuel Rodríguez harangued the people: "We still have a homeland, citizens!" San Martín managed to regroup his mauled troops. On April 5, 1818, he inflicted devastating defeat on Osorio on the plains of Maipó, almost at the gates of Santiago. At the close of the battle there occurred one of those incidents which somehow imprint themselves on the imagination of posterity. Believing the issue to be still in doubt, the wounded O'Higgins galloped on to the scene with reinforcements. "Glory to the savior of Chile!" he exclaimed, embracing San Martín. Overcome with emotion, the great Argentine replied: "Chile will never forget the name of the illustrious invalid who, today, presented himself on the battlefield!" Such was the "embrace of Maipó," never to be forgotten by Chileans.

Maipó was a devastating blow to the Spanish empire. It assured Chile's recently proclaimed independence. But although the heartland was never again threatened, royalist resistance continued in the south, where the cause was taken up by a remarkable guerrilla chief, the cruel and licentious Vicente Benavides. His predatory bands were everywhere. This was a vicious little war of lightning raids, ambushes, the sacking and burning of haciendas, and frequent atrocities; it further devastated the province of Concepción, already the victim of the scorched-earth tactics of both patriot and royalist armies. Benavides was eventually captured while trying to escape to Peru. He was hanged, drawn, and quartered (February 1822). The *guerra a muerte* as it was later called, slowly petered out, not without leaving widespread banditry in its wake. The South long remained troubled.

After Maipó, O'Higgins and San Martín turned their attention to the promised liberation of Peru. A small Chilean naval squadron was assembled: its first commander, Manuel Blanco Encalada, yielded his place at the end of 1818 to no less a figure than Lord Thomas Cochrane, one of the most famous and audacious British naval captains of the time. Driven out of his beloved Royal Navy by a reactionary government, he had been recruited by the new Chilean agent in London. Cochrane quickly struck up a cordial friendship with O'Higgins and an equally cordial loathing for San Martín. His leadership of the squadron in two forays during 1819 won Chile command of the sea; his astonishing capture of royalist-held Valdivia (January 1820) filled patriot hearts with delight. Only the island of Chiloé now remained in Spanish hands.

The emancipation of Peru was to have been a common enterprise by Chile and Argentina; a solemn alliance between the two states was signed in January 1819. But with the shadow of civil war now falling over the River Plate provinces, it fell to Chile to organize and finance (and to a large extent man) the *expedición libertadora*. The remnants of the army of the Andes were fused with the new Chilean Army. The expedition sailed from Valparaiso in August 1820 – some 4,500 soldiers, sixteen troop transports, and seven warships. O'Higgins, watching it leave the bay, perhaps sensed that this was his finest moment; certainly nobody could deny his penurious government the fullest share of credit. The rest of the war, inevitably, was observed from afar. In July 1821 San Martín entered Lima, declared Peru's independence, and was acclaimed as Protector of the new state. But with royalists still in control of much of the Peruvian interior, his triumph was less than complete. In July 1822 he sailed northward to Guayaquil to meet Simón Bolívar, whose brilliant campaigns had recently liberated Venezuela and New Granada from Spanish rule. Following that celebrated interview, San Martín, in a gesture that has been variously interpreted, chose to retire into private life, leaving Bolívar and his Colombian Army to complete the liberation of Peru. Chile played no real part in these later campaigns, which assured the independence of Peru and Bolivia (the old Upper Peru) – but a number of Chilean soldiers were present at Ayacucho (December 1824), the battle which sealed the final doom of the Spanish empire on the American mainland.

The infant Chilean nation's heroic age was now at an end. Even so, it was several years before the outside world took much notice of the new State of Chile. The first countries to extend diplomatic recognition were minor powers like Portugal (August 1821) and the United States (March 1822). Of greater practical importance was the attitude of Great Britain and France. Neither Antonio José de Irisarri nor Mariano Egaña, Chile's envoys in Europe (1819–24 and 1824–26, respectively) made any real headway on this score. In 1824 the British sent consuls to the new Spanish-American states and in 1825 recognized three of them (Mexico, Colombia, Argentina), but not Chile. Doubts about the political stability of the country persisted for several years in the chancelleries of Europe. These attitudes eventually softened. France extended recognition in September 1830; Great Britain intimated its willingness to do the same in July 1831, though the British consul in Santiago did not become chargé d'affaires for another ten years. Spain remained unreconciled to the loss of her former colony until a treaty concluded in April 1844, but for much of the rest of Europe the new Chilean nation-state now existed in theory as well as in fact.

The legacies of revolution

In matters of political belief, and perhaps still more of political hope, independence marks the deepest fault-line in Chilean history. Chilean nationality may have been formed in the colonial era; the modern nation as such dates its birth very precisely from the creole revolution. Chileans' habits of political *behavior* were to be influenced for generations to come by attitudes and practices inherited from the colonial past, but the framework of political *ideas* was now radically transformed. The traditional creole allegiance to the absolute monarchy now vanished, along with the principle of colonial subordination. With Spain's defeat, royalism as a political option could no longer be articulated. Neither was a local form of constitutional monarchy much advocated as a possible framework of government. There were those in Spanish America who thought it might prove a remedy for the problems of the new states. The most eminent of the monarchists, San Martín, even sent a mission to Europe in a vain effort to find a suitable prince to govern Peru. O'Higgins deftly disentangled Chile from all such schemes – which anyway came to nothing. Chile was thus to be a republic (as were all the former Spanish colonies; Agustín de Iturbide's attempt to set up an "empire" in Mexico was short-lived), though not until 1823 did a Chilean constitution use the word.

The new creole political outlook was formed by the standard doctrines of liberalism, derived from the Enlightenment and the American Revolution, and by the powerful fusion of liberalism and nationalism which was the French Revolution's double-edged gift to the world. Such ideas were no doubt imperfectly understood by the great majority, but the attitudes of politicians and writers were transformed by this new framework of discourse. All Chileans in public life now proclaimed their belief in the rights of man ("natural and imprescriptible rights: equality, liberty, security and property," as the 1822 constitution put it), in representative government, in the division of powers, in equality before the law, and in republican virtue. Precisely how far and how fast such principles were to be translated into practice was to be the main agenda of Chilean politics for the rest of the century and beyond.

Nationalism was also a key part of the new outlook. Schemes of Spanish-American union or confederation, it is true, were occasionally mooted during the wars of independence. O'Higgins once expressed the hope that Chile, Peru, and Argentina might some day form a "great confederation similar to that of the United States."[1] Such an arrangement was never even remotely likely. Chileans adopted the outward badges of separate nationality with alacrity. The national flag, in the revised form (red, white, and blue) we know today, was first flown at the independence ceremonies in 1818. The words of the national anthem were written in 1819 and the music a year later – though the words were later replaced, the brisk anti-Spanish sentiments of the first text proving embarrassing when Chile and Spain were reconciled diplomatically in 1844. The national coat of arms went through several versions before assuming its final shape in 1834, with the well-known condor, huemul,[2] and national motto (added in 1910), *Por la razón o la fuerza* ("By right or by might"). The same thing was happening all over Spanish America; the dream of union remained a dream, though frequently invoked.

Dreams were important in this revolutionary period. A new range of emotional public attitudes came into play, some of them persisting well beyond the revolutionary era. The entire Spanish inheritance was now vehemently condemned as reactionary and obscurantist by creole publicists: Spaniards themselves were constantly referred to as *sarracenos* ("saracens") or *godos* ("goths"), nicknames long remembered and sometimes revived. Great Britain, France, and the United States now became the models by which Chilean progress was to be measured; the very notion of "progress" itself was an important component of the revolutionary mystique. *But how could progress best be secured?* The new politicians of the 1820s generally believed that legislation on its own was effective: good laws, above all a good constitution, would automatically work wonders. A definite strand of utopian optimism was attached to the new weave of patriotic sentiment: the national future, it was felt, was bound to be luminous. Certain features of the past, too, were glorious – not least the history of the Araucanians and their long battle against Spanish imperialism – "What are the demi-gods of antiquity alongside our Araucanians?"[3] It was unfortunate that the Frontier was still immovably in place, and that the Mapuche, recalling the treaties struck at the colonial *parlamentos,* had tended to favor the royalists during the war.

Such gaps between fact and fancy were by no means confined to the way creoles now idealized the Araucanians. Given the Chilean social structure, with its small, cohesive upper class and its huge mass of illiterate rural poor, there was bound to be difficulty in introducing the liberal utopia overnight. (And it was not as if France or England or even

---

[1] Simon Collier, *Ideas and Politics of Chilean Independence 1808–1833* (Cambridge, 1967), p. 218.

[2] *Huemul:* type of deer found in Chile and other Andean countries of South America.

[3] *La Clave,* No. 22, October 11, 1827. Unless otherwise indicated, newspapers and magazines cited in the notes were (or are) published in Santiago.

the United States were quite as liberal and democratic as some Chilean ideologues liked to think.) The electoral laws of the period, and for decades afterward, reflected this fact by confining the franchise to a very narrow segment of the population. The political benefits of independence were thus largely restricted to the upper class. For the great mass of the population the new order brought little in the way of immediate improvement in material circumstances, let alone political influence. The revolution in this sense was a conservative revolution, unaccompanied by dramatic change in society.

It is very difficult to see how it could have been different. The stability of the countryside, and the absence of sharply defined ethnic castes, left very little room for the kind of tensions and upheavals felt, for instance, in Mexico – a richer and more complex society – after 1810. The final abolition of slavery (July 1823) was a noble gesture and José Miguel Infante's finest hour, but there were only some 4,000 slaves: Chile was not Peru, still less Brazil. The ending (in several laws) of the separate status of Amerindians was also without practical effect. There were very few indigenous communities north of the Frontier for rapacious landowners to dispossess; it was not yet feasible to invade the well-watered lands of Araucania itself. Chile in this respect was very different from Ecuador, Peru, or Bolivia. In the pursuit of equality before the law, O'Higgins abolished the outward and visible signs of aristocracy: the public display of coats of arms, and titles of nobility (March and September 1817). Yet he was frustrated in his attempt (June 1818) to do away with *mayorazgos*. In fact, these were mostly of symbolic value – cherished by their holders, denounced as "feudal" by reformers. Thirty years later they were abolished without controversy or even very much comment.

The wars of independence enabled some individuals, through military prowess, to move up the social scale. The snobbish creoles of Santiago might have sneered at "the bastard-orphan Riquelme," but had Bernardo O'Higgins left a family, it would have been socially very reputable. Similarly, revolutions often give scope to adventurers who in settled times remain obscure. A few of the Liberals of the 1820s can be seen in this light, contributing a minor note of social radicalism. But at the end of the day, it was the "Basque-Castilian aristocracy" of late-colonial times that moved very firmly into place as the governing class of the new republic, its position strengthened by the revolution.

Thus, despite ideological change, the main social landmarks of colonial times remained as conspicuous as ever. The Church, too, retained its traditional influence, its official status written into the constitutions of the period. True, the flagrantly royalist partisanship of the hierarchy and clergy (with exceptions such as Camilo Henríquez) meant that relations between Church and state after independence were mildly troubled. The bishop of Santiago, Rodríguez Zorrilla, was twice banished – by O'Higgins in 1817, and again in 1824. For its part, the Church did not accept that the new Chilean state had inherited the *patronato,* the old imperial supervisory power. A papal mission to Chile (1824), led by Fr. Giovanni Muzi, tried to negotiate the issue, to no avail: the future of the *patronato* was left in limbo. (The secretary of this mission, Fr. Giovanni Mastai-Ferretti, later became Pope Pius IX. He never forgot the sights and sounds of Chile, as many Chilean visitors to Rome were later to discover.) In the 1820s also, the government interfered with the religious orders and confiscated their somewhat limited properties. Such episodes apart, the underlying power of the Church remained scarcely untouched by the revolution – something noted disapprovingly by those foreign visitors to Chile who happened to be Protestants.

That there were Protestant visitors at all symbolized one of the most far-reaching changes brought by independence: the ending of colonial commercial restrictions. In January 1811, four ports were opened to foreign trade; after the wars, commercial traffic rose very fast, and by the end of the 1820s more than 200 ships were anchoring in Valparaiso each year – more than four times the level of 1810. British, French, American, and other foreign vessels quickly supplanted their Spanish and Peruvian competitors; Chilean vessels, bought from foreigners or constructed in the modest yards at Nueva Bilbao (renamed Constitución in 1828) or Talcahuano, also increased. With the abrupt decline of the previously significant trans-Andean trade, the sea was more than ever Chile's highway to the outside world, and the highway now led in all directions. As a result, the maritime nations of the North Atlantic, starting with Great Britain, gained an importance in Chilean trade they have never since lost.

The value of Chile's external trade roughly doubled between 1810 and the mid-1830s. This heightening of commercial potential had varying implications for the different sectors of the economy. Agriculture, by any standard, was badly disrupted by the wars. Concepción province, in particular, did not really recover until after the 1830s – which saw both the dreadful earthquake that so impressed Charles Darwin and a serious smallpox epidemic a bit later. (As late as 1840 a minister of the Interior publicly noted the slow pace of the southern recovery.) The wars of independence dislocated the traditional grain export to Peru. Alternative markets (Argentina, Brazil, Uruguay) were no real substitute. The growing demand for ship's provisions at Valparaiso and other ports coupled with a general rise in the price of pastoral produce meant that agricultural exports rose in value by the 1830s, but only modestly.

The northern mines were altogether less affected by warfare. Indeed, they flourished in the new commercial climate. Helped by new discoveries at Agua Amarga, near Vallenar (1811), and Arqueros, near Coquimbo

(1825), silver production probably doubled between 1810 and 1830. Smuggling (to evade official restrictions on specie export) persisted, and an exact figure is thus hard to estimate – perhaps 100 metric tons per year at the end of the 1820s. Copper, for which there was growing international demand, was also mined on a much larger scale than previously, much of it sent for a few years to British India and China. Three companies were formed in London to exploit this apparent mining bonanza. But their engineers and machines did not adapt well to the conditions of the Norte Chico, where traditional Chilean mining methods proved far more effective. Of the three companies, only one survived to rebuild its fortunes in later years.

The newly arrived British consul, reporting in 1825, described Chile's trade as generally "steady and profitable."[4] A first rush of imports reached its peak in 1820–21, but the limited Chilean market was soon saturated, as it was so often in late-colonial times. By the mid-1820s, imports ran at around twice the level of 1810, rising again in the 1830s. The trading community itself, clustering in fast-growing Valparaiso (seat of the main customs-house after 1820), became markedly cosmopolitan: the abrupt departure of Spanish traders gave new opportunities for Chileans and foreigners alike. Chileans were by no means inconspicuous – men such as O'Higgins's protegé Felipe Santiago del Solar, who won the supply contract for the Peruvian expedition, or Diego Antonio Barros, father of Chile's greatest historian, or the already well-established Agustín de Eyzaguirre, who in 1819 formed the first real Chilean shipping company and dispatched cargoes of copper to Calcutta. The new foreign traders had little of the political and family influence of such men, but their superior connections to the North Atlantic trading world gave them an edge over their local competitors. Foreigners came either as individual merchants trying their luck, or as representatives of overseas trading houses establishing offices in Chile, a classic example here being Antony Gibbs & Sons, a British firm which opened its Valparaiso branch in 1822. The foreigners did not have it all their own way: they were a long way from home, they could easily misjudge the market, and their merchandise was handled on a risky consignment basis. Those that stayed the course were able to win local respectability. John James Barnard, first secretary of the British traders' association at Valparaiso (1819), was consulted by the government on commercial matters. Joshua Waddington, who arrived in Chile in 1818, soon became a man of substance, the head of one of the largest consignment firms, and the owner of the finest estate in the

---

[4] C. R. Nugent to George Canning, March 17, 1825. R. A. Humphreys, ed., *British Consular Reports on the Trade and Politics of Latin America 1824–1826*. Camden 3rd Series, Vol. LXIII (London, 1940), p. 933.

Aconcagua Valley. His son Guillermo was the first Chilean cabinet minister with an English surname (1852).

Chilean traders sometimes viewed this influx of foreigners with alarm, even complaining on occasion through the no longer very influential Consulado. Other creoles adopted the strategy of forming partnerships with the newcomers, as in the case of the long-running firm of Juan Antonio Santa María and George Lyon. Sometimes, of course, the foreigners themselves settled permanently in Chile and founded Chilean dynasties. The most celebrated example, undoubtedly, was that of George Edwards, an English ship's doctor who settled in the Norte Chico in 1807. His own business ventures were never very successful, but one of his grandsons was the richest man in Chile.

With Great Britain entering her century of global hegemony, the discernible British presence in the new Chilean nation was hardly surprising. For the next ninety years, warships of the Royal Navy's South American Squadron were more often than not stationed off Valparaiso. Their commanders enjoyed generally good relations with the Chilean authorities. But the new influences playing on Chilean (especially upper-class) life were neither exclusively British nor exclusively commercial. France was beginning to exert her cultural sway, not least through imported reading matter. Some of the new buildings in Valparaiso (whose population rose to around 20,000 by 1830) reflected foreign architectural styles. Upper-class women adopted a few European fashions, while among both women and men tea began to replace the more traditional *mate* as a popular drink. Foreigners also played a part in the limited educational and cultural improvements of the time, some of them banding together in 1828 to form a philharmonic society in Santiago – the precursor of other notable societies of this kind. (One wholly delightful import of the 1820s which owed nothing to Europeans was a dance known at first as the *zamacueca* and later on simply as the *cueca*. It came from Peru: for whatever reason, Chileans took it to their hearts and eventually made it their own national dance.)

Since customs revenues were now increasingly important, the patriot governments were strongly interested in developing trade. The decree of 1811 imposed what amounted to a 30 percent *ad valorem* tariff on most imports. O'Higgins raised this much higher in 1817, 1818, and 1822, but the general trend of tariffs over the period as a whole was downward, although governments also tried to protect domestic economic activity, without much effect. Colonial neo-mercantilism still provided the inescapable framework for economic ideas. Foreigners were prohibited from entering the retail trade, but this was a dead letter in Valparaiso and even (to a lesser extent) in Santiago. Foreigners were also excluded from the coasting trade (*cabotaje*), though here again this went largely unenforced.

The protectionist impulse, however strong, had to be reconciled with the state's need for revenue at a time (we must remember) of administrative dislocation.

The dilemma was naturally compounded by the wars themselves. Here, O'Higgins's achievement was little short of heroic. By a variety of emergency methods (including the seizure of royalist assets and what amounted to forced loans) he raised public revenues to levels (2.3 million pesos in 1818 and again in 1822) which they were not to reach again for fifteen years. He even managed to keep the public debt within reasonable bounds; his successors were less effective. In 1822, through the Chilean agent Antonio José de Irisarri, O'Higgins also contracted a loan for £1 million in London. Opinion in political circles was hostile, but O'Higgins overrode all opposition. Part of this money (only £675,000 in effective capital) was immediately re-loaned to newly independent Peru, a gesture of solidarity that brought little but trouble. In Chile itself there was trouble enough as a result of the London loan. With falling customs revenues from declining trade, the government found it impossible to service the debt. In return for a contract to do so, it transferred the *estanco,* the lucrative state tobacco monopoly, to a Valparaiso trading house run by Diego Portales and José Manuel Cea. This was no solution: the strong-arm methods Portales and Cea had to use to enforce the monopoly (itself always unpopular) won widespread hostility; nor were they able to meet the repayments. In September 1826 the contract was abruptly rescinded. The affair of the *estanco* became one of the noisiest issues of the decade. The aggrieved Portales turned his attention to politics. There was much for him to consider.

The quest for political order, 1817–30

All over Spanish America, in the 1820s, the early hopes raised by independence were brutally shattered by episodes of confusion and bloodshed. Chile conformed to the common pattern, but in milder fashion. The first new government, the Supreme Directorship of Bernardo O'Higgins, lasted six years. "If ever there was a Good Patriot and an Honest Man it is O'Higgins,"[5] wrote an unlettered but eloquent Englishman serving in the new Chilean navy. Others saw him as rather lacking in guile. Remembering the patriot squabbles of 1810–14, he was convinced that Chile needed a period of firm rule – authoritarian, but not arbitrary. (The nominated Senate created by the brief provisional constitution of 1818 proved quite capable of questioning the Supreme Director's actions.) In this sense, O'Higgins was a reluctant dictator. He seems to have been

---

[5] John Spry to John Thomas, January 13, 1824. Archivo Nacional, Santiago: Archivo Vicuña Mackenna, Vol. 88, fo. 80–1 (O'Higgins papers).

genuinely interested in improving the lot of his fellow Chileans, not least the poor. "If they will not become happy by their own efforts," he once burst out, "they shall be made happy by force. By God! they *shall* be happy!"[6] He naturally (almost as a matter of course) restored the Instituto Nacional and the National Library. Like his father the viceroy, O'Higgins had a strong practical streak. He himself sketched out the plans (1818) for the new poplar-flanked main avenue of Santiago, by the mid-nineteenth century a very agreeable boulevard, later to bear his name. His regime also saw the completion of the Maipó (San Carlos) Canal, an old colonial irrigation project to the east and south of Santiago. Its waters still rush into the Mapocho.

As long as the war continued, the upper class accepted and applauded O'Higgins's authoritarian rule. After 1820, however, it became more restive. O'Higgins's handful of anti-aristocratic measures, already mentioned, were undoubtedly irritants. The personalist nature of the regime precluded wider upper-class participation in government. O'Higgins's circle of intimates tended to consist of fellow soldiers and helpful traders (some of them foreign); the Santiago elite could never quite see this Frontier landowner as one of its own. Some of O'Higgins's measures toward the Church (permission granted for a foreign Protestant cemetery, the prohibition of burial in churches, interference with ecclesiastical discipline) provoked predictable disquiet. There were more specific complaints. In the early years of the regime, with San Martín still much in evidence, there was suspicion of O'Higgins's Argentine connections; he was certainly a member of the shadowy "Lautaro Lodge," the semi-masonic secret society founded by San Martín. More seriously, he was also blamed for the violent ends which befell some of his main adversaries. Carrera's brothers Juan José and Luis, on their way to Chile to foment revolt, were shot at Mendoza in April 1818. (O'Higgins in fact pleaded for clemency, but too late.) The guerrilla chief Manuel Rodríguez – a turbulent spirit who once reputedly told O'Higgins, "If I were a ruler and couldn't find anyone to start a revolt against me, I would start one myself!" – was murdered six weeks later, having led one disturbance too many. O'Higgins's arch-foe, José Miguel Carrera, survived somewhat longer. He never returned to Chile, and plunged with fierce abandon into the provincial warfare then raging in Argentina. He, too, was eventually captured and shot, like his brothers at Mendoza (September 1821).

After five years in power, O'Higgins decided to introduce a full constitution. Largely written by his deeply unpopular minister José Antonio Rodríguez Aldea, it tactlessly included provisions enabling O'Higgins to stay in office for another ten years. This was unacceptable to upper-class opinion. A severe earthquake in Valparaiso (November 1822)

---

[6] John Miers, *Travels in Chile and La Plata*, 2 vols. (London, 1826), II, 36–37.

gave the clergy a chance to denounce the foreign heretics so clearly to
blame for the catastrophe and so notoriously favored by the Supreme
Director. The final blow to the regime was struck by General Ramón
Freire, the Intendant of Concepción. He had borne the brunt of the
vicious *guerra a muerte,* and his province was still prostrate after nine years
of war and banditry. Freire's pronunciamiento against the "monstrous
foetus" of the new constitution (November 1822) was the signal for the
northern province, Coquimbo, to follow suit. (Lord Cochrane, then on
the point of leaving Chile, refused to be drawn into the conflict.) The
inevitable conspiracy was soon hatched in Santiago. On January 28, 1823,
in one of the classic scenes of Chilean history, O'Higgins agreed to
abdicate. Six months later a British warship took him into exile in Peru.
He never returned to Chile. In 1824 he accompanied Simón Bolívar
during the final campaign for Peruvian independence, but was not given
a command. He spent much of his remaining years at Montalván (an
estate in the Cañete Valley given him by Peru), dying in Lima in October
1842. Not until 1869 were his remains taken back to Santiago, where
they long rested in a marble sarcophagus beneath the tall trees of the
General Cemetery he himself had founded. (In 1979 the tomb was
transferred to a new and rather ugly mausoleum in the main square.) For
Chileans he remains and will always remain quite simply the Liberator,
the father of his country, the supreme national hero.

O'Higgins's successor as Supreme Director, inevitably, was the victorious Freire. "His countenance," wrote an English clergyman who met him
soon afterward, "bespeaks great mildness and benevolence."[7] It was a fair
impression. Freire was a tolerant, liberal-minded soldier, eager to please
the contentious politicians who surrounded him, their contentiousness
enhanced by the growth of a flourishing tradition of polemical journalism: between 1823 and 1830 over a hundred "newspapers" (many very
ephemeral) were printed. The new climate also allowed free play to
factionalism in the small political class. For the moment it was the
self-styled Liberals who were center-stage, their Conservative opponents
tending (with certain exceptions) to remain in the wings.

For the next few years Chile drifted gently from one political experiment to the next. The first and most improbable of these was the
Constitution of 1823. Its author, Juan Egaña, was one of the two or three
best-read creole intellectuals of the time. He had probably read (and
written) far too much. His moralistic conservatism (based on an extreme
admiration for ancient Greece and Rome, the Incas, and imperial China)
struck a somewhat discordant note at a time of mounting liberalism. The

---

[7] [Hugh Salvin], *Journal written on board of His Majesty's Ship Cambridge from January 1824 to May
1827* (Newcastle, 1829), p. 130.

constitution was far too complex to be applied to Chile (or anywhere else), but neither the congress which abrogated it (December 1824) nor its successor the following year (boycotted by Concepción and Coquimbo) contributed anything new to the quest for new institutions. In October 1825 Freire dissolved by force what was left of congress and set off to liberate the island of Chiloé, where he had been repulsed the previous year by the talented royalist commander, Colonel Antonio de Quintanilla. This time the patriots succeeded: in January 1826 Quintanilla surrendered, and the last Spanish forces on Chilean soil withdrew.

By the time Freire returned from Chiloé a new fashion was enrapturing Liberal politicians. The man of the moment was José Miguel Infante, now obsessed with the idea of federalism. Under his sway, the constituent congress of 1826 introduced elected assemblies in the provinces[8] and debated a draft federal constitution. The moment was hardly ideal for such radical changes. Intermittent local disturbances, and growing indiscipline in the army had combined to create an atmosphere of uncertainty. Congressional hostility to the executive (regarded as a sacred duty by Liberals) was at its height. Neither of Freire's two successors as President (the title of Supreme Director now lapsed) could stand the pressure. In January 1827, Colonel Enrique Campino, the ringleader of the most scandalous mutiny of this agitated time, rode his horse into congress in order to terrify the deputies, most of whom were duly terrified. General Freire briefly returned to power to restore a semblance of order.

It was clear by now (to the politicians at least) that yet another constituent congress was needed – the fourth in five years. With the help of a distinguished Spanish Liberal, José Joaquín de Mora, it produced a new constitution (August 1828), an elegant document long admired in retrospect by Chilean Liberals. It retained the federalist-inspired provincial assemblies, few of which were functioning effectively. General Francisco Antonio Pinto, the new President, was a generous, philosophical man, eager to consolidate a stable Liberal regime. With a prominent Conservative, Francisco Ruiz Tagle, as his finance minister, and with support from General Joaquín Prieto, commander of the all-important Concepción garrison, his chances seemed excellent. Unfortunately for Pinto, the Liberals themselves (*pipiolos,* "novices," as they were nicknamed) continued to engage in factionalism, while the federalist fiasco had stiffened the Conservative opposition.

In fact partisan bitterness showed every sign of running out of con-

---

[8] In addition to Santiago and Concepción (the colonial intendancies) and Coquimbo, the first "new" province (1811), the government created five additional provinces in January 1826: Aconcagua, Colchagua, Maule, Valdivia, and Chiloé. A dozen or so more were established later, as a result of both territorial expansion and subdivision.

trol – as was to happen on a number of future occasions in the republic's history. The anti-aristocratic and anticlerical rhetoric of some *pipiolos* and the *de facto* abolition of *mayorazgos* in the 1828 Constitution offended the traditionally minded Conservatives – the *pelucones,* "big wigs," as they were termed by Liberals. The followers of the exiled O'Higgins (General Prieto included) dreamed of an authoritarian restoration, and were doubt-less irritated by the solemn repatriation of the remains of the Carrera brothers (June 1828). The fiercest opposition, however, came from a third group, the so-called *estanqueros,* politicians associated with the ill-fated *estanco* contract and led by Diego Portales. Their strident and simple demand was for strong government, and an end to disorder. *Pelucones, o'higginistas,* and *estanqueros* alike were eager to uproot the delicate flower of Liberalism. The most numerous and respectable section of the upper class clearly favored a less adventurous approach in matters of govern-ment.

President Pinto had no real stomach for the fight he knew was coming, and withdrew from office. The pretext for the inevitable showdown was provided in September 1829, by an irregularity in the election of a vice president by the Liberal-dominated congress. In Concepción, General Prieto ordered his army to march northward. In Santiago, the Liberal regime gradually disintegrated in confusion, no longer able to control the course of events. In mid-December the Liberal ("Constitutional") army fought an indecisive action with Prieto's troops at Ochagavía, a few miles from Santiago. This resulted in a truce, and General Freire was invited to take command of both armies. The deal was short-lived. In January 1830, resentful over the Conservatives' tightening grip on government, Freire broke with Prieto and left Santiago, rallying the Liberal army at Valpa-raiso. This was a fatal decision, for the Conservatives quickly consolidated their hold on power. Their hastily convened "Congress of Plenipotentiar-ies" annulled all the acts of the 1829 congress; the *pelucón* Francisco Ruiz Tagle became President; and on April 6, 1830, Diego Portales, who had thrown in his lot with the Conservative army as it neared Santiago, took over two of the three ministries, thus establishing himself as the most powerful figure of the new regime.

Eleven days later, not far from the confluence of the Lircay and Claro rivers, near Talca, Freire's army of some 1,700 men succumbed to Prieto's superior strength. Upward of 200 men were killed in the action. Only in retrospect, of course, was Lircay seen as one of the truly decisive battles of Chilean history. But so it was to prove. It was more than thirty years before the defeated Liberals even partially returned to power in a Chile that by then looked rather different.

3

The conservative settlement, 1830–41

If one day I took up a stick and gave tranquillity to the country it was only so that the bastards and whores of Santiago would let me get on with my work in peace.

– Diego Portales (1831)

The Conservative coalition that took power in 1830 was the first of three successive political combinations that governed Chile over the next six decades. Its twenty-seven-year lease on power helped lay the foundations of a tradition of political stability unique in nineteenth-century Spanish America – where mutinous armies, caudillo dictatorships, palace revolutions, and civil wars were constant and commonplace. Thanks to this tradition, as Tulio Halperín has observed, Chile came to enjoy "unrivalled political prestige among the Spanish American republics."[1]

There was nothing inevitable about this. Chile's unusual tradition was created by Chileans, not gods. Yet the ex-colony did possess certain built-in advantages from the viewpoint of consolidating a viable nation-state, and, at the risk of recrossing ground already covered, it is worth reminding ourselves of some of them. Post-colonial Chile was a compact, manageable land, with no more than 700 miles separating the northern limit of settlement from the Araucanian Frontier along the Bío Bío, and with the bulk of the population concentrated in the northern Central Valley. The settlements farther south, around Valdivia and on the island of Chiloé, were unimportant appendages of the new republic, as was (to look ahead a bit) the penal colony established on the Magellan Straits after 1843, partly to confirm the Chilean claim to the area. All constitutions from 1822 onward had mentioned Cape Horn as the southern extremity of the country.

There were roughly one million Chileans in 1830. Over the next forty years the population doubled, the fourth national census (1875) giving a possibly conservative total of 2,075,971. This was not a large population, and in many respects it was homogeneous. As we have seen, few if

[1] *The Aftermath of Independence in Spanish America* (New York, 1973), p. 14.

51

any Amerindians survived in separate communities north of Araucanian territory. The small black-mulatto trace in the population effectively vanished within a few decades of the abolition of slavery. Chile was thus essentially a land where the small creole upper class coexisted with the great mass of the laboring poor, mostly mestizo and mostly rural. The rural poor remained a largely passive factor in society and politics until well into the twentieth century. This simple social structure was not complicated by sharp divisions of economic interest within the upper class. Nor was regional diversity of much significance by the standards of Colombia, Argentina, or Mexico. The outlying northern and southern provinces may have felt neglected by Santiago (and regional feeling at times ran strong), but they were ultimately unable to counterbalance the hegemony of the capital and its rich hinterland. The two armed rebellions of the 1850s were to show this very clearly. Concepción, whose military edge was vital in the overthrow of O'Higgins in 1823 and of the Liberals in 1829–30, was not able to repeat the exercise in 1851. Similarly, the northern rebellions in 1851 and 1859, despite brief success, were to no avail against a determined government.

Do we need much more in the way of further hypothesis to explain the apparent smoothness with which Chile was stabilized after 1830? Perhaps not. The much admired national "idiosyncrasy" of (generally) orderly and civilized politics certainly stemmed in part from a convenient geographical and social endowment. It nonetheless had to be created, and it was. As always, the human factor was vital.

Diego Portales

There is undoubtedly a case for seeing Diego Portales (he was 37 in 1830) as the key figure of the Conservative settlement. He was later transformed by his admirers into what a writer of the 1870s (perhaps echoing the famous line in *Romeo and Juliet*) called "the demi-god of our mythology or political idolatry."[2] Modern scholars have rightly reacted against this kind of semi-deification. Portales was no demi-god. His very distinctive character – sardonic, highly strung, charming, and domineering by turns – was only too fascinatingly human. He was the son of a distinguished patriot and cousin to the head of the Larraín family. His personal vocation lay in commerce: the six or seven hundred surviving letters from his pen give a vivid picture of the day-to-day concerns of a Valparaiso trader of the 1820s and 1830s. Away from his business, he was a devotee of light-hearted sociability, fond of guitar-playing and

---

[2] Justo Arteaga Alemparte, "Los candidatos en candelero" [1876], in *"Diógenes" y otros escritos*, ed. Ricardo Donoso (Santiago, 1956), p. 408.

female company. The public face was very different: the sarcastic hedonist became the austere servant of the state. His political ideas were simple. "A strong, centralizing government whose members are genuine examples of virtue and patriotism" – such was the ideal he sketched to his business partner Cea in March 1822.[3] He had no very exalted opinion of the "Basque-Castilian" elite to which he belonged. "Nobody," he once complained, "wants to live without the support of the white elephant of government."[4] Nonetheless, the "families of rank" were the only class available for the task of governing the republic.

Once Portales became minister (holding the two portfolios of Interior and External Affairs, and War and Navy), nobody was allowed to stand in his way. Even before assuming office he secured the removal of the excessively conciliatory first *pelucón* president, Francisco Ruiz Tagle (his own cousin), in favor of the more compliant José Tomás Ovalle. When Colonel (later General) José María de la Cruz, a veteran of Chacabuco and Maipó, proved too independent as a new minister of War and Navy, Portales edged him aside. President Ovalle's untimely death in March 1831 (a new town in the Norte Chico was named after him) gave the minister a chance to neutralize the still hopeful *o'higginistas* by elevating their principal figure, General Prieto, to the presidency.

In August 1831, after sixteen months in office, Portales relinquished the Interior ministry (retaining War and Navy for one further year) and retired to Valparaiso, where he remained, acting for a while as governor of the port, until 1834, when he moved to the countryside to try his hand at farming. Yet even in retirement from politics, he remained the most powerful figure in the country. In April 1832, dissatisfied with the incumbent Interior minister, he maneuvered an old friend, Joaquín Tocornal, into the position. "Portales," sourly wrote an *o'higginista*, "has got a million people in his pocket."[5] His aversion to holding high office (as distinct from power) seems to have been genuine enough. He could have had the presidency for the asking, but never asked. This in itself could well have helped to inhibit the development of a caudillo tradition in Chile. Whether it did or not, no such tradition ever really took root.

The impact of firm government was unmistakable after April 1830. One of Portales's first acts as minister was to cashier 136 army officers who had supported Freire in the civil war. The name of ex-president Pinto was rather spitefully added to the list a few weeks later. Such stern

[3] Letter of March 1822. Ernesto de la Cruz and Guillermo Feliú Cruz, eds., *Epistolario de don Diego Portales*, 3 vols. (Santiago, 1937), I, 177.

[4] To Antonio Garfías, December 10, 1831. Cruz and Feliú Cruz, I, 353.

[5] Ramón Mariano de Aris to Bernardo O'Higgins, December 9, 1832. Benjamín Vicuña Mackenna, *D. Diego Portales,* 3rd ed. (Santiago, 1974), p. 86.

treatment of the military was unprecedented. Persecution of the *pipiolos* now became the order of the day. The lively if opinionated press of the Liberal years soon withered away, though *El Mercurio,* the Valparaiso newspaper founded in 1827, survived (not for the last time) by judicious adaptation. The inevitable Liberal conspiracies (some hatched by the cashiered army officers) were swiftly uprooted and the ringleaders punished. The government evinced a harsh attitude toward crime, and made new efforts to suppress banditry, still rife in the south. Early in 1832, in the mountains near Chillán, General Manuel Bulnes finally hunted down the redoubtable bandit brothers, Juan Antonio and Pablo Pincheira, whose raids had inspired terror since the mid-1820s. Meanwhile, the Conservative politicians of Santiago were piecing together the political system whose subsequent staying power was to be so remarkable. We must now look at this.

The Conservative political settlement

The Conservatives were accused at the time (and even more later on) of having mounted a "colonial reaction," of having destroyed the hopeful revolution set in motion in 1810. Portales himself saw Chile as a land where "social order" was "maintained by the weight of the night"[6] – by which he seems to have meant tradition and inertia. The republic had to find a framework of legitimacy comparable to that of the Spanish empire, a framework which had to be strictly imposed until respect for authority, shaken by the upheavals of independence, once again became a habit – another of Portales's graphic phrases called this "the mainspring of the machine."[7] It was obviously impossible to revert to monarchy. What was needed, therefore, was a fusion of colonial authoritarianism with the outward forms of republican constitutionalism. Such a system, Portales himself maintained, would be capable, eventually, of leading in a more genuinely liberal direction. Here he was not far wrong.

The formal institutions of the new regime were laid down in the Constitution of 1833. A "grand constituent convention" was summoned in the spring of 1831 to reform the 1828 Constitution. It entrusted the task to a small committee, and on reassembling in October 1832 examined a number of alternative drafts. (Portales himself seems to have taken almost no interest in the matter.) The most influential of these was submitted by Mariano Egaña, son of Juan Egaña, a corpulent *pelucón* popularly known as "Lord Callampa" ("Lord Mushroom"). His most

---

[6] To Joaquín Tocornal, July 16, 1832. Cruz and Feliú Cruz, II, 228.
[7] To Garfías, May 14, 1832. Cruz and Feliú Cruz, II, 203.

extreme ideas (including indefinite re-eligibility of the president, and a hereditary senate) were disallowed. One of those consulted about the final version was Andrés Bello, the eminent Venezuelan polymath who had settled in Chile in 1829. The new constitution went into effect in May 1833. It was not amended at all for thirty-eight years; not until 1891 was there a breakdown in its regular operations.

The constitution was strongly presidentialist. The president (elected indirectly, in the American manner) was allowed two consecutive five-year terms – this in practice led to the four "decennial" administrations of 1831–71. Presidential powers over the cabinet, judiciary, public administration, and armed forces were very extensive. (Nineteenth-century cabinets were small, with the four ministers of Interior-External Relations, Finance, War-Navy, and Justice-Education-Religion between 1837 and 1871, when a separate foreign ministry was created.) The executive also held considerable emergency powers: Congress could vote "extraordinary faculties," effectively suspending the constitution and civil liberties, and if Congress was in recess (most of the year, in practice) the president could decree states of siege in specific provinces, subject to later congressional approval – never denied. Emergency powers in one form or other were in force for approximately one-third of the period between 1833 and 1861.

Formally speaking, executive control over the legislative branch was substantial but far from absolute. A presidential veto could in theory be overridden by a two-thirds majority in the Senate and Chamber of Deputies. The Congress was also given the power to vote the British-style "periodic laws": approval of the budget (annually) and taxation and the military establishment (every eighteen months). In theory, therefore, a hostile Congress (an unlikely prospect, for reasons to be noted) was able to deny funding to the president. In due course this was attempted, but without explosive consequences before the crisis of 1890. These congressional powers eventually gave rise to a wholesale "parliamentary" reinterpretation of the constitution, as we shall see. But until the 1860s and 1870s, leaving aside a handful of memorably agitated sessions, congressional life was rather low key and often dull, with short and sometimes inquorate sittings. In the year 1838 Congress did not meet at all. The "parliamentary anaemia" of this period was real enough.

The 1833 Constitution was markedly centralist. Gone were the federalist-inspired provincial assemblies of 1828. The provincial Intendant, appointed by the president, was now defined as his "natural and immediate agent" (a phrase retained in the 1925 and 1980 Constitutions). The provincial intendancies were in many ways the nexus of local administration. The Intendants and their subaltern *subdelegados* and *gobernadores* (the colonial terms remained in use) were given absolute veto powers over the elected municipal councils. The hegemony of Santiago was thus reinforced, at the expense of local initiative.

The Conservative settlement, needless to say, did not rest exclusively on the 1833 Constitution. It depended even more perhaps on certain well-tried political techniques and methods. Straightforward repression (and not merely during times of emergency powers) was a recurrent theme for thirty years. By the more advanced standards of our own era, it was not unduly savage. Leaving aside its use (not extensive) as a criminal sanction, the death penalty was normally applied in cases (e.g., military mutinies) where the opposition turned to violence, and usually only a handful of ringleaders were shot. Imprisonment, internal exile ("relegation"), or banishment were the standard penalties for active dissidence. After the mutiny of June 1837, a moment of great danger for the regime, ten men were executed, sixteen relegated to Juan Fernández, others banished, and still others reduced to the ranks. (Just after the mutiny the Intendant of Aconcagua had eleven refractory militiamen shot, but this cruel episode, long remembered, was not typical.) Adversaries of the regime sometimes agreed to go into voluntary exile, depositing bonds with the government for surety – a kind of gentlemen's agreement.

The military restiveness and indiscipline of the 1820s had not boded well for stability. Portales undertook a serious reorganization of the country's militias. By the middle of 1831 the national (also known as the civic) guard numbered around 25,000. It more than doubled later on. Portales himself was a punctilious battalion commander in both Santiago and Valparaiso. The national guard was officered from the upper class, its rank and file recruited from artisans, small-time traders, and others of modest condition. Portales saw their regular Sunday drills as "moralizing" measures. The Argentine Domingo Sarmiento, writing at the end of the 1840s, suggested (interestingly) that the national guard had "helped powerfully to create the Chilean nationality."[8] The *cívicos* were a credible counterweight to the regular army (rarely larger than 3,000 prior to the War of the Pacific), and twice they helped save the regime from overthrow, in June 1837 and April 1851. They had one further function of supreme importance: they enabled the government to win elections.

Here in fact we come to one of the secrets of nineteenth-century Chilean stability: electoral "intervention," the wholesale fixing of elections by the executive. Not that it was a secret: all opposition parties without exception denounced it vehemently right through to 1891. This particular feature of the Conservative settlement long outlasted the

---

[8] "De las instituciones militares en Chile," *La Crónica,* No. 38, October 14, 1849.

hegemony of the Conservative party. The two governing combinations that followed were no less skilled in these manipulative arts. It was a Liberal president who, when asked in 1871 by a Conservative minister whether Chile would ever have "real" elections, replied: "Never. . . . Your trouble is that your head is in the clouds."[9] It was another Liberal president who wrote in 1885: "I have been called an interventionist. I am. . . . I want an efficient, disciplined parliament that will collaborate with the government's hopes for the public good.'[10] For the sixty years after 1830, therefore, Congress was for the most part chosen by the executive. The president, to use a phrase familiar in the 1860s, was the Great Elector.

His "electorate" was very small. The electoral law of 1833 imposed strict property qualifications for voters, but spread the net wide enough to include artisans and craftsmen – many of whom, as we have noted, served in the militias.[11] Literacy was a further qualification, but this rule was not applied (largely to swell the government vote) until the early 1840s. In the congressional elections of 1846 some 24,000 votes were cast (3,000 for the opposition). Eighteen years later (1864) the total was actually 2,000 votes lower. By the mid-1870s around 80,000 men were entitled to vote, though only 30,000 or so did so in the presidential contest of 1876. We doubt whether retrospective psephology can tell us much about nineteenth-century Chilean voting behavior: it is quite impossible to estimate what proportion of the figures cited was accounted for by fraud.

A full catalogue of the various kinds of intervention would make interminable if picturesque reading. The system lent itself to abuse at every stage. Voters registered toward the end of the year prior to an election, and were issued with registration certificates popularly known as *calificaciones*. These were presented at the voting tables in each parish at election time (March for congressional, June for presidential elections). Polling took place over two days, allowing the government time to estimate its position and take remedial measures when necessary. The fundamental strategy for both government and opposition (when it fought) was to amass as large a quantity of *calificaciones* as possible. Government officials were naturally expected to vote correctly. National guard commanders sometimes "took care" of their men's certificates until polling day, when the *cívicos* were marched to the tables to do their

[9] Abdón Cifuentes, *Memorias,* 2 vols. (Santiago, 1936), II, 69–70.

[10] Domingo Santa María to Pedro Pablo Figueroa, September 8, 1885. F. A. Encina and Leopoldo Castedo, *Resumen de la historia de Chile,* 8th ed., 3 vols. (Santiago, 1970), III, 1987.

[11] In Santiago province the qualification was a property worth 1,000 pesos, a working capital of 2,000 pesos, or a trade or craft yielding 200 pesos a year. Lower scales applied in other provinces. The voting age was 21 for married men, 25 for bachelors. Women, of course, did not vote.

republican duty. The national guard was thus an appreciable factor in every election. This largely explains the periodic efforts by the opposition to influence (sometimes through specially tailored newssheets) or mobilize the artisanate. But there were any number of means (personation, intimidation, temporary arrest, bribery) to prevent opposition voters from casting their votes. Where it could, the opposition responded in kind: in the more animated elections, *calificaciones* were bought and sold with commercial fervor, their market value rising and falling as the day went on.

By no means all elections were actually contested. In seven out of the eleven congressional elections between 1833 and 1864 the opposition either abstained or scarcely bothered to fight. On these occasions the machinery worked smoothly and silently and the government's triumphs were overwhelming. Prior to each election the government's lists of official candidates was dispatched to the Intendants, who were expected to mobilize their subaltern agents. How they did so varied from place to place. In 1850, the minister of the Interior was told that in Valdivia it was normal for the Intendant to visit his subordinates, "to greet them with warm signs of appreciation, to shake them warmly by the hand, to offer them a cigar and a glass of wine – they like this a lot, as they normally drink *chicha*."[12] Delivering the vote was a vital aspect of the Intendant's work. In 1849 Manuel Blanco Encalada, then Intendant of Valparaiso, allowed the national guards to vote as they wished. The opposition won. Blanco Encalada was subsequently vilified in the government press. Yet Intendants could at times go too far in the other direction. Elections were occasionally disallowed in Congress. When (also in 1849) the young Intendant of Colchagua, Domingo Santa María, interpreted the president's instructions to win the election "at all costs" a trifle too enthusiastically, this was seized on by his enemies as the pretext for his dismissal. Thirty years later he became the Liberal president whose views on disciplined congresses were quoted earlier.

With the Senate chosen on a single national list by an electoral college, the efforts of an opposition had in practice to focus on the directly elected Chamber of Deputies. Here, by dint of hard work and local influence, it was possible to elect a handful of deputies, though not until the 1860s was it more than a handful, and even after the 1860s never a majority. It should be added, however, that the Great Elector took reasonable pains to select able congressmen. The holding of a public job and congressional membership were not yet incompatible; some of the most competent public servants thus played a part in legislation. Andrés Bello, for instance, served three useful terms (twenty-seven years) in the Senate.

---

[12] Juan Miguel Riesco to Antonio Varas, November 20, 1850. *Correspondencia de Antonio Varas*, 5 vols. (Santiago, 1918–29), III, 245.

Over and above its more down-to-earth methods, the Conservative regime of the 1830s did what it could to enlist support from the Church. "You believe in God," Portales is said to have told Mariano (in some versions Juan) Egaña; "I believe in priests." The limited anticlericalism of the 1820s was reversed; their properties were returned (or compensation paid) to the religious orders (September 1830). From August 1832 the president and cabinet again attended important religious ceremonies, and at certain festivals the National Guard was on hand to spread the Chilean flag in the dust as a carpet for the priest bearing the sacred host. (President Prieto, a pious man, took this seriously. His successor did not, and many such practices were quietly abandoned in the 1840s.) Portales also established censorship of the theater and for imported books: one of its first victims was a novel by Madame de Staël. Book censorship was strongly criticized by Andrés Bello, and it rapidly became a dead letter, though the relevant committee remained in existence until 1878.

Somewhat after this, the government acted to regularize Chile's still somewhat anomalous ecclesiastical status by proposing to the Pope the creation of a new archdiocese of Santiago, independent of Peru, along with two new sees (Coquimbo and Chiloé). The first archbishop of Santiago, Manuel Vicuña, was installed in 1841. The whole tangled question of the *patronato* was for the moment discreetly sidestepped by simple procedural formulas. For the time being, Church and state found a modus vivendi to the advantage of both. This remained true until the 1850s, and could well account for the absence of a distinctive clerical strand in Conservative thought, such as it was, before the political realignment of 1857–58.

The political settlement we have outlined here clearly had its harsher side. For three decades it was operated in a definitely authoritarian spirit, much resented by virtually all the country's livelier imaginations. It was fundamentally a pragmatic creation. Doctrinaire reactionaries like Mariano Egaña contributed something, certainly, but most intelligent Conservatives seem to have taken a more instinctive view of their role. An article in the newspaper *El Orden* in 1845 contained a limpid and almost Burkean expression of the basic Conservative approach.

There are in nations certain habits, prejudices and facts to which there is much attachment, and only the slow and gradual action of civilization can make them disappear. If one tries to uproot them by force, a perilous reaction can supervene . . . The Conservative hand touches such circumstances with caution . . . Thus it is that no abuse, no prejudice which seems to have played its part in the common well-being will disappear, or be destroyed, until the majority is ready for this. . . . [13]

[13] *El Orden*, October 26, 1845.

This can easily be read of course as a rationalization of vested interests. (Could not the same be suspected of many traditions of conservative philosophy?) Yet it undoubtedly represented the fundamental approach of the *pelucones* in these early years of the new republic. In political terms it must also be recognized that the Conservative system did, in the end, adapt sufficiently well for the country to move into an altogether more liberal (and Liberal) phase. How this occurred will be dealt with in Chapter 5.

The economic settlement

Alongside the political settlement of the 1830s there went a consolidation of the country's finances and economic policies. The key figure here was Portales's friend and fellow-trader Manuel Rengifo (Finance minister, 1830–35, 1841–44). His importance can easily be exaggerated; to some extent he built on administrative changes made in the despised 1820s. Yet he remains the most important Finance minister of the early republic. Portales nicknamed him "Don Proyectos" ("Mister Plans"). Rengifo's main aims were to balance the budget and to stabilize commercial policy. From August 1830 all public payments were channeled through the Finance ministry. With the help of Victorino Garrido (a Spaniard who had settled in Chile and become more *pelucón* than the *pelucones*), he slimmed down the public administration, reducing expenditure by about one-sixth. (It was Rengifo who brought the army's size down from 3,500 to 2,800; he would have liked it to be 1,000.)

His main tax reform was the replacement of the colonial *alcabala del viento* (a duty on agricultural produce) by a direct 3 percent tax on landed income. (In practice, many haciendas were consistently undervalued; landowners were easily able to outwit the inexperienced valuers.) Thanks in part to rising customs revenues, the budget was balanced by 1839. (Revenues were 2.3 million pesos that year.) Rengifo also halved the domestic public debt, allowing generous terms for debt-registration, paying off government notes (issued profligately in the 1820s), and creating a sinking fund. The settlement of the foreign debt (the London loan of 1822) had to await his return to office in the 1840s. For the time being Chile came first.

Rengifo's commercial philosophy was liberal rather than neo-mercantilist, and his instincts favored the expansion of trade. The commercial legislation of 1834 confirmed the downward trend tariffs had taken since O'Higgins's high-tariff experiments. The blanket *ad valorem* system was replaced by flexible duties on imports: those competing with certain Chilean products paid the top rate (35 percent), but the average level was around 25 percent. Duties on imported wheat were tied to a market-determined sliding scale. Most export duties were eliminated, apart from 4 percent on wheat and 6 percent on minerals. The most important stimulus to trade, however, lay in the regularization of an innovation fitfully attempted by all governments since 1813: the public or bonded warehouse (*almacén fiscal*). Here traders were allowed to store merchandise at Valparaiso at low cost, subsequently importing or re-exporting it when the market was favorable. Valparaiso, in Rengifo's view (and Portales's), needed to become a dominant Pacific port. The permitted storage period was extended from three years to six in 1833. Rengifo ensured that there was sufficient warehouse space to cope with demand (he also instituted a building program) and that the *almacenes* were properly supervised. These measures did much to capitalize on Valparaiso's geographical position as the obvious port-of-call for ships entering or leaving the Pacific by way of Cape Horn. In fact, the city now became not merely Chile's principal port but also the focal point of a vast regional market embracing Bolivia, Peru, and Ecuador. In the mid-1830s about two-thirds of Peru's imports passed through the *almacenes fiscales* of Valparaiso.

The expansion of Chile's own foreign trade in the 1830s (its value by 1840 was roughly three times higher than in 1810) was not solely due to Rengifo's incentives. In May 1832 the woodcutter Juan Godoy discovered impressive new silver deposits at Chañarcillo, near Copiapó, and the most spectacular *mineral* in Chilean history was born. "For many years to come," predicted José Joaquín Vallejo in 1842 (by which time Chañarcillo had already yielded 12 million pesos), "it will continue to be one of the most solid foundations of the wealth of this republic."[14] The growing bonanza in silver and copper confirmed the Norte Chico as nineteenth-century Chile's classic mining zone, its population now increasing faster than that of the rest of the country. This created a new (if limited) market for the agriculture of the Central Valley, which by 1840 contributed only one-quarter of Chilean exports. Mining was now the real pacesetter.

By the start of the 1840s, 300 ships were calling at Valparaiso every year. The important law of October 1835 confirmed the Chilean monopoly of the coasting trade (*cabotaje*), which in the 1830s accounted for about half the traffic in and out of the ports. A further law (July 1836) tried to increase the number of Chilean sailors in Chilean-registered vessels. How successful these measures were has long been debated. Certainly the merchant fleet nearly doubled in size in the decade after Rengifo's law (61 ships in 1835, 101 in 1844), yet many foreign ships simply switched to the Chilean flag in order to enter the trade, while the number of British captains aboard coastal vessels occasioned much com-

---

[14] "Mineral de Chañarcillo," *Obras de don José Joaquín Vallejo*, ed. Alberto Edwards (Santiago, 1911), p. 67.

ment at the time. The myth of a vigorous Chilean merchant navy conjured into existence by Rengifo scarcely stands up to close scrutiny. Irrespective of its makeup, however, the merchant fleet did play a vital part in Chile's trade.

A little-noticed (and also fairly brief) "trans-Pacific" chapter in Valparaiso's commercial history deserves to be mentioned here. From the mid-1820s onward several traders (mostly foreign) had been shipping pearl and mother-of-pearl from Tahiti and other central Pacific islands to Valparaiso (mostly for re-export to France). This had some picturesque consequences. The Chilean peso ("bird money," as it was known, from the condor on the coin) became one of the currencies circulating in the Polynesian islands (when Robert Louis Stevenson bought his land in Samoa in 1890, the price was in Chilean pesos); acacias and carob trees from Chile took root at various far-flung points round the Pacific. In the 1830s quantities of Chilean wheat were sent (mostly in British ships) to New South Wales – a rehearsal for the much more substantial export of the 1850s. Two or three hundred Chilean peons crossed to Australia as indentured laborers – this, too, was a tiny foretaste of a more notable migration over a century later: by the 1970s the Chilean community in Australia numbered tens of thousands.

Despite the gradual expansion of trade, the overwhelming fact of Chilean life in the 1830s was its poverty. Even in the upper class, the scale of family wealth was in no sense noteworthy. Charles Darwin was told in the mid-1830s that "some few of the great landowners" had annual incomes of between £5,000 and £10,000 (roughly 25,000 to 50,000 pesos). He also sensed that the "inequality of wealth" was greater in Chile than in Argentina. Those Chileans who still remembered the captaincy-general (Juan Egaña died in 1836, Manuel de Salas in 1841, José Miguel Infante in 1844) would have found nothing strikingly unfamiliar in the Chile of Portales and Rengifo. The signs of new life were most obvious in Valparaiso (with the country's only daily newspaper before 1842); even so, foreigners often found the port ramshackle and disagreeable; its heyday was yet to come. Santiago had grown in size (to around 70,000 in the mid-1830s) but, O'Higgins's improvements aside, still wore the look of the late-colonial capital. Communications within the country were still difficult, although the highway from Santiago to Valparaiso was more crowded than previously. Only two mails each month linked Santiago and Concepción. (In 1834 four monthly mails to Coquimbo were introduced, a reflection of the new saliency of the mining zone.) In 1832, when a scarlet fever epidemic struck the capital, no more than nine competent doctors could be found to combat it; four were British. There was almost nothing in the way of literary life. Between

1836 and 1838, Santiago was without a theater. The University of San Felipe had become so moribund since independence that the government simply abolished it (April 1839), despite protests from its distinctly underemployed professors.

Nobody was more aware of Chile's poverty than Rengifo himself. His celebrated ministerial report of 1834 not only summarizes his view of the economic position, but also provides a lucid statement of the economic vision of the new Chilean governing class. The wars of independence, according to Rengifo, had plunged Chile into "a frightful languor" which could be overcome only by the expansion of trade. He saw two ways in which government could promote growth: first, "laws which remove obstructive impediments to industry and which protect property and its free use," and second, "laws which regulate taxation with moderation and discernment." (By "industry" Rengifo meant work in general.) He pointed to Valparaiso, "transformed by the liberality of the laws into the ...largest market in the Pacific." Yet Valparaiso, for all its bustle, was only one of the faces of Chile in the 1830s. The acuteness (and limitations) of Rengifo's vision are best revealed in his approach to the agrarian question.

Among the obstacles which hold back the development of our industry we can point to the accumulation of lands in the hands of the few. A great hacienda is never completely cultivated; nor can it ever be cultivated well.... The unduly extensive haciendas of the countryside do not yield the produce which they could yield if they were subdivided, and the nation loses considerable revenues as the result of this disproportionate distribution of the land. Even so, heaven preserve us from trying to excise this evil by resorting to coercive measures of a kind which might prejudice the free use of property. Any intervention by the public power in acts of private interest would, far from hastening, actually impair the creation of public wealth.

The views held by "Don Proyectos" on the efficacy of trade and the sanctity of property were not to be seriously challenged in the nineteenth century. He himself had been dead a hundred and twenty years before "coercive measures" were first applied to the haciendas.

The war with the Peru-Bolivian Confederation

The first sign of serious political disaffection after 1833 came not from the defeated Liberals (whose conspiracies were easily suppressed) but from within Conservative ranks. The so-called *filopólitas* (the name was that of their newspaper, *El Philopolita*, 1835) were a group whose core consisted of the formerly Liberal *estanqueros* Diego José Benavente and Manuel José Gandarillas, together with Manuel Rengifo and the powerful Errázuriz family – *los litres,* Portales called the family, alluding to a tree in whose shadow nothing was said to grow. President Prieto's first term was due to end in 1836, and Rengifo probably harbored presidential ambitions. The *filopólitas* were especially hostile to the clerically minded minister of the Interior, Joaquín Tocornal. Prieto was offended by their anticlerical tone, and in the end acted. On September 21, 1835, Rengifo arrived at his desk to learn that Portales was once again in the cabinet Rengifo bowed out; the dreams of the *filopólitas* melted away, and Prieto was re-elected with barely a murmur.

Portales's second ministry was largely taken up with the question of Chile's deteriorating relations with Peru. There were several points at issue. Peru had not repaid the Chilean loan (part of the London loan Chile had not repaid either) and did not appreciate Chilean requests for reimbursement of the costs of the expedition of 1820–21. In 1832 the Chilean government doubled the tariff on imported Peruvian sugar, in retaliation for a new Peruvian duty on Chilean wheat. Peru responded by imposing a surcharge on foreign merchandise arriving from Valparaiso's bonded warehouses. This blow to Valparaiso's commercial hegemony prompted Portales to comment that Chile might have "to go against them with an army."[15] In 1835 the tariff war was ended by a treaty, but this reconciliation was immediately overshadowed by political developments. During 1836 Marshal Andrés Santa Cruz, the ambitious president of Bolivia, overcame his main enemies in Peru, Generals Gamarra and Salaverry, and united the two nations in a new Peru-Bolivian Confederation with himself as Protector. Chile was now faced with a potentially powerful northern neighbor. Most Chileans were probably indifferent to this, but Portales was not.

Portales's patriotic sense was very pronounced. He sometimes said that he wanted Chile to become the England of the Pacific.[16] In his dealings with foreign consuls over claims arising from the 1829–30 civil war, he was polite but firm. "We are poor, but we are a nation," he told the French consul La Forest, whose house had been attacked.[17] Popular xenophobia (shown in minor but ugly ways in 1829–30) did not extend to the upper class, but Portales was well aware of it: in 1833, when governor of Valparaiso, he allowed an American whaling commander, the demented Captain Paddock, to go to the gallows for multiple murder,

[15] To Garfías, August 30, 1832. Cruz and Feliú Cruz, II, 272.

[16] In popular usage the phrase changed to "the England of South America." In his more fanciful moments, Portales spoke of lending Chile to England for a few years, as a means of improving the country. Vicuña Mackenna, *D. Diego Portales,* p. 199.

[17] Quoted in Mario Barros, *Historia diplomática de Chile, 1541–1938* (Barcelona 1970), p. 98.

despite appeals for mercy from the foreign traders. "Let us do justice to foreigners," he wrote, "let us give them all possible hospitality, but never to the extent of placing them above Chileans."[18]

Matters soon came to a head. In July 1836 the exiled General Freire led a small expedition to Chile from Peru in an attempt to overthrow the Conservative regime. Freire was captured, put on trial, and banished to Australia, but Peruvian complicity in this venture seemed to Portales a sufficient *casus belli*. Under Victoriano Garrido's command, two Chilean ships went north and seized three Peruvian vessels from Callao. Santa Cruz immediately arrested the Chilean envoy in Lima. Garrido and the Protector patched up a hasty agreement, but this was unacceptable to Portales. Mariano Egaña, with plenipotentiary powers, was next sent to Peru with an ultimatum requiring the dissolution of the Confederation. This was predictably rejected, so Egaña declared war and sailed home. Portales took a ruthlessly simple view of the impending conflict: "The Confederation must disappear forever. . . . We must dominate forever in the Pacific."[19]

In its opening months the war seems to have been very unpopular in Chile. The forcible enlistment of soldiers was widely resented. Inevitably, the opposition sought to capitalize on the discontent. The regime once again resorted to emergency powers, this time of an almost absolute nature – measures reflecting the vehemence of Portales's character as well as the danger from conspiracies. All exiles returning to Chile without permission were now to be shot within twenty-four hours. A "law of permanent courts-martial" (February 1837) provided for summary justice with no appeal. Its main victims were three Liberals (two of them prominent landowners) shot at Curicó on April 7, 1837, on the orders of Antonio José de Irisarri, then the Intendant of Colchagua. Such drastic repression merely fueled the flames of conspiracy. The plotters' web now centered on Colonel José Antonio Vidaurre, known as a troublemaker in the 1820s but now the trusted commander of the Maipó battalion (soon to be given regimental status). Summoned to Santiago to answer disquieting allegations of disloyalty, Vidaurre is said to have told Portales: "If I ever make a revolution against you, your excellency will be the first to know."[20] The story seems suspiciously neat.

At the start of June 1837, with the expeditionary force building up at Valparaiso, Portales decided to inspect the Maipó regiment in its quarters at Quillota. It was a journey later invested with legendary coloring: tradition long maintained that two angels vainly tried to restrain the

---

[18] To Tocornal, January 16, 1832. Cruz and Feliú Cruz, I, 393.

[19] To Manuel Blanco Encalada, September 10, 1836. Cruz and Feliú Cruz, III, 453–54.

[20] Vicuña Mackenna, *D. Diego Portales,* p. 372.

horses drawing the minister's carriage. At Quillota Portales was taken captive, thrown into irons, and forced to accompany Vidaurre's now mutinous regiment as it moved off toward Valparaiso to strike the decisive blow. The defenders of the port (led, ironically, by Vidaurre's own cousin, Colonel Juan Vidaurre, later allowed to add Leal, "loyal," to his surname) repulsed the rebels without difficulty – but too late to save Portales. In the early hours of June 6, near the Cerro Barón on the outskirts of Valparaiso, the "omnipotent minister" was taken from his carriage and done to death with thirty-five bayonet thrusts. A modest obelisk marks the spot today, in a tranquil suburban setting high above the wide sweep of the bay.

The revolt was broken; its leaders were caught and executed, and Vidaurre's head was exhibited on a pike at Quillota. The awesomely solemn state funeral accorded Portales's remains in Santiago (his heart was claimed by Valparaiso) made an evidently profound impression. "Chilean order," said the grief-stricken Tocornal, minister of the Interior once again, "triumphed on the Barón heights even as the religion of Jesus Christ triumphed at Golgotha." Whatever may be thought of the parallel, he was right; the Conservative settlement *was* somehow strengthened. Moreover, as the newspaper *El Mercurio* pointed out six months later, "the horrendous crime... increased the popularity of the war."[21] Yet by no means did all Chileans feel that Portales's death had been an unmitigated disaster. "He was an extraordinary and talented man, and he idolized the homeland," wrote the magistrate who went through the dead man's effects, "but he was becoming more and more corrupted, without (in my view) being aware of this himself."[22] Those who remembered him in the flesh were for many years surprisingly restrained in their tributes. Only much later (starting in the 1850s) did a true cult develop. The Chilean reaction to "strong men" in politics has always been ambiguous; only when safely dead and buried are they truly admired, and then often for the wrong reasons.

The expeditionary force finally set sail in September 1837, an army of 2,800 men under Manuel Blanco Encalada. In mid-October he occupied the southern Peruvian city of Arequipa. This was a wrong move. Santa Cruz corraled the Chileans and forced Blanco Encalada (after a meeting at the village of Paucarpata) to sign a treaty guaranteeing both the with-drawal of the expedition and recognition of the Confederation. By mid-December the Chilean army was home again – minus its horses, sold to

[21] *El Mercurio*, Valparaiso, No. 2727, January 2, 1838.

[22] J. A. Alvarez to Manuel Montt, June 12, 1837. *Revista Chilena de Historia y Geografía*, No. 27 (1917), p. 197. We are grateful to Sergio Villalobos R. for drawing our attention to this fascinating letter.

Santa Cruz, a detail that aroused much indignation. The government instantly repudiated the Treaty of Paucarpata; Blanco Encalada was court-martialed and acquitted by a one-vote margin. Much of the blame for the deal with Santa Cruz was placed on Antonio José de Irisarri, who had gone with the expedition as Blanco Encalada's adviser. He wisely never returned to Chile.

By this stage, the war had aroused the attention of the great powers. Portales himself had hoped that the Chilean offensive might be "an example that would make us stronger in the eyes of the European nations."[23] British and French partiality to the Confederation was very apparent throughout the war. The England of the Atlantic took a very disapproving view of the would-be England of the Pacific. The British consul in Santiago pressed for an armistice and Chilean acceptance of British mediation. One of his meetings with the government (December 1837) seems to have been rather violent, with the consul threatening a bombardment of Valparaiso and even the cunning Tocornal losing his normal composure. In 1838, annoyed by Chile's refusal to make peace, the British government delicately threatened to intervene by force to end the war, but nothing came of this.

A second, much larger Chilean expedition was now built up, and placed under the command of General Manuel Bulnes, with General José María de la Cruz as chief of staff. Some of the officers cashiered in 1830 were allowed to resume their ranks. A small naval squadron, under Captain Roberto Simpson, took the offensive at sea, winning the one naval battle of the war (Casma, January 12, 1839). The expedition itself – 5,400 men – left Chile in July 1838. Meanwhile General Orbegoso, president of the North-Peruvian State (one of the Confederation's three divisions), chose this moment to break with Santa Cruz, and, to underline his independence, demanded the withdrawal of the Chileans on their arrival in Peru. Bulnes fought off Orbegoso's attacks and occupied Lima. But the Chileans were unable to capture the vital Callao fortresses, and the unhealthy climate thinned their ranks. Two and a half months later Bulnes and Cruz withdrew their army to the Callejón de Huaylas, a majestic Andean valley farther north. Santa Cruz, after reoccupying Lima, set out in hot pursuit. On January 6, 1839, his men attacked Bulnes's division as it crossed the river Buin. Amidst rain, hail and thunder, the Chileans saved the day and continued their march. But their position was now fraught with peril. Outnumbered by the enemy, and low in supplies, the expedition was quickly faced with the choice of surrendering or fighting. Bulnes chose to fight. Against all odds, and thanks to a risky cavalry charge, the battle of Yungay (January 20, 1839) was a devastating

---

[23] To Ventura Lavalle, May 20, 1837. Cruz and Feliú Cruz, III, 503–04.

Chilean triumph. Of the 9,000 soldiers on the battlefield, around 2,000 were killed. Santa Cruz fled to Ecuador,[24] and the Confederation, as Portales had wished, vanished forever from the American scene.

Victory in this war undoubtedly enhanced the international prestige of Chile. It reinforced the commercial hegemony of Valparaiso. The country's finances bore the strain with remarkable ease. It seems likely, also, that the war helped to consolidate the growing sense of Chilean nationality. This is somewhat difficult to gauge. Victory undoubtedly gave many ordinary Chileans, especially in the towns, a chance to breathe the heady air of patriotic euphoria. One of the most popular of all Chilean songs was written (the words by Ramón Rengifo, Manuel's brother) to celebrate the news of Bulnes's triumph.

> *Cantemos la gloria*
> *del triunfo marcial*
> *que el pueblo chileno*
> *obtuvo en Yungay.*
>
> Let us sing the glory
> of the martial triumph
> the Chilean people
> won at Yungay.

The reputations of Generals Bulnes and Cruz shone with increased luster, while ballads and puppet shows long commemorated the deeds of two less exalted but undeniably popular figures: the hero of Buin, Ensign Juan Felipe Colipí (son of one of the friendly caciques of Araucania), and the pretty, diminutive Candelaria Pérez, "Sergeant Candelaria," who had attached herself to the army in Lima and fought bravely at Yungay.

The great victory parade held in Santiago in December 1839 was the most splendid popular celebration since independence. Politically, the government now felt able to adopt a more relaxed policy toward the opposition. Bulnes himself requested the reinstatement of all officers cashiered in 1830. One or two brief and feeble spasms of Liberal agitation failed, this time, to provoke the government to heavy-handed action. In March 1840 the opposition even elected a small handful of deputies to Congress. All eyes now turned (in a way that was to be an absolute constant in Chilean history from that day to this) toward the impending presidential election. Joaquín Tocornal, whose eight years in office had

---

[24] In 1843 Santa Cruz tried to return to Bolivia, but was arrested in southern Peru. Chile secured possession of the famous captive, and in May 1844 he was installed in moderate comfort at Chillán, guarded by Colonel Benjamín Viel, an officer of French birth, with whom (perhaps remembering Napoleon and Sir Hudson Lowe) he quarreled incessantly. Two years later he was allowed to leave for Europe, where he died in 1865.

given him the ascendancy in the Conservative leadership he was to retain until his death in 1865, was eager for the presidency. But not even Tocornal could override the wishes of President Prieto, who sensed that the popularity of the "peerless hero" Bulnes could be turned into an asset for the regime. The Liberal opposition put forward the name of ex-president Francisco Antonio Pinto. To avert a possible alliance between Tocornal and Pinto, the government approached the Liberal leadership, such as it was, and offered an orderly election and conciliatory policies to come. The happy coincidence of Bulnes's betrothal to Pinto's eldest daughter, Enriqueta, set the seal on this gentlemen's agreement. (It *was* a coincidence; they married for love, not politics.) Bulnes's triumph at the polls was a good deal more predictable than his victory at Yungay. He began his first term of office (September 18, 1841) with a general amnesty, as if to show that the Conservative settlement, tested in war, was now secure in peace. The illusion lasted most of the next decade.

PART II

The rise of a republic, 1830s–1880s

While consolidating itself as a nation-state, Chile enjoyed both substantial commercial expansion and the eventual development of a tradition of tolerant upper-class politics. Exports of copper, silver, and wheat enriched the upper class and enabled the republic to grow and to initiate modernization, though with its traditional social structure changing only slowly. Chile came to be regarded abroad as the "model republic" of South America, an opinion widely shared by educated Chileans themselves (Chapter 4). The early Conservative hegemony gradually gave way, in some memorable mid-century struggles, and with the tradition of strong presidential rule maintained, to a pattern of Liberal-dominated politics which included competition between four major parties, prefiguring the vital role of parties in later times. A severe economic crisis in the 1870s was followed by Chilean victory over Peru and Bolivia in the War of the Pacific (Chapters 5 and 6).

GOVERNMENTS

1831–1841	General Joaquín Prieto
1841–1851	General Manuel Bulnes
1851–1861	Manuel Montt
1861–1871	José Joaquín Pérez
1871–1876	Federico Errázuriz
1876–1881	Aníbal Pinto*
1881–1886	Domingo Santa María

*son of the president of 1827–29

4

A time of progress, 1830s–1870s

Everyone is shouting that Chile is the model republic of South America. What on earth can the others be like?

– *El Copiapino*, No. 3021, June 5, 1858

Bulnes was the second president to serve a full ten years. He was followed by two more, Manuel Montt (1851–61) and José Joaquín Pérez (1861–71). During these years, as we shall see in Chapter 5, the peace was twice disturbed by armed rebellion, but for most of the time settled conditions prevailed, and the country enjoyed noticeable commercial expansion. Steamships appeared in the ports, railroads inched across the northern desert and the Central Valley, telegraph wires linked the towns, banks and joint-stock companies were founded, and cities were improved. Educated Chileans saw this as a time of progress. This key nineteenth-century concept was fully assimilated by the country's leaders and opinion-formers. Santiago's first daily newspaper was called *El Progreso:* over the next hundred years this was the most popular title for newly founded Chilean newspapers.[1] In retrospect, the period of the "early republic" can also be seen as a distinct economic cycle, as the products of the mines and haciendas flowed to the outside world. Only with the crisis of the 1870s was this phase of export-led expansion exhausted.

Government policy and practice

The main emphases of the economic settlement of the 1830s were maintained by virtually all the Finance ministers of the ensuing period. Not only did they see trade as the motor of economic advance (and as the principal source of revenue), but they were also, to use a modern phrase, "fiscal conservatives," who believed in balancing the budget whenever possible. Later generations of Chileans were to ask themselves whether a

---

[1] The card catalogue of the newspaper collection in the Biblioteca Nacional, Santiago in the 1980s, shows around 110 newspapers with this title.

different strategy would have produced greater economic independence or more balanced growth. It is rather hard to see what kind of alternative approach would have worked. Would Paraguayan-style autarky, for instance, really have improved the lot of poorer Chileans? (It did little for poorer Paraguayans.) The "commercial league" of Latin American nations ("to free their industry from the European yoke") suggested by the Conservative Antonio García Reyes in 1844 might perhaps have been a more promising tactic, but it could hardly have been promoted by Chile on its own.[2] The country's rulers did not have especially sharp instruments of policy: double-entry accounting, for instance, was not introduced into the public administration before the 1880s. Their outlook was inevitably influenced by the interests of their own class. Mine-owners and hacendados were well served by the government's economic decisions. This does not mean that the decisions themselves were foolish. Associating the country with the rising tide of international trade could well have been the only strategy likely to yield any results whatsoever.

This did not imply a gadarene rush to free trade. The liberalizing impulse in economic policy was clear enough from independence onward, yet the state retained a definite interest in stimulating or protecting domestic economic activity: the "neo-mercantilist" legacy was strong. The state took a hand in developing roads, railways, and ports, and in enlarging the exiguous educational system. Its efforts here were not superhuman, but neither were they contemptible. The tariff structure (in those days the most visible symbol of economic policy) reflected pragmatism rather than doctrinaire liberalism or protectionism. Free-trade ideas, it is true, enjoyed a definite vogue among intellectuals from the 1850s onward. In 1857 *El Mercurio* even described them as a "national doctrine," noting that in Chile (unlike England) "everyone is in favor of the good principle."[3] The French economist Jean-Gustave Courcelle-Seneuil, who lived in Chile (and advised the government) between 1855 and 1863, schooled a whole generation of liberal economic theorists, including Miguel Cruchaga Montt and the talented Conservative Zorobabel Rodríguez. Yet it may be doubted whether theoretical ideas were as important in policymaking as practical issues. When in 1852 the Chamber of Deputies discussed export duties on minerals (retained throughout the period, to the annoyance of miners), it was protested that such taxes were unmodern and "anti-economic." This drew from Interior minister Antonio Varas a typical comment: "Would that the products of national industry could be freed from all imposts; but . . . it is one thing to write

---

[2] García Reyes to Chamber of Deputies, December 20, 1844. Valentín Letelier, ed., *Sesiones de los Cuerpos Legislativos de la República de Chile*, 37 vols. (1887–1908), XXIV, 663.

[3] *El Mercurio*, No. 9142, December 26, 1857.

a book, and quite another to apply its doctrines to the government of a state."[4]

Rengifo's customs ordinance of 1834 embodied what was for the most part to be the standard policy of successive governments. There were several later adjustments to the original structure. Rengifo's own second customs ordinance (1842) had the effect of lowering tariffs. In 1851 more than 100 items were exempted from taxation altogether – mostly raw materials and machinery that might be useful in mining or manufacturing. Thirteen years later, however, a new Finance minister, Alejandro Reyes, secured a comprehensive reform which went further still. Reyes was something of a doctrinaire liberalizer. He established a basic *ad valorem* tariff of 25 percent, and eliminated all but 29 of the duty-free items, though machinery (now taxed at 15 percent) could be imported duty-free with special permission. The new law also ended the domestic monopoly over the coasting trade. This customs ordinance of 1864 has often been represented as the high-water mark of liberalization in nineteenth-century Chile, and it has not had a good press. In any case, a new customs ordinance was passed in 1872. This wore a more familiar look, with a longer list of non-dutiable items – including machines, though oddly enough many industrial parts and raw materials were still taxed at 15 percent. Like most tariff laws of the period, it combined fiscal advantage with attention to local interests.

The growth of trade, on which so many hopes were pinned, proved very satisfactory. The number of ships calling at Chilean ports rose to about 4,000 per year by 1870, a more than tenfold increase since 1840. The value of foreign trade showed a fivefold increase between the mid-1840s and the mid-1870s, from roughly 15 million pesos to 75 million per annum.[5] Imports slightly outpaced exports until around 1860; during the 1860s exports were slightly ahead. This commercial expansion was not continuous. At the end of the 1850s there was a serious recession, caused by two poor harvests, the loss of overseas markets for wheat and flour, and slackening silver production – all this exacerbated by the international recession of 1857. The Chilean crisis of the later 1850s led to some famous bankruptcies, but was soon over, and growth resumed in the 1860s. There were other times, notably from the later 1840s to the mid-1850s and again from the later 1860s to the mid-1870s, when the expansion of trade was very rapid indeed, and the country experienced boom conditions.

The government was thus confident that it could rely on a generally

---

[4] Chamber of Deputies, September 24, 1852.
[5] The Chilean peso was worth approximately 45 old pence (18.75 new pence) in sterling, or just under the U.S. dollar; it retained its value, with slight fluctuations, over the whole period.

buoyant source of income. Revenues did indeed rise, from around 3 million pesos in the early 1840s to over 16 million in 1875. Prior to the late 1850s, Finance ministers had no difficulty in balancing the budget. After 1860, however, spending began to outpace the growth of trade, and it became harder to cover expenditure from "ordinary" (i.e., legislatively authorized) sources. Internal taxation declined as a proportion of the state's revenues; there was a marked reluctance to impose taxes on property or incomes (internal tax rates actually fell during this period); and even though the state was now making money from some of its own services (e.g., railways), the books could no longer be balanced without recourse to borrowing. Between 1861 and 1879 ten major internal loans were contracted, to the tune of over 21 million pesos. In 1858 Chile took out its first foreign loan in thirty-six years (with Barings of London), and between 1861 and 1879 there were half a dozen more, amounting to over 40 million pesos.[6] Given the strict policy of keeping up payments (Chile's creditworthiness was admirable), the public finances were beginning to look less solid by the 1870s.

One reason for this was that the state's obligations were gradually enlarging. The public administration (still tiny by later standards) doubled in size, from just over 1,500 to 3,000 between the mid-1840s and the 1870s. (The armed forces, always the second largest item in the budget, were kept, as we have seen, at a generally low level.) New demands on the public purse included education, railway-building, and (in the early 1870s) warships. Dramatic as the growth of trade had been by the 1870s, it was not enough, now, to sustain the greater scale of the government's operations – especially since Chile's governing class showed little inclination to impose taxes on itself.

The export economy: mining and agriculture

From the viewpoint of foreign trade, the goose that laid most of the golden eggs was mining. The export economy would have looked very different without the northern provinces of Coquimbo and Atacama (the latter created in 1843). As we saw in Chapter 1, the principal metals of late-colonial times had been gold, silver, and copper. The annual production of gold in the 1870s (270 kilograms or so) was only a quarter of what it had been half a century earlier. This did not matter: there was plenty of silver and copper. How much was actually mined? Figures can be only approximate: the level of smuggling is impossible to quantify. Pierre Vayssière's careful estimates suggest an annual average output of

---

[6] Luis M. Ortega, "Change and Crisis in Chile's Economy and Society, 1865–1879" (Univ. of London, Ph.D., 1979), p. 357.

silver rising from around 33,000 kilograms in the 1830s to over 123,000 kilograms in the 1870s. The bulk of this came from Atacama, while annual copper production increased from around 14,000 metric tons in the 1840s to more than 46,000 in the 1870s[7] – at which point Chile was regularly accounting for between one-third and one-half of the world's supply. From the 1840s onward a high proportion of copper was exported in the form of "Chili bars," smelted locally.

Mining lured a large number of workers, traders, speculators, and prospectors. Many upper-class Chileans (not to mention others) felt moved to try their luck there in hopes of a quick fortune. It has even been argued that mining, with its sudden gains and losses, was somehow peculiarly appealing to the Chilean psychology. Be that as it may, the passionate hunt for new sources of wealth was a constant in the north, as *cateadores* (mine-hunters) spread out across the arid hills and into the uninhabited wastes, the so-called *despoblado,* lying between Copiapó and the Bolivian frontier, wherever that was. (It was first fixed at 24°S in 1866, rather casually, and in any case Bolivia subsequently disavowed the treaty.) None of the discoveries made between 1840 and 1875 quite equaled Chañarcillo. The silver-strike at Tres Puntas, north of Copiapó, in 1848 was the most famous of the mid-century years; there were plenty of smaller finds. The last really dramatic "silver rush" of the period, provoking the migration of thousands of people (many of them from the Norte Chico), occurred at the start of the 1870s at Caracoles, across the border in Bolivia. Caracoles[8] yielded around 1,000 metric tons of silver in its first ten years, after which it soon declined.

Several of the nineteenth-century prospectors have been written up somewhat hagiologically by Chilean historians – Diego de Almeida, for instance, or José Antonio Moreno, whose quests were certainly wide-ranging and obsessive. Most *cateadores* were of humbler origin – originally woodcutters, maybe, or muleteers – and their discoveries were intuitive, not based on geological expertise. By no means all happy strikes, however, depended on far-flung reconnaissance; familiar *minerales* sometimes produced surprises. José Tomás Urmeneta (here we must introduce the most spectacular case of all) worked an unproductive mine at Tamaya, near Ovalle (Coquimbo province), for eighteen poverty-stricken years before finding (October 1852) the richest vein of copper ever known in the Norte Chico. *El loco del burro,* "the madman on a donkey," as he had been known locally, was soon a millionaire, joining the ranks of a handful of men whose families enjoyed the largest fortunes of the early republic.

In spite of the great increases in production, many features of the late-

---

[7] P. Vayssière, *Un siècle de capitalisme minier au Chili 1830–1930* (Paris, 1980), pp. 110–15.

[8] Literally, "shells"; it was so named because of the large number of marine fossils found in the area.

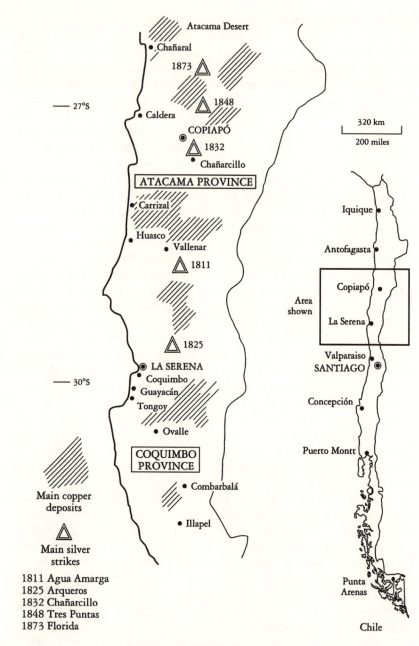

Chile: Principal Mining Zones, 1820–79

colonial mining pattern were perpetuated in the north throughout the nineteenth century: individual or family entrepreneurship, simple technology, the short-term marginal activity exemplified in the old *pirquén* system. In the mines themselves oil-lamps appear to have replaced candles for underground illumination. By the 1860s at least, some of the larger enterprises had adopted up-to-date technology. Urmeneta did this at Tamaya (one of its adits extended for two kilometers), as did another prominent capitalist, José Ramón Ovalle, at Carrizal Alto. (About one-third of the copper produced in the mid-1870s came from these two districts.) These were exceptional cases; they only mildly complicate our standard picture of the nineteenth century as the classic "artesanal" phase in the history of Chilean mining. The great majority of mines were still small (and shallow), and relied more on the labor of *barreteros* and *apires* (or in rarer cases, animal-power) than on steam-engines. According to one report from the area (probably incomplete), only one mine in twenty-three in the Norte Chico in the early 1870s used steam-engines at all.[9]

The biggest technical changes came in processing rather than extraction. In the case of silver, the old colonial "patio" process, used in the *trapiches*, was largely displaced by the so-called Cooper method, a variation on the "barrel amalgamation" common in Europe. The new system still required heavy inputs of mercury; only toward the end of the century was it replaced by the more efficient Kröhnke amalgamation process. In copper-smelting the vital innovation, the introduction of reverbatory furnaces (*hornos de reverbero*) around 1830, is usually credited to Charles Lambert, a highly successful entrepreneur of Alsatian background who settled in Chile in 1825. The new method was known in Chile as the "English system" – it had long been in use at Swansea, South Wales, then the copper-smelting capital of the world and a port to which large quantities of Chilean ore were shipped. Starting toward the end of the 1840s, partly owing to a British tariff change (1842) that reduced the advantage of Swansea, partly because sheer distance militated against the bulk shipping of ore, several large-scale Chilean smelters were established: at Guayacán (La Herradura bay, Coquimbo) and Tongoy in the north, both of which by the 1860s formed part of Urmeneta's empire, and at Lirquén and Lota in the south. From now onward most copper was sent abroad either in pure bar form, or (about one-third of the total export in the years 1855–75) in semi-processed mattes, with a copper content of roughly 50 percent. The big northern and southern smelters were the country's first real industrial enterprises.

As so often with industrialism, there was a price to be paid. The new copper smelters, large or small, needed constant inputs of fuel. Those in

[9] Leland R. Pederson, *The Mining Industry of the Norte Chico, Chile* (Evanston, Ill., 1966), pp. 191–92.

the mining zone soon exhausted the far from plentiful timber resources of the north. The long-term effect was to disturb the ecological balance and to speed up the southward advance of the desert. By the 1870s at least a few people were aware of this. The alternative to wood was coal, deposits of which were to be found near Concepción – on Talcahuano Bay and (especially) along the Gulf of Arauco. These deposits were worked more or less systematically from the 1840s; in 1852, Matías Cousiño, an entrepreneur as famous as Urmeneta, began his operation at Lota. By the mid-1870s there were more than 6,000 coalminers in the south: the Lota company had the first internal telephone system in Chile. A new industry was thus born. Its output was modest by European standards, but despite its vulnerability to competition from imported Welsh coal, Chile's more than held its own in the longer run, partly because a mixture of local and foreign coal was found to work well in the northern smelters. The southern smelters, for their part, assumed increasing importance toward the end of the century, largely because of integration with the collieries.

Most mining entrepreneurs at this stage were Chileans, many from families already established in the Norte Chico – the powerful Gallo clan, for instance, founded by an eighteenth-century Genoese immigrant, and linked to other northern dynasties like the Goyenecheas, Mattas, and Montts. Miguel Gallo, one of the great beneficiaries of Chañarcillo, seems to have been Chile's first millionaire; he died in 1842. A number of foreigners (Britons and Argentines in particular) also did well. One or two copper concerns were British-owned. The most successful miners often reinvested their profits in new mines, also buying haciendas in the Central Valley and mansions in Santiago. Most entrepreneurs did not fall into this category. Most, indeed, were dependent on a group of middlemen known as *habilitadores,* who supplied credit and equipment in exchange for ore or a stake in the mine concerned. As a valuable recent study by Eduardo Cavieres has illustrated, the import-export houses of Valparaiso were heavily involved with the *habilitación* business, with a complex and tangled web of interests throughout the mining zone. The most spectacular *habilitador* of all was Agustín Edwards, son of the first Edwards in Chile. By the 1860s, as a result of numerous profitable speculations, Edwards was one of the richest capitalists in Chile. In 1871–72 he carried out a long-remembered coup: he stockpiled as much metal as he could lay hands on, drove the world copper price up by 50 percent in eight months, and realized a personal profit estimated at 1.5 million pesos.

Important as the mines were to Chile's export economy, relatively few Chileans worked in them. In the 1860s something like four-fifths of the population lived in the hacienda-dominated countryside. The ownership of a hacienda (or *fundo,* as it increasingly came to be called) was by now the clearest emblem of membership of the national elite. The tax records of 1854 show that some 850 landowners received about two-thirds of all agricultural income in central Chile. At least three-quarters of all agricultural land was occupied by estates, most of them including large tracts of land lying fallow from year to year. There was plenty of surplus labor in the countryside, as well as unused land within the haciendas, should these ever be needed. Until around 1850 or so they were not.

The main problem for Chilean hacendados in the 1840s was still lack of markets. The now revived grain trade with Peru was not very extensive. Around 1850, however, the prospects for the haciendas improved dramatically, as new opportunities suddenly opened up. The first of these was heralded by the news reaching Valparaiso in August 1848 that gold had been discovered on the American River in California. As the only major wheat-growing country on the Pacific coast, Chile was in a position to meet the food requirements of the swelling gold-rush population. Hacendados and traders took up the challenge. Exports of wheat and flour to California rose from around 6,000 metric quintals in 1848 to a peak of nearly 500,000 in 1850. To cope with the demand for flour, a technically modern milling business sprang into existence almost overnight around Tomé (on Talcahuano Bay) and along the Maule River, where the rich, young, politically ambitious grain-trader Juan Antonio Pando installed his "La Unión" mill, the largest yet seen in Chile. By the early 1870s there were around 130 mills of modern design in Chile.

A brief digression is in order here, for the California episode was to loom large in the Chilean collective memory, thanks in part to the literary efforts of Benjamín Vicuña Mackenna and Vicente Pérez Rosales. Quite apart from its boost to the haciendas, it prompted a considerable exodus of people, as Chileans of all sorts flocked northward to try their luck in the gold-fields – not only men, for a number of *chilenas* went too, gold-diggers in a somewhat different sense. At the height of the rush there were thousands of Chileans in California. Some of them struck it rich and never returned home; as always, the majority fared much less well. And Chileans soon suffered discrimination and even violent assault from Americans, both in the gold-fields and in San Francisco. Some turned to lawlessness, as was supposedly the case with the celebrated Chilean bandit Joaquín Murieta, romanticized by later generations as a symbol of Latin resistance to Anglo-Saxon arrogance – a myth in no way diminished by the fact that Murieta, if he existed at all, was probably Mexican. The legend was powerfully revived in 1967 by Pablo Neruda and Sergio Ortega in their beautiful cantata *Fulgor y muerte de Joaquín Murieta.*

One further effect of California must be noted here. So many Chilean ships were lured to the Golden Gate (as it had just been named) that the government was obliged to allow foreign vessels temporary access to the hitherto restricted coastal trade – a prefiguration of Reyes's law of 1864. It might be remarked here that the fate of the Chilean merchant marine was not really linked to the decisions of 1849 and 1864. In the 1850s it grew substantially. But during Chile's brief war with Spain in 1865–66 (which we shall describe in Chapter 5) Chilean vessels simply switched flags to avoid trouble from Spanish warships. Not until 1885 did Chilean tonnage again reach the levels of the mid-1860s. In 1922, to look ahead a bit, the coastal trade once again became a national monopoly.

The California export-boom was ephemeral. By 1855 the new thirty-first state of the Union was self-sufficient in (and even exporting) wheat and flour. But as luck would have it, a second gold-rush came to the rescue of Chilean hacendados, with the discoveries at Bendigo and Ballarat, Victoria, in 1851. Australian farms fell idle as men made off to the diggings. Once again, ships laden with wheat and flour made their way over the Pacific. Chilean exports to Australia reached their peak (nearly 2.7 million pesos' worth) in 1855; thereafter they swiftly fell off. It was California all over again: two or three years of high profits, followed by an effective closure of the market – an important factor in the recession of the late 1850s.

Nevertheless, this was by no means the end of the story. For ten years or so after the mid-1860s, Chilean haciendas were able to send large quantities of wheat and barley to the English market. Exports rose to a peak of 2 million metric quintals in 1874. This somewhat surprising development was due to high world prices and improvements in maritime transport, as well as the fact that Chilean grain, coming from the southern hemisphere, could reach England before the northern harvests. These advantages were lost as soon as larger-scale producers (e.g., the American Midwest) were in a position to edge Chile out of the international marketplace. In 1878 *The Economist* in London stopped quoting the price of Chilean wheat.

The keys to the mid-century agricultural export booms were thus geography (Chile's southern Pacific location) and spare capacity in the countryside. Agriculture, rather like mining, responded well to the stimulus of expanding markets, *but on its own terms,* without greatly altering Chilean ways of doing things. "Chilean hacendados," as Arnold Bauer puts it, "produced for export by merely extending the existing system."[10] Yet there *were* changes in the countryside, most visibly of all, perhaps, new irrigation works, with the construction of reservoirs (like the 157-hectare lake at Catapilco in the 1850s) and canals. Some of the canals

---

[10] *Chilean Rural Society from the Spanish Conquest to 1930* (Cambridge, 1975), p. 70.

were very long – sixty kilometers in the case of Joshua Waddington's in the Aconcagua Valley (built in the 1840s), 120 kilometers (taking in three tunnels and an aqueduct) in the more spectacular case of the Canal de las Mercedes, promoted in the mid-1850s by several hacendados (including the then president, Manuel Montt); it took thirty years to build. Efforts were also made at this period to improve livestock by bringing in foreign breeds, and to domesticate new crops, such as rice; the results were initially modest. A few success stories nevertheless deserve to be singled out. The introduction of Italian bees in the 1840s transformed (indeed, virtually created) Chilean apiculture, soon enabling the country to achieve self-sufficiency in honey. Chileans, as we have seen, had drunk their own rough wines since the sixteenth century; starting in the 1850s (Silvestre Ochagavía is usually credited with being the pioneer) several landowners planted French vines for the first time. Chile's isolation meant that they survived the phylloxera plague that began to devastate European vineyards in the 1860s. Pinot and cabernet grapes, it was found, did particularly well in the Central Valley soil and sunshine. Such was the origin of a splendid tradition which in the fullness of time was to produce some of the western hemisphere's noblest wines – the only wines in the world, some believe, to preserve the authentic pre-phylloxera French taste.

The government paid something more than lip-service to agricultural improvement. From the 1840s onward it maintained a model farm and experimental station of sorts, the Quinta Normal de Agricultura in Santiago. Likewise, the *Sociedad Nacional de Agricultura* (SNA, National Agricultural Society) – twice abortively founded (1838, 1855) before finally getting going in 1869 – attempted to foster improvements; it did not become the landowners' pressure group as such until the early twentieth century. Some *agricultores progresistas,* "progressive farmers," strove valiantly to innovate, but they were clearly a minority. Leaving aside irrigation schemes, high capital investment in agriculture was a rarity. The cultivated area tripled (perhaps even quadrupled) during the export booms; the number of estates increased, as some of the huge properties of former times were subdivided (there was still plenty of scope for this); *inquilinaje* was expanded, with new families settling within estates; new forms of sharecropping developed, especially in the coastal cordillera. But none of these things implied deep change. Farming methods remained traditional; there was little mechanization, certainly in comparison with neighboring Argentina; oxen were still universal in the countryside until the 1930s. The patriarchal rural world (for so many, the real Chile), the world of *patrón* and inquilino, was strengthened rather than undermined by the export economy.

The outward and visible signs of progress

The most immediately visible symbol of progress was the revolution in transportation that accompanied (and was a necessary condition for) the expansion of overseas trade. In the 1830s Chile was still more than three months from Europe by sailing ship. In 1840 two 700-ton paddle-steamers, *Chile* and *Peru,* arrived from England to start regular sailings between Valparaiso and Callao. The man responsible, the remarkable American entrepreneur William Wheelwright, had recently organized the Pacific Steam Navigation Company, a British line whose passenger ships were to be a familiar sight on Chile's coast until the 1960s. From the mid-1840s, when the PSNC[11] extended its route to Panama, it became possible (with good connections) to reach Europe in under forty days. In 1868 direct sailings began between Valparaiso and Liverpool by way of the Magellan Straits. Other European (and more modestly, Chilean) companies soon competed with the mighty PSNC, whose tonnage in 1874 equaled that of the U.S. Navy. Steamers did not yet eclipse sailing ships, still much used for bulk cargoes. Indeed, the final great age of sail was now dawning, with its beautiful clippers and four-masted barques.

Steam also, of course, revolutionized transportation on land. The first Chilean railroad (with fifty-one miles, the first substantial line in Latin America) was laid in 1851 to connect Copiapó and the port of Caldera. It was built by the ubiquitous Wheelwright, and financed by a group of rich miners and traders, including the formidable and politically combative Doña Candelaria Goyenechea (widow of Miguel Gallo), Agustín Edwards, Matías Cousiño, and members of the Subercaseaux, Ossa, and Montt dynasties. It was later extended farther into the mining zone, where other private railroads were built in due course. The all-important link between Santiago and Valparaiso, on which work began in October 1852, was originally a mixed (half-government, half-private) venture. It ran into difficulties both with the route and with the shareholders, so in 1858 the government bought out the private interests. The 114-mile wide-gauge line was finally completed in 1863, its last (80-mile) section constructed at breakneck speed by another very remarkable American, Henry Meiggs. A third major railroad began to push southward down the Central Valley in the late 1850s; this *Ferrocarril del Sur* was another mixed venture later (1873) taken over by the state. August 1862 saw the first train to San Fernando, eighty-seven miles south of the capital. A railroad from Talcahuano to Chillán (to link up with the Central Valley

---

[11] The famous initials were later to prompt several long-running jokes, e.g.: *Pésimas Son Nuestras Comidas* (Our meals are terrible), and *Pasajeros Nunca Ser Contentos* (Passengers never happy).

line) was constructed between 1869 and 1874. By the mid-1870s, therefore, Chile had a rail network of nearly a thousand miles, more than half of it owned by the nation.

The state naturally took a hand in the development of telegraphy, the third classic nineteenth-century innovation. A Santiago-Valparaiso telegraph was installed in 1852 – yet another venture by the amazing Wheelwright, whose multiple services to Chile won him a statue in Valparaiso (1877), most appropriately, since he had earlier promoted gas-lighting and water schemes there. This first telegraph was a private company, though assisted by state subsidies; the government shouldered the main burden of creating a national network, as part of a fully organized postal service. (Rowland Hill's simple principle went into effect in Chile in 1856; two years later Chileans mailed 662,998 letters.)[12] By 1876 the state telegraph's forty-eight offices and 1,600-mile network spanned the length of the country. International connections had to be privately promoted. Santiago and Buenos Aires were linked by a line thrown over the Andes by the Chilean brothers Juan and Mateo Clark (1872). Two years later, when the Brazilian submarine cable was laid, Chile was placed in direct touch with the Old World. On August 6, 1874, for the very first time, *El Mercurio* printed European news straight from Europe. (Back in 1838 the same newspaper ran the story of Queen Victoria's coronation over four months after it happened.) A Havas Reuter's office, a true symbol of this first "information revolution," was set up in Valparaiso in 1875.

To what extent did the export booms develop the domestic Chilean economy? The question is obviously fundamental. With mining and agriculture so dominant, there might seem to have been little space for manufacturing industry. Certainly industrialization *per se* was not a priority for Chilean governments until much later. Before the 1850s at least, local manufacturing remained predominantly artesanal. In the countryside, as the French scholar Gay noted, the peasant had "to be at one and the same time his own weaver, tailor, carpenter, mason, etc."[13] The import of British cottons made some difference here, although the 1854 census still counted 9,000 weavers in Santiago and Valparaiso provinces. By the same token, however, the export economy itself, as we have seen, summoned up copper smelters and flour mills, and the expansion of the domestic market gave opportunities to would-be industrialists, many of them immigrant entrepreneurs. Their efforts marked the modest beginnings of Chilean industrialization.

---

[12] *El Araucano,* No. 2092, July 23, 1859.

[13] Claudius Gay, *La agricultura chilena,* 2 vols. (Santiago, 1973), I, 159.

According to the detailed investigations of Luis Ortega, the Chile of the mid-1870s had upward of 120 industrial establishments – "industrial" in the sense that they all used steam-power, paid money wages, and employed more than ten workers. (The Guayacán and Lota smelters, of course, had several hundred men apiece.) Plants supplying food and drink included the Viña del Mar sugar refinery (opened, with the president on hand, in 1873) and a number of modern breweries – Carlos Andwandter's at Valdivia brewing the tastiest beer of the time. Textile mills, a paper factory (at Limache), and at least ten mechanized printing shops were also operating. Fire-bricks for the smelters were being made at Lota and Coronel from the mid-1860s onward. Most impressive of all was a small metallurgical and engineering industry – plants turning out machinery, spare parts, military matériel, and rolling-stock for the railroads (which also had workshops of their own). One short-lived but noteworthy state-run enterprise, the *Fundición Nacional* (National Foundry), set up in 1865–66 at Limache, later turned out such items as steam engines, steam pumps, locomotive boilers, a steamship propeller, bells, and ploughs. The foundry was closed in 1874, partly on the grounds that it competed with private plants – recognition that this advanced branch of industry was making a mark in Chile. One or two intellectuals regarded the advent of industry with disquiet: Andrés Bello's feelings on the matter, he once implied, were those of Goldsmith in *The Deserted Village*. (But where were the real Chilean equivalents of "sweet Auburn"?) Others, looking ahead rather than backward, began to wonder whether industry might be a means of lessening dependence on exports.

The expanding pace of economic activity was naturally reflected in monetary and commercial practices. The gold, silver, and copper coins (decimalized in the early 1850s) that were the sole legal tender until 1860 were never sufficient to meet the demands of growing trade, and had a habit of flowing out of the country altogether during recessions, as in the late 1850s. The shortage of low-denomination coins was chronic. Employers sometimes used tokens (*fichas*) as unofficial currencies, sometimes (like those issued by José Tomás Urmeneta) very handsomely designed. The main sources of credit prior to the 1850s were private lenders ("capitalists" like Blest Gana's fictional Don Dámaso Encina) or the Valparaiso commercial houses. An early banking venture, mounted by Antonio Arcos in 1849, was a failure, partly because of personal distrust of Arcos (a Spaniard known for his shady deals during O'Higgins's regime), partly because the Valparaiso traders wanted the business for themselves. The first permanent note-issuing banks, the Banco de Ossa and the Banco de Valparaiso, were formed in the mid-1850s. A general (and rather liberal) banking law was enacted in 1860. Fifteen years later there were at least eleven banks in Chile, with an effective capital of more than 22 million pesos. Meanwhile, the Caja de Crédito Hipotecario, a land mortgage bank founded in 1856, funnelled a new flow of credit to the countryside – in practice to the hacendados.

Commercial organization also changed after 1850, most notably with the appearance of *sociedades anónimas,* joint-stock companies, regulated in a law of 1854. The first *sociedades anónimas* were the railroad companies. By the later 1870s at least 200 such enterprises had been formed at one time or another – predominantly in mining, banking, insurance (the first Chilean company dates from 1853), railroads, and utilities. This emergent corporate pattern illustrates certain peculiarities of Chile's burgeoning capitalism. While relatively little capital went into agriculture or manufacturing, the attraction of speculative mining ventures was powerful. The Caracoles bonanza prompted the formation of twenty-seven new companies by October 1872. "Caracoles fever," indeed, provoked an unprecedented speculative spree, a bubble that burst only too soon.

Mining, by the 1870s, included a new business whose origins must be noted here, for it was soon to loom tremendously over Chile's history. Deposits of sodium nitrate, much in demand in Europe as a fertilizer, had been exploited for some time now in the Peruvian desert province of Tarapacá. Chilean capital, nothing if not expansionist, was heavily involved here: fully one-quarter of all Tarapacá's nitrate production was Chilean-controlled in 1871–72. On the Bolivian littoral, farther south, Chileans were even more overwhelmingly conspicuous. The silver-mines at Caracoles were worked almost entirely by Chileans. Nitrate deposits in the Atacama desert had been opened up in the mid-1860s by the Chilean entrepreneurs José Santos Ossa and Francisco Puelma, who secured generous concessions from the then Bolivian dictator Mariano Melgarejo. The insignificant coastal hamlet of La Chimba suddenly blossomed into the thriving new city of Antofagasta, almost completely Chilean in population. By the mid-1870s the original Ossa-Puelma concern had been transformed into a powerful Chilean-British (in fact mostly Chilean) corporation, the *Compañía de Salitres y Ferrocarril de Antofagasta* (Antofagasta Nitrate and Railway Company). Its shareholders included a number of leading Chilean politicians.

The true nexus of Chilean capitalism at this period was the bustling port of Valparaiso, with its forest of masts in the bay, its handsomely stuccoed Customs House, its *almacenes fiscales.* Here, at the heart of a distinctly cosmopolitan trading community, several dozen import-export houses held the commanding heights of Chile's export economy. The typical such enterprise was the commission house, chiefly interested in profiting from commissions on imports and exports, but also with a powerful hold over both miners and hacendados. Foreigners were especially prominent in this business, with the British well to the fore –

representatives of what has been called (adapting Philip Curtin's phrase) "the last true large-scale trade diaspora before the coming of the multinational corporations."[14]

What we might term the British connection was fundamental to Chile in the early republic, with between one-third and two-thirds of all exports going to Great Britain and one-third to one-half of all Chilean imports coming from there. (Imports from France also ran at fairly high levels, a reflection of upper-class tastes.) Direct British investment at the period was mostly confined to government bonds, though we should not ignore the regular investments made in the British trading houses. In the widest sense, of course, Great Britain's hegemonic position in the international trading system of the nineteenth century influenced the general development of Chile's export economy *simply because it was there.* The steamers, telegraphs, railways, and joint-stock companies all played their part in solidifying Chile's links with the fast-expanding world market. The decision to follow this path, for better and worse, was a Chilean decision. This may have been a way of avoiding more serious choices, but who can really say?

The slowly changing face of society

Most educated Chileans in the early 1870s, looking back over the previous forty years or so, were convinced that their country had risen in the world. In some ways it had. But what effect did economic expansion have on Chilean society as a whole? Its impact was unquestionably somewhat uneven. The chief beneficiaries of progress were clearly the upper class, and others connected with the expansion of trade; to what extent poorer Chileans benefited is rather less clear. By the 1850s, after the first export boom, some upper-class Chileans were able to live very opulently. We might do worse than mention the case of Emeterio Goyenechea (mine-owner, trader, and landowner), who in October 1856 held the most sumptuous banquet yet seen in Santiago. Eight hundred guests; fountains playing; special lighting effects; two national guard bands in attendance – *le tout Santiago* was there, "statesmen, rich capitalists, literati, lions, dandies...." Goyenechea's bash was as much a talking point, that week, as the politically contentious "affair of the sacristan" (which we will come to in Chapter 5), just then reaching its tense climax.[15]

The rich, in fact, now got richer – much richer than their colonial predecessors. As Vicuña Mackenna put it, "there were no mining millionaires before Chañarcillo, and no landowning demi-millionaires before

---

[14] Eduardo Cavieres, *Comercio chileno y comerciantes ingleses 1820–1880* (Valparaiso, 1988), p. 227.

[15] *El Ferrocarril,* Nos. 253 and 255, October 17 and 20, 1856.

California."[16] A famous, often quoted list of fifty-nine millionaires (the highest fortune being 16 million pesos) published in *El Mercurio* in 1882 was almost certainly incomplete, and in any case its author (probably Vicuña Mackenna) revealingly noted: "if we had to take into account all those who have 200,000 pesos or more, we would fill the entire newspaper."[17]

Chile's nineteenth-century upper class was essentially what Claude Gay called "a moneyed aristocracy, whether by hereditary right, or by having won a fortune in trade, or by having found an even greater fortune in the exploitation of mines."[18] Older families undoubtedly continued to pride themselves (as many still do) on their colonial lineages: "there are probably few countries in the world that outdo us in musty old aristocratic tendencies," claimed a writer in 1859.[19] But the new magnates of mining or banking had no difficulty entering high society – if indeed they had ever been far removed from it in the first place. No upper-class Chilean found mining or trade to be socially demeaning; rather the contrary. Thus the miners and traders who, elsewhere, might conceivably have formed a *bourgeoisie conquérante*, challenging or displacing an old landed aristocracy, were here in Chile fully assimilated into the national elite from the outset, though undoubtedly modifying it in the process, just as Basque immigration had modified the late-colonial elite. Upperclass economic interests overlapped and often interlocked, miners becoming landowners, landowners investing in mines, and so on. The tradition of landownership in particular gave a high degree of coherence to this dominant social group.

It would be misleading to suggest that the upper class was fully homogeneous, either then or later. Possibly its most significant internal divide lay between Santiago and the provinces. The hesitant feelings of a *provinciano* visiting the capital for the first time are well portrayed in some of the literature of the time. And there were always impoverished upper-class families, clinging to their status with pathetic tenacity. Nonetheless, most people at this privileged level shared certain common values – a sense of social superiority, an often contemptuous view of the lower classes, a strong attachment to landownership, and, not least, a recognition of the claims of family (i.e., the extended family). Family connections criss-crossed the upper class, playing a vital role in business and social life – and politics. In the one hundred years after 1830, the impressively extended Errázuriz clan gave the republic three presidents

[16] *Don Diego Portales,* 3rd ed. (1974), p. 71.

[17] "Los millonarios de Chile viejo," *El Mercurio,* No. 16,547, April 26, 1882.

[18] *La agricultura chilena,* 1, 102.

[19] *El Ferrocarril,* No. 1173, October 6, 1859. (He had obviously not visited England.)

(one admittedly provisional), one archbishop, and upward of fifty congressmen.

Higher upper-class incomes undoubtedly encouraged conspicuous consumption – Sr. Goyenechea's party being a case in point. The "great object of life" on acquiring wealth, according to an American visitor, was to "remove to the capital, to lavish it in costly furniture, equipage and splendid living."[20] There was a high demand for imported luxury goods. Thanks to the steamship, foreign travel became much easier than before: the generation born around 1830 (a notable one) was the first to go in for lengthy trips to Europe to any extent. Political exile, as in the 1850s, could sometimes be combined with a Grand Tour. Travelers inevitably returned with new fashions and ideas. Foreign influences continued to alter upper-class lifestyles. England set the tone in masculine attire (the *frac* or frock-coat now becoming obligatory) and in sport (the conventions of the English turf, for instance, replacing traditional Chilean horseracing styles, in Santiago anyhow, by the end of the 1860s). Tea-drinking continued its advance at the expense of *mate*. The Club de la Unión, the Santiago gentlemen's club founded in 1864, and a future upper-class redoubt, imitated the models of London. France, also, perhaps even more than England, was a great source of new trends – in female dress, in furniture, literary taste, political rhetoric, and (in the Catholic Church) devotional practice. This creeping Europeanization of taste is perhaps the real key to understanding the political liberalization that set in after 1861. It seems more than possible, too, that it widened the psychological gulf that lay between the rich and poorer classes, whose more modest way of life remained altogether more traditional.

Class distinction, needless to say, was quite unavoidable. On the new steamships, for instance, servants paid half-fare, "peons and day-laborers" quarter-fare for a passage on deck.[21] In the countryside, the *patrón* or his *mayordomo* expected, and mostly received, deferential attitudes from inquilinos and peons. Yet the demonstration effect of changing upper-class *mores* undoubtedly filtered through to other classes. Between the upper class (*gente*, "people"; later on *gente decente*, "decent people") and the laboring poor (*el pueblo*, "the people"), a distinct if also miscellaneous middle social band grew noticeably larger with economic expansion. The owners of small businesses and farms, the clerks of the trading houses and government offices, engineers from abroad, lower-ranking military officers – these and others formed this embryonic middle class. The snobbish (and untranslatable) term *medio pelo* was used by the upper class to describe the "middling folk" of the time, and it was still being used

---

[20] Mrs. G. B. Merwin, *Three Years in Chile* (Carbondale, Ill., 1966), p. 63.
[21] *Almanaque nacional para el año 1854* (1854), p. 43.

well into the twentieth century. "The *medio pelo*," it was observed in 1872, "forms a separate caste; he does not fraternize with the people, whom he disdainfully calls *rotos,* but neither is he admitted into society."[22] *Medio pelo* lifestyles were a scaled-down version of those of the upper class: the latter smoked imported cigars, while the former consumed the local product. (Both classes were absolutely addicted to smoking, even today much less frowned on in Chile than in the neo-puritan United States.) The upper fringe of this middle band certainly included frustrated social climbers, yearning for upper-class status. By the later 1850s these constituted a recognizable type and were becoming known as *siúticos,* a neologism (of uncertain derivation) often attributed to José Victorino Lastarria.

The artisans, craftsmen, and tradesmen of the cities formed a further identifiable social group – a group referred to by educated Chileans as *la clase obrera,* "the working class." They evidently wished to distinguish themselves from the laboring poor: "to call artisans *rotos* is to offend them," claimed a propaganda-sheet of 1845.[23] Here, too, the influence of upper-class lifestyles was felt – something noticed by the sharp-eyed Lieutenant Gilliss, an American visitor whose account of mid-nineteenth-century Chile is singularly comprehensive. Observing the "mechanics and retail shopkeepers" of Santiago, he noted:

in public, fine dress is a passion with them, and a stranger would scarcely suspect that the man he meets in a fine broad-cloth cloak, escorting a woman arrayed in silks and jewelry, occupied no higher rank in the social scale than that of tinman, carpenter or shopman whose sole stock-in-trade might be packed in a box five feet square. They will go to any lengths to obtain fine clothes and fine furniture, or to attend the theater on holidays, yet constantly live in the utmost discomfort.[24]

The flood of foreign imports after independence by no means drove artisans out of business. They certainly resented commercial policy: in September 1861 an artisan delegation coupled its loyal greetings to the incoming President Pérez with the request that he immediately impose a 70 percent duty on all imported manufactures![25] In fact, however, the rising incomes of the rich and the incipient middle class enabled the artisanate to expand and even to share (modestly) in the new prosperity. Artisan participation in certain political episodes (1845–46, 1850–51) was salient enough – but it reflected a subaltern rather than an independent role. From the 1850s onward, in a somewhat different (but for the

[22] Recaredo S. Tornero, *Chile Ilustrado* (Valparaiso, 1872), p. 465.

[23] *El Artesano del Orden,* November 16, 1845.

[24] J. M. Gilliss, *The United States Naval Astronomical Expedition to the Southern Hemisphere during the years 1849–'50–'51–'52, Vol. I, Chile* (Washington, D.C., 1855), p. 219.

[25] *La Discusión,* No. 247, September 11, 1861.

artisans, more immediately beneficial) development, a number of mutualist associations began to be formed, to provide artisans and craftsmen
with greater security. A remarkable self-taught carpenter, builder, and
architect, Fermín Vivaceta, the son of a widowed laundrywoman, did
much to foster these societies (his first was in 1862); by the end of the
1870s around forty of them had been legally registered.

The effects of economic expansion on *el pueblo,* the laboring poor –
"the confused labyrinth of the masses," to use a phrase from 1845[26] –
were discernibly less positive than they were for the better-placed social
groups. In the countryside, as we noted in Chapter 1, there was a
clear distinction between the inquilinos of the haciendas, an incipiently
independent peasantry, and the "floating" population of peons. A variety
of pressures – the exactions of hacendados and traders, forced enrollment
in the Army, new official restrictions – seems to have reduced the scope
of independent peasant cultivation and trade in the early republic. On
the haciendas themselves, as the export booms got under way, *inquilinaje*
itself was tightened, with greater labor services usually being required
from the tenants. This did little to alter the inquilino's primitive way of
life: his dwelling was rudimentary, his bucolic diversions were rough-
and-ready, and his opportunities for self-improvement were very limited.
Yet in many ways the inquilino was the stablest element in the countryside. Haciendas could (and did) change hands; the tenant families often
remained the same from generation to generation.

The rural peons were a different matter, both inured to and degraded
by chronic underemployment and poverty, and the worst-affected when
crop failure brought famine, as it did in the Chillán area at the end of the
1830s. Some remained vagabonds, subsisting on cattle-rustling and similar thieving. Information about rural wages at this period is hard to
interpret (payments were often made in kind), but the demand for extra
hands created by the export booms may have brought a slight all-round
rise. According to Bauer, 20 to 25 centavos per day was common in the
1840s, 25 to 30 per day in the 1870s. With the spread of cereal cultivation, some peons were attracted onto the haciendas as resident workers,
usually on less favorable terms than had been the case with inquilinos.
Others drifted into the poorer districts in the towns, thus swelling the
ranks of the *rotos,* the urban laborers, though often, too, chancing their
luck as small-time traders.

As in colonial times, the simple lack of stable work meant that peons
(rural and urban alike) were forced to wander in search of subsistence.
The educated classes stereotyped them as feckless and improvident (and
certainly they liked drinking and gambling), but when work was to be

---

[26] *Gaceta del Comercio,* Valparaiso, No. 1175, November 21, 1845.

had they were very hard workers – as was often appreciated by foreigners. One outlet for them was the expanding mining zone of the north. There were possibly as many as 30,000 mine-workers there by 1870 or so, at which point many moved on to Caracoles. Wage-rates in the mines were higher than in the countryside. According to Lieutenant Gilliss, a *barretero* earned 25 pesos per month in 1850, an *apir* about half this. The isolated, ramshackle mining camps were socially more volatile than the countryside. Discipline was harsh. The theft of metals (*cangalla,* as it was known) was universal, but meant at least a flogging if detected. Occasionally the camps exploded in spasms of anomic, alcohol-fueled violence, the first such disturbance occurring at Chañarcillo as early as 1834. Political agitation from outside could sometimes spark off explosions. In October 1851, when civil war was raging farther south, the workers at Chañarcillo comprehensively sacked their settlement, the little "town" of Juan Godoy. The local *subdelegado* afterward wrote to the Intendant of Atacama:

As to the origin of the mutiny . . . it seems unquestionable that its authors had something political in mind. But in their stupidity they did not see that the mob they had to use to get the disorder going would not be so easy to rein in, would not be prevented from robbing and pillaging – natural for that brute mass which has no aspirations of its own.[27]

Yet there were a few definite stirrings of class consciousness in the mines. In 1865, when the bosses at Chañarcillo imposed a new set of regulations which implied a lowering of wages, the workers staged (and won) what seems to have been the first real strike in the mining zone.

New opportunities for at least some peons came with the road-building schemes instituted in the 1840s. Some 700 workers were employed on the Chillán-Tomé road, said to be the most important single project of the period – laid in the mid-1850s to speed the transportation of wheat to the Tomé mills. Railway-building required very much larger gangs of men. Henry Meiggs, for instance, had as many as 8,000 working for him on the Santiago-Valparaiso line. He was one of those foreigners who recognized the merits of Chilean workers, as he made clear at the inaugural banquet at Llay Llay in October 1863: "I have, it is true," he said, "treated them like men, not like dogs, as is the custom here. . . . I would prefer to work with five hundred Chileans than with a thousand Irishmen."[28] At the end of the 1860s Meiggs embarked on a series of ambitious railway-building ventures for the Peruvian government. True to his word, he turned first to Chile when recruiting his labor force. As

[27] Letter of November 3, 1851. Ministry of Interior archives: Intendancy of Atacama, Vol. 86.
[28] Ramón Rivera Jofré, *Reseña histórica del ferrocarril entre Santiago y Valparaiso,* 2nd ed. (Santiago, 1963), pp. 121–22.

many as 25,000 peons flocked northward over the next few years. By mid-1871 this highly visible outflow of labor (not to mention violent affrays in Peru in which Chileans figured prominently) was causing public concern. Landowners complained of a "shortage of hands" in the fields, though there is little evidence that peon wages rose or that cereal production fell during these years. Restrictions on emigration were considered in Congress and in the press. No controls were imposed: in the years that followed Chilean peons continued to go abroad, some to work on Ferdinand de Lesseps's abortive Panama Canal, others (many more) to embrace an altogether more promising agrarian future across the mountains in booming Argentina. The Peruvian episode, however, does seem to have focused educated Chileans' attention more closely on the laboring poor than had been true earlier on.

Foreigners and natives

How best to improve the condition of the poor? In terms of public debate, only the merest glimmerings of a "social question" can be found before the 1870s. The far-sighted Santiago Arcos (rebellious son of the would-be banker) had one solution: divide up the haciendas and give every Chilean a stake in the land. But Arcos was well known to be a wild revolutionary (albeit a charming one) who deserved to be (and, in due course, was) locked up. Most upper-class Chileans took the less inconvenient view that the best way to "moralize" the lower orders was to bring in European immigrants. "A phalanx of peaceful immigrants, of industrious settlers," wrote Marcial González in 1848, "brings in its customs and habits more civilization than the best books, more wealth than a thousand ships loaded with manufactures."[29] Immigrants, by and large, were warmly welcomed. The census of 1854 counted around 20,000 foreigners (three-quarters of them bachelors) in Chile – over half of them Argentines, along with nearly 2,000 British, more than 1,600 French, and about 700 Americans. The census of twenty-one years later put the total at around 25,000 – including 4,000 British, 3,000 French, and 900 Americans, the number of Argentines having by then fallen. Among the foreign colonies, the British were perhaps the best-organized, above all in Valparaiso, where they had their own favorite district, Cerro Alegre, their own schools, their own newspapers, their own benevolent society (1854), and, by the early 1860s, that vital need, a cricket club.

The influence of foreigners was out of all proportion to their numbers. Americans installed the new flourmills; Americans and British worked on

---

[29] *La Europa y la América o la emigración europea en sus relaciones con el enprandecimiento de las repúblicas americanas* (1848), p. 18.

railroad-building and later on often drove the locomotives; immigrants set up many of the industrial enterprises of the 1860s and 1870s. Europeans also found work as artisans, mechanics, and tradesmen, not least in the more upmarket trades. (Thirty-six of the forty-six dressmakers counted in 1854 were French; there were also 133 English carpenters in Chile that year.) Britons and others were to be found as engineers, mechanics, and mine-workers in the northern provinces and in the southern coalfields. It is impossible to say how many foreigners stayed in Chile (and became Chileans) and how many went home. What is certain is that they left a permanent mark on the country, many of them founding dynasties and enlarging the cluster of non-Hispanic surnames both in the upper class (which relatively few immigrants reached quickly) and in the small middle class. It must also be noted here that foreign experts were sometimes hired by the government to undertake scientific tasks: the Frenchmen Claude Gay, compiler of a thirty-volume account of the country (1844–71), and Amado Pissis, who mapped the republic from 28°10'S to 41°58'S (it took him more than twenty years), are two famous examples. The role of foreigners in education, medicine, and the arts was a notable one in the early republic.

Although large-scale European immigration did not materialize (there was hardly room for it in the hacienda-crowded Central Valley), the efforts of a German immigrant, Bernardo Philippi, and the redoubtable Vicente Pérez Rosales did succeed, in the 1850s, in attracting a small German migration into the sparsely populated forest lands around Valdivia and Lake Llanquihue, to the south of Araucanian territory. The 3,000 Germans who were there by 1860 proved a hardy breed, clearing the forests, breaking new ground, and establishing what Jean-Pierre Blancpain has called a "pioneer micro-society." Their presence left a distinctive stamp on the southern provinces, still very much there. "We shall be honorable and hardworking Chileans," said Carlos Andwandter, who arrived in the first large group (1850).[30] So it proved, from that day to this.

With new settlements to the south, with railroads pressing toward the Frontier from the north, Araucania itself now lay under mortal threat from its traditional *huinca* (white) adversaries. Until the 1850s, Chilean governments continued the old colonial policy toward the Mapuche: the army kept watch on the Frontier, and friendly caciques like Lorenzo Colipí (he died in 1838) were subsidized. The agricultural export boom upset the equilibrium of the Frontier: it pushed settlers south of the Bío Bío (at least 14,000 by 1858). The new province of Arauco (theoretically covering the whole of Araucania) was created in 1853. During the 1859

---

[30] Vicente Pérez Rosales, *Recuerdos del pasado*, 4th ed. (1929), p. 424.

civil war, rebel leaders stirred the Mapuche into assaulting the new trans-Bío Bío settlements. An old Frontier hand, Colonel Cornelio Saavedra (Intendant of Arauco, 1857–59), now proposed the gradual occupation of Araucanian territory by moving the official frontier south by stages, establishing new lines of forts.

The issue was kept alive by a curious and semi-comic episode that occurred soon afterward. Orélie-Antoine de Tounens, an obscure but persuasive French adventurer, entered Araucania, won the confidence of several caciques, and proclaimed that the territory was henceforth to be the Kingdom of Araucania and Patagonia, with himself as monarch. King Orélie-Antonio I's reign was sadly short. Betrayed to the Chilean army, he was repatriated to France as a madman.[31] Immediately after this episode, Saavedra was given the go-ahead to mount the final *huinca* invasion of Araucania.

It took more than twenty years. The first phase, under Saavedra himself, saw the establishment of new fortified settlements such as Mulchen and Angol (1862), the latter becoming a bustling frontier town of 7,000 by 1873. The first new frontier-line, along the Malleco River, was finally secured in 1868, by which time new forts had also been extended down the coast. So far the *huinca* advance had been reasonably trouble-free, but the Araucanians, led by the active cacique Quilapán, now mounted the inevitable counter-attack, Mapuche assaults and Chilean punitive razzias alternating until 1871. All this still left the Araucanians with a considerable swathe of territory. Only in 1878 (Saavedra was by then minister of War) was a more southerly line of forts established along the Traiguén River. Further advances were delayed by the outbreak of the War of the Pacific, after which troops were sent south to finish the job. The final Mapuche offensive (November 1881) was rapidly overwhelmed. The railroad and the telegraph had done their work. With the re-foundation of Villarica (one of the seven trans-Bío Bío "cities" lost after the Mapuche offensive of 1598) in January 1883, the long saga of Araucanian independence finally came to its close.

In the meantime, settlers were flooding into the new territory thus laid open. Unscrupulous land-grabbing at the expense of the Mapuche was an altogether predictable feature of this "new frontier," and remained so for the next few decades, despite the government's efforts to regularize purchases of Amerindian land in the imperfectly enforced laws of 1866

---

[31] Orélie-Antoine returned to Araucania in 1869; a price was placed on his head, and he prudently withdrew. A third attempt (1874) was nipped in the bud by the Argentine authorities. On yet a fourth occasion (1876) the man who would be king set out for his lost domain, only to fall sick in Buenos Aires. His appointed successors in France (he himself was a bachelor) continued the dynasty into the twentieth century, conferring honors and decorations on anyone who took the trouble to collect them.

and 1874. (The Mapuche themselves were eventually assigned around 475,000 hectares, by no means enough for the entire community.) Among those who exploited the new frontier very profitably was José Bunster, a man of Anglo-Chilean background who had seen his lumber business destroyed in the upheavals of 1859. From the mid-1860s, Bunster set up new timber mills in the south, and went into large-scale cereal-cultivation. His nickname, "the king of Araucania," was closer to reality than the noble title claimed by poor, deluded Orélie-Antoine. Realities (for the now pauperized Mapuche, very harsh realities) were to be more important than dreams as "civilization" extinguished a way of life many Central Valley peons might well have envied.

Cities and culture

The most striking contrast, in the Chile of the early republic, was between town and country. Civilization, the magic term so often invoked in discussions of the "Araucanian question," was more evident in the cities than anywhere else. In fact, we are really talking only about two cities, Santiago and Valparaiso, whose populations in 1875 were 150,000 and 100,000 respectively. Most other Chilean towns grew much more slowly; few had much to offer in the way of civic life or architectural attraction. Copiapó was the capital of a rich mining province, but despite certain improvements by 1850 or so (gas-lights, a pleasant *alameda,* a few paved streets, a new theater), it did not strike most visitors as very special. Concepción, devastated by the February 1835 earthquake, still looked fairly devastated ten years later; the wheat boom had an eventual tonic effect on the city. Of the string of Central Valley towns, only Chillán and Talca had any real pretensions. None of the places mentioned had more than 20,000 inhabitants even in 1875.

Valparaiso, "the façade, the portico of our republic," as it was described in 1849,[32] was usually the first (sometimes the only) place in Chile to be seen by foreigners. All the world's sailors went there: it lodged itself in the imagination of far-away Europe.

> A ship from Valparaiso came,
> And in the bay her sails were furled.
> She brought the wonder of her name
> And tidings from a sunnier world.[33]

As a port, Valparaiso was less than ideal. It was no safe haven. A strong north wind could dash ships against each other or on to the foreshore.

---

[32] Francisco de Paula Taforó, Chamber of Deputies, July 4, 1849.
[33] Oliver St. John Gogarty, "The Ship."

After heavy rain, thick mud flowed from the ravines that pitted the encircling hills. In spite of such inconveniences, the city progressed. A decent theater, daily newspapers, gas-lighting, a proper fire-brigade (the first in Chile) – Valparaiso had all of these things before Santiago. The streets on the narrow shelf of land nearest the port, with their (by Chilean standards) tall buildings, came to have a faintly British stamp; this contrasted (and still does) with the altogether more Chilean atmosphere of the Almendral district along the foreshore to the north. (Still farther north, the village of Viña del Mar began in the 1870s to show signs of its future development as an ocean resort.) After a foreign bombardment in 1866 (see Chapter 5), some lavish rebuilding took place. Francisco Echaurren, the tough-minded Intendant of 1870–76, sponsored further improvements, including a few public urinals (nicknamed *echaurrinas*). Those who had known Valparaiso in Portales's day found it a much more handsome town forty years later.

Before 1850 or so, the capital itself still had an essentially colonial appearance. The immigrant Polish scientist Ignacio Domeyko, who first saw it in 1840, was impressed by the "image of order and tranquillity" imparted by its low, one-story, adobe-built houses, with their barred windows and secluded patios.[34] The countryside still came right into the city: only a block away from the Moneda, in the early 1840s, there stood a dairy to which thirty or forty cows came each day. The urban throng, so Gilliss tells us, included

peons from the country with panniers and baskets of fowls, fruits and vegetables; bakers and milkwomen, with huge trunk-like receptacles slung one on each side of a mule, or stout tin cans similarly arranged; . . . water-vendors distributing to families their daily supplies from the turbid fountains; . . . a drove of pack-mules or a train of carts just entering from the port. . . .[35]

No new public buildings of distinction appeared in the 1830s or 1840s. The flow of new wealth soon altered this static picture. The city's first gas-lights began burning in 1857; horse-drawn trams ran from that year, too, supplementing the 4,500 or so coaches and carriages (great upper-class status symbols) already circulating. Part of the city center had piped drinking water by the end of the 1860s. Efforts to provide the capital with a fire-service like Valparaiso's were unavailing until a dreadful conflagration in the church of La Compañía (December 1863) that killed 2,000 worshippers. Immediately after this appalling holocaust, a volunteer fire-brigade was formed; in future years the *compañías de bomberos* became socially very respectable institutions.

A more visible sign of change was the feverish construction that set in

---

[34] *Mis viajes*, 2 vols. (Santiago, 1978), I, 494.   [35] Gilliss, p. 177.

after 1850, as rich families provided themselves with new, European-style mansions. Several noteworthy public buildings date from this period: the Teatro Municipal (1853–57), inaugurated with a performance of Verdi's *Hernani;* the University (1863–74); and, grandest of all, the splendid new Congress (1857–76). The theater burned down in 1870 (the first time a *bombero* died in action) but was immediately rebuilt. French architects such as Claude-François Brunet Debaines (the disciple of Garnier who founded Chile's school of architecture in 1849) and Lucien Hénault were well to the fore here, though they were very ably complemented by Chileans like Fermín Vivaceta, among whose many jobs was the tower we now see on the church of San Francisco, Santiago's oldest, and a central market (still standing) which was an early example of iron architecture.

Contemporaries were much impressed by these changes. When Domingo Sarmiento revisited Santiago in 1864 after a nine-year absence, he was ecstatic: "What a transformation! So many palaces! What architectural majesty and beauty!"[36] By far the greatest effort to improve the capital came in the early 1870s, under the dynamic leadership of Benjamin Vicuña Mackenna. The visionary Intendant's reach exceeded his grasp; not all his schemes bore fruit; yet no individual has ever made a greater impact on the capital – with new avenues, the paving of streets, a fine public park (the Parque Cousiño, since 1972 the Parque O'Higgins), and, most famously of all, the transformation of the Cerro Santa Lucía, hitherto an unsightly, rocky hill, into the most delightful of urban follies. Vicuña Mackenna himself was buried there in 1886.

Although the British diplomat Horace Rumbold was struck, in the 1870s, by "the general air of aristocratic ease and opulence" in Santiago,[37] he also noticed the sharp contrast between the smart central district and the altogether poorer areas lying its fringes. The physical expansion of Santiago was not limited to new *barrios* such as Yungay and Matadero: the *ranchos* (shacks) of the poor, and later on *conventillos* (one-family rooms grouped in rows on either side of a patio) spread out in several directions from the historic urban core. Most *ranchos* were pushed out of the city center by the late 1860s; Vicuña Mackenna's half-completed plan for a *camino de cintura* ("ring road") was designed to separate the city proper from the "African encampment" (his words) surrounding it. Such measures did not even begin to attack the problem. Besides, the renting of property to the poor was excellent business for the rich.

The growth of Santiago's population seems to have brought a deterioration in public health. Mortality rates were very high. Infant mortality in particular was appalling: probably only half the children born at this period reached adulthood. The city's water-conduits (*acequias*) were little

[36] To José Posse, May 20, 1864. Allison W. Bunkley, *The Life of Sarmiento* (Princeton, 1952), p. 413.

[37] *Further Recollections of a Diplomatist* (London, 1903), p. 22.

more than open sewers, while according to a provincial newspaper in 1852, *santiaguinos* were to be seen "at every time of day in the most crowded places baring their bodies to perform their needs."[38] Tuberculosis and syphilis (not surprisingly, given widespread prostitution) were commonplace; epidemics of typhoid occurred in the mid-1860s and again in the mid-1870s; there were outbreaks of smallpox in 1862–63, 1868, and 1872–73. Notions of public hygiene were beginning to gain ground by the 1870s (a respectable medical profession was by now taking shape), but hospital care for the poorer classes remained grossly inadequate, with (in 1875) around 1,000 beds in a population of 150,000. In any case, a deep-rooted fear of hospitals (a universal phenomenon before the advent of modern medicine) was part of the urban culture. In the countryside the question did not even arise.

With so many paupers in the city, did the Santiago elite ever really fear urban disorder? This is a moot point. There were occasional near-riots during periods of political tension. In 1839 an American balloonist failed to make his promised ascent; the angry crowd in the Plaza de Armas had to be driven away by the cavalry. In general, however, the capital was adequately (and rather roughly) policed by its poorly paid corps of daytime *vigilantes* and nocturnal *serenos* – the latter's tasks included the shouting of the time and (until 1843) an invocation to the Virgin Mary. Policemen were already popularly known as *pacos,* as they still are. We do not have detailed studies of crime patterns: theft seems to have been very common, murder perhaps rather less so. (Capital punishment, then as later, was by means of firing squad; executions, not very frequent, were well-attended.) A new penitentiary was constructed in the mid-1840s; this enabled the government to abolish the horrid wheeled cages (introduced by Portales in 1836) used to house certain criminals and to move them to their road-mending tasks. The new prison proved inadequate; it was now that the Magellan Straits settlement began to be used as a penal colony.

An important feature of urban life was the growth of the press. *El Mercurio* (founded in Valparaiso in 1827, a daily from 1829) was now the proud "dean" of the Chilean press, with (by the 1850s) its special Santiago edition and its "steamship" supplements (partly in English) for distribution up the coast to Panama. It published its 10,000th issue in December 1860. Even at this early stage *El Mercurio* tended to see itself as uniquely qualified to pronounce on the national destiny. Santiago had to wait until 1842 for its first daily, and in the mid-1850s was again without one. The gap was filled after 1855 by *El Ferrocarril* (its title, "The Railroad," reflecting the obsession of the moment); this distinguished newspaper ran until 1911. The 1860s saw further good-quality dailies:

[38] *El Copiapino,* No. 1362, July 23, 1852.

El Independiente (1864–91, Conservative) and *La República* (1866–78, Liberal). The size of their pages grew monstrously large, as many historians working through them know to their cost. The magazines of the period tended to have rather short lives, the longest-running being the militantly clerical *Revista Católica* (1843 onward). *El Correo Literario* (1858) was the first Chilean magazine to carry political cartoons.[39] Little is known about the exact circulation of these various organs; in the 1840s and 1850s the government actually subsidized a few.

Newspapers and magazines presuppose readers. What progress did literacy make in the early republic? According to the census, literacy rose from 13.5 percent in 1854 to 23 percent in 1875, this increase undoubtedly reflecting a gradual improvement in education. This was a particular obsession of President Montt's: during his tenure the number of primary schools rose from 571 to 911 (648 of which were state schools). Training colleges for teachers (*escuelas normales*) were established, in 1842 for men, in 1854 for women. Montt's law of 1860, establishing free primary education (non-obligatory but open to all) remained in effect until 1920. By 1875, according to Eduardo Hamuy's calculations, 17 percent of the appropriate age-group was receiving some kind of primary instruction. Secondary education, meanwhile, expanded through the foundation of state *liceos* (sometimes called *institutos*), some twenty-seven by 1879 (two of these for girls), and by the proliferation of private schools, some run by religious orders, others, like Valparaiso's Mackay School (1857), emerging from the foreign communities. Educational practice was to some extent influenced by ideas put forward in 1843 by Ignacio Domeyko: he urged a general, humanistic education in place of the narrow, professionally oriented training which was the Chilean upper-class ideal. These ideas were first applied in that key secondary institution of the period, the Instituto Nacional. This proud creation of the founders of the nation is popularly believed to have educated three-quarters of all Chile's leaders between 1830 and 1891.

By the 1840s, the Instituto was the only place in Chile where secular higher education (in practice mainly professional training) could be obtained. The abolished colonial University of San Felipe was now replaced by the new University of Chile, inaugurated with solemn ceremonial in September 1843. Its first Rector, Andrés Bello, was by now the most eminent intellectual in Latin America. Poet, grammarian,[40] educationalist, philosopher, jurist, scientific popularizer, tireless public servant – he

---

[39] Done by Antonio Smith, the son of a Scottish father and a Chilean mother; he later won a very respectable reputation as a painter.

[40] In 1844 Bello persuaded the University to adopt and sponsor a comprehensive reform of the orthography of Spanish. It was far too radical to take root, but two specific features ("i" instead of "y," and "j" instead of the soft "g") passed into common use in Chile, and were not abandoned until around 1910.

virtually molded the intellectual tradition of his adoptive land, and single-handedly, over twenty years, wrote its civil code, formally adopted in 1855. The University's model was the Institut de France. Initially, therefore, it was a deliberative and supervisory body, entrusted with overseeing the entire educational system. Not until after Bello's death (1865) did it actually teach its own students in its own building. Notwithstanding the immense prestige of figures such as Bello and Domeyko, its work accurately reflected the educational priorities of the upper class: of the 859 degrees (*licenciado* and *bachiller*) approved between 1843 and 1857, no less than 556 (65 percent) were in law; 104 were in medicine; only fourteen were in mathematics and physical science. A decree of February 1877 established a supremely important precedent by admitting women to professional courses and hence to the university. Not until the twentieth century did women take much advantage of this.

The cultural achievements of the early republic, it has to be said, were not impressive, though a fine arts school (1849) and a conservatoire (1850) helped lay the foundations for future achievements, and would-be painters benefited from the stays in Chile of two notable foreign masters, the Bavarian Johann Mauritz Rugendas and the Frenchman Raymond Quinsac Monvoisin. Upper-class taste favored imported Italian opera, whose reign was a long one; Spanish *zarzuela* companies also started visiting Chile in the later 1850s. The so-called "movement of 1842" is usually taken to mark the beginnings of national Chilean literature. While Lastarria and others passionately advocated French romanticism, Andrés Bello's essentially neoclassical approach was at least as strong an influence on the writers who now made their mark – the most valuable writings of the 1840s being the delightful, precisely targeted *costumbrista* articles of José Joaquín Vallejo ("Jotabeche") – "the Chilean Larra" – and the poems of Salvador Sanfuentes. The outstanding literary figure of this time, however, was a novelist, Alberto Blest Gana, an admirer of Balzac and Stendhal. The novels of his early manhood (he wrote more in old age) include the still popular *Martín Rivas* (1862), a well-drawn picture of the Santiago of 1850. Its hero is a kind of Chilean Julien Sorel.

The most interesting feature of the emerging cultural panorama was the leading role given to history. Here the cardinal influence of Bello (in favor of careful research and narrative method) "marked the character of Chilean historiography for a hundred years," as Sergio Villalobos puts it.[41] The immediate result was a brilliant generation of historians – above all, Miguel Luis Amunátegui, Benjamin Vicuña Mackenna, and the great Diego Barros Arana. The incandescence of Vicuña Mackenna contrasts

---

[41] Sergio Villalobos R., *Historia del pueblo chileno*, Vol. I (1980), p. 16.

with the sobriety of Barros Arana. They were all well established by the 1870s.

We are tempted to relate this enthusiasm for history to the growth of national sentiment. It is not easy to assess how far a sense of *chilenidad* ("Chilean-ness") had penetrated the general population, especially the rural population, even by the 1870s. The inquilino, it was asserted in 1861, "never designates his nationality as Chilean, but by the name of the hacienda to which he belongs."[42] Country people still frequently used the term "Chile" to mean Santiago – something still done in jest by middle-class Chilean executives posted away from the capital. It may be that patriotism filtered only slowly into the haciendas in the early decades after independence. We have no real way of telling. In the towns, by contrast, patriotic feelings seem to have been enjoyed by all classes. They were to some extent fostered by the government: Chile's new (and invented) traditions were punctiliously observed, not least in mid-September when the national holidays were joyously and alcoholically celebrated. The *fiestas patrias* were undeniably popular. More permanently visible celebrations of the nation's history were to be found in the statues that now began to adorn the capital – Freire (1856), Carrera (1858), Portales (1860), and O'Higgins (1872). There were to be many more later.

That patriotic sentiment was frequently voiced by politicians and others can be appreciated by the quickest of glances at the speeches and newspaper editorials of the time. It was often tinged with pride – "our cardinal sin," as was suggested in 1878.[43] Political stability and apparent material progress seemed ample motive for self-congratulation. "Chileans!" apostrophized a newspaper in 1858, "People of invincible spirit! Privileged race in Spanish America!"[44] Indeed, the notion of Chile as a *república modelo*, "model republic," an example to her turbulent neighbors, became increasingly widespread in educated circles. The use of this catchphrase was sufficiently common for it to be denounced in 1861 as "a mania, ... a pretty quixotic pretension."[45] Quixotic or not, it was certainly a pretension. The backward Spanish colony had become a proud little nation.

---

[42] "Atropos," "El inquilino en Chile," *Revista del Pacífico*, V (1861), p. 102.

[43] Rafael Vial to Antonio Varas, December 17, 1878. *Revista chilena de historia y geografía*, No. 29 (1918), p. 344.

[44] *La Actualidad*, No. 34, March 11, 1858.

[45] *La Discusión*, No. 77, February 22, 1861.

5

The Liberal impulse, 1841–76

"Even so," said Don Dámaso, "every citizen should be concerned with public affairs, and the rights of the people are sacred." Don Dámaso, who ... belonged to the opposition that day, spoke this phrase with great emphasis. He had just read it in a Liberal newspaper.

— Alberto Blest Gana, *Martín Rivas* (1862)

Bulnes and the re-emergence of Liberalism

It was unlikely that the Conservative settlement would survive indefinitely without alteration. In the middle years of the century a fierce and at times bloody battle was waged between the upholders of its initial authoritarian style and those who favored a more liberal and tolerant approach to government. In the end, the liberal impulse proved overwhelming. But not until nearly forty years after Portales's death did the Liberals, as a party, finally displace the Conservatives as the leading element of a governing combination. Nor, obviously, were they the same Liberals who had been excluded from power in 1830.

The conciliatory approach with which Bulnes began his presidency in 1841, and which he maintained for most of his decade in office, gave excellent results. With the tolerant *pelucón* Ramón Luis Irarrázaval as chief minister, Liberalism as a coherent political force came close in these years to being killed by kindness. Many prominent Liberals (ex-president Pinto among them) were reconciled with the regime. There was, it is true, the occasional flurry of excitement amidst the general tranquillity. In 1844 the romantic young student Francisco Bilbao, in the pages of the monthly *El Crepúsculo*, scandalized the political class with his high-flown attacks on Chilean society and the Church. Copies of the offending article were collected and burned (in private, for fear of disturbances). Bilbao himself was fined, and expelled from the Instituto Nacional. He soon went abroad.

A few youthful demonstrations in favor of a popular hot-head hardly constituted an upheaval. Only a few weeks later, in fact, President Bulnes felt able to absent himself from Santiago for nearly six months, partly to restore his health, partly (mostly, some said) to attend to his estates in the south.[1] Irarrázaval stood in as vice-president (i.e., acting president), while the Interior ministry was taken over by Manuel Montt, already regarded as the rising hope of the sterner and more unbending Conservatives. Montt's reputation as a hard-liner was much enhanced in the mildly agitated months before Bulnes's re-election, when unreconciled Liberals (notably Pedro Félix Vicuña and Colonel Pedro Godoy) mobilized support, including artisan support, against the government. A street disturbance in Santiago (September 1845) was enough to rally the political class behind Bulnes, in a hastily constituted Sociedad del Orden (Society of Order), set up to propagandize on the government's behalf. Vicuña and his associates responded by forming a Sociedad Demócrata (Democrat Society) and, for their artisan followers, a somewhat shadowy Sociedad Caupolicán, of which little or nothing is known.

In March 1846, overreacting to (or more probably simply exploiting) some confused revolutionary declamations in a poorly printed newssheet (put out by a typographer, Santiago Ramos), the government imposed a state of siege and arrested a number of Liberals, including Vicuña. These events coincided with the congressional elections. In Valparaiso (where Vicuña was a candidate) a serious riot broke out, with the loss of at least twenty lives. Conservative propaganda naturally capitalized on this deplorable instance of anarchy. Bulnes was duly re-elected as president, without opposition. A stiff new press law was rushed through Congress. The Liberals now saw Montt, the architect of this minor spasm of repression, as their most formidable adversary. He was.

For the moment, however, the era of good feelings returned. Bulnes appointed one of his cousins, Manuel Camilo Vial, as Montt's replacement. Ambitious, bad-tempered, but also tolerant, the new chief minister enjoyed a smooth tenure for his first two years. But his evident fondness for accumulating offices (for himself and his relatives) soon provoked a current of hostility within the Conservative party itself. When it was learned that Vial's list of candidates for the 1849 congressional elections omitted several of the dissident *pelucones*, hostility turned into active agitation. Despite the government's best efforts, four of the Conservative rebels were elected to the new legislature.

It may be that Vial presumed too much on his cousin's patience. The episode has never been fully elucidated. Bulnes suddenly decided to dismiss him. (He effectively withdrew from politics.) The new cabinet (June 1849) included two popular dissidents, Manuel Antonio Tocornal (son of Joaquín) and Antonio García Reyes. The recently elected Con-

---

[1] In 1839, while in Lima with the expeditionary force, Bulnes had bought Las Canteras, Bernardo O'Higgins's estate.

gress, for obvious reasons, was packed with Vial's supporters, who took a jaundiced view of the new ministers. From the ranks of this *vialista* majority a new liberal opposition gradually began to form, describing itself for a while as the *partido progresista* ("progressive party"). Such a development was, perhaps, hard to prevent. The younger generation, the first generation brought up under Conservative rule, was increasingly drawn to new ideas, and was especially enthused by news of the French revolution of 1848 – to which even President Bulnes paid tribute when opening Congress that year. In other circumstances the well-liked Tocornal and García Reyes might have contained the new political trend within the Conservative ranks. The circumstances of their appointment made this impossible.

The man of the moment for the *progresistas* was José Victorino Lastarria, the outstanding Liberal publicist of his time. The congressional sessions of 1849 were in some way his finest hour. He had a touch of vanity – *lo tengo y lo luzco* ("I have it and I show it"), he said of his own talent – but was an effective parliamentarian. In August 1849, gaining in confidence, the opposition put forward a presidential candidate for 1851: the elderly Ramón Errázuriz, whose respectability outweighed his distinctly unconvincing liberal credentials. A short-lived Club de la Reforma ("Reform Club") formed in October 1849 was a further sign of the Liberal revival, though in Congress itself, the *vialista* phalanx was beginning to shrink as ministerial pressures made themselves felt. In January 1850 the opposition made the first serious use of the ultimate parliamentary weapon by trying to delay the budget in the Chamber of Deputies. There was a dramatic rhetorical contest between Lastarria and Montt, the personifications of liberty and authority. The motion failed by a single vote.

Lastarria's own diary provides a good account of the triumphs and setbacks of this time and of his own failure to inject organizational and ideological coherence into the re-emerging Liberal party. Other men, however, were determined to widen the campaign against the Conservative regime. The *Sociedad de la Igualdad* ("Society of Equality"), founded in March 1850 by Santiago Arcos and Francisco Bilbao (who had witnessed some of the scenes of 1848 in Paris), stands out as an unusual enterprise in that age of upper-class politics. Designed to spread education to the "working class" (i.e., the artisanate), the *Sociedad* quickly closed ranks with the opposition, assuming a very hostile attitude to the supposed presidential aspirations of Manuel Montt. Montt's candidacy was still by no means a certainty, but the *Sociedad de la Igualdad's* marches and demonstrations, and the radical language of its propaganda, brought it much closer. Both Bilbao, a hyper-lyrical romantic, and Arcos, a clearer-headed social thinker, were enraptured by accounts of the French

Revolution. "Liberty, equality, fraternity" became the society's motto, "citizen" its preferred mode of address. Its leaders took nicknames from the 1790s: Bilbao was "Vergniaud" (appropriately, for he was a good orator), Arcos (less appropriately) was "Marat."

In April 1850 Tocornal and García Reyes left the cabinet, and Bulnes appointed Antonio Varas as Interior minister. He was very much Montt's protegé, and the move was correctly interpreted by the opposition as a stiffening of the government's position. Every week now brought a new excitement. On August 19 a meeting of the *Sociedad de la Igualdad* was assaulted by men with clubs, some of them police agents; the society's membership tripled in five days. In a famous incident, an *igualitario* spat in the face of the Intendant of Santiago. (He was later sent to prison for six months.) Such happenings scandalized the somnolent society of the capital, and ensured that the Conservative candidacy would go to Montt, despite the reservations of the more conciliatory *pelucones*. At the beginning of November local *igualitarios* in San Felipe briefly seized the town. The government declared the long-awaited state of siege, arrested and exiled several well-known Liberals (including Lastarria), and dissolved the *Sociedad.* It faded away with barely a murmur of protest. The opposition, thought Lastarria when he returned from his brief spell abroad in February 1851, had disintegrated completely.

Its rescue came, unexpectedly, from the southern provinces, which had remained aloof from the political excitements of Santiago. In February 1851 the leading citizens of Concepción proclaimed General José María de la Cruz, their popular Intendant since 1846, as presidential candidate. Cruz was both a Conservative and Bulnes's cousin. Despite these inconveniences the Liberals, jettisoning poor Ramón Errázuriz, took up his candidacy as their own. The more impetuous Liberals also made efforts to suborn the military. On Easter Day (April 20), the Valdivia battalion made a vain attempt to seize the artillery barracks at the foot of the Cerro Santa Lucía. Awakened at daybreak with the news, Bulnes mounted his horse and directed the suppression of the mutiny. Colonel Pedro Urriola, leader of the revolt, was killed. At the end of the battle, 200 men lay dead. "A terrible morning," wrote Antonio Varas.

With yet another state of siege in force, General Cruz was summoned to Santiago. He received embarrassing displays of public support. The elections, held soon afterward, produced the predictable majority for Montt – except in the south. The opposition issued a manifesto detailing electoral abuses, though it may be doubted whether these were more flagrant than usual. When Cruz went south again at the end of July, the eyes of the capital turned nervously toward the provinces. By the time of Montt's inauguration on September 18, La Serena was in revolt. The next day, as the new president made his way to the customary military parade, a messenger galloped into town with the news that Concepción had risen in favor of General Cruz. Within hours of laying down the presidency, Bulnes was on his way south to defend the Conservative regime in its hour of mortal danger.

The revolt of La Serena (September 7, 1851) had been staged by local, *serenense* Liberals. They were soon joined by Liberals escaping from Santiago, among them José Miguel Carrera (son of the famous patriot leader), who assumed command as rebel Intendant of Coquimbo province. Another was the young Benjamín Vicuña Mackenna, whose father, the irrepressible *pipiolo* Pedro Félix Vicuña, was now General Cruz's right-hand man in Concepción. And whatever minor forays might be mounted from the north, it was in the south that the real danger lay. Cruz was a national figure, a hero of the 1836–39 war second only to Bulnes. The Concepción and Frontier garrisons could supply hardened soldiers and militiamen – and Cruz, an old Frontier hand, knew how to neutralize the Araucanians at his rear.

One of the rebels' first actions, both in north and south, was to seize two small steamships, one of them British-owned, with the aim of keeping the two wings of the revolution in contact. With the consent of the government, the British naval squadron recaptured both ships and placed Coquimbo under blockade. (Stephen Sulivan, the British minister and a nephew of Lord Palmerston, was a fervent supporter of Montt.) The rebels were furious with the British: "if those infamous gringos rob us at sea, we should cut off their heads on land!"[2] trumpeted Pedro Félix Vicuña (who, after the April 20 mutiny, had not hesitated to seek refuge aboard a British warship). They were even more furious with Montt for having sanctioned foreign interference in a Chilean quarrel.

Early in November, Bulnes advanced to the Ñuble River. The first clash of the two armies, at Monte de Urra (November 19), probably favored Cruz. The decisive battle of the campaign was fought on December 8 near the confluence of the Maule and Loncomilla rivers. It was a grim, ferocious battle in which about 1,800 soldiers were killed. *But who won?* This has been argued about ever since. What is clear is that when Bulnes made preparations for further action, a few days after the battle of Loncomilla, Cruz accepted defeat. (One reason might have been that Cruz, himself a landowner, was concerned by the level of unofficial guerrilla activity and banditry now welling up in the south.) The Treaty of Purapel, which the two cousins signed on December 14, embodied honorable terms: rebel soldiers were allowed to rejoin the national army with their ranks (and pensions) unchanged. Bulnes also promised Cruz

---

[2] Agustín Edwards, *Cuatro presidentes de Chile*, 2 vols. (Valparaiso, 1932), I, 82.

that he would try to secure a general amnesty; this was something Montt refused to concede.

Meanwhile, troops under the command of Colonel Juan Vidaurre Leal and Victorino Garrido had laid siege to La Serena. The city's stubborn resistance, long remembered as heroic, ended only on December 31. Even then, the excitements of the year were not quite over. A further revolt in favor of Cruz suddenly broke out in Copiapó (then denuded of troops which had gone south to La Serena): its leader was Bernardino Barahona, a trader from Huasco, one of his lieutenants being "a Pinochet from Aconcagua."[3] Their moment of glory was brief. Garrido soon quelled this last spasm of rebellion. Then, in January 1852, news reached Valparaiso of a horrific mutiny in the Magellan Straits penal colony, where the sadistic Lieutenant Miguel José Cambiaso had imposed a sanguinary reign of terror on the little settlement, ostensibly on behalf of Cruz. Cambiaso and seven others were executed at Valparaiso in April 1852. The Liberals, indignant over other shootings after the civil war, refrained from including their names on their lists of the martyrs of oppression.

The crisis of 1851 was the worst faced by the Conservative regime in more than twenty years of power. General Cruz had come too close to winning for comfort. As it was, the government weathered the storm. Manuel Montt, his will to rule so bloodily demonstrated, was left for the time being in unchallenged command of the republic.

Montt and the Conservative defection

Manuel Montt's enemies (and he had many) always freely admitted his exceptional intelligence and exemplary industry. His ideals, however, were uncompromising and inflexible. He never asked himself whether the authoritarian tradition (in which he had been personally schooled by Portales himself) was still appropriate for the Chile of the 1850s. He was a man of few words, outwardly unemotional and dry. As his great friend Sarmiento tells us, there were those who seriously believed that Montt had never laughed in his entire life. "All head and no heart," was Bulnes's private verdict. Inseparably linked to Montt's name (they have been together on their monument in Santiago since 1904) is that of Antonio Varas, his Interior minister from 1851 to 1856 and again in 1860–61. Varas shared the president's authoritarian approach, but had an altogether more passionate nature, which perhaps complemented Montt's icy self-control.

The Montt administration began with a much-trumpeted emphasis on

[3] Roberto Hernández, *Juan Godoy o el descubrimiento de Chañarcillo*, 2 vols. (Valparaiso, 1932), I, 183.

material progress. The railway and the telegraph were to be the prime instruments of civilization. "You have wished," said Montt at a banquet in September 1851, "to place me at the head of a phalanx of workers... so that we may build peace and prosperity.... God be with the workers!"[4] The commercial boom that continued during Montt's first term made it easier, perhaps, for the political class to forget its recent dissensions. Montt himself may have seen his emphasis on "material interests" as a means of distracting Chileans' minds from political concerns. If so it was a tactic that failed. For the Montt decade was decisive in reshaping the political landscape: overshadowing everything else in the 1850s was the sudden defection of a large element (probably the majority) of the Conservative party. Rather unexpectedly, the pretext for this great defection was provided by the Catholic Church.

Ever since 1830 the government had taken the Church to be a negligible factor in politics: the state in practice maintained the *patronato,* whatever the Church's reservations. In 1845 the talented and ambitious Rafael Valentín Valdivieso became archbishop of Santiago. A militant and ultramontane temper spread through the hierarchy and clergy, fostered by the active Valdivieso himself. A powerful section of the Conservative party had always been strongly attached to the Church, and Montt bore this in mind in 1851 by appointing the devout and opulent Fernando Lazcano to his cabinet. Lazcano's tenure was brief: his attempt to impose an exclusively clerical regime on the Instituto Nacional caused open mutiny among its students. Two years later, when the possible reestablishment of the Jesuit order in Chile was being debated in Congress, an open rift appeared between the Senate, the redoubt of traditional Conservatism, and the Chamber of Deputies, where Varas's following predominated. (Varas's own religious position was suspect to the orthodox.) By the end of Montt's outwardly tranquil first term, a fissure was opening up in the Conservative party.

It was widened beyond repair by a trivial incident which grew into a great political issue. In a case arising out of the dismissal of a junior sacristan, two canons of Santiago cathedral, at odds with their superiors, lodged an appeal with the supreme court – a procedure open to them under the *patronato* but frowned on by Valdivieso, by ultramontane opinion, and by the Papacy itself. The supreme court upheld the appeal. Archbishop Valdivieso defied the ruling, and was threatened with banishment. Montt stood firmly by the supreme court. Public excitement was deftly played on by the clergy. Devout society ladies pledged that they would tie themselves to the wheels of the coach bearing Valdivieso into exile. More seriously, a handful of Liberals (among them Federico Errá-

---

[4] *La Tribuna,* September 9, 1851.

zuriz, the archbishop's nephew) began plotting a *coup de main* on the strength of public sympathy for the defiant prelate. A compromise was hastily found; the archbishop and the canons backed down, but the damage was done.

Conservatives had other motives for disaffection. Montt's refusal to grant an amnesty after 1851 was seen as unnecessarily harsh. He had never been forgiven by the Conservatives of the south. Moreover, in their choice of public officials and congressmen, Montt and Varas were less interested in upper-class pedigrees than in merit, which annoyed many *pelucón* families. The "new men" whose careers were thus promoted were later to form a brilliant political generation, but in the 1850s they were undeniably new and in some cases obscure. The prospect of Varas in the presidency in 1861 was also distinctly unwelcome. For many Conservatives, the president's sternly regalist attitude in the "affair of the sacristan" was the last straw. It was soon clear that a large Conservative defection was in the making.

It was first revealed in the congressional sessions of 1857, when the Senate, absolutely without warning, insisted on passing an amnesty bill – quickly gutted by Montt's amendments. It was soon evident that the dissident *pelucones* were informally aligning themselves with the Liberals, whose leaders (skillfully steered by Federico Errázuriz and Domingo Santa María) were ready to take advantage of this stroke of luck. Outside the charmed circles of politics, the public was bewildered, as was shown in an "imaginary conversation" printed around this time:

"Hello, great man, what's new?"
"Hm. The *pelucón* party has turned Liberal."
"Marvelous!"
"Well, it's not quite like that: in fact, the Liberal party has turned *pelucón*."
"My dear fellow, I don't understand."
"Nor do I."[5]

But Montt did. The embryonic Conservative-Liberal alliance next resorted to the old tactic of January 1850 by delaying the budget, in order to force Montt into changing his cabinet. Montt saw this as an illegitimate use of the Senate's powers, and even thought of resigning: Varas composed at least four drafts of a resignation message. In the end, Jerónimo Urmeneta, brother of the mining millionaire, agreed to form a new ministry that would include two Liberals (October 1857). But, after inevitable disagreements with Montt, the Liberals resigned, and the hopes of concord between government and opposition were once again shattered.

[5] *El Mercurio*, Valparaiso, August 29, 1857.

On December 29, 1857, a manifesto announced the creation of a new "National party" to support the government in the forthcoming elections. So far, despite their common detestation of Montt, the Liberals and defecting Conservatives had not coalesced in a formal alliance. The vital meeting took place at Ramón Subercaseaux's *chacra* in January 1858, with the Conservatives led by the cunning veteran Joaquín Tocornal (whose son Manuel Antonio was also prominent in the defection), the Liberals represented by Federico Errázuriz, Domingo Santa María, and Angel Custodio Gallo. The new alliance, which soon came to be termed the Liberal-Conservative Fusion (*Fusión Liberal-Conservadora*), was mocked by Montt's supporters as artificial and unstable. For the next fifteen years, at least, it was neither. As Edward Gibbon once observed, "party spirit, however pernicious or absurd, is a principle of union as well as of dissension."

The battle-lines were thus drawn. The Fusion claimed to represent "opinion." It is probably true that the majority of the political class was now opposed to Montt, with the discreet influence of the clergy not to be disregarded. The Nationals retained a section of the upper class, and attracted the support of some of the new magnates of mining and trade – the "metal bar aristocrats," as the publicist Ambrosio Montt called them. Electorally speaking, the Nationals controlled the machinery of the state. Despite this, the Fusion won at least fifteen seats in the new Chamber. The sessions of 1858 were as agitated as those of 1849. The opposition once again tried to obstruct the budget: this time the Chamber simply voted to cut off the debate, on which the Fusion deputies walked out (November 19–20, 1858). Outside Congress the agitation, now beginning to assume some of the features of 1850, showed no sign of abating. The press showered crude invective on Montt. In October that year a comet appeared: for many, it seemed a "malign messenger of imminent misfortune."[6]

Matters were brought to a head by a group of younger Liberals associated with a radical newssheet, *La Asamblea Constituyente*, whose strident theme was the need for instant constitutional reform. On December 12, 1858, five of these men (Angel Custodio Gallo, Benjamín Vicuña Mackenna, Isidoro Errázuriz, the brothers Guillermo and Manuel Antonio Matta) summoned a so-called "constituent assembly" to a concert hall in Santiago. The meeting was broken up by soldiers. More than one hundred and fifty reformers marched defiantly to prison. Once again the government declared a state of siege and closed down several newspapers (including *El Mercurio*). For the second time in eight years, Chile was on the brink of armed rebellion.

---

6 *El Mercurio*, Valparaiso, October 16, 1858.

This time there was no 1851-style southern defection; the army remained loyal to Montt. The Fusion's "revolutionary committee" (Errázuriz and Santa María were key members) thus had to improvise forces of its own. Nowhere did these have much success. A feeble mutiny in Santiago petered out immediately. A more serious effort in Valparaiso was swiftly suppressed. San Felipe, also in arms, was cruelly sacked by government troops: the young lawyer Abdón Cifuentes lost his first frock-coat in the affray. At Talca (the longest episode), the rebels withstood days of bombardment before capitulating. In the countryside, guerrilla bands (*montoneras*) organized by Fusion hacendados fared slightly better, José Miguel Carrera returning to the fray at the head of the most successful of these. By the start of May 1859, however, the *montoneras* had been dispersed. Farther south, insurgents briefly captured Tomé and Talcahuano and staged a vain attack on Concepción, while a further rebel force from the Frontier marched on Chillán: its defeat at the battle of Maipón (April 12, 1859) marked the end of the war in the south.

By mid-March 1859 the national army numbered more than 5,000. The government banished several of its more dangerous adversaries: in March a British sea-captain was paid 3,000 pesos to dump the Matta brothers, Angel Custodio Gallo, and Benjamín Vicuña Mackenna in England – a mistake, given their literary talents. Another group of rebels, on their way to the Magellan Straits, hijacked their ship (the *Olga*) and diverted it to Peru. Two of them made their way back to Chile to join the one insurgent force that seemed to stand a chance of defeating Montt, Pedro León Gallo's "Constituent Army," which had taken control of the mining zone and was mounting an altogether more serious challenge than was possible farther south.

The mining magnates of Atacama had been among Montt's strongest backers in 1851. But the powerful Gallo clan (Montt's cousins by marriage) had fallen out with the president and had embraced a radical form of Liberalism. On January 5–6, 1859, rebels seized Copiapó and acclaimed Pedro León Gallo (brother of Angel Custodio) as Intendant of Atacama. His miracles of improvisation over the next few weeks became legendary: an army of 1,000 men recruited, arms (including cannon) manufactured, "constituent pesos" (highly prized by modern numismatists) minted – and all this followed by a 300-mile march through the desert, victory over the government's forces at Los Loros (March 14, 1859), and a triumphal entry into La Serena. Here Gallo was presented with a trayful of pastry models of his staff officers; whether he ate them or not is not recorded. The Fusion leadership in Santiago was less euphoric: it was embarrassed by the radical rhetoric of the northern movement and distinctly ambivalent about its success.

Montt entrusted the final reckoning with Gallo to General Juan Vidaurre Leal and a division of 3,000 soldiers. The *constituyentes* made their last stand on the slopes of Cerro Grande, a hill just south of La Serena. There they went down to defeat (April 29, 1859). Gallo and many of his followers fled across the mountains to Argentina. The wits of Santiago fashioned an anagram from his name: *No llegó al poder* ("He did not come to power"). The north was soon pacified. In one of several minor disturbances after the end of the war, at Valparaiso on September 18, General Vidaurre Leal lost his life.

The large number of minor actions in this civil war, as well as government reticence, makes it difficult to estimate the casualties. At Cerro Grande, the largest battle, the government lost around 100 dead or wounded,[7] and the Constituent army presumably more. In the urban actions the worst fighting took place at Talca and Concepción. Numerous death-sentences were passed in the subsequent repression, but relatively few carried out; an estimate by the opposition soon afterward claimed thirty-one executions in 1859. As in the past, many were sent (or simply went) into exile. It is impossible to say how many Chileans lost their lives in the two civil wars of Montt's presidency. We hazard the guess that the total was probably around 4,000. It could not have been much less.

The Liberal-Conservative Fusion

Montt's victory in war was followed by defeat in peace. Hundreds of Chileans were now in exile; their families longed for an end to dissension. The Fusion leaders discreetly made it known to Montt that he had still not conquered "opinion" – and clearly "opinion" was undergoing a sea-change. The commercial crisis of the late 1850s was reaching its peak; the general mood of anxiety and discontent was palpable. For the opposition, there now loomed up the appalling prospect of Antonio Varas in the Moneda. Was further rebellion and upheaval the inevitable future of Chile?

Early in 1860 Jerónimo Urmeneta asked to be relieved of the Interior ministry. In his hour of need, Montt turned to the one man he could always depend on, and Antonio Varas returned to head the cabinet (April 1860). The minister of the Interior was barred, by an unspoken rule of politics, from arranging his own presidential candidacy. Varas's decision was correctly seen as the renunciation of his claim. Effusive tributes were paid to his unselfishness. "The spirit of Washington," declared the newspaper *El Ferrocarril*, "has knocked on Sr. Varas's door."[8] Varas himself

---

[7] Fernando Ruz T., *Rafael Sotomayor Baeza* (Santiago, 1980), p. 76.
[8] April 20, 1860.

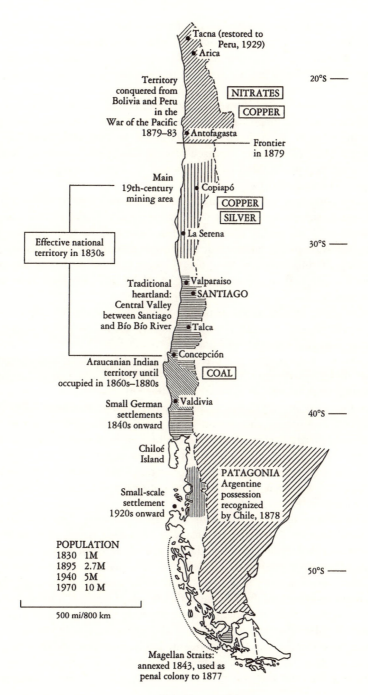

Tacna (restored to Peru, 1929)
Arica

20°S

Territory conquered from Bolivia and Peru in the War of the Pacific 1879–83

NITRATES

COPPER

Antofagasta

Frontier in 1879

Main 19th-century mining area

Copiapó

COPPER

SILVER

La Serena

30°S

Effective national territory in 1830s

Traditional heartland: Central Valley between Santiago and Bío Bío River

Valparaiso
SANTIAGO

Talca

Concepción

Araucanian Indian territory until occupied in 1860s–1880s

COAL

Small German settlements 1840s onward

Valdivia

40°S

Chiloé Island

Small-scale settlement 1920s onward

PATAGONIA
Argentine possession recognized by Chile, 1878

POPULATION
1830 1M
1895 2.7M
1940 5M
1970 10 M

50°S

500 mi/800 km

Magellan Straits: annexed 1843, used as penal colony to 1877

Chile: Territorial Expansion

went imperturbably about his business. Upholding the authoritarian tradition to the last, he introduced a new "civil responsibility law," a stern measure requiring political rebels to provide financial compensation to victims of rebellions. It never had to be applied, and was repealed in 1865.

The National party, however, was determined to maintain Varas's candidacy, and the opposition suspected a ruse, but Varas's decision was genuine enough, as he finally made clear to the National leadership in January 1861. The Fusion realized at once that a silent revolution was occurring in politics: Montt could uphold the authoritarian tradition no longer. The National party's choice for the presidency fell on an elderly, tolerant patrician, José Joaquín Pérez. "Gentlemen," he is supposed to have said, "the young lady you are offering me is very pretty, but a bit of a coquette. I will think about it." Think about it he did, but not for long. He was elected unopposed, the Fusion abstaining. At the banquets marking his inauguration, he spoke eloquently of his desire for national reconciliation and for "a government of all by all," whatever that may have meant.

One thing it did mean. Within a month of taking office President Pérez introduced a comprehensive amnesty law. The exiles began to trickle home. From the viewpoint of the Fusion, however, the silent revolution could not be complete until both the cabinet and Congress were under its control. Pérez's first cabinet naturally had a National coloring, and he was in no hurry to alter this: he was never in much of a hurry to do anything, as politicians rapidly discovered. But the insistent pressure of the Fusion soon produced the desired result. In July 1862, amid scenes of delirious public enthusiasm, Pérez took the decisive step and appointed a ministry drawn largely from the Fusion – with Manuel Antonio Tocornal at Interior, and Lastarria at Finance (though he was soon replaced by the politically more astute Domingo Santa María).

The events of 1861 mark an important dividing line in Chilean political history. Later generations were to reflect more generously on Montt and Varas, but the political class as a whole viewed their departure from office with undisguised relief. The new president's style was very different. His tolerance may have stemmed, as was said at the time, from supreme indifference. José Manuel Balmaceda described him as "drunk on indolence." Yet these qualities were precisely those needed to induce a mood of calm after the agitations of the previous decade. Admirers of strong government have often presented this elderly patrician in a poor light. In fact he deserves as much credit as any nineteenth-century president for consolidating the national "idiosyncrasy" of civilized politics. Abdón Cifuentes, no mean judge, thought of him as "one of the cleverest rulers Chile has ever had."[9]

With what was now the National opposition still very much in control of Congress, the Tocornal ministry was hampered by the kind of obstructionism the Fusion itself had used against Montt. The sessions of 1862 and 1863 were thus fairly contentious. But all the ministry had to do was to wait for the elections of 1864, when the normal processes of intervention yielded a handsome majority for the Fusion. The displaced Nationals – *monttvaristas*, as they were now nicknamed – were no longer alone in opposition. The radical wing of Liberalism, whose divergence from the Liberal mainstream had shown up in the agitation of 1858 and Pedro León Gallo's "constituent revolution," rejected the Liberal-Conservative alliance on principle. These "red" or "radical" Liberals were soon referred to simply as Radicals. The province of Atacama (where the first Radical *asamblea*, or "assembly," was formed in December 1863) was long the main redoubt of the new party. The Radicals proclaimed uncompromisingly liberal-democratic opinions, heightened later on by a note of fervent anticlericalism. This derived in part from a close connection between Radicalism and freemasonry, another notable development of these years: in April 1862 Chilean freemasons formed their own independent Grand Lodge. It was the start of one of the more profound subterranean influences in politics. The number of lodges grew from ten in 1872 to more than one hundred by the 1950s.

As it happened, the immediate course of politics after the triumph of the Fusion was interrupted by an unexpected international crisis. In April 1864 a Spanish naval squadron suddenly seized the guano-rich Chincha islands, off Peru, in reprisal for the alleged maltreatment of Spaniards in that republic. There was an instant upsurge of anti-Spanish feeling in Chile: *El Ferrocarril* even printed a Sunday edition to express its indignation. Tocornal, thought to be insufficiently zealous on this score, was replaced as Interior minister by Alvaro Covarrubias. Although Chile declared her neutrality in the conflict, Spanish warships were denied coaling rights in Chilean ports. The Spanish minister in Santiago, the sociable Santiago Tavira, aggrieved by hostile demonstrations, demanded redress. An understanding was soon reached, but Tavira had not reckoned with the commander of the Spanish squadron, Admiral José Manuel Pareja, who bore a personal grudge against Chile – he was the son of the Brigadier Pareja who had left his bones in Chillán in 1813. The admiral, with authorization from Spain, demanded further "explanations" from Chile and a twenty-one-gun salute. To this ultimatum there could be

9 Abdón Cifuentes, *Memorias*, 2 vols. (Santiago, 1936), I, 66.

only one reply. On September 25, 1865, amidst scenes of patriotic jubilation, the Republic of Chile declared war on the Kingdom of Spain.

Neither side could really hope to win, or for that matter lose. Chile quickly found allies (Peru, Bolivia, Ecuador); Pareja had none. His squadron was stronger than the tiny Chilean navy, but not strong enough to maintain an effective blockade. On November 26, 1865, the Chilean corvette *Esmeralda* (under Captain Juan Williams Rebolledo) captured the Spanish gunboat *Covadonga* after a twenty-minute cannonade. The humiliation was too much for Admiral Pareja, who shot himself. The battle of Abtao (February 7, 1866), when a small Chilean-Peruvian flotilla fought off two Spanish frigates, was a further reverse for the aggressors. Before withdrawing from the Pacific, Pareja's successor, Admiral Casto Núñez Méndez, decided to punish Chile by bombarding defenseless Valparaiso. The trading community asked the foreign warships stationed in the bay to intervene, but to no avail. The British minister, William Taylour Thomson, told a deputation of irate British traders that "the general interests of England" outweighed "those of a portion of her commerce."[10] On Easter Saturday (March 31) 1866 the citizens of Valparaiso withdrew to the surrounding hillsides to watch the three-hour Spanish bombardment. About 2,500 shots were fired. Huge plumes of smoke rose from the devastated buildings, which included the bonded warehouses. Commercial losses, according to *El Mercurio*, totaled nearly 15 million pesos.

The bombardment of Valparaiso was condemned around the world as a wicked outrage, which it was. As far as Chile went, it marked the end of this strange little war. It was some time before diplomacy laid the conflict formally to rest. Peru and Spain signed a peace treaty in Paris in 1879. Chile and Spain did likewise in Lima in 1883 – at the close of the next war Chile was to fight.

"Parties have disappeared in Chile," said Manuel Montt at the start of the Spanish war. It was never quite true: the National-Radical opposition was not averse to criticizing the conduct of the war. Yet there was no question of the benevolent Pérez failing to secure re-election in 1866 in the traditional way. The candidacies of General Bulnes (for the *monttvaristas*) and Angel Custodio Gallo (for the Radicals) were not even very seriously promoted, and the congressional elections of 1867 predictably reinforced the Fusion. Despite the general tranquillity, the emotions aroused by the Montt presidency were by no means forgotten, as was shown in the noisiest political episode of the 1860s: the impeachment of the supreme court. Montt was now its president. This was simply a quest

---

[10] W. C. Davis, *The Last Conquistadores: The Spanish Intervention in Peru and Chile 1863–1866* (Athens, Ga., 1950), p. 301.

for vengeance. Pérez disapproved of the move, as did other leading politicians, but the Fusion majority in the Chamber voted in favor, and in September 1868 the case was forwarded to the Senate. Public passion ran high. The best pamphleteers of the moment (Martín Palma and Zorobabel Rodríguez among them) exercised their talents with vigor. The Senate dismissed the charges in May 1869.

Toward the end of the 1860s the issue of constitutional reform, that old dream of the Liberals, finally rose to the top of the political agenda. In 1865, just before the war, there had been a lengthy debate over Article 5, which gave Catholics the exclusive right to public worship, though in practice the authorities had usually turned a blind eye to the mostly foreign Protestant churches of Valparaiso. Instead of a constitutional amendment, Congress enacted an "interpretative law," in effect declaring official religious toleration. The debates over Article 5 can be seen as a dress rehearsal for wider discussions of constitutional reform. The 1867–70 Congress pronounced that some thirty-four articles were in principle "reformable." Under the 1833 Constitution, only the next legislature could make the decision to amend. The elections of 1870 thus acquired a special importance.

The tide of reform now ran strongly. The Fusion wanted it, while the opposition had an obvious stake in bringing electoral liberty into the discussion. In 1868–69 many younger *monttvaristas* joined with Radicals and independent Liberals to form a network of "Reform Clubs" (*Clubes de la Reforma*) in Santiago and the provinces, holding a national convention in September 1869. The *reformista* program favored electoral freedom, an expanded franchise, "the principle of industrial liberty," and a general reduction of presidential power. Here, in fact, was the main agenda for the next phase of Chilean politics.

The vigorously contested elections of 1870 were probably the least "intervened" the country had yet seen, the opposition winning forty seats in the Chamber. The new Congress contained one of the most brilliant groups of parliamentarians in Chilean history, including five future presidents. The superb pen-portraits of the congressmen drawn by the Arteaga Alemparte brothers in *Los constituyentes de 1870*, a true political classic, bring them to life in vivid fashion. Much was expected of this so-called "constituent" congress of 1870–73; rather little was delivered. The only constitutional amendment to pass (though an important one) was the prohibition of immediate presidential re-election. The run of "decennial" administrations thus came to an end.

By now, in any case, the main question was once again the presidential succession. The death of the front-running Conservative, Manuel Antonio Tocornal, in 1867 opened the way for the ambitious Liberal, Federico Errázuriz. His connections with Archbishop Valdivieso and his well-calculated friendliness to the Conservatives gave him the edge over other contenders. The opposition (Nationals, Radicals, dissident Liberals) selected the mining magnate José Tomas Urmeneta. Both camps held modest nominating conventions, an innovation in Chile. During the election itself the government ostentatiously strengthened the garrisons near Urmeneta's estates. Errázuriz predictably won a large majority (226–58) in the electoral college. Some of Urmeneta's followers urged him to organize an armed revolt. The idea was repudiated by the Radicals Manuel Antonio Matta and Angel Custodio Gallo.

The "new politics"

The British minister Horace Rumbold was later to remember Federico Errázuriz as "A very creditable specimen of the Chilean patrician class ... [with] essentially a despotic temperament."[11] Unlike his predecessor, Errázuriz was an active president, as strong-willed in power as he had been in his implacable opposition to Montt. Although his closeness to the Conservatives had helped him to office, he was not destined to enjoy their continued support for long, for the inner contradictions of the Fusion now at last came to a head. The issue driving Conservatives and Liberals apart was "freedom of instruction" (including examination) in the country's numerous private schools, many of these Catholic. This was anathema to Liberals, Nationals, and Radicals, who wished all examinations to remain under the supervision of the Instituto Nacional and University of Chile. The decree on "freedom of examination" issued in January 1872 by Abdón Cifuentes, the Conservative minister in charge of education, provoked immediate Liberal-Conservative tension and strong opposition from Diego Barros Arana, the eminent (and very anticlerical) historian who headed the Instituto Nacional. Student disorders at the Instituto, impassioned debates in Congress, the dismissal of Barros Arana – these noisy events resulted in Cifuentes's resignation (July 1873), the Conservatives' withdrawal into opposition, and the disintegration of the Fusion.

The break was in some ways unavoidable. The Conservatives' clerical attachment had grown stronger during the 1860s, and a clash with the mounting forces of anticlericalism was bound to occur sooner or later. In fact, what are usually termed *las cuestiones teológicas,* "the theological questions," began at precisely this juncture to assume an inordinate importance in politics. The questions had less to do with theology as such than with the proper demarcation of the civil and ecclesiastical spheres. Two contentious rows at the start of the 1870s brought them

---

[11] Horace Rumbold, *Further Recollections of a Diplomatist* (London, 1903), p. 32.

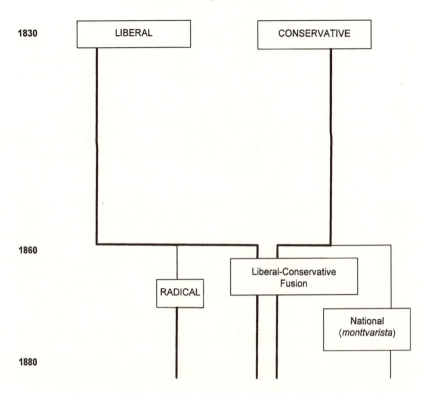

Chart 5.1. Main political parties, 1830–80.

center-stage. The Church's refusal (on ostensibly moral grounds) to marry a minor politician and to bury a popular veteran of the independence period pointed to the need for a civil marriage law and for separate non-Catholic plots in public cemeteries (a change decreed in December 1871). The passage of the new Penal Code (1874) provoked outbursts of pious and impious passion, with fisticuffs both inside and outside Congress. The parallel judicial reform (which abolished the procedures used in the "affair of the sacristan") also incensed Conservatives, but here the government had cleared the bill beforehand with the Vatican, thus cutting the ground from under their feet.

Now that they were in opposition, the Conservatives had as strong an interest in constitutional reform as anyone else. Not surprisingly the Congress of 1873–76, more productive than its predecessor, enacted a whole series of amendments. These included direct election to the Senate, the right of association (not mentioned in the 1833 constitution), modification of the emergency powers, and the introduction of "limited incompatibilities," that is, the exclusion of certain classes of public official from

Congress. Such changes were a blow, but not by any means a body-blow, to presidential power. For many politicians, however, an even greater issue was electoral reform. Should not the franchise be widened? Should not Chile be rid of the demeaning spectacle of "managed" elections? Lengthy debates in 1872–74 yielded some important changes here. The issuing of *calificaciones* was now transferred from the municipalities to supposedly more independent *juntas de mayores contribuyentes*, committees of prominent local taxpayers. However, attempts by reformers to secure the *voto acumulativo* (a primitive form of proportional representation) for all elections – municipal, congressional, presidential – were stubbornly resisted by Errázuriz. Then, in September 1874, Eulogio Altamirano, his loyal Interior minister, suddenly produced a compromise allowing the *voto acumulativo* in elections to the Chamber of Deputies. The new electoral law, the most significant since 1833, made literacy the sole voting qualification (though for men alone).

While Congress debated these reforms, Errázuriz was constructing the new governing coalition that was needed after the disintegration of the Fusion. He could rely on a solid congressional contingent of Liberals – *liberales de gobierno* ("government Liberals"), as they were to become known – and he knew how to enlarge it, but he needed also to find new allies. Since a rapprochement with the Conservatives was unthinkable, these could only come from the ranks of Radicals and dissident Liberals. The vital deal was made at a secret meeting between the president and the Radical "patriarch" Manuel Antonio Matta – held in a private house, as Matta refused to go to the Moneda. The new Liberal-Radical alliance was formalized only in mid-1875, with the appointment as foreign minister of José Alonso, the first Radical to enter the cabinet. By then it was clear that a political shift comparable to that of 1861–62 had been accomplished. Indeed, the pattern of politics now settled into the basic shape it was to retain until the crisis of 1891.

We need to look at this changing political pattern a little more closely. The interplay of political parties was now much more prominent than before. The "parties" themselves were still no more than loose agglomerations of upper-class politicians and their clientèles. Neither their congressional nor national identity was very clear. When in October 1876 the Radical deputy and noted freemason Dr. Ramón Allende Padín (grandfather of President Salvador Allende) proposed that congressmen should vote automatically along party lines, the view was widely repudiated. The parties had little in the way of formal national organization. The Radicals, it is true, had a growing network of local *asambleas* – rising to more than forty by the late 1880s – but these were not centrally coordinated. No party held a national conference until December 1878, when the Conservatives assembled thirty-eight local delegations in Santiago. Yet despite their amorphousness, the parties were an essential point of reference in all political talk – as were their well-known internal divisions. Some Conservatives (the so-called *pechoños*), accepted leadership by the Church; others (the most prominent) preferred a more independent Catholic stance. The Radicals, for their part, experienced dissension over the Errázuriz-Matta deal, the Gallo brothers disapproving. By the mid-1870s the National party consisted chiefly of the following of Antonio Varas, whose views grew more liberal with age; many younger *monttvaristas* had drifted (by way of the Reform Clubs) into the swelling Liberal ranks. Most importantly of all, the Liberals themselves divided between a majority supporting the government and a heterogeneous minority identifying at times with the opposition, at times with the president. The new Liberal-centered governing combination was inherently less stable than its two predecessors.

The ideological differences between the parties were more apparent than real. Nearly all Chilean politicians in the 1870s could have said "We are all Liberals now!" The idea that the 1833 Constitution was "parliamentary" rather than presidentialist was steadily gaining ground. (The constitutional amendment of 1871 was obviously the first important step in this direction.) Congressional practice reflected the growing trend (and would reflect it even more under Errázuriz's successor) with greater use of the *interpelación* (formal questioning of ministers, first incorporated into the Chamber's standing orders in 1846 on Manuel Antonio Tocornal's initiative) and to a lesser extent the formal *voto de desconfianza* ("vote of no confidence"). An *interpelación* had priority over other business, and could be extended over several sittings.

The president's power over Congress, as we have seen, ultimately rested on his manipulation of elections. This showed no signs of abating after the reforms of 1874. But it did become more difficult. With more seats regularly contested than previously, the executive had to resort to wider forms of fraud, intimidation, and violence – all glaringly exposed in Congress and in the press (not notably inhibited by the stiff law of 1846 or the more liberal law passed in 1872). Electoral intervention was increasingly held to be an archaic survival that squared ill with the general liberalization now occurring. Early in 1875 the rising politician José Manuel Balmaceda (one of the young *monttvaristas* who had passed into the Liberal camp) published a set of eloquent articles on this theme. Somewhat less publicly, the naval officer Arturo Prat, then studying for a law degree, chose as his thesis topic the ways in which the law of 1874 might actually be made to work.

For the moment, such hopes were in vain. The presidential election of 1876 showed, very clearly, the precise limitations of the "new politics." Early in 1875 Benjamín Vicuña Mackenna, until recently the Intendant of Santiago, decided to run for the presidency. Vicuña Mackenna has some claims to be regarded as the most remarkable Chilean of his century. We have already noted his role as a revolutionary in 1851 and 1858. He was much else besides, not least a prolific and lyrical historian. He evidently believed that a strong democratic appeal to "opinion" would give him the prize. His campaigning tours and his incandescent speeches summoned up a current of electoral excitement unprecedented in Chile.

Whether the nation (or rather the very much smaller "political nation") was ready for such politics we cannot tell. Errázuriz was not. His choice had fallen on Aníbal Pinto, the somewhat colorless son of the Liberal president of the 1820s, and son-in-law of the recently deceased General Cruz. Errázuriz, true to form, prepared the ground with consummate care, making conciliatory overtures to the Nationals and neutralizing an alternative Liberal candidacy (that of the historian Miguel Luis Amunátegui) by mounting an elaborate convention to rubber-stamp Pinto's nomination. To this Liberal Alliance convention, which he dubbed "the convention of notables," Vicuña Mackenna responded with his own "convention of the people," a gesture that was less useful electorally than the tacit alliance he had made with the Conservatives.

But the big battalions were against him. The congressional elections (March 1876) were as flagrantly "intervened" as usual. Bedeviled by problems with his own "Liberal Democrat" supporters and his Conservative allies, Vicuña Mackenna withdrew from the unequal contest a few days before the poll. Afterward, it is believed, he was approached by some army officers who offered to stage a coup d'etat for him. "A government imposed by force of arms," this truly great Chilean is said to have replied, "can never be pleasing to the people."[12] Aníbal Pinto was inaugurated as president on September 18, 1876. Errázuriz, who described the election as his own "last battle," died less than a year later at the age of 52.

---

[12] Eugenio Orrego Vicuña, *Vicuña Mackenna, vida y trabajos*, 3rd ed. (Santiago, 1951), pp. 331–32.

6

Crisis and war, 1876–83

Señor Pinto will assume the reins of government at a peculiarly critical moment in the history of his country, a time of severe commercial depression, and when several social and financial questions press for a prompt resolution, and with the prestige of the previous administration to rival. The country will expect much from him – more, probably, than will be realized. . . .

– *The Chilian Times*, September 2, 1876

Economic crisis

The fates were not at all kind to President Pinto. During his first months in office, the world price for copper fell by 20 percent and Chilean copper exports by 16 percent: the drop for semi-smelted metal was as much as 50 percent. Silver exports remained at barely one-third of their 1874 level. Unfortunately the climate also turned belligerent: between 1876 and 1878, the country's croplands underwent months of drought punctuated by indecently generous rainfall. In 1877 a sudden trebling of precipitation washed away roads, submerged rail lines, and destroyed livestock and crops. By 1878, exports of wheat and flour had dropped by well over one-third since 1873. Approximately 300,000 laborers were thrown out of work, the pace of business slowed, and the price of food soared.

Since Chileans were unable (like the Americans and British of the 1980s and 1990s) to curb their appetite for imported goods, the trade deficit widened, and in consequence specie had to be exported in record quantities. Eventually the combined impact of the ravaged export economy, the commercial slowdown, and the flight of funds weakened the country's financial institutions. Some of the defects of the earlier banking legislation now showed up. Legally permitted to lend more than their assets, the bankers had invested in a series of highly speculative schemes (including one to convert copper into gold) that could not endure the cold light of examination. In October 1877 the Thomas Bank collapsed; nine months later, in July 1878, President Pinto learned that every bank except one lacked the funds to cover its deposits.

The prospect of a general run on the banks in an already decimated economy convinced even the most obdurate supporters of laissez faire that it was time to act. In July 1878 Congress passed a measure which forced citizens to accept the notes issued by private banks as payment for debts. Financial institutions were henceforth relieved of the obligation to convert their privately printed bank notes into gold or silver. The public had little choice but to accept the new law: some of the banks had no specie left in their cash tills. It was a case of any port in a storm. Paper money was the only way to preserve what little had been left intact by the vagaries of the weather and the international economy.

The "law of inconvertibility" saved the banks, but it hardly alleviated the plight of the government. Declining exports and imports drastically reduced the state's income. Anxious to make up his budgetary shortfall, Pinto imposed a 10 percent surcharge on all import duties. He also slashed the budget ruthlessly, dismissing public employees, beaching naval vessels, and disbanding numerous Army and National Guard units. But the crisis clearly demanded a more vigorous solution. With mines closed down and fields lying fallow, the unemployed flowed into the towns in quest of work. The towns simply could not absorb them. The Church and various charitable organizations opened soup kitchens (*ollas de Pobre*), but these could provide only temporary assistance. The situation became sufficiently bleak for one newspaper to claim that the only way to avoid starvation was for a man to become a "thief and a decent woman a prostitute."[1] Some 50,000 Chileans emigrated, while others turned to crime: bands of unemployed peasants raided *fundos,* and in the cities assaults became commonplace, many citizens fearing to venture out. All the signs pointed to an incipient social crisis, with several commentators warning of a possible rebellion, spearheaded either by frustrated peasants and workers or by the embryonic urban middle class.

Congress's initial reaction to the crisis – far and away the worst crisis since independence – was to treat the symptoms rather than the underlying causes. It authorized the flogging of thieves, as a deterrent to would-be criminals. The threat of the lash, however, could not intimidate the starving. More thoughtful social observers suggested that the state should encourage manufacturing industry. New factories would not only provide employment, thereby allaying social tensions; they would reduce Chile's vulnerability to the vagaries of the weather and free the economy from the tyranny of the "European markets."[2]

In July 1878, in response to what seemed to be growing protectionist pressure, Congress enacted a revised tariff code. Henceforth, luxury items and imports competing with domestic products paid a 35 percent tax,

---

[1] *Mefistófeles,* April 20, 1878.
[2] *Industria Chilena,* October 16, 1876.

with tools, machinery, and industrial goods seen as useful in developing the economy paying only 15 percent. Goods which did not fall into either category paid either a 25 percent levy or a specific value-related tax. Congress went further than this: in the same year, it approved a more revolutionary measure, the *herencia,* a tax on gifts and estates. While certainly a progressive reform (it affected only the affluent), the *herencia* could not solve the country's economic dilemma on its own. Late in 1878, the government proposed the so-called *mobiliaria,* a tax on income and invested capital which, like the *herencia,* fell upon the wealthy. Congress, however, rejected this proposal, leading *The Chilian Times* to observe tartly that "the capitalist may breathe freely again."[3]

Although the steps taken might seem modest in retrospect, the passage of the new customs legislation and the *herencia* represented an important shift in fiscal policy. From now onward the state was to intervene more firmly to protect local industries and to levy taxes on the rich. It remained to be seen, however, if these two particular measures could provide the revenues needed to fund the government.

International crisis

Beset by increasingly serious economic problems, Chile also became embroiled in a series of diplomatic confrontations – one of which, at least, was to have crucial economic repercussions. The first portents of impending international crisis came from the north, from Bolivia. Two main issues caused friction here: first, the delineation of the border, and second, the status of those Chileans, mainly miners, who lived on the Bolivian littoral. Since it ran through the Atacama Desert, one of the world's driest wastelands, neither country had seemed unduly concerned over the exact location of the frontier. The discovery of silver, guano, and finally nitrates suddenly made the Atacama extremely valuable. Both nations now began to vie vigorously to control the desert they had previously neglected. In 1874, after a great deal of acrimonious wrangling which almost degenerated into war, the Frontier was fixed at 24°S. To secure this agreement, Chile abandoned its claims to a portion of the Atacama Desert. In return, Bolivia promised not to raise the taxes on the *Compañía de Salitres y Ferrocarril de Antofagasta,* the Chilean nitrate company now operating (as noted in Chapter 4) in the Atacama.

Bolivia was not Chile's only potential enemy. During the 1870s, the Argentine government, having tamed its unruly provincial caudillos, launched campaigns to "pacify" its Indian population. This thrust into the interior brought Argentines into an unwelcome contact with Chile,

---

[3] *The Chilian Times,* Valparaiso, August 31, 1878.

for Chileans had been filtering into the largely unpopulated wilds of
Patagonia – and had, of course, been on the Straits of Magellan since
1843. Argentina demanded that Chile recognize its sovereignty over
both areas. Chilean opinion, for the most part, appeared willing to cede
Patagonia, but to lose control of the Strait would expose the country to
the risk of an Argentine naval attack as well as deny it access to the
Atlantic. The government was strongly urged by the press to reject the
Argentine claims.

Pinto selected the historian Diego Barros Arana to negotiate a settlement. The choice proved unfortunate. Barros Arana violated his instructions, agreeing to cede Patagonia and to grant Argentina partial control
of the Straits. Barros Arana's largesse provoked rioting in Santiago. War
suddenly seemed imminent, but Pinto accepted a formula proposed by
the Argentine consul-general (given plenipotentiary powers by Buenos
Aires), and in December 1878 the two countries signed the "Fierro-
Sarratea" treaty: this postponed the question of sovereignty for future
discussion, but permitted joint Argentine-Chilean control of the Straits.
Although Pinto managed in this way to avert a war, his handling of the
Argentine crisis damaged his already shaky reputation. The opposition
seized on the boundary issue, depicting the president as a craven weakling
who had surrendered to Buenos Aires.

Pinto's problems were soon compounded by a revival of friction with
Bolivia. In December 1878, the Bolivian dictator Hilarión Daza, a barely
literate sergeant who had shot his way into the presidency, increased the
taxes on the *Compañía de Salitres y Ferrocarril de Antofagasta*. This clearly
violated the 1874 agreement, but Daza fully expected that Chile would
again "strike its flag as it did with Argentina."[4] Should the Moneda
resist, he could invoke a secret treaty signed in February 1873, in which
Peru had promised to help Bolivia in the event of a war with Chile. The
combination of Peru's not insubstantial fleet, in conjunction with the
allied armies, Daza concluded, would bring easy victory.

Pinto had little room to negotiate. The *Compañía de Salitres*'s share
holders had suborned a number of newspapers, which shrilly demanded
that the government enforce its treaty obligations. Opposition politicians,
who used the border dispute with Bolivia as an issue during the 1879
congressional election campaign, warned Pinto and his Liberal followers
not to surrender to the Bolivian dictator. Both the unscrupulous politicians and the jingoistic press organized demonstrations in Santiago and
Valparaiso to invigorate the national mood. These tactics had their effect.
Inflamed by "patriotic gore," the public, which had already demonstrated

---

[4] H. Daza to S. Zapata, February 6, 1879, in Pascual Ahumada Moreno, ed., *La Guerra del Pacífico*, 9
vols. (Valparaiso, 1884–90), I, 93.

a distinct willingness to fight during the Argentine crisis, amplified the demands of the "hawks." Watching a patriotic mob marching in front of his house, Antonio Varas, then briefly minister of the Interior, told the president that unless he moved against Bolivia "[the people] will kill you and me."[5]

In February 1879, motivated by either anger or fear, Pinto ordered the Army to seize Antofagasta as well as the territory ceded to Bolivia under the 1874 treaty. Pinto would have been content to stop at Antofagasta, but he could not. The press and the opposition alike demanded that he order the Army north of the old border in order to protect Chilean positions. Pinto refused, perhaps believing that Daza would accept a return to the *status quo ante*. But Daza did not: two weeks after the Chilean occupation of Antofagasta, Bolivia declared war.

Pinto, like most other Chilean politicians, had known for years about the "secret" Peruvian-Bolivian alliance. He hoped, however, that Lima might be persuaded to remain aloof from the conflict. For a while such an outcome even seemed likely: Peru's president, Manuel Prado, offered to mediate. At the same time, however, the Peruvians showed obvious signs of readying their navy and army – actions not lost on the Chilean press, which demanded that Pinto move against Lima before it was too late. The president labored mightily to avoid a conflict, even offering Peru economic concessions in return for neutrality. He was overwhelmed by the strength of public opinion, and finally demanded that Peru state openly whether it planned to honor the 1873 treaty. When the answer came, in the affirmative, in April 1879, Chile declared war on both Bolivia and Peru.

Pinto had good reason to hesitate before involving Chile in a war with its northern neighbors. Years of budget-cutting had deprived the Army of one-fifth of its men; the Navy had decommissioned warships; the territorial reserve, the *Guardia Nacional,* had shrunk in size by more than two-thirds. Chileans now faced two enemies whose combined armed forces outnumbered them two to one. Equipped with outmoded weapons (which posed more of a danger to the user than the prospective target), lacking medical and supply corps, the Army was now called upon to fight a war far from the country's heartland, and without decent lines of communication. For Chile to triumph, control of the sea was essential: only this would enable the Army to attack the enemy on its home ground. Without it Chile was exposed to invasion, blockade, or (as Spain had shown in 1866) bombardment. Peru's navy (Bolivia did not have one) possessed two ironclads, as well as support vessels; the Chilean fleet also included two ironclads but these, like most of the Navy's other

---

[5] Quoted in Mario Barros, *Historia diplomática de Chile,* p. 332.

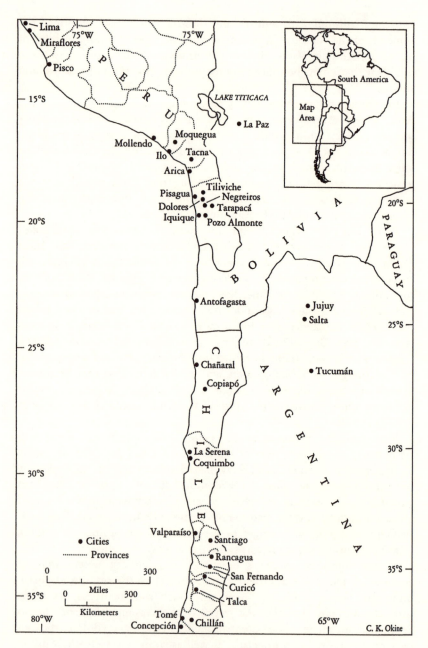

Peru-Bolivia-Chile, January 1879

ships, were in poor condition. The immediate outlook did not look promising.

The War of the Pacific

Hoping to win the maritime supremacy so urgently needed, Pinto requested the Navy's commander, Admiral Juan Williams Rebolledo, to attack the enemy fleet at Callao, its fortified home base. Williams refused. Instead he blockaded Iquique, the port through which Peru exported nitrates (its principal source of revenue), in the belief that the Peruvian president would have to either order his fleet south or face financial ruin. Thus the Chilean squadron idled off Iquique harbor, waiting for the Peruvian attack. Public opinion, soon tiring of Williams's passive waiting-game, demanded that he strike at the enemy. Anxious to enhance his popularity (Williams planned to capitalize on his command to make a bid for the presidency in 1881), the admiral finally decided to attack the Peruvian ironclads, the *Huascar* and the *Independencia,* as they lay at anchor in Callao. Without informing the Moneda, he sailed north, leaving two wooden ships, the *Esmeralda* and the *Covadonga,* to maintain the blockade of Iquique.

Williams's expedition was a fiasco: the Peruvian ships had already left when the Chilean squadron arrived. (Evidence indicates that Williams chose to attack Callao knowing full well that the ironclads had already sailed.) When the admiral at last slunk back to Iquique, he learned that the Peruvian fleet had taken advantage of his absence to break the blockade. Not only had the Peruvian admiral, Miguel Grau, successfully reinforced Iquique, but he had also sunk the *Esmeralda* in the first memorable sea-battle of the war (May 21, 1879). The battle of Iquique provided Chile with the supreme hero of the war, Captain Arturo Prat, whose death in a hopeless attempt to board the *Huáscar* gave the country an impeccable symbol of patriotic sacrifice and duty. The only bright spot in this disaster was that during a high-seas chase of the *Covadonga,* the *Independencia*'s captain ran his ship aground – thus almost halving Peru's effective naval strength.

Rather than take advantage of this unearned advantage, Williams sulked in his cabin, nursing a bruised ego and an imaginary illness. By now the government desperately wished to dismiss him, but the admiral's allies in the Conservative party successfully insulated their potential future candidate from retaliation. During the winter of 1879, meanwhile, Chile continued to suffer naval reverses: in July the Peruvians captured a fully loaded troop transport, the *Rímac,* an event that provoked massive riots in Santiago; Admiral Grau successfully terrorized the northern ports while another Peruvian warship, the *Unión,* threatened Chilean supply lines through the Magellan Straits. Finally, in August 1879, and again without informing the government, Williams broke off the blockade of Iquique. This time not even Williams's most ardent defenders could protect him. He was replaced by Admiral Galvarino Riveros, who immediately set about refitting his ships. In October the Chilean fleet trapped Grau off Punta Angamos. After a brutal exchange of fire (in which Grau perished), the Chileans captured the *Huáscar*. It was later taken to the naval base at Talcahuano, where it is still on display.

Chile was now master of the sea-lanes. The way to the north was open. But if the Navy was ready, the Army was not. Its 74-year-old commander, General Justo Arteaga, possessed neither the physical nor the mental resources to mount an expedition to Peru. Like Williams, Arteaga also enjoyed the protection of political allies and therefore seemed beyond retribution. In a rare moment of lucidity, fortunately, he resigned before he could do too much damage. His successor, Erasmo Escala, proved only marginally more effective. A fervent Catholic (he often ordered his troops to attend religious ceremonies) with close ties to the Conservative Party, the new commander seemed temperamentally incapable of working with anyone who challenged his authority or questioned his judgment. But for political reasons Pinto could ill afford to replace him. Instead he ordered Rafael Sotomayor and José Francisco Vergara, both civilian politicians (the first a National, the second a Radical), to assist (and by implication to supervise) Escala, especially by providing logistical support.

In November 1879 Escala's troops landed at Pisagua, in the Peruvian province of Tarapacá. The assault, while successful, was not without its flaws: an error of navigation put the fleet off course, and the officer in charge of the invasion botched the landing. But the Chileans emerged as paragons of military virtue in comparison with their opponents. The Allies had planned a counterattack which called for Daza to strike from the north while the Peruvian General Juan Buendía would attack from the south, thus crushing the Chilean expedition between the allied armies. The plan misfired badly. Daza, whose incompetence (already amply displayed) decimated his units as they marched from La Paz to the coast, simply deserted. Rather than advance through the desert to the south (admittedly difficult), the Bolivian dictator ordered his men to fall back on their base in Arica. Buendía, unaware of Daza's defection, continued to drive northward expecting to rendezvous with the Bolivians. The Chileans, of course, knew nothing of these events. Escala remained close to the coast, keeping a watchful eye on the north, assuming that an attack would come from that quarter. Anxious to secure a dependable supply of water for the expedition, Rafael Sotomayor ordered his colleague Vergara (now serving as an active officer) to capture the oasis of

Dolores. Vergara had accomplished this mission when one of his patrols, reconnoitering the area, ran into the advance guard of Buendía's army.

Although unpleasantly surprised, the Chilean commander, Colonel Emilio Sotomayor, managed to position his men on a convenient hill, the Cerro San Francisco, before the enemy struck. A skillful use of artillery as well as sheer fortitude gave the Chileans the battle (November 19, 1879). The Bolivian soldiers, despondent and thirsty, made off for the altiplano. The Peruvians retired in more orderly fashion to the village of Tarapacá. Rather than pursue his exhausted opponents, Escala ordered his men to attend a Mass of thanksgiving. Having fulfilled their religious obligations, the Chileans finally attacked, and a force under Vergara advanced on Tarapacá. This time, it was the Peruvians who routed the Chileans, inflicting serious casualties (including more than 500 dead) in a singularly bloody battle (November 27). Notwithstanding this victory, Peru now abandoned Tarapacá province, enabling the Chileans to occupy Iquique and its nitrate-rich hinterland.

Success in the Tarapacá campaign did not prevent squabbles in the victors' camp. Escala, for his part, had fallen under the spell of a coterie of Conservative aides, who assured him that he could parlay his military triumphs into a presidential candidacy. He frequently quarreled with Sotomayor (who was increasingly exercising military command) and with anyone who doubted his military genius. In March 1880, apparently to impress his importance on the government, Escala threatened to resign. To the general's great surprise, Pinto called his bluff and accepted the resignation.

Under a new commander, General Manuel Baquedano, Chile launched its third northern campaign in February 1880, landing an expedition at Ilo with the aim of capturing Tacna province. With no Peruvian counterattack in sight, and remembering Escala's ineptitude, Pinto reluctantly ordered Baquedano to move inland. Baquedano had to surmount desperate supply problems, but swiftly captured Moquegua and defeated the Peruvians at the battle of Los Angeles (March 22). Despite its success, the opening of the campaign lacked a little luster: during one surprise attack, a unit got lost and had to ask the local people for directions.

Anxious to capture Arica, Tacna's port and a vital strategic point, Baquedano marched his men overland, a journey which took a heavy toll of lives. After about one month the Chileans reached Campo de la Alianza, a fortified Peruvian position on the outskirts of Tacna. Although Vergara (Sotomayor had recently died suddenly) urged Baquedano to outflank the strongpoint, the general insisted upon a frontal assault. Baquedano's soldiers triumphed (May 26), but at a very high cost: three out of every ten Chilean soldiers were either killed (nearly 500) or wounded (around 1,600). Despite these heavy casualties, the army moved on to Arica, and captured its strongly fortified Morro, the Gibraltar-like rock that loomed (as it still looms) over the port, in one of the most rapid and heroic assaults of the war (July 6). From start to finish it took fifty-five minutes, around 120 Chileans dying in the attack.

Victory in the Tacna campaign did not cause unalleviated delight in Chile. The public, learning of the cost in blood of Baquedano's sledge-hammer tactics, was outraged. Indeed, one journalist was so appalled that he suggested Santiago hold "a dance of death" rather than a victory ball to celebrate the triumph at Tacna.[6] Public anger was further exacerbated by news that the Peruvians had sunk two more ships, the *Loa* and *Covadonga* (July–September 1880). Demands for an assault on Lima now grew irresistible. Fulfilling these demands proved difficult. Most of the Army's supplies were exhausted: civilians like Vergara had to labor hard to find men and equipment, and the means to transport an expedition to the new battle zone. Thanks to prodigious efforts, Baquedano's troops were poised by January 1881 to attack the Peruvian capital. As during the Tacna campaign, Vergara suggested that Baquedano try to outflank the Peruvian defenses to minimize the casualties, while allowing Baquedano to capture the city. The general, apparently a disciple of the *élan vital* school of military tactics, rejected this advice. As one admirer subsequently noted, only a frontal assault would allow the Chileans to demonstrate their virility.

On January 13, 1881, Baquedano's troops duly demonstrated their virility by breaking through the Peruvian positions at Chorrillos. As some of the victors mopped up pockets of resistance, others amused themselves by pillaging the locality and terrorizing its inhabitants. Two days later the Chileans attacked and overwhelmed the Peruvian defenses at Miraflores in a second bloody battle. (Chilean casualties for these two battles included at least 1,300 dead and more than 4,000 wounded; Peruvian losses were higher.) By the evening the Peruvian government had fled and the first Chilean units (one composed of Santiago policemen) entered Lima itself. For the third time in sixty years, the former viceregal capital lay at the feet of a Chilean army.

The fall of Lima did not end the war. Chile demanded the cession of Tarapacá, Arica, and Tacna as war reparations and as a buffer for Chile in case Peru decided to stage a *revanche*. Nicolás Piérola, who had replaced President Prado in 1879 and who now moved his government to the mountains, refused to cede an inch. Like Mexico's Juárez, he promised to wage a war of attrition to expel the occupying army. Chileans might dismiss Piérola as a bombastic fool, but they were nevertheless in an uncomfortable position. They could hardly withdraw from Peru without a peace treaty. But neither could they secure a peace treaty without convincing or coercing a Peruvian government to accept their demands. Francisco García Calderón, the hapless lawyer who became the president of Chilean-controlled Peru in February 1881, was as adamant as Piérola (still at the head of *his* government) in his refusal to contemplate territorial concessions.

While the Chilean government tried to force a settlement, Peruvian resistance stiffened. Bands of irregulars, *montoneros,* now appeared; under the leadership of seasoned officers like Andrés Cáceres they harassed and attacked the occupying army. A punitive expedition was dispatched into the Peruvian interior in hopes of crushing these guerrillas. Increasingly many Chileans began to fear that their great military victory was destined to prove pyrrhic.

A complicating factor at this point was the role of the United States, which had earlier (October 1880) attempted to mediate between the belligerents.[7] The U.S. Secretary of State, James G. Blaine, wished to use the War of the Pacific to blunt what he saw as British imperialism while extending what some might term the American variety. Blaine decided he could best accomplish these goals by encouraging García Calderón's refusal to cede territory. The Chilean government eventually tired of this game and jailed García Calderón, an action that infuriated Blaine. For a short while it even seemed possible that the United States and Chile might go to war. The crisis was ended by the assassination of President James A. Garfield (September 1881). The new president, Chester A. Arthur, replaced Blaine with Frederick Frelinghuysen, who quickly abandoned his predecessor's truculent foreign policy. Henceforth the United States was not to oppose Chilean demands for territory.

But if the diplomatic situation improved, Chile's military situation did not. Early in 1882, the government sent another expedition into the Peruvian highlands. Adrift in a hostile environment, cut off from their supplies, and constantly under attack from guerrilla bands, the Chilean army completely failed to pacify the interior. After months of fruitless wanderings in the mountains, the troops were ordered to withdraw to the coast. As they retreated, Cáceres struck his most devastating blow. At the battle of La Concepción (July 9, 1882) the Peruvians annihilated an entire Chilean detachment of seventy-seven, not only killing the soldiers but also mutilating their remains.

---

[7] In the chancelleries of Europe, there had been talk of intervention by the great powers to end the war, but the German Chancellor, Bismarck, effectively blocked all such suggestions.

The disaster at La Concepción brought home to the Chilean public the fact that its soldiers were still engaged in a bloody war. As the casualties mounted, as the men succumbed to the sniper's bullet or to disease, the press questioned why Chilean youth had to die "in places... which could have been left alone without compromising the cause of Chile."[8] Why, others demanded, was the nation wasting its blood and its treasure on a war which threatened to become the "cancer of our prosperity"?[9] As one provincial newspaper concluded: "The thing is to make peace, be it well done or not."[10]

A number of prominent Peruvians, too, had tired of the war. One of these, Miguel Iglesias, who established his own new government (with Chilean support) at Cajamarca, appeared willing to negotiate. While willing to give up Tarapacá, he balked at ceding Tacna. The government in Santiago, anxious to extricate the nation from the diplomatic morass, was now willing to make concessions. It stuck to its demand for Tarapacá, but proposed to occupy Tacna and Arica for ten years, following which a plebiscite would determine the final ownership of the territory. Although Iglesias accepted these terms, Cáceres would not – and he was still at large. Another Chilean expedition marched into the interior, determined to hunt him down. After months of hazardous maneuvering, the Chileans finally defeated him at the battle of Huamachucho (July 10, 1883). With Cáceres thus subdued, Iglesias duly signed a peace treaty, at Ancón on October 20. Nine days later, Chilean troops occupied the last pocket of *montonero* resistance, the beautiful city of Arequipa.

Bolivia still formally remained a belligerent, though had taken no part in the war since the Tarapacá campaign. The Treaty of Ancón, however, persuaded even the most truculent Bolivians to seek peace. Although vanquished, the country managed to obtain generous terms: the "indefinite truce" signed in April 1884 granted Chile only the right to temporary occupation of the Bolivian littoral. The armistice with Bolivia marked the end of the War of the Pacific, almost exactly five years after it had begun.

The Chilean capture of Lima in January 1881, we should note here, provided an incidental diplomatic dividend. With Peru out of the war, Argentina could ill afford to press its claims to the Straits of Magellan. In July 1881 Chile and Argentina signed a treaty which confirmed both Argentine sovereignty over Patagonia and Chilean control of the Straits. In addition, both nations agreed to demilitarize the waterway, while Argentina undertook never to block the Atlantic entry into the Straits.

---

[8] *El Independiente,* April 30, 1882.   [9] *El Mercurio,* Valparaiso, July 26, 1882.
[10] *El Correo de Quillota,* Quillota, September 28, 1882.

Soldiers and civilians

Apologists for the defeated Allies have traditionally described Chile as the Prussia of the Pacific – a predatory land looking for any excuse to go to war with its hapless neighbors. Common sense alone indicates otherwise. Chile's armed forces in 1879 were both small in size and poorly equipped. Moreover, too many officers owed their high ranks to political connections rather than to technical proficiency. The incompetence of men like Williams and Escala forced the government to become involved in the conduct of the war and to provide the logistical support. Some professional soldiers resented this intrusion, calling upon their political allies to protect them from the government's attempts to direct the war. This political intervention, by insulating inefficient officers, almost certainly prolonged the war.

Relations between the military and civilian society often proved acrimonious. The officers resented institutions such as freedom of the press, particularly when it was used to describe the conduct of the military in unflattering language. In San Felipe, for example, piqued subalterns destroyed a newspaper office in retaliation for a critical editorial. Baquedano had journalists jailed for pillorying his skills. A more egregious incident occurred in 1882, when Admiral Patricio Lynch, then military governor of Lima, claimed (in effect) that he was above the law when he arbitrarily abridged a Chilean colonel's civil rights. Unimpressed by Lynch's arguments, the Chilean supreme court overruled him.

The War of the Pacific forced the Army into the lives of civilians to an extent not seen before. When the first rush of patriotic enlistments tapered off, the armed forces resorted to impressment. Although this was clearly illegal, public officials tolerated (and in some cases even encouraged) such activities as long as the recruiters confined themselves to dragooning the town drunk, the petty criminal, or the vagrant. Eventually, however, the military began to seize respectable peasants, artisans, and miners. "It is a curious illustration of democratic equality and republican freedom," noted one journalist, "to force Juan, who owns not a cent, to fight in defense of Pedro's property, while the latter declines to raise an arm himself, because he is not so poor as his fellow citizen."[11] A large part of the country's male population lived in fear: farmers refused to bring produce to market; charcoal-burners stayed at home; the young, the infirm, and even the aged – all became targets. In one case, the appearance of recruiters caused a group of inquilinos to jump into a river to avoid capture. Nor was this solely a rural phenomenon. One deputy reported seeing armed soldiers pursue a man down a Santiago street, beat

[11] *The Chilian Times*, Valparaiso, April 5, 1879.

him to the ground, and then march him under the lash to the local barracks.

If some Chileans protested against these activities, others did not – notably those who did not have to serve. Indeed, one particularly patriotic deputy offered to send all of his inquilinos off to war. Occasionally hacendados objected. They did not oppose conscription; they simply did not want their supply of labor disrupted. In one case local landowners decided among themselves who should remain and who should serve. The local newspaper complimented them on their judgment, observing that such actions protected the civil liberties of all.

Once conscripted, a soldier had to accept harsh discipline and endure wretched conditions. Officers and NCOs handed out lashes more liberally than food. Rations themselves were monotonously bleak: hard tack, jerked beef, onions. The military's supply system often broke down, forcing soldiers to supplement their rations from their own pocket. Not only were the soldiers' wages low, but the men frequently did not receive their pay because the pay department functioned spasmodically at best, and they often had to write home to ask for money. Garrison life offered only slightly more comfort than the field: isolated in provincial towns, the troops fell easy prey to greedy shopkeepers who watered their liquor and cheated them at every turn.

The Chilean soldier suffered almost as much at the hands of his government as the enemy. Since the Army had economized by abolishing its medical corps, the military had neither the staff nor the facilities to care for the wounded or the sick. While civilians could supply the Army's need for surgeons and equipment, they could not compensate for the military's medical incompetence and lack of foresight. General Escala neglected to take ambulances when he attacked Pisagua. Instead of being dealt with in field hospitals, the wounded were often sent back to Chile, sometimes above deck on freighters. As a result, many soldiers arrived home either dead or with gangrenous wounds. Injured soldiers sometimes had to march to the hospitals while enemy prisoners made the same journey by coach. Until protests stopped the practice, government officials insisted that the war-wounded pay for their own medical care; the military also stopped paying a soldier's wages or family entitlements while he was hospitalized. If the war-wounded merited such cavalier treatment, the war dead received approximately the same veneration as that accorded to a medieval leper. While it is true that the remains of the more conspicuous heroes were deposited in ornate tombs, the less celebrated were dumped naked into graves with indecent haste. This state of affairs became so disgraceful that a Valparaiso workers' society began to send delegates to accompany each corpse to its final resting-place.

The maimed, and the families of the war dead, fared only slightly better than the dead themselves. The heirs of officers received some protection, but initially the government made no provision to pay pensions to the families of enlisted men. Not until the casualties started to mount, in late 1879, did Congress belatedly address the problem. Its decisions were distinctly niggardly. The mother of a private killed in battle, for example, was awarded 3 pesos per month. Worse still, the pension legislation excluded the survivors of men who died of natural causes or from accidents. Since more soldiers succumbed to the bacillus rather than the bullet, Congress could hardly be faulted for being profligate with taxpayers' money. Small wonder that patriotism was a luxury in which few Chileans could afford to indulge and that those who did derisively dismissed their rewards, in the time-honored phrase, as *el pago de Chile,* "Chile's reward."

Economy and society during the war

The War of the Pacific was the most significant national experience for Chile since independence. What were its effects on the country's economy and society? Its impact on agriculture, mining, and manufacturing was obviously variable. In the countryside, hacendados carped about "a shortage of hands," but they had been doing so long before 1879. Even if the war *did* drain men from the fields, we cannot be sure that it negatively affected production. In 1880, when the Army was already quite large, there was a slight increase in land under cultivation. The 1880 harvest proved a generous one. Agricultural production declined in 1881 and 1883 – after the fall of Lima and the start of demobilization. While many rural laborers served in the Army, their absence clearly did not seriously damage agriculture. Some hacendados apparently purchased or rented farm machinery; others hired women or used prisoners of war.

Such changes in the countryside as can be detected in these years seem to have little to do with the war. In September 1880 Congress abolished the *estanco* (a measure that had been talked about for years), and this undoubtedly stimulated domestic tobacco production. Some crop diversification seems to have taken place. None of these things signified deep change either in traditional working methods or in the hacendados' place in the countryside or the wider society.

Exports of copper continued to fall during the war, but, again, it is difficult to attribute this to the war itself. Miners were certainly drawn into the Army, and many were attracted to the conquered northern provinces and into the newly flourishing nitrate industry. But the real causes of the decline of copper mining were less the shortage of labor than "structural" factors: failure to update technology; excessive reliance on the wasteful *pirquén* system; the poor quality of the remaining ore; the continuing slump in world prices; foreign competition. Only the most efficient mines now prospered; the rest simply closed down. Indeed, by 1884, when the war was over, the *Sociedad de Minería* openly wondered whether Chile's copper mines would survive at all. Silver production also declined in 1879 and 1880, hobbled by low international demand and foreign competition, though it rose again in the early 1880s, when there was a minor flurry of new investment in the Norte Chico.

Although many of Chile's small manufacturing plants had suffered in the depression of the 1870s, some managed to survive. Only a few of these (Carlos Klein's foundry at Rancagua, for example) were able to provide logistical support to the Army and the fleet. The country imported most of its armaments and ammunition from abroad, particularly after the Army's arsenal blew up in March 1880. And, while the textile mills and shoemaking plants made uniforms and boots, they were never able to equip the entire Army and Navy. The initial effect of the war on manufacturing was negative, with a number of plants closing down in 1879, as workers joined the Army. Moreover, given that soldiers earned less than civilian workers, purchasing power declined, with inevitable effects on demand. After 1881, however, the number of plants grew again, as did their range of products: food, shoes, sweets, soap, sacks, ready-made clothing.

This surge in industrial output is attributable less to the war than to general factors. Chilean towns, for instance, expanded dramatically between 1875 and 1885 – Santiago's population rose by around one-half (to 190,000). Antofagasta, Iquique, Valparaiso, and Concepción-Talcahuano all experienced substantial growth. Not only was there a construction boom, but several municipalities undertook improvements. Meanwhile the government itself embarked on a certain amount of highway construction, and completed a number of railroad lines. All such projects stimulated the economy, both by using locally manufactured goods and by providing employment. The newly annexed northern provinces also became a market for the products of the Central Valley. A final factor to be taken into account is the tariff protection accorded by the government. In addition to imposing higher customs duties, the authorities demanded their payment in specie. Paper money was acceptable only if the importer paid the difference in value between the paper peso and the *peso fuerte* ("strong peso," i.e., specie). The difference itself fluctuated, but in some months the surcharge equaled 40 percent. On top of the regular import duties, this sometimes meant an effective 75 percent tax on foreign goods.

Conscription seems to have affected Chile's social life far more than its economy. The absence of young men ardently pursuing young women in the traditional evening *paseo* gave observers the impression that small towns had become social deserts. (Judging from the birth rate, however, enough young men remained.) Some welcomed the war, since the dragooning of the criminal population brought tranquillity after the crime wave of the later 1870s. Conversely, the peace treaty and demobilization meant that within months the number of crimes dramatically increased once again. Socially ambitious mothers also rued the return of peace, which deprived them of the chance to marry off their daughters to eligible bachelor officers.

The struggle against Bolivia and Peru was not in any sense a total war. Conscription did not affect the upper class, the *gente decente*. There was no rationing. The poor suffered during the war because they were poor, not because there was nothing to buy. The rich rarely endured privation. Social patterns remained more or less intact. Like migratory birds, the better-off still flocked to the coast or the mountains in the summer, and kept up the Santiago social round during the winter. The opera seasons of the war years were somewhat lackluster, but the number of masked balls and parties did not dwindle. Indeed, if anything, the social pace may have intensified, with party-giving becoming a patriotic, morale-raising distraction from the rigors of the war.

The lower classes, meanwhile, continued to amuse themselves in traditional ways – in the *chinganas,* or at cockfights, floggings, executions, and religious festivals. Military victories to some extent alleviated the monotony: proud citizens exploded almost as much gunpowder in celebrating Chile's triumphs as the soldiers did in winning them. Town-dwellers probably suffered more inconvenience than their rural counterparts. (After the war, however, many inquilinos apparently refused to return to the haciendas, exchanging the tyranny of the landowner for a precarious existence in the city.) Because of the "inconvertibility" crisis of 1878, the country literally ran out of money during the early months of the war. Until the government began to print paper and mint coins (the latter was delayed when the ship bringing new machinery sank), citizens had no means to purchase food. The rich, of course, could get credit; the less fortunate often had to leave such cash as they had in a store, and draw on it. Some stores printed *fichas,* scrip which they then used as change. A number of companies followed suit, issuing *fichas* of cardboard or metal to pay their workers. Unscrupulous storekeepers used the system to cheat the poor by discounting *fichas* issued by their competitors. Even after the government began to issue new money, many *fichas* remained in circulation – some so filthy that people feared to handle them.

Food prices soared during the war. One newspaper estimated that by 1881 the cost of flour had risen by one-seventh, sugar by one-fifth, and coffee, tea, and clothes by three-quarters. Meat (including *charqui*), cheese, and fats all increased in price by 50 percent. This inflationary surge can be attributed to the expansion of the money supply, to the Army's purchasing demands, and also to a cycle of poor weather. Not only did the costs rise, but there were numerous complaints in the press about storekeepers who adulterated milk, oil, and coffee, gave short weight, or sold parasite-infested pork.

Urban life was not only more expensive than it had been before; it was also more unpleasant. As we noted in Chapter 4, the expansion of Santiago and other cities had brought a deterioration in public health by the 1870s, especially with the spread of the *conventillos* – "dens destitute of every convenience . . . where the laws of health and decency are entirely ignored," according to a newspaper of 1876,[12] a year which saw yet another murderous epidemic of smallpox. In 1881 there was another appalling outbreak. These epidemics strained the country's medical facilities to the breaking point. Several cities hastily built pest-houses, where most of the smallpox victims died. Town-dwellers became well accustomed to the sight of the open wagons that carried the corpses (limbs often exposed) to the cemeteries. The government launched vaccination programs after 1876, but these met with resistance. An unholy combination of Liberals and Conservatives opposed any legislation to make vaccination mandatory. "The ravages of smallpox are nothing," stated one deputy, "in comparison to what would transpire from that other plague which bears the name of *authoritarianism*."[13] The same politicians also opposed the government's attempts to regulate prostitutes, on the grounds that they restricted freedom of trade.

The war and fiscal policy

While the effect of the War of the Pacific on the economy may have been limited, it drastically altered the country's fiscal system. As we have seen the nineteenth-century governments had relied upon customs duties, particularly the import tax, to fund their activities. During the period 1870–75, for example, the levy on imports produced almost half of all ordinary revenues. The remaining revenue came from the *estanco,* the *alcabala* (a transfer tax), *patentes* (business licenses), and the *agrícola,* the impost on landed property introduced by Rengifo in the 1830s. Since these levies were unable to fund the government during the economic crisis of the 1870s, they were unlikely to finance the war effort. The Moneda obviously needed to find new sources of revenue. Failure to do so spelled probable defeat in the war.

In May 1879, in desperation, Congress passed the *mobiliaria,* the

---

[12] *The Chilian Times,* Valparaiso, January 29, 1876.
[13] Chamber of Deputies, July 18, 1882, p. 271.

income tax it had rejected the previous year. But the new tax on its own could not defray the cost of the war. Still urgently in need of cash, the government appealed to the banks, seeking to borrow 6 million pesos in return for a number of tax concessions. The banks, needless to say, had nothing to lend but the privately printed notes that had precipitated "inconvertibility" in the first place. With the government's supply of specie almost exhausted, Pinto authorized the printing of paper notes, which the public had no choice but to accept.

Although subsequent generations were to deplore this act, feelings at the time were altogether less condemnatory. The bankers were disliked for exploiting debtors and for restricting credit to small cliques. There were many who saw paper money as a means of emancipating the country from the hands of the greedy few. Some legislators, however, urged caution. The Radical, Enrique MacIver, likened paper money to the mercury used in curing syphilis: in small quantities it might be salutary, but too much could kill the patient. But having discovered this new economic resource, the Moneda now frequently sought congressional approval to print money in order to finance the war effort.

Even the government recognized, however, that it could not indefinitely manufacture paper notes without finding some means of redeeming them. Salvation was at hand: the conquest of the Bolivian littoral and Tarapacá had given Chile a monopoly on the world production of nitrate. One of the first acts of the Chilean commander occupying Tarapacá was to force the nitrate *oficinas* to reopen and to produce; and produce they did; by 1883 over 7,000 men were laboring in the *salitreras* (as compared with 2,000 in 1880); exports doubled (to 589,000 tons) in the same three years. The new export tax imposed in September 1879 (US$1.60 per quintal) seemed likely, therefore, to guarantee a copious flow of revenue.

Although the Moneda could tax the *salitreras,* it did not own them. The nitrate enterprises of Tarapacá belonged in theory to the Peruvian government, which had nationalized them in 1875. In exchange for the owners' titles, the Peruvian authorities had issued interest-bearing trust-deeds or "certificates." The Chilean government faced two alternatives. It could either assume responsibility for the Peruvian nitrate debt,[14] in which case the Chilean state would replace Peru as the proprietor of the *salitreras.* Alternatively, it could refuse to liquidate the Peruvian debt, and recognize the holders of the certificates as the rightful owners of the enterprises. The question was studied by two legislative committees in 1880–81. Both rejected the idea of state ownership. In June 1881 Congress duly granted title to anyone who could demonstrate ownership of

---

[14] Peru had taken out loans on the strength of Tarapacá's nitrate holdings, and its foreign creditors were pressing for a settlement.

75 percent of each certificate. (It also required a cash deposit.) The following year, the government auctioned off *salitreras* which had not been claimed by their new owners. These measures enabled private entrepreneurs to take control of what was now to become the principal source of revenue for the Chilean state. Foreigners (notably the British) as well as Chileans seized the opportunity with alacrity, among them John Thomas North, the Yorkshire-born "Nitrate King," whose spectacular personal holdings in Tarapacá were soon to cause concern in Chile (and suspicion in the City of London).

Although the decisions of 1881 were much criticized later on, they seemed appropriate enough at the time. Public opinion granted the state a limited right to intervene in the economy (by fostering manufacturing, for example) but the government ownership of the means of production was regarded as beyond the ideological pale. Moreover, the sheer cost of purchasing the nitrate certificates also deterred those who might have favored state ownership. It was estimated that Chile would have to assume a debt of around £4 million – an enormous sum for a country still bogged down in a war. The return of ownership to private hands relieved the Moneda of an immense fiscal and bureaucratic burden, while by the same token the imposition of an export duty on nitrate promised a fiscal bonanza. As President Santa María, the first great beneficiary of the new policy, was to put it: "Let the gringos work the nitrate freely. I shall be waiting for them at the door."[15]

Politics and the war

A contrast is usually drawn between Chile's institutional continuity during the war and the political upheavals that occurred both in Bolivia and Peru. There is little doubt, however, that the Chilean political system was strained by the depression of the 1870s and by the growing congressional assertiveness we described in Chapter 5. As already noted, the border dispute with Argentina provoked anti-government rioting in 1878, and rioting again threatened to erupt early in 1879. The most dangerous such episode occurred after the capture of the *Rímac,* when the government had to call in troops to subdue the demonstrators. Had Chile experienced another serious military reverse soon afterward, Pinto might have suffered the same fate as his Bolivian and Peruvian counterparts, Daza and Prado.

At the level of Congress, the outbreak of hostilities by no means stopped partisan bickering. Rather than declare a political truce in the interests of prosecuting the war, the Chamber of Deputies spent the first,

[15] Arturo Alessandri, *Revolución de 1891* (Santiago, 1950), p. 204.

crucial months of 1879 in arguments about the congressional elections. The Conservative party, for instance, made a specialty of introducing votes of censure in hopes of bringing down ministries and winning portfolios for itself. Such legislative in-fighting occurred repeatedly throughout the war. In 1881 a group of deputies attempted to cut off funds for the war effort, as a means of pressuring Pinto to reshuffle his cabinet. The future champion of executive privilege, José Manuel Balmaceda, introduced a motion (September 1880) to censure Pinto's ministers on the grounds of his disagreement with the war policy, and also expressing the unusual view that cabinets should reflect the political composition of the legislature. Balmaceda's motion did not prosper, and it seriously annoyed some of his colleagues, but it was an eloquent sign of the growing "parliamentary" thrust in Chilean politics. Pinto himself did not possess the sort of personality that enabled him to tame his legislative critics. Mild-mannered, self-effacing, gentle, very honorable – he lacked the interest of his predecessor (or his successor) in directing electoral intervention.

As Pinto's term of office drew to its close, the Conservative party, systematically excluded from the wartime cabinets, and which yearned to control the Moneda again, believed that its hour had finally come. Hoping to capitalize on his reputation as the victor of Lima, the Conservatives nominated Manuel Baquedano as their presidential candidate. The general's campaign revolved around the issue of his personal credibility. Baquedano proudly admitted that he knew virtually nothing about Chile's civil and legal institutions. He claimed to be utterly apolitical – non-partisan, olympian in vision, above the madding crowd. But Manuel Baquedano was no Manuel Bulnes. It was 1881, not 1841. The politicians, whose participation in the war had in a real sense made victory possible, were unlikely to relinquish power to the cocked hats.

Domingo Santa María, Pinto's minister of the Interior in 1879–80, had not sought the presidency. Baquedano's candidacy, however, convinced him otherwise. Santa María disliked the general, and his opposition to the "candidate of the sword" won him support from government Liberals, Nationals, and a strong Radical faction. Baquedano for his part attracted both dissident Liberals and Radicals, and Vicuña Mackenna's following, which, like the Conservatives, had been kept out of Pinto's cabinets. Santa María concentrated his fire on the general's military reputation and political inexperience. Others who remembered the bloody triumphs of Tacna and Lima argued that an officer who had squandered the lives of the nation's youth did not deserve the presidency. His political inexperience, his critics alleged, might lead him to assume dictatorial powers or to rely too heavily on the advice of the Conservatives. The press, unrestrained by gentility (or serious libel laws), attacked

Baquedano personally, describing him as a fool and lampooning his manner of speaking: he had an unfortunate speech impediment. In full awareness that he would lose, and angered by the tasteless abuse of the press, the general gave up the unequal struggle and withdrew. Santa María's election was thus a foregone conclusion, and he took office in September 1881.

The War of the Pacific tested Chile. Congress's intense partisanship protected incompetent officers; its sterile debates on electoral malpractice and its frivolous censure motions consumed the time of ministers – time which they could have profitably used to prosecute the war more expeditiously. Yet despite all the strains the political system still functioned: elections, however tainted, were held according to timetable; the Moneda did not silence its critics in the press or in Congress; freedom of speech and assembly continued to be enjoyed and abused. These were worthy achievements and demonstrated, too, how much the country had changed since its earlier war against the Peru-Bolivian confederation. Clearly it had changed dramatically in other ways as well. The already well-developed Chilean sense of superiority was much enhanced by victory. A new set of heroes took its place in the national pantheon.[16] Most important of all, the war had given the country new territory – territory whose rich store of nitrate promised a constant and buoyant source of revenue. Everything seemed set fair for the most hopeful of futures.

---

[16] Few of the war heroes, however, with the major exceptions of Arturo Prat and the victims of La Concepción, seem to have lodged themselves as permanently in the Chilean imagination as the heroes of the wars of independence.

PART III

The nitrate era, 1880s–1930s

Victory in the War of the Pacific was followed at home by the triumph of "parliamentary" ideas over presidentialism in the civil war of 1891. Underlying the politics of the next three decades was a cycle of renewed export-led growth on the strength of the trade in nitrates, accompanied by inevitable social diversification, the main symptoms of which were an emergent (if still small) middle class and a militant labor movement. The so-called Parliamentary Republic failed to address the new social dilemmas of the period (Chapter 7). Failure also marked the first, would-be reforming presidency of the charismatic Arturo Alessandri. Between 1924 and 1932 the country experienced both military intervention and authoritarian rule, which had the effect of somewhat diminishing oligarchic predominance in politics. In the 1930s, Alessandri restored the Chilean tradition of institutional continuity, but in a changed political landscape. Export-led growth, meanwhile, was halted by the rise of synthetic nitrates after World War I and by the Depression of the 1930s, which prompted greater state intervention in the economy (Chapter 8).

GOVERNMENTS

1881–1886	Domingo Santa María
1886–1891	José Manuel Balmaceda
1891	Junta
1891–1896	Admiral Jorge Montt
1896–1901	Federico Errázuriz*
1901–1906	Germán Riesco
1906–1910	Pedro Montt†
1910–1915	Ramón Barros Luco
1915–1920	Juan Luis Sanfuentes
1920–[25]	Arturo Alessandri

*son of the president of 1871–76   †son of the president of 1851–61

1924–25	Military Juntas
1925–1927	Emiliano Figueroa Larraín
1927–1931	General Carlos Ibáñez
1931–1932	Juan Esteban Montero
1932	Brief governments [Socialist Republic]
1932–1938	Arturo Alessandri

7

The Parliamentary period, 1882–1920

Chile . . . is corroded to the heart by the poison of nitrate. Nitrate has been for Chile like the famous wine of the Borgias: among the grains of the fertile nitrate is hidden the poison that enervates, rots and kils. . . .

– *El Diario.* Buenos Aires, quoted in *El Mercurio de Valparaiso.*
December 29, 1907

*The elements that make up the Alliance – are they **homogeneous?***

– Ramón Barros Luco (1918)

Santa María and Balmaceda

President Santa María, in addition to having to deal with the end of the War of the Pacific, was also obliged to contend with a political scene that was (as we saw earlier on) fast losing the coherence it had earlier enjoyed. Congressmen were increasingly attracted by "parliamentary" ideas: the diminution of executive power, congressional control of the cabinet, and free elections. Santa María, whatever he may previously have done or said, wished to uphold presidential power. He was able to do so only by providing the factions of his undisciplined Liberal party with a common enemy, and by ruthless electoral intervention, amply in evidence at the polls in 1882, which were marked by both violence and bribery – "for every independent voter," claimed the newspaper *La Época,* "there are two or more who sell their vote."[1] The president himself was hostile to what he termed "medieval prejudices," and was eager to reduce the still powerful role of the Church in Chilean life. The pattern of his presidency was set at the outset by a conflict between Santa María and the Papacy itself. Following the death of Archbishop Valdivieso in 1878, the Pinto government had proposed his replacement by a priest of Liberal background, Francisco de Paula Taforó. When in 1882 an apostolic delegate (Mgr. Celestino del Frate) arrived to assess the position, only to advise

[1] *La Epoca,* April 19, 1882.

149

Pope Leo XIII to reject Taforó, Santa María sent the delegate his pass-
ports, and relations between Chile and the Holy See were abruptly broken
off. The reaction was fierce among Chilean Catholics, and not least in the
Conservative party, which Santa María was in any case doing his level
best to keep out of Congress by the usual methods.

Santa María now decided, with the congressional majority behind him,
to enact (and he duly enacted) what he saw as long overdue secularizing
legislation, depriving the Church of its monopoly over marriages and the
registration of births, marriages, and deaths. These two proposals became
law, not without a good deal of noise, in January and July 1884 respectively. Much more controversial was the law that secularized all public
cemeteries (August 1883). The Church, which had previously extended
its blessing to such cemeteries, now declared them unholy. The often
macabre and grotesque scenes that resulted (Catholics sometimes spiriting corpses away for illegal burial in churches, while coffins loaded with
stones were interred in the cemeteries) were long remembered in Chile.
Something like a "religious war" raged during these years. There is the
possibly apocryphal tale of the society lady who told Santa María that she
no longer said the Rosary because to do so would mean repeating his
name – that of the Virgin Mary. With the atmosphere then prevailing,
the story seems quite credible.

Not even the anticlerical crusade could altogether pacify an increasingly fractious Congress. The congressional elections of 1885 were once
again manipulated with much violence. As a result, relations between the
executive and the parliamentary opposition in the years 1884–86 were
among the most bitter of the century. Santa María was determined to
secure the presidential succession for his loyal minister of the Interior
(April 1882–September 1885), José Manuel Balmaceda, and the election
of June 1886, as the British minister reported, saw "a good deal of
disorder and not a little loss of life, revolvers, knives and stones having
been freely used. At one [voting] table, six people were killed and
thirty wounded."[2] The juggernaut could not be halted. The opposition
candidate José Francisco Vergara (supported by dissident Liberals and his
own Radical party) withdrew from the race. On September 18, 1886,
Balmaceda, who had just turned 46, was inaugurated as president.

No one could have been better prepared. Balmaceda's political initia-
tion had been in the Reform Clubs of the later 1860s; as we have seen,
he had been an eloquent critic of electoral intervention and presidential
abuses. He was an oligarch of oligarchs. His commanding personality, his
rhetorical gifts, and his great abilities were not disputed by his oppo-

---

[2] Minister Fraser to Lord Rosebery, June 19, 1886. Public Record Office, London: FO 16/242, No.
47 Diplomatic.

nents. Moreover, the new president's immediate re-establishment of relations with the Vatican (and the filling of the archiepiscopal vacancy by the well-liked Mariano Casanova) did much to abate the "religious war." The auguries seemed promising for a notable presidency.

Balmaceda's instincts, as he announced at the outset, were to reunite "the Liberal family," as he put it, and to press ahead with his own imaginative vision for national improvement. It was this that set Balmaceda apart from his immediate predecessors (and immediate successors) and made him an inspiration to later generations. With substantial new wealth now flowing in from nitrate exports, he conceived the idea of using the concomitant revenues for a great program of national renovation, with large-scale public works, educational improvements, and (this is sometimes overlooked) military and naval modernization. In 1887 a new ministry of Public Works was created: by 1890 it accounted for more than one-third of the budget. New schools, new government buildings, the first section of the trans-Andine railroad, the dry-dock at Talcahuano, the canalization of the Mapocho river, the long bridge over the Bío Bío, the Malleco viaduct – Balmaceda was to leave his imprint on Chile in no uncertain fashion. Yet the public works program, dramatic as it was, also carried political dangers. There were politicians who felt that it should not have priority over a return to metallic currency. More seriously, by enormously expanding presidential patronage, it heightened fears of executive predominance, while also creating a scramble for jobs and contracts, something which could (and did) exacerbate the political tussles of the moment. And these were growing fiercer by the month.

Here, Balmaceda's lofty conception of the presidential role ran into the growing determination of the parties to tame both the cabinet and the presidency itself. He began with two Liberal-National ministries (Santa María's formula), and attracted dissident Liberals into a third, but the limited intervention Balmaceda allowed in the elections of March 1888, which also roused the Conservatives to fury, soon destroyed this promising coalition. The fourth cabinet (April 1888) consisted purely of "government" Liberals, which won Balmaceda the hostility of the now excluded National party, but which, when its base was somewhat broadened (November 1888), brought a few months of stability. But the congressional opposition, stronger than ever, had by this stage become deeply suspicious of Enrique Salvador Sanfuentes (minister of Finance and Public Works in 1888–89), who seemed to be (and was) Balmaceda's choice as heir to the presidency. Balmaceda's own impatience at criticism and obstruction made it hard for him to compromise. Caught up in his own visionary schemes of progress, he seemed disinclined to politick in the way an Errázuriz or a Santa María had done.

Partly in order to bolster up his position in the nation at large, the president had started to make visits to the provinces. In February 1889 he went south as far as Los Angeles, to inspect some of his cherished public works. In March he sailed north on the warship *Amazonas,* to see the now flourishing nitrate zone for himself. At a dinner in Iquique on March 7, he spoke at some length about the future of the nitrate industry. He alluded to the dangers of a foreign monopoly (while denouncing monopolies in general), pleaded for Chilean capitalists to take up the challenge, and expressed the hope that, some day, all Chilean railways might be state-owned. Balmaceda, in fact, was seriously concerned by the way in which the extensive interests in Tarapacá of the English "Nitrate King," John Thomas North, were coming to constitute something approaching a state within a state. The government was seeking to undermine the transportation monopoly enjoyed in the province by North's Nitrate Railways Company. (North happened to be visiting Chile at this time: he and Balmaceda met on three occasions in March and April 1889.) North was eventually to lose the monopoly – but after Balmaceda's time.

Such provincial jaunts had little effect on the politicians in Santiago. By the middle of 1889 Balmaceda had lost his majority in the Senate. A combination of two groups of opposition Liberals with the Nationals and Radicals (an alliance Balmaceda nicknamed the *cuadrilátero* or "quadrilateral") now threatened to deprive him of the Chamber as well: the *cuadrilátero* was briefly enticed into a new cabinet, Balmaceda's eighth. It lasted barely two weeks (October–November 1889). From now on, with the help of a further defection from the ranks of the government Liberals, the opposition had a majority in both houses of Congress. Nearly all of Balmaceda's initial popularity was by now dissipated. The opposition had overwhelming support in the political class as a whole, and during the year 1890 the sense of impending crisis grew and grew. It was, in a sense, a replay of 1858, only with different characters and on a much larger scale.

Early in 1890 the president made overtures to the Conservatives, to no avail. Indeed, the Conservatives, seeing this as their way in from the political wilderness, were happy to join the coalition against Balmaceda. The president's next move was to withdraw Sanfuentes from a presidential candidacy by making him minister of the Interior (May 30). This did not calm the opposition: when Congress met in June, it both censured the new ministry and voted to delay passage of the "periodic" taxation law. No taxes could be collected; no public officials could be paid. Deputations of senior politicians and the new Democratic party appealed to Balmaceda to compromise, but found him in a distinctly uncompromising mood.

As if this were not enough, the president also had to contend with a sudden wave of strikes (the first serious strike wave in Chilean history), which paralyzed the port of Iquique and spread from there to the nitrate pampa, to Valparaiso, to Concepción, and to the coalmines at Lota. On the nitrate pampa a number of company stores were looted; in Valparaiso there was a riot. Where this labor unrest could not be contained by fraud (employers agreeing to terms and then disregarding them), it was repressed by soldiers and police, the bloodiest affray taking place in Valparaiso, where at least fifty people were killed. The nationwide alarm of the upper class did not, however, translate into support for Balmaceda: the political crisis continued.

Archbishop Casanova now offered his mediation, and for a short while it seemed as if the resulting deal might hold firm: Congress approved the taxation law, and on August 7, Balmaceda named a new cabinet, under Belisario Prats, and gave it freedom of action. The truce, if that is what it was, did not last. Eight weeks later Prats resigned. Balmaceda named his thirteenth (and last) cabinet, which included the amiable Claudio Vicuña (as minister of the Interior) and the far less amiable Domingo Godoy, a former criminal judge for whom the opposition was more detestable, if anything, than the criminals he had once had to sentence.

Meetings and demonstrations had been constant throughout the year so far – as also had been strident and virulent attacks on Balmaceda in the predominantly hostile press. With the Vicuña-Godoy ministry, the atmosphere became appreciably more tense and ominous. Both Balmaceda and the opposition anticipated a dramatic turn to the conflict (dictatorship, a coup d'etat, armed revolt) and made their plans accordingly. Balmaceda, for his part, was obdurately determined to uphold the presidential tradition. Congress and the parties – Nationals, Conservatives, Radicals, and the several opposition Liberal groups – were equally determined that their ideas of Parliamentary government and electoral freedom should prevail. In many ways Balmaceda was more farsighted than his adversaries: he intuited rather accurately what a Parliamentary regime would be like in Chile. But his own proposals (June 1890) for constitutional reform (clearer delimitation of executive and legislative powers; local autonomy; a six-year presidential term) fell on deaf ears in the agitated atmosphere then prevailing.

In December, Balmaceda went south to inaugurate work on the Talcahuano dry-dock. In Concepción he was the target of an extremely hostile demonstration. The scene on his return to Santiago was witnessed by a future president: "there broke out a formidable storm of deafening whistles, followed by an infernal squeal of injurious insults to the president. Balmaceda went pale...."[3] Only a few days later, an attack on the Conservative Club in Santiago by municipal agents yielded the first

[3] Arturo Alessandri, *Revolución de 1891* (Santiago, 1950), p. 73.

purely political fatality of this horribly tense year. The funeral of the young victim, Ignacio Ossa, became yet another huge demonstration against the government.

With all the inexorability of Greek tragedy, events moved rapidly to their predictable outcome. Congress, closed since October, had failed to approve a budget for 1891. On the first day of the new year Balmaceda issued a manifesto, announcing that he would keep in force for 1891 the "essential laws" approved for 1890. "Neither as a Chilean, nor as head of state, nor as a man of principle," he declared, "could I accept the political role the parliamentary coalition sought to impose on me." On January 4, he decreed that the previous year's budget would be renewed. The opposition, for its part, had made its plans. An all-party committee had already sounded out the Navy (which proved sympathetic) and the Army (which did not). In the closing days of December, the Conservative, Abdón Cifuentes, drafted an Act deposing Balmaceda. Among other things it accused the president of high treason, and assigned Captain Jorge Montt of the Navy the task of helping Congress to restore the constitution. The document was clandestinely signed by nineteen Senators and seventy deputies. (The text was not published until several months later.) On January 7, 1891, most of the warships of the Navy sailed out of Valparaiso Bay, carrying as passengers a small number of opposition leaders, including the president of the Chamber, Ramón Barros Luco, and Waldo Silva, vice-president of the Senate. Opposition politicians remaining in Santiago went into hiding.

Neither Balmaceda's decree nor the Congress's "Act of Deposition" were in any way constitutional. As Thomas Hobbes once observed, "in matter of government, when nothing else is turned up, clubs are trumps."[4] For the fourth time in the nineteenth century, a Chilean civil war was at hand: this one was to be the most serious of all.

The Civil War of 1891

It was in some ways a strange war. The Navy, as we have seen, sided with Congress. Balmaceda's only real strength at sea was in the form of two new torpedo-boats, the *Condell* and the *Lynch,* which were on their way to Chile at the start of the war. They were to give him his single naval victory – the sinking of the cruiser *Blanco Encalada* off Caldera (April 23). The Army remained loyal to Balmaceda, and was immediately rewarded with a pay increase of 50 percent. But the Army could hardly

---

[4] "A Dialogue between a Philosopher and a Student of the Common Laws of England," in *The English Works of Thomas Hobbes,* ed. William Molesworth, Vol. VI (London, 1840), p. 122. We are grateful to Professor Paul Sigmund for directing us to the source of this remark.

attack the Navy, and the Navy could inflict little damage on the Army. In the longer run, no doubt, the Congressionalists had the advantage: as in Chile's two wars with Peru and Bolivia, command of the sea conferred the ultimate edge. The Chilean fleet was (certainly by South American standards) a powerful one, with two cruisers and several smaller but well-armed vessels. It immediately showed its power by seizing thirteen steamers. In mid-January, Captain Montt declared a blockade of the nitrate ports and Valparaiso, and thereafter raided several points on the coast, taking off men, arms, and provisions.

The first major Congressionalist success came on February 6, with the capture of Pisagua. Later that month, partly through the mediation of the British admiral Sir William Hotham, Balmaceda's troops surrendered Iquique. Finally, on March 6, a bloody five-hour battle at Pozo Almonte gave the Congressionalists the nitrate zone: Antofagasta was occupied soon afterward. With this base secured, a government was rapidly improvised, under a Junta consisting of Captain Montt, Ramón Barros Luco, and Waldo Silva. While it could draw on the rich revenues of the nitrate zone, it desperately needed arms from abroad, and the quest for these now began – in the only place it could begin, abroad.

Balmaceda, for his part, urgently needed ships. Two French-built cruisers were almost ready for delivery to Chile, but Congressionalist agents in France very effectively thwarted this. Their counterparts in the United States were less effective: although they cleverly defied the American authorities in spiriting a cargo of arms southward from San Francisco aboard the steamship *Itata,* the U.S. government compelled the Iquique Junta to return the arms. (The evident support of the United States for Balmaceda during the war may have been reinforced by memories of the Confederacy's bloodily frustrated bid for independence thirty years earlier.) In the end, however, the Congressionalist agents in Europe, by prolonged cloak-and-dagger methods, succeeded in sending arms for 10,000 men to Iquique. These arrived in July. By then the Junta had secured the services of General Emil Körner, recruited in 1886 from Germany to modernize the Chilean Army. He had fallen out with Balmaceda, and made his way north aboard a British steamer. Several other disaffected officers found their way to the north, as did numerous young men, eager for the impending fray. Körner's expertise was invaluable as the Congressional government built up its army.

Balmaceda's government, meanwhile, still controlled the greater part of Chile. Free of his Congressional opponents, Balmaceda was now able to refashion the political system in line with his own ideas. In March 1891 a "Liberal Convention" nominated Claudio Vicuña as presidential candidate and in April a Constituent Assembly was elected, albeit without opposition. At the opening of this assembly, the president retailed his own version of the causes of the war, saying nothing very new. The Congress itself debated (often vigorously) such matters as constitutional reform, a plan for a state bank, and other measures. In a strange way, perhaps, given the circumstances, it testified to those Chilean concepts of legality and constitutionality that even the civil war could not destroy. But there was also a new tone in these debates. Much rhetoric was now expended on attacking foreign interests, bankers, and the upper class in general. Balmaceda himself had little to lose by such propaganda, but little to gain, either.

One thing, however, this Congress *was* able to do was to secure the dismissal of the unpopular Domingo Godoy, Balmaceda's minister of the Interior. His persecution of the opposition had been implacable: opposition newspapers were shut down, the University was closed (as was the Club de la Unión), opposition haciendas were attacked, and banks were strictly controlled (to prevent funds being shifted north). Godoy wished to intensify the repression, but in May he was replaced by the more idealistic Julio Bañados Espinosa. War, however, creates its own savage logic. With oppositionists trying to cut telegraph wires and disrupt rail traffic, some bloody encounters were inevitable: the execution of twenty to thirty young men, Congressionalist supporters gathered at the Lo Cañas hacienda near Santiago (August 19–20), was the worst such episode.

Even though, as late as mid-August, the British minister reported (far too blithely) that the war had been notable for its "absence of action, coupled with an extraordinary activity of imagination,"[5] nemesis for Balmaceda was drawing closer. Three days after this dispatch, the Navy landed a 9,000-strong Congressional army at Quinteros, thirty miles north of Valparaiso. In two extremely bloody battles at Concón (August 21) and La Placilla (August 28), the latter fought on the heights above Viña del Mar, Balmaceda's troops were routed. In Valparaiso, wild scenes of rejoicing quickly degenerated into looting and arson: marines restored order, killing some 300 people. Balmaceda, realizing that all was lost, transferred his authority, such as it now was, to General Manuel Baquedano, and took refuge in the Argentine legation, a block away from the Moneda: the Argentine minister himself opened the door to receive him. Baquedano was unable to restrain mob violence in Santiago, and the houses of prominent *balmacedistas* were attacked, looted, and vandalized. On August 31 the Congressional army entered the city, the Junta took charge, and order was gradually restored.

---

[5] Minister Kennedy to Lord Salisbury, August 17, 1891. Public Record Office, London: FO 16/265.

Balmaceda was too proud a man to surrender. He rejected any thought of exile. During his three weeks in the legation he wrote farewell letters to his family, to his friend Bartolomé Mitre in Argentina, and to his collaborators Claudio Vicuña and Julio Bañados. This last was his political testament. In lyrical prose, he defended his cause and predicted its ultimate triumph. On the morning of September 19, the day after the formal expiry of his presidential term, he took a revolver and shot himself through the head.

Having won the war, at the cost of at least 6,000 lives, the victorious Congressionalists now had to restore the constitution. In a very real sense they were, in the words of the German minister to Chile, Baron Gutschmidt, "the classes which have governed Chile up to now."[6] They were to go on governing Chile for another thirty years.

Parliamentary Republic: economic aspects

The period in Chilean history that falls between the 1891 Civil War and the 1920s is commonly called the Parliamentary Republic. We do not suggest an alternative label; the period certainly possesses an underlying unity when perceived in retrospect, and this is particularly true with respect to the economy. We need to examine some of the principal trends, bearing in mind that toward the end of the Parliamentary period, the Chilean economy was also affected by the shock waves set up by the First World War.

Agriculture, manufacturing, copper mining

The years immediately following the War of the Pacific were flourishing ones for Chilean agriculture. The country developed a pastoral economy, particularly in the South, the main area for sheep-raising. Sheep-raising also developed on a notable scale in the far South, in Magallanes, whose real economic history began after the War of the Pacific.[7] Farmers also created dairy businesses which provided milk and its byproducts to the expanding urban market. Some haciendas went in for cultivating alfalfa and hay, to feed not only their own herds of cattle, but also the horses used in the towns. Increasingly, too, local manufacturers began to process

---

[6] Quoted in Gonzalo Vial, *Historia de Chile 1891–1973*, vol. 2 (Santiago, 1982), p. 7.

[7] Sheep were taken to the Magellan Straits territory from the Falkland Islands early in 1877. A bloody mutiny of artillerymen in November that year led to the end of the settlement's use as a penal colony.

the fruits of the countryside, turning fruits into jams, tobacco into cigarettes, grains into crackers or beer, noodles and hides into shoes or other leather goods – for sale to town-dwellers and the nitrate workers of the north.

In other ways, however, the agricultural impetus began to falter. Cereal production, which had been so large a component of the nineteenth-century export economy, now entered into slow but ever deepening decline. Between 1910 and 1920 wheat harvests sometimes did not increase very much over those of the previous decade and were only slightly larger than those of two decades earlier. Occasionally there were bumper crops, but, with two exceptions (1908 and 1909) wheat and flour exports rarely equaled the peaks of the previous century. A variety of purely temporary problems hamstrung Chilean cereal growers. There were the usual vagaries of climate, and the periodic outbreak of plant blights often stunted output. The new pastoralism to some extent displaced wheat farmers from the northern Central Valley to the less fertile south. More seriously, foreign competition from Australia, Canada, the United States, Argentina, and Russia flooded the international marketplace with wheat, inevitably lowering prices. The opening of the Panama Canal (which gave Australia easier access to the all-important British market) accelerated the process of decline. Virtually driven from North Atlantic markets, Chilean hacendados had to fall back on exports to Peru and Bolivia. Only occasionally now (when Chilean harvests were good and those of competing nations poor) would Chile venture, somewhat tentatively, into the North Atlantic market; in bad years, which seemed to arrive with depressing frequency, the country was obliged to import food.

In some ways, the underlying problem for agriculture was quite obvious. In 1900, haciendas still encompassed three-quarters of the land, and accounted for about two-thirds of all agricultural produce and most of the commodities destined for export. This long historical trend showed no signs of altering during the first years of the twentieth century: in 1917, a mere 0.46 percent of all properties owned more than half of all land. At the other extreme of the agrarian spectrum, *minifundios* also multiplied – close to 60 percent of all "farms" were occupying less than 1.5 percent of the land. As the poor divided their land into smaller and smaller plots, the rich, through either purchase or marriage, increased their holdings so that it could plausibly be claimed in 1919 that "in Chile there exists a greater monopolization of agricultural land than in any other country of the world."[8] Given their dominance over the land

[8] Moisés Poblete Troncoso, *El problema de la producción agrícola y la política agraria nacional* (Santiago, 1919), quoted in Thomas Wright, *Landowners and Reform in Chile* (Urbana, Ill., 1982), p. 125.

and already assured of a domestic market, the hacendados had little incentive to produce.

If agriculture remained hidebound, manufacturing did not. The Parliamentary Republic has often been presented as a time of conspicuous consumption – the rich frittering away their wealth on imported playthings. The rich did indeed indulge their taste for English woolens and French perfumes, but this is not the whole story. While imports of consumer goods rose by 250 percent between 1885 and 1910, purchases of foreign-made machines increased still more (by almost 300 percent), and those of foreign raw materials, the grist for the newly acquired equipment, soared by more than tenfold. These figures point to the fact that manufacturing was doing rather well. Indeed, between 1880 and 1900 industrial output grew at an annual rate of 2.1 percent, rising during the next decade to 2.9 percent.

In part, Chilean manufacturing expanded in order to satisfy the needs of a growing urban population and the nitrate workers of the north. Equally important, however, were the industrialists who formed the *Sociedad de Fomento Fabril* (Manufacturing Promotion Society), SOFOFA, in 1883. This society promoted Chilean participation in international expositions, sponsored the establishment of technical training institutes, and pressured the government to erect tariff walls behind which entrepreneurs could nurture their infant industries. The government paid some attention to this last demand. In 1897 it revamped the 1878 Customs code, levying higher duties on a wider range of imports while reducing taxes on raw materials and machinery. In addition, the Moneda imposed specific taxes on items competing with local products, while subsidizing certain activities (the raising of beet-sugar, or the manufacture of sulfuric acid) considered of benefit to the country. By 1915 Chile had 7,800 plants (most of them very small) employing about 80,000 workers and satisfying about 80 percent of domestic consumer needs. This industrial expansion, of course, was uneven: manufacturers produced more than half of the country's processed foods but met less than half the demand for shoes, beverages, paper, chemicals, or textiles. Of greater significance, factories were now producing steel and capital goods, such as railroad cars and ships.

The First World War had a tonic effect on Chilean manufacturing. The initial lack of shipping, which restricted exports, by the same token sharply curtailed the flow of imports. Even when transportation once again became available, local manufacturers had little competition to fear, since the belligerent nations had geared their economies to war production. Few countries (with the important exception of the United States) were in a position to manufacture consumer goods for export. There were other factors that helped industrialists. In 1916, Congress enacted a new tariff law (described by the U.S. Department of Commerce as being one of the continent's most protectionist) which increased the levies on imported goods by 50 to 80 percent, and called for higher imposts on specific items – a 250 percent tax on imported jam, for example. This new measure provided local manufacturers both protection and incentive. The combination of higher tariffs, minimal foreign competition, and the inflating peso (which increased the cost of imports) allowed local industries to thrive. By 1918, the output of the plants producing consumer goods had soared by 53 percent. More significantly, the production of durable and intermediate goods rose by almost 59 percent. A foreign visitor of around 1920 noted the range of products now made in Chile: "metal goods, furniture, dried and tinned fruit; wines, beer, mineral waters, butter and cheese, lard, candles, soap, boots and shoes, wheat flour, Quaker oats, woven woollen and cotton cloths, pottery, chemicals, brown paper, bottles and other glass utensils, sugar and tobacco." The same visitor admiringly noted the Valdivia shipyards, "turning out vessels of over 3,000 tons."[9]

Chile's traditional copper mining industry enjoyed distinctly uneven fortunes during the Parliamentary period. By the mid-1880s most of the copper mines had exhausted their richest deposits. To exploit the remaining veins of low-grade ore would have required substantial new investment for the sinking of deeper shafts and for up-to-date machinery. Rather predictably (given their speculative propensity) Chilean capitalists preferred to put their money not in the copper mines but in the new nitrate industry, where the dividends were higher and the risks lower. Thus within a decade of the onset of the War of the Pacific, Chilean copper production plunged from 46,421,000 kg. to 24,931,00 kg. and Chile's share of the world market fell from around one-third to less than one-tenth. By 1911 the share had fallen to less than 4 percent.

An unlikely savior now appeared. In 1904 the American William Braden introduced the flotation process into Chile – the technology which had enabled the American copper industry to prosper. Purchasing El Teniente, an enormous deposit of low-grade copper ore near Rancagua, Braden revolutionized Chilean copper mining. Developing El Teniente, however, proved so costly that in 1908 Braden sold the mine to the Guggenheim family. Three years later the Guggenheims bought Chuquicamata, in the Atacama Desert, which eventually became the world's largest open-cast mine. It took five years and US$100 million before Chuquicamata began to turn a profit. The Guggenheims subsequently transferred El Teniente and Chuquicamata to the Kennecott Copper Company. A year later, in 1916, another American corporation, Anaconda

---

[9] L. E. Elliott, *Chile today and tomorrow* (New York, 1922), pp. 228–30.

Copper Company, began to develop a third great mine, at Potrerillos, to the northeast of Copiapó. Thanks to the massive investments in both equipment and infrastructure, these three American-owned mines, known collectively as the "Gran Minería," increased Chilean copper production by almost 300 percent, and its share of the world market from 4.3 to 10 percent.

The new copper mines relied less upon labor than modern technology. The mining camps were isolated enclaves, existing on the periphery of the local economy. Although they paid wages and bought food, the American companies remitted most of their earnings abroad, either to pay dividends or to buy new machinery – "leaving us only the hole," as one newspaper ruefully noted in 1920.[10] The First World War accelerated the growth of the new copper industry. Between 1914 and 1918 production almost tripled and exports more than doubled. Wartime sales of copper soared to 132 million gold pesos in 1917, an increase of more than 400 percent over the levels of three years earlier. Clearly the reviving copper business was coming into its own, and in fact by 1917 it accounted for almost 19 percent of the country's exports.

The evident success of the American-owned companies gave rise to mixed reactions in Chile. While some denounced American penetration – Ricardo Latcham's book *Chuquicamata, estado yanqui* (1926) was perhaps the classic expression of this view – others dismissed such complaints as "socialism" or "Boxerism," praising the working conditions in the mining camps, the alcohol-free environment, and noting that "American genius and capital has created … wealth which did not exist before, and it is fair that he who creates the wealth should enjoy it."[11]

Nitrates

Although copper mining revived, with promise for the future, it was the nitrate trade above all that was the real motor of the Chilean economy for nearly half a century. The role it played in the country's history was controversial at the time and has remained so ever since. It is not hard to see why.

Nitrates were an economic windfall for Chile, and such windfalls (as the British have discovered more recently with North Sea oil) can very easily be mishandled. The literature on the subject is often reproachful, the reproach itself usually directed at the foreign interests who controlled so large a part of the business. (In 1895, British companies accounted for about 60 percent of all nitrate exported; it should also be pointed out that the Chilean stake in the industry rose appreciably over the years,

---

[10] *El Sur,* Concepción, April 22, 1920.   [11] *El Mercurio,* November 7 and December 19, 1915.

controlling 60 percent of production in 1918.) Would a nationalized nitrate monopoly have been more suitable for Chile? This has often been a popular counterfactual scenario. As we saw in Chapter 6, the government refused to take this course, mostly because it seemed cheaper and more efficient to allow foreigners to assume the task of production. (Its own railroads, we might note in passing, were not only overstaffed, but also very much part of the network of political patronage.) A nationalized monopoly might possibly have earned more money for Chile, but since we have no way of telling how efficient or successful such a monopoly would have been, the question seems otiose. As for what *was* earned, it has been estimated that by 1924 the *salitreras* had generated around 6.9 billion gold pesos, and that about one-third of this total found its way into the government's coffers. Taxes appear to have accounted for about half of the production cost; a further quarter went into wages. Thus a very high proportion of the profits on nitrate remained in Chile, though nobody can pretend that they were distributed evenly.

There is a second counterfactual scenario which seems somewhat more plausible. Why did the state not use its tax windfall to diversify the economy and thus provide alternatives when the nitrate boom ended? (A number of Chileans did, in fact, express fears that a synthetic form of nitrate might eventually destroy the industry, as in due course happened.) Such a policy would have required the state to retain (and probably increase) taxes on income, estates, and gifts. But since such taxes fell principally on the better-off, Congress preferred to abolish them in favor of (in effect) taxing the foreign consumers of nitrate. It is for this reason that Chile can plausibly be described, during the nitrate era, as a kind of *rentier* republic. Moreover, the political paralysis of the Parliamentary regime militated against decisive innovations in economic or social policy. It was not difficult to conceive of alternative policies (indeed, the suspicion that the nitrate windfall was being mishandled began very early) but almost impossible, as President Alessandri was to find after 1920, to carry them into practice.

All such arguments lay in the future back in the 1880s. At the time the advantages seemed to outweigh the disadvantages. The growth of the nitrate trade was spectacular. Even before the War of the Pacific had ended, Chileans and foreigners alike flocked to Antofagasta and Tarapacá to dig the nitrate from the ungenerous desert. The first step consisted of jamming dynamite into holes drilled by the miners into the sun-baked overburden. When detonated, the explosives shattered the surface layer (the *costra*) and exposed the nitrate deposits. Once pried from the desert, the ore was loaded onto carts or railcars for transport to refineries, and the Shanks process (originally devised to produce carbonate of soda) was used to extract nitrate from the *caliche*. The refining method was labor-

Table 7.1. The nitrate industry, 1880–1920.

	Oficinas	Workers	Production[a]	Export[a]	Price[b]
1880		2,800	224,000	224,000	47.05
1885		4,600	436,000	436,000	33.68
1890		13,000	1,075,000	1,063,000	23.88
1895	53	22,500	1,308,000	1,238,000	25.92
1900	51	19,700	1,508,000	1,454,000	25.05
1905	90	30,600	1,755,000	1,650,000	36.40
1910	102	43,500	2,465,000	2,336,000	32.93
1915	116	45,500	1,755,000	2,023,000	33.12
1920	101	46,200	2,523,000	2,794,000	49.66

[a] 1,000s of metric tons. [b] US$.

Source: Carmen Cariola and Osvaldo Sunkel, *Un siglo de historia económica de Chile 1830–1930* (Madrid, 1982), pp. 126–27; Thomas O'Brien, "Rich Beyond the Dreams of Avarice: The Guggenheims in Chile," *Business History Review*, 63 (1989), p. 134; A. Lawrence Stickell, "Migration and Mining: Labor in Northern Chile in the Nitrate Era, 1830–1930" (Unpub. Ph.D. diss., University of Indiana, 1979).

intensive. When the plant's giant crushers had pulverized the hand-sorted *caliche,* it was poured into holding vats where the powdered ore was mixed with water and then heated up. The hot, nitrate-rich liquid then flowed into a series of tanks where the *salitre* was first separated from the liquid, concentrated, and then spread out to dry. Finally, the workers loaded the now powdered nitrate into burlap bags for shipment to Europe aboard the gracious "nitrate clippers" – the last great generation of sailing ships, and among the most spectacular ever built.

Working on the nitrate *pampa* was both arduous and dangerous: often carrying sacks weighing more than 140 kg. (300 lbs.), miners constantly had to thread their way between explosions, falling debris, and moving carts or railcars. The refineries were no less perilous. Laboring in plants filled with steam or dust, workers had to avoid falling into the massive grinding machines or the vats filled with scalding liquids. The accident rate, in a business singularly reluctant to introduce safety measures, was predictably high. Given the lack of medical facilities, most accidents were either fatal or permanently disabling.

Lured by the prospect of well-paying jobs, thousands of men migrated from the Central Valley to the northern *salitreras*. Between 1875 and 1907 the population of the Norte Grande grew from 2,000 to 234,000. Iquique, the principal nitrate port and commercial entrepot, became Chile's fourth largest city, Antofagasta its seventh largest. A whole new society sprang up on the *pampa* and in the burgeoning ports. It was

Table 7.2. Nitrate exports, 1913–20.

	Production	Exports	Value[a]
	[1,000s of tons]		[Pesos of 18*d*]
1913	2,772	2,738	318,908
1914	2,463	1,846	212,380
1915	1,755	2,023	232,679
1916	2,912	2,980	338,529
1917	3,001	2,776	472,146
1918	2,859	2,919	510,855
1919	1,703	803	127,077[a]
1920	2,524	2,746	535,604[a]

[a] Includes export of iodine as well as nitrate.

Source: Juan Ricardo Couyoumdjian, *Chile y Gram Bretaña durante la primera guerra mundial y la postguerra, 1912–1921* (Santiago, 1986), pp. 271, 274–75; *Sinopsis estadística de la República de Chile* (Santiago, 1919), p. 96.

inevitably a society marked by deep class division. Iquique's commercial elites (including a large foreign element) built themselves gracious homes and indulged in a frenetic social life. The men who dug the *caliche* lived in mining camps out on the arid *pampa*. Their shanties, often constructed of chunks of desert and roofed in zinc, afforded little or no protection against the extremes of temperature for which the Norte Grande is notorious. Without running water or even sewers, the miners and their families easily succumbed to ever-present epidemic diseases or tuberculosis.

While the managers of the *salitreras* enjoyed access to imported delicacies, the great mass of the nitrate miners had to satisfy their appetites at the *pulperías,* company stores which often sold shoddy goods at inflated prices. Some of the *pulperías* made enormous profits (sometimes as much as 30 percent), but, isolated in the camps, the miners had perforce to deal with them. Indeed, since many workers received their pay in *fichas,* tokens, or chits, they were obliged either to patronize the company store or to sell their scrip, at a heavy discount, to local merchants. Despite the dangerous work and often wretched living conditions, men in the thousands (sometimes men and their families) continued to flock to the north. Squalid as it was, living in the *salitreras* proved less lethal than the *conventillos,* the filthy, teeming tenements of Santiago, Valparaiso, and Concepción, which, as we shall see, almost literally killed their inhabitants.

Table 7.3. Ownership of the nitrate industry (based on percentages of exports).

	1895	1897	1906	1911	1912	1913	1918	1921
Britain	59.6	42.4	40.6	25.07	36.95	35.06	36.53	34.49
Chile	12.8	15.6	21.0	31.02	38.53	49.09	60.07	58.71
Germany	8.0	13.1	19.8	23.79	15.1	15.02	0.063	4.32

Source: El Mercurio (Valparaiso), October 19, 1912; Roberto Hernández, *El salitre* (Valparaiso, 1930), p. 160; Juan Ricardo Couyoumdjian, *Chile y Gran Bretaña durante la primera guerra mundial y la postguerra 1914–1921* (Santiago, 1986), p. 237. These figures are based on joint stock companies. The ownership of a company and the nationality of the stock-holder may not be the same.

Laboring in the *salitreras* was more remunerative as well as healthier. Virtually all Chilean urban workers earned more than their rural counterparts, but they received less than the nitrate miner. A government report of 1913 noted that the average nitrate miner commanded higher wages than any other type of Chilean worker, including those in the metallurgical plants or on the state railroads – the elites of the embryonic industrial workforce. The better paid miners (unlike most industrial laborers) were even able to accumulate a bit of capital. They received free housing (such as it was) and paid substantially less for food than the urban worker (sometimes two to three times less) – even when it was bought from the much-denounced *pulperías*. Thus bachelors (and sometimes family men) could save enough money to purchase plots of land or small businesses when they returned to the Central Valley.

Nitrates were a speculative commodity, and the health of the industry depended not only on domestic output but also on the economic fortunes of Chile's main customers – Germany (always one of the most important buyers), the United States, France, and Belgium. Since nitrate was essential in the manufacture of explosives, political conditions also could affect the price. The price in fact varied erratically, falling, for instance, from US$52 per ton in 1894 to US$41 in 1898 and then spiraling up to US$76 nine years later. During economic downturns, not surprisingly, the producers formed temporary cartels, the so-called Nitrate combinations (the first was organized in 1884), which limited production in order to maintain prices. Once this aim had been achieved, the combinations were dissolved, and the companies resumed their normal competition.

By 1914, however, the nitrate industry seemed less secure than before. After years of paying artificially high prices, European consumers began to turn to alternative fertilizers such as British sulfate of ammonium. An even more ominous threat now appeared: in 1913 the Haber-Bosch processing plant at Oppau (Ludwigshafen) in Germany went into production, pouring out tons of synthetic nitrates – the worst nightmare of all. The outbreak of the First World War, however, prevented the spread of this process and thus temporarily preserved the Chilean nitrate monopoly.

Although the war was to give a distinct boost to the *salitreras,* its immediate impact was highly disruptive. The British naval blockade shut off traditional markets such as Germany and Belgium – which before 1914 had taken more than a quarter of Chilean nitrate exports. Happily for Chile, the murderous demands of the Western Front meant that the Allied powers still needed nitrates in order to produce explosives. But while the Allied powers clamored for *salitre,* they now lacked the ships to transport it to Europe. Huge heaps of nitrate piled up in the Chilean ports. Inevitably, under the circumstances, production contracted: between mid-1914 and early 1915 monthly output fell by more than two-thirds, and prices almost halved. Many *salitreras* closed down, prompting a mass exodus of unemployed workers to the Central Valley cities. The government did what it could to help, with free transportation from the north, soup kitchens, and employment in public works.

By the middle of 1915 the situation changed notably for the better. The Allied powers reallocated ships to Chile, and the Chilean government itself leased some of its naval transports to private companies. Although shipping costs were now much higher (by 700 to 800 percent), as was the cost of labor, burlap sacks, maritime insurance, and imported coal, the *salitreras* prospered once again. Indeed, for the first time in years the government auctioned off additional nitrate lands in order to increase production. Ironically, however, the nitrate business earned much less from the bonanza than might have been expected. The Allied powers, soon joined by the United States, created the Nitrate of Soda Executive, a central purchasing agency, which eliminated competition among the Allied countries and forced Chileans to lower nitrate prices. While this tactic saved the Allies a fortune, it obviously reduced profits for the *salitreras* and hence the government's tax revenues.

Inflation and monetary policy

Nitrates, monetary policy, and inflation, already intertwined during the War of the Pacific, became more intimately connected in the ensuing decades. Nitrates and inflation, indeed, could fairly be described as the true leitmotifs of the Parliamentary Republic. Inflation was hardly new to Chile. What made it so endemic during this period? For years a fashionable explanation for the Chilean infatuation with inflation was that it was a plot of the landed aristocracy to bilk the nation. According to this scenario, the hacendados, who made up a substantial portion if not a majority of the legislature, deliberately inflated the money supply, so that they could redeem their mortgaged land in worthless paper pesos. While this conspiratorial theory has appeal, it tends to be far too one-dimensional. (As René Millar has noted, landowners were often the most vehement supporters of the gold standard.) In the late 1870s, as we saw, the government had turned to paper money because the country had literally run out of specie: an authorization of paper money was the only way to rescue the banks. And until the nitrate tax began to enrich the Moneda's coffers, paper money financed the war effort. By expanding the money supply and thereby reducing interest rates, the flood of bank-notes also stimulated the economy and encouraged investment. Thus there were many Chileans, not simply the landowners, who fell in love with the paper peso. Devotees of the "funny money" soon had plenty more of it to love: during the 1891 Civil War, Balmaceda issued an additional 20 million pesos in government paper – a 50 percent increase in the money supply.

Many Chileans argued during Balmaceda's presidency that the government should use the new, copious revenues from nitrate to return to the gold standard. In 1892, the Montt administration won congressional permission to borrow over £1 million in order to withdraw some 10 million paper pesos from circulation, and to purchase gold and silver for conversion into specie. To demonstrate the government's financial soundness, the "conversion" guaranteed to redeem the paper pesos at a rate of 24 pence, although the current rate at the time was 18 pence. The advocates of conversion, the so-called *oreros,* argued that the reduction in money supply alone would drive up the international value of the peso to 24 pence. The plan misfired. Just as the government began withdrawing the 10 million pesos, there was a fall in the value of Chilean bonds and of the peso itself. Foreign investors began to withdraw their funds, seeking to convert their deposits into gold. Worse still, Chilean depositors besieged the banks to withdraw their funds. The banks could not meet all these demands, and the prospect of a general collapse forced the government to abandon its conversion efforts.

Despite this initial setback, the government tried a second time. In 1895 it borrowed £2 million to buy up the paper pesos, this time at a rate of 18 pence. By 1897, some 44 million paper pesos had been incinerated, leaving 15 million paper notes (12 million of them issued by banks) in circulation. Chile thus successfully returned to the gold standard, but not without pain: it was expensive; contraction of the money supply increased the cost of borrowing; and four banks were forced out of business. Furthermore, the conversion occurred at a most unpropitious moment. In the mid-1890s Chile's border dispute with Argentina threatened to pitch both nations into war. The resulting arms race was financially crippling: between 1894 and 1896, the defense budget soared from

13 million to 48 million pesos. Matters were made much worse by the fact that imports of foreign consumer goods had greatly increased since the 1880s. Although the country enjoyed a trade surplus, the government could not amass sufficient gold to pay for both guns and butter. (For its military expenses alone it had to take out a loan for £4 million.) At precisely this moment there was anyway an economic downturn: added to poor wheat harvests, the international price of copper and nitrates began to fall. The nitrate producers themselves formed a Combination in the usual manner. This meant that just when the government needed money (to carry on the arms race and the "metallic conversion" simultaneously) its principal source of revenue contracted. Soon enough there was another run on the banks, and foreigners once again withdrew their investments. Literally running out of specie (in 1898 Chile exported 9 million pesos in gold coin, twice as much as was minted that year) and faced with the collapse of the banking system, the government not only abandoned the gold standard, but pumped about 50 million paper pesos into the economy.

Few seemed to mourn the demise of the gold standard. It is easy enough to see why: the "conversion" of 1895–98, by deflating the currency (by around 20 percent), had driven up both the cost of living and interest rates. The return to paper money, by contrast, made capital available, gave an element of protection to the manufacturer, and raised commodity prices, benefiting hacendados and mineowners. Even the leaders of the artisan-based Democratic party sang the praises of paper money, considering it as a stimulant to employment and higher wages. Subsequent events seemed to reassure the *papeleros,* the advocates of paper money. Interest rates fell; manufacturing expanded; higher prices for nitrates, copper, and wheat brought renewed prosperity.

Unfortunately the good times did not last, and the temptation to go on printing money was not resisted. During 1905–6 the supply of government paper rose from 55 million to 80 million pesos, while financiers, their strong-rooms bulging with money, went on a lending spree: 360 million pesos to around 230 new companies. Just as in the United States in the 1920s, investors rushed to buy stock in corporations whose business they knew nothing about. (One man earned 25,000 pesos on stock he both bought and sold during a train journey between Santiago and Valparaiso.) In 1906 this house of cards collapsed: most of the ill-conceived new ventures were swept away. By a terrible coincidence, an earthquake devastated Valparaiso. The collapse of the stock market and the destruction of the country's leading port spurred Congress to authorize the emission of additional millions of paper pesos. What in 1898 had been a temporary expedient was a habit by 1907 – the money supply reached 150 million paper pesos that year, a threefold increase since

1903. Some Chileans continued to hold out against paper money. The municipality of Limache, for instance, inveighed against paper money in 1907, describing it as "the most odious of despoilers, for it exploits the hunger of more than four million Chileans, who form the richest country in the world."[12] This opinion was shared by the Valparaiso Chamber of Commerce: "The people does not want a single paper peso more; it wants, it desires, a healthy and effective currency, an unchangeable measure of value."[13] Whether "the people" wanted it or not, it was what "the people" got. These were voices crying in the wilderness. Paper money had become the Parliamentary Republic's economic opium, an easy way to dreams.

If monetary policy reflected this complaisant approach, so too did the abandonment of the fiscal reforms of 1878–79. During the 1880s (1884, 1888, and 1889), Congress granted tax relief to the rich by abolishing the imposts on income, gifts, and estates, preferring to rely on the export tax on nitrate imposed during the War of the Pacific. After just one decade (1879–89), the export taxes rose from 4 to 45 percent of the country's ordinary revenues.[14] Indeed, from the late 1880s until 1930 the nitrate industry generated more than half of all ordinary revenues – and employed more people than any other industry. In short, for forty years *salitre* almost single-handedly propelled the economy and supported the Chilean government.

The collapse of nitrate prices in 1914, although temporary, forced Chile to restructure its tax policies. Faced with suddenly dwindling revenues, the government reduced public salaries by 10 percent and imposed taxes on alcohol, tobacco, gifts, estates, and stock-transfers, as well as on the export of borax. The Moneda also revamped the Customs code, increasing levies on imports as well as imposing special surcharges on existing duties. Stop-gap measures of this kind, however, were of little use in the emergency. The situation became so critical that Congress, after years of delay, did what had been considered unthinkable for so long: it authorized the taxation of income, capital investments, and property. But with the persistence of budget deficits, with a desperate need for revenue to provide temporary subsidies to the faltering nitrate industry, the temptation to turn yet again to paper money proved irresistible.

In the short term the government had to resort to the printing press to bail out the banks, which were once again in trouble, partly because of their inveterate habit of lending more than they held in their coffers. The onset of war precipitated a run on the banks, which as usual could not

---

[12] *El Mercurio,* Valparaiso, August 2, 1907.
[13] *El Mercurio,* Valparaiso, July 21, 1907.
[14] This sum excludes revenues derived from the state-owned railroads.

meet their depositors' demands. (One institution lost two-thirds of its deposits overnight.) Faced with a possible general crisis, the government lent the banks approximately 30 million pesos. As a direct result the money supply grew to 225 million pesos. When the nitrate companies repaid their subsidies, the money supply soon contracted. But in 1918, with another large deficit in prospect, Congress authorized a 20 million peso bond issue. In that year over 227 million pesos were circulating through the economy.

This surge in the money supply did not appear particularly critical. The trade balance improved dramatically: exports exceeded imports by about sevenfold. The mining sector was generating millions in revenues and wages; manufacturing was rapidly expanding; even the haciendas prospered. The prospects looked very bright. By 1918, the peso's international value rose by around 25 percent, making it possible for Chile to return, at last and without fuss, to the coveted gold standard.

Yet the country's finances still remained precariously dependent on money generated by export taxes. In 1918–20, the customs house contributed almost half of all the ordinary revenues; direct taxes, which fell mostly on the upper class, oscillated between 3.6 and 10 percent of the total. (The rich paid less in taxes between 1891 and 1924 than they had in the 1870s and 1880s.) Thus the postwar collapse of the nitrate market forced the government to create new taxes, to levy further surcharges on old ones, and to increase tariffs on imports, particularly those considered luxuries, by a minimum of 50 percent. Discovering that these levies could not generate sufficient revenues, the government borrowed some US$60 million. Neither the new taxes nor the new foreign loans could cover the deficits. There were new issues of bonds, which had the same impact as paper money. Between 1918 and 1924, the amount of government paper in circulation rose from 227.6 to 336 million pesos; by 1925 it reached 400 million pesos.

Parliamentary Republic: social aspects

Population, immigration, social change

By 1918, Chileans numbered an estimated 3,900,000, or almost double the country's population at the end of the War of the Pacific. This figure might well have been a conservative one. Although the Civil Registry had existed since the mid-1880s, many people neglected to register their children's births. Sometimes this was a consequence of sloth, sometimes a consequence of poverty. The Registry's employees often demanded a tip for their services, and not a few families chose not to have to pay the state to certify what they already knew – that their offspring existed. Similarly, people did not always avail themselves of the new right of civil marriage. There were several reasons for this. The Church deeply resented the loss of its monopoly over marriages and burials. Indeed, some priests attributed the devastating cholera epidemic of 1886 to the passage of Santa María's reforms – an altogether too typical contribution to the "religious war" then raging. The law on civil marriage was itself defective: while it recognized only civil marriages, it did not prohibit Church-sanctioned unions, nor did it require (as it does now) all who wished to have a religious ceremony to undergo a civil marriage beforehand. Hence the Catholic hierarchy, led by Bishop Joaquín Larraín Gandarillas, urged its flocks to marry only in church and to ignore the Santa María law. Not until 1897, and then only at the behest of the Papacy, did the Chilean clergy instruct the faithful to undergo a state marriage after receiving the sacraments of the Church. By 1905 the marriage rate had returned to its pre-1885 levels.

Despite this, the number of illegitimate births (which increased by almost 60 percent between 1848 and 1901) continued to soar. Indeed, during the early twentieth century well over one-third (in Santiago, more than half) of all Chilean children were born on the wrong side of the blanket, indicating that a substantial number either disdained marriage or seemed incapable of sustaining long-term unions. The Church branded all children born of civil marriages as "bastards" – an opinion which enraged the adamantly anticlerical Radicals in particular.

Although the population increased, it was never enough to satisfy the demand for labor – at least in the opinion of would-be employers. Hacendados, manufacturers, and *salitreros* frequently lamented that there were too few men willing to work their fields, plants, or mines, and too few women willing to be maids. It is hard to know what to make of such claims, for the newspapers of the period also constantly complained about widespread vagrancy and the hordes of beggars choking the streets.

Labor shortages, if they existed at all, may well have been related to the boom-bust cycle of the *salitreras*. In times of apparent labor scarcity, however, there were frequent calls for the encouragement of immigration. Certain nationalities were welcome, others less so. Just as Chileans had earlier discouraged the immigration of Jews and Italians (considered to be congenitally dishonest moneygrubbers and criminals, respectively), they now rejected the Japanese as well, citing the dangers of the Yellow Peril – and not forgetting blacks, whose presence, the politician Malaquías Concha believed, "would enervate the vigor and corrupt the intelligence and character and intelligence of the nation's inhabitants."[15] They were later to change their mind about Italians, who constituted around 3

---

[15] Chamber of Deputies, August 10, 1905.

percent of the population in 1920. Jews, it appears, never managed to overcome the antipathy. Owing to traditional anti-Semitic stereotypes, the pseudo-scientific writings of Nicolás Palacios and others, and the credence given to the *Protocols of the Elders of Zion* (still being cited after the Second World War), they were never really welcomed as immigrants. Indeed, in 1940 some Chileans blamed "Bolívar's failure, the crime of the Carreras, the assassination of Portales, the suicide of Balmaceda . . . and Chile's present problems" on a Jewish-directed Masonic plot.[16]

In an attempt to foster immigration, the government created the *Agencia General de Colonización* (General Colonization Agency) in 1888. Despite its efforts, and those of SOFOFA, which sought to attract skilled technicians to Chile, relatively few immigrants actually came – between 1889 and 1907, for instance, only 55,000 arrived, while Argentina in the same period received well over 2 million. Those who did immigrate increasingly came on their own account, and not, as occasionally in the past, as part of government-sponsored immigration schemes. Ironically, although some Chileans had opposed colonization projects because they did not want immigrants (such as the Germans) to create ethnic enclaves, this is sometimes precisely what happened. South Slavs ("Yugoslavs") from the Austro-Hungarian empire settled in strength in both the far South and the Norte Grande. In 1907 the two largest national groups were the Bolivians and Peruvians (some brought in as "virtual slaves," according to one newspaper), who constituted 37 percent of all foreign-born residents of Chile.

Immigration only marginally changed Chilean society. Most immigrants ended up as laborers in the fields or the mines. Some, however, found their place in the now gradually expanding middle class – one of the chief symptoms of the marked social diversification of Parliamentary times. It is not difficult to see why the "middle band" of society now began to grow. The demands of international trade and finance had created a host of new white-collar jobs; the growing national bureaucracy (by 1919 there were 27,000 public employees, nine times as many as in 1880) added to the ranks of the embryonic new social class – as did schoolteachers, journalists, and the officers of the armed forces. We do not have a clear picture of middle-class incomes for this period, but the impression gathered from many scattered sources is that they were on the low side, and they deteriorated with inflation. Positions in the bureaucracy were also very much a part of the network of political patronage.

It is perhaps important not to place too much emphasis on "the rise of the middle class" – that old cliché of so many history books. An essayist of 1908 could still plausibly claim that the outstanding social division in

---

[16] *La Nueva Edad*, No. 36, January 7, 1940. During the 1930s, the Foreign ministry apparently issued secret orders to its consuls to deny visas to Jews wishing to settle in Chile.

the country was between an upper class and a lower class (the two "separated by a great distance") and that "the rudiments of a middle class beginning to appear in certain cities and industrial centers" had not yet "reached the point of forming an appreciable category."[17] Certainly distinctive middle-class attitudes were slow to take shape. Chile's "middling folk" still for the most part aspired to imitate their supposed social superiors, though clearly this became less true toward 1920.

Life for the upper class, always good, got much better. The *gente decente* embraced hedonism with almost religious devotion. So many headed for the beaches in the summer that the railroads did not have enough rolling stock to cope with the demand. In winter they assiduously did the rounds of the Santiago social season. The most affluent members of the upper class decamped for long periods to France, to Paris or the Riviera. (It is said that, in 1891, Chileans in Paris could not find a ballroom big enough for them all to celebrate the fall of Balmaceda, but this is surely a myth; the Paris of the period had plenty of large ballrooms.)[18] Those who could not travel did the next best thing, by copying Parisian clothes, manners, and customs. But if French cultural influence still held sway among the upper class, it was now challenged from Germany, whose impact on the Army and educational system we will examine shortly.

Those not fortunate enough to be on the upper rungs of the social ladder were another matter entirely. Our observer of 1908 describes them harshly:

uneducated souls who cannot read or write, lacking in intellectual and . . . moral culture, . . . living a largely nomadic life without knowing the advantages of the family, and whose material life is pitiful, for they dress and eat badly and live in abominable dwellings.[19]

In the countryside the "uneducated souls" included the *minifundistas* and the ubiquitous inquilinos, as well as the equally ubiquitous *gañanes,* the day-laborers or peons. The inquilino and his family could at least subsist, but all that the rural underclass of *gañanes* could achieve was survival. Without access to land or stable employment, they did what they had always done, and moved on, flocking now to the northern *salitreras* in quest of work – and to the cities.

Urban life: splendors and (especially) miseries

By 1907 around two-fifths of all Chileans lived in communities of more than 2,000 people. Santiago's population that year reached 332,000, a

---

[17] Armando Quezada Acharán, *La cuestión social en Chile* (Santiago, 1908), pp. 11–12.

[18] According to Ramón Subercaseaux, the Chilean colony in Paris at the time was around 300: *Memorias de ochenta años,* 2nd ed., 2 vols. (Santiago, 1936), I, 447.

[19] Quezada Acharán, *La cuestión social,* pp. 11–12.

threefold increase since 1865; Valparaiso's was 162,000, more than double its 1865 level; there were more than twenty-two towns of more than 10,000 (as compared with six in 1865). As might be expected, urban population growth was uneven. The south and far south (Valdivia, Llanquihue, and Magallanes provinces) and the northern mining zone (Tarapacá and Antofagasta) grew more rapidly than other parts of the country for much of this period. Once the nitrate boom ended, however, the northern *pampa* lost much of its population to the south, particularly the Central Valley cities.

In its physical extent, despite its rising population, the Santiago of the 1910s was not so dramatically different from the city over which Vicuña Mackenna had presided forty years earlier. Although the turn of the century brought signs of development in what were later to be the eastern suburbs (Providencia became a separate municipality in 1897), the capital had not yet expanded very far beyond its historic core. Its main axis, the well-treed Alameda, was now lined for most of its length (from the Alameda Station to what is now the Plaza Baquedano) with handsome stores and mansions, those on its south side having a nearly uniform roofline height of about ten meters. The public architecture of the period, drawing mostly on French styles, was especially notable: the Central and Mapocho stations (1900, 1913), the National Library (finished in 1924), the Palacio de Bellas Artes (1910), the Club de la Unión (1924) – such buildings have a real charm, not least when compared with the drab office-blocks of the Barrio Cívico, so proudly constructed in the 1930s. In its outward appearance, downtown Santiago was perhaps never more agreeable than at the start of the twentieth century.

Outward appearances are rarely the whole story. Urban life at this period, whether in Santiago or in the smaller cities, may have been more stimulating than that of the countryside, but it was also more hazardous. The major cities and the provincial towns lacked adequate drinking water and sewage systems. Most sections of Santiago and Valparaiso were without piped water until after 1900; the remaining larger towns had to wait another decade. A newspaper report of 1905 alleged that in La Serena, for instance, "the water that leaves the spigot is . . . pure mud."[20] But who cared about such things? The upper class, we might note here, seemed almost as nonchalant about personal cleanliness as the poor. The first bathroom (complete with tub and piped-in hot water) did not reach Santiago until 1900: it was greeted with great curiosity by high society.

Interestingly, in some towns the benefits of electricity arrived even before municipally supplied water. Santiago started installing electric lights in 1886, Temuco in 1890, and Valparaiso a decade later. If smaller

---

[20] *El Mercurio*, Valparaiso, March 28, 1905.

towns such as Lota and Tocopilla had early access to electricity, this was because the local mining companies hooked them up to their private generators. Gas-lighting persisted in other provincial cities (such as Copiapó) for many years. Santiago electrified its tram system in 1900. Within three years the Chilean Electric Tramway had grown to almost 97 kilometers of track, and it continued its expansion into outlying districts, covering most of the city by 1910. Some of the tramcars were double-deckers in the British style, the upper deck being known as the *imperial*.

Migrants to the city often had cause to regret trading the bucolic squalor of the countryside for the horrors of the infamous *conventillos,* of which there were at least 2,000 in the Santiago of the 1900s and 1910s. In 1905 *El Mercurio* described Valparaiso as "infected, fetid, pestilent, with its streets covered with a thin layer of fermenting filth" and as "a port from which any man who values his life should flee."[21] Less than four years later the same newspaper commented: "The Spanish language, so rich in its words, does not have words sufficient to describe such a pigsty with accuracy."[22] As late as 1920 Santiago still lacked access to adequate amounts of drinking water. During the summer people literally had nothing to drink. The government did not start building a sewer system for the capital until 1903, and generally failed to keep up with the needs of the expanding city. Not surprisingly, garbage was simply often thrown into the streets. Sometimes it was collected and burned, drenching nearby neighborhoods with the not-so-fragrant odor of incinerating waste and animal remains. Some of Valparaiso's inhabitants simply turned the port's hillside ravines into combination privies and refuse dumps.

Living conditions were every bit as bad. Cramming up to eight people into a single, unventilated room (five by eight meters), the *conventillos* became fetid incubators of disease, their inmates perishing from tuberculosis, respiratory illnesses, or in some cases simple asphyxiation. In 1906 Congress created the *Consejo de Habitaciones de Obreros* (Council for Workers' Housing) with the mandate to ensure the safety of existing housing and, if need be, to replace unsafe accommodations. It never received adequate funding to do its job.

Given the deplorable housing conditions, contagious disease abounded: smallpox, diphtheria, whooping cough, meningitis, and measles decimated town-dwellers. And because, as already mentioned, almost all towns lacked running water or sewer systems as late as 1910, typhoid became another killer. Epidemic disease, it might be said, became one of the few equalizing forces in Chilean life. Cholera, yellow fever, and bubonic plague democratically annihilated rich and poor alike. Between

---

[21] *El Mercurio,* Valparaiso, July 7, 1905.   [22] *El Mercurio,* Valparaiso, March 18, 1909.

1909 and 1914 more than 100,000 Chileans perished from disease each year. Smallpox alone killed 10,000 annually. Men succumbed more frequently than women. Just as consistently, those less than one year old constituted between one-third and two-fifths of all those dying in a given year, some because they had been abandoned (25,000 in Santiago alone between 1870 and 1910), some by infanticide. This grim pattern of disease and mortality eventually prompted the lethargic Parliamentary governments to initiate programs to vaccinate the population. Curiously, we might think today, more than a few citizens refused to be vaccinated. The government's efforts to prevent contagion also failed: in Valparaiso, people confined against their will to a pest-house successfully petitioned the courts to order the health authorities to release them from quarantine.

Disease was not the only menace. Crime still abounded, not only in the countryside (where the Army was sometimes called in to help) but also, and perhaps especially, in the cities. No one, not even nuns or policemen, could escape the scourge. Valparaiso's hospitals admitted so many patients with knife wounds that they could not accommodate all of the merely diseased. It was claimed by a newspaper in 1902 that Chile had the highest homicide rate in the world. Since jails failed to contain the criminals (one inmate was discovered to be counterfeiting money), citizens called for the authorities to revive the flogging of malefactors. The criminals seemed as unstoppable as disease, often forcing the rich to hire bodyguards.

Despite its various threats, both natural and man made, urban life had far more attractions than life in the countryside: opera, plays, and parties for the better-off, more modest consolations for the poor. The rich (and *arrivistes*) attended the opera, sometimes more to be seen than to listen, still strongly preferring the international repertoire. (The Chilean composer Eliodoro Ortiz de Zárate had no success with his two operas, the first to be written by a Chilean, and staged in 1895 and 1902. *El Mercurio* even insinuated that he was trying to impose an *arte de medio pelo* on the opera-going public.)[23] The poor, for their part, flocked to the *cantinas,* many illegal, which seemed to be everywhere. Valparaiso had approximately 1,500 bars in 1909 (up from 1,151 three years earlier), one for every thirty-five *porteños,* not counting women, who, according to *El Mercurio,* did not drink,[24] and children. Many of these establishments entrapped workers on their way home, extracting their pay before it reached their families. Alcoholism became so pernicious (it is estimated that around six out of ten workers religiously celebrated San Lunes, "Saint Monday," each week) that a temperance league (*Liga contra el Alcoholismo*)

[23] Mario Cánepa G., *La Ópera en Chile* (Santiago, 1976), pp. 110–12, 137–44.
[24] *El Mercurio,* Valparaiso, December 18, 1906; June 15 and July 13, 1909.

was formed just before 1900, and in 1902 Congress enacted a *Ley de Alcoholes* which (for the first time) made drunkenness a criminal offense. The league and the law – not forgetting a vain legislative proposal in 1914 to close all bars on Saturday evenings – were as destined to failure as all such attempts in Chilean history. (These go back a long way: as early as 1558 the cabildo of Santiago launched what would now be thought of as an anti-drinking campaign.)

The brothel, which was legal if licensed, seemed almost as ubiquitous as the bar. In 1916 Santiago had 543 legal bordellos as well as some 10,000 *casas de tolerancia* operating outside the law. Despite efforts by the police and the municipal medical authorities, venereal disease was endemic, in part because the law did not allow municipalities to regulate the location of brothels. In 1897 the Chilean Navy's surgeon-general reported that commanders of foreign naval squadrons would not allow their men ashore for liberty in Talcahuano, Valparaiso or Coquimbo, because these ports had become hotbeds of venereal disease. In 1900 more than 21 percent of infants who perished before the age of six were victims of congenital syphilis. Within ten years, however, there was relief for afflicted adults, as the Wasserman test and Dr. Ehrlich's "magic bullet" reached Chile. Soon enough fullpage advertisements praising Salvarsan 600 were appearing in the Valparaiso press. Such publicity would have been deemed outrageous in the United States or the Great Britain of the period.

Surviving childhood did not necessarily mean a long life. Urban workers labored long hours, with little protection against injury or unemployment. (Deaths from industrial accidents amounted to more than 2,400 in 1910 alone.) Railroadmen, for instance, suffered an accident rate twenty-five times that of their counterparts in imperial Germany. Workers were obliged to endure draconian discipline, often at the hands of capricious foremen who levied fines for such major infractions as falling sick. Thanks to the combination of poor living and working conditions, the death rate was twice that of Western Europe, and in 1920 the average Chilean life span was thirty. Attempts to improve working conditions by legislation usually ran into opposition: a proposal in 1904 to ensure that workers got at least Sunday off was interpreted by the congressman Eduardo Suárez Mujica as an attempt to curtail the freedom of both workers and employers.[25]

Dismal as social conditions were for the majority, Chileans could not escape the impact of modern technology, uneven as this might be. There was a 15 percent increase in the use of the telephone between 1914 and 1918, while resort to the telegraph correspondingly declined. Cities like Chillán and Concepción strung telephone wires to communicate with

---

[25] Chamber of Deputies, November 26, 1904.

each other. Phones served those who could use them better than the mail service: in the early years of the century it often took eight days for a letter to reach Valparaiso from Santiago (if it got there at all). Mail from the capital to the Norte Grande often took three months to arrive. There was a shower of complaints to the press on this issue. As one critic noted, "the mail service which the primitive Indian used was a thousand times better than the one currently implanted in the midst of civilization."[26]

The automobile made its appearance in the early 1900s. By 1906 there were sixty in Santiago. Those Chileans who could, embraced the new form of transportation with enthusiasm: one car was even built locally, and reached a speed of ten kilometers per hour. Despite the relative lack of paved streets, cars became so popular that in 1907 the government called for regulating motor traffic, including issuing licenses. Three years later a speed limit of 14 k.p.h. was imposed. Neither innovation seemed to lessen the spirited way in which Chileans drove their cars (as they still often do). In 1914 there were complaints in Congress about low driving standards. In 1920 it was even alleged that foreign visitors feared to cross the streets, as automobiles sped by "as if they were running races on a special racetrack."[27]

The airplane came in 1910. It was an innovation quickly embraced by the military, sometimes with disastrous results. Some of the earliest military aviators took off straight into oblivion. Chileans still sometimes describe themselves as *más perdido que el teniente Bello* ("more lost than Lieutenant [Alejandro] Bello"), a wry allusion to a pilot who flew off into the mountains, never to return, in 1914. A British military instructor of the period, despairing of the aviators' tendency to take unauthorized jaunts, described his Chilean students as "aerial chauffeurs." In fairness, it must also be noted that it was a Chilean aviator, Lt. Dagoberto Godoy, who was the first pilot to cross the high Andes by air (December 1918), in a British-made Bristol – a notable feat, justly remembered.

The "German bewitchment": the Army and education

The armed forces as a whole did not fare much better in Parliamentary times than poor Lieutenant Bello. It is true that German instructors (first hired in 1885) made a serious effort to modernize the Chilean Army – and, of course, to Prussianize it. Bearing German arms, wearing German-style uniforms (including the *pickelhaube* helmet), and marching like Germans, Chilean soldiers became a carbon copy of their Prussian counterparts, albeit somewhat darker in hue – according to General Emil Körner. Körner had become chief of the general staff after the 1891 civil

---

[26] *El Mercurio*, Valparaiso, April 18, 1908.   [27] *El Mercurio*, November 9, 1920.

war. Between the mid-1890s and the First World War, some 130 Chilean officers received training in Germany. Several dozen German officers (some of whom stayed in Chile) became instructors in the military school and in the war academy (founded by Balmaceda), where German was the chief foreign language taught. (The Navy, still treasuring its time-honored British connections, pointedly refrained from teaching German to its cadets.) In some ways, therefore, the German impact on the Chilean Army was marked, not only in weaponry and uniforms but also, we might add, in military music: the splendid Badenweiler, Ferbelin, and Nibelung marches (and many others of Teutonic origin) still mingle with such sturdy and enduring Chilean products as the "Canción de Yungay" and "Al Séptimo de Línea" (this last, probably by Gumersindo Ipinza, surely as exciting a march as has ever been composed) at military parades, not least the splendid review held during the *fiestas patrias* on September 19 each year.

At a deeper level, however, Prussianization was more a matter of style than substance (though style should never be underrated). The government spent substantial funds (generally over 20 percent of the budget) on the military, but these did not always bear fruit. In fact, the Army's much-vaunted German reforms failed to take root. The conscription law of 1900, for instance, snared only the poor or friendless (who were often one and the same). For some of the recruits, admittedly, military service was a boon: the Army at least provided its conscripts with a basic education as well as military training. But since the government failed to develop much of a means of mobilizing troops after they were discharged, it proved next to impossible for the Army to call men to the colors. (When the First Division's reserves were mobilized in 1920, only one-third responded.) The officer corps (despite its Prussian training) seemed to spend much of its time trying to avoid service in the north, where the living was bad and costs were high. Serving in the military was not a prized career: it was extremely difficult to obtain promotion, and officers remained frozen in rank and pay grade for years. Personnel problems were not the only ones that plagued the military. The Army only belatedly developed technical services, and the few men it assigned to its transport, engineer, and signal corps possessed inadequate equipment. It still relied on civilian provisioners to feed the troops, even when they went on maneuvers. These deficiencies became painfully clear during the mobilization of 1920 (see Chapter 8), when men arrived without equipment, with carts without wheels, and without enough horses, because many had been scalded to death during the trip. All this sounds distinctly un-Prussian.

Education fared altogether better than the Army in Parliamentary times. Here, too, the impact of Germany was notable, not only as the chief inspiration of the leading educators of the time (the great Valentín

Letelier being the foremost), but also as a source of teachers, a handful of whom were attracted to the University of Chile's new Instituto Pedagóg-ico (Letelier's brainchild), established in 1888; some of them taught in the *liceos*. The "German bewitchment" did not go unchallenged, but it cannot be denied that it was a strong one, or that it played its part in a serious effort to upgrade and modernize Chilean education. The historian Gonzalo Vial describes this as "a work of titans," and he is not far wrong.

By 1918 there were some 336,000 primary students, almost a three-fold increase since 1900. About two-fifths of the population was literate by 1907, and half by 1920, a substantial gain over the figure for 1895, when illiteracy still ran at almost 70 percent. The number of children attending school continued to rise, although a majority of those enrolled did not reach graduation. Attempts to make education compulsory foun-dered, in part because some legislators (doubtless the same ones who had opposed forced vaccination) saw mandatory education as the state's usurpation of parents' natural rights. School attendance did not become compulsory until 1920, and even then the law was not rigorously en-forced. As far as secondary education went, the gains were somewhat less impressive. By 1918 only about 45,000 students attended secondary schools, about half of which were privately owned. While more boys attended school than girls, there was nevertheless a dramatic increase in the number of female students during this period.

University enrollments reached around 4,000 in 1918, most of the surge in numbers occurring after 1910. The venerable University of Chile now had competition. In 1888 the archdiocese of Santiago created (not without misgivings) the new Catholic University of Chile. Formed to provide a counterpoise to the growing anticlericalism of the period, it eventually grew to incorporate the sciences as well as the humanities, and it has made a distinguished contribution to higher education ever since. Further south, the University of Concepción opened its doors in 1919 – a bastion of secularism founded by the philosopher Enrique Molina, its rector for thirty-seven years thereafter.

Growing literacy meant that the Parliamentary period was a flour-ishing one for the press. The provincial press, in particular, was far more developed than it is today, with virtually every town of any size publish-ing at least one newspaper, and usually more than one. Most such provin-cial newspapers reflected a particular religious or political bias: there were socialist papers in the *salitreras,* and, in the cities, anarchist papers that were intermittently closed down for offending the more sensitive. Illus-trated magazines also appeared: *Sucesos* in 1902, *Selecta* in 1909, the no-table *Pacífico Magazine* in 1913, and Santiago's more durable *Zig-Zag,* whose owners, the Edwards family, also published over twenty-five other magazines.

A glance at culture (1880s–1920s)

The final decades of the nineteenth century saw the fine flowering of the historians schooled by the great Andrés Bello. Diego Barros Arana's *Historia general de Chile* was published, in sixteen thick volumes, between 1884 and 1902. Barros Arana died in 1907, the last of the great nineteenth-century "triumvirate," and nobody of quite the same caliber succeeded him. The outstanding Chilean scholar by this stage was José Toribio Medina, a man of astonishing range (history, bibliography, geography, numismatics, biography, natural history) and an insatiable collector of books and manuscripts – donated (despite offers from Harvard and Brown Universities in the United States) to Chile's own National Library on Medina's death in 1930. The nineteenth-century historiographical tradition, perhaps not surprisingly in view of its strength, long held sway in twentieth-century Chile: as late as the 1960s a memorable scholar, Ricardo Donoso, was still plowing the old furrow with distinction, while Guillermo Feliú Cruz continued the bibliographical tradition of Medina, with whom, in fact, he had served his scholarly apprenticeship.

The first stirrings of "revisionism" in historical writing became noticeable only toward the end of the 1920s, in the work of Alberto Edwards, an admirer of Burke and Spengler, and of strong nineteenth-century Chilean rulers like Portales and Montt. Edwards himself was one of the liveliest minds of the period, and the author, too, of detective and fantasy stories. (His fictional policeman, Román Calvo, "the Chilean Sherlock Holmes," is a memorable creation who deserves a revival.) Edwards's ideas were to influence those of Francisco Antonio Encina, the controversial but bestselling historian of the mid-twentieth century. Later developments can be only lightly sketched here. History as a discipline was to be somewhat eclipsed in the 1950s and (especially) 1960s, with the growth in Chile of the modern (and for a time much more fashionable) social sciences. It was to be renewed fairly decisively in the 1970s and 1980s. As examples of the vitality of our Chilean colleagues' professional activity at the end of the twentieth century, we could mention the diversity of theoretical approaches on offer and the variety of topics studied, the arrival of the modern biographical genre in Cristián Gazmuri's large-scale life (1998) of the first President Eduardo Frei, the opening of a valuable new Archive of the Twentieth Century, and the serious efforts being made (at, for instance, Patricia Arancibia's CIDOC at Santiago's Universidad Finis Terrae) to assemble the taped reminiscences of recent historical actors.

But we are getting far ahead of the story, and must move our focus firmly back to around 1900. Greater literacy, the spread of education, the new prominence of journalism as a profession – these all had their effects on cultural activity, which ceased at this point to be an upper-class preserve (though even in the nineteenth century it had not been exclusively so). Indeed, it has been argued that with the new century there came a new social type, the *intellectual* – the writer Augusto D'Halmar (who in 1904–5 ran a short-lived "Tolstoyan" colony near Santiago; it was not very Tolstoyan) has sometimes been seen as the prototype of the new breed. Certainly imaginative literature, building on the splendid example of Alberto Blest Gana, showed definite signs of life after 1900 or so, with a number of serious writers taking up "creole" themes (rural, regional, sometimes explicitly social) in reaction to the European models that had predominated in the somewhat anaemic literature of earlier times. "Creolism" in one form or other is probably the most easily identifiable *general* cultural trend after the turn of the century. In the 1900s and 1910s Baldomero Lillo and Mariano Latorre more or less invented the Chilean short story, a form much cultivated since, and by the 1920s a novelist of real distinction, Eduardo Barrios, was making his mark – though his masterpiece, *Gran señor y rajadiablos* (Grand Gentleman and Rapscallion), was not published until 1948. This was very much in the "creolist" line, although the line itself had more or less run into the sands by the 1930s.

The reputation of Chilean prose writers in the Spanish-speaking world, however, has generally been less striking than that of the country's poets, and this was certainly true in the first half of the twentieth century. Why poetry should have formed so important a part of Chilean cultural achievement is hard to say. Perhaps, on this score, Chile *is* the England of South America. The English are often regarded as the most phlegmatic of European peoples, yet their tradition of lyric poetry is easily the finest in the western world. Chileans, for their part, have often been described (rightly or wrongly) as the most phlegmatic of Latin Americans. Could it be that in both cases poetry is a necessary release? Who knows? Whatever the reason, the Chilean record is very clear. Here we have to reckon with figures of genuine and justifiable celebrity. Vicente Huidobro published his first poems in 1911, at the age of eighteen; his "Creationist" aesthetic was soon to give him an acknowledged place, in Europe as well as Spanish America, in the general ferment of modern poetry. (He was also a man of firm if changeable political views: it is largely forgotten in Chile that he was a candidate in the presidential election of 1925, winning precisely thirty-three votes.) These years, too, saw the steadily growing fame of the young Lucila Godoy Alcayaga, a schoolteacher from Vicuña in the Elqui valley (a museum devoted to her life and work stands there today), whose verses began to make an impression in the 1910s. From the names of two favorite poets (the Italian Gabriele d'Annunzio and the Provençal Frédéric Mistral) she constructed the pen-name by which she will always be known, for Gabriela Mistral is one of the glories of Chile –

> *Presidenta y bienhechora*
> *de la lengua castellana*
>
> President and benefactress
> of the Spanish language,

– as another great figure, Violeta Parra, was to describe her on her death in 1957. From the 1920s onward Mistral lived much of her life abroad, in the consular service, and in 1945 she became the first Latin American (and fifth woman) to win the Nobel Prize for Literature. One of the students in the *liceo* at Temuco, when she was principal there in 1920, was a railwayman's son called Neftalí Reyes. She gave him Tolstoy and Dostoyevsky to read. Such encounters are rightly the stuff of which legends are made. The boy, as the world knows, later adopted a pseudonym of his own, borrowing the surname of a Czech writer he knew nothing about. Many years later he was to place a flower on Jan Neruda's monument in Prague.

The "creolist" tendency mentioned in connection with prose-writing was also well reflected in painting. Here two very noteworthy figures straddle the years to either side of 1900: Pedro Lira, often described as "the first Chilean master," very much in the academic tradition (romantic landscapes, rural "characters," upper-class portraits), and, younger by ten years, the astonishing Juan Francisco González, a singularly prolific artist who devised what might be called a Chilean version of impressionism (though he himself disliked the label). González's "Limache" and "Melipilla" phases (the first from 1888 to 1900, the second from 1920 until his death at the age of 80 in 1933) were his most creative. The "creolist" tendency as such, however, came more obviously into its own with a younger group of painters, usually referred to (in conventional Hispanic fashion) as the "generation of 1913" – the year they first established themselves. This period, we should note, also saw the first generation of talented Chilean sculptors, whose contributions to the statuary of Santiago are still easy enough to appreciate.

A further sign of the new interest in the "creole" and the local was the effort now made to investigate folk poetry and popular traditions in general (Julio Vicuña Cifuentes and Ramón Laval were the real pioneers here). Comparable efforts with folk music had a direct artistic influence on what can be seen as the first generation of serious Chilean composers, notably Pedro Humberto Allende, the respected pioneer of modern music in the country, whose first works appeared in the 1910s. (The score of his cello concerto won approval from Débussy.) By the 1930s several important figures had emerged, among them Próspero Bisquertt and Carlos Isamitt, who, like Allende, were musical "nationalists," while the most notable member of the group, Domingo Santa Cruz, as his nickname ("the Chilean Hindemith") suggests, assimilated modern European influences to good effect.

Perceptions of national decline

Chilean culture had always had something of a critical edge. A number of the writers who appeared in the early twentieth century (Baldomero Lillo, Mariano Latorre, Nicomedes Guzmán, Joaquín Edwards Bello, Fernando Santiván) drew attention to miserable social conditions, often depicting the *roto,* the miner, the urban worker in their writings. What is interesting, however, is that certain intellectuals around now took issue with the entire recent course of Chilean history. What has sometimes been called a "literature of national decline" now made its appearance. The tone of these writings was set by a remarkable speech (soon afterward printed) made on a long remembered evening (August 1, 1900) at the Ateneo club in Santiago by the Radical politician Enrique Mac-Iver. "It seems to me," he said, "that we are not happy. We note a malaise that is not confined to one class of people nor to particular regions.... The present is not satisfactory, and the future is cast in shadow." Mac-Iver deplored what he saw as a decline in public spirit, contrasting with the previous energy and public-mindedness of Chilean leaders. The great wealth derived from nitrate seemed to him to have been "a devastating torrent which...destroyed the public virtues that made us great."[28] Mac-Iver offered no very concrete solutions to the "moral crisis" he adumbrated so eloquently, and, indeed, most of the writers who addressed this theme were better at analyzing ailments than prescribing cures.

We cannot review the "literature of national decline" in more than summary fashion: more than a score of writers can be associated with this trend. Some of its representative figures – Nicolás Palacios, author of *Raza chilena* (1904), and Francisco Antonio Encina, for instance – appealed to racialist ideas of no great interest today, but nonetheless ably diagnosed what they saw as failings in the upper class: its taste for conspicuous consumption, its disinclination to put its energy into industrial or commercial work, its contempt for the laboring classes, and so on. Far and away the most passionate work in this line, a book which caused a sensation when it was published (under the pseudonym of Dr. Julio Valdés Cange), was *Sinceridad. Chile íntimo en 1910,* by a provincial

---

[28] "Discurso sobre la crisis moral de la República," reprinted in Hernán Godoy, ed., *Estructura social de Chile* (Santiago, 1971), pp. 283–91.

schoolteacher, Alejandro Venegas, then 39. He had traveled the length and breadth of Chile, collecting impressions, becoming increasingly angry at the state of his beloved homeland.

We have armies, warships, fortresses, cities and ports, theaters and racetracks, clubs, hotels, public promenades, monuments, and...opulent magnates, lords of true dominions, who live in splendid palaces...; but at no great distance from the theaters, gardens and lordly residences there lives the people, that is to say nine tenths of the population of Chile, plunged in the most fearful economic, physical and moral poverty, and degenerating rapidly through overwork, poor diet, lack of hygiene, extreme ignorance, and the grossest vices.[29]

Venegas himself was eventually broken by the outcry over his book; he retired early and ended up running a dairy in Santiago and, later, serving in a grocery store in Maipú. But he has hardly been forgotten. Nor is he likely to be.

Many of the darts fired by Venegas and the other writers in this vein were well aimed. There is any amount of evidence to show that the Chilean upper class of Parliamentary times went in for spending on a sometimes spectacular scale. Lengthy trips to Europe (some, in 1910, reported as costing more than £20,000 in hotels alone), lavish mansions in town and (sometimes) country, coaches and carriages and, later, automobiles, extensive consumption of food and drink (the wines mostly imported rather than bought from the admirable vineyards of the Central Valley) – this was, indeed, for the upper class, something of a Belle Époque, well described in Luis Orrego Luco's novel *Casa grande* (1908). Such a lifestyle was not uncommon in Europe at the period (one thinks of Edwardian England), and the Chilean upper class continued to regard Europe as the fount of taste and wisdom. To some extent this was inevitable (Europe *was* still the center of the world), but a preference for the foreign as opposed to the local often – far too often – implied contempt for the local. One of the solid virtues of the literature of decline is its belief in the merits of the local, in the potential of ordinary Chileans. Given the right measures, it was held, this potential could reverse the national decline.

Indictments of the upper class were inevitably indictments of the Parliamentary Republic, which we can see in retrospect as the last phase of genuinely oligarchic rule in Chile. On this score, it is important to remember that despite the frivolous upper-class politicking, governments were not entirely supine. The thirty years after Balmaceda's fall saw impressive "longitudinal" railway construction (by 1913, it was possible to travel from Iquique to Puerto Montt by train). The evidence of our

---

[29] *Sinceridad* (Santiago, 1910), p. 250.

eyes is also helpful here: as we have already hinted, nobody wandering around Santiago, even today, can fail to appreciate that this was the last period in Chile (to date) of consistently pleasing public architecture.

It is similarly important to recognize that, oligarchic as it was, and despite some terrible lapses, the Parliamentary Republic preserved the liberal freedoms, to the extent that a modern historian, Julio Heise González, can describe it as having been "a magnificent school of civic values for the Chilean people."[30] There is much to be said for this view. At the same time, it is difficult to disagree with Harold Blakemore's verdict that Parliamentary leaders "stand condemned ... in their apparent inability not so much to recognize a society in transition, for most were aware of changes taking place, but to reform their institutions so as to cater for them."[31] It is certainly true that a stronger, more coherent political system might have been able to legislate more effectively on the "social question." A comparison with Argentina is interesting here. In Argentina, during this period, politics was altogether more polarized than in Chile, yet social legislation was more extensive. "In every major area," as Karen Remmer has pointed out, "Argentine public policy exhibited more support for less privileged groups than Chilean policy."[32] The diagnosticians of national decline were probably unaware of this: it would have given further point to their arguments.

The course of foreign affairs, too, seemed to confirm that Chile's national fortunes were in decline. In October 1891, an incident outside the True Blue Saloon in Valparaiso prompted an angry crowd to set on some American sailors enjoying shore leave from the USS *Baltimore,* then in port. Two died; others were beaten or arrested. The U.S. government demanded an apology and compensation. President Benjamin Harrison, infuriated by an injudicious cable from Manuel Antonio Matta (then foreign minister) to Chile's minister in Washington, issued what Chileans saw as an ultimatum. For a few short weeks the prospect of war seemed real. It quickly faded. Matta was replaced, and the government both apologized and agreed to pay reparations – in what a secretary at the American legation called "a very humiliating letter for these proud people to send."[33] The "Baltimore affair" cooled Chilean attitudes toward the United States, at least for a while. It also gave rise to a long-standing Chilean legend – it is a legend pure and simple – that the warship *Chacabuco* was ordered to San Francisco to salute the Stars and Stripes, and that a patriotic young lieutenant, Carlos Peña, shot himself dead

[30] *Historia de Chile. El período parlamentario, 1861–1965,* 2 vols. (Santiago, 1974–82), I, 271.

[31] Leslie Bethell, ed., *Cambridge History of Latin America,* Vol. V (Cambridge, 1986), p. 553.

[32] *Party Competition in Argentina and Chile* (Lincoln, Neb., 1984), p. 205.

[33] Joyce S. Goldberg, *The Baltimore Affair* (Lincoln, Neb., 1986) p. 128.

while lowering the Chilean flag. How many Chileans believed this, and for how long, it is impossible to say.

With Argentina, matters were altogether more serious. The 1881 treaty had agreed that the frontier between the two countries should follow the line of the highest Andean peaks and the watershed between Atlantic and Pacific. It became apparent by the early 1890s that the two lines did not always coincide. The issue was further complicated by arguments over the Puna de Atacama, Bolivian territory occupied by Chile in the War of the Pacific, but which Bolivia now unilaterally ceded to Argentina (December 1895). In April 1896 Chile accepted the cession in principle, on the understanding that Argentina would accept British mediation as a last resort on the border issues. But no progress was made on the delineation of the frontier, and by mid-1898 war fever was taking hold in both Chile and Argentina. Both countries were now openly engaged in an arms race, with new warships being ordered from European yards. (The high expenditure was a main reason for Chile's abandonment of the gold standard that year.) The Chilean and Argentine presidents, rising above the bellicosity of public opinion, resolved the issue in the short term by means of a meeting of plenipotentiaries. To give symbolic reinforcement to this agreement, they both sailed down to Punta Arenas for a friendly meeting (February 1899). While dinner was in progress aboard the Argentine cruiser *Belgrano,* the lights suddenly went out. The presidents exchanged graceful compliments, alluding to their respective national flags: "The sun of Argentina will light us!" "And so will the star of Chile!"

Such was the much-celebrated *abrazo del Estrecho,* the "embrace of the Straits." It had little real effect on subsequent events. The plenipotentiaries, meeting two months later, agreed to accept a decision from the American minister in Buenos Aires, William J. Buchanan, who awarded most of the Puna de Atacama to Argentina. Once again, the Chilean president was pilloried by the press and in Congress as the man who "gave away the Puna." To make matters worse, a number of minor incidents on the Frontier soon reinflamed Chilean war fever: Chile ordered two new battleships, as did Argentina. (Their navies were the sixth and seventh largest in the world at the time.) A complicated series of private and public initiatives (from a Chilean deputy, an Argentine business-man, and the foreign ministries of Europe, as well as from the Moneda and Casa Rosada) finally brought Chile and Argentina back from the brink. The "Pacts of May" (signed in Santiago on May 28, 1902) committed the two nations to seek arbitration in future disputes and to limit naval armaments. Later that year King Edward VII handed down his boundary award. It reflected the English taste for compromise: 54,000 square kilometers went to Chile, 40,000 to Argentina. The crisis was over.

In 1904 a large statue of Christ the Redeemer was erected high in the Andes, as a token of perpetual amity between the Chilean and Argentine peoples. In that same year (October 20, 1904) Chile finally signed a peace treaty with Bolivia. The price of ownership of the former Bolivian littoral was to be the construction of a railway from Arica to La Paz. It was opened in May 1913.

Neither the Pacts of May nor the Bolivian deal, we should note, signified diplomatic triumph for Chile. The terms accorded Bolivia were far more generous than the Bolivians would have believed possible at the time of the 1884 truce. And the perpetual peace with Argentina was secured at the cost of formally confining Chile's sphere of influence to the Pacific.

What had gone wrong? What had happened to the "model republic," the country whose heroes had won the War of the Pacific? Clearly the perceptions of national decline we have mentioned were related to something real. As we have seen, the accusing finger was pointed, as often as not, at the upper class, at the national leadership. And it is to the political record of the Parliamentary period that we ourselves must now finally turn.

Consolidation of the Parliamentary regime

It is important to remember that the typical shapes and forms of the Parliamentary Republic were not consolidated overnight. Many of its conventional practices took time to crystallize. Nor can we ignore some of the differences between the Parliamentary presidencies – so often lumped together indiscriminately and dealt with in broad generalizations. If we cannot avoid generalizations, we can at least see that they are qualified.

The resumption of constitutional government after the 1891 civil war was swift. Congressional elections were held in October 1891, and Admiral (as he now became) Jorge Montt, leader of the Congressional Junta in 1891, duly won the presidency (unopposed) toward the end of that year. He was not a politician. He was more than prepared to let the real politicians have their say – and they were more than eager to take advantage of his hands-off approach. The parties thus became the main arbiters of who was to be in the cabinet. Congressional control was also enhanced by a number of small constitutional amendments (1891–93), one of which (stemming from an initiative made in 1888) extended the idea of "incompatibility" very comprehensively: no public official could now sit in Congress, and the executive was thus deprived of a weapon that had previously been very useful. The most important new law (it was an old ideal of the Conservative, Manuel José Irarrázaval, who was much impressed by the cantonal system of Switzerland) was that of the

Table 7.4. Composition of Chamber of Deputies, 1891–1918.

	Lib	Con	Rad	L-D	Nat	Dem
1891	31	40	23	n/a	—	1
1894	27	28	16	22	—	2
1897	28	26	16	22	—	2
1900	31	25	14	22	—	3
1903	27	20	17	27	—	3
1906	16	27	16	20	12	3
1909	15	23	19	15	18	5
1912	23	29	21	27	13	5
1915	20	28	26	21	16	5
1918	29	26	32	15	5	6

Key: Lib = Liberals; Con = Conservatives; Rad =
Radicals; L-D = Liberal-Democrats (balmacedistas); Nat =
Nationals (counted as Liberals 1891–1903); Dem =
Democrats.

comuna autónoma, or "autonomous municipality" (December 1891): this removed the roughly 200 municipalities into which Chile was now divided from central supervision. The comunas were also given control over elections, with consequences we must mention shortly.

The "sacred union" of Liberals and Conservatives, forged in the civil war, and with which the Montt presidency began, was soon over: the parties naturally wished to resume the old game. As for the defeated balmacedistas, their return to political life was not long delayed. Initially, to be sure, their persecution by the new government was fairly harsh. Some were murdered. Many of them went into exile – one such exile being the scholar José Toribio Medina. The public administration was purged – 5,000 dismissals is a figure often given, though it seems a little high. (The revived Club de la Unión expelled all known balmacedistas.) As late as 1913 the Chamber of Deputies refused to authorize a statue of Balmaceda, who had to wait until 1947 for his (rather ugly) monument. Yet the immediate post–civil war rancor soon subsided: as early as Christmas 1891 there was a partial amnesty; two more followed in 1893 and a final comprehensive amnesty in August 1894. A number of amateurish plots were nipped in the bud: in a distinct echo of April 1851, no less than three of these (December 1892, April 1893, February 1894) had as their aim the seizure of the artillery barracks in Santiago. In Talca, in November 1893, meanwhile, the balmacedistas organized themselves into a new political party. The Liberal Democrats, as they styled themselves (some had advocated "Republican" as the party label), won immediate success in the congressional elections of March 1894 – to the tune of four senators and twenty-two deputies. They swiftly established themselves as recognized players on the stage, without, however, their leaders reviving Balmaceda's presidentialist philosophy. If anything could be said to distinguish the Liberal Democrats from other parties from this point on, it was their appetite for posts in the public administration – understandable, given the purge of 1891.

As Admiral Montt's term neared its end, party competition intensified. The Radicals, Liberal Democrats, and a section of the Liberal party selected the doctrinaire anticlerical Vicente Reyes as their candidate (January 1896). A larger section of the Liberal party, together with dissident Radicals and Liberal Democrats, agreed (in April that year) to support Federico Errázuriz Echaurren, son of the president of the 1870s. "Errázuriz the Little," his enemies called him (on the analogy of Napoleon and Napoleon III), but, despite a so far undistinguished political career, he had something of his father's manipulative streak, and understood intuitively how the rules of the game were changing. In order to win he needed Conservative support. This was not easy to secure. A threat of withdrawal made in a telephone call to Ramón Subercaseaux, a prominent Conservative, did the trick. (Was this the first time the telephone determined a Chilean presidential candidacy?) The Conservatives agreed to a "Coalition" with Errázuriz's Liberals. From now on this term was to be used to denote political combinations involving the Conservative party: those without them were usually known as the "Alliance" (*Alianza*) or "Liberal Alliance." The Alliance-Coalition counterpoint was to remain a constant of Parliamentary politics until 1920.

The 1896 election proved hard-fought and close, with violence (three *errazuristas* were killed at a meeting in Melipilla) and bribery playing their part. Uncertainty over two key votes in the electoral college placed the decision in the hands of Congress. Tension was heightened by the fact that four of Errázuriz's relatives (three brothers and a cousin) sat in Congress at the time. Would they be allowed to vote? (In the end three of them did.) A "Tribunal of Honor" was set up to check the validity of the electoral votes: it awarded Errázuriz a narrow victory, which was duly ratified by the Congress. Having voted, the pro-Reyes congressmen staged an ostentatious walk-out. The auguries were thus not good for the new presidency. In fact, although Errázuriz had twelve changes of ministry during his time in office, he managed to maintain a Coalition coloring in most of them, the most successful being the cabinet headed by the Conservative, Carlos Walker Martínez (April 1898–June 1899).

Errázuriz's presidency, we can see in hindsight, merely confirmed the shape and form of the political system now developing. Doubts were already being expressed about its efficacy. "It is hard to confess," wrote

Francisco Valdés Vergara in 1894, "but those of us who made the [1891] revolution, with the best of intentions, have caused damage that is greater than the benefits promised."[34] The role of the parties was to be fundamental in the new "parliamentary" regime. No great ideological fissures divided them, with one very important exception: the constant struggle between clericalism and anticlericalism. The great redoubt of the former was the Conservative party, while anticlericalism, widespread in other parties, was, in its most doctrinaire form, the particular badge of the Radicals, tied as many of them were to freemasonry and in many cases free thought. Anticlerical and, indeed, anti-religious attitudes were increasingly common in the upper class, especially among men. Women were a different story. (There was nothing unusual in the devout wife of a freethinker giving religious names to her children, as in the case of the boy born in 1908 who was christened Salvador Isabelino del Sagrado Corazón de Jesús Allende.) That anti-Catholicism had a strong popular following, too, is shown in the excitement aroused by the renegade priest Juan José Julio Elizalde – known as "Pope Julio" – whose spellbinding anticlerical oratory implicated him in several minor sensations in the first part of the twentieth century and sometimes provoked discussion in the cabinet itself.

This continuation (at a lower level) of the "religious war" of Santa María's time provoked discord on an infinity of issues, many rather trivial. The Radicals pressed (as they had done since their first national conference in 1888) for the separation of Church and state. Education was a particular bone of contention: while Conservatives strove to maintain independence for Catholic schools (and the new Catholic University), anticlericals aspired with equal zeal to implant what they called the *estado docente* – state supervision and control of the entire educational system. This partly accounts for the Radical party's extraordinary predominance in the schoolteaching profession in the first half of the twentieth century. By the same token, Conservative distrust was one reason why Congress delayed so long in legislating for obligatory primary education – enacted, as already mentioned, only in 1920.

With executive "intervention" out of the way after 1891, elections were now fought more widely and more fiercely, despite the smallness of the electorate. It was now up to the parties to manipulate the process as best they could. They did very well indeed. The municipalities controlling elections became an immediate target for politicians: networks of local political bosses now emerged, indispensable experts in fixing the electoral registers and in delivering the vote, while in the countryside landowners made full use of their inquilinos at election time. While part

---

[34] Quoted in Mario Góngora, *Ensayo histórico sobre la noción de Estado en Chile en los siglos XIX y XX* (Santiago, 1981), p. 30.

of the electorate was "captive" in this way, part of it was not, and bribery now became far more common than in the days of government intervention. The price of votes, as far as we can tell, kept steadily in pace with inflation. Some notes made by Manuel Rivas Vicuña, indefatigable Liberal politician, about the Alliance campaign in 1918 show us the influence money had by then acquired, and how completely politicians took this for granted.

We found that the Radical candidate for Arauco, frightened by the war-chest brought in by Francisco Huneeus, the Conservative, was thinking of withdrawing his candidacy. In a rapid journey to Santiago, we arranged a credit for him and sent him back into the campaign . . . From Aconcagua, Luis Claro informed us that without an extraordinary help with funds he could not face the struggle against the president of the Conservative Party, don Alberto González Errázuriz, his rival for the senate seat. . . . An urgent call came from San Fernando. Sr. Valderrama could not withstand the campaign of Sr. Lyon in Colchagua, and asked for another district. . . . We arranged for Sr. Valderrama to deliver half a million pesos to don Ernesto Barros Jarpa, a sum he would carry in a suitcase to deal a surprise blow against Sr. Ariztía in Llanquihue. Difficulties mounted up in Cautín; the Radical candidate Suárez withdrew. The situation for Sr. Valderrama was not good in Llanquihue, and Sr. Barros Jarpa returned with the suitcase to Cautín, where Sr. Valderrama's candidacy was proclaimed on the eve of the election.[35]

Half a million pesos was worth about £22,500 at the time, or around US $100,000. By the 1910s, high-spending politicians were nicknamed "Dreadnoughts," in honor of the new battleships lately ordered for the Navy. It is hardly surprising that in 1915 a wit suggested that the government simply "establish a wholesale house where the entire election could be purchased" rather than continue to "go through the present farce."[36]

If electoral bribery was a Parliamentary constant, so too was "bureaucratic corruption" – the parties demanding their share of posts in the now expanding public administration. The Radicals and Liberal Democrats were especially zealous in this respect: the price of the *balmacedista* presence in the Coalition of Errázuriz's time was (as their leader publicly declared later) 10 percent of all public jobs. The extent to which, at the higher levels of politics, congressmen and ministers exploited their position for personal or business gain is much less easy to decide: the belief that this happened was widespread, but Congress habitually refused to investigate specific cases.

In a classic essay published in an early issue of the *American Political Science Review* (more readable then than it has since become), an American scholar compared Parliamentary Chile to eighteenth-century England.

[35] Quoted in Gonzalo Vial, *Historia de Chile*, Vol. I, tomo 2 (1981), p. 590.
[36] *El Mercurio*, July 28, 1915.

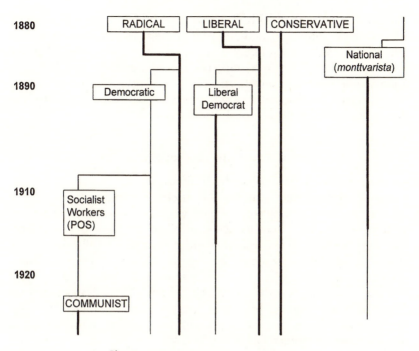

Chart 7.1. Main political parties, 1880–1930.

"Here, too," he wrote, "an aristocracy of birth and wealth has unques-
tioned control of social and political life."[37] The parallel is an apt and
attractive one, but as far as politics goes it must not mislead us. A
Chilean minister of the Interior, though often referred to as a "premier,"
had none of the authority of a British prime minister. The length of
eighteenth-century British cabinets was measured in years, that of Chilean ministries in months and sometimes weeks. Factionalism within the
parties was endemic, and stable congressional majorities were impossible.
The ground was constantly shifting. It was this, more than anything else,
that made the composition of cabinets a matter of such obsessive interest
to Parliamentary politicians. Given its indiscipline and fissiparousness,[38]
the Liberal party, often considered as the pivot of Chilean politics at this
period, was in no real sense a pivot at all.

   Federico Errázuriz was the first Chilean president to resign and then
die (July 1901) before the end of his term, and a vice-president took

---

[37] Paul S. Reinsch, "Parliamentary Government in Chile," *American Political Science Review,* Vol. III
(1908–09), pp. 507–8.
[38] The main internal division was between "moderates" and "doctrinaires," the latter being more
anticlerical.

charge. The political wheel had by this stage turned in the direction of a new Alliance, formed in mid-1900 by Liberals, Liberal Democrats, and Radicals. Their nominating convention in 1901 chose neither of the main contenders (Claudio Vicuña, the Liberal Democrat, and Fernando Lazcano, the moderate Liberal), and a judge, Germán Riesco, was selected in their place. In what was seen as a quiet election, he easily defeated the Coalition candidate, the National, Pedro Montt.

Riesco, Montt, and the "social question"

Germán Riesco, a brother-in-law of Errázuriz, was a man of upright character with a strong taste for domesticity. In some ways he was the ideal Parliamentary president, someone who, in a phrase often attributed to him, was a "threat to nobody."[39] Riesco had little interest in influencing the composition of cabinets; there were seventeen during his five years, the pendulum swinging between the Alliance and the Coalition. Among party leaders who *were* strongly interested in these matters, none was more notable than the rising chief of the Liberal Democrats, Juan Luis Sanfuentes (younger brother of Enrique Salvador Sanfuentes) – one of the great "kingmakers" of the Parliamentary period. This kingmaker, unlike many, was eager to be king himself, but his time had not yet come. In the meantime he won notable ascendancy in the political elite, and what many have seen as an excessive influence over the public administration.

By this stage there was increasing disquiet in political circles with the way the Parliamentary regime was working, a disquiet often reflected by the press. As *El Mercurio* caustically commented in 1903: "This is not parliamentarism, nor a regime, but the most reckless anarchy, produced by the irresponsible dictatorship of some 150 congressmen."[40] The idea of a "strong man," a leader who could restrain cabinet instability, began to have a certain appeal. The obvious man for the role was Pedro Montt, son of the still-remembered "strong man" of the 1850s. In 1906, he won enthusiastic support from his own National party, from most Liberals, from the Radicals, and even from a group of Conservatives. (These were known as *montanas:* a certain Sr. Montana sold fake jewelry in a shop in Calle Estado at the time.) His victory in the election was overwhelming. The weeks before his inauguration, however, were indelibly marked by a horrendous national catastrophe. On the evening of August 16, 1906, a violent earthquake shook the whole of central Chile and almost destroyed Valparaiso – the second great Pacific port to be devastated that year. At

---

[39] What he actually said was that the "unification of the Liberal parties" was not a threat; public memory simplified the phrase.

[40] December 25, 1903.

least 2,300 people lost their lives. It was months before the city was even partially rebuilt. The disaster, as mentioned earlier, imposed an unwelcome financial burden on the new government. It was also a blow from which Valparaiso never fully recovered. A second blow to the port, the opening of the Panama Canal, was to fall eight years later.

Pedro Montt, on whom so many hopes were pinned, was not Manuel Montt's son for nothing. He was an honest, hardworking, and somewhat unimaginative man, an avid reader of technical works but not much else. A friend once lent him *War and Peace;* it was returned unread. "More a statistician than a statesman," someone called him. His administration was as vigorous as the times would allow. Yet he, too, was soon trapped in the partisan and ministerial complexities that had dogged his predecessors, and found no way to retrieve the situation. Like Errázuriz Echaurren, he was the victim of failing health. The Parliamentary Republic's one more or less serious effort at self-regeneration thus came to nothing.

This was little short of tragic, for urgent dilemmas now faced the government. The first decade of the new century was marked by disturbing symptoms of social unrest. It would, of course, be silly to say that the "social question," as it is always called, suddenly "emerged" during these years. The gap between rich and poor had always been there. The plight of the poor in town and country alike had attracted a certain amount of attention since at least the 1870s. What made the "question" altogether more acute in the first decade of the new century was that workers on the nitrate *pampa* and in the cities were no longer willing to wait for their supposed betters to remedy their problems. (Even Enrique Mac-Iver, for all his insight, refused to admit that there *was* a "social question" at all.) Up until 1914 the Parliamentary governments passed just two laws dealing with social issues: the law of February 1906 creating the *Consejo de Habitaciones Obreras* (which Alejandro Venegas denounced as a paper organization), and a measure providing for the six-day week, which was not mandatory for all workers.

The new working class, meanwhile, was beginning to organize. Among artisans, mutualist associations had expanded continuously since the 1860s: by 1910 there were more than 400. After the turn of the century, however, more modern-looking labor unions ("resistance societies") began to appear – the first such unions being formed by metalworkers, railwaymen, tramdrivers, and printers. In various cities, starting in Iquique in 1900, unions and mutualist societies combined into *mancomunales* ("labor brotherhoods"). Many of these early unionists were influenced by anarchist ideas. (Spanish translations of anarchist writings were easily available and in cheap editions.) Employers and politicians might talk of "foreign agitators," but the new labor movement was largely home-grown. Its effects were soon visible to all. Between 1902 and 1908, a period of strong union growth, there were around 200 strikes, about half of which, according to Peter deShazo's analysis,[41] were won by the unions concerned. However, the challenge they mounted in the general strike of May–June 1907 in Santiago and Valparaiso was, on balance, a failure, and the labor movement then went briefly into decline.

The Parliamentary governments tried on the whole to remain aloof from these struggles between workers and employers. But they tended to view large-scale movements (especially if these were accompanied by mass demonstrations) as incipient rebellions, and at times reacted brutally. In May 1903 the Pacific Steam Navigation Company stevedores and other port-workers, on strike in Valparaiso, tried to prevent scabs from taking their place. A full-scale riot broke out, repressed by the Navy and Army with the loss of a hundred lives. In October 1905 it was Santiago's turn. A protest meeting over the high price of meat (attributed to a new duty on imported Argentine cattle) degenerated into an orgy of looting and burning: many of the statues in the Alameda were destroyed. Since the Army was away on maneuvers, order had to be restored by the city's twelve fire companies and some 300 upper-class "white guards," armed by the government with rifles. There were around 200 fatalities. In Antofagasta in February 1906, marines exacted a further toll in lives during a railwaymen's strike. The most horrific such episode took place in Iquique in December 1907, when thousands of striking nitrate workers (and their families) converged on the port in great order and dignity to seek redress of grievances. The city was paralyzed. Two cruisers were dispatched to the north, and the local military commander, the hard-faced General Roberto Silva Renard, ordered an attack (with machine guns) on the Santa María school, where the strikers were concentrated. The number of dead will never be known for sure, but it ran well into the hundreds. General Silva was later stabbed (December 1914), not fatally, by a Spaniard whose brother had died at Iquique.

Whether (as is sometimes maintained) the Iquique massacre permanently deepened the psychological chasm between rulers and ruled in Chile must remain a matter for debate. An investigative committee was proposed in Congress – and never appointed. For their part, anarchist workers eschewed political (as opposed to union) action. Those with socialist views, however, were more inclined (in line with their European counterparts) to try to insert themselves into the political system. Two tiny (and very ephemeral) Socialist parties appeared at the end of the 1890s. The Democratic party (founded in 1887), the smallest party in Congress, had consistently won artisan support, and seemed for a while the natural home for labor militants, who for a few years constituted its "advanced" wing. Among such Democrats, none was more notable than

Luis Emilio Recabarren, a Valparaiso-born typesetter whose tireless organizing activities up and down Chile (and contacts with foreign socialists on trips abroad) gave him a unique place in the early labor movement.
In 1906 he was elected to Congress as deputy for Tocopilla: he refused to
swear the formal oath and was excluded – one deputy (a Radical) expressing horror at his ideas of "social dissolution." Over the years, Recabarren
came to believe in the need for a separate working-class party. In June
1912 he broke finally with the Democrats and formed a new *Partido
Obrero Socialista* (Socialist Workers Party). Unlike its predecessors, it
lasted, its *seccionales* or branches gradually spreading across the country.

Such were some of the social portents when, in September 1910,
Chileans celebrated their Centenary – a century had passed since that first
dieciocho. Pedro Montt was dead: he had traveled to Europe in hopes of a
cure for his ailments, dying in a hotel room in Bremen on August 16,
1910. Worse still, the vice-president succeeding him had also died, so it
fell to a second vice-president, Emiliano Figueroa Larraín, to preside over
the lavish ceremonies. The fireworks, the parades, the gala nights at the
opera, the horse races, Santiago's first sight of an airplane (a Voisin
biplane), the new Palacio de Bellas Artes – the scenes of the centennial
year were long remembered. Yet not even the Centenary could disrupt
the flow of Parliamentary politics. At the Alliance nominating convention
in September (observed by some of the foreign delegations in town for
the festivities), Juan Luis Sanfuentes's hopes were thwarted by the rival
candidacy of the dynamic young business and financial magnate, Agustín
Edwards – the third of his name in Chile. Sanfuentes, for his part,
thwarted Edwards's prospects. Since neither man could reach the 60
percent of votes required under the rules, a compromise candidacy had to
be arranged. It was given to the 75-year-old Ramón Barros Luco. The
Conservatives immediately sent him a letter of support. All parties, for
once, were agreed. For the first time since 1891 a Chilean president was
elected unopposed. The "party truce" won much applause, but in its way
it was a striking symbol of the strange emptiness of Parliamentary
politics.

The decline of the Parliamentary Republic

Ramón Barros Luco holds a special place in the Chilean folk-memory for
two reasons. He gave his name to a popular variety of sandwich (beef and
cheese), which he ordered from (and at) the Confitería Torres, a café in the
Alameda opened in 1877 and closed (sadly) in 2002. And to Barros Luco
is attributed a famous remark (whether he ever made it or not is beside the
point): "there are two types of problem: those that solve themselves and
those that have no solution." He had several times held cabinet office –
sufficiently often, in fact, for Manuel Montt's widow to nickname him

"the Moneda cat." No great initiatives were to be expected from this elderly patrician – the oldest Chilean ever to become president. He himself had a simple style, often strolling with his wife in the Parque Cousiño in the evenings. He affected (though did not feel) an olympian indifference toward cabinet-making, even if he did refuse to accept ministers from the Democratic party on the grounds that they lacked social standing.

It would be wrong, however, to suggest that Barros Luco's five years were simply a period of marking time. There was now growing indignation over the extent of political corruption, opportunely mobilized by a new cross-party, *Liga de Acción Cívica* (Civic Action League), which pressed Congress for reform. In 1914–15 changes in the electoral law deprived municipalities of control over elections: from now onward the electoral registers were to be freshly compiled every nine years, which reduced the extent to which they could be falsified.

Local political squabbles were at this point somewhat overshadowed by a conflict far away, for in August 1914 Europe was plunged into the hideous catastrophe of the Great War. Chile, where sympathies for the Allied and Central Powers were well balanced, remained neutral throughout the war, as did all important Latin American nations (with the notable exception of Brazil). Chilean warships (including a battleship) under construction in England were temporarily transferred to the Royal Navy. The country, of course, was remote from the fighting, but on one occasion the fighting came very close indeed. On November 1, 1914, some forty miles off the coast near Coronel, British and German warships waged their first great naval battle – a British defeat (more than 1,500 men lost their lives) terribly avenged five weeks later off the Falkland Islands. Both Great Britain and imperial Germany violated Chilean territorial sovereignty: with no Chilean warships in the area at the time to enforce the rules of neutrality,[42] the German light cruiser *Dresden* was cornered (March 14, 1915) by the British at Más Afuera in the Juan Fernández islands and was scuttled. The British apologized, the Germans did not.

Chilean newspaper readers (it is a fair guess) found the course of the war more engrossing than the continuing ballet of Parliamentary politics, but the ballet continued nonetheless. With the 1915 presidential election, Juan Luis Sanfuentes at last came into his own, as candidate of the

---

[42] The *Dresden* was not allowed more than twenty-four hours in a neutral port, and exceeded the limit; the British were not allowed to attack. One of the *Dresden*'s officers who subsequently escaped from internment in Chile (on Quiriquina Island in Talcahuano Bay) was Lt. Wilhelm Canaris, later an Admiral, head of German intelligence in World War II. He was executed for plotting against Hitler.

Coalition. The kingmaker became king. It was not an easy victory: amongst the *electores* he had a one-vote lead over his Alliance rival, but Congress ratified his position by 77 votes to 41. Sanfuentes has at least one claim to fame among the Chilean heads of state. He was easily the largest man ever to become president: at his inauguration he had to bend very low to receive the presidential sash. The presidency, he was afterward to say, gave him few moments of pleasure. Parliamentary politicking was worse than ever: he had seventeen cabinets, their average duration being three and a half months. Sanfuentes himself favored Coalition ministries, and mostly got them until the 1918 congressional elections, in which the Alliance made some notable gains – much to Sanfuentes's annoyance.

The Parliamentary Republic was now decomposing fast. We need not fall into the old cliché of historians that the nation was "seething with discontent." History is never quite that simple. Nevertheless, there were many indications by this point that Chile was approaching a conjuncture of sorts. Some were obvious even to the politicians. The Alliance convention of 1915, for example, drew in far more representatives of the parties' grass roots then ever before – "the artisan's blouse, the flashy tie of the Radical assemblyman, the farmer's rough shoe, the sturdy walking-stick of the election agent," as Rivas Vicuña put it,[43] were all on display. (The veteran Radical, Enrique Mac-Iver, disturbed by the sight of so many *siúticos,* kept muttering, "This is a meeting of madmen!") In the 1918 elections, both the Radicals and the artisan-backed Democratic party made impressive gains, the Radicals becoming the biggest delegation (32 deputies) in the Chamber. Part of this success is attributable to the fact that many Radicals were now seeing themselves as more and more a middle-class party.

The embryonic middle class was ready to flex its muscles. But although in 1918–19 an ephemeral "Middle Class Federation" attracted a certain amount of comment, the middle class, distinctly heterogeneous in nature, could not really mobilize in the way the labor movement could. After 1917 the unions enjoyed rapid growth, with a corresponding increase in strikes (more than 130 between 1917 and 1920). A Chilean section of the industrial-syndicalist IWW (Industrial Workers of the World) was organized in 1919, gaining particular strength in Valparaiso though much weakened by government repression the following year. Of greater importance in the longer term was the *Federación de Obreros de Chile,* FOCH (Federation of Chilean Workers), a largely mutualist organization founded in 1909 by a Conservative lawyer. The old *mancomunales* of the north, expertly steered by Luis Emilio Recabarren and his POS,

---

[43] *Historia política y parlamentaria de Chile,* 3 vols. (Santiago, 1964), I, 550.

now began to assume control in the FOCH, which by 1919 was predominantly (though by no means exclusively) socialist in character. Here it is impossible to overlook the impact of the Russian Revolution of 1917 and the triumph of the Bolsheviks. The repercussions were worldwide: in Chile, as in so many other places, workers were enthused and heartened by these epoch-making events.

The workers did not entirely lack allies. Students, too, were becoming increasingly radical in their outward postures. FECH, the student federation founded in 1906, was not initially reforming in outlook, though it had displayed militancy on several notable occasions. In 1909, for instance, it had forced the resignation of the director of the medical school in the University of Chile, and four years later, in a noisy episode, it caused an unpopular papal nuncio to leave the country, ridiculing him by snatching his monsignorial hat and parading it on a donkey down the Alameda the following day. In this affair the students had been backed by anticlerical politicians in Congress. By the late 1910s, however, FECH was actively supporting working-class demands, and expressed its solidarity with the unions during a one-day general strike in Santiago in September 1919.

There was one immediate cause for these manifestations of social discontent: the end of World War I and the sharp recession that immediately followed. Galvanized by the crisis, working-class protest reached new levels: to protest the high cost of food – beans, it was reported, became "almost a luxury item"[44] – a rapidly formed *Asamblea Obrera de Alimentación Nacional* (Workers' Assembly for National Nourishment), representing most sections of organized labor, staged a huge demonstration in Santiago in November 1918, followed by mass meetings in other cities. The government responded by enacting a new Residence Law enabling the authorities to deport foreign agitators (a few such were deported) and by imposing (in February 1919) a two-month state of siege in Santiago and Valparaiso, the first in twenty-five years. The protesters, however, were undaunted, and continued to hold mass meetings. From now on, the labor movement was to be a permanent actor on the Chilean stage.

It remained to be seen whether the political system could adapt successfully to the social pressures so obviously building up after 1918. The Radical and Democratic parties canalized some of the discontent, undoubtedly, but something more was needed. Could a leader be found to embody the confused and contradictory hopes of middle-class and working-class Chile?

It probably never (before March 1915) occurred to Arturo Fortunato

---

[44] *El Mercurio,* October 15, 1920.

Alessandri, a vigorous but conventional Parliamentary politician, six times elected Liberal deputy for Curicó, that he might be just such a leader. In 1915 Alessandri (he was 47 that year) agreed to stand for the Senate in Tarapacá. The district was an apparently impregnable Liberal Democrat fief, run by a classic local caudillo: Arturo del Río, lawyer, businessman, newspaper proprietor, and (from 1909) Senator. Alessandri's unusually dynamic campaign was marked by violence (the candidate himself carried a Smith & Wesson), but also by an undoubted upsurge of popular enthusiasm. He won two-thirds of the vote, and was given a triumphant reception on his return to Santiago. From now on he was always to be known as the "Lion of Tarapacá" – taking over the nickname from a journalist-poet in Iquique who had opposed the del Río machine and thus helped pave the way for the new Lion.

Alessandri's performance in 1915 changed him into a would-be president. He now made no secret of his hopes (in sharp contrast to the discretion favored by previous presidential aspirants) and actively promoted them during a brief spell as minister of the Interior after the Alliance's triumph in the 1918 congressional elections. The more traditionalist Liberals, who had come to loathe Alessandri's passionate style, withdrew from the Alliance in November 1919 to form their own Liberal Union (*Unión Liberal*).

Thus in 1920 two Liberal nominating conventions had to be held. The Liberal Union (Liberals, Liberal Democrats, Nationals) nominated the gentlemanly Luis Barros Borgoño, nephew of the great historian Diego Barros Arana, in whose house he had grown up. The Conservatives pledged their support, and the Coalition renamed itself the National Union (*Unión Nacional*). The Alliance (Liberals, Radicals, Democrats) selected Alessandri on the second ballot. His acceptance speech was imbued with vague but undeniable reforming ardor. He warned that (unlike Riesco or Barros Luco) he *would* be a threat – "to reactionary spirits, to those who resist just and necessary reform." The day after Alessandri's "proclamation" the *Unión Nacional* placed an advertisement in the press with the alarming title HANNIBAL AD PORTAS ("Hannibal at the Gates"), accusing Alessandri, quite absurdly, of "advanced communist tendencies." The ancient Romans would not have displayed such panic. This particular Hannibal, unlike the real one, both reached the gates and marched through them.

8

The Lion and the mule, 1920–38

I am still the Lion. Ibáñez is the mule.

–Arturo Alessandri (1927)

The backwash of the First World War and the 1920s

The end of the First World War ushered in a period of economic and social disturbance in many parts of the world. Chile was no exception. The coming of peace in far-away Europe severely dislocated the Chilean economy, placing additional burdens on a political system which had already demonstrated its inability to deal with less serious dilemmas. These postwar difficulties brought into sharp relief some of the underlying constraints on the economy: overdependence on raw material production, inadequate fiscal and monetary policy, built-in inertia in agriculture. In the end, a combination of economic necessity and political upheaval pushed both the Chilean state and the economy in new directions.

The first and most dramatic effect of the Armistice was to paralyze the *salitreras*. The Allies' Nitrate of Soda Executive abruptly dumped its once valuable stocks on the open market, driving down prices. The result was entirely predictable: in 1919, exports fell by 66 percent. Although recovering dramatically in 1920, production and exports fell again the following year, this time by half. Over 10,000 miners and members of their families fled to Santiago, infecting the city with despair – and smallpox. The government responded as it had in the past, offering subsidies and buying up the surplus nitrate, while the private producers created the *Asociación de Productores de Salitre de Chile* which, like the Nitrate Combinations of old, used quotas to stabilize prices. Once the surpluses had disappeared, nitrate prices and therefore employment did indeed rise – for a while.

Copper production, which had increased between 1914 and 1918, fell in the early postwar years. Here, however, the underlying trend was upward: by the end of the 1920s, the Gran Minería's output (accounting for 90 percent of all copper produced) reached 317,000 tons, approxi-

Table 8.1. Nitrate exports, 1918–24.

	Production (1000s of tons)	Exports (1000s of tons)	Value (US$M 1960)
1918	2,859	2,919	312.6
1919	1,703	803	83.6
1920	2,523	2,746	403.5
1921	1,309	1,193	106.4
1922	1,071	1,252	114.2
1923	1,905	2,242	194.0
1924	2,403	2,333	199.8

Source: Stickell, "Migration and Mining: Labor in Northern Chile in the Nitrate Era, 1830–1930," p. 340; Cariola y Sunkel, *Un siglo de historia económica de Chile*, p. 127.

mately 16 percent of the world market. The copper mines, moreover, began to contribute more to the Chilean economy. In 1925 the government imposed a 6 percent tax on the companies. This impost, in conjunction with another levy, raised the tax rate on copper mining to 12 percent. Moreover, the implementation of new social welfare laws increased the American companies' effective contributions to the central government. Not only did copper now begin to replace nitrates as the Moneda's favorite source of revenue, but more of the Gran Minería's profits remained in Chile than had earlier been the case.

If the First World War gave a boost to the emerging Gran Minería, it also allowed the most indolent hacendados to prosper. Chilean landowners, seeking to fill the void left by the involvement of European and Allied nations in the war, rushed to cultivate more land. Unfortunately, the lack of transport which handicapped the nitrate producers also prevented the haciendas from shipping their produce to Europe. Worse still, the government, anxious to prevent shortages, turned on the hacendados by restricting the export of foodstuffs during the first years of the war. While protecting the consumer, this prohibition hurt the countryside, but the government could not be persuaded to rescind the measure.

Perhaps building on its wartime momentum, agrarian production increased more between 1920 and 1930 than it had over the previous decade; land under cultivation rose by more than half. As always, growth was uneven, some lines doing better than others. Viticulture thrived: production of wine and *chicha* more than doubled in the 1920s (to 327,800,000 liters). The pastoral economy flourished: the number of cattle rose by 10 percent, and there was a still larger increase in the sheep, goat, and pig populations. The staple crops also did well: there were significant increases over the decade in the output of barley (89 percent), maize (90 percent), potatoes (50 percent), and the old mainstay, wheat (50 percent). The use of sowing machines, threshers, reapers, and harvesters now began to spread more widely; by 1930 there were over 600 tractors in Chile.

Yet the hacendados' stranglehold on the Chilean countryside seemed, if possible, even stronger than in the past, leading the veteran politician Malaquías Concha to lament (in 1921): "There is no liberty possible if an entire country's land belongs *to a single individual or to a limited number of people.*"[1] In 1924, one-tenth of all properties covered more than nine-tenths of the land. Some of these properties, admittedly, were ranches whose boundaries contained useless mountain terrain. Even so, in the Central Valley heartland, a mere 0.45 percent of all properties encompassed 52 percent of the area. This highly inequitable land-tenure system seemed resistant to modernization. Machines cost money; inquilinos did not. Landowners, moreover, did not have to fear competition: the growth of urban population ensured a steady market for the produce of the haciendas. Hence with only a relative effort and not much in the way of capital investment, the estates could profit. Only later, when the intrinsic inefficiency of the hacienda system became more obvious, would Chilean governments feel obliged to address the problem: agrarian reform was not yet on the agenda of politics.

Having prospered and flourished during the war, Chilean manufacturers naturally sought to protect and consolidate their recent gains. They pressured the authorities to modernize highways, extend the rail system, and expand the ports. They also persuaded the government (whose appetite for revenue was always healthy) to increase the taxes on foreign imports. In 1921 Congress raised import duties by 50 percent and levied special taxes (sometimes up to 100 percent) on a range of specific items. Whether the result of these laws or not, manufacturing grew dramatically between 1920 and 1928, with significant increases in the output of textiles (by over 250 percent), shoes (140 percent), and beverages (120 percent). Indeed, by the end of the 1920s Chilean manufacturing covered a much wider range of products than ever before, and was now turning out both machinery and consumer durables. This newly acquired depth was to provide a good foundation for the country when the Depression struck.

In retrospect, the Parliamentary period should properly be called the "golden age of borrowing." Between 1891 and 1924 the Moneda's indebtedness had risen by 300 percent.[2] Congress had repeatedly turned

[1] *El Mercurio*, May 15, 1921. Italics in original.

[2] In the period 1870–91 the increase had been only 60 percent.

to foreign and domestic banks in order to finance budget deficits. This process intensified after the war. Between 1920 and 1922, the external and internal debts rose by £6 million and 200 million pesos respectively. Mortgaging future generations in this way might have had some validity if the expenditures had somehow benefited the nation. An enormous portion of the borrowed money, sometimes as much as two-fifths, went to pay the salaries and pensions of civil servants. In 1924 Congress (albeit almost literally at saber point) finally enacted a tax on income, the amount varying according to profession or occupation. Although not progressive, this levy increased direct taxation as a share of government revenues by more than half. In 1925 a further impost was enacted, the *global complementario*, which added a surcharge, varying between 0.05 and 0.70 percent, to the existing taxes. By exempting those earning less than 10,000 pesos annually, this measure introduced a scintilla of equity into the tax system.

Despite such gains as the growth of agriculture and manufacturing (and the emergence of the Gran Minería), the fundamental factor in the Chilean economy remained its dependence on the exploitation of natural resources. This dangerous reliance on foreign markets was highlighted with special clarity by the sharp recession that followed the First World War, whatever the recoveries later on. It was against a background of large-scale unemployment and social unrest that the country faced its first great political turning point of the century.

Alessandri's first presidency

Arturo Alessandri fought the presidential election of 1920 with great vigor. Chile was Tarapacá writ large. His rhetorical gifts were considerable: no other Chilean politician of the twentieth century has equaled him in this respect. He was the nearest any modern Chilean politician has ever come (in a political culture resistant to such things) to being a "charismatic leader." The magic of his name was sufficient, nearly forty years later, to help one of his sons win the Chilean presidency. Stories about his speechmaking abound. He could hold a crowd as few others have been able to do. One of his secrets was the inclusion of carefully placed demotic expressions in his oratory – as when he described the Chilean upper class as *la canalla dorada* ("the gilded canaille") or his supporters as his *querida chusma* ("beloved rabble"). His speeches no longer read well, if they ever did. His repeated and far from original catchphrase, *"El odio nada engendra; sólo el amor es fecundo"* ("Hatred creates nothing; only love is fertile"), however unexceptionable as a sentiment, seems politically vacuous – but it clearly moved his audiences. Everything was in the timing and delivery. The man himself remains controversial.

Yet whatever our verdict, he was a larger-than-life figure. Winston Churchill once remarked of Joseph Chamberlain that he was a man who "made the weather." Something of the sort could be said about Alessandri, the elected leader who held power longer than anyone else in Chilean history.

His frontal assault on the Parliamentary Republic generated unprecedented excitement. René Millar's close analysis of the 1920 election shows that all traditional methods of Parliamentary campaigning were used, but that at the same time a significant section of the electorate – in both middle class and working class – "felt strongly attracted by Alessandri's personality and by the direction of his campaign, to the point of identifying with him and unreservedly backing him."[3] To this extent the "revolt of the electorate" in 1920 was real enough. The result was very close, Alessandri just leading in the electoral college but slightly behind on the popular vote. The National Union was clearly tempted to bar his way by fair means or foul. Alessandri, determined not to be robbed of victory, kept up the pressure with repeated mass demonstrations, which the Union saw as heavy with implied menace.

This extraordinary election still held surprises. Three weeks after the poll, there was a sudden general mobilization and a dispatch of troops to the north to face an imminent attack from Bolivia – which never materialized. The public christened it "Don Ladislao's War" – the Conservative Ladislao Errázuriz being the minister of War responsible. Was it the intention to provide a patriotic distraction for the already excited population? The evidence is unclear.[4] Patriotic emotions certainly ran high, inevitably entangled with the politics of the moment. A mob (incited by Union politicians) assaulted the Santiago headquarters of the pacifist-inclined FECH: books were taken out and burned, the bar drunk dry. In Punta Arenas, the anti-war sentiments of workers led to a union headquarters being attacked and burned, with the loss of twelve lives.

Alessandri refused to be intimidated. Several politicians (including Barros Borgoño) appealed for calm. The precedent of 1896 was invoked: a Tribunal of Honor was set up to check the electoral votes. While it was meeting, one of its members, the elderly Liberal Fernando Lazcano, as if to add to the drama, had a heart attack and died. (He had earlier been a mentor to the young Alessandri but was by 1920 his bitter adversary.) The Tribunal eventually declared that Alessandri had "the better right"

---

[3] René Millar C., *La elección presidencial de 1920* (Santiago, 1981), p. 213.

[4] The Santiago garrison was largely *alessandrista*, a reason for sending it elsewhere; on the other hand, the colonel who set off the alarm about the imaginary Bolivian irredentist attack was himself a fervent supporter of Alessandri. Alessandri's memoirs show that he himself later believed that the mobilization was decreed in good faith.

to be president. On December 23 he was duly installed, amidst scenes of delirious public enthusiasm.

It was a false dawn. The many Chileans who had pinned their hopes on immediate social legislation and constitutional reform (Alessandri's two main themes, strongly reiterated in his message to Congress on June 1, 1921) were soon sadly disappointed. Old habits die hard, and Parliamentary habits were deeply entrenched. Alessandri had to face the stubborn obstructionism of National Union congressmen, especially marked in the Senate, where the Conservatives Ladislao Errázuriz and Rafael Luis Gumucio led determined offensives, while in the Chamber, Manuel Rivas Vicuña was scarcely less eloquent. Alessandri's own Liberal Alliance proved far less coherent and malleable than he would have liked. The Parliamentary rules had not yet changed: the president had little room for maneuver. Despite his early efforts to maintain ministerial continuity, he was forced to reconstruct his cabinets almost as often as his Parliamentary predecessors. The record of Congress was not completely negative: in 1923 it approved (in principle) the introduction of an income tax. But it failed to make progress with social legislation; the Labor Code presented by Alessandri in 1921 quickly floundered (and was made to flounder) amidst the complexities of parliamentary procedure.

Appeals to the electorate gave Alessandri little relief: in the elections of March 1921, the Alliance improved its position in the Chamber but failed to break the Union stranglehold on the Senate. Three years later, Alessandri himself broke with tradition by campaigning strongly in the south (no previous president had campaigned while in office) and by uses of executive power that were somewhat reminiscent of the bad old days of "intervention." The Alliance won both houses. A Mapuche entered the Chamber of Deputies for the first time. Many (perhaps most) of the new congressmen were from the middle class, which Alessandri had actively promoted in staffing government posts. This apparent advantage was undermined by the narrowness of his Senate majority and, more important, by fractiousness in the Alliance itself. A section of the now powerful Radical party (7 senators, 37 deputies in 1924) turned against the president, accusing him of personalism. A particularly fierce speech on this topic was made by the Radical deputy Pablo Ramírez in July 1924. As in Balmaceda's time, the central political struggle seemed to be defining itself as a struggle between a forward-looking president and an obstructive legislature – a Congress unable or unwilling to act. To rally his supporters, Alessandri dramatized the situation with his silver tongue, with no great result. The euphoria of 1920 gradually shifted into a mood of disappointment and frustration. The Parliamentary Republic had not, after all, been broken. Who would cut the Gordian knot?

There were those who in any case were quickly disillusioned with

Alessandri. Organized labor got little from him. Initially, it is true, he mediated personally in one or two strikes, securing favorable settlements for the workers. But he soon became impatient with their demands, and was adamantly opposed to the feeble attempts now being made to extend unionization to the countryside. Hacendados, in any case, had no difficulty countering these: Alessandri publicly expressed his support for them in May 1921. It was to be another forty years before the rural poor entered the political scene as actors in their own right.

For the urban working class, the situation was exacerbated after 1920 by the serious downturn in the nitrate industry. (Between December 1920 and December 1921 monthly production fell from 222,315 to 75,443 metric tons; exports fell by half.) By 1922 seventy *oficinas* had closed down, and at least 20,000 unemployed workers had moved south, where they urged Congress, "if there is any patriotism in the hearts of its members," to approve public works projects.[5] They were easily recruited for demonstrations and meetings by the FOCH and by Recabarren's followers. On the nitrate pampa itself, at the San Gregorio *oficina*, a battle between troops and strikers in February 1921 left more than forty dead (one of them the English manager). This event merely served to deepen working-class estrangement from the Alessandri presidency. Recabarren had been elected to Congress as one of two POS deputies in 1921, and was continuing to press his strategy of electoral action.

His conversion to Marxism was now complete. In January 1922, meeting at Rancagua just after a FOCH convention in the same city, his POS voted to turn itself into the Communist Party of Chile and to apply for membership of the Comintern. (Recabarren himself committed suicide in December 1924.) The FOCH fell rapidly under Communist control. At this stage, however, it by no means represented the trade union movement as a whole: its main strength was in the coal mines of the south and the nitrate ports; its dues-paying membership probably amounted to no more than 20,000. In the leadership of strikes in the early 1920s, FOCH was less important than the Chilean section of the IWW, which recovered from the repression of 1920, and was still very active, especially in Valparaiso. Many other unions remained anarcho-syndicalist in outlook, and resisted Recabarren's political emphasis. (FECH, the student federation, was also strongly influenced by anarchism by this stage.) Ideological dissensions, however, were only one factor that weakened organized labor after its upsurge of activity in 1918–20. Employers' associations grew steadily after 1920 and became more aggressive, as was shown in the failure of the IWW-sponsored general strike in Valparaiso in February 1922. High unemployment in any case made it much easier for employers to hire scabs.

[5] *El Mercurio*, February 24, 1921.

Alessandri's vision for Chile certainly allowed a space for organized labor, but he insisted that it should be a regulated space, that appropriate labor legislation should be introduced to replace the laissez-faire framework that had so far prevailed. Many educated Chilean minds were by now perplexed by the problem, spurred by an acute awareness of social change in Chile and of course, taking note of the European perturbations that followed the First World War. State intervention in labor matters was viewed with increasing favor among intellectuals. Such concerns, however, were not well reflected in Congress, which continued to play the Parliamentary game as if nothing had happened in 1920. There was, admittedly, a growing movement in favor of some kind of constitutional reform. On February 1, 1924, the parties of the Alliance and the Union signed an agreement in favor of changes in parliamentary procedure, to limit votes of censure to the Chamber of Deputies, to institute closure of debates by simple majority, and to curtail the use of delaying tactics on budget legislation. The party leaders also agreed to introduce a congressional *dieta* or salary (as in the U.S. Congress since its start, or the British House of Commons since 1908): a rate of 30,000 pesos was proposed for Senators, 15,000 pesos for deputies. A constitutional amendment was required for this: in order to speed things up, the government sought an "interpretative law" of the kind that had been used in 1865 on the issue of freedom of worship. This perfectly reasonable scheme aroused intense public hostility, largely because it was the only law to emerge from the *Unión-Alianza* agreement, apparently taking precedence over the social legislation Alessandri had proposed.

As the winter of 1924 came to its end, the stalemate between president and Congress showed no sign of relaxing. Yet this was no simple replay of 1891. Alessandri's popular support was much wider than Balmaceda's had been. The new social forces needed to find a way into the system. How could the deadlock be broken? The answer came with surprising speed. The Gordian knot was cut, not by politicians, but by the armed forces. It was they rather than Alessandri who finally buried the Parliamentary Republic. In ten extraordinary days in September 1924, the armed forces first shook, then destroyed, Alessandri's presidency, and imposed military rule on Chile. The rules of the game suddenly changed – as did the game itself.

Military intervention and a new Constitution

Army officers' awareness of the defects of Parliamentary government was probably as acute as that of any group of Chileans. They had come into very obvious contact with the "social question" through their intermittent role in containing urban disturbances and labor militancy. Moreover, the law of obligatory military service in 1900 brought them into regular contact with the poorer classes, for conscripts were always predominantly workers or peasants. Quite apart from this, dissatisfaction with the Parliamentary Republic's military policies impelled a number of officers, toward 1910, to form a secret "Military League" (*Liga Militar*) with clearly political intent. The short-lived League contemplated a military coup to place the historian Gonzalo Bulnes (then writing his classic account of the War of the Pacific) in the Moneda. Bulnes was in on the plan but then refused to go through with it. A more serious conspiracy, partly motivated by exaggerated military fears of "Bolshevism" and labor militancy, was detected by the government in 1919, its leading figures being Generals Guillermo Armstrong and Manuel Moore. Sixty or so officers were found guilty; nearly half of these were punished.

Alessandri's failure to make headway with his program undoubtedly swelled the ranks of the disaffected in the Army. In their hatred of Alessandri, Union politicians did not hesitate to seek the support of senior officers. Another secret society was formed – TEA, "firebrand" (also an acronym for "tenacity, enthusiasm, abnegation") – with the ultimate aim of ridding the country of Alessandri. Senior officers, however, were one thing. Officers of middle and junior rank were much less interested in a conservative restoration than in securing national "reorganization" under firm leadership. Soon after the opening of the new Congress in June 1924, groups of such officers began meeting regularly at the *Club Militar* (in the Alameda), with much indignation being voiced over the proposed congressional *dieta*. Prominent in these meetings were the effusive, emotional Major Marmaduke Grove, deputy director of the Military School, and the cool, taciturn Major Carlos Ibáñez, commander of the Cavalry School. We shall hear plenty more of both.

On the evening of Tuesday, September 2, a group of about fifty officers crowded into the Senate gallery and loudly applauded those senators speaking against the *dieta* bill. The scene was repeated the following night. When asked to withdraw by the minister of War, the officers did so, but defiantly, with an ostentatious rattling of swords. On September 4, the inspector-general of the Army, General Luis Altamirano, informed the cabinet that the high command supported the officers concerned. The commander of the all-important Santiago garrison, General Pedro Pablo Dartnell, made it known that no disciplinary action would be taken. Faced with this incipient mutiny, Alessandri agreed to receive a military delegation at the palace the following day. Overnight, at the Cavalry School, Major Ibáñez and his aide, Captain Alejandro Lazo, drew up a list of demands: these included the suppression of the *dieta*, an immediate income tax law, enactment of Alessandri's labor code, improvements in military conditions, and the dismissal of three cabinet ministers (the minister of War among them). Ibáñez also suggested the formation of a "military and naval committee" (*Junta militar y naval*) to watch over events. All his suggestions were accepted at a meeting of officers at the *Club Militar* on the morning of Friday, September 5. The new committee then went to see the president.

The two-hour meeting was tense and at times heated, Alessandri refusing to dismiss the three cabinet ministers. The cabinet resolved the issue for him by immediately resigning. With little room for maneuver at this point, Alessandri appointed General Altamirano as head of a new ministry. After the weekend, on Monday, September 8, Altamirano appeared before Congress and demanded the passage of a package of eight laws, including Alessandri's labor code. With barely a word of protest, the laws were passed, signed, and promulgated, all in a matter of hours. Events rapidly took a more serious turn. Despite its success in intimidating the legislators into action, the military-naval committee announced that it would remain in existence until administrative and political "purification" was complete. For Alessandri, now virtually a captive of the military, the position was intolerable. He resigned the presidency and at around 3:00 A.M. on September 9 moved into the United States embassy, at the suggestion of the ambassador, William M. Collier. On the evening of the next day, Alessandri boarded a special train at the Mapocho station to start his journey into exile, with Italy his ultimate destination. The tenth day of this extraordinary drama – September 11 – saw the installation of a governing Junta consisting of General Altamirano and his cabinet colleagues Admiral Francisco Nef and General Juan Bennett.

With the creation of the Junta, which was greeted with remarkable calm by the public, the initiative once more passed to the senior officers, whose main connections were with the National Union. The would-be reformers in the military-naval committee suspected very quickly that the ground was being prepared for a conservative restoration, most probably to be embodied in the presidential candidacy of the arch-Conservative, Ladislao Errázuriz. The Navy, for its part, strongly supported the Junta, and when its officers withdrew from the committee, the committee dissolved. Its most active members (Ibáñez and Grove as always to the fore) now turned to conspiracy. Their resolve was sharpened with the formal announcement of Errázuriz's candidacy (January 8), which also brought a demand for the return of Alessandri from the Radical and Democratic parties. On Friday, January 23, 1925, the conspirators struck: troops surrounded the Moneda, Altamirano and Nef (Bennett was out of town) were arrested, and a new Junta was installed under General Pedro Pablo Dartnell. The Naval high command, however, put up a show of fierce resistance to the new government. For two or three days there was acute tension, dissipated only by signs of indiscipline on the lower deck, the timely mediation of Agustín Edwards, and the inclusion of an admiral

(Carlos Ward) and a civilian (Emilio Bello Codesido) in the Junta. The key position of minister of War was taken by Colonel (as he now was) Ibáñez. Telegrams were sent to Alessandri, now staying in Italy, inviting him to return and resume his presidency.

The second Junta, pledged as it was to restore the "revolution" betrayed by the senior officers in September 1924, knew that its power-base was distinctly fragile. It had to surmount an early moment of danger: a revolt by the Valdivia infantry regiment (February 27) was quickly tamed, after which Ladislao Errázuriz and a dozen or so other Union politicians (clearly implicated) were banished for eighteen months. Faced with such enemies, the Junta sought allies in the wider society. Its attitude toward labor, for instance, seemed favorable. It responded sympathetically to a large-scale rent strike in the *conventillos* that began within days of the January 23 coup. A new rent law (February 13, 1925) set up housing committees (*tribunales de vivienda*) with the power to lower rents. Landlords, however, were able to modify the composition of these committees in ways favorable to themselves. (This had the effect of splitting the rent-strike movement, with Communists trying to work through them in quest of new support, anarchists continuing resistance.) Clearly the military reformers could act only within certain limits.

Alessandri arrived back in Santiago on March 20. Jubilant crowds escorted him from the Central Station to the Moneda, from whose balcony he instructed them once again about the difference between hatred and love. There were those who wished to rename the Alameda after him, and the Junta had so decreed: Alessandri modestly suggested that if any name were to be attached to the city's main avenue it should be that of O'Higgins – and it was in this manner that the avenue gained its modern name (pompously lengthened in 1979). Alessandri's mind, needless to say, was on more important matters. Realizing that he was in power again on military sufferance, he prudently retained Colonel Ibáñez as minister of War. He resisted all suggestions that Congress (dissolved in September 1924) should be recalled, preferring to govern by decree, using this opportunity to enact (among other things) his long-cherished scheme for a central bank (August 25, 1925). Although he was willing to make symbolic gestures toward organized labor (May 1 now became a public holiday), he reverted to the old methods of countering serious unrest: in May, when strikes broke out in Tarapacá, the Navy landed troops, and a savage massacre of nitrate workers occurred (June 3) at the La Coruña *oficina*, the number of victims running into the hundreds.

Alessandri's unavoidable priority during these months was constitutional reform. On April 7 he named a Grand Consultative Commission of 53 members (it more than doubled in size later) representing all political parties, including the Communists.[6] A smaller subcommittee worked on the actual draft, holding some thirty-five sessions. The proposed text was presented to the full Commission on July 23, when Alessandri himself spoke. The Radical, Conservative, and Communist members opposed the draft; Alessandri's words did not deter them; the day was saved by a pointed speech from General Mariano Navarrete, the military delegate, who politely conveyed the Army's opinion that the text should be approved. It was. A plebiscite was held on August 3: the turnout was poor (45 percent), but 93 percent of those who bothered to vote deposited the red voting slips that signified acceptance of the new Constitution. It was duly promulgated at a ceremony on September 18. A new Congress was elected in November.

The Constitution of 1925 was by no means a complete return to presidentialism. It did, however, shift the balance back toward the executive. The president was now to be elected every six years (by direct popular vote), the Congress every four (under a system of proportional representation). The "periodic" laws were eliminated: only the budget now had to be approved annually, and, in the event of delay, the president was given the right to do what Balmaceda had done on January 4, 1891. Congressional votes of censure (a matter of practice, not law) were nullified. The previous congressional right to validate its members' electoral credentials was now transferred to an independent tribunal. Legislation declared "urgent" by the president had now to be dispatched expeditiously. The procedure for constitutional amendment (so laborious in the 1833 document) was greatly streamlined. Provincial assemblies (abolished in 1833) were restored: this provision, however, was never acted on. The first of several "transitory dispositions" of the Constitution separated Church and State, the government agreeing to pay the Church a subsidy of 2.5 million pesos for five years. Determined to lay this old issue to rest, Alessandri had put his time in Rome to good use, arranging the deal directly with Pope Pius XI and Vatican officials. It was accepted only with reluctance by the Chilean hierarchy and clergy. It is difficult to see that it altered the place of the Church in Chilean life.

The new constitution, while enhancing presidential power, did not in any way affect or diminish the role of the political parties. As will be seen, this role was if anything strengthened in the years that followed. We might speculate here that the legacy of the Parliamentary years was a

---

[6] The Commission (with additions) included 26 Radicals, 16 Liberals, 14 Conservatives, 14 Democrats, 10 Liberal Democrats, 6 Communists, and 2 Nationals. The remaining thirty or so members were independents of various kinds.

very deep one. Party spirit had come to seem inseparable from the Chilean way of life, and competition between parties as natural as the air Chileans breathed. The parties, in fact, were becoming fundamental "building blocks" of society – their networks linking Santiago and the provinces, their influence often extending into spheres other than politics. Once the 1925 constitution began to function properly (after 1932), the parties found it a perfectly congenial framework within which to operate.

For the time being, however, it did not function properly. Chile's time of troubles was not yet over. With Alessandri's term due to end in December 1925, a new president had to be elected. Alessandri himself favored a single candidate, possibly his Liberal friend Armando Jaramillo. Meanwhile, there was a sudden groundswell of support for the minister of War, Colonel Ibáñez, with whom Alessandri's relations had now become very strained. Nobody, of course, could yet see how this mutual antipathy would overshadow the next two decades of Chilean history. At the end of September, Ibáñez received a petition signed by members of most parties, urging him to stand for the presidency. He accepted the invitation. Since this seemed to be an official candidacy, the cabinet resigned – all its members except Ibáñez. The colonel published an open letter to Alessandri, refusing point-blank to resign and insisting that all presidential decrees henceforth carry his signature as well as the president's. This request, technically legal (since Ibáñez was now the only minister in office), can be seen only as a deliberate provocation. Alessandri's response was immediate: he appointed his old rival of 1920, Luis Barros Borgoño, as minister of the Interior, named him vice-president, and then on October 2, 1925, resigned the presidency for a second time. But he would be back.

The Ibáñez regime, 1927–31

If Carlos Ibáñez remains one of the more enigmatic figures of Chilean history, the main reason is that he was (unlike his great rival Alessandri) a man of few words. "I have always believed," he once (doubtless more than once) said, "that one should speak only when one has something to say"[7] – not a philosophy that has ever won much support among politicians, Chilean or otherwise. Ibáñez's army career had been a successful and conventional one; he had been known as "Boots" Ibáñez at the military school. Unlike his contemporaries, he had experienced combat: in 1906, when on secondment in El Salvador as a military instructor, he took part in a brief battle between that country and Guatemala, and was decorated by the Salvadorans. Ibáñez was proud of this exploit. There

---

[7] Luis Correa Prieto, *El presidente Ibáñez* (Santiago, 1962), p. 105.

was little in his record to suggest that he was likely to become a national leader. He himself was to say, repeatedly, that this role had been forced on him by "the circumstances and my enemies." His behavior after September 1924, however, shows that this cannot possibly have been the whole truth.

After Alessandri's second resignation, Ibáñez was the most powerful man in Chile. But his position was not yet unassailable. Several high-ranking officers discouraged his presidential candidacy. *Reculer pour mieux sauter* – Ibáñez understood the principle perfectly: he was a master of the tactical resignation which is somehow never accepted. He nonetheless insisted that the parties find a common candidate. Their choice fell on the Liberal Democrat, Emiliano Figueroa Larraín (the vice-president of 1910), who was elected (October 1925) with 72 percent of the vote. His unexpected contender, Dr. José Santos Salas, a former army surgeon and popular minister of Social Welfare under the second military Junta, polled surprisingly well, backed by (among others) the Communist party – which elected five deputies and one senator to the new Congress.

Although by no means the colorless personality he is often made out to be, Figueroa Larraín was far too much the traditional Parliamentary politician to make a success of the presidency. He was anyway not much interested in the job. Congressional in-fighting and attacks on the government once again became the order of the day. In these circumstances, further moves by Ibáñez were inevitable. In February 1927 he maneuvered himself into the ministry of the Interior (this was the real start of his government), and not long afterward his efforts to purge the judiciary forced Figueroa Larraín to take leave (thus making Ibáñez vice-president) and then to resign. Ibáñez now had political support from nearly every quarter, and was elected president on May 23, 1927, with 98 percent of the vote (on an 83 percent turnout). Just before his inauguration on July 2, a new minister of the Interior, President Balmaceda's son Enrique, handed him the presidential sash entrusted to him by his father with the request that it should be placed only on a true national leader. Ibáñez, said Enrique Balmaceda, *was* that long-awaited leader.

There were many who agreed with this judgment. Public support for Ibáñez seems to have been substantial, at least while economic conditions favored him, as they did until 1930. After the upheavals of 1924–25, after the apparent relaxing of the bonds of discipline in Chilean society, the appeal of a "strong man" was undeniable: many parallels were drawn with O'Higgins, Portales, and Manuel Montt. The historian Alberto Edwards, whose classic essay *La fronda aristocrática* appeared in 1928, asserted that Ibáñez's "great service" to Chile lay in his "radical reconstruction of the fact of authority."[8] The regime Ibáñez began constructing in February 1927 was unquestionably authoritarian. Ibáñez himself was by no means unhappy when described as "the Chilean Mussolini." Restrictions were placed on the press. Informers proliferated. Upward of 200 politicians (from Conservatives to Communists) were banished or "relegated": Alessandri (partly for making the remark we have used as the epigraph for this chapter) was expelled in October 1927, settling eventually in Paris. Vowing to extirpate "Communism and Anarchism," Ibáñez ordered the repression of the Communist party (it was outlawed in March 1927, and many of its leaders were sent to Más Afuera) and a ruthless assault (including murders) on the labor movement, from which it did not recover until the 1930s, although many workers joined the "legal unions" that were now sponsored by the new regime: these may have had as many as 50,000 members by 1930.

The politicians were by now thoroughly chastened. Congress, in an uncharacteristically submissive mood, delegated many of its prerogatives to the cabinet, where Ibáñez had a powerful collaborator in Pablo Ramírez, his strong-minded finance minister – Alessandri's assailant of 1924. He was given decree powers in August 1927. (Ramírez was a man of humor: he said that he would like to shoot all landowners so as to stimulate their successors to higher production.) At the end of 1929, Ibáñez insisted that the party leaders devise a single list of candidates for the 1930–34 Congress, thus making an election unnecessary. This was the so-called "Thermal Congress": Ibáñez approved the list while at the thermal spa near Chillán. His own efforts to create a party (CRAC: Republican Confederation for Civic Action) were not very serious. For all his drive to reform and reorganize, Ibáñez was not attracted by the "corporatist" schemes advocated by some of his supporters.

With his powers thus greatly reinforced, Ibáñez imposed a permanent mark on Chile. In one respect, the comparison with Balmaceda seems very apt: a large-scale program of public works was now set in train. Between 1928 and 1931, the Moneda invested almost 760 million pesos in a variety of useful projects: drains, roads, bridges, barracks, prisons, airfields, port facilities, 500 kilometers of branch-lines for the railways, the new south façade of the Moneda, the presidential summer residence (Cerro Castillo) at Viña del Mar. The public administration (much expanded in the mid-1920s as the new labor legislation came into effect, and as the state began to intervene more actively in the economy) was rationalized and overhauled: a new *Contraloría General* (General Comptrollership) was created in 1927 to watch over the bureaucracy and the constitutionality of fiscal measures. Ibáñez also succeeded in bringing a

---

[8] *La fronda aristocrática*, 7th ed. (Santiago, 1972), p. 266.

degree of order to the vexed question of property rights in the provinces between the Bío Bío and Puerto Montt, where the conflicting claims of the state, private landowners, and the Mapuche had been hopelessly tangled for decades, the losers being the Mapuche, one-third of whose assigned land had by this time been usurped. Farther south still, settlement was started in the empty Aysén territory.

In the diplomatic sphere, Ibáñez was able to resolve the long-standing wrangle over Tacna-Arica, which had bedeviled relations with Peru since the War of the Pacific. It had become the western hemisphere's Schleswig-Holstein Question. Ibáñez re-established diplomatic relations with Peru (in effect suspended since 1910) and, partly through the good offices of the United States, finally secured a direct deal (June 1929). Tacna now reverted to Peru, Arica remaining in Chile, which paid Peru US$6 million. The new frontier was satisfactorily delineated by 1932.

Ibáñez did not neglect his most obvious sources of power. A major reform of the police was undertaken in 1927, with the fusion of all local forces with the Carabinero Regiment (founded in 1906). The new 19,000-strong national police force, Carabineros de Chile, with its high standards of smartness and discipline, came in time to be seen as the finest in Latin America. In the short term it was naturally a bastion of the Ibáñez regime. But it is fair to note, too, that in all its subsequent history, Carabineros has[9] shown particular veneration for its founder. Meanwhile, the Army (25,400 men, 1,200 officers in 1928) was kept under strict control by a loyal minister of War, General Bartolomé Blanche. (Ibáñez himself was not promoted to the rank of general until 1930.) The temper of the Navy, whose high command was quietly purged, was sweetened by the six modern British-built destroyers which arrived in 1929. The decisive innovation of these years, however, was the creation of FACH, the Chilean air force (March 1930). Planes and officers were transferred from the military and naval aviation branches which had grown up over the previous seventeen years. Among the early responsibilities of the FACH, it might be noted here, was the operation of the country's first airline, the *Línea Aeropostal Santiago-Arica* (March 1929) – from 1932 onward known as LAN (*Línea Aérea Nacional*) or LAN-Chile.

The backcloth for much of Ibáñez's time in power was prosperity. Economic conditions had so improved by the mid-1920s that more than forty nitrate *oficinas* reopened; and employment on the *pampa* reached its all-time high (60,000). This prosperity proved ephemeral. There was no way of returning to the good old days, because foreign competitors,

---

[9] As readers of crime reports in Chilean newspapers will know, Carabineros is always treated as a singular noun.

Table 8.2. Nitrate industry, 1925–34.

	Oficinas	Workers	Production (metric tons)	Exports (metric tons)	Price (US$ per ton)
1925	96	60,800	2,532,000	2,518,933	44.55
1926	91	38,118	2,016,698	1,668,169	43.12
1927	67	35,778	1,614,084	2,271,482	42.59
1928	69	58,493	3,164,824	2,832,899	37.18
1929	38	44,464	3,233,231	2,896,946	36.78
1930	21	44,100	2,445,834	1,785,728	34.20
1931			1,225,900		28.82
1932	11	8,535	694,496	243,391	22.32
1933	13	8,486	437,655	669,232	18.87
1934	17	14,133	812,368	587,703	18.80

Source: A. Lawrence Stickell, "Migration and Mining: Labor in Northern Chile in the Nitrate Era, 1830–1930" (Unpub. Ph.D. diss., University of Indiana, 1979), p. 341; Sergio Ceppi et al., *Chile: 100 años de industria* (Santiago, 1983), p. 174; Thomas O'Brien, "Rich Beyond the Dreams of Avarice: The Guggenheims in Chile," *Business History Review*, 63 (1989), p. 134.

especially Germany, began using the Haber-Bosch process to produce synthetic ammonia. This nitrate-substitute quickly glutted the market, depressing prices and slashing the nitrate producers' profits.

It seemed for a while that the Chilean nitrate industry might go out of business altogether. However, the Guggenheim interests (engaged in the industry since 1916) now introduced a new technique (using refrigeration) to speed up the extraction of nitrate. Since the new technology increased tenfold the yield from cheap, low-grade ore, the Guggenheims believed that they could compete with the synthetics. But despite their innovations, which also enabled them to extract iodine and sodium sulfate from nitrates, and an investment of over US$130 million, the Guggenheims were not able to revive the *salitreras* for very long. Thanks to the export tax, Chilean nitrates still cost more than the synthetics. Over and above this the German government, anxious to protect its own flourishing chemical industry, prohibited the importation of *salitre* from Chile. Thus, by the late 1920s, the Chilean share of the world market fell to less than a quarter.

Arguing that the export duty seriously handicapped their ability to sell nitrate, the Guggenheims pressured the government to rescind the levy. But here the dream of achieving prosperity through tax cuts and new technology clashed with Ibáñez's own priorities. The dictator saw the nitrate industry as a source of both revenue and employment. Rather than become adversaries, the Guggenheims and Ibáñez decided to go into partnership: in 1931, they formed COSACH – *Compañía de Salitre de*

Chile (Nitrate Company of Chile). The new corporation, half state-owned, was to issue bonds to acquire all the remaining *salitreras*. Once guaranteed a monopoly, COSACH would process the ore and market the refined nitrates. In return for abrogating the export tax, the Chilean government was to receive US$80 million over a four-year period; after that, it would share in the profits or losses of the new corporation. Chileans were, additionally, to constitute at least 80 percent of COSACH's workforce. Seeking to reconcile Ibáñez's economic nationalism with the Guggenheims' need for profit, COSACH failed to benefit either party. Per capita output rose dramatically for a while, but the new cost-saving technology soon slimmed down the workforce COSACH sought to protect.

By the mid-1920s, just before the Ibáñez regime began, the government had enlisted the advice of Edwin Kemmerer, the American "Money Doctor of the Andes," who was asked to overhaul the country's fiscal and tax systems. In short order Kemmerer (an economics professor at Princeton) restored the gold standard, created a Central Bank, and reformed the notoriously inefficient rail system. He also made the tax system more efficient but somewhat fairer, abolishing numerous tax exemptions, and compounding this audacity with a new 6 percent tax on virtually all types of economic activity and a special 6 percent levy on the copper companies. The combination of Kemmerer's tonic measures and the return of political stability encouraged foreign investment. Manufacturing, as we have seen, continued to grow. Nitrates seemed to be holding their own, and copper, like some astrological sign, was in the ascent – as was the share of revenues provided by internal taxes. (By 1926 internal taxes generated 215 million pesos, approximately half of what customs duties yielded.)

Despite this improvement, the customs house still remained the mainstay of the tax system, and neither customs duties nor the new direct taxes provided adequate revenues. Ibáñez, like his predecessors Alessandri and Figueroa Larraín (who between them increased the country's debts by £2 million and approximately US$70 million), turned to large-scale borrowing. In fairness, by no means all of the loans contracted by Ibáñez and Pablo Ramírez were used to patch up gaps in the fiscal fabric. More than his predecessors (more even than Balmaceda), Ibáñez was an economic nationalist who believed that government "should resolve and execute, not postpone, the solution of the nation's problems."[10] Hence the public works programs and spending on infrastructure already mentioned, which were notable enough.

In 1927–28 Ibáñez founded two useful development banks, the *Caja de Crédito Agrario* (Agrarian Credit Bank) and the *Caja de Crédito Minero*

---

[10] Patricio Bermedo, "Prosperidad económica bajo Carlos Ibáñez," *Historia*, 24 (1989), p. 62.

(Mining Credit Bank). Because they lacked sufficient collateral, smaller farms (unlike the haciendas) had traditionally had little access to capital. The *Caja de Crédito Agrario*, however, accepted land, crops, livestock, or equipment as security for long-term, low-interest development loans, and also provided inexpensive fertilizer, seeds, and livestock. The *Caja de Crédito Minero*, like its agrarian counterpart, provided funds for small-scale mining operations. Typical of Ibáñez's economic nationalism, it favored local interests, lending money only if Chileans owned 75 percent of the mine in question. (Foreigners could obtain credit only if they had lived in Chile for more than five years and on condition that 75 percent of the wages they paid went to Chilean nationals.)

The *Instituto de Crédito Industrial* (Industrial Credit Institute), created in 1928, used pension funds as well as government money to stimulate manufacturing. Accepting plant equipment as security, it also lent money to industrialists, providing technical advice as well as financing the modernization or expansion of plants. As with the other banks, the *Instituto* enjoyed substantial success, funneling credit to the metallurgical sector as well as to plants turning out furniture, textiles, food, and beverages. In 1928 Congress "authorized" Ibáñez to raise tariffs (by between 35 and 50) percent on imports competing with local production. He was empowered to reduce levies on essential imports, such as medicine, by up to 25 percent, and by up to 50 percent on materials benefiting the metallurgical, mining, or nitrate industries. At its discretion, the Moneda was also allowed to grant specific exemptions on raw materials or foreign machinery needed in local manufacturing.

The most questionable side of Ibáñez's economic management was that he mortgaged the country's future. By 1930 Chile owed American, British, and Swiss banks a total of £62 million – more than twice the foreign debt of 1920. At the time these loans were made, however, the Chilean economy seemed more than capable of supporting the increased debt. In 1928–29, nitrate revenues were ample. Domestic taxes were by now providing the government almost 30 percent of its income, nearly as much as the customs house. The government's fiscal policies thus seemed sound: there was a balanced budget and a trade surplus; the Chilean peso had stabilized, as had the money supply; bank reserves remained above the minimum levels required; and the gold supply seemed adequate for the nation's needs.

No authoritarian ruler, however successful in delivering prosperity, can expect to be immune from attempts at overthrow. Alessandri, the "king over the water," was behind most of the conspiracies against Ibáñez. The first of these was hatched in a hotel in Calais (January 1928), by Alessandri, Colonel Marmaduke Grove (who had fallen out with Ibáñez), and two other Chilean officers: the "Pact of Dover," as it became known (on the strength of a sighting of Alessandri and others in that English port by a Chilean agent a few days later), led to the "relegation" of a number of *alessandristas* (including Alessandri's son Eduardo) to Easter Island, but had no other consequences. In September 1930, Grove, General Enrique Bravo (one of the Calais conspirators), and others flew in a red Fokker trimotor from San Rafael, Argentina, to Concepción, in the belief that the garrison would rise against Ibáñez. It did not, and Grove and Bravo, too, soon found themselves on Easter Island. Ibáñez, it must be said here, was not above orchestrating completely fictitious plots against himself: a much-publicized attempt to blow up the Maipó railway bridge while his train was crossing it (December 1930) was the most celebrated instance.

In the end, General Ibáñez was defeated not by Alessandri's remorseless plotting but by the Wall Street crash and the onset of the Depression. Its effects were felt in Chile in the second half of 1930.

The fall of Ibáñez and the months of turbulence

Like a degenerative disease, the U.S. stock market crash progressively eroded Chile's economic prosperity. As the international economy slumped, the price of copper and nitrate went into something like free-fall. Between 1929 and 1933 copper output plummeted from 317,000 to 163,000 tons. This abrupt decline, while clearly painful, was compounded by a drop in the price from 17.47 to 7.03 cents per pound: the value of the country's most lucrative export fell from US$111 million to US$33 million. Faced with a glutted market and dwindling demand, copper miners had to absorb yet another blow: in 1932 the United States imposed a 4-cent-per-pound import tax. Between 1931 and 1933 (not surprisingly) exports of Chilean copper to the United States fell from 87,000 to 5,000 pounds. The copper price itself fell to 5.6 cents per pound in 1932, before slowly rebounding. Quite predictably, employment levels followed the same appalling downward spiral.

The Depression administered the *coup de grâce* to the already enfeebled *salitreras*. In 1930–31 nitrate production roughly halved. Unemployment, already substantial because of the Guggenheims' new technology, rose to new heights. Starting in late 1930, around 29,000 people fled from the north as if it were a pest-house. By 1932 the output of the remaining eleven *salitreras* (now employing no more than 8,000 workers, where there had been almost 60,000 only three years earlier) had declined to one-fifth of its 1929 level; in the same period, foreign sales dropped by more than 90 percent. By 1932–33, in fact, not only had the total volume of Chile's exports fallen by 64 percent from the levels of 1928–29; their purchasing power had declined by a staggering 84 percent.

Ibáñez did not have to confront the crisis immediately. Money from the foreign loans was still pouring in. For a few months it was business as usual; imports actually increased in 1930. By the start of 1931, however, the inflow of American capital had stopped. With its principal export earners prostrate and no Wall Street bankers to come to the rescue, the man in the Moneda at last had to face reality. In February 1931, Ibáñez was given emergency powers (which he hardly needed) to deal with the crisis. He and his advisors first tried traditional nostrums, slashing expenditures while raising import taxes by approximately 71 percent. But no matter how quickly and deeply he cut spending, Ibáñez was quite unable to cover the deficit, which reached 31 percent in 1931. Servicing the foreign debt and purchasing essential imports soon devoured the gold reserves. Eventually, the government had no choice: it went off the gold standard and stopped payments to its foreign creditors.

These actions, like the budget cuts and tax increases, came too late. The economic situation worsened by the week. In desperation, Ibáñez appointed (July 13, 1931) a new cabinet (a "cabinet of national salvation") with "independent" ministers: Pedro Blanquier took the Finance ministry, and a well-liked Radical, Juan Esteban Montero, became minister of the Interior. Montero immediately insisted on the lifting of restrictions on the press, with predictable results. Blanquier's announcement of the colossal budget deficit caused widespread consternation. Then, finding that they could not work with Ibáñez, the two ministers resigned. The streets suddenly filled with crowds. Students at the University of Chile and Catholic University went on strike. The professional associations, starting with doctors and lawyers, declared their solidarity with the students. The inevitable street disturbances were countered by the police in the usual rough way: at least a dozen people were killed. The movement became uncontrollable. For the first time in Chilean history, a government was forced to yield to civil protest.

Alberto Edwards (who died soon afterward) has left a striking description of Ibáñez's final meeting with his ministers: " 'Yes, I am resolved,' said Sr. Ibáñez, 'this cannot continue.... What have I done to deserve such hatred?' And his eyes . . . misted over."[11] His request for leave to go abroad was denied by a suddenly assertive Chamber of Deputies. Since his last cabinet had by now resigned, Ibáñez named the president of the Senate as vice-president. Early the next day (July 27, 1931) he was driven to Los Andes, from where he took the trans-Andine train to exile in Argentina. A day later, Congress declared the presidency vacant, and the vice-presidency was handed over to Juan Esteban Montero, hastily reappointed as minister of the Interior.

Montero was the man of the moment. Likeable and honest, he some-

---

[11] Quoted in Arturo Alessandri, *Recuerdos de Gobierno*, 3 vols. (Santiago, 1967), II, 444.

how came to embody the hopes of many of those who wanted a return to proper constitutional rule. The professional groups so instrumental in Ibáñez's fall swept him immediately into a presidential candidacy – supported by Conservatives, Liberals, and Radicals. Alessandri, who now returned with other exiles to great acclaim, made a show of reluctance (at a meeting in which he once again alluded to the asymmetry of love and hatred), but soon agreed to run. In order to free himself for the campaign, Montero temporarily delegated the vice-presidency to his minister of the Interior, Manuel Trucco (August 20, 1931).

Trucco was faced almost immediately by a naval mutiny.[12] Reacting to publicized cuts in public administration salaries (announced by the newly reappointed Finance minister, Blanquier), sailors on warships at Coquimbo imprisoned their officers and issued a series of demands, some professional, some semi-revolutionary in tone. Mutiny also broke out at the Talcahuano naval base, from where a rebel flotilla sailed north to Coquimbo. The naval communications school at Las Salinas near Valparaiso and the air-base at Quinteros were also seized, though soon recaptured, as was the Talcahuano base. There remained the rebel squadron in Coquimbo Bay: on September 6, a far from effective air attack (one of the attacking planes was shot down) intimidated the mutineers into sailing their ships to Valparaiso and surrendering.

Montero won the election (October 4, 1931) easily, with 64 percent of the popular vote, as against Alessandri's 35 percent. He could do little, however, to dispel the unquiet climate of the moment. Soon after his inauguration in December, some Communists tried to seize the Esmeralda regimental barracks in Copiapó. They fled after a half-hour shootout with police. When the news reached Vallenar (where rumors of a Communist plot had kept local society away from the Christmas ball at the Gran Hotel), the Carabineros dynamited the local Communist headquarters and then dragged several known Communists from their homes and shot them. More than twenty people died in this grim episode.

Montero took over a country later to be described by the League of Nations (in its *World Economic Survey 1923–1933*) as the nation most devastated by the Depression. A run on the banks had so depleted the money supply (by August 1931 it had contracted by 40 percent) that for the first time in decades consumer prices fell. But low prices were a cruel joke for men out of work. The government attempted to palliate the effects of high unemployment by creating a *Comité de Ayuda a los Cesantes* (Unemployed Aid Committee), which provided housing and food. It also reduced rents and local taxes by 20 percent and 80 percent respectively. The government, however, needed relief as much as its citizens. Although

---

[12] By coincidence the British naval mutiny at Invergordon broke out a couple of weeks later.

Chile ended 1931 with a trade surplus, the country still lacked revenues, forcing Montero to borrow from the Central Bank to cover the budget deficit.

Politically, too, for all the good feelings with which it had started, the Montero government quickly floundered, caught in the web of the subterranean rivalry of *alessandristas* and *ibañistas*. At least three pro-Ibáñez plots were uncovered in the early months of 1932, one of them masterminded by the ambitious journalist Carlos Dávila. He was a little-known figure who had been Ibáñez's ambassador in Washington (during which time he had earned a Ph.D. at Columbia University in New York). At the start of June 1932, Dávila and some *ibañista* officers combined forces with the irrepressible Air Commodore Grove (whom Montero had reluctantly put in command of the FACH) and the socialist lawyer Eugenio Matte – leader of yet another conspiracy and recent founder of a small socialist party, *Nueva Acción Política (NAP)* – in a joint move to overthrow the government. This ill-assorted band of rebels went into action on Saturday, June 4. Aircraft from the base at El Bosque, Grove's redoubt, took off to "buzz" the Moneda and to drop leaflets on the city. Faced with the imminent coup d'état, Montero turned to Arturo Alessandri for advice. Alessandri drove to El Bosque and conversed with Grove. It was afterward alleged (by Grove) that he encouraged the revolt, telling Grove: *"No afloje, Coronel"* ("Don't weaken, Colonel!"). This remark was always denied by Alessandri himself. Back at the Moneda, Alessandri told Montero that the coup could not be resisted. As evening fell, a battalion of soldiers took over the Moneda. Grove, Dávila, Matte, the *ibañista* General Arturo Puga, and others arrived by car and rushed up the stairs to the second floor to confront Montero and his assembled cabinet. Realizing that the Army would not defend him, Montero surrendered.

The victorious revolutionaries now proclaimed the "Socialist Republic of Chile" and set up a Junta consisting of General Puga, Dávila, and Matte. Grove became its minister of Defense. In its initial declaration to the public, the Junta declared that "the liberal economy" had failed; the state would henceforth assume a strongly directive role. Over the next few days, the activity of the new regime was frenzied. It dissolved Congress and, among other measures, decreed a three-day bank holiday (followed by strict controls on withdrawals), halted evictions from low-rental properties, and ordered the *Caja de Crédito Popular* (a savings and loan bank for those of modest means, founded in 1920) to return clothes and tools which had been pawned there. The moment was one of "lyrical illusion" for a number of revolutionary committees that hastily formed, in the hope, perhaps, that they might become Chilean soviets. By the same token, the better-off were greatly alarmed. However, the Junta in its initial form lasted less than two weeks. Grove had no time for Dávila, Dávila no time for Grove. Dávila was playing the deeper game: on June 13 he resigned from the Junta, but in less than three days, aircraft having once again buzzed the palace, army leaders had reinstalled him as president of a new Junta, while Grove and Matte were on their way to banishment on Easter Island. Within a matter of days a state of siege was declared to cover the entire country. Strict press censorship was introduced, while radio stations were allowed to transmit only official bulletins.

It was now widely rumored that the way was being prepared for the restoration of General Ibáñez. But here there was an odd twist in store. On July 6, Ibáñez himself arrived at Santiago's newly constructed Los Cerrillos airport on board PANAGRA's regular Wednesday flight from Buenos Aires, traveling incognito – not that this fooled anybody. In a house near the Moneda he conferred with Dávila and several military chiefs. The Army as a whole, however, was not prepared (or was persuaded not) to back him. On July 8, therefore, Dávila declared himself Provisional President of the Socialist Republic. Ibáñez went back to Buenos Aires, Dávila soon afterward giving him the consolation prize of the ambassadorship there.

Dávila now pressed ahead with his plans to reorganize the Chilean economy along strongly *dirigiste* lines: his vision was one of a series of large public corporations running agriculture, mining, industry, transportation, foreign trade, and so on, coordinated by a national economic council (which he actually set up). All this was a chimera. Dávila had no real support outside (and by no means wholehearted support within) the Army, the true arbiter of events. Alessandri's following had its own simple agenda. The *ibañistas* were unwilling to forgive the betrayal of their hero in July. Nor, in the febrile atmosphere of mid-1932, could further military conspiracies be prevented. On September 13, with the now familiar sight of aircraft buzzing the Moneda once more, Dávila's "Hundred Days" (and the Socialist Republic) came to an abrupt end: he transferred the provisional presidency to his minister of the Interior, the *ibañista* retired General Bartolomé Blanche. Blanche immediately ordered presidential and congressional elections, scheduling them for October 30.

General Blanche's intentions seem to have been honest and straightforward enough, but nevertheless he was soon surrounded by a cloud of suspicion. Was he planning to retain power himself? Was he thinking of restoring Ibáñez? By this stage, a strong mood in favor of civilian government was spreading fast: shadowy paramilitary "republican militias" were being organized in Santiago and elsewhere; the military had by now become deeply unpopular, and knew it. At the end of September, a group of civic leaders in Antofagasta persuaded the local military commander, General Pedro Vignola, to pronounce in favor of civilian government. Blanche sent a destroyer to blockade Antofagasta, but the movement caught on in several other provinces, notably Concepción, and the pressure was sufficient to compel Blanche to hand over power to the president of the supreme court, Abraham Oyanedel, who assumed office as vice-president (October 2) to steer the country through the imminent elections.

Candidacies had been organized during Blanche's brief tenure. Radicals, Democrats, and Liberals reconstituted a Liberal Alliance and nominated Arturo Alessandri. The Communists (as they had done in 1931) put forward their leader Elías Lafertte. The Conservatives and Liberal Democrats also fielded candidates. Marmaduke Grove, still languishing on Easter Island, was placed on the ballot by various socialist groups. When the election came (October 30), with recent events still very fresh in the memory, Chilean voters turned to the one candidate whose name offered the prospect of future stability, of a return to normal, despite the now common saying that you either loved him or feared him but never quite believed him. Arturo Alessandri won 54 percent of the popular vote. The Conservative and the Liberal won 12 percent each, Lafertte a mere 1.2 percent. The surprising runner-up was the "socialist" Grove (18 percent), the effusive "Don Marma," despite the fact that he arrived back from Easter Island only on election day. The Socialist Republic had failed (in reality it had never really started), but socialism in one form or other was now very firmly on the Chilean agenda. It has never left it since.

The newly elected Congress opened on December 19, 1932. On Christmas Eve, Arturo Alessandri was inaugurated as the first president in more than sixty years to begin a second term.

Alessandri's second presidency, 1932–38

In a country still ravaged by the Depression, still in political ferment, Alessandri's greatest achievement from 1932 to 1938 was to restore stability, laying the foundations for four decades of widening democracy. His methods (which included occasional use of emergency powers) were rough but effective. A loyal Defense minister, Emilio Bello Codesido (well liked by the military), and a thoroughly professional commander-in-chief, General Oscar Novoa, saw to it that the Army refrained from further political meddling. As a useful precaution against such meddling, Alessandri himself gave distinctly controversial encouragement to the so-called "Republican Militias" (*Milicias Republicanas*) – the paramilitary units secretly organized amidst the alarms of 1932, and recruited from the upper and middle classes. In May 1933 some 20,000 militiamen (including a smart motorcycle unit; they even had an airplane at their disposal) marched past the president. They were demobilized only in mid-1936, their weaponry passing to the Army, whence much of it had come in the first place.

With the return of normality, it became clear that the upheavals of 1924–32 had reshaped the political landscape, with middle-class (and, increasingly, working-class) politicians playing a far greater part than in Parliamentary times. The Conservatives, Liberals, and Radicals remained strong, with the Democrats still a respectable small party. Conservatives and Liberals were now more and more identifiable as the political Right,[13] while the Radicals were by this stage a classic center party that could, in the proper circumstances, ally with either the Right or the Left. For there *was* now a genuine political Left in Chile, small but growing. In April 1933 various tiny left-wing groups combined to form the new Socialist party of Chile, its main founders being veterans of the "Socialist Republic" like Marmaduke Grove and Eugenio Matte. Matte died in January 1934: his Senate seat was won (in a celebrated by-election) by Grove, the effective leader of the party over the next few years. Proclaiming revolutionary Marxist principles (though the picturesque Grove often boasted that he had never read Marx), the Socialists nonetheless showed an eager willingness to play the political game as understood in Chile. They entered into immediate and successful rivalry with the Communist party, which was then at a disadvantage, having been weakened by a Trotskyist defection (the *Izquierda Comunista* or Communist Left; in 1936 it joined the Socialists) and also by the policy of the Comintern, which insisted on an exclusivist and intransigent line in its member-parties.

Among other new groups that appeared in the 1930s, two need to be singled out: the National Socialist Movement (founded in April 1932) and the *Falange Nacional* (a separate party from 1938), the latter starting as a group of dissident young Conservatives inspired by the "social" encyclicals of the Papacy and by the thought of the French Catholic philosopher Jacques Maritain, whose lectures were heard with admiration by the young lawyer Eduardo Frei in the Paris of 1934. If the *falangistas* were later to grow into the most successful Chilean political party of the second half of the twentieth century, no such fate awaited the *nacistas*, the National Socialists, and their impressively eloquent "creole Führer," Jorge González von Marées, who was partly of German descent. They were a local reflection of the fascism then so spectacularly in the ascendant in

---

[13] The terms "Right" and "Left" had been used (somewhat artificially) in the Parliamentary Republic. They were now fully integrated into standard Chilean political discourse – often (from the 1930s to the 1950s) in a plural form, i.e., *las derechas, las izquierdas.*

Europe. Their dark-hued shirts, their paramilitary style, and their eagerness to engage in sometimes bloody affrays with their opponents (usually Socialists) gave them a highly visible place in the agitated politics of the 1930s. The street battles of *nacistas* and young Socialists (who also had their "militias") eventually prompted Alessandri to introduce (February 1937) the singularly tough *Ley de Seguridad Interior del Estado* (State Internal Security Law), which, in addition to banning the use of political uniforms, armed the government with a comprehensive range of new powers to regulate meetings and publications. The bill was bitterly resisted inside and outside Congress by Socialists, Communists, Democrats, many Radicals, and (of course) *nacistas*. It was never repealed: later governments found it far too useful.

Alessandri himself, it has to be said, was sometimes tempted to use the new law to settle personal scores. A notorious instance occurred in January 1938, when police seized all copies of issue number 285 of the satirical magazine *Topaze* – one of the finest such magazines anywhere in the world this century. A cartoon had infuriated the president. Although the courts exonerated the editor and returned the copies, agents staged a midnight raid on the magazine and burned them, Alessandri later candidly admitting responsibility. The Lion's claws could be sharp at times.

Alessandri began his second term with a cabinet that included Liberals, Conservatives, Radicals, and Democrats. Liberals and Conservatives, indeed, were to be the mainstay of his administration. The Radicals, however, found themselves increasingly interested in an alliance with the Left (in which they were certain to be the senior partners) and in April 1934 left the government, returning only (and then only briefly) in September 1936. The Radical withdrawal did not embarrass Alessandri in electoral terms (government parties did well in the municipal elections of April 1935, the first in which women were allowed to vote), but it undoubtedly helped to accentuate the dividing line between Right and Left, whose ideological battles, fought out in the press, in the streets, and on the floor of Congress, were far more serious than those of the pious and the impious in Parliamentary times. There were several episodes that deepened this Left-Right divide. In June–July 1934, a violent protest movement by evicted peasant-squatters in Cautín province (the "Ranquil rebellion") was repressed by Carabineros, who massacred at least one hundred peasants. A few weeks later, the Socialist newspaper *La Opinión* was assaulted. In February 1936, when the railwaymen went on strike, Alessandri sent in the Army, following which he closed Congress (then in extraordinary session) and decreed a three-month state of siege.

These happenings, all of which created a public furor, disguised the fact that a large part of the now reviving labor movement found no difficulty in working within the framework of the legislation enacted in and after 1924 (usefully codified by Ibáñez in 1931). The number of legal unions (other unions were non-legal rather than illegal) grew fast, their membership rising to more than 100,000 in 1938. Their confederation (1934) soon joined forces with what little was left of the old Communist-controlled FOCH to form a new *Confederación de Trabajadores de Chile* (Workers Confederation of Chile) or CTCH: the majority of delegates to its opening convention (December 1936) were Socialists or Communists, whose competition for adherents in the labor movement was vigorous. While trade unionism thus made progress in the cities, with close links to the two Marxist parties, it was still barred without much difficulty from the countryside by the hacendados: the tenacious organizing efforts (remarkable for the period) of the Trotskyist deputy Emilio Zapata made relatively little headway.

Meanwhile, Alessandri's economic policies, largely crafted by his acerbic but brilliant minister of Finance, Gustavo Ross, were pulling Chile out of the Depression. Alessandri and Ross did not, in fact, deserve all the credit. World prices for raw materials rose in the mid-1930s, reviving the copper industry, whose output rose from 103,000 metric tons in 1932 to 413,283 in 1937. There was even a flicker of new life in the few remaining *salitreras.* In 1933 Alessandri abolished the Ibáñez-Guggenheim brainchild, COSACH, replacing it the following year with a new *Corporación de Ventas de Salitre y Yodo* (COVENSA: Nitrate and Iodine Marketing Board), which gave the state effective control of what was left of the industry, and 25 percent of all profits.

Alessandri raised the levies on the copper industry from 12 to 18 percent, and (somewhat controversially) subjected the industry to a differential exchange rate system. Henceforth the companies were obliged to sell their dollars to the government at an artificially high official rate (initially 19.35 pesos to the dollar); the government then resold the dollars on the open market. As the difference between the official and free market rates widened, this device acted as a hidden tax. The combination of higher taxes and exchange differentials increased the government's income from the copper mines by approximately 500 percent. Attacking the copper companies proved not only lucrative but also politically popular.

Although the circumstances were different, Alessandri seemed as committed to economic nationalism as his arch-rival Ibáñez had been. He increased tariffs by 50 percent and later doubled them. He also imposed a surcharge on import duties unless they were paid in gold; the tariff eventually equaled 300 percent. A whole range of new methods (multiple exchange controls, quotas, import licenses, the rationing of scarce foreign exchange) came into play to foster and protect domestic industry. Chilean manufacturers responded well. The number of factories more than doubled; the industrial workforce almost doubled. Well protected behind the high tariff walls, Chilean factories were able to satisfy 97 percent of the country's consumer needs, thus reducing imports. As before, the producers of durable and intermediate goods grew more rapidly, rising almost 50 percent, while the output of industries manufacturing only consumer goods actually declined slightly.

A particularly successful device for stimulating the economy was a law of 1933 which temporarily suspended taxes on all construction projects, providing they were completed by the end of 1935. This measure made the construction business one of the most vibrant of the 1930s, and, as always, the construction boom benefited a whole host of ancillary businesses. It was clearly assisted by the government's encouragement to pension funds to invest in housing, and more directly still by its decision to promote public works. The construction of the Barrio Cívico, the uninspiring gray slabs that still surround the Moneda, gave the heart of Santiago a new face (if that metaphor is allowed). Far and away the most popular of such efforts, however, was the building of a national football stadium, completed in 1938, for soccer had by now become one of the great twentieth-century enthusiasms of the Chilean people.

Agriculture, arguably the most backward of the nation's economic sectors, seemed the most resilient during the Depression years. Between 1929 and 1938 the amount of land under cultivation rose by approximately one-fifth; the total value of agricultural products increased by almost 10 percent. Cereal production modestly edged upward, as did the output of barley, beans, and potatoes; maize crops fell off, but Chileans now turned increasingly to rice cultivation (a fourfold rise between 1933 and 1938). These increases in production can be attributed in part to the spread of technology: the number of tractors more than doubled between 1930 and 1936. The outlook for agricultural exports, however, remained poor: the hacendados stood no real chance of competing with the farmers of Canada, the United States, and Australia who had saturated the world's wheat markets. As had been true now for several decades, the only serious markets for the fruits of the countryside were in Chile's own growing cities. The government, however, did not neglect the agrarian sector. A new *Junta de Exportación Agrícola* (Agricultural Export Committee) began operations in 1932 (some two years after its formal creation). Its two fundamental aims were to help the haciendas and farms by maintaining minimum price levels and to promote exports through subsidies. Alessandri gave the Junta powers to control the cultivation, sale, import, and export of wheat.

While helping the farmers, the government also threw its protective mantle (somewhat tentatively) over the consumer. The short-lived Socialist Republic had created a *Comisariato General de Subsistencia y Precios*

(General Commissariat of Subsistence and Prices) with authority to fix the price of staple foods. At the same time the government assumed powers (including the right of seizure) over virtually any enterprise involved in the production, transportation, or sale of essential foodstuffs – as well as any land inefficiently cultivated or lying fallow. The more conservative Alessandri might have been expected to disband the *Comisariato*. But with a League of Nations report indicating that more than 75 percent of all Chileans were either undernourished or seriously malnourished, clearly the Moneda had to try to balance the equities, if only to protect itself politically. Thus the Alessandri administration retained price controls, limiting profits on staples to between 15 and 35 percent. It could be said that the countryside was, in this sense, sacrificed to the urban worker. But Alessandri had too strong a respect for the landed elite (on which he now relied politically) to consider a serious reform of the haciendas.

Part of the economic recovery of the mid-1930s can be attributed to Chile's ability to restrain the demands of its international creditors. The government obdurately refused to pay the interest which had accumulated between 1931 (when, as we saw, the moratorium began) and 1935. Ross went one step further by buying up Chile's depressed bonds at bargain rates. Some 15 million pesos were spent in order to withdraw over 139 million in bonds, thereby reducing the government foreign debt by 31 percent. This tactic not only lowered Chile's interest payments, but saved millions for the state – an obvious boost to the recovery.

Alessandri's handling of the domestic debt was altogether less adroit. During the Socialist Republic, in only a few weeks, Central Bank loans had risen by more than 400 percent. Alessandri seemed almost as generous: between 1932 and 1937, Central Bank lending increased by half, and the total means of payments doubled. It was only a matter of time before the old Chilean nemesis, inflation, made its reappearance. And in fact, by the time Alessandri left office, wholesale prices had risen by one-third.

But when all is said, the achievement of Alessandri and Ross is unquestionable. They restored prosperity to Chile: by 1937 agricultural and manufacturing production had surpassed their 1929 levels. They balanced the budget by reducing expenditures and raising taxes, notably customs duties, and imposing a new 5 percent sales tax. Unemployment fell steadily: the men who once flocked to the ephemeral make-work schemes of the Socialist Republic now labored productively in the factories or on the construction sites. Important structural changes, in fact, occurred during Alessandri's second term. The nation's industrial sector was both growing and diversifying. Chilean factories not only produced more consumer goods (food, beverages, tobacco, clothing, and shoes), but they also begun to manufacture durable and intermediate products (textiles, paper, chemicals, and metallic and non-metallic products). Thus, even before the advent of the Popular Front, local factories could satisfy up to 70 percent of the country's demand for durable and intermediate items.

But politics, not least the competition of the parties, was more than ever an essential part of Chilean life, and, as we have noted, no longer simply at the level of the traditional political class. In the mid-1930s, the newly salient Left, still struggling for votes, took a decisive step forward. The Communists had by now shifted from their intransigent position and were promoting (in line with the Comintern's new policy, designed to combat the rise of Nazism in Europe) the formation of a Popular Front of all left-wing and "progressive bourgeois" parties. The Radicals came to see this as the best way of realizing their dream of a Radical-dominated coalition. The party's leadership (not without some heart-searching) agreed to join the Front in June 1936, although the decision was not ratified by the party's national convention (on a 316–138 vote) until May 1937. The Socialists, for their part, had to overcome dislike for both Radicals and Communists, but they disliked Alessandri even more. The new CTCH was also brought in, largely as a way of enhancing the Front's electoral strength. Despite its lackluster performance in the congressional elections of 1937 (the only real gains were made by the Socialists), the new alliance held together, Communists and Socialists abating their revolutionary rhetoric (and programs) in the interests of the larger cause. All attention was now focused on the presidential election of 1938.

The nominating conventions of the Popular Front and of the Right were held in April 1938. At the first of these, ten ballots were needed before the persistent and ever-popular Marmaduke Grove (whose supporters chanted "*¿Quién manda el buque? / ¡Marmaduke!*" or "Who commands the ship? / Marmaduke!") dramatically withdrew in favor of the inevitable Radical, Pedro Aguirre Cerda, an affable and unassuming lawyer and vineyard owner (hence his nickname, Don Tinto, "Mister Red Wine"), who had thrice been minister of the Interior in the first Alessandri administration. The Liberal-Conservative convention, with equal inevitability, selected Gustavo Ross, who had left the Finance ministry in March 1937 to prepare for the presidential candidacy he coveted above all else. Ross's assertive personal demeanor did not win him many friends. Alessandri (who always dreamed of recapturing the Radicals) did not really want him as his successor. The opposition loathed "the minister of hunger," as they called him. His contempt for ordinary Chileans was well known: in June 1935 he had said that a few million pesos should be spent to encourage massive "white immigration" – a remark that won condemnation in the Senate. The Right saw him as a likely "strong man." And Ross, personally very wealthy, was prepared to spend a fortune for the presidency. His campaign was conducted in the spirit of a man who argued that "the impoverishment of those above does not enrich those below."[14]

Most disconcertingly from the viewpoint of the Popular Front, a third contender for the prize now appeared – no less a figure than General Ibáñez. He had returned to Chile in 1937, much to Alessandri's annoyance. His following, organized in June 1938 as the *Alianza Popular Libertadora* (People's Liberation Alliance), attracted a number of dissident Socialists and received the enthusiastic support of González von Marées's *nacistas*, who in fact provided most of the impetus for his campaign. Ibáñez was an unknown quantity, but his reappearance served to heighten tension as the election season approached.

Political tempers were thus already well and truly frayed when, on June 1, 1938, Alessandri went to Congress to deliver his final annual message. As he rose to speak, the Radical senator Gabriel González Videla, against all protocol, attempted an interruption. He was shouted down by Conservatives and Liberals. The Popular Front congressmen then walked out in protest. As they did so, González von Marées (one of the three *nacista* deputies) fired his revolver at the ceiling. The two Gonzálezes were roughly handled by the police who removed them from the hall.

Much worse was to follow. On Sunday, September 4, 30,000 of Ibáñez's followers staged an impressive demonstration in Santiago. At around noon the next day, groups of *nacistas* seized both the University of Chile and the Caja del Seguro Obligatorio, a tall (by Santiago standards) office building just across the street from the Moneda. Here the rebels killed a Carabinero and entrenched themselves on the seventh floor. At the University, an artillery piece blasted open the main doors, and the *nacistas* (who had lost six dead) surrendered. The twenty-five survivors were herded across to the office building, where the group on the seventh floor also soon surrendered. Both groups of *nacistas* – sixty-one young men in all – were then shot dead by Carabineros. There were many who believed that Alessandri himself had given the order for the massacre. We do not know for sure. It is likely that, in the heat of the moment, he uttered something that was interpreted as such.

Alessandri never lacked courage. It says something for him that even at this time of fierce political passions he continued to take his regular

---

[14] Edecio Torreblanca, *Ante la próxima elección presidencial* (Santiago, 1938), p. 42.

walks in the Alameda, accompanied by his Great Dane, Ulk – perhaps the most renowned Chilean pet since the days of Andrés Bello's cat, the not very originally named Micifuz.[15]

The shocking massacre of the *nacistas* prompted a final twist to the election campaign, in which Ross's copious wealth seemed to be gaining ground over enthusiasm for the Popular Front. General Ibáñez, who had not been party to the attempted putsch, withdrew his presidential candidacy and advised his supporters to vote for the Popular Front – a nasty sting for Ibáñez's hated rival, Alessandri. It was just enough to tilt the balance in favor of Aguirre Cerda. The election (October 25, 1938) was a cliffhanger: on an 89 percent turnout, Aguirre Cerda won 222,720 votes (50.2 percent) to Ross's 218,609 (49.3 percent). Thanks to General Ibáñez and the *nacistas*, Chile had elected the only Popular Front government outside Europe.

Ibáñez's political career, as we shall see, was not yet over. As for Alessandri, he soon left on a visit to Italy, where he told Mussolini's foreign minister, Count Ciano, that he would probably return "fairly soon" to power. He never did. But it was not for want of trying. He never gave up. At the time of his death[16] at the age of 81 (August 24, 1950), he was back in the Senate, and, needless to say, its president. He was, when all is said, an extraordinary man.

---

[15] A very common cat name in Southern South America. Ulk's stuffed cadaver is on display in the National Historical Museum in the Plaza de Armas, Santiago.

[16] In circumstances comparable, some believe, to those of President Félix Faure of France in 1899.

PART IV

Industrial advance and the dawn of mass politics, 1930s–1960s

Between the 1930s and the 1960s, Chile underwent a widening of the democratic tradition, in which the franchise expanded and vigorous party competition continued, with the Marxist Left now an established actor. Fourteen years of Radical party ascendancy (1938–52) were followed by the election of the former dictator Ibáñez and, in 1958, a right-wing administration headed by Jorge Alessandri (Chapter 9). From the 1930s onward, the state took an increasing hand in the economy, as export-led growth was supplanted by "inward-directed" development, although the export of copper remained a vital economic factor. The impulse to industrialize yielded some initially impressive results, the innovative state development agency CORFO spurring industrial advance. Urban progress, however, was not replicated in the hacienda-dominated countryside. By the 1950s economic growth had slackened off, and the pressure for "structural" reform was mounting. The way was now opened to parties with strong reforming platforms (Chapter 10).

GOVERNMENTS

1932–38	Arturo Alessandri
1938–41	Pedro Aguirre Cerda
1942–46	Juan Antonio Ríos
1946–52	Gabriel González Videla
1952–58	General Carlos Ibáñez
1958–64	Jorge Alessandri*

*son of the president of 1920–25/1932–38

9

The Radicals, the General of Hope,
and the Lion's Son, 1938–64

The political crisis has reached an unbearable point. Economic and moral bankruptcy, the result of a long period of political activity undertaken at the service of the privilege and greed of a partisan circle, has greatly accelerated the process of decomposition.

– President Carlos Ibáñez (1953)

The successful restoration of constitutionalism by Arturo Alessandri after 1932 was perhaps the first step toward widening the Chilean democratic tradition. Politics itself was no longer the exclusive preserve of the traditional upper class; the parties themselves increasingly conducted their rivalries within a framework of mass politics. Too much should not be made of this. The widening of democracy still had some way to go in the 1930s and 1940s. With women (until 1949) and illiterates (until 1970) denied the vote in national elections, the electorate did not seriously expand much before the 1960s. Moreover, the 1925 Constitution had institutionalized proportional representation, and the complex system adopted (invented by the Belgian, Victor D'Hondt, in the late nineteenth century) both encouraged party fragmentation and limited the ability of insurgent parties (particularly those of the Left) to challenge the existing order. In addition to this, the government long refused to reapportion electoral districts to take account of changes in population. This clearly benefited the countryside, controlled by the Right, at the expense of the cities, where the Left was much stronger. The venerable tradition of vote-buying continued well into the 1950s. Indeed, in the 1930s several Radical politicians defended the practice on the grounds that it was the only protection they had against the frauds perpetrated by the Right.

The parties maintained (albeit within a broadening framework) much of the character that had been theirs in Parliamentary times, owing their congressional seats less to "the indisputable merit of their leaders" than to "the resources they control,"[1] as a jaundiced writer put it in 1938. This may not in itself have guaranteed the status quo, but it did mean

---

[1] Carlos Sáez Morales, *Y así vamos . . .* (Santiago, 1938), p. 79.

Table 9.1. Congressional strengths, 1937–65.

	DISTRIBUTION OF CHAMBER OF DEPUTIES SEATS, 1937–65						DISTRIBUTION OF SENATE SEATS, 1937–65					
	Comm	Con	F/PDC	Lib	Rad	Soc	Comm	Con	F/PDC	Lib	Rad	Soc
1937	6	35	—	35	29	19	1	6	—	6	6	3
1941	16	32	3	22	44	15	2	5	—	4	6	1
1945	15	36	3	34	39	15	3	5	—	7	7	2
1949	—	33	3	35	42	9	—	3	1	6	6	1
1953	—	18	3	23	19	12	—	4	—	5	4	1
1957	—	23	14	32	36	24	—	4	1	5	5	1
1961	16	17	59	28	39	12	4	2	2	5	7	4
1965	18	3	82	7	20	12	2	—	11	—	3	3

Key: Comm = Communist party; Con = Conservative party; F/PDC = Falange/Christian Democrat party (1957–); Lib = Liberal party; Rad = Radical party; Soc = Socialist party.
Source: Germán Urzúa Valenzuela, *Diccionario político-institucional de Chile* (Santiago, 1984), pp. 31, 42, 53, 73, 92, 147, 176.

Table 9.2. Breakdown of congressional seats according to political bloc.

	LEFT Communist + Socialist	CENTER		RIGHT Conservative + Liberal
		Rad	F/PDC	
1937	25	29	—	70
1941	31	44	3	54
1945	30	39	3	70
1949	9	42	3	68
1953	12	19	3	41
1957	24	36	14	56
1961	28	39	59	45
1965	30	20	82	10

Source: Atilio Borón, *La evolución del regimen electoral y sus efectos en la representación de los intereses populares: el caso de Chile* (Santiago, 1971), cuadro 3; Germán Urzúa Valenzuela, *Diccionario político-institucional de Chile* (Santiago, 1984), pp. 58–61.

that change was likely to come slowly to Chile. Until the passage of the important electoral reforms of 1958 and 1962, Conservative and Liberal politicians, relying heavily on the still easily manipulated inquilinos of the haciendas, consistently controlled between 30 and 40 percent of the popular vote. The Left, cheated of its fair share of congressional seats by the D'Hondt system, attracted between 15 and 28 percent of the electorate.

If the Liberals had acted as the (highly unstable) pivot of politics during the Parliamentary regime, this role now fell to the Radicals, who finally came into their own with the election of 1938. The single most important (and in a real sense the most popular) party between the 1930s and the early 1960s, the Radical party combined delicately balanced and often competing interests. Its ideological variations were notorious, but concealed (or often did not conceal) an underlying interest in office-holding and the dispensation of patronage. In the now classic Chilean game of coalition-building, the Radicals proved themselves to be past-masters. Their reward was the fourteen years of ascendancy they enjoyed between 1938 and 1952. But their maneuvering ability carried its own price: arguably it served to prevent the implementation of consistent policies, but more seriously it eventually discredited the party in the eyes of the voters, who came to see the Radicals' gyrations as self-seeking attempts to perpetuate themselves in office. This led in due course to a "revolt of the electorate" comparable (in some ways) to that of 1920. In 1952 the voters turned to the former dictator, Carlos Ibáñez, and in 1958 to the "independent" Jorge Alessandri, the "Lion's Son" – men who outwardly professed no ideology beyond simple patriotism, and who promised to restore economic order.

Pedro Aguirre Cerda, 1938–41

As we have seen, the Popular Front victory which brought the Radicals to power was in some ways an accident. Had the *nacistas* not rebelled, Ross would have bought his way into the Moneda. Born out of both convenience and desperation, the Front was an improvised confederation of often mutually antagonistic elements, unified more by a loathing of the Right than by any shared purpose. Once the inherent defects within the alliance were exposed, it disintegrated. Certainly Don Tinto must have realized that his narrow electoral victory hardly constituted a strong mandate for change. His program called for the state to stimulate the economy, improve the lot of rural and urban workers, and (at least by implication) employ the expanding middle class in the bureaucracy. In fact, union membership did now increase (as did the number of strikes and their duration), while the number of public employees rose by nearly one-sixth between 1937 and 1941. But though he had promised to help the rural poor, by redistributing the land and creating agrarian unions, he dared not keep his word: Don Tinto had to guarantee that his urban constituents (who, unlike the inquilinos, could vote freely and had to buy, not raise, their food) would remain loyal. A serious assault on the agrarian system could well have increased the price of basic foods and thus derailed Aguirre Cerda's economic strategy. Hence the president backed away from his campaign promise to bring justice to the country-side in return for *latifundista* support for, or at least toleration of, his urban programs and industrialization.

In fact nothing that he could do was likely to endear him to the Right. The new president aroused the same hatred among the rich as Franklin Roosevelt did in the American upper crust. Roosevelt's critics loathed him for being a traitor to his class. In Aguirre Cerda's case it was precisely because he did not belong to the upper class (and perhaps because he was a mestizo and physically unattractive) that better-off Chileans despised him, though he was better educated than most of them. The conservatives described him as a *roto;* some even refused to shake his hand.

Social slights on their own accomplished little, and the most obdurate conservatives were not above conspiring with *ibañistas* and disaffected army officers to overthrow the government by force. In August 1939 General Ariosto Herrera (with the support of Ibáñez) launched an abor-tive putsch. In general, however, Liberal and Conservative politicians preferred to use their congressional majority (67 seats in the Chamber of Deputies and 23 in the Senate to the Popular Front's 65 and 18) to impede Aguirre Cerda's legislative program. Their obstructionist tactics included the impeachment of ministers (as always), and rendering the chambers inquorate through non-attendance.[2] However, Aguirre Cerda enjoyed one bit of perverse good luck. Normally his call for increased state involvement in the economy would have encountered insuperable legislative resistance. But in January 1939 an earthquake devastated the town of Chillán and much of the area between the Maule and Bío Bío rivers. At least 5,600 people died, and 70,000 remained homeless. It was the worst such catastrophe since 1906. The need to rebuild the rav-aged communities of the south led Aguirre Cerda to create a new state development agency, CORFO (*Corporación de Fomento*), to oversee the reconstruction program. From the first, CORFO was also assigned a longer-range role: to foster Chile's energy sources and to promote indus-trialization (see Chapter 10). Congress approved the new agency by the narrowest of margins.

[2] The Center (Agrarios, Nacistas, Falange, and Democrats) elected fifteen deputies and four senators.

In many respects, Aguirre Cerda had almost as many problems with his putative allies as he did with his adversaries. The Socialists, whose mistrust of the Radicals was always marked, considered his reforms too tame. The Socialists also fought with the Communists, aspiring both to control of the union movement and the leadership of the Left. Here we should note that the Second World War, now in progress, had a far greater effect on Chilean politics than had been true in 1914–18. Stalin's non-aggression pact with Hitler (August 1939) exacerbated Socialist-Communist hostility. The Communist Party scrupulously followed Moscow's directives: thus the same party leaders who had originated the idea of the Popular Front now denounced it vociferously, encouraging strikes in the unions they controlled, and almost reverting to their earlier policy of "intransigence."

Meanwhile the Socialists (not for the last time) underwent an internal schism. The left of the party bolted, under the leadership of César Godoy, to form the new Socialist Workers Party (April 1940). This rift reduced the Socialist voting bloc in Congress by one-third. The Radicals, too, suffered from internal divisions: the party's left wing opposed what it perceived as Aguirre Cerda's drift to the right; the more conservative wing, without consulting the president, tried to forge an alliance with the Conservative and Liberal parties.

The Popular Front finally fell apart early in 1941, with the withdrawal of the Socialists and the labor movement, although they remained in the government. But if the Front did not survive, the new structure of political alliances did: indeed, the Chilean political system virtually demanded it. Thus the Left and Center cooperated in campaigning for the 1941 congressional elections, the Radicals, Communists, and some smaller groups forming one voting bloc, the Liberals and Conservatives coalescing into another. The Socialists, still bereft of the Godoy faction, acted alone. The Radical-Communist alliance proved to be profitable. The Radicals won six seats in the Senate and forty-four in the Chamber. The Communists did even better: their representation rose from one senator to two and from six deputies to sixteen. Only the Socialists suffered, losing two seats. One is tempted to blame their loss on the schism within the party, but a more likely culprit was the D'Hondt system, which deflated their score by eleven seats while giving the Radicals an additional fourteen.

The Radical-Left coalition, although it had won 50 percent of the vote, was in a more precarious position in the new Congress than this figure might imply. The activities of the minister of the Interior, Arturo Olavarría Bravo, who (on his own admission) cheerfully extorted money from Santiago's Jewish community and who just as cheerfully persecuted the opposition press, so antagonized the Radical party's left wing that it withdrew support from the government. A further distraction was the continued bitter rivalry between Communists and Socialists. Here, however, world history came to the rescue. In June 1941 Hitler invaded the Soviet Union. The Communists' view of the war as no more than an imperialist struggle was revised with lightning speed. The imperialist struggle was now a great anti-Fascist crusade, a holy war in which everyone (even Socialists and Radicals) could find a place. The Socialists were thus able to re-forge their alliance with the Communists and Radicals in a *de facto* continuation of the Popular Front. All this meant much plainer sailing, politically, for Aguirre Cerda, but he himself was by now seriously ill with tuberculosis, and toward the middle of November 1941 he resigned. Within a fortnight he was dead.

He died a disappointed man. In hindsight, we can see that Aguirre Cerda's government made substantial contributions to Chile: it integrated the Marxist parties into the political system; it built schools and low-cost housing; it encouraged the formation of agricultural settlements, and even redistributed some land; above all, it created CORFO. Yet Aguirre Cerda himself seemed less than pleased with his own performance.

I promised to take the people out of their misery, to raise their social, economic, and moral level. Apart from the intelligent and constructive action of some of my ministries, we have wasted time in long debates and discussion without having ever reached practical and effective solutions of our great problems. It wounds my soul greatly because I am sure that the people, whom I love so much, will conclude that I have deceived them.[3]

Aguirre Cerda had good cause for such despair: in order to bring change to Chile he had compromised with the traditional power structure, placating the hacendados by abandoning land reform. He pleased the industrialists by permitting them to retain a monopoly on the country's industrial base. He rewarded the urban middle class by giving them jobs in the burgeoning bureaucracy, and by granting them disproportionately higher social security benefits and wages than those of the poor. In short, everyone but the needy shared in the bonanza. These concessions served to perpetuate (and in some cases to aggravate) the structural flaws in Chilean society. But not too many Chileans could see this at the time.

Juan Antonio Ríos, 1942–46

The jockeying for power that followed Aguirre Cerda's death revealed the porous quality of Chilean political memory. Despite his earlier dictatorship and his penchant for conspiracy (as mentioned, he had supported General Herrera's abortive rising in 1939), Carlos Ibáñez emerged as one

---

[3] Arturo Olavarría Bravo, *Chile entre dos Alessandri,* 4 vols. (Santiago, 1962–65), I, 555.

of the principal contenders for the vacant presidency. His strongest oppo-
nent was Juan Antonio Ríos, a landowner on the conservative wing of
the Radical party. Although the Radicals had once expelled him (for
collaborating with the Ibáñez regime), he managed to defeat a more
liberal adversary and win the party's nomination. He promised a government that would represent all Chileans.

The uncharismatic Ríos probably did not deserve to win the February
1942 election. But thanks to a feeling that a vote for Ibáñez was a vote for
Fascism, and the public's willingness to believe the propaganda of this
supposed "soldier of liberty,"[4] he triumphed with 55.7 percent of the
vote. The Democratic Alliance, his electoral coalition, like Aguirre Cerda's, had potentially volatile components: Radicals, Communists, Socialists, *alessandrista* Liberals (Don Arturo had neither forgiven nor forgotten
Ibáñez's role in the 1920s). And as with Aguirre Cerda, once the common
bond (in this case, loathing of Ibáñez) disappeared, the tenuous alliance
frayed and disintegrated.

President Ríos honestly attempted to fulfill his campaign promise. His
first cabinet (of "national unity") consisted of five Radicals, three Socialists, two Liberals, and two Democrats. Within six months the government had fallen apart. Ríos fell back (October 1942) on a "Democratic
Alliance" cabinet (Radicals, Socialists, Democrats, and independents), but
this too soon ran into difficulties, mostly owing to the president's refusal,
despite pressure from the Left, to break off diplomatic relations with the
Axis. The president's own party, divided by internal fighting, also proved
particularly uncooperative. Unfortunately, Ríos could not compensate for
defections on the right by picking up political support from the left: the
Socialists, as so often obsessed with their own internal ideological tussles,
attacked him for being too conservative and withdrew from government
early in 1943. The political situation became disagreeably reminiscent of
the Parliamentary regime. In June 1943 Ríos appointed a non-partisan
"administrative" cabinet, reverting three months later to a Radical-
Liberal-independent formula. At this point Ríos came increasingly under
pressure from the Army (which according to one diplomatic report was
on the point of rebelling) and his presumed political colleagues. In 1944
the Radical party, under the influence of its left wing, demanded that
Ríos sever relations with Franco's Spain, extend recognition to the Soviet
Union, expel all Liberals from his government, and form a cabinet either
consisting exclusively of Radicals or one which mirrored the composition
of the Democratic Alliance. When Ríos refused, the Radical Party expelled any members who agreed to serve in his government. Ríos thus
became, for the time being, a president without a party. In November
1944 he named a second "administrative" cabinet.

---

[4] Quoted in Luis Palma Zúñiga, *Historia del partido Radical* (Santiago, 1967), p. 226.

Given the level of political in-fighting, it is no surprise that the opposition did well in the 1945 congressional elections. When the last stuffed ballot box was counted, the Liberal and Conservative parties, who accused Ríos of corruption and being "soft on Communism," won 41 percent of the vote, which translated into twelve seats in the Senate and seventy in the Chamber of Deputies. The Radicals suffered a mild setback, while the Communists and (especially) the Socialists fared altogether worse.

The Left's electoral debacle complicated Ríos's political situation. After two abortive tries, he forged a cabinet (May 1945) drawn from the Radical, Democrat, Falange, and Authentic Socialist parties (this last was Marmaduke Grove's following, self-removed from the Socialist mainstream). This uncongenial mixture still did not give him a majority in the lower house. Other problems swiftly developed. The conclusion of the Second World War marked the return of the Communists to the anti-government camp, a stance they seemed to relish.

Terminal cancer forced Ríos to resign the presidency in January 1946. For the remainder of the year Alfredo Duhalde, a member of the conservative wing of the Radical Party, stood in as vice-president. His brief moment of glory was by no means tranquil. Capitalizing on their power within the unions, the Communists fomented a wave of strikes. A demonstration in the Plaza Bulnes in Santiago (January 1946) turned violent, leaving scores of injured and a handful of dead. (One of the dead was an 18-year-old Communist, Ramona Parra.) In protest against police brutality, several ministers (including a few Radicals) resigned from the cabinet, weakening the caretaker government. Juan Antonio Ríos himself died late in June 1946, at his villa in the foothills of the Cordillera, forcing the country to undergo its second presidential election in five years.

Although one critic, writing soon afterward, described the Ríos government as "directionless," the president as "a nonentity," and his advisers as "political hermaphrodites,"[5] it is possible to take a more generous view. Ríos set in motion plans to construct the country's first steel mill; he organized the petroleum industry and created an electrical monopoly. And by bringing Chile into the Allied camp (relations with the Axis were broken off in January 1943), he secured a place for his country in the United Nations.[6] Ríos was also the first Chilean president to visit the United States (October 1945). Politically, however, as we have seen, he was plagued, as Aguirre Cerda had been, by party indiscipline and

---

[5] Oscar Bermúdez, *El drama político de Chile* (Santiago, 1947) pp. 143–44.

[6] Chile proclaimed a state of war with Japan in February 1945 and signed the Declaration of the United Nations immediately thereafter, but the country never actually declared war on Germany. Argentina (albeit less than five weeks before Hitler's suicide) declared war on Japan, and on Germany "as the ally of Japan."

constant in-fighting. His aim, he once stated, was "a government of the Left, but of a Left of order, of tranquillity and respect for the legitimate rights of citizens."[7] Such an aim was well beyond the possibilities of the moment, even had Ríos managed to secure a stable political base, which was never remotely likely.

Gabriel González Videla, 1946–52

Four men sought to replace the unfortunate Ríos: Gabriel González Videla, the candidate of the Radicals and Communists; Eduardo Cruz Coke, who ran on behalf of the Conservative Party and its breakaway faction, the Falange; Bernardo Ibáñez (no relation to the general), the nominee of the Socialists; and Fernando Alessandri, son of Don Arturo, who was backed by the Liberal party, in conjunction with splinter groups and small parties such as the Democratic Radicals (composed of Radical dissidents such as Arturo Olavarría Bravo), the Authentic Socialists, the old Democratic party (now in terminal decline), and the newly formed Agrarian Labor party, which was soon to come into its own, albeit briefly.

González Videla, 47 years old, a man of the Radical Party's left wing, had actively supported Aguirre Cerda in the days of the Popular Front and had served as his minister to France. His flamboyant left-wing stance so antagonized many of his fellow Radicals that they abstained from voting in the nominating convention, and bolted when González Videla emerged as winner, forming the Democratic Radical party. Their defection did not really damage González Videla, whose electoral strategy was to enlist the ever-useful support of the Communists.

The Communists, in fact, put a great deal of effort into González Videla's campaign. At his "proclamation" as candidate, the poet Pablo Neruda (a recent convert to the party and a newly elected senator) contributed a stirring ballad.

> *En el norte el obrero del cobre,*
> *en el sur el obrero del riel,*
> *de uno a otro confín de la patria,*
> *el pueblo lo llama Gabriel.*

> In the north the copper worker,
> in the south the railroad worker,
> from one end of the country to the other
> the people call him "Gabriel."

Perhaps for the first time in a presidential election, there was another powerful candidate who also espoused social reform, though in a very

---

[7] Quoted in Palma Zúñiga, *Historia*, p. 228.

different way. Eduardo Cruz Coke, a physician influenced by Christian Socialism, advocated improved medical care for the poor and an end to inflation, though, unlike González Videla, he did not present an elaborate economic program. Nor did Fernando Alessandri. Bernardo Ibáñez, the Socialist, ran more to show the flag than with any expectation of winning.

In the September 1946 election González Videla won 40.1 percent of the vote. His two principal opponents gleaned less (Cruz Coke, 29.7 percent, and Alessandri, 27.4 percent). Since González Videla had not obtained an absolute majority, Congress had to determine the election. Cruz Coke's refusal to concede the contest forced González Videla to begin the sordid process of bartering for votes in the legislature. In his barely concealed lust for power, he promised all things to all men: he won the votes of the Liberals by vowing to include them in his cabinet and pledging firm opposition to unionization in the countryside. Yet even while dickering with the Liberals, González Videla took care to cement his alliance with the Communists, the most strident proponents of agrarian reform, promising them, too, a place in his cabinet. "I assure you," he said, "that there is no power, human or divine, that can break the links which bind me to the Communist party and the people."[8] In the short run González Videla's duplicitous strategy worked: Congress elected him president by 136 votes to 46. It does not seem to have occurred to him that a cabinet composed of mutually antagonistic Radicals, Liberals, and Communists was hardly a guarantee of future tranquility.

The situation was undoubtedly complicated by the end of the Second World War and the onset of the Cold War. The Communist party was now able with good conscience to return to its happy prosecution of the class struggle. The party's control of the labor unions enabled it to make particularly effective use of the strike weapon. With members now in key government posts, the Communists won their own unions wage increases while preventing other unions from striking. The 1947 municipal elections revealed the wisdom of these tactics: the Communists won 16.5 percent of the vote, becoming the third most popular party in the country (behind the Radicals and the Conservatives).

The political consequences of the Communist advance were immediate. The Liberals and the Radicals quickly came to feel that the Communists were deriving most of the benefits from participating in González Videla's cabinet, and duly withdrew from the government. The president was suddenly faced with a major political crisis. Bereft of congressional support, and himself fearing that the Communists had become altogether too powerful, he asked the three Communist ministers to resign (April

---

[8] Florencio Durán Bernales, *El partido radical* (Santiago, 1958), p. 426.

1947). The Communists complied, fully expecting González Videla to reappoint them to a new cabinet. His failure to do so infuriated them. Traditionally, Congress provided the main forum for expressing political dissent. The Communists, however, did not disdain "extraparliamentary" methods. With their unions as shock-troops, they took the dispute into the streets and openly challenged the government, perhaps emulating their counterparts in Western Europe. In June 1947 a strike of Santiago bus drivers quickly degenerated into violence: four men died and twenty were wounded. González Videla declared Santiago an emergency zone and suspended civil liberties, which drew predictable diatribes from the Communist press.

The most violent of these confrontations occurred in the southern coalfields, which were twice paralyzed by strikes, in August and October 1947 – winter and early spring, the best time to exert leverage on a country where coal was the principal fuel. On both occasions the government resorted to emergency powers, even sending troops to re-establish order. González Videla himself made a dramatic appearance in the coalfields (November 1947), and with a certain amount of help from the Socialists and by expressing sympathy for the strikers' demands, he managed to persuade the workers to return to the pits.

No sooner had peace been restored to the south than a strike broke out at the Chuquicamata copper mine. The workers' leaders requested that González Videla arbitrate the outstanding issues. Once the president agreed to this request, the mine owners reluctantly accepted his authority to settle the dispute. This agreement might have ended the strike, but it did not. The Communists seized control of a disorderly union meeting and secured repudiation of the arbitration deal. A furious González Videla declared a state of siege, jailing the local Communist labor organizer. Following the restoration of order the miners accepted arbitration and returned to work.

Blaming the Communists for fomenting labor unrest and fearing that the party, with the support of the Soviet bloc embassies in Santiago, would create further domestic turmoil, González Videla broke off diplomatic relations with the Communist countries. He also decided to create a strongly anti-Communist government. While this decision can principally be seen as reflecting González Videla's need to escape from an intolerable political situation (largely, it must be said, of his own making), it is doubtless also true that he was more than conscious of American attitudes. U.S. Assistant Secretary of State Spruille Braden had earlier opposed the extension of credits to Chile on the grounds of González Videla's connections with the Communist party, and the president was anxious to see a renewal of American largesse.

So the die was cast. In July 1948 a "Cabinet of National Concentration" took office, consisting of Radicals, Liberals, Socialists, Conservatives, and Democrats. One of the new government's first acts was to introduce legislation outlawing the Communist party. Entitled (with presumably unconscious irony) the Law for the Permanent Defense of Democracy, this measure banned the Communist party, struck more than 20,000 Communists from the voting registers, and barred others from participating in the union movement. (The Communists, and plenty of others, were always to refer to the law as the *Ley maldita,* the "accursed law.") González Videla, at least, did not repeat the tactics of the Ibáñez regime: the government might "relegate" Communists to the nitrate pampa (a detention camp was opened at the old nitrate port of Pisagua, by now virtually a ghost town), but he did not order any of them killed. Many, however, were forced into hiding – one of them Pablo Neruda, who was expelled from the Senate. González Videla claims, in his memoirs, to have given the police the order: "Search for him and *don't find him.*" Whether this is true or not (it probably is), Neruda soon made his way across the southern mountains into an exile which did nothing to diminish his mounting fame. It is never altogether wise to antagonize major poets. Thanks to Neruda, González Videla is likely to be remembered in future times more for his repression of the Communists than for anything else he may have done.

In fact, it could be argued that organized labor suffered more than the outlawed Communists. This was a time for the settling of old scores: the unions were purged, strikes by public sector employees were prohibited, and a variety of new controls on unions were imposed. Not until the early 1950s did the labor movement begin to overcome such difficulties, with the creation in 1953 of the *Central Unica de Trabajadores* (CUT), from then until 1973 the country's principal federation of unions.

Outlawing the Communists did not make them disappear, nor did it end their sometimes violent struggle. In June 1949 a meeting of a Communist "front organization" at the Teatro Caupolicán in Santiago led to an exchange of gunfire which left four policemen and twenty civilians wounded. A more serious episode occurred two months later. Students in Santiago had organized to protest a government increase in bus fares. Some believed that the Communists hoped to fan this demonstration into an urban *jacquerie* not unlike the one which had devastated Bogotá, Colombia, following the assassination of Luis Gaitán in April 1948. Although the government called up both the police and local army units, violence nonetheless erupted. Fearing a repetition of Santiago's bloody riots of 1905, the Moneda ordered armored units and other reinforcements into the capital. Only when faced with this overwhelming display of force did the rioting cease.

The repression of the Communists may have relieved the pressure on

González Videla from the Left, but it did not assure political calm. There were now some disturbing signs of disaffection in the Army. In 1948, in what came to be known derisively as the "Pigs Feet Plot," a retired General, Ramón Vergara Montero, with the complicity of a number of civilians and active-duty officers, sought to persuade González Videla to assume dictatorial powers and to crush "Marxism." Should González Videla demur, the would-be rebels planned to make Carlos Ibáñez president. Although he subsequently disclaimed involvement in the plot, Ibáñez was far from innocent: there is no doubt that his name was used by the conspirators in hopes of winning converts in the armed forces. The conspirators (including Ibáñez) should probably have concentrated on their pigs' trotters rather than try to overthrow the government. For one of the would-be rebels' wives, apparently infatuated with Don Gabriel, became an informer (October 1948), and the conspiracy was crushed before it could do much harm.

González Videla's triumph over the military plotters did not, however, end his political problems. Faced with rising inflation, his minister of Finance, Jorge Alessandri, instituted an austerity program. Early in 1950, when it was clear that belt-tightening had not strangled inflation, the government froze wages and prices, a move which angered trade unionists. The inevitable demonstrations, which began with white collar workers, quickly spread to the transport sector. Even the traditionally elitist bank clerks joined in. As the pressure on González Videla mounted, support from his cabinet waned and finally evaporated. In February 1950 the president dismissed his ministers, replacing them with a "Cabinet of Social Sensitivity" (if nothing else, González Videla's presidency was notable for the labels it gave its cabinets) consisting of Radicals, Democrats, Social Christians, and the Falange. Notwithstanding numerous reshuffles, it lasted until after the 1952 presidential election.

González Videla's political traumas should not be allowed to obscure his positive achievements: his government supervised the construction of a steel mill and a smelter; it rebuilt the city of La Serena in a charming pseudo-colonial style (from this point of view, it has similarities with Santa Barbara, California); it extended social security legislation to more people. In 1949, women finally received the right to vote. Regrettably there was a darker side not simply to the González Videla administration, but to all of the three Radical presidencies. Fraudulent voting had not abated; the Moneda still dispensed jobs to pay off old debts and to win new favors. A more ominous tendency now also emerged: the party system started to disintegrate. Eighteen parties, many of them shards of once monolithic organizations, fielded candidates in the 1949 congressional elections. Fourteen parties won seats: the Liberals, and the Conservatives, who suffered the fewest divisions, accumulated almost 40 percent of the vote, the Radicals approximately 22 percent. The Left, consisting of three fractious Socialist parties and gutted by the banning of the Communists, attracted a paltry 9 percent of the electorate. The remaining seats, nearly one-third, went to new parties or splinter groups from existing parties.

This new 1949 congress was not only fragmented. Its composition did not accurately reflect political reality. There had been no re-districting since the 1920s. The D'Hondt system continued to deny voters a fair choice of deputies and senators. Electoral bribery was still rife – in the words of Eduardo Cruz Coke in 1952, "the major vice of our electoral system."[9] Since the congressmen obtained their seats through fraud there was little need for them to adjust their ideologies (assuming they had them) to meet the needs of their constituents. The proliferation of new and often short-lived parties brought no relief. Whatever their intentions, the fledgling new parties were like sparklers which quickly burned themselves out.

Thus, by 1952, Chile seemed to be suffering a crisis of political faith. The Right, without fresh intellectual leadership and obsessed with the threat of "Marxism," seemed more than ever rooted in the past – extolling the virtues of the soil and the humble peasant whose right to vote it still denied. On the Left, the Communists waited, their noses pressed to the window, for their moment to re-enter the sweetshop of politics. The Socialists squandered their energies in mindless squabbling. The Radicals had promised but failed to bridge the political gap. Somewhere, they became more obsessed with retaining their power than using it. After fourteen years, the Chilean electorate had its fill of Radical mismanagement, corruption, and false promises. The voters were ready for someone "above" politics, a wise father, a man on horseback. That man was Carlos Ibáñez.

The General of Hope, 1952–58

As we have seen, Ibáñez had never ceased to dream of returning (by fair means or foul) to the Moneda. In 1952, after two decades of being a political leper, he achieved his ambition. Ibáñez began his political comeback in 1949, when he was elected a senator for the newly created Agrarian Labor party (PAL, *Partido Agrario Laborista*), an amalgam of several fringe groups. New and hence untainted, the PAL apparently appealed to those who were disenchanted by the traditional parties.

---

[9] Eduardo Cruz Coke, *Geografía electoral de Chile* (Santiago, 1952), p. 55.

Unencumbered by a rigid ideology (the party's 1947 conference called for "a functional democracy of an economic type"),[10] the PAL seemed suddenly to be the wave of the future. Four years after its formation, its candidates captured fourteen deputyships and two Senate seats in the 1949 congressional elections.

The presidential election of 1952 gave the general and the aspiring PAL politicians the chance to make a marriage of convenience. The PAL provided Ibáñez with the key to the Moneda. With the general as its champion, conversely, the PAL could transform itself into a genuine force in national politics. The PAL, coalescing with the inevitable splinter groups from the established parties into a new coalition, the National Alliance of the People (ANAP), nominated the former dictator as its presidential candidate, an offer Ibáñez graciously accepted.

His chances did not look especially promising. The field in 1952 was crowded. The Radicals selected Pedro Enrique Alfonso, a former congressman and government official, who promised assistance to agriculture and industry, vowing to end inflation by cutting spending, strengthening the power of the Central Bank, and imposing wage and price controls. The Liberal and Conservative parties nominated Arturo Matte, the son-in-law of Arturo Alessandri and a former minister under Ríos. Matte pledged that he would place economic policy in the hands of technocrats rather than politicians. The Left, meanwhile, put forward Salvador Allende, the rising star of the Socialist party, who had served as Aguirre Cerda's minister of Health when he was 31. Supported by his own section of the Socialists (the party was once again divided) and by the Communists (debarred from running their own candidate), he articulated a radical program: state control of the copper mines as well as of important industries, agrarian reform, public works programs, and the implementation of a progressive tax system.

His adversaries may have had well-conceived platforms, but Ibáñez's ideology was ill-defined, not to say obscure. He deliberately made his lack of a coherent political philosophy into a virtue, describing *Ibañismo* as "an organic force, almost sentimental."[11] Chileans, in his view, did not need parties – only a "noble and disinterested sense of patriotism and social justice."[12] This line had an obvious appeal in 1952. As the magazine *Topaze* noted, the general's supporters, "guided more by instinct than by any rationale, doctrine, or values, cried out to Ibáñez as one would cry

---

[10] Cristián Garay, *El partido agrario laborista 1945–1958* (Santiago, 1990), pp. 44, 53, 69.

[11] Quoted in Donald Bray, "Peronism in Chile," *Hispanic American Historical Review,* 47:1 (1967), p. 67.

[12] René Montero Moreno, *La verdad sobre Ibáñez* (Santiago, 1952), p. 201.

out to a policeman when in danger of being attacked."[13] And there were many politicians who regarded him as a savior, someone who represented "the beginning of a new era for Chile, one in which political puritanism, administrative decency, and social justice would be imposed – a regime so supremely important that it would last longer than a presidential term."[14]

Ibáñez, with his long record of doublespeak, did nothing to dispel these illusions when he began his campaign, and retreated into the shadows of vague generalization. (He did not read his political platform until after it had been published.) He promised the earth: economic planning, the centralization of banking, agrarian and tax reform, control of the copper companies, an end to inflation. He never made it clear how he would fulfill such promises. All it needed, he implied, was willpower: "Since I am not accustomed to promising that which I cannot fulfill," he stated, "I will not deceive the country. I solemnly declare that I will stop this inflation. I will be able to do it because it is my will."[15]

Ibáñez enjoyed certain advantages over his adversaries. He looked austere (he invariably stressed that he was an early riser), and the public believed his speeches about virtue. If his opponents had the poor taste to mention his earlier dictatorship, the general's supporters had a ready answer: Ibáñez had only reluctantly assumed dictatorial powers, and because he had had no alternative. And there were many in 1952 who seemed prepared to forgo constitutional protection for an honest, reform-minded government. As was noted by Ibáñez's campaign manager ("generalissimo," as Chileans would say), there were those who sincerely "believed that only a dictatorship could deal with Chile's problems, by sweeping aside all the obstacles standing in its way."[16] A pro-Ibáñez newspaper espoused similar sentiments: "[Chileans] want a dictatorship, if we understand by this a strong government with wide public support which could purify the country and lift it from its present prostration."[17]

When the election came, and for whatever reasons, Ibáñez devastated his opposition, capturing 46.8 percent of the vote. Matte came second, with 27.8 percent, and Alfonso third, with 19.9 percent. (Allende got 5.5 percent.) The Radical party had clearly suffered an enormous defeat.

[13] *Topaze*, September 12, 1952, quoted in Jean Grugel, "Populism and the Political System in Chile: *Ibañismo* (1952–1958)," *Bulletin of Latin American Research*, 11:2 (1992), p. 176.

[14] Olavarría Bravo, *Chile entre dos Alessandri*, II, 63.

[15] *Ibid.*, I, 390.

[16] *Ibid.*, II, 120.

[17] *El Estanquero*, January 19, 1952, quoted in John L. Pisciotta, "Development Policy, Inflation and Politics in Chile: An Essay in Political Economy" (Ph.D. diss., University of Texas, 1971), p. 171.

The magnitude of his victory surprised even Ibáñez. Among other things, he had shattered the landowners' control of the southern provinces. For the first time in Chilean history, the inquilinos had refused to vote as their *patrones* demanded. Given the extent of this popular mandate, legislative ratification of Ibáñez's victory was no more than a formality.

The General of Hope might have won the hearts and minds of the people, but Congress was another matter. Only nineteen deputies and three senators supported him. In order to strengthen his legislative position, Ibáñez needed to sweep the 1953 congressional elections. He urged his partisans to merge. They did not. In fact, some twenty political organizations claimed to represent the true spirit of *ibañismo* at the polls. Although the general's followers won fifty-three seats in the lower house and thirteen in the Senate, this was nothing like good enough: the opposition still controlled Congress. In this, his first test, he had failed to transform the political pattern.

Ibáñez's first cabinet typified the eclectic nature of his support: a combination of quasi-Marxists, Agrarians, and Ibáñez devotees who fundamentally had little in common. Given the inherently confused nature of his coalition, and the fact that Ibáñez himself had no clear vision of how he would accomplish his goals, problems were sure to arise. A conflict immediately broke out between Juan Rossetti, the minister of Economy, who advocated a policy of austerity, and Guillermo del Pedregal, the minister of the Interior, who favored an ambitious construction program. This internal bickering favored the opposition (the Right, the Falange, and the Radicals, who, in varying degrees, loathed the president). Ibáñez made little attempt to hide his disdain of politicians, whom he considered lazy and greedy. In his heart of hearts, no doubt, the general would have preferred to run the country like a barracks. Given this mutual antipathy, it was only a matter of time before Ibáñez and the politicians came to blows, if only figuratively.

In 1954 a strike of copper miners spread to other areas of the economy, forcing Ibáñez to declare a state of siege first in the north and then in Santiago and Valparaiso. Events began to display a faint similarity to those which had led to Ibáñez's overthrow in 1931. The general reacted as he had in the good old days, imposing press censorship and ordering the arrest of political dissidents. He also sought congressional authorization to suspend several constitutional guarantees. But these were not the good old days: Congress not only refused Ibáñez's request, but ended the state of siege.

Stymied by the civilians, Ibáñez turned his eyes on the military, perhaps secretly aspiring to emulate his world-famous Argentine counterpart, Juan Domingo Perón.[18] The officer corps (or part of it) proved receptive. Even before he took office, some dissatisfied army officers had formed a secret lodge, PUMA, *Por Un Mañana Auspicioso* ("For an Auspicious Tomorrow"), prepared to use force if necessary to ensure that the politicians did not cheat Ibáñez of the presidency. Restive Army and Air Force officers, many of whom had sworn a personal oath of allegiance to Ibáñez, later created another military lodge, *Línea Recta* ("Straight Line"). In February 1955 Ibáñez invited some *Línea Recta* members to tea – mostly colonels yearning to become generals. Over the teacups the group explained their organization's goals: the enforced retirement of certain senior officers (to free the way for promotions), and dictatorial powers for the president, so that he could restore economic order and save Chile from "international Communism." Typically, Ibáñez reacted ambivalently, neither committing himself to the movement nor repudiating it. When the colonels' superiors learned of the tea party, they were furious. Two generals resigned, and others demanded that the members of *Línea Recta* be punished for insubordination, a request Ibáñez refused. News of all this soon reached the public, and the affair quickly became a national scandal. The incident seemed to confirm the prevailing opinion that the leopard had not changed its spots – once a conspirator, always a conspirator. The military eventually convened a court martial which dissolved *Línea Recta* and dismissed some of its members.

Dealing with the army proved much easier than vanquishing inflation – Chile's principal enemy, according to Ibáñez. As perhaps befitted a general, he tried to end the economic crisis by ordering wage and price controls. Labor invariably bore the brunt of such measures, and there was soon a wave of strikes. Ibáñez imposed a state of siege, arrested union leaders, and "relegated" them to a camp in the northern desert. Jailing people did not end inflation; it merely turned the country against Ibáñez. When the Agrarian Labor party lost a by-election in 1955, the PAL, no longer wishing to be associated with the man who had given it its chance of office, withdrew from the government. While Ibáñez's supporters fell into disarray, his enemies remained steadfast. The Radicals made opposition to Ibáñez's legislative program party policy. Meanwhile the Left consolidated its long-divided strength. In March 1956 the Socialist, Democratic, and Communist parties created the new *Frente de Acción Popular* (FRAP), which attracted into its orbit those left-wingers who had

---

[18] Perón paid a visit to Chile in February 1953, arousing applause from the public but a more muted response from politicians. Argentina has influenced twentieth-century Chile in slang, and certainly in popular music (both the tango and "neo-folklore" were extremely popular in the country), but *never* in politics.

supported Ibáñez (the small Popular Socialist and People's Democratic parties).

Thus within four years of taking office, Ibáñez found his support evaporating. The Radicals, FRAP, and the Conservatives swept the 1956 municipal elections, while the Agrarian Labor party suffered enormous losses. The more important 1957 congressional contest confirmed the anti-Ibáñez trend. The Radicals almost doubled their congressional representation, winning thirty-six seats. The Falange and the Conservatives both did very well. The PAL lost half of its congressional seats, and was never to recover. Obviously the General of Hope no longer counted for very much in the eyes of voters.

The last months of the Ibáñez government proved turbulent. The student federation, FECH, organized a campaign to protest an increase in bus fares and the high cost of living. The demonstrations, and the government's response, with heavy use of the police and Army and mass arrests, prompted widespread riots and looting (April 1957). When the fighting had subsided more than twenty people were dead, and parts of downtown Santiago were in a shambles.

As so often in Chilean history, all eyes now turned toward the forthcoming presidential election. Although the Center parties, the Radicals and Christian Democrats (as the Falange had now become), had increased their popularity, they nonetheless feared that a right-wing candidate would win the Moneda. Consequently they joined forces with the Left to create a temporary alliance in Congress in order to frustrate conservative hopes. The alliance introduced legislation to repeal the *Ley maldita* and thus re-legalize the Communist party, and also pushed through an electoral reform law to extend the franchise while eradicating opportunities for fraudulent voting. (It also banned "electoral pacts" in elections to the Chamber: such pacts had always encouraged the proliferation of opportunistic small parties.) This particular reform not only improved the Left's political chances, but also dealt a more or less final blow to the Right's traditional control of the inquilino vote. The number of voters rose by one-third in the 1958 presidential elections, and many of the newly registered voted for the Left.

Salvador Allende, the candidate of FRAP, now sought the presidency for the second time. His platform included nationalization of the copper mines, agrarian and fiscal reform, an end to inflation, a stimulus to industrialization, and all-around improvement in the living standards of the poor. The newly founded Christian Democrat party put forward Senator Eduardo Frei, who directed his appeal to both sides of the political spectrum, stressing his commitment to agrarian reform while emphasizing legality and democracy. The Radicals, for their part, tried to form a coalition with the Left, but this tactic failed. The Left was tired of

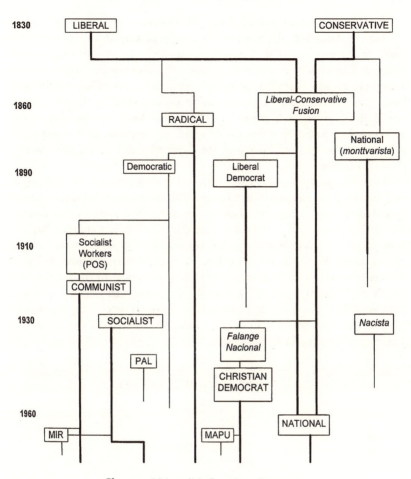

Chart 9.1. Main political parties, 1830–1970.

the Radical party's empty rhetoric. Likewise anathema to the Right, the Radicals were forced to go it alone, selecting the somewhat colorless Luis Bossay as their standard-bearer.

The Liberal and Conservative parties nominated Jorge Alessandri. It was an intelligent choice. The son of Don Arturo, he had won a national reputation for his attempts (while Finance minister in 1947–50) at ending inflation. Like Ibáñez, Alessandri had a reputation for personal rectitude, somehow enhanced by his simple habits and lifelong bachelor status. Like Ibáñez, he, too, was not formally affiliated with any political party. An engineer and businessman, he seemed the ideal candidate, a "mechanic" who could fix the economy and stimulate growth. His name alone commanded respect.

Yet Alessandri barely won the 1958 election, with 31.6 percent of the vote to Allende's 28.9 percent – a margin of around 33,000 votes. Indeed, his victory could well have been an accident. A defrocked priest, Antonio Zamorano, *el cura de Catapilco,* who also entered the race with a vaguely radical platform, attracted votes (41,000) which might well have gone to Allende, though we have no real way of telling. Bossay, the Radical, won 15.6 percent of the vote, but less than Frei (20.7 percent). The Radicals, although they did not know it, were about to be eclipsed as the "natural" party of the Center by the ambitious, efficient *demócratacristianos.*

Ibáñez's campaign symbol in 1952 had been a broom – he had promised to sweep the nation clean, to purge the bureaucracy and end inflation, speculation, and corruption. The broom was never more than a fantasy. Unlike his great rival Arturo Alessandri, Ibáñez was not able (perhaps he was simply too old) to make a real comeback. The 1950s were not the 1920s. Even those who voted for him in 1952 became disillusioned with the General of Hope. Chilean voters wanted to return to the comfortable world of the parties – but not completely. Alessandri's election showed that they had not quite lost their taste for men who were supposedly "above" politics. As for Ibáñez, he did not long survive his second presidency. He died in April 1960.

The second Alessandri, 1958–64

> *Ha ganado la elección*
> *el hijo del León*
>
> The election was won
> by the Lion's son!

So went a popular cry of the time.[19] The second Alessandri's election did not, of course, mean a break with the status quo, but it did perhaps represent the status quo's last chance at self-reform. It remained to be seen whether the "Great Engineer" could do better than the General of Hope. Alessandri's first ("independent") cabinet included "apolitical" technocrats who gave promise of bringing professional expertise to government. The 1960 municipal elections seemed to indicate public approval for Alessandri's approach. Though the Radicals emerged as the largest single winner, the Liberal and Conservative parties won almost 30 percent of the vote. FRAP, which had come so close to triumph two years earlier, suffered substantial losses. The Christian Democrat party,

---

[19] It is believed that some voters, especially in the countryside, thought that Don Arturo himself was running.

meanwhile, increased its share of the vote to nearly 14 percent. Soon after the elections, however, the government had to confront a classic Chilean catastrophe: a major earthquake (May 1960) at Concepción and through the provinces south to Chiloé. Tidal waves assaulted the coast, and at least five volcanoes erupted – among them the beautiful Volcán Osorno. At Valdivia, swamped by the tidal wave, the level of the Calle Calle River was raised by six feet. In its toll in lives (at least several hundred) and damage, the disaster was certainly comparable to those of Chillán in 1939 and Valparaiso in 1906.

By 1961 Alessandri's political position had worsened, partly because of economic disarray (to which the earthquake contributed) and the renewal of inflation (see Chapter 10). The decline in the president's support became clear in the congressional elections of that year. Although the Right and the Radicals between them still managed to elect well over half of all deputies, the Left's share of the popular vote jumped to 22 percent, and the Christian Democrats continued to gain ground. Fortunately for Alessandri the Chamber of Deputies (thanks in part again to the D'Hondt system) did not reflect the opposition's full strength. By inviting the Radicals into his government (August 1961), thus abandoning his previously "independent" stance, the president was able to retain easy control of both houses (84 out of 147 deputies, 26 out of 45 senators). The Radicals, Liberals, and Conservatives later (October 1961) created a formal coalition under the name of *Frente Democrático* (Democratic Front).

Political change, however, *was* in the air. In 1962, Congress passed a further electoral reform, even more important than that of 1958. It outlawed "electoral pacts" in senatorial elections and simplified both voter registration and the ballots used in voting. Thanks to the reforms of 1958 and 1962, the electorate grew from 1,156,576 in 1958 to 2,915,114 in 1964, a very rapid expansion. Many if not most of the new voters were poor – some, indeed, living in the now burgeoning shanty-towns or in the shadow of the hacienda's "big house." This set up a distinct challenge to the parties. Who would capture the new vote? Moreover, the new voters themselves, given their circumstances, seemed likely to place new demands on the political system itself.

These demands were difficult to satisfy. The resurgence of inflation in 1961 infuriated the workers, who struck for higher pay in the northern copper mines, in the Huachipato steelworks, in the ports, in the banks, and on the railroads. (The strike wave was the immediate cause of Alessandri's reconstruction of the government in August.) Later in 1961 the schoolteachers went on strike. Early in 1962 the government found itself in a bitter confrontation with the doctors. Not all the demonstrations of the time ended peacefully. In November 1962 the angry inhabitants of the José María Caro shantytown vented their frustration by trying to blockade the north-south railroad. The police intervened. Shoving led to stone-throwing which, in turn, led to violence. When the tear gas cleared, five people were dead, and more lay wounded.

Politics, however, was very far from being the sole topic of conversation in the Chile of 1962. This was the unforgettable year when the national mania for soccer achieved its apotheosis, for the World Cup itself was played in Chile. The country rose to the occasion: many foreign visitors were extremely complimentary about the way the tournament was organized. Although the Chilean team defeated such giants as the Soviet Union, Italy, and Yugoslavia, its way to the final was barred by the (in those days) omnipotent Brazilian eleven. Even so, there was much cause for rejoicing in the streets. As a popular *tonada* of the moment put it,

> *fuimos tercero en el mundo,*
> *y eso para nuestra tierra*
> *es gloria mundial . . .*

> we were third in the world,
> and that for our land
> is worldwide glory . . .

Few Chileans have ever enjoyed such admiration as Eladio Rojas, who scored the vital goal, and who naturally had a *cueca* written in his honor.

But the euphoria of the *Mundial* soon faded. The 1963 municipal elections revealed the extent of the country's disenchantment with the Alessandri administration.[20] The high abstention rate (almost one-quarter) could well have indicated disgust with the traditional political parties and their "business as usual" attitude. Those who did go to the polls, moreover, voted against the Alessandri coalition. The Right (Liberals and Conservatives) won only 23.6 percent of the vote, a substantial decline as compared with its performance two years earlier. Although the Radicals held more or less level, they were now supplanted by the Christian Democrats (22 percent) as the largest single party. The Communists and Socialists, the big battalions of FRAP, won 23.5 percent. Clearly a fundamental shift, a sea-change, was occurring. The electoral reforms of 1958 and 1962 had done their work: between them the

---

[20] Alessandri remained *personally* popular to the end. He was often to be seen walking (without bodyguards) between the Moneda palace and his apartment on the Plaza de Armas, usually wearing the famous scarf that was his trademark.

Christian Democrats and FRAP now commanded a larger share of the electorate than did the parties of the Democratic Front.

Alessandri's basically conservative philosophy did not allow him to make serious policy concessions to the opposition. Worse still, as the president's power-base narrowed, the opposition became more vocal in its denunciations of the government. Flushed by their recent success at the polls, the Christian Democrats made much of the running, clearly hoping to establish themselves as the principal opposition party, a development not viewed with any great enthusiasm by the Left.

And once again there was a presidential election on the horizon. The Liberals and Conservatives, still yearning to preserve the status quo, hoped that their alliance with the Radicals in the Democratic Front would hold and in June 1963 accepted, not without some misgivings, a Radical candidate, the vigorous orator Julio Durán.[21] The Christian Democrats (also in June) selected the 52-year-old Eduardo Frei, the obvious choice, to lead them into battle. FRAP had made its decision the previous year, and gave Salvador Allende his third shot at the presidency. This was to be a more formidable challenge than that of 1958 (1952 scarcely counts). FRAP had by now had time to organize; the Communist party was fully back in business. The program Allende and FRAP presented to the electorate was elaborate: the nationalization of large monopolistic corporations and the banks; agrarian reform (with the state taking about one-third of the land); extended social security; the enfranchisement of illiterates; votes at eighteen.

By the close of 1963 it looked as though the contest would be three-cornered, the three candidates representing clearly defined political blocs. On any analysis of recent voting patterns, Durán and the Democratic Front seemed the probable winners, with Allende and Frei likely to come in second and third respectively. Fate decided otherwise. In March 1964 the congressional seat for Curicó became vacant on the death of the incumbent deputy, Oscar Naranjo. As its candidate in the by-election the Democratic Front unwisely chose Rodolfo Ramírez, a man associated with the local "country club set" and an ally of the landowners. FRAP much more intelligently nominated the former deputy's son and namesake, a young doctor known for his charitable work. The Christian Democrats, initially uncertain whether to run or not, eventually joined in.

Since Curicó was a traditional rural district, many saw it as a conservative "safe seat." The Radicals were so certain of triumph that they

---

[21] Durán, like Richard Nixon, was somewhat given to spreading his arms wide when making speeches. An irreverent nickname for him was "Dolipen" – a well-known deodorant of the period.

announced that the by-election should be considered "a national plebiscite" on Alessandri's policies. This tactic badly backfired. A vigorous campaign gave FRAP 39.2 percent of the vote to the Right's 32.5 percent. The Christian Democrats, although coming in third, nonetheless won 27.7 percent, a considerable improvement over their previous performance in the district.

The Curicó by-election forced an immediate political realignment. The Democratic Front rapidly disintegrated, the Liberals and Conservatives fearing that the Durán candidacy was not strong enough to fend off the victory of Allende in the presidential election. The Radicals, for their part, decided to retain Durán as their candidate, if only as a "salute to the flag," but also perhaps hoping that concessions could be extracted from either Frei or Allende if the election had to be decided in Congress. For the Liberals and Conservatives it was really Hobson's choice. They had little sympathy for the ambitious reform programs espoused by Frei and the Christian Democrats, but absolutely none at all for the socialist vision of Allende and FRAP. Frei was *el mal menor,* the lesser evil. Liberal and Conservative voters were advised to support him, though Frei refused to make concessions to the Right in return.

The 1964 presidential election was one of the hardest-fought of recent times. It generated great enthusiasm and no little venom. The Christian Democrat campaign sought to reassure the Right by stressing Frei's own strong democratic leanings while predicting that, if elected, Allende would allow the godless Communists to steal or murder its children. (This tasteless "campaign of terror" permanently soured the hitherto very warm personal relations between Frei and Allende.) Attempting to neutralize such propaganda, Allende's supporters made overtures to the Radicals, even offering ministerial posts in return for their support. Durán apparently accepted the offer, but then at the last moment he reneged. Some believed that Frei (and the United States) offered the Radical politician a better deal.[22]

With the election itself (September 1964) the Radicals' happy dreams of deals in smoke-filled rooms melted away. Frei won with 56.1 percent of the vote, Allende receiving 38.9 percent and Durán a mere 5 percent. Frei carried Santiago and Valparaiso, and even did well in districts (the mining areas, for instance) where the Left's strength was traditionally concentrated. It was a singular triumph. Chileans were to argue for years

---

[22] Federico Gil and Charles J. Parrish, *The Chilean Presidential Election of September 4, 1964,* Part 1 (Washington, D.C., 1965), pp. 36–39. The United States, through the CIA, funneled US$2.6 million to the Frei campaign, apparently without Frei's knowledge; he also received assistance from the West German CDU.

about the real nature of the huge vote for Frei, Christian Democrats naturally claiming that it was due to the attractiveness of their philosophy, others suspecting it had more to do with fear of Allende. But one thing was quite clear in September 1964: for the first time in Chilean history, a serious new party with a serious new agenda had risen in less than a decade to break the mold of traditional politics. For once a cliché is justified: things were never to be the same again.

10

The industrial impulse, 1930s–1960s

...a New World country with the social organization of old Spain, a twentieth-century people still preserving a feudal society; a republic based on the equality of man, yet with a blue-blood aristocracy and a servile class as distinctly separated as in any of the monarchies of the Old World. Throughout Chile's history this situation has existed. It is this social heritage that forms the background for the present-day problems of the Chilean people.

– George McBride (1936)

Underlying the competition of the parties during the Radical presidencies, and those of Ibáñez and the second Alessandri, there was the whole issue of *economic development,* as we now call it. The Chilean population was growing, and Chileans were no longer willing to accept the limited horizons of their parents and grandparents. They needed to find a place in Chile, or face the prospect of emigration – like those thousands who had earlier departed for the *guaneras* of Bolivia, the railroads of Peru, the pampas of Argentina, or M. de Lesseps's Panama Canal. They were as affected as anyone else by the twentieth-century "revolution of rising expectations," aspiring to share the lifestyles enjoyed by other peoples – not least as images of the "developed" world reached them through the movies. Hollywood, as was often been remarked, was one of the true revolutionary forces of the twentieth century.

The Radicals first, and Ibáñez and Alessandri after them, wished to complete the process of economic change begun in the 1930s, with the aim of modernizing the economy and raising living standards. The options available to Aguirre Cerda and his successors were, however, limited. The Gran Minería, which had only just begun to emerge as the engine of the economy, could achieve only so much: the mines could generate revenues, but they employed relatively few workers, and hence could not soak up the growing number of underemployed and jobless. Nor, while the hacienda system continued, was there any way of increasing employment in the countryside – even if such an idea had been considered at all, which it was not. Industrialization offered an apparent solution to the dilemma. Industry promised a source of employment while simultaneously modernizing the economy.

Achieving this goal, as we shall see, proved extraordinarily difficult. There was no modern Portales to impose reforms, and even if there had been, the political system had changed too dramatically to accommodate a Portales. The government, particularly in the early stages of the new "development strategy," had to strike a balance, building up and satisfying the needs of urban, industrial interests while not offending "the feudal society," to use George McBride's phrase – in other words the traditional landed elites whose political domination of the countryside still gave them a veto power over major reforms of which they disapproved. This, perhaps, was the economic equivalent of what Oscar Wilde called "the tyranny of the weak." And in this sense (as became obvious a little later) the resolution of the problems of agriculture was crucial. It is here that we must start our survey of Chilean economic and social fortunes from the 1930s to the 1960s, the essential background to the political events we described in Chapter 9.

The economy during the Radical ascendancy

Agriculture at mid-century

With only about one-thirteenth of the land area cultivated, logic might have dictated that Chilean farmers should work their properties intensively in order to maximize profits. Instead, only a quarter of agricultural holdings were actively farmed in the 1930s; the rest either provided fodder for livestock or lay fallow. Indeed, the primitive state of Chilean agriculture forced an American visitor to lament in the 1930s that the large estates were "operated now almost as they were in colonial times."[1] This was an exaggeration, but a pardonable one in the circumstances. Without improvements, agricultural output increased by a mere 2.4 percent a year, more slowly than the annual 3 percent rise in population. On a per capita basis, agricultural production actually fell slightly between 1935 and 1945, while the agricultural trade deficit of Chile, once the premier farming nation on South America's Pacific Coast, increased almost sixfold between 1940 and 1954.

While there were several obvious reasons for this decline -- the government policy of holding down consumer prices, inflation, and defective infrastructure – a growing trend among economists (and others) was to blame agricultural stagnation on the traditional land-holding system, which remained as skewed as ever. A study in 1939 revealed (though it should hardly have come as a surprise) that less than 1 percent of all agricultural properties occupied approximately 68 percent of the land. At

[1] George McBride, *Chile, Land and Society,* 2nd ed. (Port Washington, N.Y., 1971), p. 178.

the other end of the spectrum, 47 percent of land-holdings consisted of plots of less than five hectares, an area too small to be economically viable. Moreover, with agricultural stagnation, rural living standards declined. The wages (including perquisites) of the rural labor force could barely sustain life. When daily wages did increase, inflation eroded any real gains. With rare exceptions, noted one report, "the wages and perquisites of these two [main] classes of workers [inquilinos and casual laborers, *afuerinos*] cannot provide basic necessities, such as food." In some areas only 16 percent of peasants regularly ate meat, milk, and fresh vegetables; the remainder did not. A 1945 government study understated the position when it observed that those "who constitute our peasant class, approximately a million and a half people, are not able to participate significantly in the process of consuming the products of our national industries."[2]

In 1939 Marmaduke Grove, the Socialist leader, estimated that some 340,000 Chilean rural workers received barely enough food to subsist and were living in hovels "that do not appear to have been constructed for human beings."[3] Grove's cure for the problem was simple: "The Chilean soil . . . should be . . . the natural right for all Chileans who wish to work it and who are capable of doing so."[4] He advocated a three-point program: henceforth individuals should not be allowed to turn farmland into a source of rental income; they should *work* their properties. The government should seize any farm lying fallow. And, most important, the state should divide the haciendas and redistribute the land to the peasants. Such policies, "Don Marma" argued, would spur higher production, lowering the price of food to the consumer while increasing agricultural exports and reducing the disparity between "those who have everything and those who have nothing."[5] Reform of the land-holding system, in short, would transform Chile:

> Neither men without land, nor land without men
> Is the cry of the Socialist Party
> The land for he who wishes to work it!
> Death to the latifundio, to the absentee landlord,
>   and to the exploitation of the peasantry![6]

The political realities of the period prevented the Popular Front from following Grove's suggestions. Aguirre Cerda (who had himself become a landowner) realized that agrarian reform would cost him the support of

---

[2] *Plan Agrario* (Santiago, 1945), pp. 21–22.

[3] Marmaduke Grove, *Reforma agraria* (Santiago, 1939), p. 58.

[4] Ibid., p. 6.   [5] Ibid., pp. 16, 24.   [6] *Acción,* Copiapó, April 1942.

his Radical Party's right wing, while he also needed Conservative and Liberal acquiescence in his urban and industrial programs. In hindsight the bargain can be seen as Faustian. The thrust for rural unionization that occurred in the Popular Front years was also successfully neutralized by landowners. Some 200 unions were created, mostly on the initiative of Socialists and Communists. Under pressure from the still-powerful *Sociedad Nacional de Agricultura* (SNA), Aguirre Cerda suspended the formation of further such unions. Similarly, congressional moves in favor of unionization in 1944 were stymied by President Ríos.

True to form, González Videla adopted a double policy on this issue, both encouraging the Right to produce a restrictive rural union bill and lifting Aguirre Cerda's prohibition. More than 400 unions were founded in a matter of months, usually by the Communist party; these immediately demanded changes in their labor contracts. Once again, however, political reality intruded. González Videla's break with the Communists meant a safe passage for the Right's new farm labor bill (1947), which banned agricultural strikes and very severely limited the scope of unionization in the countryside. The subsequent repression of the Communists dealt a further blow to rural unions.

Without union protection, the prospects for rural laborers seemed wretched. Landowners continued to maltreat their workers when so minded, flouting the 1931 Labor Code with a variety of subterfuges – stalling, seeking exemptions, sometimes bribing government inspectors. Using their positions in Congress, the landowners also prevented government agencies from enforcing the law by cutting off funding. The often illiterate inquilinos, whose relations with their *patrones* were usually based on a verbal understanding, had few means of obtaining redress from the bureaucracy. Even with the spread of written contracts in the countryside, the situation did not change fundamentally.

The government, however, did nor completely neglect the countryside. The state mandated that inquilinos receive family allowances and the protection of minimum wage legislation; and government inspectors were charged with ensuring adequate housing conditions. Landlords, however, sometimes managed to subvert the intention of the law by replacing inquilinos with sharecroppers, who did not receive social security or family benefits.

The landowners' tactics were successful in the short run, but the day of reckoning could not be delayed indefinitely. In hindsight the Radicals' failure to act seems shortsighted, however understandable: an attack on the estates would have diminished the hacendados' economic clout and shattered their grip on the inquilino vote. The opponents of agrarian reform only temporarily frustrated the drive for change. Once the electoral reforms of the 1950s and 1960s enfranchised the rural workers, it became only a matter of time before reformist political parties would take up their cause. Agrarian reform thus emerged as one of the most important issues of the 1960s – as did the question of foreign ownership of the copper mines.

Mining

Long before President Salvador Allende called copper "Chile's life-blood," the Radical presidents had discovered the economic virtues of the red metal. Taxes on the American-owned copper companies, as we saw in Chapter 8, were first imposed by Arturo Alessandri: by 1939 they stood at 33 percent. The government's income from these levies (as well as from the exchange differential on the dollar) soared from 5.3 million pesos in 1938 to 25 million pesos in 1942. Unsurprisingly, the copper companies became favorites of the tax collector: the fact that they were foreign-owned meant they could be taxed without antagonizing local economic interest groups.

There were always those who advocated going beyond simple taxation. As early as 1940, for example, Jorge González von Marees, the *nacista* leader, called for the state to nationalize the mines in order "to liberate ourselves from the Yankee tutelage we endure today, and to adopt more decidedly nationalistic attitudes in the area of economics."[7] While the government had no intention of acting on González's proposals, his call for nationalization revealed a hostility toward American control of the mining industry which was to grow with the years.

When the outbreak of World War II reduced the sale of copper to Europe, Aguirre Cerda – despite the Popular Front's carping about "Wall Street exploitation" – insisted that the United States increase its purchases of Chilean copper and nitrates. Initial American reluctance was soon dispelled by Pearl Harbor. Henceforth Washington became the suitor, seeking both Chilean minerals and bases. Under a new agreement the United States agreed to purchase Chilean copper at a fixed price of 12 cents per pound, and to abrogate its import levy of 1932. Chile, moreover, was to keep 65 percent of the profits. Since the Moneda still required the copper companies to buy their dollars at an artificially high rate, its income increased dramatically. Nationalists were subsequently to complain that the 12-cent purchase price was too low and that the United States owed Chile approximately US$500 million.

Although production dropped off after 1945, the Korean War ended the postwar slump. In June 1950 Washington and the copper companies

[7] Jorge González von Marées, *El mal de Chile* (Santiago, 1940), p. 171.

set the price of copper at 24.5 cents per pound. The government, furious that it had not been consulted, demanded that the United States negotiate a new contract. The Washington Treaty of 1951 raised the price of copper to 27.5 cents per pound. The Chilean government also obtained the right to market 20 percent of all copper mined in Chile at the prevailing world price – then at around 54.5 cents. The following year, the government decided unilaterally to purchase the entire output of the copper mines at the price fixed by the New York market (then quite low) and then sell the red metal directly to buyers. Under this arrangement Chile would reap any windfall profits generated by the war.

By the 1940s and 1950s, copper had fully replaced nitrate as Chile's principal revenue-earner. Once again the country's prosperity balanced precariously on the export of a raw material. As in the case of *salitre,* the government's use of the copper revenues can be questioned, at least in retrospect. Instead of diversifying the economy or expanding the country's infrastructure, the Moneda spent more than two-thirds of the taxes to finance general expenses or to subsidize imports. Unlike the nitrate *oficinas,* the copper mines themselves did not offer the major new source of employment needed by an expanding population. So where were the new jobs to come from? The countryside promised no solution. In the past, the *salitreras* had given an outlet for at least some of the rural poor. Any expectation that the copper mines might fulfill a similar role were soon dispelled: modern technology increased production but at the cost of reducing the labor force. (Thanks to mechanization, employment in the Gran Minería fell from 18,390 in 1940 to 12,548 in 1960.) It is really not so surprising that the Radical governments pinned so many of their hopes on industrialization.

Industrialization

Chile's manufacturing base, as we saw in Chapter 8, both survived the Depression and flourished because of it. Exchange controls, higher protective tariffs, and the onset of the Second World War dried up the flow of imports and confronted Chileans with the choice of substituting their own manufactures or doing without. Clearly the establishment of CORFO in 1939 proved crucial in this process of "import-substitution industrialization" (ISI), as it has so often been called. CORFO set itself three prime goals: to enhance national energy supply, in order to power new industries and improve living conditions; to endow Chile with a steelworks, vital for any future industrial advance; and to establish new industries.

Assuring ample energy supplies was an essential step in modernization: as late as the 1930s, many Chileans still relied on firewood for fuel and heat. In 1944, to generate low-cost power, CORFO created ENDESA (*Empresa Nacional de Electricidad,* National Electricity Enterprise), which began tapping the country's enormous hydroelectric potential by constructing plants (Pilmaiquén in 1946, Abanico and Sauzal two years later) and laying the groundwork for a national grid. This program proved successful: by 1965, electrical power satisfied 27.3 percent of all energy needs (up from 11.6 percent in 1940), and ENDESA by then supplied power across the whole national territory. The rolling black-outs and rationing Santiago had known until the mid-1950s were now no more than a memory. The state also fostered the expansion of the coal industry by establishing two new companies and providing funds to modernize existing mines. Coal production rose during the 1940s and the first half of the 1950s, after which it slackened off.

The most significant such change, perhaps, occurred in oil production. The Second World War demonstrated the danger, as well as the cost, of depending on imported petroleum. In December 1945, working with a team of American specialists, CORFO discovered plentiful oil reserves in Magallanes. After 1950 the government-owned ENAP (*Empresa Nacional de Petróleo,* National Petroleum Enterprise) coordinated the development of the oil industry, and built a refinery at Con Con. Thanks to CORFO, the oilfields satisfied three-quarters of the country's petroleum requirements by the 1960s. Dependence on foreign oil was thus greatly reduced, and Chile began exporting byproducts such as butane and propane gas.

In addition to making the country almost self-sufficient in energy, CORFO made striking progress with its second objective, by constructing Chile's most ambitious industrial complex yet: the steel mill of the Pacific Steel Company (CAP, *Compañía de Acero del Pacífico*) at Huachipato. It went into production in 1950. Located on San Vicente Bay, near Concepción, it had easy access to the sea (over which came the iron ore of the Norte Chico), to local coal, and to cheap hydroelectric power. The plant had an inevitably tonic effect on the local economy, and over the years the Concepción-Talcahuano area became one of the country's major industrial centers.

With respect to manufacturing in general, CORFO's stimulus to "import substitution" was considerable (though its charter in theory permitted the promotion of "substitution" only in capital goods). In 1940, for instance, it lent money to MADEMSA (*Manufacturas de Metales,* Metal Manufactures) which produced home appliances and a host of other products using local metals. MADECO (*Manufacturas de Cobre,* Copper Manufactures), also with support from CORFO, began producing copper tubes, alloys, and brass fixtures. Loans to other companies permitted the establishment of plants producing wire, electrical goods, motors, radios, and automobile tires, as well as a couple of cement factories. CORFO

Table 10.1. Employment of Chileans by economic sector
(percentages).

Sector	1940	1952	1960
Agriculture	35.0	29.7	27.7
Mining	5.4	4.8	3.8
Manufacturing	16.9	19.1	18.0
Construction	3.3	4.8	5.7
Transportation & Communications	4.2	4.5	4.9
Services	24.3	23.1	24.5
Commerce	9.2	10.4	9.2
Unspecified	1.7	3.6	6.2

Source: World Bank, *Chile, an Economy in Transition* (Washington, D.C., 1980), p. 12.

also encouraged chemical and pharmaceutical companies to utilize the chemicals derived from oil refining and steel production. On a less grandiose scale, it helped to fund a sugar-beet mill and to expand meat packing and fish canning, also stimulating the manufacture of clothes and of shoes. In line with its charter, the agency eventually sold its shares in all such enterprises to private interests, investing the capital in the creation of new industrial plant. It should be mentioned here that although CORFO's priority was industrial development, it did not entirely ignore the countryside: it created the Mechanized Agricultural Equipment Service (SEAM), which imported and then rented tractors to small-farm owners.

In its initial phases, the industrialization program seemed successful. Between 1940 and 1952 the number of Chileans employed in manufacturing jumped by almost 18 percent. The output of the country's industries rose as well. The new factories, moreover, increasingly relied upon local raw materials. By 1957 the factories obtained 74.4 percent of their raw materials from domestic sources (up from 65 percent in 1940).

Although initially import substitution thus seemed to work (purchases of foreign consumer goods certainly declined sharply), certain weaknesses became evident soon enough. By the early 1950s, the industrial base was overconcentrated in furniture, food, clothing, textiles, and footwear. Nor were all the new industries necessarily efficient. Even during its period of greatest expansion (1940–52) the manufacturing sector's annual increase in production did not match that of agriculture. Cossetted by tariffs and high exchange rates, industrialists did not need to fear foreign competition. Hence locally made consumer goods often proved more expensive than those produced either in the United States or (more to the point) in other Latin American countries. By the late 1960s a Chilean-made stove

Table 10.2. Government expenditures and revenues, 1939–58 (millions of pesos [unadjusted]).

Year	Income	Expenditure	Surplus/Deficit
Pedro Aguirre Cerda			
1939	1,807	1,777	30
1940	2,082	2,202	−120
1941	2,496	2,761	−265
Juan Antonio Ríos			
1942	2,954	3,052	−98
1943	3,378	3,960	−222
1944	4,089	4,472	−383
1945	5,531	5,741	−210
1946	6,198	6,697	−499
Gabriel González Videla			
1947	9,979	9,611	368
1948	14,379	13,027	1,352
1949	16,395	15,416	979
1950	18,887	20,637	−1,750
1951	26,008	27,641	−1,633

Source: John L. Pisciotta, "Development Policy, Inflation and Politics in Chile 1938–1958: An Essay in Political Economy" (Unpub. Ph.D. diss., University of Texas, 1971), pp. 259–60.

cost nearly three times as much as a foreign import, a refrigerator more than six times as much. Industrial goods were equally expensive: during the same period a locally made electric motor cost 300 percent more and an abrasive wheel 170 percent more than their foreign-made equivalents.

Nor did industrialization bring the anticipated all-around rise in living standards. While industrialists reaped substantial profits, their workers for the most part did not. The most highly paid laborers were those employed by the petroleum and basic metal industries – a mere 5 percent of the industrial workforce. Most industrial laborers by the early 1950s were earning about three times as much as their rural counterparts, which is not saying very much. Urban working-class incomes rose altogether more slowly during this period than those of white-collar workers or professionals.

In fact, for all the achievements of the Radical years, the creation of consumer-oriented industries neither stimulated the Chilean economy over the long run nor provided the longed-for alternative source of employment. The government reacted as it had during the Parliamentary Republic, by expanding the public administration. Between 1939 and

Table 10.3. Cost of living increases in Santiago (percentage variation).

1936	8	1944	11
1937	12	1945	8
1938	4	1946	15
1939	1	1947	33
1940	12	1948	18
1941	15	1949	18
1942	25	1950	15
1943	16	1951	22

Source: Merwin I. Bohan and Morton Pomerantz, *Investment in Chile* (Washington, D.C., 1960), p. 236.

Table 10.4. Money supply, 1952–64 (millions of pesos).

Year	Money supply	Annual change
1952	26.2	—
1953	37.2	+42
1954	53.4	+44
1955	91.8	+72
1956	128.8	+40
1957	164.8	+28
1958	221.5	+34
1959	293.7	+13
1960	383.4	+29
1961	431.5	+33
1962	556.7	+31
1963	746.3	+35
1964	1,129.2	+51

Source: World Bank, *Chile, an Economy in Transition*, p. 41.

1953 the number of government employees rose by more than half. (By 1969 the state, in fact, was the country's largest employer.) The Radicals, to be fair, hardly initiated the tradition of bureaucratic expansion: the nineteenth-century press had sometimes inveighed against *empleomanía,* the desire for public posts. In the Congress of 1926 a deputy had

Table 10.5. Government deficits (millions of 1969 escudos).

	Expenditures	Revenues	Deficit
1952	5,302	3,937	−2,365
1953	5,501	3,848	−1,653
1954	5,238	3,858	−1,380
1955	5,621	4,146	−1,475
1956	5,298	4,357	−941
1957	5,532	4,424	−1,108
1958	5,554	4,353	−1,201

Source: Ricardo Ffrench-Davis, *Políticas económicas en Chile*, 1952–1970 (Santiago, 1973), p. 329.

complained that "our youth are educated to become public employees."[8] While it cannot be denied that the state's enhanced role in the mid-twentieth century necessitated a larger bureaucracy, or that the officials of CORFO (for instance) served their country well, the suspicion remains that the expanded public administration was (to adapt the celebrated phrase about the British empire) in part a system of indoor relief for the Chilean middle class.

Fiscal policy and inflation

The Radical governments soon discovered that foreign borrowing and the tax on copper were not sufficient to meet the cost of both the industrialization program and the normal (and now expanding) operations of the state. The Moneda spent the copper levies to meet its general expenses (including those of CORFO) or to subsidize imports such as food or fuels. In theory, no doubt, higher taxes levied on the wealthy might have been used to fund the government and the income from copper to develop the economy. This was seen as either too dangerous politically or simply not feasible. Rather than increase taxation or impose an austerity program, the Radicals, like their predecessors, found a happy way out: inflation.

Inflation, as we have seen, had by now become a deeply ingrained habit in Chile. Between 1939 and 1942, the money supply almost doubled, wholesale prices soared by 91 percent, and the cost of living rose by 83 percent. These increases can be traced directly to government borrowing from the Central Bank. Four-fifths of these funds went to cover the government's deficits; the remaining portion was used by agen-

[8] Quoted in Germán Urzúa Valenzuela and Anamaria García Barzelatto, *Diagnóstico de la burocracia chilena 1818–1969* (Santiago, 1971), p. 60n.

cies like CORFO. This became a pattern: no matter how much revenue the state received, it managed to spend even more, with inevitable inflationary consequences. As the cost of living rose, the Left and Center parties backed legislation to increase wages by 20 percent – as a defense against inflation and (so it was claimed) as a stimulus to consumption and hence industrialization. Unfortunately the wage increases themselves (30 percent in 1941, 36 percent in 1942) exceeded the actual rise in the cost of living, and hence accelerated the inflationary spiral. The government itself virtually institutionalized inflation when in 1941 it created autonomous boards ("Mixed Wage Commissions") which automatically increased wages to match increases in the cost of living. The government also empowered development corporations (chiefly CORFO) to issue promissory notes, which banks were able to use as collateral to increase their lending. Between 1939 and 1941, for example, loans to the general public rose by 15 percent annually.

The Ríos administration refused to halt inflation, fearing that such a policy might hamper economic growth, though Ríos was less open-handed than his predecessor, and a constitutional amendment (November 1943) somewhat limited Congress's power over public expenditure. It was, however, the Second World War rather than Ríos's economic wizardry that brought the renewed prosperity of these years. Mineral production, stimulated by the American demand for copper, rose by approximately 10 percent; the output of the manufacturing sector, functioning for the first time without foreign competition, climbed by almost half. In 1943 GNP surged by 10.4 percent, and it averaged over 8 percent for 1944 and 1945.

González Videla enjoyed worse fortune than his predecessor, thanks to declining international demand for copper and political unrest, both of which had adverse effects on the economy. GNP fell by 14 percent in 1947, but the country managed to get back on the path of economic growth; by 1951 GNP had risen to over 150 million pesos. Yet if González Videla did not exactly lead Chile to the economic Promised Land, at least he became the first president to try to confront the issue of inflation head on. His minister of Finance (1947–50), Jorge Alessandri, devised a plan to reduce spending while raising taxation. His policy produced the first consecutive budget surpluses since the mid-1930s, and almost halved inflation. Alessandri's further proposal to impose a wage-price freeze, however, brought an angry public reaction (not least from the trade unions) and his own resignation.

Ironically enough his successor, Carlos Vial, called for many of the same nostrums as Alessandri: restrictions on the money supply and government expenditures, along with a wages-and-prices freeze. Congress rejected the reforms. By this stage such a response was entirely predictable. Labor wanted higher wages. Business did not want higher taxes. Both sides now had powerful political allies. Congress cravenly capitulated to public pressure and authorized pay increases to civil servants well in excess of the rate of inflation. This measure, which increased salaries by between 20 and 90 percent, absorbed 25 percent of the national budget for 1952. Clearly an inflationary psychology was fast gaining sway: Chileans were coming to expect higher and higher *reajustes* ("readjustments") at regular intervals. And certainly the González Videla government had no difficulty printing money. Given such largesse, the Moneda recorded some of its highest deficits in 1950 and 1951. By now it seemed clear to many that the political parties possessed neither the skill nor (more to the point) the will to stop inflation. This feeling was a contributory factor in the election of Ibáñez in 1952, as the belief spread that only a "strong man" could restore economic order.

The economy under Ibáñez

The General of Hope did no better than his predecessors; most would argue he did much worse. In fairness, it has to be said that circumstances hardly favored him. The end of the Korean War in 1953 brought a sharp drop in copper prices, leaving Chile with large stocks of metal it had difficulty unloading. Agriculture was more stagnant than ever, its per capita production continuing to decline (by an annual average of 0.5 percent between 1945 and 1954). Worse still, the country's industries were falling short of meeting the demand for consumer goods: in 1957 (leaving aside tobacco, textiles, non-metallic minerals, and paper products) more foreign-made goods were imported than in 1945–46 – purchases of foreign shoes, for example, were three times higher than in 1945. Exports suffered a similar fate. New products for sale abroad (chemicals, paper, printing stock, and metallurgical items) did not make up for the decline in traditional exports (foods, beverages, textiles). Between 1953 and 1956, annual industrial growth fell by 60 percent as compared with the previous three-year period and, while it rose again in the years up to 1960, it still remained below the level of 1953.

As manufacturing stagnated, the industrial labor force shrank by around 5 percent. In the 1950s as a whole, even agriculture took on a higher proportion of new labor than industry. Newly discharged factory workers could sometimes find employment in smaller shops (between 1940 and 1960, the number of Chileans working in artisan workshops or in firms with five employees or less actually increased from 140,000 to 207,000) or get taken on in the building trade, whose labor force grew by nearly one-third in these years; there was a mild construction boom during Ibáñez's presidency, though its economic effects were nothing like those that marked the earlier boom in the 1930s.

Although revenues fell, the government refused to cut expenditures, setting up a depressingly repetitive pattern which can be sketched as follows: (1) first the resulting deficit led to a devaluation of the peso; (2) this in turn sent up the price of imports and the cost of living; (3) demands for wage increases quickly followed; (4) the ensuing economic crisis forced the government to spend further funds to bail out the industries hardest hit by the wage increases and the depreciating peso; (5) these expenditures further devalued the peso. And so the "inflationary cueca" went on, made worse by restrictions on interest rates, which, by falling behind inflation, actually declined in real terms – provoking a spasm of borrowing and lending.

Obviously this economic merry-go-round had to stop. But to do this effectively the pockmarked Ibáñez would have needed the charisma of his friend Juan Domingo Perón (a good inflation fighter, as it happens), coupled with the wisdom of a John Maynard Keynes. Ibáñez at least tried. But his congressional following was incoherent and his fiscal arsenal hopelessly inadequate. Despite the changes we mentioned in Chapter 8, the tax system still rested essentially on two imposts: one on imports, the other on exported copper (which generated approximately 40 percent of the country's foreign exchange). Initially Ibáñez used existing laws to increase revenues, imposing a surcharge on income tax and reforming the Gran Minería's exchange rate. Desperately in need of funds, he also imposed a new sales tax, although much of the yield from this was devoured by inflation.

Copper remained Ibáñez's most promising fiscal resource. But the existing tax (coupled with the hidden tax implicit in the differential exchange rate) was becoming prohibitive for the companies themselves. In 1954, for example, the Los Andes company (Anaconda) paid 92.2 percent of its profits to the government, while Kennecott paid 79.7 percent. The companies, increasingly dissatisfied with their lot, hesitated to modernize the mines, and as a consequence Chile's share of the international market declined from 21 to 14 percent between 1948 and 1953.

Dimly aware that it ran the risk of killing the goose that laid the golden eggs, the government tried to strike a balance between national requirements and the companies' profits. In 1955 it proclaimed a *Nuevo Trato* ("New Deal") which greatly simplified the tax structure. Henceforth, the companies were to pay the state 50 percent of their profits, subject to a 25 percent surcharge in the event of production falling below the levels of 1949–55. The state also retained the right to market copper directly. Given this choice between carrot and stick, the companies now invested an average of US$22 million to US$40 million annually in their Chilean holdings. Production soared by nearly one-third between 1953 and 1958. The Gran Minería also began purchasing more locally manufactured products.

Copper revenues on their own were never enough: Ibáñez therefore considered domestic tax reform. None of his eight Finance ministers had very much success on this score. The second, Felipe Herrera, had the temerity to suggest that "the powerful" should pay their proper share of taxes, and was driven from office. His successor, Guillermo del Pedregal, authorized a huge wage increase in the belief that it would bring social tranquility and hence increased production. This solution proved short-lived. When inflation reached 70 percent and strikes broke out, Ibáñez turned to the *Falange* leader Eduardo Frei, whose formula (tight money, an end to automatic pay *reajustes,* and fiscal and agrarian reform) debarred him from even taking office. The next minister, Jorge Prat, proposed an austerity program (including both higher taxes and the suspension of the right to strike) which aroused the immediate animus of Congress.

By the mid-1950s Chile seemed to have returned to the worst days of the Parliamentary Republic: the country wallowed in crisis while the politicians temporized. In 1953 the cost of living rose by 50 percent, the following year by 58 percent, and in 1955 by 88 percent. The situation became increasingly desperate: unemployment almost doubled; plant utilization fell to the lowest levels since the mid-1930s; GNP plummeted by 8 percent; there was a wave of strikes, as workers tried to protect themselves; speculation increased; the peso lost two-thirds of its value in less than a year. Those who could not buy dollars hoarded goods.

Since little was to be expected from the political parties, Ibáñez turned for advice to foreigners. In late 1955 the Klein-Saks mission arrived in Santiago to mastermind a plan for economic stabilization. Klein-Saks was an American consulting firm, known for its laissez-faire bias, which had earlier done an apparently successful job on the Peruvian economy. The firm enjoyed close ties with Washington, which seemed to open the prospect of American loans should the mission's deflationary strategy be adopted. Congress, however, enacted only a few of the Klein-Saks proposals. By a one-vote margin the Senate limited the 1956 *reajuste* to 50 percent of the rise in the cost of living, although, to cushion the blow, increased benefits (including higher family allowances) were authorized and a minimum wage was instituted.[9] Congress also restricted credit and

---

[9] A minimum salary for certain classes of *empleados,* white-collar workers, had been introduced in 1937. Both the *sueldo vital* (minimum salary) and *salario mínimo* (minimum wage) became, in later years, *units* in the calculation of wage and salary increases rather than genuine minimum wages or salaries.

abolished the byzantine system of exchange controls. The government, however, did not substantially reduce spending; nor did it get Congress to enact much-needed tax reforms. Although Congress refused to implement the entire Klein-Saks program, it did enough to secure an American loan of US$75 million, and the mission itself achieved one important goal: it at least broke the inflationary fever of the mid-1950s. There was a negative side to this: the construction industry slumped with the contraction of the real estate market, while the end of exchange controls exposed local manufacturers to the harsh breezes of foreign competition. New credit restrictions reduced purchasing power. While inflation fell (to 38 percent in 1956 and 17 percent in 1957), unemployment rose. The poor, as always, bore the social costs of deflation.

Having endured these painful economic withdrawal symptoms, the government prematurely retreated from the austerity program. It may have had little choice: a sudden decline in the value of copper (from 47 to 21 cents a pound in 1957) resulted in two higher deficits. A drought in the Central Valley drove up the cost of food. Construction fell by half, to its lowest level since the 1930s. Faced with this economic decline and high unemployment, the government authorized a 20 percent "readjustment." Together with easier bank credit this revived inflation (33 percent in 1958). Not everybody saw this as a loss. The loyal *ibañista* politician Rafael Tarud, for instance, denounced less than adequate *reajustes* as inhuman. The solution, he suggested, lay in reducing the privileges of "those elites who have remained tragically backward in their understanding of the social dilemma."[10] More and more Chileans were now inclined to think the same.

By the time Ibáñez left the Moneda both he and the country were exhausted after the worst inflationary episode in Chilean history. The lessons read into this episode by economists and politicians were diverse. The Klein-Saks deflation (however imperfect and temporary) probably heightened rather than diminished the growing demand for "structural" reform and for programs in which the state would have to take a stronger hand than in the past. But even more than this, the second Ibáñez administration demonstrated just how difficult it was to implement serious economic reform (in whatever direction). Price and wage controls, for instance, might have slowed the inflationary spiral. But they would have antagonized both the businessmen (who, predictably, would have been happy enough to see wage controls) and the salaried employees and workers. The country's political leadership, therefore, faced a predicament: it was unable to stabilize the economy without offending business, agriculture, or urban labor. Successive Congresses and presidents solved

---

[10] Rafael Tarud, *Contra el despojo de los reajustes* (Santiago, n.d.), pp. 6, 26.

the problem by doing little or nothing. The result, as the Ibáñez debacle indicated, was something perilously close to chaos.

Jorge Alessandri's economic policies

Jorge Alessandri represented the last chance for the traditional political establishment to cure or at least alleviate the economic ailments of Chile. Perhaps the inequities were too entrenched; perhaps the political parties lacked the grit, the imagination, or the wisdom to address the painful issues. Whatever the reasons, the economic situation did not change fundamentally during his six years: the problems which had long warped Chile's national development – the inequitable land-holding system, the reliance on revenues from mining, the generally regressive tax system, the chronic inflation – all remained stubbornly in place. Notwithstanding this, the second Alessandri was a good manager, and he did his best.

The agrarian question

Pressure for agrarian reform mounted in the 1950s. The Left had (at least in theory) long demanded it, and other groups now added their voices to the chorus. In 1962 the Catholic Church created its *Instituto de Promoción Agraria* (Agrarian Promotion Institute), which distributed a few of the Church's estates to landless peasants. The Kennedy administration in the United States, both at the Punta del Este meeting (1961) and through its Alliance for Progress, advocated agrarian reform as a basic building-block in what Arthur Schlesinger Jr. later called the Alliance's "grand project for the democratic modernization of Latin America."[11] Chilean Conservatives and Liberals, who (as we have seen) had long thwarted all attempts to weaken their hold on the countryside, had no particular desire to be democratically modernized – by the United States or by anyone else. But the Radical party, desperate to regain the presidency, now came to see espousal of agrarian reform as a means of winning the rural vote, and (as we noted in Chapter 9) the Right depended on Radical help to fend off the growing challenge from the Left and the Christian Democrats. With great misgivings, therefore, the Right came to accept the premise of land reform.

Conservatives, Liberals, and Radicals argued at length about the question of compensation for estates to be taken over. The 1925 Constitution allowed the state to expropriate property, but in return for cash payments. The Radicals proposed payment by a combination of cash and long-term bonds, and the Right reluctantly swallowed this concept of "deferred

---

[11] Arthur Schlesinger Jr., *A Thousand Days* (Boston, 1965), p. 186.

compensation." In August 1962 Congress duly enacted an agrarian reform law (Law 15.020). It authorized the state to buy land with 20 percent cash-down payments and interest-bearing bonds due in ten years. Nobody (except perhaps the most antediluvian) considered the 1962 measure either revolutionary or punitive. With few exceptions, the state was empowered to redistribute only abandoned or inefficiently cultivated property, or corporately held land lying fallow, of which there was relatively little.

In addition to authorizing land reform, however, the new law made a serious effort to improve rural living conditions. Landowners were now required to invest a portion of their profits in improving inquilino housing. Agrarian wages were to reflect inflation. Workers were to be given long-term contracts if so desired, and to receive their wages entirely in cash (rather than, as previously, in cash and perquisites). More significant in the long run (as we shall see) were the new bureaucratic organizations now established: the *Corporación de Reforma Agraria* (CORA, Agrarian Reform Corporation), to oversee the process of expropriation; the *Consejo Superior de Fomento Agropecuario* (CONFSA, Higher Agrarian Development Council), to ensure the efficient development of the expropriated lands; and the *Instituto de Desarrollo Agropecuario* (INDAP, Agrarian Development Institute), to provide technical assistance and credit to the countryside.

Despite its shortcomings (eloquently adumbrated by the Left, the Christian Democrats, and even agricultural experts from the Organization of American States), the legislation of 1962 did achieve certain goals. It established the *principle* of reform once and for all, and it imposed certain minimal responsibilities on landowners. In practice, however, it barely touched the countryside: a mere 60,000 hectares (more than two-thirds of which already belonged to the state) was distributed to around 1,000 peasants. As one observer of the time cynically observed, the chief beneficiaries were not the landless so much as the bureaucrats hired to administer the new law.[12]

Copper

Between 1958 and 1964, partly because Anaconda brought its new El Salvador mine on line (to replace the now exhausted Potrerillos), the value of Chilean copper exports surged from US$232 million to US$363 million. Tax revenues from copper (varying in line with prevailing prices) nearly doubled. The companies themselves launched a "Buy Chilean" program, which greatly increased their purchases of locally made prod-

---

[12] *Hispanic American Report*, 16:2 (1963), p. 164.

ucts. Chile's share of the world copper market, however, remained at around 14 or 15 percent, roughly its level at the time of the *Nuevo Trato* of 1955. This failure to increase "market share" was attributed by many to inadequate investment in the Gran Minería by the companies. Although Anaconda and Kennecott sank US$203 million into the mines during Alessandri's presidency, this was seen as nothing like enough by their increasingly vocal critics, who began to call into question the usefulness of the *Nuevo Trato* agreement.

The companies had their own reasons to distrust the *Nuevo Trato*. Following the earthquake of May 1960, the government levied special new taxes on copper (in violation of the agreement) to finance reconstruction in the South. Two years later Congress increased the taxes yet again, which pushed the tax rate on El Teniente and Chuquicamata to more than twice the level paid by copper companies operating in Northern Rhodesia (Zambia after 1964). Given the political invective directed against them, and under pressure from their stockholders to diversify production globally, the companies were reluctant to make further investments in Chile without firm guarantees from the government. They expressed willingness to invest additional sums (perhaps up to US$500 million) and to build a refinery to produce electrolytic copper, but as a quid pro quo asked the government to freeze taxes for twenty years and to refrain from further tampering with the *Nuevo Trato*. Such a scheme seemed entirely too rigid to many Chileans (not least the Left), who saw it as depriving the state of flexibility in future economic programs. Harsher spirits viewed the companies' attempts to barter investments for tax concessions as a form of extortion, and called for a state marketing monopoly.

Alessandri's presidency saw no innovations in copper policy. The government pursued a "hands-off" approach, even tending to disregard the views of its own Copper Department (set up at the time of the *Nuevo Trato* to monitor the companies' operations) when these conflicted with those of Anaconda or Kennecott. Eventually the whole question of foreign ownership was to fuse disparate political elements into an anti-American phalanx. The Conservative Francisco Bulnes (popularly known as "the Marquis") and the Socialist Salvador Allende normally agreed about little, but concurred in suggesting that the time had come to consider outright nationalization. Thus this theme, like agrarian reform, was very firmly placed on the agenda of the politics of the 1960s.

Inflation and fiscal policy

Philosophically, Alessandri believed that the government should intervene in the economy as little as possible. While actively pursuing stabili-

Table 10.6. Inflation under Jorge
Alessandri (% increase).

1958	25.9	1962	13.9
1959	38.6	1963	44.3
1960	11.6	1964	46.0
1961	7.7		

Source: Ricardo Ffrench-Davis, *Políticas
económicas en Chile, 1952–1970*
(Santiago, 1973), p. 247.

zation policies, he also pinned his hopes on stimulating agricultural and
industrial production, in the view that inflation could ultimately best
be contained by satisfying consumer demand. Public investment might
initially be necessary to reactivate the economy; the private sector could
then lead the way in creating wealth and providing employment, spurred
on by suitably liberalizing measures.

As part of his private-sector "stimulus package," as it might now
be called, Alessandri encouraged the creation of savings-and-loan banks
(*Asociaciones de Ahorro y Préstamo*). These new institutions both indexed
interest rates to match inflation and accepted foreign-currency accounts –
an incentive (combined with a tax amnesty) to repatriate capital where
this was held abroad. The banks thus gained ample funds which could in
theory be funneled to Chilean businesses. In part to make such businesses
more competitive, Alessandri also greatly reduced import restrictions and
simplified procedures. From April 1959 it became possible to import
more or less anything, and although many items on the former "prohibited" list were subject to stiff deposits, these were reduced over the next
few months and in many cases phased out altogether. In 1959–60,
Chilean overseas trade was less constrained by bureaucratic controls than
at any time since the onset of the Depression.

Meanwhile a notable law (DFL-2), enacted in July 1959, gave a strong
stimulus to the construction of small houses. It was the most striking
initiative of its kind in many years. The "DFL-2 houses" (as they became
known) were exempted from property taxes, and the contractors who
built them were given tax relief. Alessandri additionally mounted a
public works program – including an impressive amount of highway
construction. The DFL-2 law had particularly impressive results: housing
starts quadrupled – more in 1959 than in the previous four years put
together. Although the pace of construction slackened off thereafter, it
remained well above the level of 1958. Here were solid gains.

In his efforts at stabilization, Alessandri offered what he hoped would
prove a decisive psychological stimulus by establishing a single exchange

rate and a new monetary unit, the escudo (1,000 pesos), which he vowed to keep at par with the U.S. dollar: it was in fact pegged at US$1.05 in January 1959.[13] In order to bolster confidence in the new money, all exchange controls were lifted and the opening of dollar accounts was allowed in the banks. Alessandri also made it clear, on assuming office, that wages and salaries were no longer to be "readjusted" in line with inflation but were to come from profits and improved productivity. The legacy of the Ibáñez years made the immediate application of this plan impossible: partly with a view to reactivating demand, Alessandri authorized an initial one-off *reajuste* of between 60 and 100 percent.

During Alessandri's first two years (thanks in no small part to DFL-2) economic conditions markedly improved. In 1959 the budget was balanced (for the first time since Alessandri himself had balanced it as Finance minister in 1950). The country enjoyed a positive trade balance; industrial production rose by 10 percent; unemployment fell from 9 to 7 percent (and to 5.5 percent by 1963); the rate of inflation slowed during the second half of 1959. Inflation, in fact, declined from 33 percent in 1959 to 5 percent in 1960, rising again to 10 percent in 1961. All such symptoms seemed to indicate that a page had been turned, that inflationary expectations were being dampened, and that the economy was about to flourish once again.

Alas, it was not. Alessandri's expectations of the private sector proved far too sanguine. There was no rush of new investment, nor much in the way of direct foreign investment, despite new incentives. The liberalizing measures of 1959, meanwhile, produced a veritable flood of imports, largely financed by foreign loans, but no corresponding rise in exports – whose value in any case was undermined by the fixed exchange rate. By 1961 the trade deficit widened to US$153 million. At the end of that year a financial panic led to a three-week suspension of foreign currency dealings, the introduction (January 1962) of a dual exchange rate (the US$1.05 rate being maintained for imports, with a much lower rate for capital transactions and tourism), and the reimposition of stricter controls on foreign trade (including, once again, a "prohibited list" for imports). Fearing its inevitable effect on inflation, Alessandri resisted an all-around devaluation of the escudo until October 1962, when it was devalued by 38 percent and allowed to "float" – downward. Depreciation of the currency brought renewed price increases. Inflation ran at 28 percent in 1962, at 45 percent in 1963, and at 40 percent in 1964. Alessandri had

---

[13] The new currency (with its E° sign) came into public use in 1960, though, as with the French after the introduction of the *franc lourd* by President de Gaulle, people continued to talk in terms of the old money for several years thereafter.

moderate success in restraining *reajustes,* but at the cost of depressing real wages and thus heightening popular discontent.

As so often in the past, inflation compounded the government's fiscal problems. The need to finance its early "pump-priming" investment, coupled with the demands of reconstruction in the earthquake-ravaged South, made it impossible to keep control of the deficit without recourse to large-scale borrowing: this built up levels of foreign debt which were modest by the standards of the 1970s and 1980s but which seemed alarming enough at the time. Even if Alessandri had been inclined to increase domestic taxes to finance government spending (which he was not), he would have found it easier to draw blood from a stone. The highly regressive tax system, which in 1962 still derived 64.6 percent of its income from indirect taxes, seemed impervious to change. (The government *did* take measures to improve tax collection, a not inconsiderable feat in a country where as many as one-third went in for successful tax evasion.) Sales tax was now increased by 20 percent, and in February 1964, after long delays in Congress, a major simplification of income tax was introduced.[14] These changes had no real effect on the deficit, which fell somewhat in 1963–64 mostly because public investment had by then been frozen.

At the close of Alessandri's term, therefore, the country continued to find itself in an economic quagmire, with three-quarters of its foreign reserves being used to service its debts and more than half of the remaining quarter spent on importing food. There was very little left over to fund ordinary government operations, let alone to modernize the economy. The Great Engineer, like the General of Hope, had failed. A new way would have to be sought. But could it be found?

Society at mid-century: 1930s–1960s

Social structure, new roles for women

If the Parliamentary period had been the Belle Epoque of the upper class, the years after the 1930s were when the Chilean middle class came into its own. Industrialization, the extension of education, and the growth of the public administration gave new opportunities all around. Not that the land-owning elite was driven to the sidelines. In fact, the growth of manufacturing allowed the upper class to broaden its interests quite notably. There had long been powerful financial groups in Chile (one of

---

[14] Income tax included what elsewhere would be called corporation tax. The 1964 reform reduced the previous six categories of tax to two: corporation tax and personal income tax.

the oldest being the Edwards group), and their role was if anything strengthened by the industrial impulse. Concentration of wealth may even have been enhanced as a result. In a well-known study of 1961, the brilliant young economist Ricardo Lagos (whose name will recur in our final chapter) identified eleven leading conglomerates, often interconnected, which controlled 290 of the country's 1,300 or so joint-stock companies.[15]

In politics and business, however, the upper class was obliged from now onward to coexist with (and increasingly to collaborate with) the burgeoning middle class, the chief beneficiary of the Radical years. All sections of the middle class seem to have improved their economic position. After 1938, for example, most of the country's white-collar workers received the protection of the various social security laws – a piecemeal process, occurring in stages from the 1920s onward. All Chileans may have been equal, but some were definitely more equal than others: white-collar *empleados* generally received higher unemployment and family benefits than did *obreros,* that is, the industrial working class. (The distinction between *empleado* and *obrero* was a legal one and enshrined in the Labor Code.) Nevertheless the working class, though small by the standards of Europe or North America, made discernible gains after the 1930s, both through access to social security and through unionization. (The gains were much less striking in terms of real wages, which were subject to bewildering ups and downs because of inflation.) Between 1932 and 1964 the number of unions more than quadrupled, as did membership (to 270,000 in 1964). A combination of labor militancy and inflation doubled the number of strikes over the same period.

Chilean society by the mid-twentieth century was thus more complicated and diverse than it had ever been. This was true for most of the larger and middle-sized Latin American countries at the same period, but the Chilean social pattern was distinctive in certain ways. One such distinctive feature was the greater prominence of women in the professions, the arts, and even public life, something often remarked on by foreign visitors. This is a point that warrants a brief examination.

There was something slightly paradoxical about this development, for the law, despite a number of modifications to the strongly husband-oriented Civil Code in the 1930s and 1940s, restricted the role of married women in certain (mostly property-related) matters, although by the end of the 1950s unmarried women over the age of 21 were "fully responsible in civil law."[16] In the 1950s the wearing of slacks by women in public was still considered a matter for serious debate in magazines. Neverthe-

---

[15] Ricardo Lagos E., *La concentración del poder económico* (Santiago, 1961).
[16] Felicitas Klimpel, *La mujer chilena* (Santiago, 1962), p. 51.

less, Chilean women of the upper and middle classes had begun at last to seize the opportunities opened up by Education minister Miguel Luis Amunátegui's decree of February 1877, admitting them to professional education. Of the more than 8,000 degrees awarded to women at the University of Chile (the Catholic University admitted women from 1932 onward) between 1910 and 1960, 464 were in medicine, 357 in law, 931 in dentistry, 471 in pharmacy, and 67 in architecture. (In the same period, 3,200 were in schoolteaching.) By the 1930s and 1940s, a female presence was becoming altogether more visible in the professions, in the health service, in education, in the arts, in journalism, and on the radio.

It was natural that educated Chilean women should wish at some point to invade the predominantly masculine terrain of politics. They had been specifically excluded from voting in an election law of 1884 – after some women in San Felipe had successfully (in 1875) insinuated their names into the electoral register, an episode that provoked much indignation among congressmen at the time. Largely for this reason, their part in the traditional political parties had been only a small one, although the Radicals accepted female membership as early as 1888. There had been a short-lived Feminine Civic party in the 1920s, and the more serious Feminine Party of Chile was formed in 1946, pledged to campaign for female suffrage in national elections – an aim achieved in the law of February 1949. González Videla's presidency, much maligned in so many other ways, was a fairly notable one from this particular viewpoint: it saw the appointment of the first woman cabinet minister (Adriana Olguín at Justice) and first woman ambassadors (to the Netherlands and the United Nations), and the creation of the *Oficina de la Mujer,* a national bureau for women's affairs.

The achievement of the vote might have induced a rush of female aspirants to Congress (as happened at the same period in Argentina). In fact it did not: the first woman to enter the Chamber of Deputies was Inés Enriquez Frödden, a Radical, in a by-election of 1951, but only three more followed her during the 1950s (one Feminine, one Radical, one Liberal); the number was to rise notably in the 1960s. Perhaps reassuringly, the Feminine party (which dissolved in 1953) proved as prone to faction as its male-dominated counterparts, producing a classic splinter movement (the "Progressive Feminine" party) at the time of the presidential election of 1952, when the bulk of the party supported General Ibáñez. The outstanding woman politician of the moment was the party's president, the inspirational María de la Cruz, whose raw oratory was well displayed during Ibáñez's election campaign. It was she who first described Ibáñez as the General of Hope. Elected to Ibáñez's now vacant senate seat in 1953, she fell from grace (and into obscurity) soon afterward – partly because of her effusively proclaimed enthusiasm for General Perón and his ideas, partly because of her alleged implication in corrupt practices,[17] but most of all, no doubt, because of time-honored masculine prejudice.

Why did Chilean women (of the upper and middle classes, anyway) assume professional, medical, and educational roles so readily? English-speaking feminists might find the question otiose, but it is not, given Chile's historical background and Hispanic cultural matrix. The points we feel inclined to make are suggestions rather than answers. The whole theme needs serious investigation. We can point to the fact that in countries with strong landed elites women landowners (albeit usually widows or daughters) are often highly visible – and accepted by their male counterparts. Images of strong female character from the historical past (and in folklore) can also dispose particular cultures to see female leadership as having a natural place, at least at certain times. Cases in point in Chile's own past include, in the colonial era, Inés de Suárez (Pedro de Valdivia's strong-willed mistress) and the sadistic La Quintrala, and in the nineteenth century Javiera Carrera (a prominent supporter of her three brothers at the time of independence) and Candelaria Goye-nechea – the mother of Pedro León Gallo and a generous contributor to his revolt in 1859. (By sheer force of character she prevented President Montt's soldiers from searching her house in Copiapó.) All of these women have (or anyway used to have) an established place in the Chilean collective memory. Finally, we might remark that single-sex education, the general rule in Chile for most of its history, seems to encourage academic or sporting achievement in girls more than does co-education, which possibly reinforces gender stereotypes. It is probably no accident that Great Britain (with its aristocratic tradition, its historical images of strong queens like Boadicea, Elizabeth I, and Victoria, and its formerly widespread single-sex education) has in recent times elected a woman prime minister, whereas the United States (without a traditional landed elite except in the long-vanished Old South, and with widespread co-education) still shows no signs of putting a woman in the Oval Office.

Population, health, education

The population of Chile rose from around 4.5 million in 1930 to around 8 million in 1964. Its distribution underwent a few changes that need to be noted. The largest cities, Santiago, Valparaiso (with adjacent Viña del Mar), and Concepción (with adjacent Talcahuano), retained and enhanced

---

[17] One of her peccadilloes was to give a seller of watches privileged access to the employees of the state railroad system in return for a 150,000-peso donation to the Feminine party. The *asunto de los relojes*, "the affair of the watches," was joked about for years afterward.

their traditional demographic supremacy. By contrast the collapse of the nitrate industry meant the relative depopulation of the Norte Grande. In 1930 the inhabitants of Iquique numbered only slightly more than in 1907. The northern cities (with the partial exception of Arica, declared a "free port" in the early 1950s) tended to languish. As a catchy popular song of the early 1960s put it, in foxtrot rhythm,

> *Antofagasta dormida,*
> *tus calles están desiertas.*
> *¿Cómo pudiera yo darte*
> *dinamismo siglo veinte?*
> *¡Despierta de tu letargo!*

> Slumbering Antofagasta,
> your streets are deserted . . .
> How could I give you
> twentieth-century dynamism?
> Awake from your lethargy!

Much of the increase in the national population resulted from a decline in general mortality rates, in part the consequence of gradually improving sanitary conditions. The creation of the *Servicio Nacional de Salud* or SNS (National Health Service) in 1952 and the extension of benefits under the social security system contributed to rising standards of health, as did organizations providing child care and nutritional guidance. These services, together with better prenatal care, the introduction of antibiotics, and vigorous programs to eliminate tuberculosis (the single greatest cause of death), slashed the mortality rate. Between 1930 and 1952 the life expectancy for women rose from 37.7 to 53.8 and for men from 35.4 to 49.8. Surviving the first year of life still proved difficult: proportionately more Chileans died then than at other ages – 129 per thousand in 1952, one of the worst infant mortality rates in Latin America. It was to fall by about half over the next twenty years.

Until 1925 education had absorbed almost all of the government's "social" expenditures. After that date, the budget increasingly included social security, health care, and associated expenses (housing, urban improvements, etc). By 1955 education consumed only 20.3 percent of public social spending; housing and urban expenses received 20.4 percent. The social security program, which constituted 41.4 and 51.4 percent of public social expenditures in 1955 and 1961 respectively, became the most expensive item in the budget.

Chileans lived longer now, but not necessarily better. As late as 1960 nearly half of the country's houses had no more than two rooms; rather more than half of these had no access to piped water. Recent studies have shown that the proportion of families consuming less than 2,000 calories a day was the same in 1960 as in 1935. Thus, while most Chileans at birth had the same weight and height as Americans, differences in growth rates quickly developed thereafter. Upper- and middle-class children matured at the same rate as Americans; those of the lower middle and working classes did not. Differences in height and weight between the upper and lower strata of Chilean society were thus greater than those between Americans of different social classes. Malnutrition, in fact, remained a serious problem. In Santiago province, the country's most affluent, 60 percent of the population suffered "nutritional deprivation" in 1968 and 1969, at which point just over half of all families in Chile consumed 1,600 calories daily, while around one-quarter had a daily intake of 2,100.[18]

Foreign observers, it has to be said here, were still too often struck by the misery of the poorer classes in town and countryside alike. The American writer Waldo Frank, visiting Chile in 1942, wrote: "The poverty is appalling; in its dark timelessness, it is almost Oriental."[19] Eighteen or so years later, El Loco Pepe, an Argentine bank robber soon to be famous for his ingenious attempts to escape from the Santiago penitentiary, noted when he arrived in the capital his "painful impression" on seeing "ragged women with little kids in their arms begging for charity in the city center."[20] Certainly the Argentina from which El Loco Pepe emigrated was, in the 1960s, an altogether more prosperous country than Chile.

In many societies a classic route out of poverty has always been education. In Chile, decades of government expenditure on education began to bear fruit after 1950. Literacy rose to 84.6 percent in 1960. (It was at 94 percent by 1990.) This figure obscures, however, a somewhat more dismal reality: most of those who entered the primary educational system remained there for less than five years. Even in the early 1960s only three out of every ten children got beyond the sixth year of education, and only one in every twenty-two lasted until the final year of high school. In practice, therefore, as more than one commentator noted, the educational system, although partially financed by the poor, primarily benefited the middle and upper classes.

In some ways, in fact, it could be said that the country developed a two-tier system of education. Rich families (and many of those of the upper middle class) sent their children to private schools: in the 1940s

[18] Peter Hakim and Giorgio Solimano, *Development, Reform and Malnutrition in Chile* (Cambridge, 1978), p. 8.

[19] Waldo Frank, *South American Journey* (London, 1944) p. 146.

[20] José Roberto Rubio [El Loco Pepe], *La vuelta al pago en 82 años. Las memorias del Loco Pepe* (Santiago, 1967), p. 116.

and 1950s, 28 and 35 percent of school-age youngsters attended private primary and secondary schools respectively. At the secondary level, private schools (122 in 1915, 453 in 1956) were more numerous than the state *liceos,* though with fewer students. Catholics often selected religious schools for their offspring: the Padres Franceses' Sagrados Corazones or the Jesuits' San Ignacio. The more secular-minded, particularly those who wished their children to learn a foreign language, could enroll them in the Lycée Français, the Deutsche Schule, or (for those who could see the coming worldwide hegemony of English) the Grange School, where British traditions (including rugby football) were implanted, or the American-oriented Santiago College. Provincial cities, as well as Santiago, often contained these tiny educational enclaves of foreign culture.

The number of university students now expanded (7,800 in 1940, 19,000 by 1956), as did the number of universities they attended, although in the 1950s fully three-quarters of all students did their studying at the venerable University of Chile, a monster organization by this stage beginning to suffer from academic "overstretch." In addition to the two already existing private universities (the "Católica" in Santiago, and the Concepción campus), two new foundations were established in Valparaiso in the 1920s (the Catholic University of Valparaiso and the Federico Santa María Technical University). In Santiago, González Videla created a new State Technical University[21] in 1947; many of its graduates were to find employment in the new CORFO-sponsored industrial enterprises, and it swiftly developed useful provincial branches. In 1954 Ibáñez approved the formation of a new campus at Valdivia, the Universidad Austral. It was devastated by the 1960 earthquake, but recovered.

Urbanization and urban life

At some point in the late 1930s, Chile crossed the line to become a predominantly urban nation, with a majority of its population living in cities of more than 20,000. Santiago's population now rose vertiginously, from about half a million in the 1920s to over 2 million by the early 1960s. This brought changes greater than any in its past. After the 1920s, in physical terms, the capital expanded well beyond its historic colonial core and limited nineteenth-century additions, partly in line with a *Plan regulador* ("regulating plan") devised by the Austrian town-planner Karl Brunner, contracted in 1928 to advise on the future development of the city. By then the upper and middle classes were increasingly abandoning their traditional downtown residences and relocating to the growing eastern suburbs, the so-called *barrio alto* ("upper district"), which

---

[21] Renamed the University of Santiago de Chile in the 1970s.

over the decades spread remorselessly toward the Cordillera,[22] with new districts like Las Condes, La Reina, and Vitacura (this last being named after an Inca governor of the locality at the time of the Spanish conquest). Altogether more modest districts grew up to the north of the Mapocho River, while the south side of the metropolis became a predominantly (though never exclusively) working-class area. In ways that had been less obvious in the city's past, the social classes were now to some extent insulated from each other in separate districts. Stephen Clissold described the Santiago of the 1940s as "aesthetically and architecturally undistinguished,"[23] and there is no reason to dissent: the city's charms were then, as later on, to be found in its small corners rather than in its not very monumental downtown. By the 1960s, "anti-seismic" technology was enabling *santiaguinos* to construct high-rise buildings for the first time, giving a distinctly new appearance to the capital's hitherto low-level skyline.

The expansion of Santiago, we might mention here, continued to the end of the century and beyond. Its population grew to more than 5 million by 2000, by which time traffic congestion was intense and scheduled restrictions on automobile use were a regular feature of daily life. The color (and to a large extent, the size) of buses became standardized. Supermarkets became common after the 1960s. Shopping malls appeared in the eastern suburbs (and eventually elsewhere), and urban freeways were built on the capital's outskirts. (Highway 68 from Santiago to Valparaiso was upgraded to a freeway in 2001–02.) A construction boom in the late 1970s went on (with occasional hiatuses) in later years. Whole new districts (La Florida, for instance) were developed. The main axis of Providencia, the oldest of the eastern suburbs, came to abound in boutiques, bars and restaurants. Vitacura became the scene of an impressive concentration of high-rise buildings; apartment-blocks proliferated across the *barrio alto* (a term no longer used much). Several downtown streets were "pedestrianized," and the central Plaza de Armas remodeled (not to everyone's taste). Santiago grew into a smarter, livelier and more cosmopolitan city than it had ever been in the past – but, like many big cities, it still offered striking contrasts as between old and new districts, some of them ritzily modern and others seedy and dilapidated.

The demographic explosion of Santiago in the mid-twentieth century was due not only to natural increase but also to internal migration, as lack of opportunity in the countryside forced scores of thousands of Chileans to move away from the haciendas or *minifundios* in quest of work. The contraction of the labor force in the Gran Minería, likewise, added to the throng: by 1952 some 54,000 northerners had joined the rush to the capital since the 1930s.

---

[22] By the 1990s it had more or less got there.   [23] *Chilean Scrapbook* (London, 1952), p. 89.

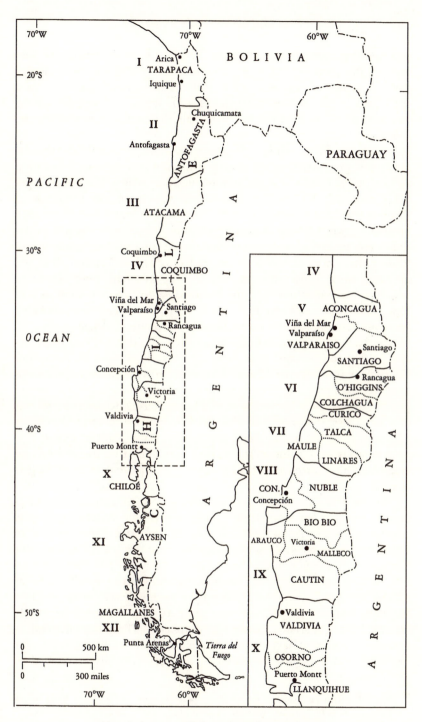

Twentieth-century Chile, with New (1974) Regions

Santiago thus came to dominate the nation's life more completely than ever in the past. By 1960 it contained 28 percent of the country's manufacturing industry and nearly half the industrial labor force. Four out of ten of all Chilean professionals, technicians, and managers lived and worked there, as did more than half the country's secretaries and clerks.

In one important respect, the capital was simply unable to take the strain of rapid expansion. Neither housing nor employment could keep pace with the flood of migrants from the countryside. The result, especially noticeable by the 1950s and early 1960s, was the formation of shantytowns in and around the city – *callampas* ("mushrooms"), as they became known. Lacking electricity, drinking water, and medical provision, these miserable settlements represented the grimmest underside of Chilean life, a true *cinturón de la miseria* ("poverty belt") surrounding and in many cases infiltrating the capital. The generally unemployed or underemployed inhabitants of the *callampas* fended for themselves as best they could – in street-vending, casual labor, domestic service. Probably half a million people lived in the shantytowns by the mid-1960s.

The extraordinary growth of Santiago left all other Chilean cities behind, although the larger ones all had their own *callampas* by the 1960s. The Valparaiso–Viña del Mar and Concepción–Talcahuano conurbations grew steadily in the mid-century decades (with populations of 400,000 and 300,000 respectively by the mid-1960s). Valparaiso's heyday as a port was now long past; the growth of Viña del Mar lessened its attractiveness as a place of residence for the upper and middle classes, and its atmosphere from now onward became more "popular" and raffish than that of its rising neighbor. Other towns remained appreciably smaller, and for the most part sleepier.

The patterns of urban life (and social life in general) in this mid-century period need more serious study and can be sketched only very impressionistically here. Although Church and state had separated in 1925, the nation remained something more than nominally Catholic. But Chileans were not now great churchgoers, if they ever had been. (In this, too, as with poetry, they *were* perhaps the "English of South America" they so often said they were.) The secular state still celebrated religious holidays, though some of these were shorn away in the 1960s (ironically enough by a Christian Democrat government). Those who married in haste often regretted having done so; there was still no divorce law.[24] The better-off could obtain an annulment; the poor generally deserted their

---

[24] Meanwhile capital punishment (still by firing squad) remained on the statute book, though happily it was applied relatively sparingly: between 1890 and 1967 there were 54 executions, an average of 0.7 per year.

spouses. Birth control devices were not difficult to buy, including the pill when this became available. Abortions were technically illegal; but they still terminated almost one in four pregnancies. Prostitution abounded, as it always had, but drugs did not.

On Saturdays and Sundays many of the urban rich still decamped for their fundos or *chacras*, or to the coast, also much frequented in summertime by the middle classes. Older ocean resorts like Viña del Mar or (on a much smaller scale) Constitución were now complemented by a string of seaside settlements, some modest, some more fashionable, along the coast to the north and south of Valparaiso. Tourism also developed on a small scale among the lakes and volcanoes of the South – a particular mecca for anglers in quest of the region's abundant salmon. In wintertime the ski slopes at Farellones (in the mountains behind Santiago) and Portillo attracted a growing crowd of youngsters, for whom, in Santiago, there were also the sporting and country clubs established (from the 1920s on) by the foreign colonies: the British, the Spaniards, the French, the Italians, and others. For the upper and middle classes, the Chile of the 1950s and early 1960s was in many ways a distinctly agreeable country in which to live.

The life of the urban working class was altogether more circumscribed – football matches (soccer was now fully and professionally organized, in British-style "divisions")[25] and *empanadas* at the weekends, or for the more genteel a stroll in the Parque Cousiño or the Quinta Normal (where Pentecostal preachers offered their spiritual wares). A regrettably large number of working-class men still devoted their day-and-a-half off to drinking themselves into a stupor, some recovering to return to their often wretched jobs on time, others staying at home to celebrate what was still the country's favorite Saint's Day, "San Lunes." Maids, the *empleadas* still universal in upper- and middle-class households in the 1960s (and beyond), generally used their Sunday afternoons (often the only rest they received after laboring in their employers' kitchens) to visit the hairdressers, go to the movies, or meet their boyfriends for a few furtive moments.

Mass media, communications, transportation

Gradually, however, horizons expanded. Patterns of popular entertainment changed greatly in the mid-twentieth century in Chile, as they did everywhere else. The old "print culture" was now challenged by the advance of the electronic media, though not supplanted: more than 4

---

[25] British readers might note that one of the professional clubs (at Viña del Mar) was, and is, called Everton.

million books (1,400 separate titles) were printed in the Chile of 1959, and a visitor that year would have found a wide variety of magazines (political, humorous, sporting, feminine, right-wing, left-wing, Catholic, masonic) and newspapers (including tabloids) available at the traditional sidewalk kiosks (*quioscos*) in the cities. At the end of the 1950s *El Mercurio* (it was to celebrate its 150th birthday in 1977) had a daily circulation of around 75,000, its national hegemony no doubt reinforced by its indispensable and comprehensive "small ads" section.

The country's 300 or so cinemas, meanwhile, showed imported American or European movies or, for those who could read the subtitles only with difficulty, the offerings of the intermittently flourishing film industries of Argentina (in the 1930s and 1940s) or Mexico (from the 1940s onward). Chilean film-making sputtered briefly into life in the 1940s (with the inevitable support of CORFO), but the impetus was not maintained; many of the movies then made were directed by Argentines, and in any case did not succeed in the wider Spanish-American market. In the 1960s about five feature films were produced annually, with the help of the two main universities and (once again) the state. Directors like Alvaro Covacevich, Patricio Kaulen, Helvio Soto, and Miguel Littin all won box-office success in Chile. Some of their films became known abroad, the best-known being Littin's *Chacal de Nahueltoro* (1970).

By 1960 Chileans owned close to one million radio sets. (Transistor radios were to spread like wildfire over the ensuing decade, not least in the countryside.) The hundred or so radio stations operating that year poured out an unremitting flow of popular music (accounting for more than half of all broadcasting time), news, sportscasts, comedy, and drama. Television came more slowly to the republic: there were still only 31,000 TV sets in 1964. Antennae did not begin to sprout in any numbers until after 1965, and we may look ahead a bit here: by 1970, 374,000 sets were in use. The viewing fare as it developed by the late 1960s was an eclectic combination: imported American or European programs and Argentine or Mexican *telenovelas*. Locally produced shows, many directed from the University of Chile or the Catholic University,[26] varied from lively political talk shows to totally undemanding variety extravaganzas such as *Sábados Gigantes* ("Giant Saturdays") – later (in the 1990s) transferred to Spanish-language TV in the United States.

Mid-twentieth-century Chileans were becoming steadily more mobile. Increasingly from the 1920s onward, motor buses linked the main cities and revolutionized urban transportation, eventually displacing the electric

---

[26] The first TV stations in Chile were run by these two universities, which also ran, as they continue to run, *professional* soccer teams, a practice denounced in a university magazine of 1962 by the historian Claudio Véliz: his strictures had no effect whatever.

tramcars which had run in Santiago since 1900. Somewhat inappropriately dubbed *góndolas* (a now vanished term) and *micros,* they were later supplemented by the fast-moving mini-buses known altogether more aptly as *liebres* ("hares"). As more people rode on buses, passenger traffic on the railroads began to decline, a tendency reinforced by the growth in internal air services. (Between 1930 and 1960 some twenty regional airports or aerodromes were opened, Santiago being served after 1932 by Los Cerrillos.) While the railroads remained important for the carriage of freight, they were challenged here, too, by the one- and two-man trucking businesses which proliferated after the 1930s and whose national role in 1972 and 1973 was to be so decisive. By the mid-1960s there were some 80,000 trucks (and around 60,000 smaller commercial vehicles) in Chile.

Partly because of the Second World War, the number of private automobiles increased only slowly after 1940, but by the mid-1960s, the number of vehicles on the road had almost tripled (to more than 300,000) – and half of these were passenger cars, not, as in the past, trucks or buses, though in 1960 more than half the cars were more than ten years old. A number of automobile assembly plants were established at Arica by the early 1960s, and during that decade locally finished Austin Minis and Citronetas (an adaptation of the classic Deux Chevaux so prominent in France a bit earlier) were a familiar sight in the streets – often, indeed, the first cars owned by young middle-class Chileans. Greater affluence permitted the better-off to abandon public transportation and to drive to work, and, needless to say, to add to the growing problem of traffic congestion in Santiago.

More cars meant more roads, although most of these, even after the completion of the north-south "Pan American Highway" in 1970, remained unpaved. Driving was not without its hazards. Santiago did not install a system of traffic lights until just before World War II.[27] Nor did traffic lights much restrain the élan with which motorists habitually drove. Pedestrians crossed the street at their peril; the incidence of road accidents was one of the highest in the world in the early 1960s. And Chileans developed their own motoring folklore. Traffic jams, for instance, were often blamed (very unjustly) on the Carabineros: *donde hay paco hay taco* ("where there's a cop there's a snarl-up") was a common saying among drivers in the 1950s and 1960s, and maybe still is.

Communications in general became smoother all around by the end of the 1950s. The postal service, after its lapses in Parliamentary times, now functioned adequately, though the retrieval of parcels from abroad

[27] Here Santiago was ahead of the much larger metropolis of Buenos Aires, which did not do so before the 1960s.

remained an infuriatingly time-consuming procedure. The national telephone system slowly modernized. By the early 1930s some 37,000 phones were in service, though most calls required the assistance of an operator. Demand invariably outstripped supply. By 1952 there was one telephone for every sixty citizens, and the instruments themselves remained difficult to obtain over the next two decades. (It was widely believed, no doubt fancifully, that political connections dictated the speed with which telephones were installed in particular households.) International long-distance might have linked Santiago with Buenos Aires as early as 1928, but even in the 1950s it was sometimes necessary to wait forty minutes to be connected between Santiago and Valparaiso, at a time when the road journey took two and one half hours. Inflation made it necessary to use tokens rather than coins in public phones, when they could be found working at all. It was generally advisable to ask to borrow a phone from a good-natured shopkeeper. By the 1960s, however, many of these quirks of the system were a thing of the past.

And for better and worse, Chile finally became more accessible to the rest of the world, its long isolation at last tempered by the airplane. PANAGRA and Air France began flying to Santiago in 1929. Not until 1935 did the German Condor Airline connect Chile to Germany, with stops at Natal, Rio de Janeiro, and Buenos Aires. (A few Chileans, one of them the notable journalist Abel Valdés Vicuña, crossed the Atlantic on the *Graf Zeppelin* during the years it flew to and from Brazil.) While the Second World War temporarily ended flights from Europe, travel to and from the United States remained open: the traveler could now fly from Santiago to Miami in three days, with overnight stops at Lima and Panama. British Overseas Airways began to serve Chile in the late 1940s, as did KLM, and other European companies soon followed suit. The national airline, LAN-Chile, did not venture out of Chilean airspace before 1946, when it started regular flights to Buenos Aires, adding Lima and Miami to its schedules in 1956 and 1958. Soon afterward a second Chilean airline, LADECO (*Línea Aérea del Cobre*, "Copper Airline"), initially serving the Chuquicamata copper mine, began to extend its operations within the country – later it, too, was to fly abroad. Air travel to and from Chile did not become really easy for Europeans or North Americans until the introduction of jet airliners in the 1960s. (As a direct result, the number of ocean liners regularly calling at Valparaiso dropped off rapidly; the once ubiquitous Pacific Steam Navigation Company withdrew its main service in 1964.)[28] LAN-Chile got its first jets, French-made Sud-Aviation Caravelles, in 1964. The jets and President Frei, we

---

[28] This was a worldwide trend: on the North Atlantic, the number of travelers on airplanes exceeded those on liners for the first time in 1958.

might say, arrived at roughly the same time. Both represented a new image of modernity; both sought to supersede the old; and both were to make their impact on Chile.

A glance at culture (1930s–1960s)

In the middle decades of the twentieth century, as earlier on, Chilean literature staked its claim to international attention mostly through poetry. These were the years when Pablo Neruda established himself as probably (for in matters of taste there can be no disputing) the leading poet of his time in the Spanish language, and as an altogether protean figure who towers over Chile's twentieth-century cultural panorama in ways nobody else will ever quite be able to do. Like Gabriela Mistral, he won the Nobel Prize for Literature (1971) – so far Chile is the only Latin American country to have taken it twice – and nobody has ever had a better claim to it. He was a prolific poet who went on writing all his life. To give an adequate assessment in a line or two is beyond our powers. For millions of Spanish-American readers (not least those who are in love) the poems of his youth, especially the *Veinte poemas de amor y una canción desesperada* ("Twenty Love-Poems and a Song of Despair," 1924), remain favorites, but the truth is that he added to his literary stature in every decade – with the series of *Residencias* ("Residences") in the 1930s, the majestic (if also uneven) *Canto general* ("General Song") of the 1940s, and the three classic volumes of "odes" of the 1950s, the brevity of whose lines disguises the fact that the underlying rhythm follows traditional Spanish seven- and eleven-syllable sequences. However achieved, the effect is marvelous. Neruda's themes are universal: both the progress of humanity and the humble artichoke find a place in his pages. Little if anything escaped his attention. He is, for twentieth-century Chileans, the master of masters, *el vate,* the Bard. Nor is it foolish, we believe, to mention his name alongside that of another Bard, whose *Romeo and Juliet* Neruda translated (rather freely, but magnificently) in 1964.

The shadow of Neruda was a huge one, and it is not surprising that it was some time before the world took note of other Chilean authors, although the local gallery of novelists and short-story writers was more than respectable by the 1950s and 1960s. From the 1930s onward, the earlier fashion for "creolism" was abandoned in favor of more modern and universal themes – a tendency strongly encouraged by the outstanding critic of the period, Hernán Díaz Arrieta ("Alone"), himself a stylist of genuine quality. Modern and universal themes, however, definitely included social themes, strongly developed (sometimes with a hard political edge) by the so-called "generation of 1938," although embodied also in the work of a slightly earlier novelist, Manuel Rojas, whose masterpiece is *Hijo de ladrón* ("Thief's Son," 1951) and also in a remarkable autobiographical trilogy (1933–38) by the nowadays unjustly neglected Carlos Sepúlveda Leyton (1895–1941). But when, in the middle of the 1960s, the celebrated "boom" in the Latin-American novel came along, none of its leading figures was a Chilean. True, some noteworthy Chilean talents (especially members of the "generation of 1957" such as José Donoso and the somewhat younger Jorge Edwards) were by that stage becoming fairly well known outside Chile, as was Nicanor Parra, a poet of great distinction who escaped from Neruda's shadow partly by embracing "anti-poetry." Yet it was only in the mid-1980s that Isabel Allende, with her mesmeric novel *La casa de los espíritus* ("The House of the Spirits"), won the kind of "superstar" status hitherto reserved for Gabriel García Márquez, Mario Vargas Llosa, and Carlos Fuentes.

A serious modern theater tradition in Chile began to grow up in the 1940s, partly inspired by the performances of Margarita Xirgú's Spanish company, whose productions of Lorca's plays are still legendary. Experimental theater programs now sprang into being in both the University of Chile and the Catholic University. (The University of Concepción soon followed suit.) The seeds of renewal thus planted did not take long to germinate, with the appearance in the 1950s and 1960s of a talented generation of Chilean playwrights (though again of mostly local renown): Fernando Debesa, Egon Wolff, Sergio Vodanovic, Alejandro Sieveking, and many more. The tradition was to continue beyond the collapse of democracy in 1973. On a lighter level, no doubt, we need to mention Isidora Aguirre's *La pérgola de las flores* (1960), far and away the most popular musical comedy of recent times in Chile.

In fact, we must always remember that, as W. H. Auden put it,

> The pious fable and the dirty story
> Share in the total literary glory.[29]

Pious fables and dirty stories (there have always been plenty of both in Chile, as everywhere else) have not, perhaps, been very well represented in literature, but popular novelists like Jorge Inostrosa (author of a five-volume evocation of the War of the Pacific, *Adiós al Séptimo de Línea*, 1955–59, later serialized at inordinate length on the radio)[30] must not be ignored. And two admirable contributors to the lighter side of life cannot possibly be omitted from even the simplest account of modern Chilean culture: Paz and Pepo. Marcela Paz's delightful *Papelucho* books (written in the form of an ingenuous child's diary) have now delighted several generations of Chilean children (and rather a large number of Chilean grown-ups). Starting in the 1950s, too, thanks to a pen of genius, that of

---

[29] "Letter to Lord Byron," Part III.   [30] It had sold 500,000 copies by the end of the 1950s.

"Pepo" (René Ríos), Chileans became acquainted with one of the two most memorable cartoon characters ever to have come out of Latin America (or anywhere else for that matter): the immortal Condorito. (The magazine of that name is now sold all over Spanish America, and many who buy it in, say, Mexico, are often unaware of its Chilean provenance.) Our admiration here is unconditional. Condorito and his friends and relations, and the goings-on in the village of "Pelotillehue" (and practically everywhere else in time and space), are authentic creations from which more about Chile, probably, can be learned than from most academic sources. Condorito's only rival in recent times in South America (and she lasted only for the ten years after 1963) has been Argentina's delightful Mafalda.

The abandonment of "creolism" by writers in the 1920s and 1930s was paralleled by similar developments in painting and music. (In architecture, however, a reverse trend got under way after the 1920s, with a new taste for traditional Hispanic designs supplanting the previous European hegemony.) The painters of the "Montparnasse group" or "generation of 1928" (Camilo Mori perhaps deserves to be singled out) sought to embrace the artistic ferment then centered on France, where several of them traveled in the 1920s. This tendency was given a somewhat unexpected boost in 1929, when General Ibáñez shut down the Escuela de Bellas Artes and packed off twenty-six painters and sculptors (including the painter Mori and the sculptor Tótila Albert) to study in Europe. They naturally returned with their allegiance to the Modern movement greatly strengthened. Meanwhile a number of painters from the architecture school at the Catholic University succumbed to the lure of Surrealism, among them Nemesio Antúnez and Roberto Matta (who settled abroad, finally in Italy, where he died in 2002), – twentieth-century Chile's most renowned artists, both of them now firmly in the Latin American pantheon.

In classical music, meanwhile, what is usually called "nationalism" (deriving its inspiration from local folk-styles) steadily lost ground to "internationalism" (the adoption or adaptation of modern European tendencies) among Chilean composers. The key figure in this development (an almost universal one in Latin America) was undoubtedly the eminent Domingo Santa Cruz, whose younger colleague Juan Orrego-Salas also advocated (and practiced) modern, international forms of composition. The institutional framework in which they could work was at first a very fragile one. We cannot talk of a really flourishing musical life in Chile (opera apart) much before the 1940s. It is worth remembering that the Beethoven symphonies had first been heard (as a cycle) in Santiago only in *1913;* and the orchestral society responsible for these concerts had soon dissolved. Much excellent work was done soon afterward by a Bach Society formed in 1917 and lasting till 1932. This led the way in the

1920s (Santa Cruz's role here deserves a very honorable mention) to the revamping of the national conservatoire (created, as we noted in Chapter 4, in 1850), and to the inclusion of music among the subjects studied in the University of Chile's new Faculty of Fine Arts (founded in 1929). The decisive step forward was taken in 1941, when Congress set up the Instituto de Extensión Musical of the University of Chile: one of its first acts was the formation – *at last!* – of a national symphony orchestra.

Notwithstanding the distinct invigoration of musical life by such measures as these, none of Chile's leading composers can really be placed alongside Latin America's "big three" of the twentieth century (the Brazilian Heitor Villa-Lobos; the Mexican Carlos Chávez; the Argentine Alberto Ginastera). But at a different level Chilean *performers* have most certainly made their mark in the musical world. The celebrated baritone Ramón Vinay, for one, became very familiar on the international operatic circuit: at Bayreuth in the 1950s he was a favorite of the Wagner family. We cannot fail to mention, either, one of the world-class pianists of his time, Claudio Arrau (like Vinay, born in Chillán), whose preeminently international profession meant that he, too, lived much of his life abroad. Toward the end of his long career (he died in 1991), his occasional visits to Chile increasingly resembled royal progresses. And why should they not have?

According to the sculptor Rodin, progress exists in the world, but not in art. At a deep level, this is surely true. Yet certain periods *do* become recognized as peculiarly fertile in artistic expression, as being *better* than others. We would venture the claim that, even as Chilean economic progress was faltering, even as social problems intensified, the country's "cultural production" was never livelier than in the 1950s and 1960s. And the impetus was not by any means lost in the bad times that lay ahead. Whatever else may be said about them (and there is plenty), modern Chileans cannot be faulted for creativity.

PART V

Democracy and dictatorship, 1960s–2000s

Between 1964 and 1973 two reforming governments, adopting different forms of revolutionary rhetoric, attempted deep structural reforms in an effort to cure Chile's outstanding social problems and slow economic growth. Whatever their immediate successes, neither the Christian Democrat "revolution in liberty" nor the Marxist parties' "transition to Socialism" succeeded in their aims. Politics on all sides became ideologically highly charged, with acute polarization of opinion setting in during Salvador Allende's presidency (Chapters 11 and 12). This growing crisis led to the breakdown of the political system in September 1973, and the seizure of power by the armed forces. Under the stern leadership of General Pinochet, a neo-liberal economic scheme was imposed on Chile, and drastic national reorganization took place. The results, inevitably, were mixed. At a time of steady economic growth, based once again on exports, the Pinochet regime was successfully challenged by the democratic opposition (led by Christian Democrats and Socialists), which, in the shape of a new and disciplined political coalition, took charge of the country in March 1990 (Chapter 13). This coalition elected three presidents in succession, attempted to correct some of the deep inequities left by the outgoing regime, and saw Chile into the twenty-first century (Chapter 14).

GOVERNMENTS

1964–1970	Eduardo Frei
1970–1973	Salvador Allende
1973–1990	General Augusto Pinochet
1990–1994	Patricio Aylwin
1994–2000	Eduardo Frei*
2000–[06]	Ricardo Lagos

*son of the president of 1964–70

11

Revolution in liberty, 1964–70

*Juan Verdejo[1] como un rey
si gobierna Eduardo Frei.*

Juan Verdejo like a king
if Eduardo Frei is governing!

– Christian Democrat slogan,
early 1960s

Catholic social reformers

In any Catholic country, a political option colored by Catholicism is always conceivable, even if many such countries do not produce one. Chile in the early 1960s was still very much a Catholic country – in spite of the strong secularist tradition of Radicals and left-wingers, the half million or so Chilean Protestants, or the fact that only one baptized Catholic in seven regularly attended Mass on Sundays. In Chile, politicians of Catholic background put together the reforming movement that won the presidency in 1964, and this produced the first great turning point of Chilean history since the 1930s. Chile's Christian Democrat party was the first such party to win power in Latin America. Domestically, it was to prove the strongest political party of the second half of the twentieth century.

As we have seen, there had been a traditional link between the Catholic Church and the Conservative party. The separation of Church and state in 1925 did something to lessen the old connection, but so, too, over a longer period, did changes within the Church itself. In the mid-nineteenth century, Pope Pius IX's intransigence had helped stiffen Archbishop Valdivieso's opposition to Manuel Montt. A century later the Church's changing outlook helped to turn certain Chilean Catholics in the direction of social reform. At first it was a mere handful, in particular

---

[1] Juan Verdejo: symbolic personification of the common man invented by the caricaturist Jorge Délano ("Coke"), and made known in the pages of his magazine *Topaze*.

a group of former students of the Catholic University, including the future Christian Democrat leaders Eduardo Frei, Bernardo Leighton, Rafael Agustín Gumucio, and Radomiro Tomic. They first joined the Conservative party (1932), then formed its youth movement (1935), and finally set up their own party, the Falange Nacional (1938).

As politicians the *falangistas* won much respect for their political integrity. In 1938, Bernardo Leighton gave up the ministry of Labor in protest when President Alessandri attacked *Topaze*. Eight years later Eduardo Frei, then Justice minister, was the first in vice-president Duhalde's cabinet to resign after the bloody affray in the Plaza Bulnes. Such gestures were admired, yet electorally speaking the Falange made little headway before the mid-1950s. Other "social Christians" (including the well-loved Dr. Eduardo Cruz-Coke) had remained within the Conservative fold. In 1949 they too formed their own separate Social Christian Conservative party, which for a year or two did better than the Falange in elections. There was no point in having two such movements in Chile, and in June 1957 they fused to form the new Christian Democrat party (PDC).

It would be very misleading to see the growth of the PDC as having been actively promoted by the Church. Two reform-minded priests, Fr. Fernando Vives and Fr. Jorge Fernández Pradel, had provided some of the impetus for the original Falange group, but the hierarchy's interest in social reform was at that stage limited. The reforming Catholic Action programs set up in the 1930s (more socially oriented in Chile than elsewhere in Latin America) involved only a tiny minority of Catholics. As late as 1947 the much-loved archbishop of Santiago, José María Caro (Chile's first cardinal), denounced the *falangistas* as insufficiently anti-Communist. This climate changed only slowly, with the assimilation of the "social encyclicals" of the Papacy – *Rerum novarum* (1891), *Quadragesimo Anno* (1931) – and the thought of modern Catholic philosophers such as Jacques Maritain. In 1947 an active and later much revered Jesuit, Fr. Alberto Hurtado (famous for his nocturnal forays in a green pick-up truck to rescue destitute children for the orphanages he founded), set up his *Acción Sindical y Económica Chilena* (ASICH, Chilean Economic and Union Action) in a new attempt to foster Catholic trade unionism. The socially conscious bishop of Talca, Manuel Larraín (a close friend of Fr. Hurtado's), lent his support to the *falangista* Emilio Lorenzini, whose efforts to organize vineyard workers near Curicó won him a prison sentence (1953). The workers then staged a much-publicized march on Santiago to secure his release. Both the Church and the Falange were by now increasingly interested in mobilizing the still almost completely "unorganized" countryside.

After its formation in 1957, as we have seen, the PDC made very rapid progress. Eduardo Frei's unexpectedly good vote in the 1958 presidential election enhanced his growing national stature. In 1939, Gabriela Mistral had seen him as the outstanding *falangista*, a man "of concrete ideas, unsentimental, but of noble nature."[2] He was serious-minded, very well read, and also tall, with a prominent nose much appreciated by the caricaturists of *Topaze* and which won him the nickname *Pinocho* ("Pinocchio"), a nickname also applied, rather confusingly, to a later Chilean notability. After 1958, Frei and the PDC embarked on a determined effort to create new networks of support, in the universities, in the *callampas*, in the countryside, and not least among the new voters flooding on to the electoral registers. PDC membership is said to have quintupled between 1957 and 1964.

But what did it stand for? The party's electoral symbol (inherited from the Falange) was an arrow with two bars across the stem – it symbolized the party's claim that both capitalism and socialism could be transcended in a "communitarian" society. Definitions of the "communitarian society" were never exactly precise. To some it meant profit-sharing schemes in enterprises, to others some kind of vaguely "organic" collaboration between workers and employers, to still others (the PDC's "left wing") the Yugoslav-style "market socialism" attracting attention during those years. Yet however indefinite its world-view, the PDC clearly embodied a serious aspiration to social reform (not least agrarian reform), combined with a fierce attachment to democracy – in short, a "revolution in liberty."

For its part, the Church now became discernibly more sympathetic to such aims. Under Fr. Emilio Tagle (archbishop of Valparaiso after 1961), the larger of the country's two seminaries trained a new generation of priests in a greater awareness of the problems of the poor. Between 1955 and 1964 half the bishoprics in Chile changed hands, the new incumbents being more favorable to reform, as was also true of Raúl Silva Henríquez, elevated to the archbishopric of Santiago in 1961. Moreover the Church now set up a whole range of new organizations to articulate its growing social thrust. At the Jesuits' Centro Bellarmino, a formidable Belgian, Fr. Roger Vekemans, heading his own research center (DESAL), masterminded a whole platform of "revolutionary reforms" for Latin America.[3] More important (for the PDC as well as the Church) was the creation of Catholic-based neighborhood committees, mothers' groups, and youth clubs in roughly half the *callampas* surrounding Santiago. In 1962 two notable pastoral letters from the bishops confirmed the new emphasis on social action and reform. All such developments were strongly affected by the international renewal of the Church, the *aggiorna-*

---

[2] Eduardo Frei, *Memorias 1911–1934* (Santiago, 1989), p. 158.

[3] Fr. Vekemans' forceful personality helped foster the impression that he was the *éminence grise* of the PDC government after 1964. Having in his own eyes failed to save Chile from Communism, he left the country within days of the 1970 presidential election.

mento brought about in the pontificate of John XXIII and at the Second Vatican Council, where the Chilean bishops made a good impression.

Frei and the PDC undoubtedly benefited from the Church's self-renewal (and its new networks), despite their sincere claim that the PDC was strictly non-confessional. This can be seen in analyses of voting behavior. The measurement of public opinion in Chile was still in its infancy: the respected (and for many years rather solitary) pioneer of such studies, Dr. Eduardo Hamuy, conducted his first serious survey (confined to Santiago) in 1958, and another was carried out prior to the 1964 election. Frei's support (leaving aside the Right's contribution to his victory) was drawn from a very heterogeneous social base: Catholics (definitely out in force), the urban middle class, and a respectable section of the working class. It seems also to be true that many of those who joined the PDC in its years of expansion were "somewhat more conservative than longer-standing party members."[4] Frei's stance – between "reactionaries with no conscience" and "revolutionaries with no brains," as he put it at a rally in Valparaiso[5] – had obvious appeal to a wide spectrum of opinion. And in 1964–65 there was an evident groundswell of sympathy for the PDC that augured well for the "revolution in liberty."

A "parliament for Frei"

Yet this sympathy was hardly universal. The parties of FRAP soon declared their opposition to the PDC government, which the Socialists dismissed, in an already well-worn phrase, as *la nueva cara de la derecha* ("the new face of the Right"). Given their electoral contribution in 1964, the parties of the Right naturally hoped that the PDC was less reforming than it sounded. Frei soon disabused them of this notion. But, far outweighed by the Right, the Left, and the Radicals in Congress, the PDC could make little early headway with its program: its first bills were nearly all rejected or entangled in committee. With congressional elections due in March 1965, the PDC staked everything on the cry of "a parliament for Frei!" Rather unexpectedly, the gamble paid off. Winning just over two-fifths of the popular vote, the PDC took eighty-two seats in the Chamber of Deputies (a majority) and increased its senators from three to thirteen – not quite enough to prevent a united opposition from blocking legislation.[6] The most remarkable feature of this electoral "earthquake" was the near-eclipse of the Right, down from one-third of

---

[4] Michael Fleet, *The Rise and Fall of Chilean Christian Democracy* (Princeton, 1985), p. 79.

[5] *El Mercurio,* September 1, 1964.

[6] Thirteen women were elected to the new Congress, a percentage (6.5%) which, though small, put to shame the British House of Commons or *a fortiori* the U.S. Congress of that period.

Table 11.1. Percentages of the popular vote won by the four main political blocs, 1958–73.

Election	RIGHT	PDC	RADICAL	MARXIST
1958 Presid.	ALESSANDRI 31.6	Frei 20.7	Bossay 15.6	Allende 28.9
1960 Municip.	29.5	13.9	20.0	18.9
1961 Congress.	30.4	15.4	21.4	22.1
1963 Municip.	23.6	22.0	20.8	23.5
1964 Presid.	—	FREI 56.1	Durán 5.0	Allende 38.9
1965 Congress.	12.5	42.3	13.3	22.7
1967 Municip.	14.3	35.6	16.1	28.7
1969 Congress.	20.1	29.7	12.9	28.2
1970 Presid.	Alessandri 34.9	Tomic 27.8	—	ALLENDE 36.3
1971 Municip.	21.9	25.6	8.0	39.4
1973 Congress.	23.6	29.1	3.8	34.8

RIGHT: Combined vote of Liberal and Conservative parties 1958–65, vote of National party 1967–69, combined vote of National and Radical Democrat parties 1970–73.

PDC: Christian Democrat vote, excluding smaller allies.

RADICAL: Vote of "official" Radical party only.

MARXIST: Combined vote of Communist and Socialist parties, excluding smaller allies, e.g., during UP period, API, MAPU, IC, PSD (these together totaled 4.5 percent in 1973).

the vote (1961) to one-eighth. The Radicals also lost ground; the Left held its own. (See Table 11.1.) Both the Socialists (with vehemence) and the Communists (more moderately) now reiterated their opposition to Frei, resentful that the PDC was staking its claim to be the party of true reform, while the Radicals, at their quadrennial conference in June 1965, began to contemplate a renewed alliance with the Left, much to the disgust of Julio Durán and his following.

Unhappily, the electoral earthquake was soon followed by a real one, the most serious for Santiago in a century. A dam-break in the Andes caused 300 deaths. Shortly afterward, Frei's troubles were compounded by the international crisis brought on by the U.S. intervention in the Dominican Republic (April 1965). This provoked angry demonstrations in Santiago. Frei had already asserted Chile's independent stance by restoring diplomatic relations with the Soviet Union and Eastern Europe (though not Cuba, with which Alessandri had broken off relations), and he now did so again: Chile, unsupported by the other Latin American delegates, condemned President Lyndon Johnson's action at the Organization of American States. The eminent troubleshooter Averell Harriman was hastily jetted down to Santiago in a vain effort to change Frei's mind.

As it happened, the American connection with Chile was again highlighted later in 1965, by the revelation that the U.S. Defense Department was sponsoring a social-science inquiry into Chile's "internal war potential." This was seen by some as a crude attempt to spy on the Chilean Left, and the resulting furor caused this grotesquely named "Project Camelot" to be abandoned. Frei was the last man to indulge in the rhetoric of anti-imperialism; in any case, the United States was providing Chile with large amounts of aid under President Kennedy's "Alliance for Progress" (around US$720 million between 1961 and 1970, the largest amount, on a per capita basis, given to any Latin American nation). Frei did, however, believe in strengthening links with Western Europe, and traveled there in July 1965 for a series of official and state visits. The triumph of the PDC had aroused much international interest, and he was well received. In London, *The Times* hailed him as "the most significant political personality in Latin America." In Paris, he had three long talks with General Charles de Gaulle. In Rome, Pope Paul VI beamed approval on the revolution in liberty. On his return to Santiago's Los Cerrillos airport, the president was acclaimed by a crowd of 100,000 people. Nationally as well as internationally, the tide seemed to be flowing his way.

Yet no reformer, as Machiavelli pointed out long ago, can expect life to be easy. With reform legislation taking its time in Congress, the more radical wing of the PDC began to stir. In March 1966, when troops killed seven workers during a strike at the El Salvador copper mine, the diatribes of the Left gained credibility, even within the PDC. The party's second national conference (August 1966) revealed a three-way division: the *oficialistas,* whose loyalty to Frei was unconditional, the *rebeldes* ("rebels"), who wanted more radical policies and greater party control over government, and the so-called *terceristas* ("thirdists"), whose criticisms of the government were more restrained, and who sought compromise within the party. For the moment the *oficialistas* had no difficulty in maintaining control.

Some of the PDC's difficulties undoubtedly stemmed from the sheer extent of its triumph in 1964–65. Its decision to govern alone, without seeking allies, was an aberrant one by the normal standards of Chilean politics. Had this been the Parliamentary period, a PDC-Radical alliance would have swiftly been cobbled together. As it was, the somewhat triumphalist attitudes, not to say hubris, of certain Christian Democrats (Radomiro Tomic and others even talked of "thirty years in power") were hardly calculated to win friends. The emollient deals and compromises of coalition politics were forgotten by this suddenly successful (and for that reason alone resented) newcomer among the traditional parties. To some Chileans, the PDC's criteria for the dispensation of patronage seemed more partisan, indeed more ideological, than had been the case when the Radicals (those past-masters in this art) had ruled the roost. The atmosphere of politics was somehow changing. The writer Cristián Huneeus, returning home in 1966 after three years in England, wondered whether it might still be possible to live in Chile "as if in the nineteenth century."[7] It was not. As another writer around this time perceptively commented: "Power has turned out to be a supermarket business. Before it used to be the corner grocery."[8]

Social reforms and economic frustrations

Four particular areas of reform had high priority for the PDC government: *promoción popular,* education and welfare, the countryside, and copper. *Promoción popular* – the fostering of networks of local, self-helping organizations, especially among the "unorganized" populations of the shantytowns – was developed vigorously from the outset, and was placed under a national supervisory council (*Conserjería nacional*). Residents' committees (*juntas de vecinos*), mothers' centers (*centros de madres*), parents' groups, youth clubs, sports associations – all of these now proliferated. By 1970, according to the government, some 20,000 "units" of this type had sprung into existence, about half of these being *centros de madres* with

[7] *Autobiografía por encargo* (Santiago, 1985), p. 88.
[8] Leonard Gross, *The Last Best Hope: Eduardo Frei and Chilean Democracy* (New York, 1967), p. 132.

an estimated membership of 450,000 women. (The government also claimed to have distributed 70,000 sewing machines to these centers.) In his last annual message to Congress, Frei asserted that such measures had given "a new form of life and hope" to hundreds of thousands of Chileans.

The Left was initially wary of *promoción popular,* seeing it as a paternalistic scheme whereby the PDC could gain a vast new clientele, to counterbalance the Left's continued predominance in the labor movement. Only in 1968 did Frei get Congress to confer official status on *juntas de vecinos.* But where the PDC led, others could very easily follow, and by the end of the 1960s the Left had made considerable inroads into the *poblaciones* ("settlements"), as the *callampas* were now more politely called. The Left was also very much to the fore in encouraging the seizure of urban land (for new *poblaciones*) by the homeless, a regular occurrence in 1969–70 and also through the early 1970s.

Such urban land seizures simply reflected a growing problem: with an expanding city population (Santiago swelled by 800,000 in the 1960s), the government could not keep up with the relentless demand for housing. It did not even meet its own targets. Even so, between 1964 and 1970 some 260,000 new houses were built (around one-third of these by CORVI, a state housing corporation set up in 1953), and about 200,000 *soluciones habitacionales* ("housing solutions") were claimed – this particular term covered the provision of sites for self-help housing projects; a specific program, *Operación Sitio* (Operation House-Site), accounted for around one-third of such "solutions." The PDC's concern for improving welfare was also shown in the fact that the number of hospitals (and beds) doubled during this period. At its highest levels Chilean medicine had long been excellent. (Heart transplants were carried out by Chilean surgeons soon after the technique was pioneered in 1967.) But medical attention remained very uneven: in 1970 there was still an overconcentration of doctors in Santiago, though medical care was by then spreading in the provinces, partly through government action.

Educational reform could not be guaranteed to help the PDC politically, whatever its longer-range effect on social mobility. Here the effort was noteworthy: as a proportion of public expenditure, education rose from one-seventh to one-fifth. (Military spending in 1970 was around one-eighth.) And, as Harold Blakemore has suggested, "the period was one of extraordinary ferment at all educational levels."[9] Something like 3,000 new schools were built: nobody driving around the Central Valley in the later 1960s could fail to notice the simple new school buildings dotting the countryside. By 1970 primary education covered 95 percent of children in the relevant age group. A number of imaginative new

---

[9] "Chile," in Nancy Parkinson, ed., *Educational Aid and National Development* (London, 1976), p. 343.

textbooks (especially at the secondary level) were introduced. The more traditionally minded might lament that history was now made part of "social sciences" in the new curricula. But we have to remember here that teaching methods and materials had scarcely changed in decades. Nothing comparable to these changes has been seen since the 1960s in Chile.

Agrarian reform marked a still stronger break with the past – in some ways it was the strongest such break since independence. Chile now had, in Brian Loveman's words, "six years of drastic change in the country-side."[10] Frei and the PDC both greatly stimulated rural unionization and began to expropriate estates in a serious way. The long-enduring rural hegemony of landowners was thus seriously threatened for the first time in the country's history.

A simplification of legal procedures (February 1965) enabled trade unions in the countryside to grow much faster than ever before. Union membership as a whole approximately doubled between 1964 and 1970: about half of this increase was accounted for by the new rural unions, for which a special law was enacted in April 1967. By mid-1970 there were about 500 of these, grouped into three "federations" (*Triunfo Campesino, Libertad, Ranquil*) with a total membership of around 130,000. The unionized labor force was still a minority in the countryside, but with the agricultural minimum wage raised to the urban level, with strikes and disputes, with labor laws enforced (albeit selectively) for the first time, it was obvious that the balance of power in the countryside was shifting. As with *promoción popular*, the PDC no doubt expected a political dividend, but once again the Left took up the challenge: one of the three new peasant federations, *Ranquil*, was part of the Left's expanding rural network.

In its early years, the PDC government used the Alessandri agrarian reform law vigorously. It expanded both CORA and INDAP (whose vehicles were soon a familiar sight on the dusty rural roads) and expropriated some 400 haciendas prior to mid-1967. But the government naturally wanted its own more ambitious plans to take legislative form. The necessary constitutional reform (Article 10.10) and the new agrarian reform bill had a protracted passage through Congress, exciting the ire of the Right in general and hacendados in particular. The reform law (Law 16.625), signed in July 1967 by Frei (in the kind of lavish public ceremony for which the PDC had a distinct fondness), made all farms of more than 80 "basic" hectares[11] liable to expropriation, the owners being entitled to retain an 80-hectare "reserve" and to compensation in the

---

[10] *Struggle in the Countryside* (Bloomington, Ind., 1976), p. 278.

[11] This meant 80 hectares of irrigated Central Valley land. Estates larger than 80 hectares but not irrigated to the same standard could thus be exempted from expropriation.

form of a small cash payment and long-term government bonds. Inefficiently run haciendas were the first to be targeted for expropriation (in 1968 CORA devised a points system to rate efficiency). By the close of Frei's period, using the old and new laws, CORA had expropriated more than 1,300 haciendas – between one-fifth and one-quarter of all properties liable to takeover. The agrarian reform was thus far from complete, but it was most emphatically under way.

Inevitably there were those who wished to go faster, an aim shared both by the *rebelde* wing of the PDC and the Left. Seizures (*tomas*) of estates by peasants, often egged on by the Left or enthusiastic INDAP agents, became very frequent in 1969–70, these two years seeing 400 *tomas*. Not surprisingly landowners sometimes resisted. When in mid-1969 more than forty *fundos* were seized in the Melipilla district, only timely intervention by Carabineros prevented a bloody pitched battle. Elsewhere bloodshed was not avoided. On April 30, 1970, Hernán Mery, a CORA regional official, was fatally injured in an affray at an estate at Longaví (near Linares) being defended by its combative owner. Agrarian reform had found its martyr. By 1970 it was proving hard to contain agrarian mobilization.

A serious agrarian reform always poses the question of how the countryside is to be organized afterward. In Chile there was no shortage of suggestions. The *rebeldes* of the PDC (exemplified by Jacques Chonchol, vice-president of INDAP) wanted sweeping reorganization all around. The peasants, especially the ex-inquilinos, did not share the aims of urban intellectuals. Initially, at least, expropriated *fundos* were not subdivided, but became *asentamientos* ("settlements") worked under an elected peasant committee and CORA. After five years, the members (*socios*) of each *asentamiento* were to decide whether to work it collectively or to subdivide. More than 900 *asentamientos* were formed by the end of Frei's term: of these around 100 had made their decision, most choosing to continue as undivided units.

The chief beneficiaries of the agrarian reform as it unfolded in the short term were, in fact, the *socios* of the *asentamientos*. With rapidly rising wages, these almost became a new privileged class in the countryside. Day-laborers and casual workers (denied *socio* status) fared much less well. Among the *minifundistas* and sharecroppers of the "unreformed sector," INDAP strove valiantly to develop co-operatives, and with some success. Landowners, for their part, responded to the threat of extinction by reorganizing the SNA (by 1970 it embraced a much wider range of rural proprietors than previously) and by promoting employers' and smallholders' unions – an early indication that conservatives as well as radicals were quite capable of actively mobilizing. Sometimes (perhaps taking their cue from similar goings-on in France) indignant farmers blocked highways in order to publicize their demands. Agricultural output rose slightly during the PDC years, in spite of the fact that 1968 saw the most disastrous drought in living memory. More of this increase came from the "unreformed sector" than from the *asentamientos,* where much of what was grown or raised was understandably consumed by the *socios* themselves.

Any ambitious program of reform is bound to be expensive. Public spending doubled between 1964 and 1970 (from E°8,453,000 to E°16,161,000 in 1969 escudos). In looking around for additional revenue it was natural for Frei to see what could be extracted from the copper industry. The aim here was to secure greater control over the American companies and to stimulate large increases in production, which in turn would enhance revenues. Rather than outright nationalization (as long advocated by the Left), Frei favored the more cautious policy of "Chileanization," as it was termed – the acquisition of a 51 percent holding in the mining companies. In return for tax concessions, these would increase both investment and production. Frei called this scheme the *viga maestra* ("master plank") of his platform. Kennecott (whose subsidiary, Braden, ran El Teniente) agreed to Chileanization immediately (December 1964). Anaconda (owners of Chuquicamata and El Salvador) showed much greater reluctance. Only in 1969, after strong demands for nationalization from the Left (and part of the PDC), did Frei renew his approach to Anaconda, which then asked to be nationalized with due compensation. The eventual deal, announced with much fanfare in June 1969, provided for immediate Chileanization, followed by a final Chilean takeover later on – what Frei called a *nacionalización pactada* or "agreed nationalization."

Chileanization failed to convince Frei's left-wing critics, although production increased and both Kennecott and Anaconda developed plans for further expansion. The government itself made several intelligent new moves here. The old "Copper Department" was upgraded as CODELCO (*Corporación del Cobre,* Copper Corporation) and given both new tasks and an expert staff. Chileans became much more prominent at the managerial level in the mines. Chile was now also taking more of a hand in refining, with the building (under Alessandri) of a new plant at Las Ventanas, north of Valparaiso (its enormous chimney still pollutes the surrounding countryside), to supplement the older works at Paipote, near Copiapó.[12] Most important of all, the government intervened in pricing policy: from 1966, in a decisive shift, Chilean copper was sold at prices quoted on the London Metal Exchange – at that point double the prices accepted by the American companies. Since copper prices were now soaring, thanks in part to the rapidly escalating war in Vietnam, this meant a large increase

[12] In the Norte Chico "Paipote" is sometimes used as a nickname for heavy drinkers.

Table 11.2. Chile 1964–70: selected indicators.

	1964	1965	1966	1967	1968	1969	1970
Per capita GDP	86.4	89.6	96.4	95.5	96.7	100	101.4
Government Expenditure (100 = 1969)	61.8	76.6	87.4	87.9	95.6	100	118.2
Fiscal Revenue (100 = 1969)	51.4	65.0	79.5	86.4	92.2	100	113.2
Balance of Payments ($M 1969)	63.1	81.3	94.3	-31.6	109.7	80.7	91.0
Imports ($M)	611.9	615.5	775.4	769.0	801.6	926.8	1202.0
Exports ($M)	593.2	683.1	865.3	874.3	911.0	1173.3	1272.0
Inflation (%)	46.0	28.8	22.9	18.1	26.6	30.7	32.5
Industrial Output (Physical)(100 = 1969)	80	87.2	95.6	96.9	98.3	100	103.5
Total Trade Union Membership (000s)	270.5	292.6	351.5	411.2	499.7	530.9	551.0
Rural Union Membership (% of total trade union membership)	0.6	0.7	3.0	11.5	16.7	19.7	20.7
Strikes	564	723	1073	1114	1124	1277	1819

Source: Ricardo Ffrench-Davis, *Políticas económicas en Chile, 1952–1970* (Santiago, 1973), Tables 35, 43, 44, 51, and 68; Barbara Stallings, *Class Conflict and Economic Development in Chile 1958–1973* (Stanford, 1978), Tables A.4, A.5, A.6, A.13.

in tax revenue: between 1966 and 1970, it ran at twice the level of the Alessandri years. On this score, the PDC government was handed a piece of very good luck. It certainly needed it.

The title of a book by the economist Aníbal Pinto, published just before the 1964 election, described Chile as "a difficult economy." It remained difficult throughout Frei's term. The PDC government had to balance the conflicting claims of reform, growth, and stability. Its aim was to promote increased production all around, to enable reform to be maintained while inflation was held down. Frei's economic teams fared no better than their predecessors in squaring the circle. The opening phase of PDC rule was marked by a sudden and welcome spurt of all-around growth, but this gave way to the less impressive final years of the decade, with lower growth rates and rising inflation, which meant fewer resources available for the PDC's reform programs.

There was, however, a conscious effort now to rationalize and to plan – the best symbol of this being the early creation of ODEPLAN (*Oficina de Planificación Nacional*), the new state planning office. To smooth the ups and downs of foreign trade, an intelligent policy of regular small devaluations of the escudo went into effect in April 1965. A number of fiscal innovations – the raising of income and sales taxes, the indexation of certain other taxes, the imposition of an *impuesto patrimonial* (wealth tax) affecting about 80,000 people, the reassessment of property values, a new drive to halt tax evasion – meant that the yield from direct taxation doubled by 1970. This, combined with the higher revenues from copper already mentioned, enabled Chile to maintain a favorable balance-of-payments position and to build up reserves. Exports roughly doubled in value, with copper still making most of the running. Efforts were now made to diversify overseas markets: by 1970 Chile was even trading again (in a small way) with Cuba. Here we must mention the initiatives of Frei and his highly personable foreign minister Gabriel Valdés to promote schemes of Latin American economic integration. These years saw the formation of the new Andean Group (1969) – Chile, Peru, Bolivia, Ecuador, Colombia, and (later) Venezuela. It would be only slightly wrong to describe the Andean Group as a Christian Democrat invention. Its promise was not fulfilled, but that is another story.

With regard to industry (for which it was hoped the Andean Group would provide new outlets) the government followed a more conservative policy, despite the PDC's proclaimed belief in "communitarian" enterprises, whatever that might mean. Even so, the business elite (only part of which was sympathetic to Frei) and its venerable pressure group SOFOFA were far from won over. This was reflected in the decline in private investment, which went down by about one-fifth in the 1960s. (Chile's investment rate had long been low even by Latin American standards.) The state was more or less obliged to play a part here. Indeed, the entire PDC program can be seen as an extension and intensification of the state-interventionist tradition that had built up since the Ibáñez regime of the 1920s. By 1969–70 the state was responsible for well over half of all industrial investment. Nor did the state neglect infrastructural improvements. Hydroelectric capacity was expanded by ENDESA's huge Rapel project (near Rancagua), from which power began to surge in 1968. (By the mid-1990s, hydroelectricity accounted for 80 percent of Chile's power.) ENTEL (*Empresa de Telecomunicaciones*), a new state enterprise, began work on a national telecommunications system. ENAP built an oil refinery at Concepción and continued to drill for oil in the far south. Transport also benefited, with the building of a new international airport at Pudahuel (Los Cerrillos was now too small), the planning of the French-designed Metro for Santiago (its first section opened in 1975 and by 2000 the blue trains of the smartly maintained network were running on three completed lines and through more than fifty stations), and the cutting of the 2.75-kilometer Lo Prado tunnel, which shortened the road journey from Santiago to Valparaiso (and Viña del Mar) by forty-five minutes. (A parallel tunnel was added thirty years later to cope with increased traffic on Highway 68). The state was also active in a number of joint ventures with foreign firms, notably the impressive petrochemical complex installed at Concepción in association with Dow Chemical, which participated on very favorable terms.

Frei and the PDC inherited and made use of Alessandri's liberal legislation on foreign investment. With multinational corporations extending their influence all around the globe in the 1960s, it is hardly surprising to find them making advances in Chile. Foreign (especially U.S.) investment in manufacturing was a striking feature of the Frei years, both encouraged and welcomed by the government. Either by establishing local subsidiaries or by buying out older established local firms (like INSA, the tire company), the multinationals entrenched themselves in the newer, most dynamic sector of industry – electronics, pharmaceuticals, automobile assembly. By 1970 some forty out of the top one hundred Chilean companies were effectively controlled by foreign interests, at which point twenty-four of the leading thirty American multinationals (as ranked by *Fortune*) were operating in the country. Foreign firms in 1970 controlled about one-quarter of all industrial capital. Since many of the new industries were capital-intensive, they had little effect on employment patterns. And although by the end of the 1960s Chile was producing virtually the whole range of consumer goods (including consumer durables such as TV sets and washing machines), many capital goods still had to be imported. The advantageous terms on which foreign firms operated, their growing saliency in manufacturing, their repatriation of profits – these aspects were much debated, not least among left-wing social scientists, of whom there were many. The name (prominently displayed on its outer wall) of an American-owned factory on the south-western outskirts of Santiago, AMERICAN SCREW CHILE, lent itself to the obvious crude joke by the linguistically knowledgeable.

In spite of genuine signs of economic advance (especially in 1965–66), the perennial Chilean problem of inflation continued to haunt the PDC government. Early stabilization policies were fairly successful; growth was high and inflation fell. Wage increases ran ahead of what the government wanted, but this did not matter immediately. Over the longer term, however, it proved impossible for Frei to devise a good relationship with the trade unions. PDC unionists effectively withdrew from the Left-controlled CUT between 1962 and 1968. Attempts to promote "parallel" unionism got almost nowhere. In 1967, Sergio Molina, Frei's Finance minister, conscious of the falling investment rate, presented an elegant but politically foolhardy plan whereby 5 percent of the *reajuste* (the now traditional annual wage-and-salary increase) was to be held back and placed in a national investment fund, to which employers were also to contribute. Employees were to receive the withheld 5 percent in the form of long-term government bonds, and were also to give up the right to strike for one year. The plan ran into immediate resistance. The opposition caustically christened the long-term bonds *chiribonos;*[13] the CUT staged a one-day general strike, during which four workers and a child were killed by police. The *chiribono* scheme faded away.

Seen in retrospect, this episode was a critical turning point for the "revolution in liberty." Inflation rose again in 1968, 1969, and 1970. With inflation outrunning growth, with the drought of 1968 pushing up the price of local and imported food, with unions once again demanding higher wages, it became increasingly hard to maintain a balanced policy – although the worst effects of slower growth were palliated by high copper revenues. In his last annual address to Congress, Frei denounced what he termed "the new feudalism," in other words, labor unions and other special interests pressing their claims beyond the bounds of what the government thought reasonable. Although constitutional amendments passed in 1969–70 *did* slightly enhance the executive's control over economic affairs,[14] there was little Frei could do to keep the barons in order.

By 1970, therefore, it seemed to some observers that "to a large extent the government had lost the control it had earlier attained over the economic situation."[15] Every age has its cant, and it was part of the cant of the late twentieth century that economic figures are to be taken as sacred. Yet figures

---

[13] *Bonos* = bonds. *Chirimoyo* (from the chirimoya fruit, which goes bad quickly) is Chilean slang for a bouncing check.

[14] These amendments also allowed for a plebiscite in cases of disagreement between president and Congress, the creation of a new Constitutional Tribunal, and the extension of the suffrage to illiterates.

[15] Ricardo Ffrench-Davis, *Políticas económicas en Chile, 1952–1970* (Santiago, 1973), p. 183.

never tell us everything. More Chileans felt comfortably off in 1970 than ever before. There were far fewer beggars in the streets of Santiago than ever before. The boundaries of the modern consumer society were clearly much wider than ever before. From the vantage point of three years later, the writer and art critic Jorge Elliott thought that "Chile in 1970 was prospering . . . , on the point of take-off toward full development."[16] Others shared this impression. Nevertheless it remains true that some of the early promise of the PDC government had faded. The old dilemmas – slow growth, inflation, maldistribution of income, the concentration of economic power – remained stubborn and intractable. In this sense Radomiro Tomic was right to insist, as he did so often in 1969–70, that a *profundización,* a deepening, of the process of reform would be necessary if the PDC succeeded in winning a second six years in office.

Radicalization, polarization, mobilization

By 1967 the prospects for a second PDC presidency were already looking somewhat thin. Opposition to the PDC had not abated. In January that year the Senate spitefully denied President Frei permission to visit the United States. The municipal elections (April 1967) gave government and opposition the chance to measure their strength. Not surprisingly there was an erosion of PDC support. The Right showed a modest revival, as did the Radicals. The parties of FRAP made more encouraging gains. Both on the Right and the Left there were at this point some interesting shifts. The Conservative and Liberal parties, bowing to the logic of the times, had finally merged (May 1966) under the name "National party." (How the illustrious shades of Montt and Varas must have smiled!) The "new" Right adopted a combative pro-capitalist stance, put across with special verve in Marcos Chamudes's highly readable fortnightly *P.E.C.* The later 1960s unquestionably saw a recovery of nerve on the part of the *momios* ("mummies") – as right-wingers were now nicknamed by their adversaries. (The term had occasionally been used by Montt's opponents back in the 1850s.)

Meanwhile the Left, while gaining ground electorally, was prone to debilitating internal squabbles. Here it is absolutely vital to remember the impact of Fidel Castro's Cuban Revolution all over Latin America. It was the biggest single political influence of the 1960s, arousing immense hopes and immense fears around the continent. It provoked guerrilla movements in a dozen countries, and radicalized large sections of left-wing opinion. In a politically-minded country like Chile, its effects were absolutely inescapable, and were especially marked on the left. In August 1965 a new Movement of the Revolutionary Left (MIR) had been founded in the

---

[16] *Chile y el subdesarrollo* (Santiago, 1973), p. 8.

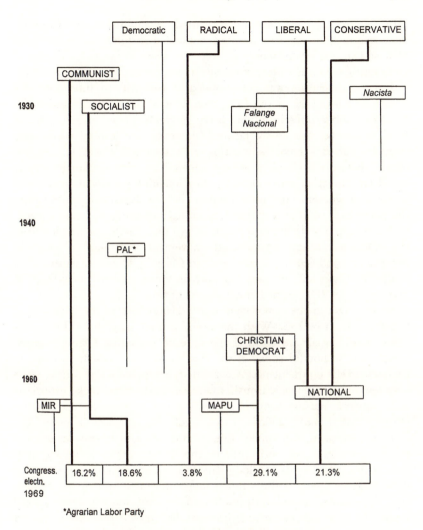

| Democratic | RADICAL | LIBERAL | CONSERVATIVE |

COMMUNIST

1930 SOCIALIST | Nacista

Falange Nacional

1940

PAL*

CHRISTIAN DEMOCRAT

1960 NATIONAL

MIR | MAPU

| Congress. electn. 1969 | 16.2% | 18.6% | 3.8% | 29.1% | 21.3% |

*Agrarian Labor Party

Chart 11.1. Main political parties, 1930–1970.

University of Concepción. Its small, active, and mostly university-educated membership adopted Guevarist views on the need for "armed struggle" to overthrow capitalism and to install a Cuban-style revolutionary system in Chile. A similarly intransigent approach also found favor in sections of the Socialist party. At its conference at Chillán in November 1967, the party redefined itself as Marxist-Leninist and declared its aim to be the creation of a "revolutionary state." Many Socialists, however, including Salvador Allende, continued to adhere to an electoral strategy, as did the Communists. These debates on the Left often assumed an acrimonious form, with the

MIR-leaning magazine *Punto Final* regularly inveighing against Communist "reformism." The Communists responded in kind, denouncing the MIR and similar revolutionary factions as *grupúsculos burgueses* ("bourgeois grouplets"), which as a piece of instant sociology was by no means unfair.

Internal dissension was not confined to the Left. In June 1967 the *rebeldes* and *terceristas* in the PDC won control of the party leadership. Relations between Frei and his party suddenly grew very strained. A PDC committee headed by Jacques Chonchol (the leading *rebelde*) had recently drafted a report advocating a "non-capitalist way of development." Beneath a cloud of windy generalities, this document clearly urged an altogether more radical policy, including nationalizations and schemes of workers' control. Although the dissidents were ousted from the party leadership at a national committee meeting in January 1968, with the help of a dramatic appearance by Frei himself, the discontent of the PDC's left wing, and its youth movement, continued to fester. In November 1968 (during a state visit to Chile by Queen Elizabeth II of England), Chonchol resigned his post as vice-president of INDAP. A division of the PDC seemed only a matter of time.

Change was in the atmosphere nearly everywhere in the later 1960s, and not just in politics. With the steady growth of global communications, many social and cultural trends were becoming visibly international. The wonderful songs of the Beatles were as popular in Chile as everywhere else on the planet. American-style hippiedom, it is true, made very few inroads: a few skirmishes between long-haired rock enthusiasts and "squares" outside Santiago's fashionable Coppelia ice-cream parlor (August 1967) hardly added up to a revolution in youthful mores. The militant feminism, experimentation with drugs, and interest in oriental religion that were so noticeable in the United States had very little impact in Chile. Beards and long hair now became much more common, certainly, and styles of dress much more informal. And in other ways, too, the country shared fully (albeit in its own way) in international trends. In 1967–68 the universities were shaken by explosions of student rebellion, starting at the Catholic University of Valparaiso early in 1967 and spreading to the Catholic University, Santiago, and to the University of Chile itself. Both these institutions and others went through a cycle of occupations, negotiations, endless meetings, and changes of rectors and deans, extending over many months. There was little originality in these student movements (as compared with those of France or the United States): in many ways, as might have been foreseen, they were (or anyway soon became) simply extensions of the wider competition of the parties. An exception here was the *gremialista* movement in the Catholic University, Santiago, which under the leadership of Jaime Guzmán wrested control of the student federation from the PDC in 1968 – the *gremialistas,* with their insistence on strict attention to student problems, were not tied to any of the major parties, although, with their roots in Catholic "integralism," they could be regarded as right-wingers. At the University of Chile the tussle was between the PDC and the Left, which won control in 1969.

It would be absurd to suppose that these youthful eruptions were simply an echo of American or European protest movements. Nor was opposition to the Vietnam War (however strongly felt) the detonator. There were plenty of local grievances on which student militancy could feed. And Latin American influences (themselves significant in shaping the ideological profile of the so-called New Left in Europe and the United States) also played their part in inducing a new mood of radicalism. General de Gaulle may have dismissed the Bolivian guerrilla episode of 1967 in a pungent phrase ("the future of the world will not be played out in Bolivia"), but there is no denying its impact in Chile. (President Frei, it is said, was much affected by the press photographs of Che Guevara's corpse.) Radicalization also undermined the "social Christian" consensus that had earlier formed around the PDC. In August 1968 priests and laymen from a newly formed *Iglesia Joven* ("Young Church") movement staged a brief occupation of Santiago cathedral. While the Catholic hierarchy continued in general to support the PDC's reforms, the Jesuit magazine *Mensaje* was developing an altogether more revolutionary tone.

If there is one cultural shift associated with radicalization that needs to be mentioned here it is certainly the appearance of the so-called New Chilean Song (*Nueva canción chilena*), later so influential throughout Latin America. In part this trend was a conscious rejection of the anodyne commercial popular music now emanating from the country's 130 or so radio stations, some of it prettified Chilean folk music, some of it of Anglo-American provenance. (Rock-and-roll had its local imitators, the most celebrated of whom called himself "Danny Chilean.") Much of the initial inspiration for the New Song came from the work of the folklorist Violeta Parra. The passionate, agitated life of this extraordinary woman ended (she shot herself) in February 1967, soon after she had recorded an album of "Last Compositions." ("They *are* the last," she told her sister Hilda). Those hauntingly beautiful songs are likely to prove the most precious legacy of the 1960s in Chile.

> Y su conciencia dijo al fin:
> cántale al hombre en su dolor,
> en su miseria, y su sudor,
> y en su motivo de existir.

> And his conscience said at last:
> sing of man in his sorrow,
> in his poverty, in his sweat,
> in his reason for being alive.

Violeta's children Angel and Isabel opened their now legendary *peña* in Santiago in 1965. Over the next few years it became the focal point for the New Song, with regular appearances by singers such as the Parras themselves, Rolando Alarcón, Patricio Manns, and, perhaps most memorably, Víctor Jara, later to meet a brutal end at the hands of the military in 1973. (Happily his recordings are with us still, a reminder of the strong flavor of those years.) Apart from singers, instrumental groups such as Inti-Illimani and Quilapayún, later so famous internationally, sprang from the fertile terrain of the New Chilean Song. The stamp of these artists was utterly refreshing, musically innovative, and politically committed.

But while revolutionary rhetoric and emotion became more salient, even within the PDC, there was no overwhelming surge to the Left in electoral terms. What was more in evidence was *polarization* – attitudes on the Right and the Left becoming more entrenched. A new period of "conviction politics" was evidently looming, fostered in no small degree by the PDC's own ideological assertiveness. The later 1960s also saw growing all-around *mobilization,* however we choose to define that term. The number of strikes rose steadily (see Table 11.1), partly because there were now so many more unions to organize them. In the countryside, as we have mentioned, the seizure of *fundos* took on a new rhythm in 1969–70, as did the occupation of urban land by the homeless, *los sin casa.* The MIR was active in encouraging such movements: in certain *poblaciones* ("July 26" in Santiago, "Lenín" in Concepción) rudimentary "popular militias" began to form. Loud student demonstrations and fisticuffs between rival political groups became disturbingly recurrent.

More seriously, there were signs (from March 1968 onward) of a campaign of minor urban terrorism – bomb attacks on the American consulate, supermarkets, the house of the popular National party senator Francisco ("the Marquis") Bulnes, and even (August 1969) the tomb of Arturo Alessandri. In 1969–70 the MIR staged a series of bank robberies ("expropriations" in *mirista* terminology), and several aircraft hijackings were attempted, one successfully. Carabineros discovered so-called "guerrilla schools" in the Maipó Valley (June 1969) and near Valdivia (May 1970). All such news stories confirmed the Right in its reiterated view that the country was falling apart. It was not – or not yet.

The congressional elections of March 1969 brought further setbacks for the PDC. It lost twenty-seven seats in the Chamber, though it raised its senatorial delegation to twenty. The Left, as compared with 1967, remained level, but the Right now made up some of the ground it had lost so spectacularly in 1965. The Nationals, in fact, established themselves as the largest party after the Christian Democrats. Almost before they had time to reflect on these results, politicians were distracted by one of those tragic blunders that dot Chilean (and not only Chilean) history: Carabineros, trying to evict some squatters from a plot of land at Pampa Irigoin, just outside Puerto Montt, killed eight people and wounded fifty more. The event occasioned one of Víctor Jara's most moving protest songs, in which an accusing finger was pointed at Frei's tough-minded Interior minister Edmundo Pérez Zujovic. The Left rained fierce attacks on Pérez Zujovic, who had taken over the ministry from the mild and conciliatory Bernardo Leighton a few months earlier. So, too, did the youth movement of the PDC. Puerto Montt was the last straw for the PDC dissidents. Within a few weeks they decided to create their own party, MAPU (*Movimiento de Acción Popular Unitaria,* Unitary People's Action Movement) – the acronym was the Mapuche word for "earth" – and to associate themselves with the Left.

In electoral terms, as it turned out, the PDC lost rather little from this excision, but the immediate trauma was real enough. For the PDC there was little consolation in the fact that the Radical party, too, was in disarray. Here the movement was in the opposite direction, with a number of right-wingers being expelled from the party. Later in 1969 they set up their own Radical Democrat party, the most prominent *demócrata-radical* being the combative and plain-spoken Julio Durán. The new party immediately gravitated toward the reviving Right.

The "Tacnazo" and the triumph of Allende

The forcefully eloquent Radomiro Tomic had for years been recognized as Frei's heir-apparent. He returned to Chile in 1968 after three years as ambassador in Washington. Tomic had long hankered after a broad alliance between the PDC and the Left – what he himself termed *unidad popular,* "people's unity" (the phrase is his if it is anybody's). For a while he made his presidential candidacy conditional upon such an alliance. The Left had no intention of playing second fiddle to Tomic. *"Con Tomic ni a misa"* ("Go with Tomic? Not even to Mass"), said the Communist secretary-general Luis Corvalán in 1968, using an old Spanish saying from someone who never went to Mass anyway. In mid-1969 Tomic changed his mind, and on August 15 he was nominated as PDC candidate for the 1970 election. Over the next few weeks, other parties announced their choices: Chonchol for MAPU, Salvador Allende for the Socialists, and Pablo Neruda for the Communists. There was never any real chance that the greatest living Spanish-language poet would end up in the Moneda: his name was a bargaining counter, for no formal left-wing alliance had yet been agreed. The Right, meanwhile, pinned its hopes on ex-president Jorge Alessandri, whose name alone was magical. No message of assent came from the old man. An unusual turn of events was to concentrate his mind wonderfully.

The last thing anybody in Chile expected in 1969 was a military coup. All the country's neighbors were currently under military regimes, but Chileans felt themselves to be immune from this particular virus. In the later 1960s, however, the military itself began to feel aggrieved. Military spending had fallen sharply since the 1950s. Frei, like Alessandri before him, paid little attention to the men in uniform, but he had not forgotten them: in September 1967, inaugurating a monument to Pedro Aguirre Cerda, he pointedly alluded to the armed forces' civic responsibilities. In April 1968 some eighty trainee staff officers presented their resignations, ostensibly on grounds of hardship. Sensing trouble, Frei appointed a retired general, Tulio Marambio, as minister of Defense. But the younger officers in particular continued to fret. During the *dieciocho* of 1969, a battalion of the Yungay Regiment deliberately turned up late for the ceremonies in order to embarrass the president.

One month later the government prematurely retired the commander of the First Army Division (Antofagasta), General Roberto Viaux, who was believed to be plotting. He was. On October 20–21, Viaux took a LADECO flight to Santiago, usurped command at the Tacna Regiment, and defied the government. "Nobody will move me from here!" declared President Frei from the Moneda. All political parties (with the exception of the Socialists) rallied immediately to the president. The CUT called for a general strike. Municipal garbage trucks were lined up outside the palace to obstruct the inevitable attack. It never came. Units from the Maipó, Yungay, Guardia Vieja, Colchagua, and Buin regiments took up positions near the red-brick Tacna barracks – as did a large crowd of sightseers in an extremely festive mood. General Viaux, *un milico con cara de milico* ("a soldier with a soldier's face"), according to one of the numerous journalists who flocked to interview him,[17] insisted that his "movement" was no more than a way of publicizing the plight of the Army – almost, indeed, the military equivalent of a strike or a *toma*. Early next day Viaux was persuaded to surrender. Had there been a secret deal? In the aftermath of the *Tacnazo* (as the episode was rapidly dubbed) most of Viaux's union-style demands were met: General Marambio and the Army commander-in-chief soon resigned, and Congress, with unseemly speed, voted a substantial pay increase for the armed forces.

For all its pronounced element of farce, the *Tacnazo* was a sobering event. It seems to have scared the Communist party: the annual *reajuste* was decided, unusually, in an agreement between the government and

---

[17] Eugenio Lira Massi, *Ahora le toca al golpe* (Santiago, 1969), p. 73.

the CUT. Within the Army, the perturbations caused by Viaux meant months of fence-mending for the new commander-in-chief, General René Schneider, and his loyal chief of staff, General Carlos Prats. In order to dispel doubts about the Army's future role, Schneider publicly stated (May 1970) that the armed forces were duty-bound to ensure a proper presidential election and to support whoever was elected – a proposition later referred to as the "Schneider Doctrine." A number of politicians (notably Julio Durán) found it intolerable that the commander-in-chief should make such statements at all.

The immediate political effect of the *Tacnazo* was to force Alessandri into the open. Aware that Viaux was being looked over in right-wing circles as a possible man of destiny (an illusion the self-publicizing Viaux did nothing to correct), the ex-president, now 73, quickly announced his own "independent" candidacy. He made light of his age (and in fact was to live to 90). With the PDC and the Right in the field, all that remained was for the Left to unite around a common candidate. In October 1969 a new left-wing alliance was formed, adopting the name *Unidad Popular* (UP). It consisted of Socialists, Communists, and Radicals, together with three smaller parties: MAPU, a new Social Democrat party (PSD), and *Acción Popular Independiente* (API, Independent Popular Action), the personal following of the old *ibañista,* Senator Rafael Tarud. By mid-December the UP parties had agreed upon a common program, more comprehensively socialist than those of FRAP in 1958 and 1964, and probably the most radical platform ever presented to the Chilean electorate. Choosing a candidate, however, proved unexpectedly tortuous. Salvador Allende was the obvious choice, but he had lost three times already and had always done badly with female voters, perhaps because of his reputation as a ladies' man. His political skills, however, were universally agreed to be in a class of their own, and in January 1970 he was finally proclaimed as the UP's presidential candidate.

The election year itself was marked by petty violence: street skirmishes, assaults on party offices, even the odd bomb attack. An attempted general strike by the CUT in support of Allende (July 8) brought further affrays. The three candidates, meanwhile, stumped the country to rally the faithful and win votes. Long noted as a powerful orator, Tomic proclaimed his vision of a "national, popular and democratic revolution," distancing himself (to the annoyance of many Christian Democrats) from Frei's record, in a clear attempt to attract Allende's national constituency. Allende, in much calmer fashion, expounded the "transition to Socialism" charted in the UP program. Alessandri, calmer still, reiterated the country's obvious need for law and order and an end to demagoguery. For the first time in Chile, television played a part in the contest: there were now twelve times as many sets in the country as there had been in 1964.

Alessandri and Tomic came across poorly in this new medium, Allende slightly better. In the final weeks of the campaign, Chileans once again gave themselves over to the happy rituals of electioneering: marches and rallies, speeches, posters, wall-slogans, campaign songs (Alessandri's was the most hummable, Tomic's certainly the least). The Right mounted a minor "campaign of terror" – press advertisements showing Russian tanks outside the Moneda – and attempted to undermine Tomic's appeal with the catchphrase *Pero no es Frei* ("But he isn't Frei"). The popular and indiscriminately populist newspaper *Clarín* (famed for its slangy head-lines, its crime stories, and the spicy advice-column signed "Professor Jean de Fremisse") attacked Alessandri without mercy, describing him as "the candidate of the rich" (which was true enough) and alleging homosexuality (which was surely not). On election day *Clarín* printed the astonishing headline: THE PEOPLE HAVE TWO WINNING CARDS – AL-LENDE OR TOMIC.

The real competition, however, was between Allende and Alessandri. Supposedly well-informed observers (including those at the U.S. embassy) were convinced that Alessandri would win. The electoral trends of recent years indicated otherwise. Only eighteen months earlier, the parties now forming the UP had won more than two-fifths of the vote. In a three-cornered contest this gave Allende the edge he needed. Yet when the election result was announced, in the early hours of September 5, it was clear that he had barely managed to defeat the challenge from Alessandri. The margin was a mere 40,000 votes.

This democratic election of an avowed Marxist (albeit one with an impeccable Parliamentary record) created immediate uncertainty. Shares fell dramatically on the Santiago stock exchange; there was an unprece-dented run on the banks; those who could not afford to buy gold laid in stocks of consumer goods; the ticket counters at Pudahuel airport saw unusually brisk business for a week or two. Since none of the three candidates had won an absolute majority, Congress was required to con-firm Allende's election. On September 9, Alessandri announced that should Congress vote for him, instead of Allende, he would immediately resign, thus paving the way for new elections. The PDC, the arbiter of the situation, was not seriously tempted by this siren-song. It agreed to support Allende on condition that the UP sign a "statute of democratic guarantees" – a somewhat otiose clarification of freedoms already in the constitution. That this should seem necessary at all, as Arturo Valenzuela has pointed out, "showed the deterioration of confidence between political leaders who had been close for decades."[18] Allende's own very conciliatory attitudes did much to lower the temperature during these difficult weeks.

---

[18] *The Breakdown of Democratic Regimes: Chile* (Baltimore, 1978), p. 49.

When some demonstrators clambered over the statue of General Baquedano in the square named after him (October 8), he and the UP instantly
supported the Army's indignant protests.

The Right, however, was seriously disappointed by the PDC's failure
to oppose the Marxist menace. A hastily organized *Patria y Libertad*
("Homeland and Liberty") movement, headed by the implacably reactionary lawyer Pablo Rodríguez, staged rallies and once or twice rained
leaflets on Santiago from light airplanes. Impetuous rightists set off a few
bombs, but were soon caught by the police. For his part the would-be
man of destiny, General Viaux, was now plotting to foment a coup to
prevent Allende from assuming office. Other generals (some on the active
list) were also conspiring, encouraged (and even supplied with arms) by
the American CIA – an ominous indication of the treatment Allende
could expect from the Nixon administration, already nervously (and
rather ridiculously) contemplating a "second Cuba." The tactic of the
plotters was to kidnap the despised constitutionalist, General Schneider,
and thus to provoke the Army into action. Viaux's group moved first (the
other dropped out), and bungled the plan. Schneider resisted the kidnap
attempt but was mortally wounded (October 22). He died three days
later. His successor as commander-in-chief, General Prats, described him
as a "hero of peace and martyr of democracy."[19]

General Prats spoke for everyone. The assassination shocked the entire
nation. Nothing quite comparable had occurred since the murder of
Portales in 1837. Public opinion rallied firmly behind Allende and the
democratic tradition. Even as Schneider fought his last battle in the
Military Hospital, Allende's election was confirmed in Congress by 153
votes to 35, the National party maintaining its opposition to the last.
When the result was read out, those who were listening to the radio
heard the Socialist deputy Mario Palestro[20] give an utterly demotic
shout of *Viva Chile, mierda!* ("Long live Chile, *shit!*"). Some people were
scandalized. Most people laughed.

---

[19] *Memorias. Testimonio de un soldado,* 2nd ed. (Santiago, 1985), p. 188.

[20] It had recently been written of Palestro that his socialism was "not the product of a complicated
intellectual process" (Eugenio Lira Massi, *La Cámara y los 147 a dieta,* Santiago, 1968, p. 62). He
and his brothers were colorful, old-style political bosses who at that time ran the strongly
working-class municipality of San Miguel (in southern Santiago) as a fief. Their style was
eminently populist.

12

The Chilean road to socialism, 1970–73

As in the classic Greek tragedies, everybody knows *what will happen, everybody* says *they do not wish it to happen, and everybody does exactly what is necessary to bring about the disaster.* . . .

— Radomiro Tomic to General Carlos Prats (August 1973)

Born into a comfortable, if not affluent, Valparaiso family, Salvador Allende (he was 62 in 1970) had originally wanted to become a physician, like his respected paternal grandfather, Ramón Allende Padín, the Radical politician and Serene Grand Master of Chilean freemasonry. (Allende himself was a loyal and lifelong freemason.) While studying medicine, he discovered firsthand the appalling conditions of the poor, and in particular their medical situation – malnutrition, infant mortality, congenital disease. Though he qualified as a doctor, politics gradually superseded medicine as his real vocation. He was active in the FECH, and was briefly jailed during the Ibáñez dictatorship. He quickly rose to prominence in the fledgling Socialist party of the 1930s, was elected a deputy for Valparaiso in 1937, and served as minister of Health between 1939 and 1942. In 1945 he became a senator, and remained in the upper house (rising to be its president in 1966) until he moved to the Moneda. He was a politician to the marrow of his bones.

There can be no denying the enthusiasm with which *allendistas* greeted the new government and which remained alive for many (if not most) of them while it ran its course. The Left had come into its own at long last. This was no mere "lyrical illusion." From the beginning, the new government strove hard to fulfill its program. It greatly increased social spending, and made a determined effort to redistribute wealth to the lower-paid and the poor. As a consequence of higher wages and new initiatives in health and nutrition, many poorer Chileans, perhaps for the first time in their lives, ate well and clothed themselves somewhat better than before. Nor did the state simply attempt to improve their physical well-being: it funded a great variety of cultural endeavors, in a real effort to take the arts (serious as well as popular) to the mass of the people. The musicians of the New Song provided their own remarkable contribution

Table 12.1. Expenditures for social programs under Allende (millions of U.S. dollars).

	1965–69 average	1970	1971	1972	1973
Health	139.4	154.2	211.6	247.8	237.2
Education	281.9	362.0	473.2	524.2	354.9
Housing	133.7	108.6	229.0	228.3	229.9
Child Assist.	.3	.7	.6	.8	.7
Social Assist.	6.9	7.8	8.4	10.6	5.3
Social Sub.	.8	1.9	1.5	.8	.3
TOTAL	562.8	635.2	924.2	1,012.6	828.5
% of total expenditure[a]	32.2	28.9	33.5	34.3	21.6

[a] excluding debt service expenses

Source: World Bank, *Chile, an Economy in Transition* (Washington, D.C., 1980), p. 165.

to the morale of the victorious Left. One cultural program, remembered by Víctor Jara's wife Joan, "brought regular performances of ballet, orchestral music, folklore, theatre, poetry and mime to the outlying working-class districts of Santiago in a circus tent or on a large, mobile open-air stage."[1] And there were many such initiatives. With illiterates and 18-year-olds now given the vote, the government's public attitudes seemed to favor wider mass participation in decision-making, with socialist egalitarianism modifying traditional hierarchical attitudes. Certainly the government was able to draw on reserves of idealism among its supporters. As the months went by, teams of *allendistas* spread out into the countryside and the shantytowns to do volunteer work on weekends. To many it seemed as if the dreams of Bilbao and Arcos, not to mention those of Balmaceda, Recabarren, and Aguirre Cerda, were about to be realized at long last in the socialist world lying ahead for Chile.

A large part of the tragedy that followed was that this vision (which most assuredly had its noble side) was never shared by a clear majority of Chileans. Almost two out of three voters had voted against Allende; his political following, substantial and enthusiastic as it was, was clearly outnumbered, and the radical nature of his program was certain to arouse opposition, not least from those whose economic interests were to be undermined. As things turned out, however, many of the president's difficulties came as much from his own coalition as from his adversaries. A crucial factor here was that while Allende and many of his followers sincerely believed that socialism (albeit in a very comprehensive form) could be built on the solid foundations of the Chilean democratic tradition, there were many others among his followers who wished to go

[1] Joan Jara, *Victor: An Unfinished Song* (London, 1983), p. 164.

outside (or as they would have said, "beyond") that tradition altogether. They were the heirs of the heady radicalization of the 1960s. As Hugo Cancino has pointed out, in a very detailed study of this period, "a wide section of the Chilean Left . . . , from the mid-1960s, began to experience a process of estrangement from Chilean reality, assuming the most orthodox, canonized, formalized versions of Marxism-Leninism."[2] As Cancino also wisely says, the Chile of 1970 was not the Russia of 1917.

This contradiction between Allende's own objectives (the essence of the "Chilean road to socialism" in its only meaningful sense) and the radical demands of the militant "ultras" within (and alongside) the coalition, who could mobilize significant rural and urban constituencies, was to provoke many of the dilemmas of the UP government. Their revolutionary aims were utopian and far-reaching. There were even those among the most militant who held the apocalyptic belief – such beliefs tend to become self-fulfilling – that it would be *better* for the future of the Left and of socialism if Allende "fell by an act of force," as some of them told an American observer in 1971 – "we are trying to create a situation of disorder and chaos to provoke the reactionaries into a coup d'état."[3] This is why, despite his vast political experience, his parliamentary skills, and his engaging personality, President Allende never quite seemed fully in control after his first upbeat year in office – and it could be argued that during his final year he was close to losing control completely.

Given Allende's overall political position, a stronger dose of gradualism might well have been advisable. Efforts might perhaps have been made to widen the UP's political base by enticing the PDC into some kind of alliance, thus isolating the obdurately hostile Right. Instead, the government forged ahead with its announced programs – accelerated agrarian reform, large-scale nationalization, the confiscation of property, and so on – which eventually alienated the PDC. When it became clear that Allende needed to modify these policies in order to survive politically, he was unable to do so. Within the coalition, the Communists and Radicals were generally a force for moderation, and supportive of the president's general approach. By contrast, Allende's own Socialists (under the sway of their firebrand secretary-general Carlos Altamirano), MAPU, and (outside the coalition) the MIR pressed ahead with their own agenda, and in so doing allowed him far too little space to maneuver, obliging the president, sometimes against his instinctive political wisdom, to adhere to policies that led, as we shall see, to ultimate disaster.

---

[2] Hugo Cancino, *Chile. La problemática del poder popular en el proceso de la vía chilena al socialismo* (Aarhus, Denmark, 1988), p. 439.

[3] Norman Gall, "The Agrarian Revolt in Cautín, Part Two," *American Field Service Reports, West Coast South America Series,* 14:5 (Chile), p. 15.

Table 12.2. UP and anti-UP vote, 1970–73.

	1969 Cong.	1970 Pres.	1971 Mun.	1973 Cong.
Total				
UNIDAD				
POPULAR vote	44.2[a]	36.3	49.7	43.9
Total opposition vote	—	62.7	48.0	55.7

[a] 1969 vote: votes of the parties which later formed the Unidad Popular coalition

However, it is always easy to be wise after the event, and we must not anticipate. For most of 1971 Allende and the UP improved their political position. The opposition was in disarray, the PDC not knowing quite what to do, but certainly not relishing any kind of collaboration with the detested Nationals. In its first major political test, the UP coalition won 49.7 percent in the municipal elections of April 1971, nearly two points more than the opposition. (Although the Socialists made the most substantial gains, perhaps because they were the "president's party," the PDC remained the single largest party, with 25.7 percent of the vote, while the Nationals did better than the Communists.) The municipal elections, however, while elating the UP, made no difference to the position in Congress. The UP controlled only one-third of the Senate and two-fifths of the Chamber. It was perhaps at this point, from a position of strength, that the president could have best made overtures to at least a section of the PDC. Radomiro Tomic even suggested that the UP and PDC field a common candidate in an imminent by-election in Valparaiso. Allende considered the idea, but was overruled by the coalition.

An alternative discussed at the time was for Allende to call a plebiscite with the aim of convoking an *asamblea del pueblo* ("people's assembly") for the purpose of drafting a new constitution. Such an assembly had been proposed in the UP's "Basic Program," which envisaged a strengthening of the presidency, a unicameral legislature, and (very sensibly) an end to staggered elections. Given the political momentum supplied by the municipal elections, the UP might well have won such a plebiscite in 1971. (The only party to propose it formally was Raúl Ampuero's breakaway People's Socialist Union, USOPO, founded in 1967, which was outside the coalition and anyway unimportant.) Allende hesitated, and in the end decided not to go ahead with the plebiscite. He himself evidently came to feel that it was one of his most serious political miscalculations.

At the time, however, the decision did not seem so very important. The heady atmosphere of the first months, victory in the municipal elections, a disunited opposition, and some very positive economic figures – all of these things seemed to indicate a rising tide of popularity both for the UP and the "transition to socialism." The government was emboldened to move ahead rapidly with its economic program. Let us now take an extended look at this, before returning to the tumultuous political ups and downs of the remaining Allende years.

Toward a socialist economy?

The nationalization of copper

Nacionalizando el cobre
dejaremos de ser pobres

("By nationalizing copper / We shall cease to be poor") – so ran a Communist party slogan of 1969–70 vintage. In December 1970 Allende introduced a constitutional amendment to nationalize the Gran Minería, and in July 1971 Congress unanimously approved the proposal. The PDC no longer had any objection. The Right, too, supported the measure partly because to reject nationalization would discredit it in the eyes of the nation and partly because it still resented the American advocacy of agrarian reform in the 1960s. The UP rationale was simple: foreign ownership of the Gran Minería was "the basic cause of our underdevelopment... of our meager industrial growth, of our primitive agriculture, unemployment, low wages, our very low standard of life, the high rate of infant mortality, and... our poverty and backwardness."[4] Copper was Chile's most valuable resource – in Allende's phrase, *el sueldo de Chile,* "Chile's wages" – and provided more than 70 percent of the country's foreign exchange. The enormous copper profits, estimated at well over US$120 million annually, could now be used to benefit the nation. Along with its high symbolic importance, nationalization would have an inevitably tonic effect on the economy. "With this decree," affirmed Luis Figueroa, head of the CUT, "President Allende has rendered justice to Chile and its history."[5]

Allende announced that the holdings of Kennecott and Anaconda were to be purchased with 30-year bonds (yielding no less than 3 percent interest) in payment. This compensation was to be based on the book value of the companies' financial interest, minus deductions for amortization and depreciation, as well as "excess profits." The last (and rather novel) provision gave Allende a powerful weapon. He alone was empow-

---

[4] *New York Times,* January 25, 1971, quoted in Eric Baklanoff, *The Expropriation of U.S. Investment in Cuba, Mexico and Chile* (New York, 1975), p. 96.
[5] *Ercilla,* October 6–12, 1971, p. 20.

ered to calculate the level of the "excess profits," and in September 1971 he defined as excessive any profit of more than 12 percent earned after 1955. Using this standard he calculated that instead of being entitled to compensation, Anaconda and Kennecott should pay the state US$78 million and US$310 million respectively. The companies not unexpectedly objected, arguing that their profits had not been as generous as Allende had estimated. Just as predictably the president and the UP rejected the corporations' claims. The copper companies had no real legal remedy in Chile against the retroactive decree and, as we shall see, took the matter to foreign courts.

Nationalization of the mines did not bring the anticipated cornucopia. Both production and profits plunged sharply. The government's supporters claimed that the United States was sabotaging production by denying the nationalized mines access to American machinery and spare parts. It *did* become difficult for the mines to obtain spare parts, although it was often possible to purchase these through third parties. (When, for example, spare tires for Lectra Haul trucks were no longer available from the United States, they were obtained, more cheaply, from Japan.) Replacements for high-ranking technicians (including numerous Chileans) who left the mines after nationalization were more difficult to find than spare parts. Some quit in protest at the government's policies, others because they were no longer paid in dollars (a traditional perquisite and a boon in inflation-ridden Chile), some because they could not adjust to the new management. Whatever the reason, the departure of these skilled officials hamstrung production, particularly in technical areas such as refining.

Political squabbles soon intruded into the mines after nationalization. Struggles between the PDC- and independent-controlled unions and Socialist and Communist mine officials led to wildcat strikes and a collapse of labor discipline. Meanwhile, as part of its employment policy, the government increased the mines' labor force – in the case of Chuquicamata by around one-third. An American observer noted that many of the new employees were "nontechnical personnel such as sociologists and psychologists and public relations men, who plunged into political work on behalf of the Unidad Popular or infantile rivalries among themselves."[6] David Silberman, a Communist mining engineer working at Chuquicamata, lamented that political affiliation rather than training governed too many hirings. As he put it: "The problems in the mines are mainly political and social."[7] Between 1967–69 and 1973 employment

---

[6] Norman Gall, "Copper Is the Wage of Chile," *Field Staff Reports, West Coast, South American Series,* 19:3 (1972), p. 7.
[7] Ibid., p. 6.

in the mines increased by 45 percent while per capita production fell by 19 percent – at Chuquicamata, by 28 percent.

President Allende himself, well aware of the difficulties, complained of poor discipline, lack of worker dedication, and work stoppages. His more militant supporters saw such dislocations as temporary, arguing that "new ways of exercising authority..., and, in general terms, the development of a new power structure" were inevitably changing "traditional schemes to which both miners and technical personnel were accustomed."[8] Even among the faithful, however, there were doubts about such assertions. According to Joaquín Figueroa (former general manager of the Andina copper mine) the mines by mid-1972 were "paying less than under the Yankee imperialists."[9]

In the days of American ownership, the Left had consistently supported the miners' demands for higher wages. After nationalization, the government expected them to moderate or perhaps even forgo such demands. The workers refused, and the Christian Democrats, who now dominated the mining unions, encouraged their discontent in order to embarrass the government. The miners struck eighty-five times in 1971 and 1972. Twice they quit the mines altogether. The most costly wage dispute lasted from April to July 1973, and occurred at El Teniente, briefly spreading to Chuquicamata. President Allende's lectures to the miners were to no avail. When the El Teniente strike broke out, he ordered the jailing of the union's leaders. Carabineros fought with striking miners in Rancagua and tried (in vain) to stop them from marching on the capital. Allende even congratulated those of his supporters who fired on the strikers when they demonstrated in Santiago (June 1973).

Recalcitrant miners were by no means the least of the government's problems. Kennecott sued the government in France, Germany, Sweden, and Italy. Both Kennecott and Anaconda also initiated legal proceedings in New York. These suits discouraged purchases of Chilean copper. Since the U.S. government had guaranteed part of Kennecott's loans, it had a financial (as well as an obvious ideological) interest in pressuring Chile on the issue, and it did so by means of a credit squeeze. Washington opposed Chilean loan applications to the Inter-American Development Bank and the International Bank for Reconstruction and Development. It also discouraged private American banks from lending funds to Chile, though in many cases official discouragement was hardly necessary.

Could this ugly confrontation over copper nationalization have been avoided? The U.S. ambassador to Chile, Edward Korry (who was later to

---

[8] Baklanoff, *Expropriation,* p. 258.
[9] "How Politicians Manage Mines," *Business Week,* August 12, 1972, p. 46.

claim that a number of key figures in Washington had been willing to seek common ground with the UP), tried to arrange a compromise.[10] Korry wanted Allende to agree that the U.S. Overseas Private Development Corporation (OPIC) would guarantee the Chilean government's bonds. This would have allowed the copper companies to sell the bonds immediately, albeit at a discount – and would have saved OPIC a small fortune in insurance. Allende considered the proposal seriously, but, faced with opposition from his Socialist ministers, he had no choice but to reject it. Yet even had there been a compromise, even had there not been retaliation from the United States, it is doubtful whether the nationalization of the Gran Minería would have yielded the expected immediate fruits, for between 1970 and 1973 the world copper price fell by 35 cents per pound. Allende, unlike his predecessor, was the victim of bad luck on this score. It cannot easily be denied, however, that the way nationalization was carried out – its severe internal dislocations, its alienation of the companies and the United States – compounded the effects of ordinary bad luck.

The acceleration of agrarian reform

While most Chileans supported or at least tolerated copper nationalization, the extension of agrarian reform proved more controversial, no doubt because it hit closer to home. The UP parties had no common conception as to the shape of the reorganized countryside of the future. The Socialists (or many of them) advocated thoroughgoing collectivization, viewing the ex-inquilinos of the *asentamientos* as potentially "reactionary kulaks." Communists and Radicals, for their part, favored cooperatives which peasants could work while still enjoying the right to private plots. These arguments over policy meant, in practice, a high level of confusion in the countryside.

Agrarian reform was, however, greatly speeded up. Jacques Chonchol, now Allende's Agriculture minister, promised to expropriate all estates larger than eighty "basic" hectares.[11] He was a man of his word: before the end of 1972 there was no farm in Chile which exceeded this basic limit. This was by no means all Chonchol's doing: the UP's "ultras" and the MIR resented the minister's use of the time-consuming, "bourgeois" PDC reform law. In order to "accelerate the reform process," the MIR organized peasants (and dispossessed Mapuche) into a *Movimiento Campe-*

---

[10] He successfully negotiated the nationalization of the Bethlehem Steel Company, the Northern Indiana Brass Company, and the Cerro Corporation's Río Blanco holdings.

[11] See Chapter 11, note 11.

sino Revolucionario ("Revolutionary Peasant Movement"), which seized more than 1,700 properties, many of them less than eighty hectares in size. These land seizures (the *tomas* we saw beginning in the later 1960s, now carried out on a much larger scale) placed President Allende in an awkward position. If the Carabineros evicted the peasants, he laid himself open to the charge of "betraying the people," but toleration of the *tomas* was bound to be exploited by his adversaries as evidence that the UP was flouting the law. To escape from this dilemma, Allende resorted to subterfuge: a little-known provision of the reform law allowed the government to seize an estate and appoint an *interventor* (temporary administrator) should a strike or stoppage interrupt work. Use of this measure enabled the government to placate the "ultras," while remaining within the letter of the law, but it did little to sweeten the opposition's temper.

Under the PDC reform law, as we saw, only the ex-inquilinos (the *socios* of the *asentamientos*) shared in the land of an expropriated hacienda; the casual laborers or *afuerinos* (about two-thirds of the rural work-force) received nothing. The radical wing of the UP urged the confiscation of all agrarian properties and the creation of new agricultural units, *haciendas del estado* ("state farms") cultivated by inquilinos and *afuerinos* alike. The peasants of the *asentamientos* vigorously opposed this proposal – the PDC had promised them the land of their *patrones;* now the UP apparently wanted to take it away. The government was not able to ignore the peasants' demands: rural unionization had gone too far, and, encouraged by the PDC, the former inquilinos adamantly insisted on the retention of the *asentamientos*. Chonchol was obliged, therefore, to tolerate existing *asentamientos,* but he clearly opposed the formation of new ones. In January 1971, to further its own plans, the government created the *Consejo Nacional Campesino* (CNC, National Peasant Council). This new umbrella organization, with subsidiary provincial and local "councils," was composed of representatives of the various peasant groups, but carefully relegated peasants to an advisory rather than a decision-making role. The tactic often failed, largely because the PDC successfully organized peasants into unions which stubbornly resisted government control.

In its drive to complete agrarian reform, the government decided to meld adjoining expropriated farms into new entities known as *Centros de Reforma Agraria* (CERAs, Agrarian Reform Centers). Each CERA was to give the state 90 percent of its profits, the government paying its members (ex-inquilinos and *afuerinos* alike) a wage while marketing their produce. However, the laws regulating the CERAs were so vaguely worded that nobody knew precisely what form the new agricultural unit was to take. The CERA, in fact, seemed more a device that allowed the government to sidestep the existing agrarian reform legislation (and the *asentamiento*) in pursuit of the objective of a "classless society in the countryside."[12] Critics soon attacked the CERA as a scheme which "merely transferred more prerogatives of proprietorship to bureaucrats while removing from the individual enterprise or group of *campesinos* control over the surplus generated in the rural sector."[13] In late September 1971, and again early in 1972, members of opposition agrarian unions and other peasant organizations marched on Santiago to demand that the state fulfill the law by dividing the *asentamientos* into individual plots. Even the CNC, the new peasant council, became unruly, demanding a cooperative system which allowed peasants at least the right to cultivate a private plot of land.

The government further complicated the agrarian situation when, in addition to the CERAs, it also established *Centros de Producción* (CEPROs, "Production Centers"). These state-owned units were founded to deal with "exceptional" forms of agriculture.[14] Their workers were state employees who received wages and social security benefits. Although accounting for only 2 percent of the communal-type farms, the CEPROs eventually covered approximately one-seventh of the land in the "reformed sector."

But whether they were called *asentamientos*, CERAs, or CEPROs, the new agrarian units changed the rural topography of Chile. Farms of eighty hectares or more, covering 55 percent of the land as recently as 1965, accounted for no more than 3 percent in 1972. Just over one-half of all rural properties now consisted of farms of between five and eighty hectares – compared with just under one-fifth in 1965. This was a fundamental alteration of the rural power structure. Much was to change over the next few years, but the traditional hacienda (and all that the hacienda meant) was never to return to Chile. It had gone – and gone with surprising swiftness, we might think, given its enduring place in history.

The countryside, however, replicated many of the problems now affecting the copper mines, with political rivalries once again playing a confusing role, and with government objectives conflicting with peasant (especially ex-inquilino) aspirations. Peasants were reluctant to allow the state to take the place of their former masters. The government seemed incapable of appreciating the peasant aspiration to *ownership*. As Emilio Lorenzini, a Christian Democrat long active in the agrarian reform movement, noted:

it does not matter who is the owner of the capital, but rather who has the power to decide, to obtain the fruits of the enterprise, and to orient national production. We

---

[12] Brian Loveman, *Struggle in the Countryside* (Bloomington, Ind., 1976), p. 293.
[13] *Ibid.*, p. 295.   [14] Stefan de Vylder, *Allende's Chile* (Cambridge, 1975), p. 188.

achieve nothing if we merely change the group which exploits the workers in the
capitalist system for . . . an *interventor* designated by bureaucrats. . . . The workers continue to sell their labor to those who control the capital. . . . Before they were stockholders; now they are bureaucrats.[15]

The combination of rural unrest, the erosion of peasant discipline, and
(as so often throughout Chilean history) poor weather had a predictable
effect on agricultural production. Between 1969–70 and 1972–73 the
amount of land under cultivation fell by around one-fifth. Harvests of
certain crops shrank – wheat by more than one-third, potatoes by more
than one-seventh, rice by 20 percent, sugar beet by 40 percent – though
other crops (barley, maize, rye) did much better, and similarly, if there
were now fewer cows and sheep, there were more pigs and chickens than
before. In general, however, disturbed conditions created uncertainty. Fear
of a *toma* or expropriation so terrified some private farmers that they
simply refused to plant, sold off machinery, slaughtered their livestock,
or (illegally) sent their animals across the mountains to Argentina. Peasants in the "reformed sector" proved almost as recalcitrant as the farmers,
devoting most of their efforts to cultivating their private plots (consuming the produce or selling it on the burgeoning black market) rather than
laboring on the communally held land. For its part the government did
its best to raise peasants' consciousness – by *concientización,* to use an oft-
repeated term of that time. This was a double-edged tactic. Having been
repeatedly reminded of their former exploitation by landowners, many
peasants were inclined to regard any government advice as an echo of the
old paternalism, and any assistance that came their way as compensation
for past injustice. Not only did they fail to repay money received as an
advance on the harvest, but they frequently used the state's technical aid
(when it was forthcoming, which was by no means always) to develop
their own private plots.

The growing agricultural difficulties were compounded by other policies. A price freeze combined with wage increases meant that domestic
food consumption soared, and to satisfy demand the government was
obliged to import more food. By 1972 it was spending 56 percent of its
export earnings on food purchases; the countryside was by now producing
only two-thirds of what Chileans consumed.

The nationalization of industry

The UP aimed to nationalize, if not the country's entire industrial base,
then at least its most significant parts. As we have seen in earlier chapters,

---

[15] *La Prensa,* November 26, 1971, quoted in Loveman, *Struggle in the Countryside,* pp. 298–99.

the Chilean state already owned or controlled much of the economic high ground: the steelworks, the oil fields and refineries, most of the railroads, the national airline, and so on. Through CORFO the state also participated in the ownership of several large manufacturing companies, controlling by 1970 something like 40 percent of national production. Nonetheless, the UP administration remained intent on eradicating *all* large private corporations – what it characterized as "the monopolies." Because it hit at long-entrenched vested interests, not least those of the country's most powerful financial conglomerates, this was the most strongly resisted aspect of the UP's economic program.

As with the copper mines and the countryside, nationalization was the subject of conflicting views within the coalition. The "Basic Program" of the UP envisioned an economy in three distinct parts: (1) the Area of Social Property, more briefly the "Social Area" (state-owned companies), (2) the "Mixed Area" (firms where the state was the majority stockholder), and (3) the "Private Area" (small businesses). The Communists and the Radicals suggested caution, urging the takeover of only those concerns exercising "monopolistic power," with exemption from nationalization for smaller companies – a course, it was argued, that would open the way to attracting political support from the middle class. The Socialists and MAPU (not to mention MIR), with their comprehensive hostility to more or less any form of capitalism, wanted the immediate nationalization of virtually all the means of production. Once again Allende was faced with a difficult ideological tussle.

In October 1971 the president submitted a proposal to transfer to the Social or Mixed Areas all companies whose net worth exceeded 14 million escudos (around US$1 million). There were some 253 such corporations (150 of them manufacturing concerns), controlling some 90 percent of total corporate assets. The government agreed to buy these companies with interest-bearing bonds equal to the 1969 book value of their assets, small-time investors receiving an adjustment for inflation, larger shareholders getting a less favorable deal. A majority in Congress, partly because it feared that this legislation would be used to control the mass media, opposed these proposals.[16] In January 1972 the companies targeted for expropriation were reduced to ninety, but this did nothing to placate the opposition.

As with agrarian reform, the government discovered a way to bypass

---

[16] A particularly contentious issue in the background here was the government's attempt to buy a 51 percent holding in the *Compañía Manufacturera de Papeles y Cartones* (locally known as the "Papelera"), the country's chief source of newsprint, and a company presided over by ex-president Jorge Alessandri. The shareholders resisted the takeover, and a long tussle ensued, with the government trying to squeeze the company by freezing the price of paper.

Congress. During the Socialist Republic of 1932, Marmaduke Grove had issued a decree (DFL 520) enabling the government to seize any industrial concern deemed "essential" to the economy – should it infringe the law. Any minor infraction could easily be interpreted in this light. Never repealed, DFL 520 had languished in the law books until a UP lawyer came across it. Grove's forgotten edict now became one of the Moneda's most powerful instruments, the chief of the so-called *resquicios legales* ("legal chinks") that so aroused opposition ire. Allende possessed a second weapon of this kind, a measure (enacted during the Popular Front period) permitting the government to requisition factories should they fail to operate efficiently, though without transferring formal ownership to the state. Together the two measures became the industrial counterpart of the rural *toma,* strikes or other disruptions of production providing the pretext for the installation of government-appointed *interventores* in the factories affected.

Not all cases required resort to subterfuge in this way; in many instances nationalization proceeded without real incident. The government had little difficulty in purchasing the shares of the major banks. It also exercised a certain selectivity when nationalizing foreign-owned corporations. Rather predictably, American concerns became a favorite target: Ford, ITT (the latter with ample reason, given its grotesque behavior at the time of Allende's election),[17] and Ralston Purina quickly became part of the Social Area. By 1973, through a combination of requisitions, seizures, and purchases of stock, the state controlled 80 percent of the country's industrial output, upward of 400 enterprises, and around 60 percent of GNP.[18]

But the nationalized or "intervened" factories were not exempt from the difficulties now affecting mining and agriculture – and for much the same reasons. *Interventores* were often selected less for their technical qualifications than for their parties' influence in the coalition, the Socialists and Communists receiving the lion's share of such posts. Some *interventores* proved to be incompetent, others venal. In addition, the government's employment policy often inflated factory payrolls, the newly hired workers sometimes refusing to obey their managers, on ostensibly political grounds. As discipline relaxed, difficulties multiplied – "corruption; stealing; absenteeism; costly carelessness in the use of machinery, including neglect of maintenance; simply not working;

---

[17] Both before and after September 1970, ITT offered the CIA money to prevent the election and installation of Allende, an example of "corporate subversion" which aroused intense indignation in Chile, not only on the Left.

[18] Alberto Baltra, *La gestión económica del Gobierno de la Unidad Popular* (Santiago, 1973), pp. 53–54.

carrying on vendettas (partly based on political allegiance)[19] – in particular, absenteeism, reaching 10 to 15 percent in some factories (and more in government offices) reduced productivity." Strikes increased, sometimes encouraged by the opposition. Between 1970 and 1972 work stoppages almost doubled, costing the country 162 million man-days.

It was, however, some time before the implications of rapid nationalization became apparent. Indeed, 1971 was a year of plenty: with prices frozen and wages increased, purchasing power (especially for those who had had little or none before) was dramatically enhanced. GNP soared by 8.3 percent; industrial production rose by 12.1 percent; unemployment declined to 3.8 percent by the end of the year. These promising figures were achieved because factories could exploit existing inventories, accumulated supplies of raw materials, and an unused industrial capacity of almost 25 percent. The good times, alas, did not last, and could not last. The extended price freeze made it unprofitable for companies to continue to produce at the same high levels. Expecting expropriation in one form or other, private factory owners refused to invest in their plants. Industrial output slowly began to shrink. In mid-1972 production remained slightly above that of 1971; during the last months of that year the decline became painfully apparent, and increasing production costs soon put the Social Area as a whole into the red – in 1972, its various enterprises ran a deficit of around 22 billion escudos, equal to 60 percent of the national revenue. As Stefan de Vylder has put it, "the Social Area became a leaking bucket, adding fuel to the money supply and the galloping rate of inflation."[20]

In many ways the process of nationalization spun out of control. In April 1971 the workers at the Yarur textile plant seized the factory, and demanded its incorporation into the Social Area. This was the first time that workers, rather than the government, had taken over a factory. The example was soon imitated. In June 1972 workers at the Perlak canning plant at Los Cerrillos also demanded to be included in the Social Area. Perlak, along with two other nearby factories, created the *Cordón Cerrillos,* the first of the so-called *cordones industriales* or "industrial belts," worker-controlled areas, effectively independent of the government. When the government did not respond, the workers concerned blocked roads near their *cordón* and occupied the ministry of Labor. Once again Allende was faced with a painful choice. Was he to accept the workers' actions or return the occupied factories to their owners? When the Moneda opted

[19] Henry Landsberger and Tim McDaniel, "Hypermobilization in Chile, 1970–1973," *World Politics,* 28:4 (1976), p. 529; *Ercilla,* September 5–11, 1973.
[20] De Vylder, *Allende's Chile,* p. 154.

for the former course, militant Socialists and *miristas* took over other factories, demanding workers' control. It seemed clear that the government's ability to steer the process of nationalization at its own pace was seriously impaired.

As industrial (and agricultural) production fell, it became more difficult for Allende to fulfill his promise to raise living standards. With industry failing to produce consumer goods in sufficient quantities, the government resorted to imports. As copper prices fell, so did the country's capacity to earn foreign reserves, and hence its ability to pay for imports. Reluctant to reduce living standards, but facing a mounting economic crisis, Allende had to choose between (in a metaphorical sense) guns and butter. Serious long-term planning (appropriate enough in a genuine "transition to socialism") might have indicated that the government use its dwindling reserves to buy raw materials and essential spare parts. In the end political calculation triumphed over economic good sense and planning for the future. Allende opted for consumer goods (including food) rather than capital goods. By the end of 1972, the country had reached an economic impasse. It faced a massive trade imbalance: exports had fallen by a quarter since 1970, while imports had risen by two-fifths. The trade deficit rose from US$18 million to US$255 million in 1971–72.

The failure of the UP's economic strategy

A key element in the UP's overall strategy for improving the lot of the country's lower-paid and worst-off – a "Keynesian" strategy, as it was often described at the time – was to provide employment, either in the new nationalized enterprises or on public works projects. In 1971 alone, for instance, funding for public works increased from 19 million to 33 billion escudos – a step, it was believed, that would not only provide jobs but also stimulate the economy through higher consumption. Like all his immediate predecessors, Allende promised to insulate the consumer from inflation by "readjusting" wages. During his first year wages increased by 55 percent (far more than the previous year's inflation of 33 percent, and well above the government's initial guidelines). Higher increases were awarded to blue-collar workers in order to narrow the gap between them and the hitherto pampered *empleados*. As noted earlier, the Moneda also dramatically increased social expenditures, particularly for health, housing, and education (see Table 12.1). Additionally, Allende increased public access to the social security system and provided enhanced state benefits, such as increased family allowances.

The inflationary implications of such policies were disregarded by government officials, who argued that the state possessed an adequate monetary brake: by imposing price controls it could restrain possible adverse economic forces until production matched demand. Indeed, when the cost of living rose by only 22 percent in 1971, the UP's economic approach seemed to have been more than justified. This mild increase, however, masked an underlying inflationary tendency. Businesses (private or public) flourished in 1971 by drawing down on their stocks of raw materials and inventory. By 1972 existing supplies had been consumed, and producers were forced to buy replacements and raw materials at much higher prices. The Moneda used its substantial reserves of foreign exchange (inherited from the Frei period) to subsidize imports for the consumer. But with export earnings in decline, the country's foreign reserves dwindled by 90 percent. It eventually became impossible for the government to continue to underwrite the consumer economy.

There were other ominous statistics: during 1971 the money supply doubled, and the amount of credit made available to both the private and the public sectors increased by threefold. Tax revenues also declined. Inevitably these factors would make themselves felt. To cover the deficit and find funds for consumer and capital goods, the government sought foreign loans. It knew better than to seek these in Washington: as already noted, the U.S. government was using its power to veto Chilean applications to international banks. The American credit squeeze undoubtedly intensified Chile's economic difficulties, but, if it added up to an "invisible blockade," as was so often alleged at the time, its effectiveness can at least be questioned. By mid-1973, as Allende's loyal foreign minister, Clodomiro Almeyda, was later to note, "Chile . . . had obtained enough normal bank credits from [Western Europe] to buy there much of the merchandise it could not purchase in the United States."[21] This amount, moreover, did not include the more than US$750 million in loans and credits from China, the Soviet bloc, and Latin American countries. Such economic assistance, however, came far too late to arrest all-around economic deterioration.

In the end, inflationary pressures simply became too strong. A declining supply of locally produced goods, along with the appearance of a strong black market, forced prices inexorably upward. No really serious effort was made to impose rationing. In an increasingly desperate attempt to maintain wage levels, the government continued to "readjust." Just prior to the congressional elections of 1973 Allende ordered the payment of a 700-escudo bonus to every worker at the next *fiestas patrias.* Such measures enhanced inflationary expectations. Between July 1971 and July 1972 the cost of living rose by 45.9 percent; inflation doubled in August 1972 and rose half as much again in September (in the same six weeks, the escudo plummeted from 150 to 300 to the dollar on the black

[21] Quoted in Joaquín Fermandois, *Chile y el mundo, 1970–1973* (Santiago, 1985), p. 395.

market); over the next year it soared by more than 300 percent. Ignoring government price controls, many people feverishly purchased consumer goods as a hedge against future inflation or to cushion themselves against the shortages which had become all too common by Allende's third year.

The UP's economic strategy thus failed virtually across the board. By mid-1973, in fact, the economy was close to collapse. The nationalized mines, the "reformed" farms, and the expropriated factories ceased to produce at precisely the moment when they were most needed. Many were later to attribute the economic debacle to the hostility of the middle and upper classes and of the United States – and the hostility was real enough, and deep. It was not the opposition, however, whatever its culpability in other ways, which took the major economic decisions. The economic dimension to the UP years can best be interpreted, perhaps, as a classic instance of the "primacy of politics." Pedro Vuskovic, Allende's minister of Economy (1970–72), admitted as much: "Economic policy is subordinate, in its content, shape and form," he claimed in March 1972, "to the political needs of increasing Popular Unity support...; a central objective is to widen support for the government."[22] Yet this central objective came nowhere near to being achieved.

Confrontation and stalemate

Although the Allende government began on an undeniably buoyant note, which carried it through much of its first year, the note could not be sustained indefinitely. The deterioration of the political atmosphere mirrored (and in some ways anticipated) the worsening economic situation. In June 1971 an extremist group, VOP (*Vanguardia Organizada del Pueblo,* Organized Vanguard of the People), assassinated Frei's former minister of the Interior, Edmundo Pérez Zujovic. The terrorists were men to whom Allende had controversially granted amnesty on becoming president, and the PDC was furious. It demanded that the president restrain and disarm the various "ultra" paramilitary groups such as VOP and MIR, whose activities it suspected Allende of tolerating. While the government quickly crushed VOP, it did little to rein in the MIR. The electoral effects of the assassination were registered in July, with a by-election in Valparaiso, when the National party agreed to support the PDC's nominee, Dr. Oscar Marín. The PDC denied there was a formal alliance but accepted right-wing support, calling for the votes of all who "repudiated violence and hatred, sectarianism and illegal armed groups."[23] Dr. Marín's

---

[22] Pedro Vuskovic, "The Economic Policy of Popular Unity Government," in J. Ann Zammit, ed., *The Chilean Road to Socialism* (Austin, Texas, 1973), p. 50.

[23] Paul Sigmund, *The Overthrow of Allende* (Pittsburgh, 1977), p. 149.

slim victory was something of a watershed: it placed the UP on the political defensive.

Political positions now began to harden noticeably. The PDC pledged itself to oppose any attempt to turn Chile into a "totalitarian society," and to introduce legislation to protect the small businessman and the landowner, by requiring the government to obtain congressional approval before transferring property into the Social Area. A number of left-wing Christian Democrats broke ranks at this point and formed a new party, *Izquierda Cristiana* (Christian Left), which immediately joined the UP coalition. The UP itself also suffered the defection of a group of Radicals, disquieted by growing Marxist influence in their party, which created the *Partido de Izquierda Radical* (Radical Left party). This excision cost the UP five senators and seven deputies, which more than compensated for the *Izquierda Cristiana*'s defection from the PDC.

For the PDC, the middle months of 1971 were something like a moment of truth. Any attempt at cooperation with the UP threatened it with a loss of identity and to confer on it the status of a political chameleon – what might unkindly be called the "Radical syndrome." The logic of traditional party competition more or less compelled it to assume an opposition stance. In September 1971 it launched a broad attack on the government. Its deputies formally introduced legislation (October 1971) requiring the government to obtain congressional approval before expanding the Social or Mixed area. It also sought to restrict the use of DFL 520, by limiting requisitions of property to a six-month period and enabling property-owners to appeal to the supreme court.

Resistance to the UP both inside and outside Congress gradually mounted. A proposed constitutional amendment from Allende (November 1971) to introduce the unicameral legislature of the UP program ran into immediate opposition. During a lengthy visit paid to Chile by the Cuban prime minister, Fidel Castro, at this same period, middle- and upper-class housewives staged their famous "March of the Empty Saucepans," parading down the Santiago streets and banging cooking pots to denounce food shortages and inflation (December 1, 1971). UP supporters assaulted the demonstrators, an incident that led the opposition to impeach the minister of the Interior, José Tohá. Before the impeachment reached the Senate, Allende transferred Tohá to the ministry of Defense – an act viewed by the opposition as a calculated snub to Congress. Electorally if not philosophically, the PDC and the Nationals now drew closer together in an informal alliance. In January 1972 two by-elections were held: the first, in O'Higgins-Colchagua, for the Senate, the second, in Linares, for the Chamber. Both government and opposition threw their full strength into these contests. The UP lost the Senate seat to a

Christian Democrat and the deputyship to the National candidate. Capturing the senatorial post proved particularly significant, since the UP had carried the district in the 1971 municipal elections.

Clearly worried by the deteriorating political situation, President Allende called a meeting of coalition leaders at El Arrayán in February 1972. The conference amply demonstrated the divisions that continued to plague the UP, with the Communists and Radicals (and Allende's own personal following among the Socialists) preaching moderation, some even suggesting a "dialogue" with the PDC, the bulk of the Socialists (led by Altamirano) and MAPU responding with the demand that the government "accelerate the revolutionary process." The El Arrayán meeting, in fact, served to underscore Allende's fundamental dilemma. More or less any policy he adopted was bound to alienate one or other of the main wings of the coalition. And quite apart from having to fight his presumed friends, the president still had to do battle with his *real* adversaries, whose attacks on the government were becoming increasingly confident and unremitting. In April 1972 the PDC won the all-important Rectorship of the University of Chile. In July the party noisily alleged that the UP had rigged recent elections in the CUT, and Congress successfully impeached Hernán del Canto, the minister of the Interior, for (among other things) permitting the smuggling of weapons into Chile aboard a Cuban airplane. Although the UP won a by-election at Coquimbo (also in July 1972), its performance there was less than sparkling.

Much of the political argument in the first half of 1972 focused on a thorny constitutional issue. In February 1972 Congress passed the PDC-sponsored constitutional amendment to prohibit legislatively unauthorized expropriations. Allende vetoed the proposal, and a majority of the legislature retaliated by voting to override the veto, an act that threatened to plunge the nation into a classic constitutional crisis. Allende claimed that Congress could override his veto only by a two-thirds majority rather than a simple majority as claimed by Congress. This difference in interpretation arose from the constitutional amendment of January 1970 which, in setting up a mechanism for plebiscites on disputed constitutional amendments, had clouded this particular issue. The arguments flowed back and forth, the opposition urging a plebiscite, and Allende insisting that the two-thirds majority was necessary (as it was for overriding his veto on regular legislation) and that the matter should be determined by the Constitutional Tribunal created by the 1970 amendment. For the moment this issue was left unresolved.

Attempts were now made by the UP (or part of it) to reach an understanding with the PDC, but none of them succeeded. In March 1972 one such effort was undermined when the minister of Economy, Pedro Vuskovic, with Socialist support, suddenly accelerated the takeover of factories, a measure that infuriated the PDC. Three months later, discussions over the constitutional deadlock were broken off, as a result of pressure from both the UP's intransigent left wing and the PDC's now equally intransigent right wing. This in itself was a fair measure of the increasing (and increasingly bitter) polarization now beginning to dominate the entire political landscape.

Congressional pressure continued to mount. In June 1972 the PDC introduced a new constitutional amendment prohibiting the seizure of farms less than forty hectares in size and demanding that the government (in line with the 1967 law) convert the *asentamientos* into cooperatives or individual holdings. With politicians once again arguing the constitutional issues, the growing conflict between government and opposition was now being regularly taken into the streets: the increasing violence of the demonstrations caused Allende to decree states of emergency in Santiago and Concepción in August and September 1972. Many suspected that the "ultras" of both Left and Right were gradually turning Chile into an armed camp – as was certainly to some extent the case, though to *what* extent remains uncertain. In line with the prevailing mood, Congress legislated to restrict the ownership of automatic weapons to the armed forces and Carabineros, and also gave the military the right to search for (and confiscate) firearms found in private hands. This new *Ley de control de armas* ("Arms Control Law"), duly signed by Allende, went into effect in October 1972.

In the same month, incensed by plans to create a state transportation enterprise, a group of truckers went on strike in the southern province of Aysén, and in so doing provoked the first great crisis of the UP years. The jailing of the strike leaders precipitated a sudden and widespread wave of work-stoppages. Other groups, notably shopkeepers and the owners of small businesses, joined the strike in sympathy, banding together into *gremios* (literally, "guilds") to defend their interests. Under an umbrella organization, the *Frente Nacional* (later the *Comando Nacional*) *de Defensa* (National Defense Front/Command), they threw their weight behind the truckers. For once in Chilean history, here was a grass-roots mass mobilization which owed little or nothing to the political parties, although both the PDC and the National party predictably endorsed the nationwide action, which was eventually joined between 600,000 and 700,000 people, including peasants, merchant sailors, doctors, lawyers, and other professionals. At the height of the stoppage more than 23,000 trucks were off the road. Given their vital role in the transportation of goods, the country suddenly found itself close to paralysis.

Mobilization by the opposition was paralleled by that of the UP's radicals, who responded by seizing factories closed by their owners in solidarity with the strikers, incorporating them into existing *cordones*

Table 12.3. Election results by party, 1969–73 (percentage of popular vote).

	1969 Cong.	1970 Pres.	1971 Mun.	1973 Cong.
UNIDAD POPULAR				
Socialist Party (PS)	12.3		22.4	18.6
Communist Party (PC)	15.9		17.0	16.2
Radical Party (PR)	12.9		8.0	3.8
Social Democrats (PSD)	0.9		1.3	—
MAPU	—	ALLENDE	—	2.5
Christian Left (IC)	—		—	1.2
API	—		—	0.8
People's Socialists	2.2		—	0.3
TOTAL UNIDAD POPULAR	44.2	36.3	49.7	43.9
DEMOCRATIC CONFEDERATION				
Christian Democrats	29.7	Tomic	25.6	29.1
		27.8		
PADENA	1.9		0.5	0.4
Radical Left (PIR)	—		—	1.8
National Party (PN)	20.1	Alessandri	18.1	21.3
		34.9		
Radical Democrats	—		3.8	2.3
TOTAL DEMOCRAT. CONFED.	—		48.0	55.7
ABSTENTIONS	26.4	16.5	25.5	18.1

Unidad Popular not running as such until 1970; **Democratic Confederation (CODE)** not running as such until 1973. People's Socialists (USOPO): Raúl Ampuero's splinter party, formally outside the UP coalition.

industriales, and creating new ones. The *cordones,* often supported by local community groups, now set up *comandos comunales* ("communal commands") which sought to keep the economy going during the strike. These "parallel" (and to an extent paramilitary) organizations became increasingly powerful – by mid-1973 there were about a dozen *cordones* around Santiago – and posed an agonizing dilemma for President Allende. In January 1973 the Moneda announced that it would consider returning some of the occupied factories to their owners. Faced with strong opposition from Socialists and from members of the *cordones,* Allende retracted the proposal.

Anxious to restore order in time for the forthcoming congressional elections of March 1973, the president cast around for means to allay what had become a monumental national crisis. At the suggestion of Radomiro Tomic, he reshuffled his cabinet (not unexpectedly, as Congress was attempting to impeach four of his ministers at the time) by inviting General Carlos Prats, the Army commander-in-chief, to serve as minister of the Interior, and offering portfolios to two other officers (November 2, 1972). Prats, like Allende a freemason, swiftly asserted himself as a key figure in the increasingly contentious political scene. He quickly settled the truckers' strike (November 1972), thus allowing the congressional election campaign to take place in a somewhat calmer atmosphere. The importance of this election was lost on nobody. A two-thirds majority for the PDC-National opposition (now formally allied in a "Democratic Confederation") would enable it to override presidential vetoes and impeach the president himself. In short, both sides had everything to play for.

Given the high rate of inflation, the food shortages, the long lines outside shops, and the rampant black market which were now part of the everyday scene, many outside observers assumed that the UP would lose heavily. A maxim of Chilean politics held that no governing party did well during a period of high inflation. But the *allendistas* remained loyal, albeit wryly – as a wall-slogan of the time put it: *Es un gobierno de mierda, pero es el nuestro* ("It's a shitty government, but it's *ours*"). The UP won 44 percent of the vote, the opposition 55 percent. In party terms, the PDC (29 percent) and Nationals (21 percent) outpolled the Socialists (19 percent) and Communists (16 percent). This hardly mattered: Allende had retained his one-third of Congress and was safe from impeachment. The 1973 elections roused a host of conflicting claims and counter-claims over the stuffing of ballot boxes and excessive delays in declaring the results. The wrangles were eloquent testimony to the atmosphere of mistrust that had by now built up between government and opposition – and the UP itself, it has to be said, had given all too many hostages to fortune on this score. But the opposition's failure to achieve its electoral goals carried an ominous implication. If parliamentary methods were ineffective, the door was already half open to rebellion.

Breakdown and tragedy

Perhaps emboldened by its electoral performance, the government next revealed plans to introduce a new educational reform, the so-called "Unified National School" (*Escuela Nacional Unificada*) or ENU. While seeking to provide children with better access to education, the measure also had a more far-reaching objective: to create *el hombre nuevo,* "the new man . . . , free to develop himself fully in a non-capitalist society, and who will express himself as a personality . . . conscious of and in solidarity with the revolutionary process, who is . . . technically and scientifically able to develop the economy in a society in transition to socialism."[24] The ministry of Education hoped to accomplish this goal by combining "traditional Chilean values" with a recognition of "the proletarian struggles for sovereignty and independence which have been virtually ignored in traditional teaching, which serves the class interests of the oligarchy."[25]

The new measure managed to alienate groups which had previously been neutral. The Catholic Church, which had hitherto shown a tolerant attitude to the UP government, now changed its stance, the bishops criticizing ENU for ignoring "Christian values" and for usurping the role of parents in education. The Church requested that the government delay the plan while it was more fully debated. The clergy were not alone in their opposition. Parents of children in private schools also objected, as did some 800 military officers, who, in their capacity as fathers, denounced the measure as an attempt by the state to indoctrinate their children. ENU provoked student demonstrations both for and against the project, in one of which a sniper killed a demonstrator. The politicians took up the cry, the PDC calling the measure parochial and ill-conceived, the Nationals describing it more luridly as "thought control." The Left denounced this attitude as typical of a "retrograde and classist ideology, the egoism of this privileged group, their intellectual myopia, and their closed-minded defense of caste interests."[26]

Faced with the hostile reaction, Allende and his minister of Education, the Radical Jorge Tapia, agreed in April 1973 to delay the implementation of ENU. But while Tapia was briefly abroad, one of his subordinates, Carlos Moreno, announced that the government would go forward with part of the legislation. This enraged the opposition, while Tapia, furious

---

[24] Joseph P. Farrell, *The National Unified School in Allende's Chile* (Vancouver, 1986), p. 96.
[25] *Ibid.*, p. 97.
[26] *La Nación,* April 25, 1973, quoted in Farrell, *The National Unified School,* p. 222.

that his aides had sabotaged his policies, tendered his resignation, which Allende rejected. Although Tapia continued to negotiate the provisions of ENU with the leaders of the PDC, the episode seemed to many a further proof that the government could not control its own officials.

But ENU was not the only issue to exacerbate political feelings. Soon after the elections, the Moneda announced that it would (contrary to the provisions of the agrarian reform law) take over farms between forty and eighty hectares in size. The government also continued to nationalize factories. The PDC responded by reviving the constitutional issue left dormant in 1972, hoping to secure the amendment limiting the Social Area. The arguments remained essentially the same, Allende wishing the dispute to be adjudicated by the Constitutional Tribunal (which in fact refused to adjudicate), the opposition invoking the need for a plebiscite, which it assumed Allende would lose.

As Congress and the president once again battled over the constitutional issue, the country seemed mired in growing paralysis. Workers continued to occupy factories, extending the *cordones industriales.* Paramilitary groups on Right and Left alike redoubled their shadowy efforts, preparing for the armed confrontation their hearts desired. The street demonstrations intensified in vehemence. The rhetoric on both sides became increasingly strident, not least in the press, which often resorted to vulgar and demeaning language – one left-wing newspaper plainly described the justices of the supreme court as *viejos mierdas* ("old shits"). Slogans proliferated on the walls, those from the left threatening all *momios* with the firing squad, those from the right plaintively urging the armed forces to intervene. On some walls the simple, menacing word *Djakarta* was inscribed – a pointed allusion to the Indonesian military's massacre of 300,000 Communists eight years earlier.

In this atmosphere of impending breakdown, the military began, perhaps inevitably, to move toward center-stage. Many officers now resented the government they had sworn to protect, though arguably the armed forces had done better in material terms under Allende than under Frei or Alessandri. The military was increasingly subjected to the disdain of the opposition. Civilians insulted the officer corps, casting doubts on its intelligence (and sometimes its virility). Meanwhile the Left added fuel to the fire by denouncing the officers, exhorting the enlisted men to mutiny, and calling for workers' militias to replace the professional armed forces. Nerves on both sides became frayed. In one famous incident (June 27, 1973) General Prats himself forced a woman's car off the side of the street after she had put out her tongue at him. He would have arrested her had not a hostile crowd intervened.

Rising military discontent was first translated into action on June 29, 1973, when the Second Armored Regiment rebelled. In some ways the rising had the quality of a comic opera. One tank crew had to refuel at a civilian gas station (they paid the attendant), and the tanks scrupulously obeyed the traffic signals while on their way to overthrow the government. With the Carabinero presidential guard holding fast, General Prats took personal charge of crushing the putsch. Moving from tank to tank, armed with a machine gun, he ordered the mutineers to surrender. Cowed by his personality, and aware that other Army units had failed to join them, they gave up. Meanwhile the leaders of the *cordones industriales,* verbally encouraged by Allende and the CUT in the tense hours while the revolt was in progress, seized more than 350 factories, which they refused to abandon even after the collapse of the putsch.

Although Allende survived the *tancazo* (as the revolt was soon dubbed), his political position now rapidly deteriorated. The president asked Congress to grant him emergency powers. Fearing that he might use the law against them, the legislators rejected the request. Allende next tried to mollify the opposition by reshuffling his cabinet, but his failure to give important ministries to the military undermined this effort at reconciliation. By this stage the Nationals had set their face against any accommodation whatever with Allende, and the PDC saw a military presence in the cabinet as the only way of upholding the constitution. (Their confidence in the military, needless to say, was seriously misplaced.) Allende did, however, now make a last-ditch attempt to reach an understanding with the PDC. He spent most of July 30 discussing (at the Moneda) the main bones of contention with the then PDC party president, Patricio Aylwin, and his vice-president, Osvaldo Olguín – both of them senators. Allende agreed to accept the PDC's demand that the government enforce the arms control law, to discuss military participation in the cabinet, and to consider limitations on the Social Area and on agrarian reform. In return, however, he asked that Congress recognize that two-thirds majorities were needed to override presidential vetoes. Both sides promised to establish special committees to pursue further negotiations. But because of pressure from the UP's intransigents, led by Carlos Altamirano, as well as from those of the PDC, the committees never met. On August 17, Allende and Aylwin were to meet again, this time secretly, at Cardinal Raúl Silva Henríquez's house in Calle Simón Bolívar, but it proved impossible to restart negotiations. The Allende-Aylwin "conversations" were the last real attempt at compromise involving both sides.

By the end of July, although it did not yet know it, the country had entered the last days of the ill-starred "transition to socialism." The economy, already crippled by the costly strike at El Teniente, was further disabled by a recurrence of action by the truckers, who claimed that the government was trying to destroy them by withholding spare parts. As in October 1972, the *gremios* mobilized for a second all-out confrontation.

This movement was if anything wider than its predecessor; the *gremios* and professional groups were joined now, for instance, by the pilots of LAN-Chile. Once again, polarization was compounded by national paralysis.

We are tempted to compare the bitter struggle of 1973 with comparable episodes in Chile's own past: the contest between Manuel Montt and the Liberal-Conservative Fusion; the mobilization of the parties against Balmaceda; even, perhaps, the resistance to Arturo Alessandri's reforms. In all three cases the outcome was some kind of upheaval: civil war or military intervention. The confrontation between the UP and the PDC-National opposition was on an altogether larger scale than any of its predecessors. The essential difference was that it occurred in the age of modern, mass politics, and, indeed, in the age of the mass media, and there can scarcely have been anybody in the country who was unaffected by or ignorant of what was happening. Families were divided; old friendships were strained to the breaking point; tempers were comprehensively lost. It was a time when many of the traditional Chilean virtues, above all the virtue of *convivencia,* the ability to respect alternative points of view, seemed totally in abeyance.

A question frequently asked later on was whether the dire emergency of 1973 was either caused or exacerbated by external meddling, specifically by the United States. Neither President Richard Nixon nor his vain foreign policy adviser (and soon to be Secretary of State) Henry Kissinger made much of a secret of their loathing of the UP government. Actuated by their unreflective view of *Realpolitik,* they were certainly the chief authors of the credit squeeze against Chile orchestrated in Washington, and the various forms of "covert action" used by the CIA in Chile in its efforts at political "destabilization."[27] Nixon's *intentions* are crystal clear, and the US$8 million allocated to the CIA for its operations against Allende (much of it used to subsidize the opposition, including *El Mercurio*) has long been a matter of public record, thanks largely to the U.S. Congress. It may be doubted, however, whether the CIA made very much difference: sad as it is to have to say this, the real "destabilization" of Chile was the work of Chileans. As Patricio Aylwin was to say, sixteen years later, "We were all responsible."

In the deadly political climate of mid-1973, events developed their own ineluctable impetus. On July 26, unknown attackers assassinated Allende's naval aide, Commander Arturo Araya. A month later another group, led by a Mexican political refugee, murdered a young Army

---

[27] It was in the Chilean context that this ugly word entered the English language. See the entry for "destabilization" in the *Oxford English Dictionary* (2nd ed.). The verb "to destabilize" is considerably older.

lieutenant. Efforts were made to suborn a FACH garrison near Viña del Mar. In a still more ominous move, MIR, MAPU, and Socialist militants tried to foment a mutiny on two warships at Valparaiso and also in the Talcahuano naval base. Carlos Altamirano provocatively (and characteristically) announced that he had foreknowledge of the abortive naval mutiny and that he supported such actions. Did he really believe that this would have no effect on military hearts and minds?

As the atmosphere of violence thickened, Allende desperately tried to hold his government together. In early August he formed a new cabinet, appointing General Prats minister of Defense, Admiral Raúl Montero minister of Finance, and FACH General César Ruiz minister of Public Works. The president's decision to reinclude the military in the government, obviously designed to conciliate the PDC, came far too late. The country had by now entered a state of political limbo. No one person or institution commanded sufficient respect to overcome the impasse. The UP's "ultras," led by the ever-tactful Altamirano, refused to negotiate with "reactionary and counter-revolutionary leaderships or parties";[28] the opposition voiced similar sentiments, though not the same rhetoric. A coalition of PDC and National congressmen, citing the government's toleration of armed paramilitary groups, its use of obscure decrees to expropriate property, and its continuous refusal to abide by the judiciary's decisions, passed a resolution (August 22) which accused the government of comprehensively breaking the law. Stopping just short of advocating a coup d'état, it nonetheless called on the military members of the cabinet to "put an immediate end to all the *de facto* situations ... which infringe the Constitution and the laws."[29] President Allende now had virtually no room for maneuver. His final proposal for a political solution to the crisis – a national plebiscite, possibly leading to a constitutional assembly – was seriously mooted among the UP parties early in September, but was overwhelmed by events.

For the military, caught between defending the government and mounting a rebellion, had finally chosen the latter course of action. "Who saves his country breaks no law" – a naval officer was to quote Napoleon's remark when the die was finally cast.[30] But by all accounts the decision did not come easily. Although some officers had contemplated a coup d'état as early as mid-1972, this sentiment took time to spread. Mounting chaos, insinuations from the opposition, the vocal demand of left-wing militants that the state replace the armed forces with "popular

[28] Arturo Valenzuela, *The Breakdown of Democratic Regimes: Chile* (Baltimore, 1987), p. 94.

[29] *El Mercurio,* August 23, 1973.

[30] Florencia Varas and José Manuel Vergara, *Operación Chile* (Buenos Aires, 1974), p. 73.

militias," and the abortive naval mutiny (with its explicit support from Altamirano) – these things finally convinced most officers that they should withdraw support from the Allende government.

Before the military could act, however, they had to force out Allende's appointees. When a delegation of generals informed Prats that he no longer enjoyed their confidence (he had earlier been the target of an unseemly demonstration by their wives), the commander-in-chief resigned (August 21). His replacement was General Augusto Pinochet, whom Allende (and Prats) believed to be as strongly "constitutionalist" as Prats. Similar changes occurred in the other armed services. Naval officers, emulating their colleagues in the Army, successfully secured the removal of the fleet's commander, Admiral Raúl Montero, whose place was taken by Admiral José Toribio Merino. The FACH commander, General César Ruiz, was dismissed by Allende himself, in a tense episode. His successor, General Gustavo Leigh, needed no winning over. The way was now open. On Sunday, September 9, after several days of intense plotting, the leaders of the armed forces, with support from the Carabineros, made their pact to overthrow the government.

The operation did not require much in the way of preparation. The Army used the pretext of the annual September 19 military parade – an event in the *fiestas patrias* almost as old as the republic itself – to mask its transfer of units into Santiago. Tuesday, September 11 (General Pinochet had initially wanted the 14th), was fixed as the date for the rebellion. As planned, the fleet sailed out of Valparaiso, ostensibly to take part in annual joint maneuvers, of many years' standing, with the U.S. Navy. Under cover of darkness the warships returned to port in order to seize Valparaiso. The FACH had already ordered its fighters to the south, out of harm's way. Before dawn on September 11 the Army went into action. By early morning it had seized "red Concepción," while the Navy took control of Valparaiso without difficulty. The heaviest fighting, no doubt predictably, occurred in Santiago, much of it between the Army and snipers. President Allende, informed of the naval revolt in the early hours, left his residence for the Moneda. Learning that their commanders supported the coup, the Carabineros defending the palace marched away, leaving the president virtually without protection.

Although the armed forces quickly overpowered their opponents in the provinces and the capital, Allende himself continued to resist. Entrenched in the Moneda with a handful of stalwarts, he refused an offer of safe passage out of the country. He broadcast a final, deeply moving speech over the one radio station which had not yet fallen into military hands. (It soon did.) Betrayed by his soldiers, the president stood fast. Following a rocket attack on the palace by low-flying Hawker Hunters of the FACH, making their raid from Concepción,[31] the infantry assaulted the burning Moneda.

Never had the palace burned before. It was the most dramatic and tragic moment in the modern history of Chile. At around two o'clock that afternoon, Salvador Allende – physician, freemason, Socialist, and president of the republic – shot himself through the head with a machine gun.

---

[31] The rockets were released just over the Mapocho Station.

13

The Pinochet years

Not a leaf stirs in Chile without me moving it.

– General Augusto Pinochet (1981)

Consolidation of the Pinochet regime

September 11, 1973 – *el once,* "the eleventh," as Chileans simply called it for years afterward – represented the worst political breakdown in the history of the republic. Perhaps because the level of national desperation had reached such heights in 1973,[1] the aftermath was far more prolonged than anyone would have believed possible. At the end of July 1989, General Augusto Pinochet broke the previous record for length of tenure among Chilean rulers (all since 1540) – until then held by Governor Gabriel Cano de Aponte at fifteen years, ten months (1717–33). By the time he left office, Pinochet had ruled Chile for eight months longer than his colonial predecessor.

The iron heel of ruthless repression was stamped down from the first moments of the new regime. Congress was closed. The UP parties were banned, other parties placed "in recess" – until 1977, when they too were banned. A strict night-time curfew was imposed and not lifted for several years. Left-wing newspapers and magazines vanished from the kiosks. The public administration was extensively purged. In the opening phase of the regime, virtually all important national institutions (including the soccer federation) were assigned to generals or admirals, colonels or captains, some of them hauled out of retirement. In the universities (also extensively purged), uniformed "delegate-Rectors" took over. The atmosphere of Chile was transformed overnight. The regime's first minister of the Interior, General Oscar Bonilla (killed in a helicopter accident in 1975), told some trade unionists visiting his office: "Stop using the

---

[1] Both authors independently (both before the coup and after) heard perfectly intelligent and rational Chilean friends express the view that they longed for a foreign (American or European) *military* intervention to end (in the first case) the sheer turmoil and (in the second case) the dictatorship.

word 'demand'; don't forget that this is a dictatorship."[2] Nobody could have put it better.

The ferocity of the coup and the severity of the new military Junta's first decrees led outside observers (especially perhaps journalists) to assume that the carnage had been enormous. What Edward Gibbon once called "the melancholy calculation of human calamities" was often, in the years afterward, a political plaything. (Radio Moscow memorably reported that 700,000 had died within two days of the coup.) To have even a few thousand killed in short order (many of them simply disappearing) was in all conscience shocking enough in a small country, and a small country unused to such convulsions: only nonagenarian Chileans could remember the 1891 civil war. Activists of the UP parties were ruthlessly hunted down; some were shot out of hand; many (at least 7,000) were herded into the national stadium in Santiago, the main center for early interrogation. Detention camps were opened up and down the country. Several dozen prominent *allendistas* (including cabinet ministers) were sent to the bleak surroundings of Dawson Island in the Magellan Straits. As in 1948, Pisagua received a batch of prisoners. So too did Quiriquina Island in Talcahuano Bay, where Bernardo O'Higgins had once grazed his cattle. Arrests were in the tens of thousands, and likewise tens of thousands of Chileans were simply banished. By the middle of 1978 there were nearly 30,000 Chileans in exile in Western Europe alone. By the end of the decade exiles could be counted in the hundreds of thousands. This Chilean diaspora was in some ways comparable to that of Spain after the civil war or Cuba's after 1959. Only in the 1980s were the exiles allowed back into Chile, and many (but by no means all) then made the journey home.

Outward peace and quiet, the *tranquilidad* frequently eulogized by the Junta and its publicists, quickly returned to Chile. To guarantee its continuation, the apparatus of a modern police state was systematically assembled. Before the end of 1973 a new secret police was formed, directly under the control of General Pinochet. This was the *Dirección de Inteligencia Nacional* (Directorate of National Intelligence) or DINA: newspapers hesitated for months before printing the ominous acronym. Commanded by Colonel (later General) Manuel Contreras, the DINA recruited the majority of its agents from the Army: some were sent for training in Brazil and South Africa. By 1977 its strength was around 10,000: its paid informers were twice or three times as many. To the DINA can be attributed most of the horrific incidents of torture documented by (in Chile) the Catholic Church and (abroad) by organizations such as Amnesty International. Its notorious torture-centers included the

[2] Quoted in Eugenio Ahumada et al., *Chile, la memoria prohibida*, 3 vols. (Santiago, 1989), III, 491.

Villa Grimaldi, a mansion in La Reina, on the eastern outskirts of Santiago – which DINA's twisted humor nicknamed "the laughter palace." In its opening months DINA targeted the MIR and the Communist party, and in this shadowy campaign no quarter was given. General Pinochet himself was reliably reported as saying: "The members of the MIR *must* be tortured. . . . Without torture they don't sing."[3] Some did sing; others were successfully "turned" (to use the picturesque language of modern espionage) by the DINA.

DINA's arm stretched, when it had to, far beyond Chile's borders. Particularly at risk were those exiled figures who might plausibly head some new post-military government. In September 1974 General Carlos Prats and his wife (self-exiled immediately after the coup d'état) were killed by a car-bomb outside their apartment block in the Palermo district of Buenos Aires. In October 1975, the popular PDC politician Bernardo Leighton was gunned down in Rome, barely surviving. (He died in 1995.) Another car-bomb took the life (September 1976) of Orlando Letelier, this time outside the Chilean embassy in Washington, D.C., where the distinguished and well-liked Socialist had earlier worked as President Allende's ambassador. This terrorist outrage in the nation's capital stung the U.S. Justice Department and FBI into action. The trail of evidence led inexorably to Santiago and the DINA. American pressure (exercised skillfully) secured the extradition of the chief DINA agent responsible (as it happened, a U.S. citizen, and later jailed in the United States), but other extraditions, including that of Contreras, were firmly refused.

The intense national and international commotion caused by the Letelier Affair (and also, apparently, strong feeling within the Army) more or less obliged Pinochet to disband the DINA. It was replaced (August 1977) by a somewhat scaled-down secret police under the name of *Central Nacional de Informaciones* (National Information Center) or CNI. By this stage the level of repression had in any case somewhat subsided. (January 1977 was the first month since the coup with no "disappearances" being reported to the Catholic Church.) Disappearances, torture, and murder were, however, to recur at regular intervals until almost the end of the military regime. A particular furor was roused in March 1985 by the murder of three Communist professionals (a teacher, a sociologist, and a retired artist); their throats were slit and their bodies dumped on a roadside on the outskirts of Santiago.

With political parties banned, with the law courts shamefully acquiescent, with society-wide surveillance by the secret police, the only institution able to retain a more or less independent profile was the Catholic

---

[3] Quoted in Sheila Cassidy, *Audacity to Believe* (London, 1977), p. 158.

Church. A month or so after the coup, Cardinal Raúl Silva Henríquez sponsored the formation of an ecumenical "Peace Committee" to provide legal aid to victims of repression and to monitor human rights violations. It was forced to close in November 1975, but the work (always difficult, sometimes heroic) went on in a new Vicariate of Solidarity (*Vicaría de la Solidaridad*) directly dependent on the Cardinal himself (January 1976). Pinochet and his colleagues were angered by the Church's criticisms, which later extended to the economic policies of the regime. Given the Church's position in Chilean life, no all-out counter-attack was possible. In April 1977, when a minister of Justice made some unusually bitter comments about the Church, Pinochet fired him.

Politics does not disappear in authoritarian regimes; it merely becomes more secret. The most notable feature of authoritarian politics in Chile after September 1973 was the irresistible rise of General Pinochet. ("Who is Pinochet?" ex-president Frei asked on the day of the coup. "I don't know him.") His position as commander-in-chief of the Army gave him the edge over his colleagues, as he quickly appreciated. The early notion that the presidency of the Junta would rotate amongst its members (himself; Admiral José Toribio Merino, Navy; General Gustavo Leigh, FACH; General César Mendoza, Carabineros) was soon shelved. By the end of 1974 Pinochet had arrogated the title of President of the Republic; the regime became an increasingly personal one. While no systematic "personality cult" of Pinochet really developed, his uniforms tended to become more splendid over the years, and in 1981 he revived (for his own use) the old colonial title of Captain General. The next step, said the wits of Santiago, was to be the restoration of the encomienda.

Although important administrative changes took place in the first years of the regime – notably the division of the republic into twelve new regions[4] – Pinochet (like Ibáñez in the 1920s) made no serious effort to consolidate a political movement of his own. After the trauma of 1973, such a movement might have had a substantial following, had it been organized soon enough, but equally it would have conflicted with Pinochet's wish to "de-politicize" the country for a lengthy period. In any case, he never lacked support in the population at large. Hostility to Allende and the UP was easily translated into admiration for their nemesis. At a deeper level, there was a real sense in which Pinochet's stern image (enhanced by the dark glasses he so often wore) touched a nerve in the Chilean culture. As he chastised the unruly and rewarded

---

[4] The new regions (1974), each under a Regional Intendant, and each covering a number of provinces, were numbered I to XII, with Santiago and its immediate hinterland becoming a Metropolitan Area. Twenty years later the regions (still usually referred to by their numbers) were taking on an identity of their own.

the obedient, was he not the old *dueño de fundo,* the old estate-owner, writ large? Did he not also have some of the cunning and resourcefulness of the traditional *huaso?* A dictator he might be, but he was at least an identifiably *Chilean* dictator. Even some of his bitterest adversaries came eventually to feel a wry satisfaction in pointing this out to foreigners. For Pinochet himself, it was a source of strength. Nor can it be denied that his gruff appeals for national reconstruction, and his invocations of (even, perhaps, his self-identification with) Diego Portales and Bernardo O'Higgins, struck a patriotic echo in many hearts.[5]

Pinochet's *huaso*-like astuteness (and suspicious mind) served him well in fending off challenges to his personal power. When his FACH colleague General Leigh tactlessly declared (to an Italian newspaper) his hopes for an early "normalization" of politics, Pinochet swiftly (and at some risk) removed him (July 1978).[6] He stood firm during the Letelier Affair, which brought strained relations with the United States, whose foreign policy was then in an unusual phase, thanks to President Jimmy Carter's positive belief in human rights – an emphasis not shared by Carter's successor, who believed (if that is not too strong a word) in "friendly dictatorships." U.S. restrictions on military aid (first imposed in December 1974 and made more comprehensive in February 1976) did not seriously inconvenience the regime: European countries, despite a few short-term prohibitions, were more than prepared (as was Brazil) to supply arms to Chile, and the country's own armaments industry was given something of a boost, as was shown by the rise of the enterprising Carlos Cardoen's plant at Iquique, which, among other things, was soon selling cluster-bombs to Saddam Hussein's Iraq.

More immediately dangerous than Jimmy Carter was a sudden flare-up of crisis in Chile's relations with Argentina, arising from a long-running dispute over three small islands in the Beagle Channel. The matter had earlier (1971) gone for mediation to the British crown. In January 1978 Argentina rejected Queen Elizabeth II's award of the islands to Chile. We may doubt whether Chilean war fever was as quite as profound as it had been in 1898 or 1900, but the tension between Santiago and Buenos Aires was serious enough, and for a few weeks the prospect of war seemed real. In December 1978 Pope John Paul II successfully imposed his mediation, and the immediate danger receded.

---

[5] A minor official cult of Diego Portales was noticeable in the first years of the regime. It faded by the end of the 1970s, probably because of the renewed focus on O'Higgins during his bicentennial celebrations (1978).

[6] Leigh was replaced by General Fernando Matthei, who served on the Junta for the remainder of the regime. The Carabinero chief, General Mendoza, resigned (August 1985) as a result of the case of the Communist professionals murdered in March 1985, and his replacement was General Rodolfo Stange.

A draft Papal award (confirming the islands as Chilean) was ready by the end of 1980. Argentina's military regime continued to drag its feet. At this point Pinochet had an unexpected stroke of good luck. Argentina's defeat by Great Britain in the brief Falklands War (April–June 1982) – during which Chile gave discreet and totally unpublicized assistance to the British – dispelled the prospect of further military adventures from that quarter. A treaty was duly signed in May 1985.

By then the Pinochet regime was well into a second phase. In July 1977, Pinochet himself announced that his intention was to move Chile toward a new, albeit "protected," democracy. A small group of conservative jurists was already working (at a somewhat leisurely pace) on a new constitution. The completed draft was submitted to the new and largely honorific Council of State (set up in 1976); its chairman, the octagenarian ex-president Jorge Alessandri, made suggestions to Pinochet that were deemed excessively liberal. (Alessandri resigned from the council in disgust.) The tenor of the final version was markedly authoritarian. Among other things it provided for an extremely strong eight-year presidency (Pinochet wanted sixteen-year terms, but was dissuaded), a Congress with more limited powers than before (and with one-third of the Senate nominated, not elected), and various institutional mechanisms to entrench military influence over future governments. Moreover, the "transitory dispositions" (very numerous) were to remain in effect for nearly a decade. Pinochet himself was to take the first eight-year term, at the end of which a plebiscite would be held to endorse (or reject) the military's candidate (Pinochet himself, as it predictably turned out) for the second term (1989–97). Only then could congressional elections be called – along with presidential elections in the event of a "no" vote in the plebiscite.

In the meantime, as in 1925, a referendum was needed to give the new constitution a semblance of legitimacy. The country was deluged with propaganda, but from one side only. Opponents of the constitution (ex-president Frei was the most vocal) were given almost no opportunities to campaign. When the day came (September 11, 1980), more than six million Chileans voted. In the circumstances, it is not altogether easy to see the result (67 percent in favor, 30 percent against) as an unarguably limpid expression of the popular will. Six months later (March 11, 1981) Pinochet assumed the presidency under the new 1980 Constitution. In a heavily symbolic gesture, he moved his office to the now fully restored Moneda palace.

The Chilean road to capitalism

When they seized power, the generals knew nothing much about economics. They had to stabilize and reactivate a badly dislocated economy, and desperately needed advice. There were economists eager to give it. They were products of the Catholic University and some of them, anyway (under a Point IV exchange agreement), of the economics department of the University of Chicago – the chief home of a burgeoning new orthodoxy of "monetarism" and unrestrained laissez-faire. The key figure of the group was Sergio de Castro, the tough-minded, rugby-playing dean of social sciences at the Catholic University in Santiago. When they became prominent, as they soon did, these "neo-liberal" Chilean economists were nicknamed *"los Chicago Boys."* Many of them were given official posts by the new regime, an important nucleus moving into ODEPLAN, the state planning office. The effect of their advice on economic policy was immediate: in October 1973, nearly all price controls were abolished, and the escudo was devalued (from 50 to 250 to the dollar) at a single, unified exchange rate.

Yet the Chicago Boys by no means won an instant victory. At a moment of steeply rising prices and mounting unemployment, their austere vision of unrestrained capitalism seemed altogether too risky to many military men, not to mention business leaders. During 1974, however, Chile began to feel the effects of the devastating international recession caused by the "First Oil Shock" – the quadrupling of oil prices following the Arab-Israeli war of October 1973. In mid-1974 the copper price started to fall alarmingly. Moreover, despite the regime's initial efforts, inflation still seemed to be largely out of control. These mounting difficulties coincided with the consolidation of Pinochet's personal power. It was at this point (March 1975) that the assertive American guru of monetarism, Professor Milton Friedman, saw fit to visit Chile: he talked to Pinochet, emphasizing the need for "shock treatment" to eliminate inflation. In April 1975, after hearing the arguments and counter-arguments of economists at a weekend conference at Cerro Castillo, Pinochet threw caution to the winds, came down decisively in favor of the Chicago Boys, conferred extraordinary powers on Jorge Cauas (his Finance minister since July 1974), and appointed Sergio de Castro as Economy minister. The steelier de Castro took over as Finance minister when Cauas withdrew in December 1976.

The Chicago Boys now came fully into their own. Their energy and dogmatism (equal to that of any Communist of former days) did not make them universally popular. They took full advantage of their alliance with Pinochet, masterminding the most drastic economic reconstruction yet seen in twentieth-century Chile. Their aims were utopian and all-embracing. They wanted to reverse the entire state-interventionist trend that had developed in Chile since the 1920s, which they blamed (rightly or wrongly) for holding back economic growth. This could best be secured, they held, by opening up the economy and by fostering the country's "comparative advantage" in export markets. To achieve these aims, market relations had to be imposed throughout society; a new entrepreneurial culture had to replace habitual dependence on the state; the state itself should henceforth be confined to its classical role as "night-watchman."

Cauas applied "shock treatment" immediately. Public spending was reduced by more than a quarter, the money supply was tightly reined in, and interest rates more than trebled. The predictable result was a deep recession, with unemployment rising to nearly 20 percent (and real wages plummeting down to three-fifths of their 1970 level). By the end of 1975, GDP was down by one-seventh, industrial production by a quarter. The inevitable hardship prompted the regime to institute a low-wage "minimum employment program" (PEM, *Programa de Empleo Mínimo*), in which, by 1976, 200,000 men were working on road-paving and similar tasks.

Notwithstanding the recession, the neo-liberal program was pressed ahead with great thoroughness over the next seven years. Privatization of the more than 400 state-owned, state-controlled, or "intervened" companies (started in 1974) was accelerated, though a hard core of large "strategic" enterprises (many now being efficiently run by military men) remained in the public sector, which ten years after the coup was still larger than it had been in President Frei's time. Meanwhile import tariffs were brought down from an average 70 percent in 1974 to an almost standard 10 percent (one of the lowest in the world) by the end of the decade – with easily predictable consequences for Chilean manufacturing, whose share of GDP fell by one-fifth between 1975 and 1982. Very liberal foreign investment laws were decreed (1974, 1977). The taxation system was revamped, with (among other things) the introduction of a European-style value-added tax (IVA). The currency was reformed (1975): 1,000 escudos became one peso (1 million of the pesos abolished in 1960). In June 1979, partly to neutralize "imported" inflation, de Castro instituted a fixed exchange rate of 39 pesos to the dollar.

In the countryside, the neo-liberal impact was overwhelming. Agrarian reform was halted in its tracks. Government spending on agriculture was slashed. The personnel of the ministry of Agriculture (including agencies like CORA and INDAP) shrank from 27,000 in 1973 to 5,000 in 1980. Just under one-third of all agricultural land in the "reformed sector" was returned to its former owners, about one-half was parceled out to peasants (though by no means all of them), and most of the remainder was auctioned off by CORA. In 1979 a new law encouraged the Mapuche to subdivide their communal lands into private plots. (Nearly one-third of the 3,000 or so communities had already done so in the 1930s and 1940s.) These various measures did not, however, lead to a restoration of the traditional hacienda: the dominant agrarian unit very soon became

Table 13.1. Real wages and salaries, 1974–81 (1970 = 100).

1970	100	1979	82.3
1974	65.1	1980	89.3
1975	62.9	1981	97.4
1976	64.8	1982	97.2
1978	76.0		

Source: Carlos Fortín, "The Political Economy of Repressive Monetarism," in Christian Anglade and Carlos Fortín, eds., *The State and Capitalism in Latin America*, 2 vols. (Pittsburgh, 1985–90), I, 163; and Alejandro Foxley, "The Neoconservative Economic Experiment in Chile," in J. Samuel Valenzuela and Arturo Valenzuela, eds., *Military Rule in Chile* (Baltimore, 1987), p. 17.

Table 13.2. Inflation, 1973–89 (% increase).

1973	605.9	1982	20.7
1974	369.2	1983	23.1
1975	343.2	1984	23.0
1976	197.9	1985	26.4
1977	84.2	1986	17.4
1978	37.2	1987	21.5
1979	38	1988	12.7
1980	31.2	1989	21.4
1981	9.9		

Source: Sebastián and Alejandra Edwards, *Monetarism and Liberalization: The Chilean Experiment* (Chicago, 1991), pp. 28, 213.

the highly capitalized, labor-intensive commercial farm, often geared to the export trade (Chile's southern hemisphere location once again playing the part we have already noted in connection with the nineteenth-century wheat booms), as were the new pine plantations of the south, which were generously subsidized by the state. While some peasants survived well in this bewildering new environment, others (about one-third of the original beneficiaries by the early 1980s) sold their *parcelas* and sometimes drifted into the swelling rural shantytowns to fend for themselves as best they could. The new "agribusinesses" had none of the paternalism of the old hacienda, and offered relatively few stable jobs. Thus the cost of Chile's

Table 13.3. GDP growth according to sector, 1975–82.

	1975	1976	1977	1978	1979	1980	1981	1982
Agriculture & Forestry	4.8	−2.9	10.4	−4.9	5.6	1.8	2.2	−2.1
Fishery	−6.7	33.9	15.4	17.9	14.3	7.5	18.1	9.4
Mining	−11.3	12.2	2.7	1.6	5.4	5.2	7.7	5.7
Manufacturing	−25.5	6.0	8.5	9.3	7.9	6.2	2.6	−21.0
Construction	−26.0	−16.0	−0.9	8.1	23.9	23.9	21.1	−23.8
Commerce	−17.1	2.5	24.8	20.0	11.0	12.4	4.3	−17.3
Financial	−4.2	9.3	14.5	20.1	28.0	22.6	11.9	−5.4
Public services	1.9	5.9	1.8	−3.1	−1.2	−3.2	−1.8	−2.9

Source: Sebastián and Alejandra Edwards, *Monetarism and Liberalization: The Chilean Experiment* (Chicago, 1991), p. 13.

Table 13.4. Percent variation
of GDP, 1971–82 (GDP per
capita in parentheses).

1971	9	(7.1)
1972	−1.2	(−2.9)
1973	−5.6	(−7.1)
1974	1.0	(−0.7)
1975	−12.9	(−14.4)
1976	3.5	(1.8)
1977	9.9	(8.0)
1978	8.2	(6.4)
1979	8.3	(6.5)
1980	7.8	(6.0)
1981	5.7	(3.9)
1982	−14.3	(−14.2)

Source: Carlos Fortín, "The
Political Economy of
Repressive Monetarism," in
Christian Anglade and Carlos
Fortín, eds., *The State and
Capitalism in Latin America*, 2
vols. (Pittsburgh, 1985–90),
I, 207.

dynamic new agriculture (which the military regime could never have brought about without the agrarian reform's extrusion from the country-side of the old landowning class) was an intensification of rural poverty – the poor now being the victims of capitalist modernization rather than of the inertia and hierarchy of the past.

In conventional economic terms, this ruthless neo-liberal "restructuring" seemed to bring results. Inflation fell from triple digits to double digits and finally to single digits (9.5 percent in 1981). The economy began to rebound from the 1975–76 recession, GDP rising by an average 7 percent per year between 1976 and 1981. Helped by a new export-promotion office (*Pro-Chile,* 1974) – not wholly approved of by the neo-liberal purists – the growth of "non-traditional" exports (those of the farms and forests) was especially impressive. Chilean apples appeared in British supermarkets, good-quality Chilean wines in American liquor stores. (By the mid-1990s the shares of one of the classic traditional vineyards, Concha y Toro,[7] were being quoted on the New York Stock Exchange.) Whereas copper had accounted for nearly nine-tenths of all

---

[7] The name gave rise to a colloquial Chilean reflexive verb: *concha-y-torearse,* "to get smashed."

exports (taking yearly averages) in the 1960s, it accounted for under half in the 1980s. Here was an obvious success story.

The privatizations of the 1970s, in town and countryside alike, gave excellent opportunities to financial conglomerates both old and (especially) new to build up large business empires on highly favorable terms (amounting in effect to a state subsidy). By the end of the decade, a handful of such conglomerates (*grupos económicos*) controlled much of the banking system, the new and unregulated finance houses known as *financieras,* and, through their numerous affiliated companies, a growing share of the manufacturing and agro-exporting sectors. With European and American banks overflowing with "petrodollars" after the First Oil Shock, the conglomerates borrowed abroad on a huge scale, using the money both to buy up companies and to make loans (very often to their own affiliates) at the much higher local interest rates. Construction boomed, as did the import business, fueled by easy consumer credit: in 1979 Chile's first credit card ("Diners Club de Chile") appeared on the scene. The country was soon awash in foreign goods: Japanese TVs and radios, Korean automobiles (the number of cars in Chile tripled between 1975 and 1982), French perfumes, Scotch whisky (now costing only slightly more than Chilean-made Pisco, the "clear brandy" from the Norte Chico that so often captivates the foreign visitor). All of this created a powerful illusion of new prosperity. Notwithstanding the colossal (mostly private) foreign debt now building up (US$17 billion by 1982), there was much optimism in the air. Chile, we were told, was to become the next Taiwan or South Korea. In August 1980 Labor minister José Piñera declared: "Chile in 1990 will be a developed country."[8]

Two years later, the Chilean economy simply imploded, in a recession even worse than that of 1975–76. First came another steep rise in the price of oil (the "Second Oil Shock" of 1979). Once again the world economy slumped, which meant slackening demand for Chilean exports – by this stage less competitive because of the fixed exchange rate, which both overvalued the peso and caused acute balance-of-payments problems. International interest rates soared as both the United States (under President Ronald Reagan) and Great Britain (under Prime Minister Margaret Thatcher) adopted harsh neo-liberal strategies of their own. In this new downturn, the two leading new conglomerates, Vial (BHC) and Cruzat-Larraín, their international credit evaporating, were buried for good under a mountain of bad debt from their often hastily acquired affiliates. Bankruptcies rose to more than 800 in 1982 (having run at around one-third that figure between 1977 and 1981). GDP fell by one-seventh; the industrial workforce shrank by one-fifth; and unemployment rose even

---

[8] Quoted in Arturo Fontaine A., *Los economistas y el presidente Pinochet* (Santiago, 1988), p. 140.

higher than in 1975–76. By early 1983 more than half a million men were employed in PEM and a second emergency scheme, POJH (*Programa Ocupacional para Jefes de Hogar:* Work Program for Heads of Households). Manufacturers and farmers alike clamored for protection: their organizations, hitherto spurned by the Chicago Boys, were to be listened to more attentively from now onward.

In mid-1982, de Castro bowed out as Finance minister, and his fixed exchange rate was quickly ditched, Pinochet himself simply telling the new minister: "I have decided to devalue." Two further devaluations brought the peso's value down by 88 percent. (Hard-currency debtors were allowed a *dólar preferencial,* a preferential rate to cushion the effects.) Early in 1983, with the banking system near collapse, the regime took direct control of ten banks and *financieras,* liquidating three altogether, the Central Bank assuming their debts. It took two years or so for a new economic policy fully to take shape – and no less than four Finance ministers. (General Ibáñez's shade must surely have smiled!) Then (in February 1985) Pinochet gave the job to the 36-year-old Hernán Büchi. It did not pass unnoticed that *his* postgraduate work had been done at Columbia, not Chicago, and in business, not economics. With his long hair and enthusiasm for jogging and bicycling, Büchi hardly looked like a Finance minister, yet he, more than anyone else, symbolized the intelligent pragmatism that now replaced the earlier, fundamentalist version of neo-liberalism.

The new pragmatism was grounded in a careful manipulation of the exchange rate and money supply, but it also (partly to hold down imports) allowed selective measures to benefit domestic-oriented agriculture and industry as well as the already much-favored exporters. Import tariffs (after a brief surge in the early 1980s) were set at slightly higher levels than in 1980, and surcharges on specific items were reintroduced, while Chilean-made components for exported manufactures were exempted from IVA. Spurred by this mix of limited "import substitution" and export promotion, Chile's factories and workshops – as well as the spreading Central Valley fruit farms and southern pine forests – helped to propel the country into a new phase of solid growth from the mid-1980s onward, with inevitable effects on employment and wages (and probably politics too). Yet the general neo-liberal framework was maintained and strengthened. During the 1980s, most national pension schemes were transferred to private companies, known as AFPs – *Administradoras de Fondos de Pensión,* "Pension Fund Administrations." (By the early 1990s the new private pension funds were worth around US$15 billion.) After 1985, in addition, a number of the "strategic" state enterprises – including CAP (steel) and SOQUIMICH (nitrates and chemicals) – were sold off in a new round of privatizations, the workers in some of these

Table 13.5. Social expenditures [US$ (1981)
1,000 million].

1972	226.2	1977	165.8
1974	182.6	1979	191.7
1975	153.2	1981	202.1

Source: Juan Pablo Arellano, "Social Policies in
Chile: A Historical Review," *Journal of Latin
American Studies,* 17:2 (1985), 405.

companies acquiring around one-third of the equity. Even after this, the
public sector retained a cluster of large corporations, including ENAP
(petroleum) and the mammoth copper corporation, CODELCO.

A particular effort was now made to tackle the gargantuan foreign
debt, and with some success: as a percentage of GNP it fell from 143
percent in 1985 to 74 percent in 1990. (Back in 1970 it had been a mere
8 percent of GNP.) On this front, Chile pioneered the innovative use of
"debt-equity swaps" (foreign investors buying debts, selling them to the
Central Bank, and using the proceeds to buy equity in Chilean companies
or to initiate new investments). Direct foreign investment, of which there
had been relatively little until now, also increased by leaps and bounds
after 1985, about two-fifths of it coming from the United States, and
much of it applied to productive purposes – unlike the speculative
borrowing of the late 1970s. A large new copper mine, La Escondida,
owned by U.S., European, and Japanese multinationals, began production
in 1990, with plans to enlarge to the size of El Teniente. Developments
such as these gave Chile a highly positive profile in the international
business press. For other Latin American countries, mired (as most of
them were) in a decade-long recession, the "Chilean model" had obvious
attractions by the early 1990s. Not for the first time in its history, this
small country seemed to be leading the pack.

The effects of the neo-liberal economic revolution on Chilean society
have been much debated. As we have seen, economic growth after the
mid-1980s was achieved at the cost of two deep recessions and levels of
unemployment that remained high until the end of the period. Urban
and rural poverty undoubtedly intensified during these years. For those in
regular employment, real wages in 1990 were probably little better than
they had been twenty years earlier, though they were once again improving steadily with the renewal of economic growth. Income distribution
became badly skewed, with many of the benefits of growth accruing to the
betteroff, while the poorest two-fifths of the population, and sections of
the middle class (dismissed bureaucrats and schoolteachers, or those caught
by increasing debt), had to cope with static or declining living standards.

Table 13.6. Unemployment, 1970–83.

(%)	Open	PEM	Total
1970	5.7	—	5.7
1974	9.2	—	9.2
1975	14.5	2	16.5
1976	14.4	5.8	20.2
1977	12.7	5.9	18.6
1978	13.6	4.3	17.9
1979	13.8	3.5	17.3
1980	12.0	5.2	17.3
1981	10.8	4.8	15.6
1982	20.4	5.1	25.5
1983	18.6	10.3	28.9

Source: Sebastián and Alejandra Edwards, *Monetarism and Liberalization: The Chilean Experiment* (Chicago, 1991), p. 137; and Carlos Fortín, "The Political Economy of Repressive Monetarism," in Christian Anglade and Carlos Fortín, eds., *The State and Capitalism in Latin America*, 2 vols. (Pittsburgh, 1985–90), I, 163.

It is not that the military regime forgot the poor (though some of its supporters did). Indeed, the poorest poor (those in "extreme poverty") were a particular concern of its planning team at ODEPLAN. By the late 1980s the regime could point with justifiable pride to significant improvements in low-cost housing, sewerage, street-paving, domestic water supply, life-expectancy (65 in 1973, 72 in 1990), child nutrition, and infant mortality (in 1970 Chile had one of Latin America's highest rates; by 1990 it had the lowest). All this was undeniably impressive. Yet in other ways the regime's economic project was socially detrimental. The old national health service (SNS) was replaced by a new "National Health Fund" (*FONASA: Fondo Nacional de Salud*), a state insurance scheme. Additionally, from 1981 onward, the regime allowed the creation of private health-care ISAPREs (*Institutos de Salud Previsional*), somewhat resembling American HMOs. These benefitted only a minority, albeit an expanding one: by 2002, some 23 percent of the population was enrolled in the ISAPREs. Other Chileans (notably the out-of-work, the sick, and the elderly) were much less fortunate. Spending on the state health services (regionalized in the 1980s) declined, as did standards of medical attention and hospital care. The decentralization of social services (and state education) to the municipalities (undertaken after 1981) had the advantage of cutting out bureaucracy, but poorer municipalities were not well placed to shoulder this new burden.

Moreover, neo-liberal "restructuring" greatly disrupted traditional patterns of employment. High unemployment itself had obvious effects on family life and family incomes. By the late 1980s, between one-third and two-fifths of the working population was engaged in "informal" occupations, including street-vending and domestic service. With the widespread use of subcontracting (by factories, farms, and the state itself), employment often became short-term or seasonal – the classic case being fruit picking and packing, which in the 1980s drew in thousands of men and women from the cities as well as the countryside. (In the countryside, temporary workers outnumbered those in stable jobs by about six to one.) In the *poblaciones,* grass-roots communal groups (often assisted by the Catholic Church, and with women very frequently taking the lead) organized the crafting and sale of artesanal wares, including the beautiful *arpilleras* (rag tapestries) later exhibited all around the world. Those for whom such survival strategies did not work sought refuge in alcohol or the now blossoming Protestant (mostly Pentecostal)[9] churches: by 1985 around one-fifth of the population was thought to be Protestant, a subterranean change whose implications for the future (if any) few bothered to evaluate.

Despite the tremendous underside of poverty, many Chileans adapted to, and thrived in, the new economic climate. A new breed of tough, modern-minded (often rather philistine) entrepreneurs took their place alongside the older generation. Chilean "yuppies" abounded. New (and old) conglomerates, more solidly based than Vial or Cruzat-Larraín, were able to grow spectacularly in the 1980s. Older, established enterprises, slimmed down by the two recessions, proved willing to compete successfully in the domestic and (increasingly) international marketplaces, and were now less inclined than before to look to the state for support or protection. Confident in their own abilities, businessmen began to see themselves (and by the mid-1980s were projecting an image of themselves) as one of the leading edges of society. Meanwhile, at a more modest level, the "information revolution," accepted with enthusiasm by Chilean business, gave scope for thousands of well-trained computer specialists. Courses in management, commercial law, and accounting

---

[9] Very much a domestic Chilean church (founded 1910), and not, like some of the Protestant churches of Central America, connected with the fundamentalist sects of the United States, though some of these, too, have sister churches in Chile.

proliferated in a series of new private universities (uninhibited by pretensions to research) and professional institutes. Higher education in general had a distinctly functional look by the late 1980s, but it undoubtedly widened the limits of the entrepreneurial culture dreamed of by the regime.

The neo-liberal technocrats probably did not engineer a deep shift in the national culture. Certain public attitudes were nonetheless shifting. The opinion survey conducted by Carlos Huneeus in 1986 shows that while the banks and conglomerates were disliked by those interviewed, small and middle-sized businesses were very well regarded indeed, though a majority wanted the economy to be mixed rather than completely privatized.[10] Proprietors of successful new small businesses, the workers owning stock in the newly privatized corporations, peasants growing *porotos* for export or vegetables for the Santiago market – all of these, perhaps, felt a growing attachment to the market economy. Even some who worked in the large "informal" sector could sometimes see themselves as small-time entrepreneurs, while others had no great desire to return to the factory floor.

The authors Joaquín Lavín and Luis Larraín claimed in 1989 that Chile had become "a more efficient society, more humane, better informed, more cultured."[11] They pointed to the modern business executives, the shopping malls of eastern Santiago, supermarkets and street-paving in the *poblaciones,* the computer courses, the renewed diversity of cultural expression, the enormous variety of consumer goods in the shops, the growth of industrial exports – such, they asserted, were the indisputable signs of an emerging new society, a *modern* society. Much of what they said was true enough. The material marks of modernization were manifold in the Chile of 1989. A different and less friendly eye, however, also would have noticed, that year, not only the obvious persistence of poverty, but also a certain social atomization, the American-style trivialization of the mass media, a tendency to rather mindless consumerism. One thing no visitor in 1989 could fail to notice was the fact, among other signs of environmental degradation, that the Santiago smog was one of the most noxious in the western hemisphere – caused partly by the sheer rise in the number of automobiles (approaching 1.5 million in Chile by the mid-1990s) and partly by an uncontrolled increase in bus traffic in a city now reaching 4 million.[12] It was, in its way, an eloquent

---

[10] Carlos Huneeus, *Los chilenos y la política* (Santiago, 1987), pp. 116–20.

[11] Joaquín Lavín and Luis Larraín, *Chile, sociedad emergente* (Santiago, 1989), p. 17.

[12] At the end of the 1980s Santiago was reputed to have as many buses as Buenos Aires, a city three times larger.

symbol of "deregulation." If, in short, the Pinochet regime had left solid foundations for future governments to build on, it had also left much to be put right. *But by whom?*

The renewal of politics

Among the effects of the acute misery induced by the economic collapse of 1982–83 was the rise of serious and increasingly vocal opposition to the Pinochet regime. It was sparked by the labor movement. After 1973, with the old CUT dissolved, trade unions had been severely hampered by both repression and numerous new restrictions. Not until 1979 did the regime introduce its own labor code (*Plan Laboral*), which severely limited the scope of unions. Their membership roughly halved between 1973 and 1983. Yet, as Alan Angell has observed, "class and political consciousness could not be abolished by decree,"[13] and resistance to the regime from labor had never entirely died out. By the early 1980s, a number of labor leaders were becoming nationally known for their independent stance – notably the textile workers' Manuel Bustos, the El Teniente copper miners' Rodolfo Seguel, and the rather older Tucapel Jiménez, leader of the public employees' union (ANEF) and earlier a supporter of the regime. Jiménez's growing popularity was clearly seen as a threat: in February 1982 he was brutally murdered by the CNI, his corpse dumped in an abandoned taxi. It was Rodolfo Seguel ("the Chilean Lech Walesa," as some called him) who next took the initiative and called for a one-day general strike on May 11, 1983. Somewhat to Seguel's surprise, the strike attracted widespread support. Santiago was paralyzed: the blare of car horns and the banging of pots and pans showed that militant opposition had returned to the streets of Chile. Over the next three years or so, there were more than twenty such days of protest (*protestas*), with strikes, demonstrations, and running battles with the police.

Although the initiative for the first few *protestas* came from the unions, it soon passed to the newly reviving political parties, as Seguel, a Christian Democrat, wanted it to. For, as he declared in July 1983, it was the duty of the parties to "assume the role that belongs to them in this society..., [to] find the point where they are in agreement and present the people with a project."[14] Neither the unions (which had their own battles to fight) nor the thousand or so grass-roots organizations in the *poblaciones* (in which the prominent role of women once again deserves to be highlighted) could easily articulate the needed national "project."

[13] *Cambridge History of Latin America*, ed. Leslie Bethell, vol. VIII (Cambridge, 1991), p. 371.
[14] Eugenio Ahumada et al. *Chile, la memoria prohibida*, III, 515.

For all the disruption of the previous ten years, the parties had never disappeared. The National party, to be sure, had patriotically disbanded itself after the coup, its membership thereafter supporting the regime. The Communists, though damaged by repression, knew how to survive in clandestinity. In 1980, in a drastic divergence from its historic "peaceful" line, inspired partly by the recent revolutions in Nicaragua and Iran, the party began espousing a tactic of mass insurrection: its new urban guerrilla group, the Manuel Rodríguez Patriotic Front (FPMR), mostly recruited in the shantytowns, was now engaging in minor terrorism – the *rodriguistas* having a notable penchant for blowing up electricity pylons and causing power cuts. The Socialist party's national networks had been far more severely dislocated by repression. Its internal fissures multiplied, especially among the exiles, whose debates were endless. The substance of these, however interesting, does not concern us here. By the early 1980s, two principal factions were consolidating: first, those unreconstructed Socialists who aspired to revive the full *allendista* program, and second, the so-called "renewed" Socialists (influenced by European social democracy and, some claimed, by the writings of Antonio Gramsci), for whom an association with the Christian Democrats was no longer absolutely unthinkable. The PDC itself, briefly disorientated by the death of its hero, Eduardo Frei (January 1982), was now reinvigorated at the hands of a new president, the fluent and active Gabriel Valdés. His techniques included the wholesale dispatch of morale-raising cassettes to local groups of the PDC faithful. (Only a few years earlier, we might note, cassettes had played their part in the downfall of the Shah of Iran and the triumph of Ayatollah Khomeini.)

In the wake of the first *protestas,* two main party-centered coalitions took shape (August–September 1983). The first, the Democratic Alliance (*Alianza Democrática*), had as its focus the PDC, the so-called "Republican Right" (right-wingers beginning to distance themselves from the regime), and "renewed" Socialists, as well as a bewildering number of smaller groups – some old (like the Radicals), some new (like the Humanists). The Communist party, excluded from the Alliance, formed its own People's Democratic Movement (MDP), along with the other main Socialist faction (the "Almeyda Socialists"), and what little was left of the MIR.

The mass mobilization of 1983–86 undoubtedly disconcerted the regime. Its response was predictably heavy-handed: each *protesta* brought its quota of deaths, injuries, and arrests, while late in 1984 police and troops mounted a series of brutal sweeps through the shantytowns. An initiative from the new Cardinal-Archbishop of Santiago, Juan Francisco Fresno, induced eleven parties (roughly the full spectrum, minus the Communists) to sign (August 1985) a "national agreement for the transition to full democracy" (*Acuerdo Nacional para la Transición a la Plena Democracia*) – a minimal consensus in favor of free elections, re-establishment of the rule of law, and recognition that the Chilean economy should be "mixed." Whatever heart-searchings this may have provoked within the armed forces (and there were evidently some), Pinochet himself would have nothing to do with the agreement. On Christmas Eve 1985 he bluntly told the Cardinal not to meddle in politics. The Captain General had recently celebrated his seventieth birthday, and was in excellent physical shape, as Chileans were pointedly reminded in a short TV film showing him doing his legendary early-morning exercises.

The final issue in 1985 of the opposition magazine *Fortín Mapocho* carried the huge headline EL DEBE IRSE EN EL 86 ("HE MUST GO IN '86"). But he did not. Despite demonstrations in the streets and uproar on university campuses, he was determined to stick to his personal timetable – victory in the plebiscite in 1988, a second term lasting to 1997. In September 1986 he survived a serious attempt at assassination (mounted by the *rodriguistas*) in which five of his bodyguards died. This providential escape, and, not least, the now reviving economy served to reinforce Pinochet's position. The opposition (or most of it) slowly began to realize, with some reluctance, that its only practical tactic was to work within the framework of the detested 1980 Constitution. The proposition that the constitution should be treated as "a fact" was first enunciated in June 1984 by the PDC veteran Patricio Aylwin. By August 1987, when Aylwin once again took over the presidency of his party, succeeding Valdés, there were many more who were prepared to contemplate "the fact" – if only because the regime itself was now actively making preparations for the plebiscite.

In February–March 1987 new electoral registers were opened, and non-Marxist political parties were permitted to re-form, on condition that they collect (at the national level) 33,500 signatures from registered voters. This was the moment of truth for the opposition. The new and youthful Humanist party (a local version of the Green parties doing so well at that time in Western Europe) was the first to start a deliberate registration drive. The PDC and other parties soon followed. (By August 1988 more than nine out of ten qualified voters were registered.) For Socialists, and other left-wingers barred from re-forming, an "umbrella" party, the PPD ("Party for Democracy"), was usefully conjured into existence. (It rather interestingly developed an identity of its own later on.) The Right, finally re-entering the political arena in a state of some confusion, eventually divided its forces between two main parties: the traditional-conservative *Renovación Nacional* (RN, National Renewal), descending from the old National party, and the technocratic, neo-liberal *Unión Demócrata Independiente* (UDI, Independent Democrat Union), led

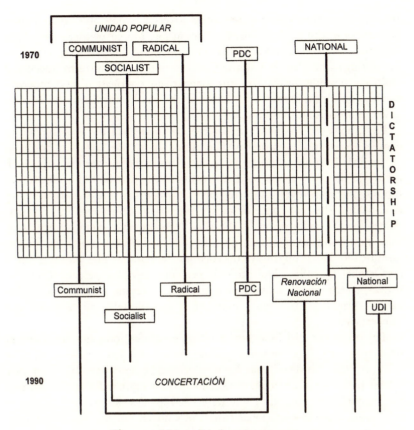

Chart 13.1. Main political parties, 1970–90.

by Jaime Guzmán, the former *gremialista* student leader, and one of Pinochet's closest advisers over the years – not that his advice had always been taken.

The "Concertacíon[15] of Parties for No" (*Concertación de Partidos por el No*) formed in February 1988 linked more than fifteen parties and movements (not including the Communists) in a common effort to win a "no" vote in the impending plebiscite. It was, we are inclined to say, the latest in a line of political combinations stretching back to the Liberal-Conservative Fusion. In one respect the parallel with the Fusion is apt: like the Liberals and Conservatives of the 1850s, the big battalions of the Concertación, the PDC, and the Socialists (who became a reunited party

---

[15] There is no adequate English translation available for *Concertación*. It really means "Concert" as in "Concert of Europe."

again in December 1989) were former adversaries now able to sink their differences in the fight against a common foe. Moreover there were both Christian Democrats and Socialists (again the parallel with the Fusion is interesting) who already saw the Concertación as a long-term governing coalition to guide the country into a new phase – a phase of re-democratization, combining broad acceptance of the market economy with a renewed emphasis on social justice.

First, however, the newly registered electorate had to be persuaded to deny Pinochet his second term. The campaign for the "no" vote bordered on genius. It brushed aside harassment from the authorities, of which there was plenty – 2,000 political arrests in the first half of 1988. It was thoroughly up-to-date in its recourse to "focus groups" (as a means of establishing the real concerns of voters) and to computers and fax machines for the monitoring of the vote.[16] Aware that there were now at least 3 million television sets in Chile, it made brilliant use of the fifteen-minute TV slots grudgingly conceded by the regime. The vote was taken on October 5, 1988. "No" won 54 percent, "yes," 43 percent. (Ninety-seven percent of all those registered – 92 percent of all qualified to vote – turned out.) It was a moment of unforgettable euphoria for the Concertación.

The result enraged Pinochet. Another plebiscite long ago, he observed soon afterward, had chosen Barrabas. (What did that make him?) He made it clear, however, that he would observe the timetable, and that proper presidential and congressional elections (under the 1980 constitution) would now be held. These were fixed for December 1989. It was at this point that the traditional rituals of Chilean politics really resumed. The Concertación, flushed with its success, was eager to devise a common list of candidates for Congress and to elect a president. A PDC candidate was as inevitable as the Radical candidate had been for the Popular Front in 1938. To the annoyance of the rest of the Concertación, the PDC itself conducted a sharp internal battle before making up its mind: Gabriel Valdés wanted the nomination, as did the rising star of the younger generation, Eduardo Frei, the son and namesake of the former president and a successful engineer and businessman. But Valdés dramatically withdrew in favor of the obvious candidate, Patricio Aylwin, whose stature had been greatly enhanced by his role as official spokesman of the Concertación during the plebiscite campaign. The Right (Renovación

---

[16] The opposition was also helped by approximately US$2 million from the Reagan administration: one reason for this largesse, it has been suggested, is that the administration, obsessed in the 1980s with bringing down the revolutionary regime in Nicaragua, wished to appear even-handed in its Latin American dealings. For a useful survey of U.S. policy toward Chile from the 1960s to the 1990s, see Paul Sigmund, *The United States and Democracy in Chile* (Baltimore, 1993).

Nacional and UDI) chose the initially reluctant Hernán Büchi, in the belief that his unconventional style might prove attractive. A third candidate entered the lists. This was the "populist" millionaire Francisco Javier ("Fra Fra") Errázuriz, whose motive for running was obscure – it may simply have been because he was, after all, an Errázuriz. He proclaimed himself a "man of the center," which he was not.

Electioneering apart, the Concertación also used the year between plebiscite and election to secure a number of amendments to the 1980 Constitution. It was helped here by the positive attitude of *Renovación Nacional* (not least its intelligent and youthful leader Andrés Allamand) and the skillful maneuvering of Pinochet's last minister of the Interior, Carlos Cáceres, who believed that the Captain General would win honor by a strict observance of his own constitution. The Concertación did not get everything it wanted, but a package was eventually agreed to, and this was approved (by 86 percent of the 7 million voters) in a plebiscite held at the end of July 1989. The package included an end to the prohibition (Article 8) on parties who were "against the family" or in favor of "class struggle," an enlargement of the elected element in the Senate, an easing of procedures for constitutional amendment, and changes in the composition of the new (and, in design, military-dominated) National Security Council. It also, as a temporary measure, limited the next presidential term to four years.

Pinochet also proved conciliatory over the composition of the board of the Central Bank, now to be independent of the government (like the Federal Reserve or the German Bundesbank) – an old dream of the Chicago Boys. The Concertación could not, however, secure changes in the new "binomial" election system[17] now decreed, or arrest a final spate of laws – the so-called *leyes de amarre* ("tie-up laws") – by which Pinochet sought to tie the hands of future governments: these included permanency of tenure for civil servants, the irremovability of the commanders-in-chief, and a few more last-minute privatizations. On one further point, too, the general was immoveable: whatever the outcome of the election, he himself was to remain as commander-in-chief of the Army until 1998.

All this hardly seemed to matter. For the first time in nearly two decades, Chileans were enjoying the recovered (and for the younger generation, wholly unfamiliar) delights of a presidential election campaign. The outcome reflected, almost exactly, the vote in the plebiscite, Aylwin winning 55 percent of the vote, his two right-wing rivals collecting 43 percent between them. In the congressional elections, the Con-

---

[17] This weighted the system toward the Right by favoring rural areas and also by the rule that in two-seat districts, the winning party could take both seats only if it had twice the votes of the losing party.

certación won 72 of the 120 seats in the Chamber, and 22 of the 38 elected Senate places.

One of Pinochet's final schemes had been the construction of a new Congress building in Valparaiso – a half neo-Babylonian, half postmodernist atrocity across the street from the bus terminal. It was part of an old deal with Admiral Merino, but doubtless seen, also, as a means of deflating the egos of politicians by removing their main forum from Santiago. This architectural monstrosity was only half-finished when, on March 11, 1990, Patricio Aylwin was inaugurated there as president of Chile.

"Re-encounter with history"

The septuagenarian Patricio Aylwin was the first Chilean president to have an English surname – and a very old one, with the original meaning of "elf-friend" (or alternatively just "good friend"). The elves (albeit creatures of Nordic rather than Latin mythology) may possibly have given him some help. It is tempting to compare him (despite many differences of character) to the emollient nineteenth-century president José Joaquín Pérez. His task was in some ways similar, in some ways much more daunting. Aylwin's clear head, his patience, his negotiating talent, his mildly ironic smile – these assets were invaluable to the country as it took its first steps back to democracy, to what Aylwin himself, in his moving televised address on New Year's Eve 1990, termed "Chile's re-encounter with its history."

The new government's task was threefold: it had to reinforce the democratic consensus and in particular to ensure smooth civil-military relations; it had to handle the delicate questions arising from the human rights abuses of the years after 1973; and it had to maintain economic growth while attending to the social inequities left by the outgoing regime. Aylwin himself warned that progress could not be swift. Nor was it in all respects, but he was helped by a generally constructive attitude among the politicians (or most of them), and he was quite prepared to negotiate major initiatives (like the tax and labor laws of 1990) with the right-wing opposition parties. In Congress, the charm and authority of Gabriel Valdés did much to smooth inter-party relations: parliamentary life in the early 1990s lacked something of the cut-and-thrust and sparkle of previous eras, but this is probably true of most modern legislatures. (In any case, Congress's role was now more restricted than it had been before 1973: 90 percent of all legislation between 1990 and 1994 was initiated from the Moneda.) The Concertación's willingness to consult the opposition stemmed in part, no doubt, from the need to ensure the reintegration of the Right (closely associated with the outgoing regime and strongly inclined to defend its achievements) into the mainstream of politics, so as to reinforce the democratic consensus. The consensus may have seemed a trifle too constricting for some, but it probably reflected the general will of most Chileans.

The Concertación knew, however, that certain debts to recent Chilean history had to be paid without undue delay. In September 1990, Salvador Allende was given a state funeral in Santiago, thousands of people saluting the coffin as it traveled along the road from Viña del Mar (where the president's remains had been unceremoniously buried the day after the coup). Allende's widow described the funeral as a moment of "reparation and reconciliation."[18] Five months earlier, Aylwin had set up a Commission on Truth and Reconciliation (*Comisión de la Verdad y de la Reconciliación*) to make an accounting of human rights violations during the Pinochet years. It was chaired by an elderly Radical ex-senator, Raúl Rettig, who forty years earlier had actually fought a duel with Allende (neither man was harmed)[19]: he was later Allende's ambassador in Brazil. The Rettig Report, submitted in March 1991,[20] laid bare a grim panorama of repression, documenting more than 2,000 deaths, and strongly criticizing the judiciary for its acquiescence during the Pinochet regime – which infuriated the unrepentant judges of the supreme court, one of whom was later dismissed by the Senate (June 1993). Aylwin introduced a compensation scheme for victims of repression, but left the question of specific prosecutions to the courts. Only a very few cases were actually taken up by the courts over the next two years, to the dismay of human rights groups and the families that had suffered. In mid-1993 Aylwin failed in a proposal to speed up trials (with witnesses allowed anonymity).[21]

The constraints here were very obvious. The Army was back in barracks, but it retained a high degree of independence vis-à-vis the new government. Despite the Concertación's hopes for its abolition, the CNI was merged into military intelligence (DINE), and a number of episodes (notably a phone-tapping scandal in 1992) seemed to indicate that political espionage was still occurring. (The records of the DINA and CNI, the Army later revealed, had been destroyed in a most regrettable fire.)

---

[18] *El Mercurio,* September 5, 1990.

[19] For details, see Carlos Jorquera, *El Chicho Allende* (Santiago, 1990), pp. 284–305.

[20] Available in English as *Report of the Chilean National Commission on Truth and Reconciliation,* trans. Phillip E. Berryman, 2 vols. (Notre Dame, Ind., 1993). In 1993, following one of the suggestions of the Report, a monument to the victims of repression, with some 4,000 names carved into a 30-meter marble wall, was constructed in Santiago.

[21] In 1993 the ex-head of DINA, General Manuel Contreras, and his principal lieutenant were tried and sentenced to imprisonment for their role in the Letelier Affair. The verdicts were upheld by the supreme court in May 1995, and later enforced.

Table 13.7. GDP growth, inflation, unemployment, 1990–94.

	GDP (% growth)	Inflation	Unemployment (%)
1990	2.1	27.3	5.7
1991	6.0	18.7	5.3
1992	10.4	12.7	4.9
1993	6.0	12.2	4.4
1994	4.3	8.9	6.0

Source: Estudios Sociales, 75 (1993), p. 59. *El Mercurio*, January 6, 1993; January 6, 1994; January 6 and February 2, 1995.

Pinochet himself, though indisputably an old soldier, was most unwilling simply to fade away, and remained impervious to the many suggestions that he resign as commander-in-chief. He wrote his memoirs (eventually extending to four volumes), and they sold briskly, but he clearly felt tempted sometimes to play the rogue elephant. Inquiries in Congress and the press into financial scandals involving Army officers (and his own son-in-law) prompted him into ordering an *acuartelamiento* (summoning of all troops to barracks) in December 1990, a piece of dramatic saber-rattling that induced a brief fit of nerves in a few over-excitable politicians (and indifference in the general public), and in May 1993 he ringed the ministry of Defense with soldiers and ordered his generals to wear battle dress to work that day. This seems to have been no more than a small (and unnecessary) reminder to Chile that he was still there. Aylwin handled all such pinpricks with great tact and patience. (He told the Spanish prime minister, Felipe González, that it was as if González were running Spain with General Franco still alive.) There were those in the president's entourage who believed that the best tactic was simply to humor the old boy. It may be misleading, though, to focus too much on the interplay of commander-in-chief and president as individuals. At other levels, civil-military relations were acquiring a more solid footing. Congress, for its part, consciously cultivated links with the armed forces. Civilians were now allowed to study alongside officers at the War Academy. Yet even if the prospect of further military intervention receded, no future Chilean government was likely to ignore the Army.

Reinforcement of the democratic consensus was undoubtedly enhanced by economic success. The Concertación's economic aims were summarized in the phrase "growth with equity": its program accepted the market economy as a reality (though with further privatizations suspended) and stressed both the containment of inflation and the continued promotion of exports, but it also placed emphasis on addressing the *deuda social,* the "social debt" inherited from the Pinochet regime. The last two years of the military regime had been mildly inflationary, with higher public spending designed to capture electoral support. Alejandro Foxley, the new Finance minister, earlier an internationally known critic of the neo-liberal model, now found himself administering the necessary corrective by reining in the money supply and raising corporation taxes and IVA. This adjustment meant lower growth in Aylwin's first year, but the economy rebounded vigorously thereafter, with investment also rising fast and the Central Bank manipulating the exchange rate as necessary. (The peso was now formally valued against a dollar-yen-Deutschmark currency "basket.") By the end of 1992, which Foxley described as "the best economic year in three decades," Chile had enjoyed eight years of continuous export-led growth. And growth continued in 1993 and 1994, making it ten years.

Aylwin's numerous official visits to foreign countries, while designed to re-establish Chilean credentials internationally, were themselves also a conscious form of export-promotion. In 1991, Japan overtook the United States as the country's biggest single export market; Japanese investment increased strongly; and the Japanese government gave Chile the best investment-risk status in Latin America. September 1991 saw a free trade pact between Chile and Mexico, which doubled trade between the two nations within a year. Longer-term hopes were now being pinned on eventual access to the projected North American Free Trade Agreement (NAFTA), ratified by the U.S. Senate at the end of 1993, and to the common market (MERCOSUR) now being set up by Brazil, Argentina, Uruguay, and Paraguay. Such strategies were more than ever necessary, for the international panorama of the mid-1990s was by no means positive, with Europe struggling with a recession, Japan's economic miracle in a more uncertain phase than previously, vast economic reconstruction facing the former Soviet bloc countries, and only modest growth in the United States. Agricultural protectionism (especially in Japan and Europe) and the likelihood of renewed competition from within Latin America (notably Argentina) presented difficult challenges to the policymakers of Santiago. But other economic "models" seemed few and far between at the time. As the Finance ministry's chief economist put it in May 1993: "We either pursue export-led growth or no growth at all."[22]

The Aylwin government did not regard economic growth as an end in itself. It slowly (too slowly for some) began to tackle the *deuda social,* continuing some of the outgoing regime's programs but also adding its own – a new "Solidarity and Social Investment Fund" (FOSIS: *Fondo de Solidaridad e Inversión Social*), for instance, now steered aid toward poorer communities, with sensitivity and skill. Social spending (on health and education in particular) rose by around one-third between 1989 and

---

[22] Joaquín Vial, quoted in *The Financial Times,* London, May 19, 1993, p. 31 (survey of Chile).

1993, by which point, according to a United Nations report, the numbers of Chileans definable as poor had fallen from two-fifths to one-third of the population. The definition of poverty, of course, constantly changes: it can reasonably be claimed that in the 1990s more Chileans were better fed, better housed, and better educated than at any time in history. In other ways, however, despite these signs of modernity, the government failed to legislate in favor of social liberalization: it set its face against, for instance, a divorce law or the removal of legal disabilities still affecting married women.[23] Indeed, we might speculate here that one of the more unexpected consequences of the Pinochet years was a certain "reclericalization" of society, the Church's role during the period having won it new respect.[24] The old lay, masonic, freethinking component of Chilean culture (so splendidly vibrant from the 1880s to the 1970s) seemed altogether less prominent in the 1990s – a matter of regret to those who prefer diversity to homogeneity.

In the area of labor, the Concertación enacted a new law (1990) to expand trade union rights and collective bargaining. The labor movement, now reunited in a new national confederation (*Central Unitaria de Trabajadores,* 1988), still had much ground to make up and was still far weaker than in the 1960s. There were modestly successful strikes at El Teniente and Chuquicamata in July and August 1991. In October 1992, doctors in the state health service rose in revolt over pay and conditions, bringing about the resignation of the witty and amusing Health minister, Dr. Jorge Jiménez.

In many ways, such episodes could be seen as no more than the symptoms of a gradually reviving democracy. Nor could the intermittent urban terrorism of these years – conducted by a splinter group from the now inactive FPMR, and a rival group, the MJL (*Movimiento Juvenil Lautaro*) – be regarded as a serious threat to democratic stability, although it could still produce its shocks, most notoriously the assassination in April 1991 of the UDI leader and senator Jaime Guzmán. A "leniency law" in September 1991 (offering terrorists favorable treatment if they turned state's evidence) and the capture of the main *lautarista* leader (July

---

[23] Capital punishment, abolished in nearly all developed countries, also remained on the statute book.

[24] Pope John Paul II visited Chile in April 1987. The canonization of Chile's first Saint (St. Teresa of Los Andes, an exemplary Carmelite nun who died in 1920 at the age of nineteen) took place in Rome in March 1993. Old-fashioned anticlericals would have been suspicious of the timing of these events. It is believed that some PDC leaders would have preferred the canonization of their favorite Jesuit, Fr. Alberto Hurtado; he may not have long to wait, for he was beatified in October 1994, several thousand Chileans (including the president) flying to Rome to witness the ceremony. Soon afterward the incumbent archbishop of Santiago, Mgr. Carlos Oviedo, received his red hat, the fourth Chilean to do so.

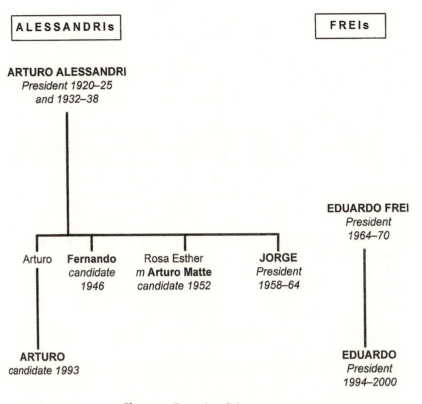

Chart 13.2. Dynastic politics, 1920–94.

1992) helped the police to stay well ahead of the men of violence. The men of violence were in any case repudiated by all sections of political opinion, including the element of the Left that remained outside the Concertación in the Communist-led MIDA (*Movimiento de Izquierda Democrática Allendista*) formed at the end of 1991 under the leadership of the former Finance minister Pedro Vuskovic.

Constitutional reform was unavoidably a political issue in the Aylwin years. On this score, however, the Right (with the help of the "nominated senators") was able to block Aylwin's most serious proposals (1992–93), which included the restoration of the president's right to dismiss the commanders-in-chief and the abolition of the nominated Senate seats. Nor could Aylwin secure changes in the "binomial" electoral system. Government and opposition did agree, nevertheless, to return the country's more than 300 municipalities (still run by Pinochet-appointed *alcaldes*) to democratic control. Municipal elections were accordingly held in June 1992, and produced results in line with the plebiscite and the 1989

election, with the Concertación winning more than 52 percent, and the
still divided Right (if "Fra Fra" Errázuriz's following is included) accounting for just over 30 percent. The Communist party (nearly 7 percent)
looked increasingly a shadow of its former self: with the Eastern European revolutions of 1989 and the dissolution of the Soviet Union itself
two years later, the party's once awesome frame of reference had by now
withered almost to a vanishing point.

Since Aylwin's term was to be four years (future terms were fixed at
six in February 1994), all the precedents in Chilean history made maneuvering for the next presidential election absolutely inevitable before the
end of 1992. The second Eduardo Frei staked a strong claim to the PDC
nomination, and by implication that of the Concertación, where the
popular and talented Socialist Ricardo Lagos (Aylwin's Education minister from 1990 to 1992) was his main rival. In what was a distinct
innovation in a political coalition, primary elections within the Concertación were finally agreed to (after a good deal of discussion and negotia-
tion, in the best Chilean style); 500,000 people voted (May 1993), and
the winner was Frei, whose ratings in public opinion polls were high. As
if to underline the continuities of Chilean history the Right selected
Senator Arturo Alessandri, a grandson of the Lion of Tarapacá (August
1993). Much to the disappointment of the Right, the Concertación
remained both disciplined and united – more so, in fact, than any of the
classic coalitions of the past. Indeed, some of its leading figures now
talked of maintaining the alliance for a decade or two – though, as the
Spanish saying has it, *del dicho al hecho, hay gran trecho* ("From the said to
the done there's a long stretch"). Frei's victory in the election (December
11, 1993) seemed a foregone conclusion, and so it turned out: he triumphed with nearly 58 percent of the popular vote (the highest percentage since 1931), the Lion's grandson winning around a quarter. For the
fifth time in Chilean history a son had followed a father to the presidency.
More important, no doubt, Frei's majority (better than Aylwin's in 1989
and his own father's in 1964) was an electoral vindication of the governing coalition. He was inaugurated (in the now finished architectural
monstrosity in Valparaiso) on March 11, 1994.

Our account must finish here, for to assess the presidency in course at the
time of writing is not really the historian's job. But a question is certainly
in order. What are the prospects for the re-established Chilean democracy? At a peculiarly dismal moment in the fortunes of the republic
(October 1975), one of the authors of this book asked the first Eduardo
Frei whether he could find reasons for hope. He replied that he had no
"rational reasons" for optimism, but several "irrational reasons," and the
chief of these was "the essence of Chilean history," as he put it – a

history that had been liberal and democratic with certain moments of constructive reform.[25] Chile's history *has* been one of constitutionalism and, at least in more recent times, widening democracy. Notwithstanding the trauma of 1973 and its prolonged aftermath, this underlying trend seems moderately clear. The Chilean electorate is perhaps wiser in the 1990s than at any time in the past – certainly *more* of it is wiser than before, although apathy amongst the young and the poor (hardly a phenomenon unique to Chile) is a matter that needs to be addressed by the politicians. Much depends also on the ability of governments to promote "growth with equity" (in the familiar Concertación phrase). The second President Frei has several times expressed the hope that Chile might enjoy southern European living standards by the year 2010. Reverence for the free market went to grotesque extremes in the Chile of the 1970s and 1980s, and President Aylwin, at the very end of his term, made some trenchant observations on this topic. The task of politicians and citizens alike (and not only in Chile, let it be said very firmly here, for this has now become a worldwide problem) is to find ways of combining the undoubted advantages of the market with greater social justice and (a pressing need in the future of us all) protection of the deteriorating global environment.

History has always had chapters that are happy, chapters that are dull, and chapters that are tragic. Our hope is that the chapter that opened in March 1990 may prove to be one of the happier ones for Chile, and perhaps, too, one of the duller ones – where constructive but undramatic work outweighs tension and excessive drama. Whether it does or not depends, as it has to, on the resolve and common sense of Chileans.

[25] Conversation with Simon Collier, Santiago, October 15, 1975.

14

Re-encounter with history, 1990–2002

I think you are a bit confused, Heredia.
Who isn't confused in these times?
– Ramón Díaz Eterovic, *El ojo del alma* (2001).

Friend of the elves, 1990–94

The coalition that assumed power in March 1990 would elect two further presidents over the next decade: the Christian Democrat Eduardo Frei, and, following him, the Socialist Ricardo Lagos. While these Concertación governments had to operate within the constraints inherited from the Pinochet regime (the 1980 constitution and the economic "model"), they strove very hard to modify its legacies. The first Concertación president, the septuagenarian Patricio Aylwin, was the first in Chile's history to have an English surname – an ancient one, with the prime meaning of "friend of the elves," or the subsidiary meaning of "good friend." The elves, albeit creatures of Nordic rather than Latin mythology,[1] may possibly have given him some help. It is tempting to compare him, despite definite differences of demeanor, with the emollient nineteenth-century president José Joaquín Pérez. His task was in some ways similar, in some ways more daunting. Aylwin's clear head, his patience, his negotiating talent, his mildly ironic smile – these assets were invaluable to the country as it took its first steps back to what Aylwin himself, in his moving televised address on New Year's Eve 1990, termed Chile's "re-encounter" with its history.

The Concertación governments' task was threefold: to reinforce the democratic consensus and, in particular, ensure smooth civil–military relations; to handle the delicate questions arising from the human rights abuses of the 1973–90 period; and to maintain economic growth while attending to the *"deuda social"* ("social debt") left by the outgoing regime. Aylwin

---

[1] Elves were, however, familiar to Chileans through the best-selling translation of J. R. R. Tolkien's *Lord of the Rings*. The movies (2001–) stemming from the book were as popular in Chile as everywhere else.

himself warned that progress could not be swift. Nor was it in all respects, but he was helped by generally constructive attitudes among politicians, or most of them. He was quite prepared to negotiate major initiatives (like important tax and labor laws in 1990) with the right-wing opposition. In Congress, the charm and authority of Gabriel Valdés, president of the Senate, smoothed inter-party relations. Parliamentary life in the early 1990s lacked something of the sparkle of previous eras. Congress's role, in fact, was somewhat more restricted than it had been before 1973. Nearly all legislation between 1990 and 1994 emanated from the Moneda. The Concertación's willingness to consult the opposition stemmed in part from the need to ensure the re-integration of the Right (still strongly inclined to defend the military regime's record) into the political mainstream, thus reinforcing the democratic consensus. Although the consensus may have seemed a trifle too constricting for some, it probably reflected the wishes of most Chileans at the time.

It was not to be expected that the emotions aroused by the Pinochet years would vanish quickly. Time alone could eventually bind up all the wounds. Disturbances and demonstrations (often on September 11, the anniversary of the 1973 coup) were a common feature of the 1990s, but not on a large scale. They did not compare with the disturbances and demonstrations of the early 1970s or mid-1980s. The government knew, however, that certain debts to recent history had to be paid without delay. In September 1990, Salvador Allende was given a state funeral in Santiago, thousands of people saluting the coffin as it traveled along the road from Viña del Mar, where the president had been buried unceremoniously on September 12, 1973. Allende's widow described the funeral as a moment of "reparation and reconciliation."[2] Five months earlier, Aylwin had set up a Truth and Reconciliation Commission (*Comisión de la Verdad y de la Reconciliación*) to make an accounting of human rights violations during the Pinochet years. As was acknowledged by President Nelson Mandela, it inspired South Africa's similar commission of 1995 onward. It was chaired by Raúl Rettig, an elderly Radical ex-senator who forty years earlier had actually fought a harmless duel with Allende.[3] The Rettig Report (March 1991)[4] laid bare a grim panorama of repression, documenting more than 2,000 deaths (the total number was around 3,000) and strongly criticizing the judiciary for its acquiescence during the Pinochet regime. This infuriated the unrepentant

---

[2] *El Mercurio*, September 5, 1990.

[3] See Carlos Jorquera, *El Chicho Allende* (Santiago, 1990), pp.284–305.

[4] Available in English as *Report of the National Commission on Truth and Reconciliation,* trans. Philip E. Berryman, 2 vols. (Notre Dame, Ind., 1993). In 1993, following one of the Report's suggestions, a monument to the victims of repression, with some 4,000 names carved into a 30-meter marble wall, was constructed at Santiago's General Cemetery.

judges of the supreme court, one of whom was later dismissed by the Senate (June 1993). Aylwin introduced a compensation scheme for the victims of repression. Some 65,000 returning exiles were helped by an office that worked from 1991 to 1994. The question of specific prosecutions was left to the courts. Progress here was slow, to the dismay of human rights groups and families who had suffered. In mid-1993 Aylwin failed in a proposal to speed up trials, with witnesses guaranteed anonymity. Something of a breakthrough came later that year, when the ex-head of DINA, General Manuel Contreras, and his main lieutenant, were condemned for their role in the Letelier Affair of 1976–77. The supreme court confirmed their imprisonment in May 1995, and it was enforced – after a series of embarrassing delays.

The initial constraints on such prosecutions were obvious. The Army was back in barracks, but it retained a high degree of independence. Despite the Concertación's hopes for its abolition, the CNI was merged into military intelligence (DINE). The records of both CNI and DINA, the Army later revealed, were destroyed in a regrettable fire. A number of episodes (notably a phone-tapping scandal in 1992) seemed to indicate that political espionage was still occurring. General Pinochet himself remained impervious to the numerous suggestions that he should resign as commander-in-chief. Unquestionably an old soldier, he was unwilling to simply fade away. He wrote his memoirs (in four volumes), and they sold briskly, but he clearly felt tempted sometimes to play the rogue elephant. Inquiries in Congress and the press into financial scandals involving army officers (and his own son-in-law) prompted him into ordering a general *acuartelamiento* (summoning of troops to barracks) in December 1990, a piece of dramatic saber-rattling that induced a brief fit of nerves in a few over-excitable politicians – and public indifference. In May 1993, while Aylwin was abroad and his affable Interior minister Enrique Krauss was standing in as vice president, Pinochet ringed the Ministry of Defense with soldiers, ordering his staff to wear battledress to work. This seems to have been little more than an unnecessary reminder to Chile that he was still there. Aylwin handled all such pinpricks with tact and patience. He told Spanish prime minister Felipe González that it was rather as if General Franco were still alive in Spain. It may be misleading, though, to focus too much on the relationship between commander-in-chief and president as individuals. At other levels, civil–military relations were acquiring a more solid footing. Congress cultivated links with the armed forces far more systematically than before.

In the labor field, the Concertación enacted a new law (1990) to somewhat expand trade union rights and collective bargaining. The labor movement, reunited since 1988 in a new national confederation, CUT (*Central Unitaria de Trabajadores*), had much ground to make up, and was still much weaker than it had been in the 1960s. There were modestly successful strikes at El

Teniente and Chuquicamata in July and August 1991. In October 1992, doctors in the state health service rose in revolt over pay and conditions, bringing about the resignation of the witty Health minister, Dr. Jorge Jiménez. Such episodes could be seen as no more than the symptoms of a gradually reviving democracy. Nor was the intermittent urban terrorism of these years – staged by a militant fraction from the now inactive FPMR, and a rival group, the MJL (*Movimiento Juvenil Lautaro*) – a serious threat to renewed democratic stability, although it could still produce its shocks, most notoriously the assassination of Senator Jaime Guzmán, founder, leader, and principal ideologue of UDI, and earlier one of Pinochet's more valued advisers. A leniency law in September 1991 (offering terrorists favorable treatment if they turned state's evidence) and the capture of the main *lautarista* leader in July 1992 (by mid-1994 the entire leadership was behind bars) helped the police to stay well ahead of the men of violence. (In December 1996 a daring helicopter raid on the high-security jail in Santiago "sprung" four imprisoned terrorists, including Senator Guzmán's assassin.) The men of violence were in any case repudiated by all sections of political opinion, including the remnant of the Left, focused on the Communist party, which stayed outside the Concertación.

Constitutional reform was an unavoidable aim for Aylwin. But the Right in Congress (helped by the "nominated senators") blocked his most serious proposals (1992–93), which included the restoration of the president's right to dismiss the commanders-in-chief and the abolition of the nominated senatorships. Nor could Aylwin secure changes in the "binomial" electoral system. His successor would have similar difficulties, and for much the same reasons. Even when politicians of the Right (mainly from Renovación Nacional) proved sympathetic to reform, the intransigent UDI usually rejected such proposals. Government and opposition did agree, however, to return the country's more than 300 municipalities (still run by Pinochet-appointed *alcaldes*) to democratic control. Municipal elections of sorts were held in June 1992. The Concertación won more than 52 percent, and the Right won just over 30 percent of the vote. The Communist party (nearly 7 percent) looked increasingly a shadow of its former self. With the Eastern European revolutions of 1989 and the disintegration of the Soviet Union, the party's once awesome frame of reference had by now withered to vanishing point. Its role in the politics of the 1990s would be rather limited.

Since Aylwin's term was to be four years (future terms were fixed at six years in February 1994), all the precedents in Chilean history made maneuvering for the next presidential election inevitable by early 1993. The second Eduardo Frei, who had by now acquired the strong interest in politics he seems earlier to have lacked, staked his claim to the PDC nomination, and indeed that of the Concertación. Here his main rival was the intelligent and popular Socialist Ricardo Lagos, the holder of a Ph.D. from

Duke University in the United States, very prominent in the plebiscite campaign in 1988, and more recently Aylwin's Education minister. In what was a remarkable innovation in a coalition, and a precedent for the future, the Concertación agreed to hold a cross-party primary election; 600,000 people voted (May 1993). Frei won 62 percent, Lagos 38 percent. As if to underline the continuities of Chilean history, RN and UDI nominated (August 1993) senator Arturo Alessandri, a grandson of the Lion of Tarapacá. But for the time being the electoral tide was flowing strongly for the Concertación. Frei triumphed (December 11, 1993) with nearly 58 percent of the popular vote (the highest percentage since 1931), the Lion's grandson winning around a quarter. For the fifth time in Chilean history a son had followed a father to the presidency. Frei's majority (better than Aylwin's in 1989 and his own father's in 1964) was a clear vindication of the governing coalition. The now finished architectural abomination in Valparaiso saw its second presidential inauguration on March 11, 1994.

Neo-liberalism with a human face?

A decade of advance

The Concertación governments continued the general line of the neo-liberal economic "model" imposed by the military regime, mostly because it was delivering the goods. Pinochet's last two years had been mildly inflationary, with higher public spending designed to capture electoral support. Alejandro Foxley, Aylwin's Finance minister (earlier an internationally known critic of neo-liberalism), now found himself administering the necessary corrective by reining in the money supply and raising corporation taxes and IVA. This adjustment meant lower growth in Aylwin's first year, but the economy rebounded vigorously thereafter. Aylwin's government completed the sale of LAN-Chile. Frei's privatized sanitation, port, and highway projects. More significantly, the post-1990 governments tried to diversify Chile's economic base. Minerals, it is true, still constituted the country's largest single export, but their share of GDP fell to 8.4 percent by 2001. Copper at that point contributed 36.5 percent of the country's export income, compared with 70 percent in the early 1970s. The state-owned CODELCO still generated about 0.5 percent of the government's revenues in 2001, but by then privately owned mines accounted for two thirds of copper exports; domestically smelted refined metal (CODELCO pioneering the way) formed an increasing proportion (almost two thirds) of all exported copper.

The so-called "non-traditional" exports, meanwhile, continued to flourish, with the products of the farms, fisheries, and forests well to the fore. Exported table fruits alone (particularly grapes) earned over US$ 1 billion in 2001. Wine production diversified spectacularly: 744 wines were "classified" in 2001, as against 165 in 1993, Chardonnays and Merlots showing the biggest growth. Since the local demand for fish and shellfish was easily satisfied, the huge surplus could be frozen or canned for sale abroad. Fish farms, located on the southern lakes, greatly expanded their output (a fivefold increase between 1992 and 2002), and Chile became the world's second largest source of salmon. (Over-fishing and the vagaries of climate, however, may indicate a less certain future for Chile's large exports of fish oil and fishmeal.) A whole range of forestry products – wood pulp, paper, mechanical and chemical pulp, veneer, plywood, fiber, and grainboards – registered dramatic increases in the 1990s, accounting for nearly one eighth of exports in 2001, while the government's reforesting program had by then expanded by one half the area of replanting.

Although the production of raw materials rose fast (by over 11 percent per year from 1985 to 1995), a more significant trend was the steady growth of "primary" and "secondary" processed goods. In 1985, unprocessed natural resources accounted for three quarters of all exports; eleven years later it was two thirds. About half the country's fishmeal, for instance, was now being used to raise salmon, while timber was converted increasingly into cellulose or chemical pulp, or, more traditionally, into doors, furniture, and paper products (including diapers). Fruits were processed as juices, tomato paste, and jam, US$ 406 million's worth of which were exported in 2000. Service industries (including tourism) also expanded steadily through the 1990s. Chile at the end of the twentieth century was no longer simply a "platform" exporting irreplaceable raw materials; increasingly, the labor of its people was enhancing the value of its exports.

"We either pursue export-led growth," said the Finance ministry's chief economist in May 1993, "or no growth at all."[5] It cannot be pretended that export-led growth benefitted everyone. Many small farms, for instance, did not participate at all in the agricultural export boom. Income distribution remained badly skewed – possibly, in the long term, neo-liberalism's Achilles heel? Moreover, changes in the international scene could make a difference. The economy withstood the "tequila effect" that perturbed many countries after Mexico's crisis in 1994, but the Asian recession soon afterward weakened one of Chile's more important markets. The uninterrupted run of high growth rates since 1985 ended in 1999, a year of "negative growth," with the years immediately following showing only modest expansion, though exports held up well. Argentina's dire economic collapse in December 2001 was a further challenge. Any economic downturn, of course, limits revenues and threatens to hobble social programs. Against this, the government both attempted to improve the yield from taxation

---

[5] Joaquín Vial, quoted in *The Financial Times* (London), May 1993, p.31 (survey of Chile).

(by vigorously pursuing tax cheats) and to expand the relentless quest for overseas markets, often through bilateral trade agreements, for which the Concertación governments had a distinct fondness. In November 2002, Chile signed a comprehensive economic treaty with the European Union, only the second Latin American government to do so. A deal with South Korea promised new outlets for agro-industrial products such as cellulose and fishmeal. Chile's astute commercial diplomacy also targeted Pacific and Asian countries such as New Zealand and Singapore. Chilean membership of NAFTA, delayed in the mid-1990s by the Republican-dominated U.S. Congress's spiteful denial of "fast track" negotiating authority to President Bill Clinton, is now assured. Following the debacle in Argentina, where Chilean interests had acquired numerous companies since the 1980s, investors began shifting their funds to Mexico, in some cases locating enterprises there, in order to gain easier access to the U.S. market.

Tackling the "social debt"

The Concertación governments did not see economic growth as an end in itself. They pledged themselves to tackle the "social debt," and to repair Chile's tattered safety net. They continued some of the military regime's social programs, while adding their own. A new "Solidarity and Social Investment Fund" (FOSIS), for instance, steered aid toward poorer communities with sensitivity and skill. The Aylwin and Frei administrations increased the funding for public health, housing, education, infrastructure, public services, pensions, and social security. In 1999, in real terms, the Moneda spent nearly double the 1990 amount on public housing. Over the same nine years, the number of people receiving direct welfare payments rose by one fifth. President Ricardo Lagos heightened this evident commitment to narrowing the gap between rich and poor. As of 2000 the state earmarked 73 percent of its social spending for the nation's worst-off 40 percent. Lagos's 2001 budget devoted 70 percent of all government expenditures to education, health, housing, subsidies, and insurance.

A particular concern was health care. The military regime, as we saw, had instituted a dual scheme of health coverage, the state system (FONASA) theoretically responsible for about 75 percent of the population, while the private ISAPREs, offering more comprehensive treatment, looked after the remaining quarter or so. All those employed paid a small tax to buy health insurance. This covered (just about) the cost of a FONASA basic health plan, but not the premiums of the ISAPREs, which could be afforded only by the better-off. The dual system led to a serious imbalance in medical care: a 2001 study, for instance, showed that infant mortality in the poor Santiago district of Independencia was seven times higher than that of affluent Vitacura. Similarly, health care in rural areas was sparser than in the cities. Progress in resolving these problems was slower in the 1990s than the Concertación might have wished. In 2002 the Lagos government introduced a new program, Plan AUGE, designed to improve FONASA's basic health package by enabling it to provide expensive treatments (such as kidney dialysis) for certain ailments, and to reduce waiting times for operations to six months. Plan AUGE also demanded that the ISAPREs offer a single health care policy to all their members, regardless of age or sex. (Initially, ISAPREs often refused to sell policies to the elderly.) Since the government did not wish to increase the existing tax (7 percent) for health insurance, general revenues would have to be used to pay for expanded health care. As of now, the legislature has yet to decide the fate of Plan AUGE.

The Concertación governments also substantially increased funding for education (the highest single increase in social spending in the 1990s), in the belief that education was one of the surest means of breaking the cycle of poverty. By the start of the twenty-first century, virtually all Chilean youngsters were literate. One in ten, however, still did not go on from primary school to a *liceo*. (The number of children enrolling in pre-school, of particular benefit to the disadvantaged, rose by 58 percent between 1990 and 2000.) The government paid attention to the predictable educational disparity between town and country, steering resources to some 900 primary schools in the neediest areas. Most poorer schoolchildren, we should note, were provided with medical and dental care, free textbooks and school supplies. In raw figures, well over one million children in primary schools received free school lunches in 2000, as compared with 680,000 in 1990. The government also began extending similar benefits to a significant number of high school students. In 2002, the Lagos administration enacted a measure requiring all children to complete high school, with financial subsidies envisaged for needy families, to prevent students from dropping out for economic reasons.

By the end of the 1990s, the Concertación had cause for self-congratulation. Its policies had improved the people's health, made education more available, reduced the percentage of the impoverished (38.6 of the population in 1990, 20.6 percent in 2000), while halving the number of poverty-stricken *households*. Two million Chileans had moved out of poverty. For the first time, the underprivileged possessed some of the paraphernalia of the "good life." Nine out of ten poor households had color TV sets; three quarters had refrigerators and washing machines; and, perhaps more surprisingly, another two fifths had telephones. Nearly all the urban poor now lived in homes with potable water as well as electricity; only one in ten such homes lacked an indoor toilet. Surveying the scene in 2000, two observers noted that "In many ways the 1990s can be considered the decade of Chile's highest economic performance this century. In fact, if the evolution of poverty and other social indicators are added, the progress achieved this decade stands unprecedented in the nation's entire history."[6]

Turn-of-the-century social symptoms

When Ricardo Lagos became president in March 2000, there were approximately 15 million Chileans. The population had increased less as a consequence of an accelerated birth rate (which in fact declined) than of a reduction of mortality rates, particularly amongst the most vulnerable: the old and very young. Here we need to take a long view, and glance back occasionally beyond 1990. In 1960 the death rate of children under the age of one was 115 per thousand. Improvements in prenatal care and immunization programs cut this to 8.9 in 2001, the lowest level in Chilean history, and a figure worthy of most "developed" countries. Since virtually all Chilean children now received vaccines for tuberculosis, diphtheria, tetanus, whooping cough, polio, and measles, the incidence of these diseases had dropped, in some cases almost to zero – an incredible change from the days when Chile enjoyed the dubious distinction of having the world's highest infant mortality rate. (Children, one year old or younger, accounted for 36,914 of the 109,785 deaths in 1937). The health of grown-ups had improved as well. Water purification programs cut the incidence of hepatitis. There were 1,112 cases of typhoid in 1998; as recently as 1982 there had been 12,000. Tuberculosis caused 5 per cent of deaths in 1953–55, but no more than 0.5 percent in 1995. The number of syphilitics in the late 1930s was between 370,000 and 380,000 – 8 percent of the population![7] – but fell to 4,705 in 2000. Life expectancy was 60 in 1970, but a *chilena* born in the early twenty-first century could hope to live to almost 79, a *chileno* to about 75. As more people succumbed to heart disease and cancer, Chile's "health profile" increasingly resembled that of the world's richest nations.

Chileans were not only healthier in 2000, but also better educated. More of them than ever graduated from high school, and many went on to technical schools or universities. Before 1981 Chile had eight institutions of higher learning. By 2002 these had subdivided into twenty-five, with an enrollment of 167,000. New private universities, as we noted in Chapter 13, opened their doors (forty-two by 2002, attended by 77,000), along with sixty-nine professional institutes and 126 technical schools. In 1996, some 262 such institutions were providing more than 350,000 students some form of advanced education.

---

[6] Francisco Javier Meneses and José María Fuentes, "The State of Economic Processes," in *Chile in the Nineties* (Stanford, Calif., 2000), p.241.

[7] Salvador Allende, *La realidad médico-social chilena* (Santiago, 1939), pp.21, 89–91, 99.

The developing mass media, too, played an increasingly important part in the pattern of life. At the start of the twenty-first century, Chileans had 211 newspapers to read. One in every three Chileans regularly scanned magazines, many more than in 1990. The magazines themselves ranged from the serious *Qué Pasa* and *Ercilla* (more popular among men than women) to the never-to-be-forgotten *Condorito*. (*Condorito's* original creator, "Pepo," died in July 2000.) Social status and gender often influenced the choice of magazine: upper and middle class women read the glossy *Paula* and *Vanidades,* while *Rock & Pop* appealed to middle and upper class youth; the poorer classes preferred entertainment magazines such as *TV Grama*. More than eight out of ten Chileans now listened daily to one of the country's 864 AM and FM radio stations (in 1959 there were 113). The old university-run and state-run television stations were supplemented after 1986 by five new private channels. Cable TV became available from 1987, and satellite TV soon after. Competition from foreign cable channels had a tonic effect on Chilean TV. By the mid-1990s, Chilean-produced shows accounted for nearly two thirds of local programs. News programs attracted some of the largest audiences, but once they ended men often turned to sportscasts, particularly of soccer, while the women followed the latest episodes of their favorite *telenovelas.* At the start of the twenty-first century, as if to show that some things never change, viewers could still watch *Sábados Gigantes,* compèred by the gruff but golden-hearted "Don Francisco" (Mario Kreutzberger), although now from a TV station in Miami, not Santiago.

Despite such signs of contemporary modernity, the Concertación governments did not legislate in favor of the social liberalization modernity perhaps demanded. It gave no encouragement to a divorce law, long overdue, though pressure for one mounted in the 1990s. Abortion remained illegal. Movies could still be censored and TV stations penalized for showing "improper" programs. Capital punishment, though not applied, remained on the statute book until finally abolished (for "ordinary" crimes) in May 2001. One reason for this social conservatism may have been a certain "re-clericalization" of society, an unintended consequence of the Pinochet years, the Catholic Church's role during the dictatorship having won it new kudos with the public.[8] The old lay, masonic, freethinking component of Chilean culture (so splendidly vibrant from the 1880s to the 1970s) seemed much less prominent in the 1990s. It showed slight

---

[8] Pope John Paul II visited Chile in April 1987. Chile's first saint (St. Teresa of Los Andes, an exemplary Carmelite nun who died in 1920 at age nineteen) was canonized in Rome in March 1993. The PDC's favorite Jesuit, Fr. Alberto Hurtado, may not have long to wait. He was beatified in October 1994, and several thousand Chileans (including President Frei) flying to Rome for the ceremony. Soon afterward, the archbishop of Santiago, Mgr. Carlos Oviedo, received his red hat, the fourth Chilean to do so. Old-fashioned anti-clericals would have been suspicious of the timing of these events.

signs of revival, maybe, with the election of an avowedly agnostic president in 2000.

Although the Catholic Church retained easily the most substantial religious following in Chile, it was complemented from the 1970s onward by a growing trend to Protestantism, mainly Pentecostal sects (American fundamentalist sects made little headway) – embraced by between one eighth and one fifth of the population. In 2002, Osorno's Pentecostal Methodist congregation built a church large enough to hold 2,500 faithful.[9] There were enough Muslims in Chile to warrant the conference they held, at Iquique's Bilal Mosque,[10] in September 2002. A 1998 opinion survey indicated the persistence of certain religious values in society. Sixty percent of the respondents were indulgent toward premarital sex, but strongly rejected infidelity, abortion, and homosexuality. Approximately 70 to 80 percent believed in the existence of God, an after-life, and miracles (57 percent believed in Hell). Six out of ten Chileans attended church only three times a year or less; Protestants being more regular churchgoers than Catholics. The Catholic Church, however, fared very well in ratings (in a 2002 survey) of the trustworthiness of institutions – trusted by 55 percent of respondents. This could be compared with radio stations (57 percent), the Carabineros (52 percent), television (43 percent), the armed forces (36–39 percent), newspapers (34 percent), the judiciary (14 percent), Congress (11–12 percent), and political parties (4 percent). Small businessmen came out ahead of the leaders of big business in public esteem, with union leaders ranking third.[11]

In 1938 the exiled Peruvian intellectual Luis Alberto Sánchez noted that Santiago's population appeared ethnically homogeneous and culturally provincial. He ignored the older foreign colonies (British, German, French, Italian) in the city. The mix changed over the years, with the arrival (in the 1930s and 1940s) of Spanish Republican exiles and a handful of Eastern European Jewish refugees. The economic changes of the 1970s and 1980s brought numerous Europeans and North Americans to work in Chile, and a somewhat greater flow of tourists, some of whom flocked to the (French-owned) ski-resort of Valle Nevado or to the trout-filled rivers of the south. With the expansion of Chile's trade to Asia, Hyundais and Daewoos jostled for space on the country's roads. With their cars came a few immigrants from Korea, China, and Japan. Ethnic groups, old and new, maintained their identities through their schools, newspapers, and social organizations as well

---

[9] *El Llanquihue* (Puerto Montt), October 11, 2002.

[10] *La Estrella* (Iquique), September 21, 2002.

[11] Opinion data from: Centro de Estudios Públicos, "Estudio Social y de opinión pública, junio de 1998," *Documento de trabajo*, No.325 (October 2001) and CERC (Centro de Estudios de la Realidad Contemporánea), "Informe de prensa sobre temas económicos y políticos," September 2002.

as the older, nationally based country clubs. In October 2002, for instance, Puerto Montt's *Frauenverein* met in the community hall of the local Lutheran church; at the other end of Chile, Croat women gathered in Iquique's Croat Club. As in so many other parts of the world, the most pervasive foreign influence on local *mores* in these years was American. In October, 2002, the news reported that Iquique's *Escuela Italiana* was teaching its students baseball. Although hamburgers have made inroads – competing with the infinitely more savory *empanada* – there are signs that North American and Chilean culinary cultures may be fusing: McDonalds is selling a *Churrasco*, a Chilean beef and avocado sandwich, marketing it as the "McChurrasco," while a small restaurant chain has advertised bagels as "the round bread".[12] Examples of this kind could easily be multiplied.

Such influences might be interpreted (quite wrongly, in our view) as a dilution of Chilean identity. For Chile's approximately 660,000 Amerindians (86 percent of them Mapuche, the largest of eight separate ethnic groups) a different trend was under way. In 2002 some Mapuche celebrated Columbus Day by demanding that the government return 70,000 hectares of former Indian-owned property and grant them the right to "share the powers of the state."[13] The more radical Mapuche groups evidently aspired to the independent status enjoyed by their forebears in the colonial era (not something any Chilean government could easily concede), and in 1998 began a series of lawsuits to recover lands they had lost. Some resorted to direct action, burning forestry company trucks and even occupying estates. A bitter conflict between Indians and the state broke out along the Bío Bío river, where the electricity company ENDESA planned to construct a series of dams for hydroelectric power. The first was opened by President Frei in 1997. The second dam, higher up the river at Ralco, provoked a chorus of protest: although the completed dam would generate 570 megawatts of energy, it would also create a 2,000-hectare lake, displacing 380 Pehuenche families. The Indians opposing the scheme, with attacks on the construction site, likened their cause to the centuries-old struggle against the Spaniards. As one Mapuche leader noted, "Today we fight against the government, ENDESA, private colonists and forestry companies, just as Lautaro did in the past. Lautaro is alive!" In November, 2002, a Mapuche teenager, Edmundo Lemún, was killed while trying to seize a privately owned *fundo*. Within days, his name began appearing as political grafitti on Santiago's streets indicating that he had become an icon in the struggle for "the national liberation of the Mapuche people."[14]

[12] *La Estrella* (Iquique), October 28, 2002.

[13] *El Sur* (Concepción), October 15, 2002; *El Mercurio de Valparaíso*, October 13, 2002.

[14] *Ercilla*, No.3186, 1–14 April 2002; *El Diario Austral de la Araucania* (Temuco), 15 November 2002.

The Ralco issue can be seen as blending "identity politics" with growing "eco-consciousness," both of which are symptomatic of current modernity. Chile's "greens," though electorally unimportant, were successful in the 1990s in alerting public opinion to some of the costs of economic growth. In 1996 there was protest against a *gasoducto* (gas pipeline) being installed through a nature reserve in the Maipó canyon, and in 1998 a row over the American Trillium corporation's plan to cut the stands of Magellan oak on Tierra del Fuego. Three years later, the Canadian Noranda corporation's plans to build a large aluminum smelter in Aysén (and dams to provide power) provoked the immediate hostility of "greens," including the *bancada verde*, the cross-party "green benches" in Congress. The "greens" had a point. Evidence of environmental contamination abounded. Sulfur dioxide (a byproduct of copper smelting) polluted the soil, industrial waste the rivers, and the fish farms' uneaten food and excreta the lakes. Smog so enshrouded Santiago, particularly in winter, that the Andes were no longer in view for much of the time, while the concentrations of lead in the atmosphere stunted the intellectual development of new-born children. The fate of Chile's rainforests (more than a quarter of all those in the world's temperate zones) and the fact that in September 2001 the Antarctic hole in the ozone layer stretched as far north as Punta Arenas – these were issues that would hardly go away.

A major cause of Santiago's noxious smog was the rise in automobile ownership. The number of private cars in the capital nearly doubled in the 1990s, while the number of bus riders fell by half.[15] (In Chile as a whole, car ownership rose by 12 percent between 1996 and 2000.) The municipality of Santiago had considerable success in reducing industrial pollution, but limiting the vehicular emission of particulates and nitrous oxide proved altogether more difficult. A partial solution could perhaps be found in introducing electric or natural gas-powered buses, and by the addition of new lines to the Metro. Daily Metro passengers (700,000 in 2000) were expected to more than double by 2005.

The pattern of transportation and communications, in fact, changed drastically between the 1970s and the early 2000s. The railroads continued their prolonged decline. The passenger service between Santiago and Valparaiso was abandoned in the late 1980s. Buses, increasingly, picked up the slack. More Chileans than ever took to the air. Between 1996 and 2001 the annual number of domestic airline passengers grew by almost one third (to 3.1 million), international travelers by two thirds (to 2 million). Only 350,000 Chileans had flown in airliners back in 1957. In the first year of the twenty-first century, thirty-two cities had airports, three of them serving international as well as domestic flights. Santiago's Comodoro Arturo

---

[15] *El Mercurio*, September 26, 2002.

Merino Benítez[16] Airport (as Pudahuel was renamed by the military regime) installed a large new international terminal in the early 1990s, and which has since been expanded.

Back in the late 1950s, like flying, the ownership of a telephone (160,000 in a population of 7 million) indicated a certain social cachet. In the mid-1990s, the long-distance phone companies competed ferociously for new customers: between 1996 and 1999 the number of telephones increased by 38 percent (to roughly 3 million). After the introduction of cellular phones, there were approximately 500 instruments (fixed or mobile) for every 1,000 citizens. Chile became one of the many countries where it was impossible to escape the irritating sound of bleating cell phones. The increase in phone lines, however, provided one distinct benefit. It enabled Chileans who owned computers (20 percent in 2000) to dial up the Internet and to use E-mail. This most dramatic of all worldwide innovations in the 1990s (in its infancy at the time of Chile's democratic restoration) was embraced energetically, enterprisingly, and enthusiastically. Many Chilean newspapers now became readable online. Like most innovations, the Internet sometimes produced untoward results. In October 2002, Carabineros in Santiago arrested a man whose two websites ("galaxy.nude.boy" and "sex.paradises") purveyed child pornography.

A very brief glance at culture (1970–2000)

The artistic "generations" of the late twentieth century which will, we hope, be adding to Chile's cultural patrimony well into the twenty-first, had a more difficult start than earlier generations. An *apagón cultural* ("cultural blackout") prevailed for several years after 1973. The military regime viewed novel artistic expression with suspicion. It tried to suppress all memory of the *Nueva Canción* of the 1960s. Víctor Jara's records were long unobtainable. Inti-Illimani, now world-renowned, returned to Chile only in 1988, after a fifteen-year exile. The stream of exiles after 1973 included other cultural luminaries, among them Ariel Dorfman, who consolidated an international literary reputation. His play (later a movie) *Death and the Maiden* (1991), acclaimed around the world, was largely ignored in the Chile of the early 1990s, probably because it cut a little too close to the bone.

No striking new trends in painting or music were easily discernible in the last decades of the twentieth century. Culture in general was not a high priority of the state (Chile has no Ministry of Culture), although in 1992 the Aylwin government set up FONDART, an agency which subsidized more than 5,000 artistic projects over the next decade. The Pinochet regime had been against protectionism in culture as well as in commerce, with

---

[16] A distinguished pioneer of aviation (of *ibañista* and Socialist sympathies).

predictable results. A conference held in Santiago in June 1993 heard rather plaintive pleas over the plight of popular music, swamped as it seemed to be by the globally dominant Anglo-American mainstream (and by Spanish and Mexican fare). Only 8 percent of the music heard on the country's radio stations, it was alleged, was Chilean in origin; barely a quarter of records and tapes sold were of Chilean music.[17] While there was a considerable undergrowth of music-making, a fair amount in the local rock idiom, nothing as distinctive as the *Nueva Canción* was on the horizon. But an undergrowth that included groups like Congreso or Ángel Parra's jazz trio (to name but two of our personal favorites) could well prove a seed-bed for the future.

In literature, the classic vehicle of Chilean culture, the outlook was more promising. Poetry, prose, and drama reflected (often indirectly rather than directly) the traumas of the recent past and the bewildering "modernity" to which the traumas had led – rampant consumerism, the fraying of the old links of community, the impact of "globalization." Among a number of interesting dramatists of the recent period (one of rather lively theater) it would probably be fair to single out the remarkable Juan Radrigán (b.1937). We might note also that a revival of film-making occurred in the 1990s, with talented directors like Pablo Perelman, Ricardo Larraín, Gustavo Graef-Marino, and Andrés Woods. As was predictable in Chile, there was a respectable output of poetry. More of it than before was written by women, and some of it by a number of serious Mapuche poets. How good were these younger poets? *"Bastante + ruido que nueces"* ("more *nothing* than ado about nothing") was the now octogenarian Nicanor Parra's comment on a poetry competition in 1994. Nobody can deny, however, the genuine quality in the work of Jorge Teillier (1935–96), simple but profound, often focusing on nostalgic visions of happy rural childhood, or in that of Raúl Zurita (b.1951), a poet of explosive lyricism, innovative and experimental, in his way a true renewer of language.

The prose writers of the 1980s and 1990s did not quite measure up to the best mid-twentieth century figures. The much-trumpeted *Nueva Narrativa* ("New Narrative") of the 1990s was perhaps less a genuine trend than a marketing catchphrase fostered by various astute publishers. Nevertheless, the number of writers at work in the 1980s and 1990s was impressive. Only a few names can be mentioned: among the men, Luis Sepúlveda (b.1949), Pedro Lemebel (b.1950), Jaime Collyer (b.1955), and Arturo Fontaine (b.1952), the last-named also a poet; and among the women, the productive Marcela Serrano (b.1951) and Diamela Eltit (b.1950), who won a certain international critical acclaim in feminist circles. José Donoso died in 1996, but other veterans of the older literary "generations" were still writing,

[17] *Silencio en la Música Popular Chilena? Seminario sobre los Problemas Actuales de la Música Popular en Chile* (Santiago, 1993), pp.21–22.

among them Nicanor Parra and Jorge Edwards. Volodia Teitelboim, a former Communist senator remembered for his broadcasts to Chile from Radio Moscow during the Pinochet years, added to his earlier reputation as a novelist with his noteworthy biographies of Pablo Neruda, Gabriela Mistral, and Vicente Huidobro, and with his volumes of autobiography. The 1990s, rather interestingly, also saw a revival of the detective genre, not much cultivated since the days of Alberto Edwards's Román Calvo stories, at the hands of two authors: Roberto Ampuero (b.1953) and Ramón Díaz Eterovic (b.1956). The "fall-out" from the recent past lightly brushes their thrillers. The inquiries of Ampuero's Cayetano Brulé, a Valparaiso-based Cuban expatriate private eye, take him up and down the Americas (and sometimes further afield). Díaz Eterovic's Heredia (with his talkative white cat, Simenon) operates mostly in a neatly evoked Santiago.

These writers, and others old and new, gave the turn-of-the-century literary scene an air of vitality, at least at the local level. The annual *Feria del Libro* (Book Fair), staged each spring in Santiago's Mapocho Station, now imaginatively converted into a cultural center, became well worth wandering around, ideally after an agreeable lunch at one of the popular restaurants nearby, in the old (1872) central market.

Frei II and Lagos, 1994–2002

The public did not see the second Eduardo Frei as having quite the rhetorical powers and political talents of his father, but he discharged his duties with due decorum and dignity. It was fortunate that the economy held up well until almost the end of his *sexenio*, and that no great international issues loomed. Indeed, Frei's term saw the liquidation (not without adverse comment from unreconstructed nationalists) of the remaining boundary problems between Chile and Argentina. These focused on two areas (Laguna del Desierto and the ice-fields and glaciers known as Campo de Hielo Sur) on the far-southern border. In February 1999, to underline Chilean–Argentine amity, Frei and the Argentine president Carlos Menem staged a centennial re-enactment of the celebrated *abrazo del Estrecho* of February 1899.

The second Concertación presidency began in an atmosphere of scandal, with the deputy sales chief of CODELCO, Juan Pablo Dávila, caught out in irregular futures trading on the London Metal Exchange, entailing losses approaching US$ 300 million. To describe such scams, the wits of Santiago proposed a new Spanish verb, *davilar.* It did not catch on. The losses caused no real economic damage. President Frei later set up a high-level commission to examine problems of corruption, which were believed at the time to be intensifying. Were they? The issue would remain a recurrent concern. We should note, however, that an international index of corruption that became well known in the later 1990s[18] sometimes placed Chile higher (i.e., less corrupt) than the United States, and far higher than any other Latin American country.

The two coalitions that now dominated the political scene, the ruling Concertación and the right-wing *Unión por Chile* (Union for Chile), as it was now called, held firm – reassuringly; history suggests that Chilean fortunes have improved with stable coalitions and worsened with constantly shifting alliances, as in the days of the Parliamentary Republic. Partisan competition in the 1990s, as vigorous as in the past, was largely confined to intra-coalition maneuvering. *Ad hoc* cross-coalition alliances occasionally formed, as in July 1997, when Concertación deputies and UDI joined forces to protest a supposed cover-up by the supreme court over drug trafficking. Within the Concertación, there were intermittent strains. The Socialists were aggrieved when Frei's first cabinet reshuffle (September 1994) deprived them of the Interior portfolio. (Frei managed to infuriate all the parties by failing to consult them about the reshuffle.) In December 1994 the abrupt dismissal of the director of the national TV channel (Channel 7) annoyed some Socialists. For their part, the Christian Democrats were angered when the PS enlisted Communist support to defeat PDC candidates in the CUT elections in 1996.

These were storms in a glass of water, in the Spanish phrase, and never really threatened the stability of the coalition. The Concertación vote (56 percent) held up well in the municipal elections of October 1996. The UDI's fluent and personable Joaquín Lavín, the popular *alcalde* of the affluent Santiago district of Las Condes since 1992, was re-elected with a remarkable 77 percent, thus definitely challenging Andrés Allamand (RN) as a main contender to lead the Right, where intra-coalition competition was fiercer, perhaps, than within the Concertación. UDI clearly aspired to displace RN as the principal right-wing party. Its coherence, discipline, very real mystique, and zealous work at the grassroots (especially municipal) level recalled, for those old enough to remember, the dynamic thrust of the PDC in the early 1960s. Certainly, UDI proved more dynamic than RN in the renewal of the Right in the 1990s. In the congressional elections of December 1997, the Concertación vote fell to 50 percent (the PS and PPD doing better, relatively, than the PDC), while the *Unión por Chile* inched forward slightly. The main loser in these elections was Andrés Allamand. To some extent the victim of his own talent, he failed to win election to the Senate, and abruptly withdrew from political life. If Allamand's star waned, that of Ricardo Lagos (then Frei's Public Works minister) waxed more brightly. His claim to the Concertación's presidential candidacy in 1999 began to seem irresistible.

---

[18] From Transparency International (http://www. transparency.org/)

The Frei government strove hard to place civil–military relations on a stable footing. A few incidents still muddied the waters. In an early test of wills, Frei asked for the retirement of General Rodolfo Stange as head of the Carabineros. It took five difficult months to secure his departure (October 1994). Meanwhile General Pinochet continued to resist all suggestions that he should resign as commander-in-chief. He finally handed over to his successor, General Ricardo Izurieta, in March 1998. In an ingenious conflation of military and academic terminology, the Army declared him Commander-in-Chief Emeritus. His immediate induction into the Senate as a life-senator, his right under the constitution,[19] was accompanied by violent confrontations between police and demonstrators outside the hideous Congress building, and undignified scenes inside – watched by the new senator with a frosty smile.

He was soon the focus of a huge international sensation. On October 16, 1998 he was suddenly arrested while on a trip to London, at the request of a Spanish judge, Baltasar Garzón, who sought his extradition to Spain for interrogation and trial. Pinochet was confined to a villa near the leafy suburb of Virginia Water, Surrey. "Tell my friends to get me out of here!" he urged his wife. His Chilean admirers trooped across the ocean to see him. He entertained former British prime minister Margaret Thatcher to a cup of tea. On March 24, 1999 the Law Lords (the House of Lords' judicial panel) ruled almost unanimously in favor of extradition in principle. British Home Secretary Jack Straw (the namesake of a famous leader of England's Peasants' Revolt of 1381) authorized the necessary legal proceedings, and in October 1999 a London magistrate approved extradition. The British government, however, yielded to the pleas of Pinochet's lawyers and supporters, and released him on grounds of ill-health. His fourteen-month captivity ended in March 2000, when he was flown home.

This unprecedented drama provoked much healthy discussion around the world on the "internationalization" of justice, an idea whose time has come. In Chile, it might possibly have produced political turmoil. It did not. Pro- and anti-Pinochet rallies were loud but small. British and Spanish flags were burned. The municipality of Las Condes huffily refused to collect garbage from the British and Spanish embassies. The Army behaved with commendable dignity throughout, merely urging the Frei government to be firm in its reiterated protests against European "interference" in Chilean affairs, a line that caused minor strains in the Concertación. Many Socialists (and some Christian Democrats) failed to conceal their relish at the prospect of a Spanish show-trial. Right-wing politicians, much less restrained than the Army, were especially vocal in their demands for action against the obviously decadent Mother Country and perfidious Albion. There was nothing the government could do, apart from symbolic gestures like the suspension

---

[19] This applied to ex-presidents who had served six years; Aylwin did not become a life-senator.

of LAN-Chile flights to the Falkland Islands. Nor was there any serious impairment of relations with Spain or Britain, whose governments
(whatever their judges did or their peoples hoped) found the Pinochet case
an embarrassment.

Pinochet's detention destroyed the myth of his invulnerability. For many
Chileans it was a psychologically liberating moment. The spell was broken.
Soon after Pinochet's return from England the supreme court abrogated his
congressional immunity. A zealous judge, Juan Guzmán, had been preparing an extensive case against him for several months. Well over 200 lawsuits
against him had by now been filed in the courts. Changes in the organization and composition of the supreme court had made prosecutions for
human rights violations much more credible than was true a few years
earlier, though not necessarily easier. A *Mesa de Diálogo* ("Dialogue Round-
Table") set up by President Frei in August 1999, consisting of military men
and civilians, but excluding party politicians, got as far as persuading the
military to provide information on the whereabouts of the remains of some
of those who had "disappeared" during the dictatorship. Though the information submitted (January 2001) proved highly unsatisfactory, the *Mesa*
could be seen as a step, even if only a faltering one, in the right direction.
The government continued to leave the matter in the hands of the courts. In
October 2002 the FACH commander-in-chief, one of whose subordinates
was found to have destroyed information on the "disappeared"), was obliged
to resign. The Right gave him no support. This was one of several straws
in the wind that indicated both easier prosecutions and the constitutional
amendments sought by a growing number of politicians.

It was never likely that Pinochet himself would actually face trial. In July
2001 he was deemed to be too decrepit. None of the leaders of RN or UDI,
contrary to their practice in earlier years, bothered to attend his eighty-sixth
birthday party in November 2001. In July 2002 the supreme court ruled
his decrepitude to be "irreversible." Pinochet's fate – as a has-been – was
more galling than that of many famous ex-dictators.

His captivity had no real influence on the presidential election of 1999 –
or 1999–2000, as it turned out. Neither of the main candidates wished to
make it an issue. In the run-up to the election, Joaquín Lavín established
himself as the unchallenged standard-bearer of the Right, the *Alianza por
Chile* (Alliance for Chile), as it was now styled. His only rival, the ambitious RN leader Sebastián Piñera, dropped out of the race in January
1999. The Concertación held a nation-wide primary election (May 1999),
in which Lagos was the clear winner with 71 percent; the PDC's candidate,
the diminutive Andrés Zaldívar, won 29 percent. RN had made attempts to
attract Zaldívar and the PDC right wing into a larger right-wing alliance –
swiftly scotched by UDI – and before his London misadventure Senator
Pinochet, who had once exiled him, discreetly tried to boost Zaldívar's

presidential hopes. The two coalitions held firm as the election approached. Claims by certain right-wing Christian Democrats and retired army officers that the Socialist Lagos would return Chile to the days of the *Unidad Popular* lacked all credibility and were plain silly. The 61-year-old Lagos's mildly professorial style contrasted with the 46-year-old Lavín's boyish brio. Lavín adopted a much lighter touch than many of his UDI supporters would probably have wished. His propaganda presented him as a competent administrator, a man almost "above party," whose eyes were fixed on the future, not the past. This attempt to capture the center ground almost succeeded. The 1999 election took its place alongside the cliffhangers of 1938, 1958, or 1970. Lagos and Lavín won 47.95 and 47.51 percent, respectively. Under the constitution this meant, for the first time in Chile, a French-style second round (January 16, 2000), which Lagos won, with 51.3 percent to Lavín's 48.7 percent. The result left the relatively youthful Lavín well positioned for a presidential bid in 2005. Chileans, needless to say, immediately began speculating about his possible contenders. Ex-president Frei, we might note provocatively, would only be in his early sixties in 2005.

"Ricardo, what have you got yourself into?" asked the 104-year-old mother of the third Concertación president on the day he was inaugurated. What President Lagos had got himself into was a more complex scene than might have been foreseen even a year or two earlier. The downturn of 1999 left him the problem of "reactivating" the economy. Moreover, the congressional elections of December 2001 confirmed the advance of the Right. The Concertación's 48 percent of the vote compared with 44 percent for the *Alianza por Chile*. The PPD won nearly as many seats as the PDC, while UDI (with 35 deputies as against RN's 22) became the biggest of the country's political parties, just as the PDC had done in 1963. Joaquín Lavín stayed in the public eye, holding the highly visible post of *alcalde* of Santiago from December 2000. This balancing of political forces must be seen as positive. In a democracy, it is right that the government should sometimes change hands. It did not, however, make Lagos's task any easier, though he bent to it with all his formidable intelligence and skill, striving to revive the economy and to make further headway with the Concertación agenda (this chapter has noted some of his actions), as Chile approached the bicentennial of independence.

At a dismal moment in Chilean fortunes, the first Eduardo Frei told one of this book's authors that he could find no "rational reasons" for optimism about the future, but several "irrational reasons." The chief of these was "the essence of Chilean history," as he put it – a history that had been liberal and democratic with certain moments of constructive reform.[20]

---

[20] Conversation with Simon Collier, Santiago, October 15, 1975.

Table 14.1. Composition of Congress: following congressional elections of December 2001.

	Chamber of Deputies [1997 figure]	Senate
		Elected
Concertación	62 [70]	20
PDC	24 [39]	12
PPD	21 [16]	3
PS	11 [11]	5
PRSD[a]	6 [4]	–
Alianza por Chile	57 [40]	18
RN	22 [23]	7
UDI	35 [17]	11
		Nominated
		10

[a] Partido Radical-Social Demócrata: the radical and Social Democrat parties merged in 1994.

Notwithstanding the terrible storms of the 1970s and 1980s, this opinion seems to us to be well-founded. The Chilean electorate is better educated in the early twenty-first century than at any time in the past, although apathy amongst the young and the poor[21] (a phenomenon hardly unique to Chile, alas) is something that needs to be addressed by politicians, as does the widespread perception, especially among the young, that there is a widening gap between *las cúpulas* (the party high commands) and the grassroots. Today's politicians are far better *informed* than their predecessors, but their predecessors perhaps had "people skills" which could do with being revived.

Much depends also on the ability of governments to attack the poverty that still remains. The second Eduardo Frei sometimes expressed the hope that Chile might reach southern European living standards by the 2010s. Reverence for the free market went too far in the Chile of the 1970s and 1980s. (President Aylwin, at the end of his term, made some trenchant observations on this topic.) The task of politicians and citizens alike is to find ways of combining the advantages of the market with greater social justice and (a need that will certainly become more urgent) protection of the environment. Such challenges have become worldwide in the age of "globalization" that, as everybody tells us, is now under way. Chileans, we are convinced, have national traditions that enable them to confront the inevitable uncertainties of the times to come with greater confidence than many other peoples. We wish them well.

[21] Only just over half those eligible to vote did so in the congressional elections of 1997 and 2001.

Table 14.2. Value added in millions of pesos (1996) 1985–97.

	1985	1986	1987	1988	1989	1990	1991	1992	1993	1994	1995	1996	1997
I	237.1	253.4	277.7	312.7	329.6	360.2	364.7	405.7	416.6	441.5	464.3	470.4	452.1
II	35.2	39.6	43.3	45.16	50.67	54.69	60.28	70.28	74.19	86.32	100.04	109.77	120.01
III	567.68	610.94	643.17	699.85	776.49	784.16	826.01	920.29	987.06	1027.35	1104.7	1140.2	1203.6
IV	86.46	91.75	96.76	102.2	94.20	85.99	109.18	139.29	146.04	155.11	166.94	160.67	177.60
V	149.02	163.54	178.49	193.82	215.41	237.01	233.38	265.22	327.5	324.03	356.17	386.85	416.87
VI	459.16	482.79	535.40	563.84	652.97	683.13	748.84	880.33	944.20	992.60	1133.11	1241.04	1356.40

I Agriculture and Forestry. II Fishing. III Manufacturing. IV Electricity, gas, water. V Construction. VI Trade, hotels, restaurants.
Source: Banco Central.

Table 14.3. Social expenditures as a percentage of total social expenditures 1989–2000.

	Health	Housing	Insurance	Education	Subsidies	Other
1989	15.8	8.0	47.7	20.2	4.5	3.8
1990	15.3	8.1	49.0	19.5	4.6	3.6
1991	16.5	8.2	46.7	20.12	4.5	3.9
1992	17.4	8.3	44.8	21.1	4.2	4.2
1993	17.8	8.3	44.3	20.9	4.0	4.7
1994	18.5	8.2	43.2	21.4	3.9	4.8
1995	18.0	8.0	42.7	22.3	3.9	5.1
1996	17.8	8.2	41.9	23.0	3.8	5.3
1997	17.9	7.3	41.6	24.0	4.0	5.3
1998	18.0	7.0	41.0	24.8	4.2	5.0
1999	17.2	6.4	42.0	24.6	4.0	5.8
2000	17.6	5.8	41.5	25.2	3.9	6.0
A	135.4	52.7	84.8	165.0	87.3	238.7

A = cumulative increase 1989–2000.
Source: Ministerio de Planificación y Cooperación.

Table 14.4. Social spending as a percentage of total government expenditures.

1989	64.8
1990	67.6
1991	67.1
1992	65.8
1993	66.9
1994	67.0
1995	67.5
1996	67.5
1997	66.7
1998	67.5
1999	68.5
2000	70.5

Source: Ministerio de Planificación y Cooperación.

Table 14.5. GDP growth, unemployment, and inflation.

	GDP growth (±%)	Unemployment (%)	Inflation (±%)
1992	12.3	4.9	12.7
1993	7.0	4.7	12.2
1994	5.7	6.0	8.9
1995	10.6	6.4	8.2
1996	7.1	6.4	6.6
1997	6.6	6.1	6.0
1998	3.2	6.4	4.7
1999	−1.0	9.8	2.3
2000	4.4	9.2	4.5
2001	2.8	9.2	2.6
2002	2.0	9.0	2.8

Source: Banco Central de Chile, Instituto Nacional de Estadística, International Monetary Fund, and Ministerio de Hacienda.

Glossary of Spanish terms

Not all terms explained in context in the course of the narrative are included here. Certain very common terms (left un-italicized here) are not italicized in the text after their first appearance there.

afuerino   casual farm laborer
alameda   tree-lined avenue
Alameda   main avenue of Santiago
alcalde   mayor
alessandrista   follower of Arturo Alessandri
allendista   supporter of Salvador Allende
almacén fiscal   public bonded warehouse (Valparaiso)
apir   mineworker
asentamiento   settlement (agrarian reform unit)
Audiencia   colonial appeal court and administrative tribunal

barretero   mineworker
bombero   fireman

cabildo   municipal council
cabildo abierto   open assembly of leading citizens
cabotaje   coastal shipping trade
calificación   voting certificate
callampa   shantytown
campesino   peasant, countryperson
cantina   bar, tavern
casa de tolerancia   unregulated brothel
chacra   small farm, usually near a town
charqui   jerked beef
chicha   fermented juice of grape, apple, or *frutilla*
chilote   inhabitant of Chiloé
chingana   popular venue for drinking and dancing
cívico   militiaman, national guardsman

Consulado   merchant guild
conventillo   tenement house
cordón industrial   "industrial belt"
cueca   Chilean national dance
cúpulas   high commands of political parties (an expression much used in the 1990s. Literally, "domes").

demócratacristiano   Christian Democrat
dieciocho   September 18 (national holiday)

empleado   white-collar worker
encomendero   holder of an encomienda
encomienda   grant of Indians to a Spanish conquistador
estancia   great estate (ranch)
estanco   state tobacco monopoly

falangista   supporter of the Falange Nacional
ficha   token
fiestas patrias   national holidays (September 18–19)
fundo   common Chilean term for hacienda

gañán   day-laborer, peon
gobernador   governor of a provincial district
gremio   (1) trade guild in colonial times; (2) association (usually of the self-employed)

habilitación   credit business (usually in connection with mining, nineteenth century)
habilitador   businessman engaged in *habilitación*
hacendado   estate owner, landowner hacienda great estate
huaso   peasant owning a horse

ibañista   follower of General Ibáñez
inquilinaje   the institution of tenant-labor on haciendas
inquilino   tenant-laborer on a hacienda
interventor   temporary administrator

latifundista   estate owner
liceo   high school, secondary school

mayordomo   estate manager
mestizo   of mixed Spanish/Indian parentage
minifundio   small peasant holding

mirista   member of MIR
momio   right-winger ("mummy")
Mundial   World Cup soccer tournament

nacista   member of the National Socialist Movement of the 1930s

oficina   (1) nitrate working; (2) office in the conventional sense
o'higginista   follower of Bernardo O'Higgins

pampa   northern desert
parcela   plot of land
parlamento   ceremonial Spanish-Araucanian parley
partido   (1) colonial administrative subdivision; (2) political party
paseo   walk, stroll (especially in the evening)
patrón   boss, landowner
patronato   the supervisory rights of the state over the Catholic Church
   (to 1925)
pelucón   Conservative (nineteenth century)
peña   informal club
pipiolo   Liberal (nineteenth century)
pirquén   system of marginal mining
población   shantytown or marginal community
porteño   inhabitant of Valparaiso
protesta   day of protest (1983–86)
provinciano   from the provinces
pulpería   company store

rancho   shack
reajuste   readjustment of wages and salaries
roto   urban laborer

salitre   nitrate
salitrera   nitrate working
salitrero   owner of nitrate business
santiaguino   inhabitant of Santiago
serenense   inhabitant of La Serena
siútico   pretentious social climber; used as an adjective, similar in meaning to conventional Spanish *cursi*
socio   member of an *asentamiento*
subdelegado   official in charge of a *partido,* provincial sub-district

telenovela   television soap opera
toma   land seizure (literally, a "take")
trapiche   ore-grinder (gold, silver)

Initials and acronyms

AFP *Administradora de Fondos de Pensión:* Pension Fund Administration (1980s onward).

ANAP *Alianza Nacional del Pueblo:* National Popular Alliance (Ibáñez electoral coalition).

ANEF *Asociación Nacional de Empleados Fiscales* National Association of Public Employees.

API *Acción Popular Independiente:* Independent People's Action (following of Rafael Tarud).

APL *Alianza Popular Libertadora:* Popular Liberation Alliance (Ibáñez electoral coalition).

ASICH *Acción Sindical y Económica de Chile:* Chilean Economic and Union Action (Catholic union movement).

CAP *Compañía del Acero del Pacífico:* Pacific Steel Company.

CEPRO *Centro de Producción:* Production Center (agrarian reform unit).

CERA *Centro de Reforma Agraria:* Agrarian Reform Center (agrarian reform unit).

CIA Central Intelligence Agency (United States).

CIDOC *Centro de Investigación y Documentación en Historia de Chile Contemporáneo* (Research and Documentation Center in Contemporary Chilean History, Universidad Finis Terrae).

CNC *Consejo Nacional Campesino:* National Peasant Council.

CNI *Central Nacional de Informaciones:* National Information Center (secret police, Pinochet regime).

CODELCO *Corporación del Cobre:* Copper Corporation.

CORA *Corporación de Reforma Agraria:* Agrarian Reform Corporation.

CORFO *Corporación de Fomento a la Producción:* Production Development Corporation.

CORVI *Corporación de la Vivienda:* Housing Corporation.

419

COSACH *Compañía de Salitre de Chile:* Nitrate Company of Chile.

COVENSA *Corporación de Ventas de Salitre y Yodo:* Nitrate and Iodine Marketing Board.

CTCH *Confederación de Trabajadores de Chile:* Confederation of Workers of Chile (trade union confederation).

CUT (1) *Central Unica de Trabajadores* (1953): Sole Workers' Center (trade union federation). (2) *Central Unitaria de Trabajadores* (1988): Unitary Workers' Center (trade union federation).

DINA *Dirección de Inteligencia Nacional:* Directorate of National Intelligence (secret police, Pinochet regime).

ENAP *Empresa Nacional de Petróleo:* National Petroleum Enterprise.

ENDESA *Empresa Nacional de Electricidad:* National Electricity Enterprise.

ENTEL *Empresa Nacional de Telecomunicaciones:* National Telecommunications Enterprise.

ENU *Escuela Nacional Unida:* Unified National School (Allende government).

FACH *Fuerza Aérea de Chile:* Chilean Air Force.

FECH *Federación de Estudiantes de la Universidad de Chile:* University of Chile Student Federation.

FOCH *Federación de Obreros Chilenos:* Federation of Chilean Workers (trade union confederation).

FONASA *Fondo Nacional de Salud:* National Health Fund.

FONDART *Fondo de Desarrollo de las Artes y la Cultura:* Fund for the Development of the Arts and Culture (1992).

FOSIS *Fondo de Solidaridad e Inversión Social:* Social Solidarity and Investment Fund (Aylwin presidency).

FPMR *Frente Patriótico Manuel Rodríguez:* Manuel Rodríguez Patriotic Front (Pinochet regime).

FRAP *Frente de Acción Popular:* People's Action Front (left-wing coalition, 1950s–1960s).

INDAP *Instituto de Desarrollo Agropecuario:* Agricultural Development Institute.

ISAPRE *Instituto de Salud Previsional:* Welfare Health Institute.

IVA *Impuesto al valor agregado:* Value-added tax.

LADECO *Línea Aérea del Cobre:* Copper Airline.

LAN-Chile *Línea Aérea Nacional de Chile:* National Airline of Chile.

MADECO *Manufacturas de Cobre:* Copper Manufactures (company).
MADEMSA *Manufacturas de Metales:* Metal Manufactures (company).
MAPU *Movimiento de Acción Popular Unitaria:* Unitary People's Action Movement.
MERCOSUR projected South American common market: Brazil, Argentina, Uruguay, Paraguay (1991). Chile joined as an associate member in 1996.
MIDA *Movimiento Democrático Allendista:* Allendista Democratic Movement (Aylwin presidency).
MIR *Movimiento de Izquierda Revolucionaria:* Movement of the Revolutionary Left.

NAFTA North American Free Trade Agreement: Canada, U.S.A., Mexico (1994)

ODEPLAN *Oficina de Planificación Nacional:* National Planning Office.

PAL *Partido Agrario-Laborista:* Agrarian Labor Party.
PDC *Partido Demócratacristiano:* Christian Democrat Party.
PEM *Programa de Empleo Mínimo:* Minimum Employment Program (Pinochet regime).
POJH *Programa Ocupacional para Jefes de Hogar:* Work Program for Heads of Household (Pinochet regime).
POS *Partido Obrero Socialista:* Socialist Worker Party.
PRSD *Partido Radical-Social Demócrata:* Radical-Social Democrat Party, the merger (1994) of the former Radical and Social Democrat parties.

RN *Renovación Nacional:* National Renewal party.

SNA *Sociedad Nacional de Agricultura:* National Society of Agriculture.
SNS *Servicio Nacional de Salud:* National Health Service.
SOFOFA *Sociedad de Fomento Fabril:* Society for Industrial Development.
SOQUIMICH *Sociedad Química Chilena:* Chilean Chemical Company.

UDI *Unión Demócrata Independiente:* Independent Democrat Union.
UP *Unidad Popular:* People's Unity (Allende coalition).
USOPO *Unión Socialista Popular:* People's Socialist Union.

VOP *Vanguardia Organizada del Pueblo:* Organized Vanguard of the People (extremist group).

Further reading

Our emphasis in this note is on reasonably accessible books and articles in English (though *not* Ph.D. dissertations, generally less accessible), but where necessary, to cover particular gaps, we have also noted a few of the more important titles in Spanish (and in one or two cases, French), and it should be remembered that most of the recent research has been published in Spanish. Those interested in specific topics, or wishing to undertake research, should start by consulting both the *Handbook of Latin American Studies* (edited by the Hispanic Division of the Library of Congress, with the volume containing the History section appearing every other year), as well as the regular "Fichero bibliográfico" in *Historia,* the pre-eminent historical journal in Chile, edited from the Catholic University, Santiago, and now into its fifth decade. All "ficheros" from 1959 to 1996 were collected in *Historiografía Chilena. Fichero Bibliográfico, 1959–1996* (2000), an indispensable reference-book. Julio Retamal A. and Sergio Villalobos R., *Bibliografía histórica chilena. Revistas chilenas, 1843–1978* (Santiago, 1993), is a comprehensive survey of Chilean periodical literature. Harold Blakemore, *Chile* (Oxford, 1988), in the World Bibliographical Series, offers a highly useful listing and discussion of materials (not just historical materials) on Chile in English. There are also specialized bibliographical essays for particular periods or episodes, such as Simon Collier, "The Historiography of the 'Portalian' Period in Chile (1830–1891)," *Hispanic American Historical Review* (hereafter cited as *HAHR*), 57 (1977), 660–90; Harold Blakemore, "The Chilean Revolution of 1891 and Its Historiography," *HAHR,* 45 (1965), 393–421; Arturo Valenzuela and J. Samuel Valenzuela, "Visions of Chile," *Latin American Research Review,* 10:3 (1975), 155–75.

General works on Chilean history currently available in English include: Brian Loveman, *Chile. The Legacy of Hispanic Capitalism*, 3rd ed. (New York, 2001), and Leslie Bethell, ed., *Chile since Independence* (Cambridge, 1993), a reprint of relevant chapters (by Simon Collier, Harold Blakemore, Paul Drake and Alan Angell) in Leslie Bethell, ed., *The Cambridge History of Latin America* (in progress, Cambridge, 1984–). John Hickman, *News from the*

End of the Earth. A Portrait of Chile (London, 1998) is useful for its account of the Pinochet period, for some of which Hickman was British ambassador in Santiago. Stephen Clissold's charming *Chilean Scrapbook* (London, 1952), though written half a century back, is recommended for its historical episodes and anecdotes, evoked in the kind of disciplined prose most professional historians should envy.

The colonial background

There is not much in English on the colonial period. H. R. S. Pocock, *The Conquest of Chile* (New York, 1967), is a useful narrative. Mario Góngora, "Urban Stratification in Colonial Chile," *HAHR,* 55 (1975), 421–48, describes the various social groups; William F. Sater, "The Black Experience in Chile," in Robert Brent Toplin, ed., *Slavery and Race Relations in Latin America* (Westport, Conn., 1974), 13–50, concentrates on the slaves brought to Chile or passing through to Peru. Eugene Korth SJ, *Spanish Policy in Colonial Chile: The Struggle for Social Justice, 1535–1700* (Stanford, Cal., 1968), includes ample information on the attempts to protect the Indian population. For the southern Frontier, see Louis de Armond, "Frontier Warfare in Colonial Chile," *Pacific Historical Review,* 23 (1954), 125–32. Later colonial developments are examined in Jacques Barbier, *Reform and Politics in Bourbon Chile, 1755–1796* (Ottawa, 1980). In Spanish, the classic account of Chilean history from the conquest to 1833 is Diego Barros Arana, *Historia general de Chile,* 16 vols. (Santiago, 1884–1902), the undisputed masterpiece of Chilean historiography of its own or any other age.

Political and cultural history

For a new study of the political dimension of the early republic, see Simon Collier, *Chile. The Making of a Republic, 1830–1865. Politics and Ideas* (Cambridge, 2003). For nineteenth-century church-state issues, see the same author's "Religious Freedom, Clericalism and Anti-clericalism in Chile, 1820–1920," in Richard Helmstadter, ed., *Freedom and Religion in the Nineteenth Century* (Stanford, Calif., 1997). Constitutional developments (with emphasis, because of the book's focus, on their authoritarian elements) are very usefully examined by Brian Loveman in *The Constitution of Tyranny: Regimes of Exception in Spanish America* (Pittsburgh, 1993), Chapter 8. Timothy R. Scully, *Rethinking the Center: Party Politics in Nineteenth and Twentieth Century Chile* (Stanford, Cal., 1992), gives an interesting overview of political history, better on the period since the 1920s than for earlier times. Two good descriptions of the political system at the point it had reached by the 1950s and

1960s are Federico G. Gil, *The Political System of Chile* (Boston, 1966), and Arturo Valenzuela, *Political Brokers in Chile* (Durham, N.C., 1977).

Simon Collier, *Ideas and Politics of Chilean Independence, 1808–1833* (Cambridge, 1967), offers a detailed account of the independence period. Stephen Clissold, *Bernardo O'Higgins and the Independence of Chile* (London, 1968), is a straightforward biography of the supreme national hero. See also Mary Lowenthal Felstiner, "Kinship Politics in the Chilean Independence Movement," *HAHR*, 56:1 (1976), 58–80. Jay Kinsbruner, *Diego Portales, Interpretive Essays on the Man and His Times* (The Hague, 1967), gives insights into the work of the "organizer of the republic." Unfortunately there is no general study of nineteenth-century Chilean political history in English. In Spanish, a general account of the period from independence to 1891 is Francisco Antonio Encina's large-scale (and also highly idiosyncratic) *Historia de Chile desde la prehistoria hasta 1891,* 20 vols. (Santiago, 1942–52), vols. IX–XX. It is not the equal of Barros Arana's great history (cited above) of the colonial and independence periods, which Barros Arana in effect continued in his superb swan-song, *Un decenio de la historia de Chile, 1841–1851,* 2 vols. (Santiago, 1905–06). For the War of the Pacific, see William F. Sater, *Chile and the War of the Pacific* (Lincoln, Neb., 1986), focusing on domestic developments rather than military history *per se.* The same author's *The Heroic Image in Chile: Arturo Prat, Secular Saint* (Berkeley, Cal., 1973), examines the myths surrounding the outstanding hero of the war.

Harold Blakemore, *British Nitrates and Chilean Politics, 1886–1896: Balmaceda and North* (London, 1974), describes the Balmaceda presidency and the events leading to the civil war of 1891. In Spanish, Julio Heise G., *Historia de Chile. El período parlamentario, 1861–1925,* 2 vols. (Santiago, 1974–82), has much interesting information. The multi-volume *Historia de Chile* (in progress, Santiago, 1981–) by Gonzalo Vial is another essential work for the period from 1891 through to the 1920s, its heavy use of anecdote adding to its readability. A useful study of "Parliamentary" times (contrasting the Chilean record with Argentina's) is Karen Remmer, *Party Competition in Argentina: Political Recruitment and Public Policy, 1890–1930* (Lincoln, Neb., 1984). For an interesting approach to the period, very good on education, see Patrick Barr-Melej, *Reforming Chile: Cultural Politics, Nationalism and the Rise of the Middle Class* (Chapel Hill, N.C., 2001). For the "Lion of Tarapacá," see Robert J. Alexander, *Arturo Alessandri,* 2 vols. (Ann Arbor, Mich., 1977), and, in Spanish, the totally indispensable account by Ricardo Donoso, *Alessandri, agitador y demoledor,* 2 vols. (Mexico City, 1952–54). Frederick Nunn, *The Honorable Mission of the Armed Forces* (Albuquerque, N.M., 1970), concentrates on the collapse of the Parliamentary regime and the upheavals that led to the rise of Ibáñez, who has not yet received a proper study either in Spanish or English. Readers of Spanish will find Carlos Vicuña, *La tiranía en Chile,* 2nd ed. (Santiago, 1988), an incomparable, gossipy account of the agitated politics of the 1920s.

Chile's elections from 1932 to 1973 are covered in César Caviedes, *The Politics of Chile: A Sociographical Assessment* (Boulder, Col., 1979). For accounts of some crucial mid-century decades, concentrating on the Left, see Paul W. Drake, *Socialism and Populism in Chile, 1932–1952* (Urbana, Ill., 1978); Julio Fáundez, *Marxism and Democracy in Chile: From 1952 to the Fall of Allende* (New Haven, Conn., 1988); and Carmelo Furci, *The Chilean Communist Party and the Road to Socialism* (London, 1984). The second Ibáñez administration is examined in Tomás Moulián, *El gobierno de Ibáñez, 1952–1958* (Santiago, 1985). Michael Fleet, *The Rise and Fall of Chilean Christian Democracy* (Princeton, N.J., 1985), gives able coverage of the trajectory of the PDC, though its title reads strangely in the mid-1990s. See also Ernst Halperin, *Nationalism and Communism in Chile* (Cambridge, Mass., 1965), and Ben G. Burnett, *Political Groups in Chile: The Dialogue between Order and Change* (Austin, Texas, 1970). In Spanish, Cristián Gazmuri (with Patricia Arancibia and Álvaro Góngora), *Eduardo Frei Montalva y su época,* 2 vols. (Santiago, 2000), a mammoth biography, is strongly recommended.

On the Allende years, much of the enormous literature (especially that published in the 1970s) can best be described as axe-grinding in nature. Arturo Valenzuela, *The Breakdown of Democratic Regimes: Chile* (Baltimore, 1978), remains probably the best single piece of writing on the convulsive politics of the time, and a cool narrative is offered in Paul Sigmund, *The Overthrow of Allende and the Politics of Chile* (Pittsburgh, 1978). See also Edy Kaufman, *Crisis in Allende's Chile: New Perspectives* (New York, 1988), and Mark Falcoff, *Modern Chile, 1970–1988* (New Brunswick, N.J., 1989), the latter from the viewpoint of an intelligent American conservative. Something of the "feel" of the early Allende years as captured by an intelligent British conservative can be found in Alistair Horne, *Small Earthquake in Chile* (London, 1972). Peter Winn, *Weavers of Revolution: The Yarur Workers and Chile's Road to Socialism* (New York, 1986), a superb piece of social history, looks at the story from the perspective of the workers in an important textile plant. See also Colin Henfrey and Bernardo Sorj, eds., *Chilean Voices: Activists Describe Their Experiences of the Popular Unity Period* (Hassocks, 1977).

Useful material on the Pinochet period is now appearing, though much remains to be done. Both Paul Drake and Iván Jaksić, eds., *The Struggle for Democracy in Chile, 1982–1990* (Lincoln, Neb., 1991), and J. Samuel Valenzuela and Arturo Valenzuela, eds., *Military Rule in Chile: Dictatorship and Opposition* (Baltimore, 1986), contain a number of splendid essays on various aspects of Chile during these critical years. Two journalistic studies of the period (suffering from the disadvantages of the genre but in their own way very informative) are Pamela Constable and Arturo Valenzuela, *A Nation of Enemies: Chile under Pinochet* (New York, 1991), and Mary Helen Spooner, *Soldiers in a Narrow Land: The Pinochet Regime in Chile* (Berkeley, Cal., 1994). Despite its disagreeably sour tone, James R. Whelan, *Out of the Ashes: Life, Death and Transfiguration of Democracy in Chile, 1833–1988* (Washington, D.C., 1989), also has interesting material. For a striking collection of photographs from the years of dictatorship, see Susan Meiselas, ed., *Chile from Within* (New York, 1990). The role of the Church under Pinochet (and also in the preceding PDC and UP periods) is well described in Brian Smith, *The Church and Modern Politics in Chile* (Princeton, N.J., 1982). The shantytowns during the dictatorship are brought to life in Cathy Lisa Schneider, *Shantytown Protest in Pinochet's Chile* (Philadelphia, 1995). For the most recent period, see Gerardo Munck, "Authoritarianism, Modernization and Democracy in Chile," *Latin American Research Review,* 29 (1994), 188–211; David Hojman, *Chile: The Political Economy of Development and Democracy in the 1990s* (Pittsburgh, 1993); and Joaquín Fermandois and Michael A.Morris, *Democracy in Chile: Transition and Consolidation 1987–2000* [Conflict Studies, 279] (London, 1995). See also Mark Ensalaco, *Chile under Pinochet* (Philadelphia, 2000). Patricia Verdugo, *Chile, Pinochet and the Caravan of Death* (Miami, 2001), published in Spanish in 1989, describes a notorious early episode in the initial repression. See also Patricia Politzer, *Fear in Chile. Chilean Lives under Pinochet* (New York, 2001), Marcelo Pollack, *The New Right in Chile, 1973–97* (New York, 1999), and Peter Siavelis, *The President and Congress in Postauthoritarian Chile* (University Park, Pennsylavia, 2000).

The armed forces

Frederick Nunn, *The Military in Chilean History* (Albuquerque, N.M., 1976) covers various aspects of the history of the Chilean military. This apart, there is hardly anything else in English. The multi-volume works by the Chilean Army's general staff, *Historia del Ejército Chileno* (Santiago, 1983–85) and Rodrigo Fuenzalida Bade, *La armada de Chile* (Santiago, 1975–80), describe, in sometimes excruciating detail, the development of these two pillars of the armed forces. Carlos Maldonado, "Los carabineros de Chile: historia de una policía militarizada," *Ibero-Americana: Nordic Journal of Latin American Studies,* 20:3 (1990), 3–31, discusses the Carabineros. William F. Sater and Holger Herwig, *The Grand Illusion. The Prussianization of the Chilean Army* (Lincoln, Nebraska, 1999) demolishes some hoary old myths, amplifying our statements in Chapter 7. In Spanish, see also Gen. Roberto Arancibia Clavel, *La influencia del Ejército Chileno en América Latina, 1900–1950* (Santiago, 2000).

Diplomatic history

For Chile's diplomatic history, see the only comprehensive work, Mario Barros, *Historia diplomática de Chile, 1541–1938* (Barcelona, 1970); a recent revision (1990) adds little. Robert N. Burr, *By Reason or Force: Chile and the Balancing of Power in South America, 1830–1905* (Los Angeles, 1965), shows that nineteenth-century Chilean foreign policy was not reactive but, in fact, followed certain principles. William F. Sater, *Chile and the United States* (Athens, Ga., 1990), traces Chile–U.S. relations in a broad sweep from independence onward. There are no comprehensive works dealing with Chilean relations with other non–South American nations. R. A. Humphreys describes Chilean attitudes toward the Second World War in his *Latin America and the Second World War*, 2 vols. (London, 1981–82), I, 22–25 and 159–64, and II, 105–19, a theme also dealt with very professionally in Michael J. Francis, *The Limits of Hegemony: United States Relations with Argentina and Chile during World War II* (Notre Dame, Ind., 1977). President Allende's diplomatic relations with the United States and the world are well described in Poul Jensen, *The Garotte: The United States and Chile, 1970–1973*, 2 vols. (Aarhus, Denmark, 1988), and in Joaquín Fermandois, *Chile y el mundo, 1970–1973* (Santiago, 1985). Material on General Pinochet's foreign policy can be found in Heraldo Muñoz, *Las relaciones exteriores del gobierno militar chileno* (Santiago, 1986). See also Joaquín Fermandois, "Chile and the Great Powers," in Michael A. Morris, ed., *Great Power Relations in Argentina, Chile and Antarctica* (London, 1990), Chapter 6, an excellent summary of the period from the 1960s onward. David Mares and Francisco Rojas, *The United States and Chile – Coming in from the Cold* (New York, 2001) provides a good overview of the diplomatic relations in the post-Pinochet period.

Intellectual and cultural history

Scholars are increasingly devoting effort to these themes. Allen Woll, *A Functional Past: The Uses of History in Nineteenth Century Chile* (Baton Rouge, La., 1982), is an admirable study of historiography in its classic phase. For an outstanding study of the key nineteenth-century intellectual figure, see Iván Jaksić, *Andrés Bello. Scholarship and Nation-Building in Nineteenth-Century Latin America* (Cambridge, 2001). Iván Jaksić, ed., *Selected Writings of Andrés Bello* (New York, 1997), is an anthology of Bello's prime texts in English. Oxford University Press's "Library of Latin America," of which the anthology is a title, has also recently published

English translations of the nineteenth-century authors Alberto Blest Gana, José Victorino Lastarria, Vicente Pérez Rosales, and José Joaquín Vallejo. Iván Jaksić, *Academic Rebels in Chile: The Role of Philosophy in Higher Education and Politics* (Albany, N.Y., 1989), examines the role of philosophers, with its focus on the twentieth century. Some excellent essays about the great turn-of-the-century scholar José Toribio Medina can be found in Maury A. Bromsen, ed., *José Toribio Medina, Humanist of the Americas: An Appraisal* (Washington, D.C., 1960). For the creation and growth of Chile's greatest university, see Sol Serrano and Iván Jaksić, "In the Service of the Nation: The Establishment and Consolidation of the University of Chile, 1842–1879," *HAHR*, 70:1 (1990), 139–71, and Sol Serrano's excellent *Universidad y nación. Chile en el siglo XIX* (Santiago, 1994). Juan Guillermo Muñoz Correa, *La Universidad de Santiago de Chile: sobre sus orígenes y su desarrollo histórico* (Santiago, 1987), studies the story of the institution that began as the State Technical University. For Chilean culture in historical perspective, see Hernán Godoy Urzúa, *La cultura chilena* (Santiago, 1982), a well-illustrated panoramic survey. Numerous English translations of Pablo Neruda's poetry are now available, for example, *Pablo Neruda: Five Decades: Poems 1925–1970*, trans. Ben Belitt (New York, 1974). See also John Felstiner, *Translating Neruda: The Way to Macchu Picchu* (Stanford, Cal., 1980), for some acute insights. For literature in general, see the relevant sections of Roberto González Echevarría and Enrique Pupo-Walker, eds., *The Cambridge History of Latin American Literature*, 3 vols. (Cambridge, 1996). Joan Jara's biography of her cruelly murdered husband Víctor Jara, *Victor, an Unfinished Song* (London, 1983), is an excellent way into the story of the New Chilean Song. For an exhaustive account of the national dance (and associated song), see Samuel Claro Valdés and others, *Chilena o cueca tradicional* (Santiago, 1994), which contains numerous texts of *cuecas*.

Economic and social history

There is a growing amount of literature on economic history. Markos Mamalakis, *The Growth and Structure of the Chilean Economy* (New Haven, Conn., 1976), and his "Public Policy and Sectoral Development," in Markos Mamalakis and Clark W. Reynolds, *Essays on the Chilean Economy* (Homewood, Ill., 1965), are perhaps the best starting points. A fundamental source is Carmen Cariola and Osvaldo Sunkel, *Un siglo de historia económica de Chile, 1830–1930* (Santiago, 1991), which contains a study of the impact of nitrates on economic development as well as an annotated bibliography (by Rafael Sagredo) that includes nearly 1,000 citations. Valuable statistics are contained in Markos Mamalakis, *Historical Statistics of Chile*, 6 vols. (Westport, Conn., 1979–89). Particular episodes and periods of economic history are covered in Luis Ortega, "Economic Policy and Growth in Chile from Independence to the War of the Pacific," in Christopher Abel and Colin Lewis, eds., *Latin America: Economic Imperialism and the State* (London, 1985), 147–71; William F. Sater, "Economic Nationalism and Tax Reform in the Late Nineteenth Century," *The Americas,* 33 (1976), 311–35; the same author's "Chile and the World Depression of the 1870s," *Journal of Latin American Studies,* 11:1 (1979), 67–99; and in the relevant sections of Bill Albert, *South America and the First World War* (Cambridge, 1988). See also P. T. Ellsworth, *Chile: An Economy in Transition* (New York, 1945), focusing on the Depression. The crucial economic dimension to the Allende years is well described in Stefan de Vylder, *Allende's Chile: The Political Economy of the Rise and Fall of the Unidad Popular* (Cambridge, 1976). Probably the best overall study of the economy in the Pinochet period is that by Sebastián and Alejandra Edwards, *Monetarism and Liberalization: The Chilean Experiment* (Chicago, 1991). See also Carlos Fortín, "The Political Economy of Repressive Monetarism: The State and Capital Accumulation in Post-1973 Chile," in Christian Anglade and Carlos Fortín, eds., *The State and Capital Accumulation in Latin America,* 2 vols. (Pittsburgh, 1985–90), I, 139–209. Joseph Collins and John Lear, *Chile's Free Market Miracle: A Second Look* (Oakland, Cal., 1995), is a useful corrective to the more starry-eyed press reports of recent economic growth.

Thomas C. Wright, "Origins of the Politics of Inflation in Chile, 1888–1918," *HAHR,* 53:2 (1973), 239–59, and Albert Hirschman, "Inflation in Chile," in his *Journeys Toward Progress* (New York, 1963), 161–223, discuss an endemic Chilean ailment. René Millar, *Historia económica de Chile* (Santiago, 1994), traces fiscal policy through to 1925, as does a classic, Frank W. Fetter, *Monetary Inflation in Chile* (Princeton, N.J., 1931). Paul Drake, *The Money Doctor in the Andes: The Kemmerer Missions, 1923–1933* (Durham, N.C., 1989), is very useful on the 1920s (see pp. 76–124). Rory Miller, *Britain and Latin America in the Nineteenth and Twentieth Centuries* (London, 1993), includes some excellent material on Britain's economic involvement in Chile, as, for more specific periods, and in obviously greater detail, do John Mayo, *British Merchants and Chilean Development, 1851–1886* (Boulder, Col., 1987), and Eduardo Cavieres, *Comercio chileno y comerciantes ingleses, 1820–1880: un ciclo de historia económica* (Valparaiso, 1988). Juan Ricardo Couyoumdjian, René Millar, and Josefina Tocornal, *Historia de la Bolsa de Comercio de Santiago, 1893–1993* (Santiago, 1993), is an impressively detailed study of the Santiago stock exchange. On Santiago, in Spanish, see Armando de Ramón, *Santiago de Chile* (Santiago, 2000). Javier Martínez and Alvaro Díaz, *Chile: the Great Transformation* (Washington DC, 1996) is an interesting overview from the 1970s to the 1990s. For aspects of the 1990s, see

Bulletin of Latin American Research, Vol. 21, No. 3 (July 2002), a special issue on Chile.

The countryside

Arnold Bauer, *Chilean Rural Society from the Spanish Conquest to 1930* (Cambridge, 1975), is a key work here, focusing on the mid-nineteenth-century Central Valley. See also Arnold Bauer and Ann Hagerman Johnson, "Land and labour in rural Chile, 1850–1935," and Cristóbal Kay, "The development of the Chilean hacienda system, 1850–1973," in Kenneth Duncan and Ian Rutledge, eds., *Land and Labour in Latin America* (Cambridge, 1977), Chapters 4 and 5 respectively. A classic portrait of an early-twentieth-century hacienda is provided in C. J. Lambert, *Sweet Waters: A Chilean Farm* (London, 1952), and an equally classic general description of the agriculture of the time is George M. McBride, *Chile: Land and Society* (New York, 1936). José Bengoa, *El poder y la subordinación. Historia social de la agricultura chilena*, 2 vols. (Santiago, 1984), explains the dark side of life in the shadow of the "big house" (which by European standards was never very big). Thomas C. Wright, *Landowners and Reform in Chile: The Sociedad Nacional de Agricultura, 1919–1940* (Urbana, Ill., 1982), studies the mind-set of the SNA, the landowners' pressure-group, as it worked to advance its interests; meanwhile, Brian Loveman, *Struggle in the Countryside: Politics and Rural Labor in Chile, 1919–1973* (Bloomington, Ind., 1976), documents the attempts of inquilinos and others to organize unions. José Garrido, Cristián Guerrero, and María Soledad Valdés, *Historia de la reforma agraria*, 2nd ed. (Santiago, 1990), concentrates on the issue of agrarian reform. For the impact of the Pinochet period on the countryside, see David Hojman, ed., *Neo-Liberal Agriculture in Rural Chile* (London, 1990).

Mining and manufacturing

The mining sector, which has so often driven the economy, is the subject of growing research. Leland Pederson, *The Mining Industry of the Norte Chico, Chile* (Evanston, 1966), examines copper and silver mining in its classic nineteenth-century locations. See also Pierre Vayssière, *Un siècle de capitalisme minier au Chili, 1830–1930* (Paris, 1980), a valuable survey, and the essays by John Mayo, "Commerce, Credit and Control in Chilean Copper Mining before 1880," and William Culver and Cornel Reinhart, "The Decline of a Mining Region and Mining Policy: Chilean Copper in the Nineteenth Century," both in Thomas Greaves and William Culver, eds., *Miners and Mining in the Americas* (Manchester, 1985), 29–46 and 68–81. Clark Reynolds, "Development Problems of an Export Economy," in Markos Mamalakis and Clark Reynolds, *Essays on the Chilean Economy* (Homewood, Ill., 1965), 203–398, concentrates on the copper region in more recent times. Thomas O'Brien, *The Nitrate Industry and Chile's Crucial Transition, 1870–1891* (New York, 1982), examines the formation of the nitrate industry, while Robert Greenhill, "The Nitrate and Iodine Trades, 1880–1914," in D. C. M. Platt, ed., *Business Imperialism 1840– 1930* (Oxford, 1977), 231–83, and Donald D. Crozier, "La industria del yodo, 1815–1915," *Historia*, 27 (1993), 141–212, discuss a byproduct, iodine. The coal-mining industry is covered in Luis Ortega, "The First Four Decades of the Chilean Coalmining Industry, 1840–1879," *Journal of Latin American Studies*, 14:1 (1982), 1–32, and in Enrique Figueroa C., *Carbón: cien años de historia, 1848–1960* (Santiago, 1987), more detailed.

Henry Kirsch, *Industrial Development in a Traditional Society: The Conflict of Entrepreneurship and Modernization in Chile* (Gainesville, Fla., 1977), focuses on the early stages of industrialization and is the only work to date on this topic in English. In Spanish, see Luis Ortega's important articles, "Acerca de los orígenes de la industrialización chilena, 1860– 1879," *Nueva Historia*, 1:2 (1981), 3–54, and "El proceso de industrializa- ción en Chile, 1850–1930," *Historia*, 26 (1991), 213–45. *Chile. 100 años de industria* (Santiago, 1993), published by SOFOFA, and Sergio Villalo- bos R., ed., *Historia de la ingenería en Chile* (Santiago, 1993), both have much useful material.

Robert Oppenheimer, "Chile's Central Valley Railroads and Economic Development in the Nineteenth Century," *Proceedings of the Pacific Coast Council on Latin American Studies*, 6 (1977–79), 73–86, intelligently opens up the theme of communications. The history of a key northern railway was chronicled in detail by Harold Blakemore in his last book, *From the Pacific to La Paz: The Antofagasta (Chili) and Bolivia Railway Company 1888–1988* (London, 1990). The build-up of the telegraph network has been described by John J. Johnson in *Pioneer Telegraphy in Chile* (Stanford, Cal., 1948). Basil Lubbock, *The Nitrate Clippers* (Glasgow, 1932), tells the story of the beautiful sailing-ships that carried Chilean nitrate to Europe. For the growth of air transportation, see R. E. G. Davies, *Airlines of Latin America since 1919* (London, 1984), Chapter 26.

Social aspects

Gabriel Salazar, *Labradores, peones y proletarios* (Santiago, 1985), analyzes the changing lives of rural and urban poor in the period to either side of independence. Vicente Espinoza, *Para una historia de los pobres de la ciudad* (Santiago, 1988), looks at urban poverty in the years after 1900. The early twentieth century's growing interest in social improvement is inter- estingly looked at in James O. Morris, *Elites, Intellectuals and the Consensus*

(Ithaca, N.Y., 1966). The early years of the labor movement are described in graphic detail by Peter deShazo in his *Urban Workers and Labor Unions in Chile, 1902–1927* (Madison, Wis., 1983), a first-class study which restores the Anarchists to their rightful place in labor history. See also Charles Bergquist, *Labor in Latin America* (Stanford, Cal., 1986), 20–80, for some suggestive ideas. Alan Angell, *Politics and the Labour Movement in Chile* (London, 1972), is an indispensable account of the labor movement in a more recent phase. On women's history, three titles in Spanish are essential: Sergio Vergara Quiroz, ed., *Cartas de mujeres en Chile, 1630–1885* (Santiago, 1987); Felicitas Klimpel, *La mujer chilena: el aporte femenino al progreso de Chile, 1910–1960* (Santiago, 1962); and Lucía Santa Cruz, Teresa Pereira, Isabel Zegers, and Valeria Maino, *Tres ensayos sobre la mujer chilena* (Santiago, 1978).

Specific ethnic minorities have received a certain amount of attention from historians. For the most important of these, the remaining "first Chileans," see José Bengoa, *Historia del pueblo mapuche: Siglos XIX y XX* (Santiago, 1984), based extensively on oral history; the decline and fall of "indomitable Araucania" is well sketched in Jacques Rossignol, "Chiliens et Indiens Araucans au milieu du XIXe siècle," *Cahiers du Monde Hispanique et Luso-Brésilien,* 20 (1973), 69–98; Louis C. Faron, *The Mapuche Indians of Chile* (New York, 1968), provides a modern description. Nineteenth- and twentieth-century immigrant groups are covered in Jean-Pierre Blancpain, *Les allemands au Chili, 1816–1945* (Cologne, 1974), a monumental work in the modern French tradition, and the same author's *Francia y los franceses en Chile* (Santiago, 1987); George Young, *The Germans in Chile: Immigration and Colonization, 1849–1919* (New York, 1974); John Mayo, "The British Community in Chile before the Nitrate Age," *Historia,* 22 (1987), 135–50; Gunter Bohn, "Inmigración de judíos de habla alemana a Chile y Perú durante el siglo XIX," *Jahrbuch für Wirtschaft und Gesellschaft Lateinamerikas,* 25 (1988), 455–93; Mario Matus González, *Tradición y adaptación: vivencia de los sefardíes en Chile* (Santiago, 1993); Myriam Olguín Tenorio, *La inmigración árabe en Chile* (Santiago, 1990); Carlos Díaz, *Italianos en Chile. Breve historia de una inmigración* (Santiago, 1988).

Local history

Local history (at various levels) has enjoyed great popularity in Chile, as elsewhere, but none of it has found its way into English. Two specimens of the genre which are worthwhile are Mateo Martinic B., *Historia de la región magellánica,* 2 vols. (Punta Arenas, 1992), and Fernando Campos Harriet, *Historia de Concepción, 1550–1970* (Santiago, 1982). Serious work on the urban history of both Santiago and Valparaiso is now in progress and may be expected to bear fruit in the not-too-distant future.

Travelers' tales

Descriptions and reminiscences of Chile by travelers or short-term residents often repay close study. Only a few of the classic travel books can be mentioned here. Maria Graham, *Journal of a Residence in Chile during the Year 1822* (London, 1824), and Captain Basil Hall, *Extracts from a Journal Written on the Coasts of Chile, Peru and Mexico in the Years 1820, 1821, 1822*, 2 vols. (Edinburgh, 1824), are two notable specimens from the early 1820s. Charles Darwin's pages on Chile in his *Voyage of the Beagle* (numerous editions) are always worth reading, as is the rest of that wonderful book. Descriptions from later in the century include Lieutenant J. M. Gilliss, *The United States Naval Astronomical Expedition to the Southern Hemisphere during the years 1849–'50–'51–'52, Vol. I, Chile* (Washington, D.C., 1855), singularly comprehensive; Mrs. G. B. Merwin, *Three Years in Chile* (New York, 1863); Robert Nelson Boyd, *Chili: Sketches of Chili and the Chilians during the War 1879–80* (London, 1881); Charles Wiener, *Chili & Chiliens* (Paris, 1888); William Howard Russell, *A Visit to Chile and the Nitrate Field of Tarapacá* (London, 1890), the account of the legendary British journalist who accompanied the "Nitrate King," John Thomas North, to Chile in 1889; and William Anderson Smith, *Temperate Chile, a Progressive Spain* (London, 1899).

The twentieth century has seen less in the way of good-quality travel literature covering Chile, but a few titles can be recommended: for the 1920s, Earl Chapin May, *2000 Miles Through Chile: The Land of More or Less* (London, 1924); for rural life in the Huasco valley in the 1930s and 1940s, E. B. Herivel, *We Farmed a Desert* (London, 1957); and, for the 1940s, Erna Fergusson, *Chile* (New York, 1943), and Claude G. Bowers, *Chile Through Embassy Windows, 1939–1953* (New York, 1958), the latter the reminiscences of a well-liked American ambassador. It is difficult to think of anything more recent that is half as interesting as Fergusson or Bowers, although Sara Wheeler, *Travels in a Thin Country. A Journey through Chile* (London, 1994) is a good read. Maybe the twenty-first century will do better than the twentieth.

The Internet

The Internet has swelled so prodigiously in recent years that any specific recommendations as to Chilean websites with a bearing on history is pointless. Those of the government and Congress, all major (and some minor) political parties, the armed forces (the Army's is excellent), the universities, and an enormous variety of institutions and organizations, not to forget websites devoted to historical or cultural figures, can be found with the help of the best search-engines and clicked on to with the greatest ease. As mentioned in Chapter 14, many newspapers can now be read in on-line versions.

Index

Namesakes are listed in order of lifetime: (1) the earlier, (2) the later.

437